SolidWorks 2010 Tutorial

David C. Planchard & Marie P. Planchard CSWP

ISBN: 978-1-58503-568-7

SDC
PUBLICATIONS

Schroff Development Corporation

www.SDCpublications.com

Schroff Development Corporation

P.O. Box 1334

Mission KS 66222

(913) 262-2664

www.schroff.com

Publisher: Stephen Schroff

Trademarks and Disclaimer

SolidWorks® Corp. is a Dassault Systèmes S.A. (Nasdaq: DASTY) company that develops and markets software for design, analysis, and product data management applications. Microsoft® Windows, Microsoft Office® and its family of products are registered trademarks of the Microsoft Corporation. Other software applications and parts described in this book are trademarks or registered trademarks of their respective owners.

Dimensions of parts are modified for illustration purposes. Every effort is made to provide an accurate text. The authors and the manufacturers shall not be held liable for any parts or drawings developed or designed with this book or any responsibility for inaccuracies that appear in the book. Web and company information was valid at the time of the printing.

Copyright© 2010 by D & M Education LLC

Examination Copies

Teacher evaluation copies for 2010, 2009, 2008 and 2007 SolidWorks books are available with classroom support materials and initial and final SolidWorks models. Books received as examination copies are for review purposes only. Examination copies are not intended for student use. Resale of examination copies is prohibited. All assemblies and components for the final ROBOT assembly displayed on the cover are located on the enclosed CD under the Chapter 5 models folder. SolidWorks 2010 Tutorial with MultiMedia CD is targeted toward a technical school, two year college or four year university instructor/student or industry professional that is a beginner or intermediate user who is looking for a step-by-step project based approach with an enclosed 1.5 hour Multi-media CD with SolidWorks model files. The physical components and corresponding Science, Technology, Engineering, and Math (STEM) curriculum are available from Gears Educational Systems www.gearseds.com. Visit www.schroff.com or www.dmeducation.net for additional information.

Electronic Files

Any electronic files associated with this book or MultiMedia CD are licensed to the original user only. These files may not be transferred to any other party without the written consent of the publisher Schroff Development Corporation or D&M Education LLC.

SolidWorks 2010 Tutorial with Multimedia CD is written for students and instructors in a technical school, community college, college or university, and also designers, engineers, and industry professionals that want to learn how to design with SolidWorks. Developed for the beginner to intermediate SolidWorks user, the book provides you a step-by-step project based approach to learning SolidWorks with 1.5 hours of video instruction and hundreds of SolidWorks models on the enclosed CD.

The book is divided into two sections. Chapter 1 though Chapter 6 explore the SolidWorks User Interface and CommandManager, Document and System properties, simple machine parts, simple and complex assemblies, design tables, configurations, multi-sheet, multi-view drawings, BOMs, and Revision tables using basic and advanced features.

Follow the step-by-step instructions and develop multiple assemblies that combine over 80 extruded machined parts and components. Formulate the skills to create, modify and edit sketches and solid features. Learn the techniques to reuse features, parts and assemblies through symmetry, patterns, copied components, design tables and configurations. Explore SolidWorks SimulationXpress, an introduction to Finite Element Analysis (FEA), SolidWorks SustainabilityXpress, an introduction to Life Cycle Assessment (LCA), and DFMXpress, an introduction to design for manufacturability. Learn by doing, not just by reading!

Chapter 7 through Chapter 11 prepares you for the Certified SolidWorks Associate Exam (CSWA). The CSWA certification indicates a foundation in and apprentice knowledge of 3D CAD and engineering practices and principles. Follow the steps in these chapters to assist you in learning the skills required to pass the CSWA.

Desired outcomes and usage competencies are listed for each project. Know your objective up front. Follow the steps in each project to achieve your design goals. Work between multiple documents, features, commands, custom properties and document properties that represent how engineers and designers utilize SolidWorks in industry.

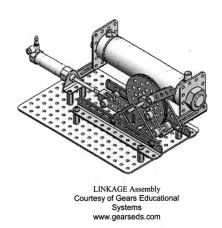

LINKAGE Assembly
Courtesy of Gears Educational
Systems
www.gearseds.com

About the Cover

Create the final ROBOT assembly illustrated on the cover. The physical components and corresponding Science, Technology, Engineering, and Math (STEM) curriculum are available from Gears Educational Systems www.gearseds.com. *Note: All assemblies and components for the final ROBOT assembly are located on the CD under the Chapter 5 models folder.*

Pneumatic Components Diagram
Courtesy of Gears Educational Systems
www.gearseds.com

About the Authors

David Planchard is the Founder of D&M Education LLC. Before starting D&M Education, he spent over 28 years in industry and academia holding various engineering, marketing, and teaching positions and degrees. He holds five U.S. patents and one International patent. He has published and authored numerous papers on Machine Design, Product Design, Mechanics of Materials and Solid Modeling. He is an active member of the New England SolidWorks Users Group and the Cisco Regional Academy Users Group. David holds a BSME, MSM and a Certified SolidWorks Associate (CSWA) Certification. David is a SolidWorks Solution Partner and an Adjunct Professor at Worcester Polytechnic Institute.

Marie Planchard is the Director of World Education Markets at DS SolidWorks Corporation. Before she joined SolidWorks, Marie spent over 10 years as an engineering professor at Mass Bay College in Wellesley Hills, MA. She has 14 plus years of industry software experience and held a variety of management and engineering positions. Marie holds a BSME, MSME and a Certified SolidWorks Professional (CSWP) Certification. She is an active member of the American Society of Mechanical Engineers (ASME) and the American Society for Engineering Education (ASEE).

David and Marie Planchard are co-authors of the following books:

- **A Commands Guide for SolidWorks® 2010**, 2009, 2008 and 2007

- **Assembly Modeling with SolidWorks® 2010**, 2008, 2006, 2005-2004, 2003 and 2001Plus

- **Drawing and Detailing with SolidWorks® 2010**, 2009, 2008, 2007, 2006, 2005, 2004, 2003, 2002 and 2001/2001Plus

- **Engineering Design with SolidWorks® 2010**, 2009, 2008, 2007, 2006, 2005, 2004, 2003, 2001Plus, 2001 and 1999

- **Engineering Graphics with SolidWorks 2010 with MultiMedia CD**.

- **SolidWorks®: The Basics, with MultiMedia CD 2009**, 2008, 2007, 2006, 2005, 2004 and 2003.

- **SolidWorks® Tutorial with MultiMedia CD 2010**, 2009, 2008, 2007, 2006, 2005, 2004, 2003 and 2001/2001Plus.

- **The Fundamentals of SolidWorks®: Featuring the VEXplorer robot, 2008** and 2007.

- **Official Certified SolidWorks® Associate (CSWA) Examination Guide** Version 2 and Version 1.

- **Applications in Sheet Metal Using Pro/SHEETMETAL & Pro/ENGINEER**.

Acknowledgements

Writing this book was a substantial effort that would not have been possible without the help and support of my loving family and of my professional colleagues. I would like to thank Professor Holly Keyes Ault and the community of scholars at Worcester Polytechnic Institute who have enhanced my life and knowledge and helped to shape the approach and content to this book.

A special acknowledgment goes to my loving wife for her support and encouragement and to my daughter, Stephanie Planchard, who supported us during this intense and lengthy project.

Contact the Authors

This is the 8th edition of this book. I realize that keeping software application books current is imperative to our customers. We value the hundreds of professors, students, designers, and engineers that have provided us input to enhance our book. We value your suggestions and comments. Please visit our website at **www.dmeducation.net** or contact us directly with any comments, questions, or suggestions on this book or any of our other SolidWorks books at dplanchard@msn.com.

Note to Instructors

SolidWorks 2010 Tutorial with Multi-media CD is targeted towards a high school, a two year college or four year university instructor/student or industry professional that is a beginner or intermediate user who is looking for a step-by-step project based approach with an enclosed 1.5 hour MultiMedia CD with SolidWorks model files. The physical components and corresponding Science, Technology, Engineering, and Math (STEM) curriculum are available from Gears Educational Systems **www.gearseds.com**. Additional information (five chapters) on the SolidWorks Certified Associate CSWA exam is provided at the end of the book, to assist the user to take and pass the CSWA exam.

Please contact the publisher **www.SDCpublications.com** for additional classroom support materials (.ppt presentations, labs and more) and the Instructor's Guide with model solutions and tips that support the usage of this text in a classroom environment.

Trademarks, Disclaimer and Copyrighted Material

DS SolidWorks Corp. is a Dassault Systèmes S.A. (Nasdaq: DASTY) company that develops and markets SolidWorks® software for design, analysis and product data management applications. Microsoft Windows®, Microsoft Office® and its family of products are registered trademarks of the Microsoft Corporation. Other software applications and parts described in this book are trademarks or registered trademarks of their respective owners.

The publisher and the authors make no representations or warranties with respect to the accuracy or completeness of the contents of this work and specifically disclaim all warranties, including without limitation warranties of fitness for a particular purpose. No warranty may be created or extended by sales or promotional materials. Dimensions of parts are modified for illustration purposes. Every effort is made to provide an accurate text. The authors and the manufacturers shall not be held liable for any parts, components, assemblies or drawings developed or designed with this book or any responsibility for inaccuracies that appear in the book. Web and company information was valid at the time of this printing.

The Y14 ASME Engineering Drawing and Related Documentation Publications utilized in this text are as follows: ASME Y14.1 1995, ASME Y14.2M-1992 (R1998), ASME Y14.3M-1994 (R1999), ASME Y14.41-2003, ASME Y14.5-1982, ASME Y14.5M-1994, and ASME B4.2. Note: By permission of The American Society of Mechanical Engineers, Codes and Standards, New York, NY, USA. All rights reserved.

Additional information references the American Welding Society, AWS 2.4:1997 Standard Symbols for Welding, Braising, and Non-Destructive Examinations, Miami, Florida, USA.

References

- SolidWorks Users Guide, SolidWorks Corporation, 2010.
- ASME Y14 Engineering Drawing and Related Documentation Practices.
- Beers & Johnson, Vector Mechanics for Engineers, 6th ed. McGraw Hill, Boston, MA.
- Betoline, Wiebe, Miller, Fundamentals of Graphics Communication, Irwin, 1995.
- Earle, James, Engineering Design Graphics, Addison Wesley, 1999.
- Hibbler, R.C, Engineering Mechanics Statics and Dynamics, 8th ed, Prentice Hall, Saddle River, NJ.
- Hoelscher, Springer, Dobrovolny, Graphics for Engineers, John Wiley, 1968.
- Jensen, Cecil, Interpreting Engineering Drawings, Glencoe, 2002.

- Jensen & Helsel, <u>Engineering Drawing and Design</u>, Glencoe, 1990.
- Olivo C., Payne, Olivo, T, <u>Basic Blueprint Reading and Sketching</u>, Delmar, 1988.
- Planchard & Planchard, <u>Drawing and Detailing with SolidWorks</u>, SDC Pub., Mission, KS 2009.
- Walker, James, <u>Machining Fundamentals</u>, Goodheart Wilcox, 1999.
- 80/20 Product Manual, 80/20, Inc., Columbia City, IN, 2009.
- Reid Tool Supply Product Manual, Reid Tool Supply Co., Muskegon, MI, 2009.
- Simpson Strong Tie Product Manual, Simpson Strong Tie, CA, 2009.
- Ticona Designing with Plastics – The Fundamentals, Summit, NJ, 2009.
- SMC Corporation of America, Product Manuals, Indiana, 2009.
- Gears Educational Design Systems, Product Manual, Hanover, MA, 2009.
- Emhart – A Black and Decker Company, On-line catalog, Hartford, CT, 2009.

There are over 200 enhancements in SolidWorks 2010. Over 90% of these enhancements were requested directly by customers.

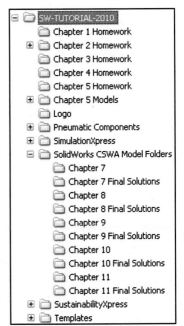

Every license of SolidWorks 2010 contains a copy of SolidWorks SustainabilityXpress. SustainabilityXpress calculates environmental impact on a model in four key areas: *Carbon Footprint*, *Energy Consumption*, *Air Acidification* and *Water Eutrophication*. Material and Manufacturing process region and Transportation Usage region are used as input variables.

All templates, logos, and needed models for this book are included on the enclosed CD. Copy the model folders from the CD to your local hard drive. Work from your local hard drive. View the MultiMedia files for additional help.

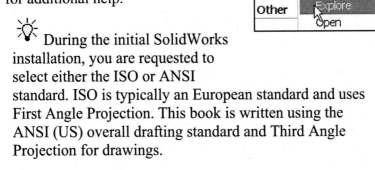

During the initial SolidWorks installation, you are requested to select either the ISO or ANSI standard. ISO is typically an European standard and uses First Angle Projection. This book is written using the ANSI (US) overall drafting standard and Third Angle Projection for drawings.

Notes:

TABLE OF CONTENTS

Introduction   I-1
About the Cover   I-2
About the Authors   I-2
Acknowledgements   I-3
Contact the Authors   I-3
Note to Instructors   I-3
Trademarks, Disclaimer, and Copyrighted Material   I-4
References   I-4
Table of Contents   I-7
What is SolidWorks?   I-15
Design Intent   I-17
Overview of Chapters   I-20
About the Book   I-25
Windows Terminology in SolidWorks   I-25

Chapter 1 - Linkage Assembly   1-1
Chapter Objective   1-3
Chapter Overview   1-4
AXLE Part   1-5
Start a SolidWorks Session   1-6
SolidWorks User Interface and CommandManager   1-7
  Menu bar toolbar   1-7
  Menu bar menu   1-7
  Drop-down menu   1-8
  Right-click   1-8
  Consolidated toolbar   1-8
  System feedback   1-8
  Confirmation Corner   1-9
  Heads-up View toolbar   1-9
  CommandManager   1-11
  FeatureManager Design Tree   1-12
  Fly-out FeatureManager   1-14
Task Pane   1-15
  SolidWorks Resources   1-15
  Design Library   1-15
  File Explorer   1-16
  Search   1-16
  View Palette   1-16
  Appearances/Scenes   1-17
  Custom Properties   1-17
Motion Study tab   1-17
New Part   1-18
AXLE Part   1-22
  AXLE Part-Extruded Base Feature   1-23
  AXLE Part-Save   1-26
  AXLE Part-Edit Color   1-27

AXLE Part-View Modes   1-28
SHAFT-COLLAR Part   1-31
  SHAFT-COLLAR Part-Extruded Boss/Base Feature   1-31
  SHAFT-COLLAR Part-Extruded Cut Feature   1-34
  SHAFT-COLLAR-Modify Dimensions and Edit Color   1-35
FLATBAR Part   1-39
  FLATBAR Part-Extruded Base Feature   1-39
  FLATBAR Part-Extruded Cut Feature   1-42
  FLATBAR Part-Linear Pattern Feature   1-44
LINKAGE Assembly   1-45
Mate Types   1-46
  Standard Mates   1-46
  Advanced Mates   1-47
  Mechanical Mates   1-47
AirCylinder Assembly-Open and Save As option   1-48
LINKAGE Assembly-Insert FLATBAR Part   1-52
LINKAGE Assembly-Insert SHAFT-COLLAR Part   1-56
Motion Study-Basic Motion Tool   1-59
LINKAGE Assembly-Basic Motion   1-59
Chapter Summary   1-62
Chapter Terminology   1-63
Chapter Features   1-64
Engineering Journal   1-65
Questions   1-68
Exercises   1-69

Chapter 2 - Front Support Assembly   **2-1**
Chapter Objective   2-3
Chapter Overview   2-4
Reference Planes and Orthographic Projection   2-5
HEX-STANDOFF Part   2-9
  HEX-STANDOFF Part-Extruded Boss/Base Feature   2-10
  HEX-STANDOFF Part-Hole Wizard Feature   2-14
ANGLE-13HOLE Part   2-15
  ANGLE-13HOLE Part-Documents Properties   2-17
  ANGLE-13HOLE Part-Extruded Thin Feature   2-18
  ANGLE-13HOLE Part-Extruded Cut Feature   2-20
  ANGLE-13HOLE Part-Linear Pattern Feature   2-22
  ANGLE-13HOLE Part-Fillet Feature   2-23
  ANGLE-13HOLE Part-Second Extruded Cut/Linear Pattern 2-24
  ANGLE-13HOLE Part-Third Extruded Cut Feature   2-26
TRIANGLE Part   2-31
  TRIANGLE Part-Mirror, Offset and Fillet Sketch Tools 2-33
  TRIANGLE Part-Extruded Boss/Base Feature   2-36
  TRIANGLE Part-First Extruded Cut Feature   2-37
  TRIANGLE Part-Second Extruded Cut Feature   2-39
  TRIANGLE Part-Mirror Feature   2-41
  TRIANGLE Part-Third Extruded Cut Feature   2-42
  TRIANGLE Part-Circular Pattern Feature   2-44
SCREW Part   2-45

SCREW Part-Documents Properties   2-47
SCREW Part-Revolved Feature   2-47
SCREW Part-Extruded Cut Feature   2-51
SCREW Part-Circular Pattern Feature   2-53
SCREW Part-Fillet Feature   2-53
SCREW Part-Chamfer Feature   2-54
FRONT-SUPPORT Assembly   2-56
  FRONT-SUPPORT Assembly-Insert ANGLE-13HOLE   2-56
  FRONT-SUPPORT Assembly-Insert HEX-STANDOFF   2-58
  FRONT-SUPPORT Assembly-Insert TRIANGLE   2-61
  FRONT-SUPPORT Assembly-Insert SCREW   2-64
Chapter Summary   2-66
Chapter Terminology   2-67
Chapter Features   2-68
Engineering Journal   2-70
Questions   2-74
Exercises   2-75

Chapter 3 - Fundamentals of Drawing   **3-1**
Chapter Objective   3-3
Chapter Overview   3-4
Drawing Template and Sheet Format   3-5
Create a new Drawing   3-7
Drawing-Document Properties   3-9
Title Block   3-10
Create a Title Block   3-11
Company Logo   3-15
Create a Drawing Logo   3-15
Save Sheet Format and Save As Drawing Template   3-18
FLATBAR Drawing   3-21
  FLATBAR Drawing-Open the FLATBAR Part   3-21
  Move Views and Properties of the Sheet   3-25
  FLATBAR Drawing-Position views   3-27
  Detail Drawing   3-28
  FLATBAR Drawing-Dimensions and Annotations   3-30
  Part Number and Document Properties   3-35
  FLATBAR Drawing-Part Number and Document Properties 3-35
  FLATBAR Drawing-Linked Note   3-38
LINKAGE Assembly Drawing-Sheet1   3-41
  Exploded view   3-45
  LINKAGE Assembly Drawing-Exploded view   3-45
  LINKAGE Assembly Drawing-Animation   3-47
  Bill of Materials   3-48
  LINKAGE Assembly Drawing-Bill of Materials   3-48
  LINKAGE Assembly Drawing-Automatic Balloons   3-50
  LINKAGE Assembly Drawing-Sheet2   3-51
  LINKAGE Assembly Drawing-Sheet2 Section view   3-53
  LINKAGE Assembly Drawing-Sheet2 Detail view   3-53
Design Table   3-55
FLATBAR Part-Design Table   3-55

FLATBAR Drawing-Sheet2   3-59
FLATBAR-SHAFTCOLLAR Assembly   3-61
Chapter Summary   3-66
Chapter Terminology   3-67
Questions   3-70
Exercises   3-71

Chapter 4 - Advanced Features   **4-1**
Chapter Objective   4-3
Chapter Overview   4-4
WEIGHT Part   4-6
  Create the WEIGHT Part   4-7
  WEIGHT Part-Loft Feature   4-12
  WEIGHT Part-Instant3D-Extruded Cut Feature   4-13
HOOK Part   4-14
  Create the HOOK Part   4-15
  HOOK Part-Sweep Profile   4-20
  HOOK Part-Swept Base Feature   4-21
  HOOK Part-Dome Feature   4-21
  HOOK Part-Threads with Swept Cut Feature   4-22
WHEEL Part   4-27
  Create the WHEEL Part   4-29
  WHEEL Part-Extruded Boss/Base Feature   4-30
  WHEEL Part-First Revolved Cut Feature   4-31
  WHEEL Part-Second Revolved Cut Feature   4-33
  WHEEL Part-First Extruded Cut Feature   4-34
  WHEEL Part-Second Extruded Cut Feature   4-36
  WHEEL Part-Circular Pattern Feature   4-39
Modify Parts   4-42
HEX-ADAPTER Part   4-42
  HEX-ADAPTER Part-Extruded Boss/Base Feature   4-45
  HEX-ADAPTER Part-Extruded Cut Feature   4-45
AXLE-3000 Part   4-48
SHAFTCOLLAR-500 Part   4-49
Chapter Summary   4-52
Chapter Terminology   4-52
Questions   4-54
Exercises   4-55

Chapter 5 - PNEUMATIC-TEST-MODULE and ROBOT Assembly   **5-1**
Chapter Objective   5-3
Chapter Overview   5-4
Assembly Techniques   5-6
PNEUMATIC-TEST-MODULE Layout   5-7
FLATBAR Sub-assemblies   5-9
3HOLE-SHAFTCOLLAR Assembly   5-9
WHEEL-FLATBAR Assembly   5-16
  Create the WHEEL-FLATBAR Assembly   5-17
  WHEEL-FLATBAR Assembly-Insert 3HOLE-SHAFT-COLLAR Assembly   5-19
  WHEEL-FLATBAR Assembly-Insert 5HOLE-SHAFT-COLLAR Assembly   5-21

WHEEL-AND-AXLE Assembly   5-25
  Create the WHEEL-AND-AXLE Assembly   5-25
  WHEEL-AND-AXLE Assembly-Insert HEX-ADAPTER Part   5-28
  WHEEL-AND-AXLE Assembly-Insert SHAFTCOLLAR-500 Part   5-30
PNEUMATIC-TEST-MODULE Assembly   5-32
  Create the PNEUMATIC-TEST-MODULE Assembly   5-33
  Modify the LINKAGE Assembly   5-33
  PNEUMATIC-TEST-MODULE-Insert LINKAGE Assembly   5-42
  PNEUMATIC-TEST-MODULE-Insert AIR-RESERVOIR-SUPPORT   5-44
  Component Patterns in the Assembly   5-46
  PNEUMATIC-TEST-MODULE-Component Pattern   5-47
  PNEUMATIC-TEST-MODULE-Linear Component Pattern   5-48
  PNEUMATIC-TEST-MODULE-Insert FRONT-SUPPORT Assembly   5-50
  Mirrored Components   5-52
  PNEUMATIC-TEST-MODULE-Mirrored Component   5-53
  PNEUMATIC-TEST-MODULE-Fix the MIRRORFRONT-SUPPORT   5-55
  Component Properties   5-56
  PNEUMATIC-TEST-MODULE-Insert WHEEL-AND-AXLE Assembly   5-56
  PNEUMATIC-TEST-MODULE-Remove Rigid State   5-58
  PNEUMATIC-TEST-MODULE-Review AirCylinder Configurations   5-59
Final ROBOT Assembly   5-64
  Create the ROBOT Assembly   5-65

  Insert the Robot-platform Assembly   5-65
  Insert the PNEUMATIC-TEST-MODULE Assembly   5-65
  Insert the basic_integration Assembly   5-67
Chapter Summary   5-68
Chapter Terminology   5-68
Engineering Journal   5-70
Questions   5-72
Exercises   5-73

Chapter 6 - SimulationXpress, Sustainability and DFMXpress   **6-1**
Chapter Objective   6-3
SolidWorks SimulationXpress   6-3
SolidWorks SimulationXpress-Analyze the Bent Bar   6-8
SolidWorks SustainabilityXpress   6-15
SolidWorks SimulationXpress-Analyze the CLAMP Part   6-15
  Material Class   6-16
  Material Name   6-16
  Manufacturing Process   6-16
  Manufacturing Region   6-16
  Transportation and Usage region   6-16
  Baseline   6-16
  Find a Similar Material   6-18
  View the Environment Impact for the Alternative Material   6-18
  Run a Report   6-19
SolidWorks DFMXpress   6-19
SolidWorks SimulationXpress-Analyze the AXLE and ROD Part   6-20
Chapter Summary   6-21

Certified SolidWorks Associate Exam

Chapter 7 - Basic Theory and Drawing Theory	**7-1**
Introduction	7-1
Goals	7-1
Objectives	7-2
Identify the correct reference planes: Top, Right and Front	7-3
Identify material, measure and mass properties	7-4
Assign and edit material	7-4
Tutorial: Assign and edit material 7-1	7-4
Tutorial: Assign and edit material 7-2	7-5
Measure tool	7-5
Tutorial: Measure tool 7-1	7-6
Tutorial: Measure tool 7-2	7-6
Locate the Center of mass, and Principal moments of inertia	7-7
Tutorial: Mass properties 7-1	7-8
Tutorial: Mass properties 7-2	7-9
Procedure to create a Named Drawing view	7-10
Tutorial: Drawing named procedure 7-1	7-11
Tutorial: Drawing named procedure 7-2	7-11
Tutorial: Drawing named procedure 7-3	7-11
Tutorial: Drawing named procedure 7-4	7-12
Tutorial: Drawing named procedure 7-5	7-12
Tutorial: Drawing named procedure 7-6	7-13
Tutorial: Drawing named procedure 7-7	7-13
Tutorial: Drawing named procedure 7-8	7-14
Engineering Documentation Practices	7-14
Document Properties	7-15
Tutorial: Document properties 7-1	7-16
Tutorial: Document properties 7-2	7-16
Summary	7-16
Questions	7-18
Chapter 8 - CSWA - Simple Part Modeling	**8-1**
Objectives	8-1
Read and understand an Engineering document	8-2
Build a simple part from a detailed illustration	8-2
Tutorial: Volume / Center of mass 8-1	8-2
Tutorial: Volume / Center of mass 8-2	8-4
Tutorial: Mass-Volume 8-3	8-7
Tutorial: Mass-Volume 8-4	8-8
Tutorial: Simple Cut 8-1	8-11
Tutorial: Mass-Volume 8-5	8-12
Tutorial: Mass-Volume 8-6	8-14
Tutorial: Mass-Volume 8-7	8-16
2D vs. 3D Sketching	8-18
Tutorial: 3DSketch 8-1	8-18
Tutorial: Mass-Volume 8-8	8-20
Tutorial: Mass-Volume 8-9	8-22
Callout value	8-25

Tolerance type   8-25
   Tutorial: Dimension text 8-1   8-26
   Tutorial: Dimension text 8-2   8-26
   Tutorial: Dimension text 8-3   8-27
Dimension text symbols   8-27
   Tutorial: Dimension text symbols 8-1   8-28
   Tutorial: Dimension text symbols 8-2   8-28
Build additional simple parts   8-29
   Tutorial: Mass-Volume 8-10   8-29
   Tutorial: Mass-Volume 8-11   8-31
   Tutorial: Mass-Volume 8-12   8-33
   Tutorial: Mass-Volume 8-13   8-34
   Tutorial: Mass-Volume 8-14   8-36
   Tutorial: Mass-Volume 8-15   8-37
   Tutorial: Mass-Volume 8-16   8-39
   Tutorial: Basic-part 8-1   8-41
   Tutorial: Basic-part 8-2   8-44
   Tutorial: Basic-part 8-3   8-47
   Tutorial: Basic-part 8-4   8-50
Summary   8-52
Questions   8-53

Chapter 9 - CSWA - Advanced Part Modeling   **9-1**
Objectives   9-1
Build an Advanced part from a detailed dimensioned illustration   9-2
   Tutorial: Advanced Part 9-1   9-2
   Tutorial: Advanced Part 9-2   9-6
   Tutorial: Advanced Part 9-3   9-9
   Tutorial: Advanced Part 9-4   9-12
Calculate the Center of mass relative to a created coordinate system location 9-17
   Tutorial: Coordinate location 9-1   9-17
   Tutorial: Coordinate location 9-2   9-19
   Tutorial: Advanced part 9-5   9-20
   Tutorial: Advanced part 9-5A   9-24
   Tutorial: Advanced part 9-5B   9-25
   Tutorial: Advanced part 9-6   9-27
   Tutorial: Advanced part 9-6A   9-33
   Tutorial: Advanced part 9-7   9-34
Summary   9-39
Questions   9-40

Chapter 10 - CSWA - Assembly Modeling   **10-1**
Objectives   10-1
Assembly Modeling   10-1
Build an assembly from a detailed dimensioned illustration   10-3
   Tutorial: Assembly model 10-1   10-4
   Tutorial: Assembly model 10-2   10-13
   Tutorial: Assembly model 10-3   10-20

Mate the first component with respect to assembly reference planes 10-30
   Tutorial: Assembly model 10-4 10-30
Summary 10-34
Questions 10-35

Chapter 11 - CSWA - Advanced Modeling Theory and Analysis **11-1**
Objectives 11-1
General Definitions 11-1
SolidWorks SimulationXpress 11-8
   User Interface 11-9
   Tutorial: SimulationXpress 11-1 11-10
Summary 11-21
Questions 11-227

Appendix **A-1**
ECO Form A-1
Types of Decimal Dimensions (ASME Y14.5M) A-2
SolidWorks Keyboard Shortcuts A-3
Windows Shortcuts A-4
Helpful On-Line Information A-5
CSWA Homework Answers A-6

Index **I-1**

What is SolidWorks?

SolidWorks is a design automation software package used to produce parts, assemblies and drawings. SolidWorks is a Windows native 3D solid modeling CAD program. SolidWorks provides easy to use, highest quality design software for engineers and designers who create 3D models and 2D drawings ranging from individual parts to assemblies with thousands of parts.

The SolidWorks Corporation, headquartered in Concord, Massachusetts, USA develops and markets innovative design solutions for the Microsoft Windows platform. Additional information on SolidWorks and its family of products can be obtained at their URL, www.SolidWorks.com.

In SolidWorks, you create 3D parts, 3D assemblies and 2D drawings. The part, assembly and drawing documents are related.

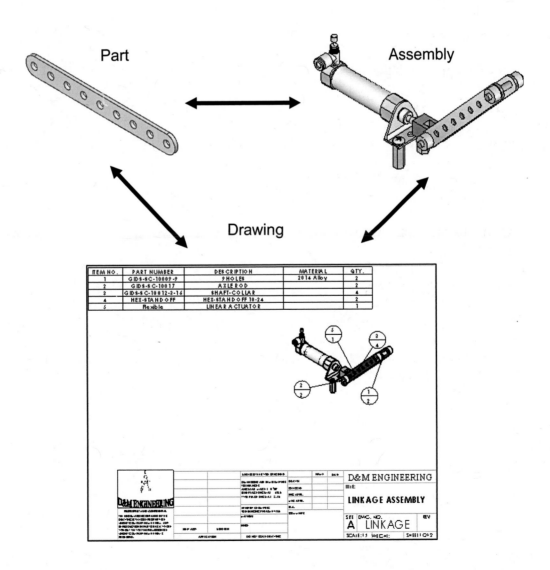

Features are the building blocks of parts. Use
features to create parts, such as: Extruded
Boss/Base and Extruded Cut. Extruded
features begin with a 2D sketch created on a
Sketch plane.

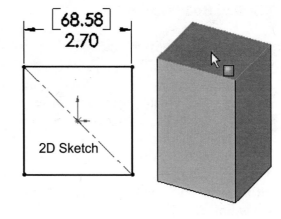

The 2D sketch is a profile or cross section.
Sketch tools such as: lines, arcs and circles are
used to create the 2D sketch. Sketch the
general shape of the profile. Add Geometric
relationships and dimensions to control the
exact size of the geometry.

Create features by selecting edges or faces of
existing features, such as a Fillet. The Fillet
feature rounds sharp corners.

Dimensions drive features.
Change a dimension, and you
change the size of the part.

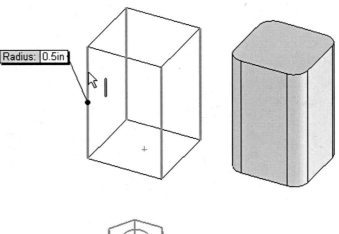

Apply Geometric relationships:
Vertical, Horizontal, Parallel,
etc. to maintain Design intent.

Create a hole that penetrates
through a part. SolidWorks
maintains relationships through
the change.

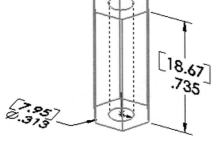

The step-by-step approach used in
this text allows you to create
parts, assemblies and drawings by
doing, not just by reading.

The book provides the knowledge
to modify all parts and
components in a document. Change is an
integral part of design.

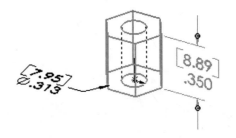

Design Intent

What is design intent? All designs are created for a purpose. Design intent is the intellectual arrangement of features and dimensions of a design. Design intent governs the relationship between sketches in a feature, features in a part and parts in an assembly.

The SolidWorks definition of design intent is the process in which the model is developed to accept future modifications. Models behave differently when design changes occur.

Design for change! Utilize geometry for symmetry, reuse common features, and reuse common parts. Build change into the following areas that you create:

- **Sketch**

- **Feature**

- **Part**

- **Assembly**

- **Drawing**

When editing or repairing geometric relations, it is considered best practice to edit the relation vs. deleting it.

Design Intent in a sketch

Build design intent in a sketch as the profile is created. A profile is determined from the Sketch Entities. Example: Rectangle, Circle, Arc, Point, Slot, etc. Apply symmetry into a profile through a sketch centerline, mirror entity and position about the reference planes and Origin.

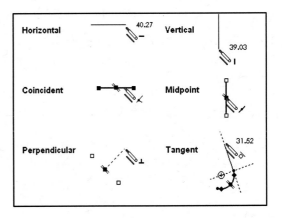

Build design intent as you sketch with automatic Geometric relations. Document the decisions made during the up-front design process. This is very valuable when you modify the design later.

A rectangle (Center Rectangle Sketch tool) contains Horizontal, Vertical and Perpendicular automatic Geometric relations.

Apply design intent using added Geometric relations if needed. Example: Horizontal, Vertical, Collinear, Perpendicular, Parallel, Equal, etc.

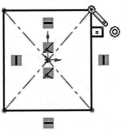

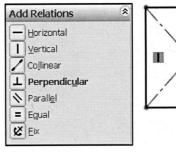

Example A: Apply design intent to create a square profile. Sketch a rectangle. Apply the Center Rectangle Sketch tool. Note: No construction reference centerline or Midpoint relation is required with the Center Rectangle tool. Insert dimensions to fully define the sketch.

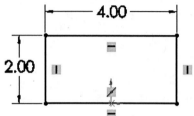

Example B: Develop a rectangular profile. Apply the Corner Rectangle Sketch tool. The bottom horizontal midpoint of the rectangular profile is located at the Origin. Add a Midpoint relation between the horizontal edge of the rectangle and the Origin. Insert two dimensions to fully define the rectangle as illustrated.

Design intent in a feature

Build design intent into a feature by addressing symmetry, feature selection, and the order of feature creation.

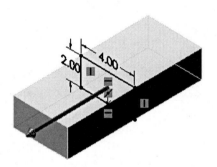

Example A: The Extruded Base feature remains symmetric about the Front Plane. Utilize the Mid Plane End Condition option in Direction 1. Modify the depth, and the feature remains symmetric about the Front Plane.

Example B: Create 34 teeth in the model. Do you create each tooth separate using the Extruded Cut feature? No.

Create a single tooth and then apply the Circular Pattern feature. Modify the Circular Pattern from 32 to 24 teeth.

Design intent in a part

Utilize symmetry, feature order and reusing common features to build design intent into a part. Example A: Feature order. Is the entire part symmetric? Feature order affects the part.

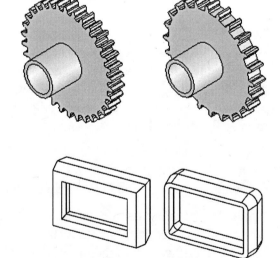

Apply the Shell feature before the Fillet feature and the inside corners remain perpendicular.

Design intent in an assembly

Utilizing symmetry, reusing common parts and using the Mate relation between parts builds the design intent into an assembly.

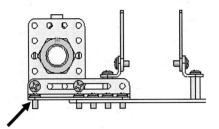

Example A: Reuse geometry in an assembly. The assembly contains a linear pattern of holes. Insert one screw into the first hole. Utilize the Component Pattern feature to copy the machine screw to the other holes.

Design intent in a drawing

Utilize dimensions, tolerance and notes in parts and assemblies to build the design intent into a drawing.

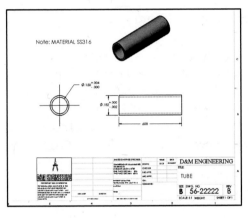

Example A: Tolerance and material in the drawing. Insert an outside diameter tolerance +.000/-.002 into the TUBE part. The tolerance propagates to the drawing.

Define the Custom Property Material in the Part. The Material Custom Property propagates to your drawing.

Create a sketch on any of the default planes: Front, Top, Right or a created plane.

Additional information on design process and design intent is available in SolidWorks Help.

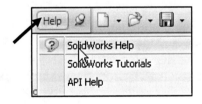

The book is design to expose the new user to many tools, techniques and procedures. It does not always use the most direct tool or process.

Every license of SolidWorks 2010 contains a copy of SolidWorks SustainabilityXpress. SustainabilityXpress calculates environmental impact on a model in four key areas: *Carbon Footprint, Energy Consumption, Air Acidification* and *Water Eutrophication*. Material and Manufacturing process region and Transportation Usage region are used as input variables.

Overview of Chapters

Chapter 1: Linkage Assembly

Chapter 1 introduces the basic concepts behind SolidWorks and the SolidWorks 2010 User Interface.

Create a file folder to manage projects. Create three parts: AXLE, SHAFT-COLLAR, and FLATBAR. Utilize the following features: Extruded Boss/Base, Extruded Cut and Linear Pattern.

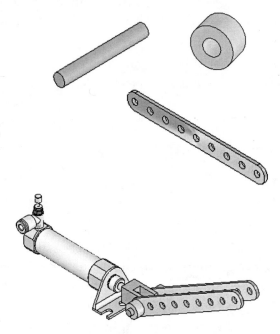

Create the LINKAGE assembly. The LINKAGE assembly utilizes the SMC AirCylinder component located on the enclosed CD in the book. Note: Copy all SolidWorks files from the CD to your hard drive. Work from the hard drive folder: SW-TUTORIAL 2010.

Chapter 2: Front Support Assembly

Chapter 2 introduces various Sketch planes to create parts. The Front, Top and Right Planes each contain the Extruded Boss/Base feature for the TRIANGLE, HEX-STANDOFF and ANGLE-13HOLE parts.

Utilize Geometric relationships in your sketch.

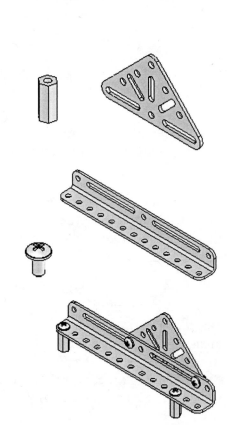

Create the SCREW part using the following features: Revolved Base, Extruded Cut, Fillet and Circular Pattern.

Create the FRONT-SUPPORT assembly. Utilize additional parts from the Web or the enclosed CD to create the RESERVOIR SUPPORT assembly in the Chapter exercises.

Chapter 3: Fundamentals of Drawing

Chapter 3 covers the development of a customized Sheet format and Drawing template.

Review the differences between the Sheet and the Sheet format. Develop a company logo from a bitmap or picture file.

Create a FLATBAR drawing. Insert dimensions created from the part features. Create the LINKAGE assembly drawing with multiple views and assemblies.

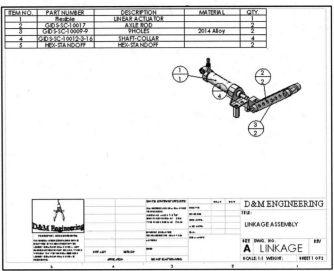

ITEM NO.	PART NUMBER	DESCRIPTION	MATERIAL	QTY.
1	Flexible	LINEAR ACTUATOR		1
2	GIDS-SC-10017	AXLE ROD		2
3	GIDS-SC-10009-9	9HOLES	2014 Alloy	2
4	GIDS-SC-10012-3-16	SHAFT-COLLAR		4
5	HEX-STANDOFF	HEX-STANDOFF		2

Develop and incorporate a Bill of Materials into the drawing Custom Properties in the parts and assemblies. Add information to the Bill of Materials in the drawing. Insert a Design Table to create multiple configurations of parts and assemblies.

Chapter 4: Advanced Features

Chapter 4 focuses on creating six parts for the PNEUMATIC-TEST-MODULE Assembly: WEIGHT, HOOK, WHEEL, HEX-ADAPTER, AXLE-3000 and SHAFTCOLLAR-500.

Apply the following Advanced model features: Plane, Lofted Base, Extruded Cut, Swept Base, Dome, Helix and Spiral, Swept Cut, Extruded Boss/Base, Revolved Cut, Extruded Cut, Circular Pattern, Axis and Hole Wizard.

Reuse existing geometry and modify existing parts to create new parts with the Save as copy command.

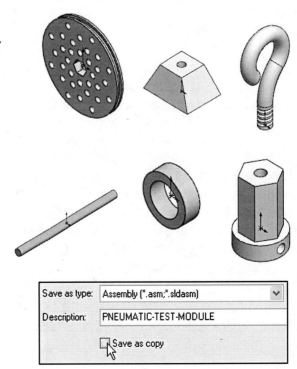

Chapter 5: PNEUMATIC-TEST-MODULE Assembly and Final ROBOT Assembly

Chapter 5 focuses on the PNEUMATIC-TEST-MODULE Assembly and the final ROBOT Assembly.

Create the WHEEL-AND-AXLE assembly. First, create the 3HOLE-SHAFTCOLLAR assembly and the 5HOLE-SHAFTCOLLAR assembly.

Insert the WHEEL part, AXLE 3000 part, HEX-ADAPTER part and SHAFTCOLLAR-500 part.

Insert the FLAT-PLATE part that was create in the Chapter 2 exercises. Insert the LINKAGE assembly and add components: HEX-STANDOFF, AXLE and SHAFT-COLLAR.

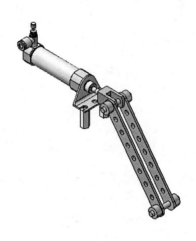

Insert the AIR-RESERVOIR-SUPPORT assembly. Insert the SCREW part. Utilize the Feature Driven Component Pattern tool and the Linear Component Pattern tool.

Insert the FRONT-SUPPORT assembly and apply the Mirror Components tool to complete the Pneumatic Test Module Assembly.

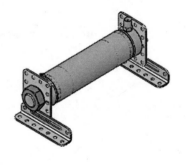

Create the final ROBOT Assembly as illustrated with the Robot-platform sub-assembly, PNEUMATIC-TEST-MODULE sub-assembly, basic_integration sub-assembly and the HEX-ADAPTER component. Add additional components in the Chapter exercises.

Learn the process to work with multiple documents between parts and assemblies and to apply the following Assembly tools: Insert Component, Standard Mates: Concentric, Coincident, and Parallel, Linear Component Pattern, Feature Driven Component Pattern, Circular Component Pattern, Mirror Components and Replace Components.
Note: All assemblies and components for the final ROBOT assembly are located on the CD under the Chapter 5 Models folder.

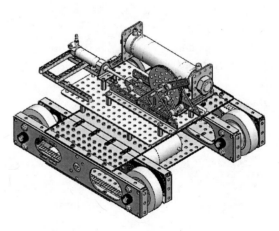

Chapter 6: SolidWorks SimulationXpress, Sustainability and DFMXpress

Chapter 6 introduces three general SolidWorks analysis tools: SimulationXpress, SustainabilityXpress and DFMXpress.

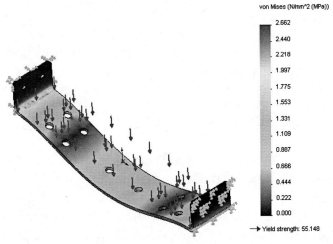

Execute a SolidWorks SimulationXpress analysis on a part. Determine if the part can support an applied load under a static load condition.

Perform a SustainabilityXpress analysis on a part. View the environmental impact calculated in four key areas: *Carbon Footprint, Energy Consumption, Air Acidification* and *Water Eutrophication*.

Material, Manufacturing process region and Usage region are used as input variables.

Compare similar materials and environmental impacts.

Implement DFMXpress on a part. DFMXpress is an analysis tool that validates the manufacturability of SolidWorks parts. Use DFMXpress to identify design areas that may cause problems in fabrication or increase the costs of production.

The book is designed to expose the new user to many tools, techniques and procedures. It does not always use the most direct tool or process.

Chapter 7 - 11: Introduction to the Certified SolidWorks Associate Exam

DS SolidWorks Corp. offers various levels of certification representing increasing levels of expertise in 3D CAD design as it applies to engineering: Certified SolidWorks Associate CSWA and the Certified SolidWorks Professional CSWP along with specialty fields in Sheet Metal, Surfacing and FEA.

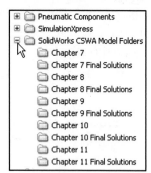

The CSWA certification indicates a foundation in and apprentice knowledge of 3D CAD design and engineering practices and principles. The main requirement for obtaining the CSWA certification is to take and pass the three hour, seven question on-line proctored exam at a Certified SolidWorks CSWA Provider and to sign the SolidWorks Confidentiality Agreement. Passing this exam provides students the chance to prove their knowledge and expertise and to be part of a worldwide industry certification standard!

The primary goal of Chapters 7 - 11 is not only to help you pass the CSWA exam, but also to ensure that you understand and comprehend the concepts and implementation details of the CSWA process.

The second goal is to provide the most comprehensive coverage of CSWA exam related topics available.

The third and ultimate goal is to get you from where you are today to the point that you can confidently pass the CSWA exam.

Review the five exam categories: *Basic Theory and Drawing Theory, Part Modeling, Advanced Part Modeling, Assembly Modeling, and Advanced Modeling Theory and Analysis.*

View the Certified SolidWorks Associate CSWA exam pdf file on the enclosed CD for a sample exam!

About the Book

The following conventions are used throughout this book:

- The term document refers to a SolidWorks part, drawing or assembly file.

- The list of items across the top of the SolidWorks interface is the Menu bar menu or the Menu bar toolbar. Each item in the Menu bar has a pull-down menu. When you need to select a series of commands from these menus, the following format is used: Click **Insert**, **Reference Geometry**, **Plane** from the Menu bar. The Plane PropertyManager is displayed.

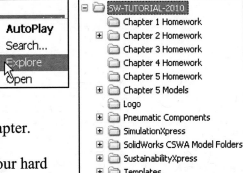

- The book is organized into Chapters. Each Chapter is focused on a specific subject or feature. Use the enclosed Multi-media CD to obtain parts and models that are used in this book and to view the features created in each Chapter.

- Copy all folders and files from the CD to your hard drive. Work from the hard drive. All assemblies and components for the final ROBOT assembly are located on the CD in the Chapter 5 Models folder.

The following command syntax is used throughout the text. Commands that require you to perform an action are displayed in **Bold** text.

Format:	Convention:	Example:
Bold	• All commands actions. • Selected icon button. • Selected icon button. • Selected geometry: line, circle. • Value entries.	• Click **Options** from the Menu bar toolbar. • Click **Corner Rectangle** ▢ from the Sketch toolbar. • Click **Sketch** ⌒ from the Context toolbar. • Select the **centerpoint**. • Enter **3.0** for Radius.
Capitalized	• Filenames. • First letter in a feature name.	• Save the **FLATBAR** assembly. • Click the **Fillet** feature.

Windows Terminology in SolidWorks

The mouse buttons provide an integral role in executing SolidWorks commands. The mouse buttons execute commands, select geometry, display Shortcut menus and provide information feedback.

A summary of mouse button terminology is displayed below:

Item:	Description:
Click	Press and release the left mouse button.
Double-click	Double press and release the left mouse button.
Click inside	Press the left mouse button. Wait a second, and then press the left mouse button inside the text box. Use this technique to modify Feature names in the FeatureManager design tree.
Drag	Point to an object, press and hold the left mouse button down. Move the mouse pointer to a new location. Release the left mouse button.
Right-click	Press and release the right mouse button. A Shortcut menu is displayed. Use the left mouse button to select a menu command.
ToolTip	Position the mouse pointer over an Icon (button). The tool name is displayed below the mouse pointer.
Large ToolTip	Position the mouse pointer over an Icon (button). The tool name and a description of its functionality are displayed below the mouse pointer.
Mouse pointer feedback	Position the mouse pointer over various areas of the sketch, part, assembly or drawing. The cursor provides feedback depending on the geometry.

A mouse with a center wheel provides additional functionality in SolidWorks. Roll the center wheel downward to enlarge the model in the Graphics window. Hold the center wheel down. Drag the mouse in the Graphics window to rotate the model.

☼ SolidWorks System requirements for Microsoft Windows Operating Systems and hardware are as illustrated.

Supported Microsoft Windows® Operating Systems (9)			
	SolidWorks 2008	SolidWorks 2009	SolidWorks 2010
Windows 7 32-bit (2)(10)	No	No	Yes
Windows 7 64-bit (2)(10)	No	No	Yes
Vista 32-bit (3)	Yes	Yes	Yes
Vista 64-bit (3)(4)	Yes	Yes	Yes
XP Professional 32-bit (5)(1)	Yes	Yes	Yes
XP Professional 64-bit (4)(1)	Yes	Yes	Yes

Computer and Software Requirements:

RAM
- **Minimum:** 1GB RAM
- **Recommended:** 2GB RAM
- **Very large models:** X64 processor and Operating System with 6GB or more of RAM when system resources exceed the 2GB limit of a 32-bit OS architecture.

☼ The book does not cover installing SolidWorks for the first time. A default SolidWorks installation presents you with several options. For additional information for an Education Edition, visit the following site:

http://www.solidworks.com/sw/docs/EDU_2009_Installation_Instructions.pdf

Chapter 1

LINKAGE Assembly

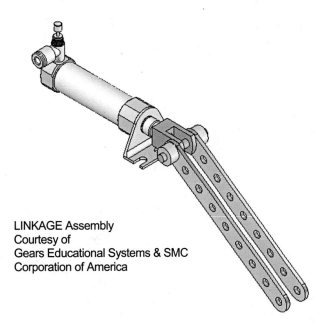

LINKAGE Assembly
Courtesy of
Gears Educational Systems & SMC
Corporation of America

Below are the desired outcomes and usage competencies based on the completion of Chapter 1.

Desired Outcomes:	Usage Competencies:

• Create three parts:
 	
  o AXLE
 	
  o SHAFT-COLLAR
 	
  o FLATBAR
	• Understand the SolidWorks default User Interface. Establish a SolidWorks session.
	
	• Create 2D sketch profiles on the correct Sketch plane.
	
	• Apply the following 3D features: Extruded Boss/Base, Extruded Cut and Linear Pattern.

• Create an assembly: o LINKAGE assembly	• Understand the Assembly toolbar. • Insert components into an assembly. • Apply the following Standard mates: Concentric, Coincident and Parallel.

Notes:

Chapter 1 - LINKAGE Assembly

Chapter Objective

SolidWorks is a design software application used to model and create 2D and 3D sketches, 3D parts, 3D assemblies and 2D drawings. The chapter objective is to provide a comprehensive understanding of the SolidWorks default User Interface and CommandManager: *Menu bar toolbar, Menu bar menu, Drop-down menu, Context toolbar / menus, Fly-out FeatureManager, System feedback, Confirmation Corner, Heads-up View toolbar and an understanding of Document Properties.*

Obtain the working familiarity of the following SolidWorks sketch and feature tools: *Line, Circle, Centerpoint Straight Slot, Smart Dimension, Extruded Boss/Base, Extruded Cut and Linear Pattern.*

Create three individual parts: *AXLE, SHAFT-COLLAR* and *FLATBAR.*

Create the assembly, LINKAGE, using the three created parts and the downloaded subassembly, AirCylinder, from the CD in the book.

On the completion of this chapter, you will be able to:

- Start a SolidWorks session and navigate through the SolidWorks (UI) and CommandManager.

- Set units and dimensioning standards for a SolidWorks document.

- Generate a 2D sketch and identify the correct Sketch plane.

- Add and modify sketch dimensions.

- Create a 3D model.

- Understand and apply the following SolidWorks features:

  o Extruded Boss/Base, Extruded Cut and Linear Pattern

- Insert the following Geometric relations: Vertical, Horizontal, Coincident, MidPoint, Parallel and Equal.

- Download an assembly into SolidWorks and create an assembly.

- Understand the Assembly toolbar.

- Apply the following Standard mates: Coincident, Concentric and Parallel.

Chapter Overview

SolidWorks is a 3D solid modeling CAD software package used to produce and model parts, assemblies, and drawings.

SolidWorks provides design software to create 3D models and 2D drawings.

Create three parts in this chapter:

- AXLE

- SHAFT-COLLAR

- FLATBAR

Download the AirCylinder assembly from the enclosed CD.

🔆 The AirCylinder assembly is also available to download from the internet.

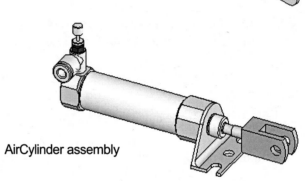

Combine the created parts and the downloaded AirCylinder assembly to create the LINKAGE assembly.

🔆 Illustrations in the book display the default SolidWorks user interface for 2010 SP1.0.

🔆 Every license of SolidWorks 2010, contains a copy of SolidWorks SustainabilityXpress. SolidWorks SustainabilityXpress calculates environmental impact on a model in four key areas: *Carbon Footprint*, *Energy Consumption*, *Air Acidification* and *Water Eutrophication*. Material and Manufacturing process region and Transportation Usage region are use as input variables.

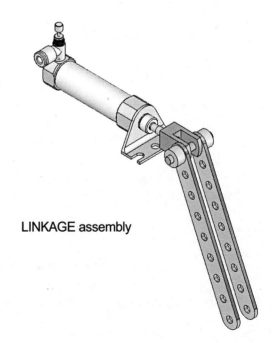

LINKAGE assembly

AXLE Part

The AXLE is a cylindrical rod. The AXLE
supports the two FLATBAR parts.

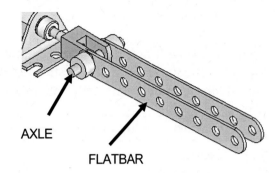

AXLE

FLATBAR

☼ Tangent Edges are displayed for
educational purposes.

The AXLE rotates about its axis. The
dimensions for the AXLE are determined from other
components in the LINKAGE assembly.

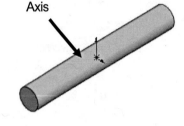

Axis

Start a new SolidWorks session. Create the AXLE part.

Apply features to create parts. Features are the building
blocks that add or remove material.

Utilize the Extruded Boss/Base 🗎 tool from the Features
toolbar to create a Boss-Exturde1 feature. The Extruded
Boss/Base feature adds material. The Base feature (Boss-
Extrude1) is the first feature of the part. The Base feature is the
foundation of the part. Keep the Base feature simple!

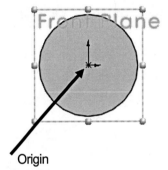

Origin

The Base feature geometry for the AXLE is a simple extrusion.
How do you create a solid Extruded Boss/Base feature for the
AXLE?

- Select the Front Plane as the Sketch plane.

- Sketch a circular 2D profile on the Front Plane, centered at
  the Origin as illustrated.

- Apply the Extruded Boss/Base Feature. Extend the
  profile perpendicular (⊥) to the Front Plane.

Utilize symmetry. Extrude the sketch with the Mid
Plane End Condition in Direction 1. The Extruded
Boss/Base feature is centered on both sides of the Front
Plane.

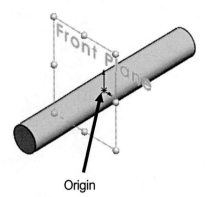

Start a SolidWorks session. The SolidWorks application
is located in the Programs folder.

Origin

SolidWorks displays the Tip of the Day box. Read the Tip of the Day to obtain additional knowledge on SolidWorks.

Create a new part. Select File, New from the Menu bar toolbar or click New ⬜ from the Menu bar menu. There are two options for new documents: *Novice* and *Advanced*. Select the Advanced option. Select the default Part document.

Activity: Start a SolidWorks Session

Start a SolidWorks 2010 session.

1) Click **Start** from the Windows Taskbar.

2) Click **All Programs** All Programs ▷ .

3) Click the **SolidWorks 2010** folder.

4) Click the **SolidWorks 2010** application. The SolidWorks program window opens. Note: Do not open a document at this time.

5) If you do not see the below screen, click the SolidWorks **Resources** 🏠 tab on the right side of the Graphics window location in the Task Pane as illustrated.

☼ If available, double-click the SolidWorks 2010 icon on the Windows Desktop to start a SolidWorks session.

☼ The book was written using SolidWorks Office 2003 on Windows XP Professional SP3.0 with a Windows Classic desktop theme.

Read the Tip of the Day dialog box.

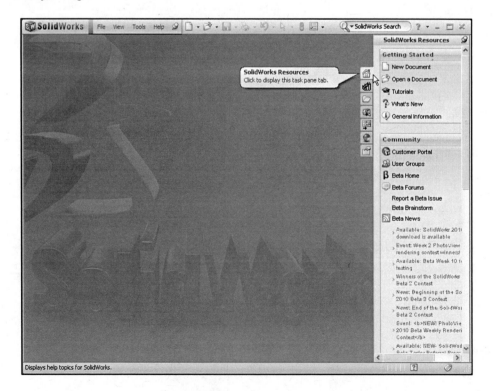

Activity: Understand the SolidWorks User Interface and CommandManager

Menu bar toolbar

SolidWorks 2010 (UI) is
design to make maximum use of the Graphics window area. The default Menu bar
toolbar contains a set of the most frequently used tool buttons from the Standard toolbar.
The available tools are: **New** ⬜ – Creates a new document, **Open** 📂 – Opens an
existing document, **Save** 💾 – Saves an active document, **Print** 🖨 – Prints an active
document, **Undo** ↺ – Reverses the last action, **Select** ⌖ – Selects Sketch entities,
components and more, **Rebuild** 🔵 – Rebuilds the active part, assembly or drawing,
Options 🗒 – Changes system options and Add-Ins for SolidWorks.

Menu bar menu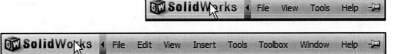

Click SolidWorks in the
Menu bar toolbar to
display the Menu bar menu. SolidWorks provides a Context-sensitive menu structure.
The menu titles remain the same for all three types of documents, but the menu items
change depending on which type of document is active.

Example: The Insert menu includes features in part documents, mates in assembly
documents, and drawing views in drawing documents. The display of the menu is also
dependent on the workflow customization that you have selected. The default menu items
for an active document are: *File, Edit, View, Insert, Tools, Window, Help* and *Pin*.

🔆 The Pin 📌 option displays the Menu bar toolbar and the Menu bar menu as
illustrated. Throughout the book, the Menu bar menu and the Menu bar toolbar is referred
to as the Menu bar.

🔆 Until a file is converted to the current version
of SolidWorks and saved, a warning icon is
displayed on the Save tool as illustrated.

🔆 Expand the drop-down menu to display additional
options and tools.

Drop-down menu

SolidWorks takes advantage of the familiar Microsoft®
Windows® user interface. Communicate with SolidWorks
either through the; *Drop-down menu, Pop-up menu, Shortcut
toolbar, Fly-out toolbar* or the *CommandManager*.

A command is an instruction that informs SolidWorks to
perform a task. To close a SolidWorks drop-down menu, press
the Esc key. You can also click any other part of the
SolidWorks Graphics window, or click another drop-down
menu.

Right-click

Right-click in the *Graphics window, FeatureManager* or
Sketch to display a Context-sensitive toolbar. If you are in the
middle of a command, this toolbar displays a list of options
specifically related to that command.

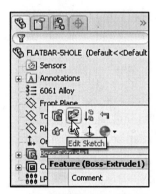

Press the **s** key to view/access previous command tools in
the Graphics window.

Consolidated toolbar

Similar commands are grouped in the CommandManager.
Example: Variations of the Rectangle sketch tool are grouped
in a single fly-out button as illustrated.

If you select the Consolidated toolbar button without expanding:

• For some commands such as Sketch, the most commonly
used command is performed. This command is the first listed and
the command shown on the button.

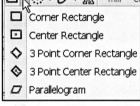

• For commands such as rectangle, where you may want to
repeatedly create the same variant of the rectangle, the last used
command is performed. This is the highlighted command when
the Consolidated toolbar is expanded.

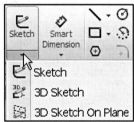

System feedback

SolidWorks provides system feedback by attaching
a symbol to the mouse pointer cursor. The system
feedback symbol indicates what you are selecting or
what the system is expecting you to select.

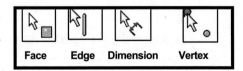

As you move the mouse pointer across
your model, system feedback is provided
to you in the form of symbols, riding next
to the cursor arrow as illustrated.

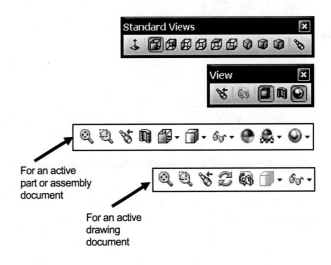

Confirmation Corner

When numerous SolidWorks commands are active, a symbol or a set
of symbols are displayed in the upper right hand corner of the
Graphics window. This area is called the Confirmation Corner.

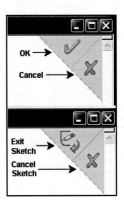

When a sketch is active, the confirmation corner box displays two
symbols. The first symbol is the sketch tool icon. The second symbol
is a large red X. These two symbols supply a visual reminder that you
are in an active sketch. Click the sketch symbol icon to exit the sketch
and to saves any changes that you made.

When other commands are active, the confirmation corner box
provides a green check mark and a large red X. Use the green check
mark to execute the current command. Use the large red X to cancel
the command.

Heads-up View toolbar

SolidWorks provides the user with
numerous view options from the
Standard Views, View and Heads-up
View toolbar.

The Heads-up View toolbar is a
transparent toolbar that is displayed in
the Graphics window when a
document is active.

For an active
part or assembly
document

You can hide, move or modify the
Heads-up View toolbar. To modify
the toolbar: right-click on a tool and
select or deselect the tools that you
want to display.

For an active
drawing
document

The following views are available: Note: Views are document dependent.

- *Zoom to Fit* : Zooms the model to fit the Graphics window.

- *Zoom to Area* : Zooms to the areas you select with a bounding box.

- *Previous View* : Displays the previous view.

- *Section View* : Displays a cutaway of a part or assembly, using one or more cross
  section planes.

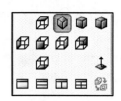

- *View Orientation* ⬚ ▾: Provides the ability to select a view orientation or the number of viewports. The available options are: *Top, Isometric, Trimetric, Dimetric, Left, Front, Right, Back, Bottom, Single view, Two view - Horizontal, Two view - Vertical, Four view.*

- *Display Style* ⬚ ▾: Provides the ability to display the style for the active view. The available options are: *Wireframe, Hidden Lines Visible, Hidden Lines Removed, Shaded, Shaded With Edges.*

- *Hide/Show Items* ⬚ ▾: Provides the ability to select items to hide or show in the Graphics window. Note: The available items are document dependent.

- *Edit Appearance* ⬤ : Provides the ability to apply appearances from the Appearances PropertyManager.

- *Apply Scene* ⬚ ▾: Provides the ability to apply a scene to an active part or assembly document. View the available options.

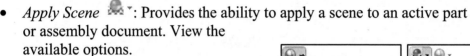

- *View Setting* ⬤ ▾: Provides the ability to select the following: *RealView Graphics, Shadows in Shaded Mode* and *Perspective.*

- *Rotate* ⟳: Provides the ability to rotate a drawing view.

- *3D Drawing View* ⬚ : Provides the ability to dynamically manipulate the drawing view to make a selection.

☼ To deactivate the reference planes for an active document, click **View**; uncheck **Planes** from the Menu bar. To deactivate the grid, click **Options** ▤, **Document Properties** tab. Click **Grid/Snaps**; uncheck the **Display grid** box.

☼ To deactivate a single reference plane in an active document, right-click the **selected plane**, click **Hide**.

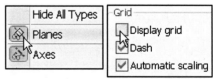

☼ Modify the Heads-up View toolbar. Press the **space** key. The Orientation dialog box is display.

Click the **New View** ⬚ tool. The Name View dialog box is displayed. Enter a new **named** view. Click **OK**. The new view is displayed in the Heads-up View toolbar.

CommandManager

The CommandManager is a Context-sensitive toolbar that automatically updates based on the toolbar you want to access. By default, it has toolbars embedded based on your active document type. When you click a tab below the CommandManager, it updates to display that toolbar. Example: if you click the Sketch tab, the Sketch toolbar is displayed. The default Part tabs are: *Features, Sketch, Evaluate, DimXpert* and *Office Products*.

Below is an illustrated CommandManager for a default Part document.

If you have SolidWorks, SolidWorks Professional or SolidWorks Premium, the Office Products tab appears on the CommandManager.

The Office Products toolbar display is dependent on the activated Add-Ins during a SolidWorks session.

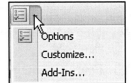

SustainabilityXpress under the Evaluate tab is new in 2010.

To customize the CommandManager, right-click on a tab and select Customize CommandManager.

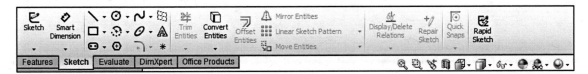

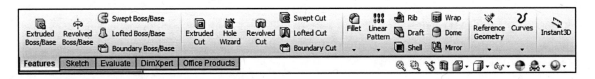

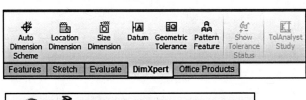

☼ To save space in the CommandManager, right-click in the CommandManager and uncheck the Use Large Buttons with Text box. This will eliminate the text associated with the tool.

☼ If you want to add a custom tab to your CommandManager, right-click on a tab and select the toolbar you want to insert. You can also select to add a blank tab as illustrated and populate it with custom tools from the Customize dialog box.

FeatureManager Design Tree

The FeatureManager design tree is located on the left side of the SolidWorks Graphics window. The design tree provides a summarized view of the active part, assembly, or drawing document. The tree displays the details on how the part, assembly, or drawing document is created.

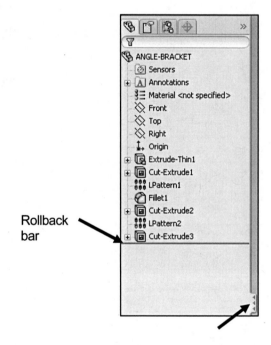

Understand the FeatureManager design tree to troubleshoot your model. The FeatureManager is use extensively throughout this book.

The FeatureManager consists of four default tabs:

- *FeatureManager design tree*

- *PropertyManager*

- *ConfigurationManager*

- *DimXpertManager*

Rollback bar

☼ Select the Hide FeatureManager Tree Area arrows tab 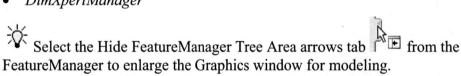 from the FeatureManager to enlarge the Graphics window for modeling.

☼ The Sensors tool ⊠ Sensors located in the FeatureManager monitors selected properties in a part or assembly and alerts you when values deviate from the specified limits. There are four sensor types: *Mass properties*, *Measurement*, *Interference Detection* and *Simulation data*.

Various commands provide the ability to control what is displayed in the FeatureManager design tree. They are:

1. Show or Hide FeatureManager items.

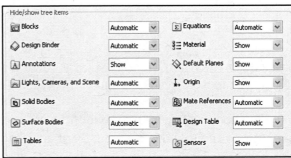

Click **Options** 📋 from the Menu bar. Click **FeatureManager** from the System Options tab. **Customize** your FeatureManager from the Hide/Show Tree Items dialog box.

2. Filter the FeatureManager design tree.
Enter information in the filter field. You can filter by: *Type of features*, *Feature names*, *Sketches*, *Folders*, *Mates*, *User-defined tags* and *Custom properties*.

Tags are keywords you can add to a SolidWorks document to make them easier to filter and to search. The Tags 🏷 icon is located in the bottom right corner of the Graphics window.

To collapse all items in the FeatureManager, **right-click** and select **Collapse items**, or press the **Shift +C** keys.

The FeatureManager design tree and the Graphics window are dynamically linked. Select sketches, features, drawing views, and construction geometry in either pane.

Split the FeatureManager design tree and either display two FeatureManager instances, or combine the FeatureManager design tree with the ConfigurationManager or PropertyManager.

Split bar

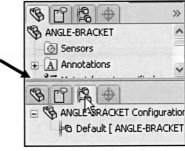

Move between the *FeatureManager design tree*, *PropertyManager*, *ConfigurationManager* and *DimXpertManager* by selecting the tabs at the top of the menu.

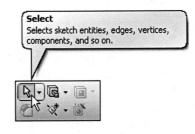

Press the **s** key to view/access previous command tools in the Graphics window.

Illustrations may vary depending on your SolidWorks version.

Split the ConfigurationManager and either display two
ConfigurationManager instances, or combine the
ConfigurationManager with the FeatureManager design tree,
PropertyManager, or a third party application that uses the
panel.

The icons in the ConfigurationManager denote whether the
configuration was created manually or with a Design Table.

The DimXpertManager tab provides the ability to insert
dimensions and tolerances manually or automatically. The
DimXpertManager provides the following selections: *Auto
Dimension Scheme* , *Show Tolerance Status* , *Copy
Scheme* and *TolAnalyst Study* .

Fly-out FeatureManager

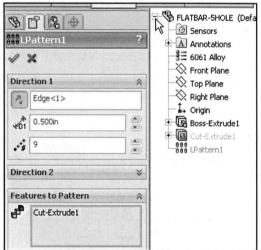

The fly-out FeatureManager design tree
provides the ability to view and select items in
the PropertyManager and the FeatureManager
design tree at the same time.

Throughout the book, you will select
commands and command options from the
drop-down menu, fly-out FeatureManager,
Context toolbar, or from a SolidWorks toolbar.

Another method for accessing a command
is to use the accelerator key. Accelerator keys
are special keystrokes which activate the drop-
down menu options. Some commands in the menu bar and
items in the drop-down menus have an underlined
character. Press the **Alt** key followed by the
corresponding key to the underlined character activates
that command or option.

Press the **g** key to activate the Magnifying glass tool.
Use the Magnifying glass tool to inspect a model and
make selections without changing the overall view.

Task Pane

The Task Pane is displayed when a SolidWorks session starts. The Task Pane contains the following default tabs: *SolidWorks Resources* 🏠 , *Design Library* 📁 , *File Explorer* 📂 , *SolidWorks Search* 🔍 , *View Palette* 🗗 , *Appearances/Scenes* 🔵 and *Custom Properties* 📋 .

🔆 The Document Recovery tab ↩ is displayed in the Task Pane if your system terminates unexpectedly with an active document and if auto-recovery is enabled in the System Options section.

SolidWorks Resources

The basic SolidWorks Resources 🏠 menu displays the following default selections: *Getting Started*, *Community*, *Online Resources*, and *Tip of the Day*.

Other user interfaces are available during the initial software installation selection: *Machine Design*, *Mold Design* or *Consumer Products Design*.

Design Library

The Design Library 📁 contains reusable parts, assemblies, and other elements, including library features.

The Design Library 📁 tab contains four default selections. Each default selection contains additional sub categories. The default selections are: *Design Library, Toolbox, 3D ContentCentral* and *SolidWorks Content.*

🔆 Click **Tools, Add-Ins…, SolidWorks Toolbox** and **SolidWorks Toolbox Browser** to active the SolidWorks Toolbox.

🔆 To access the Design Library folders in a nonnetwork

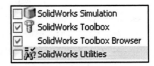

environment for a new installation, click **Add File Location** 📁 , enter: **C:\Documents and Settings\All Users\Application Data\SolidWorks\SolidWorks 2010\design library**. Click **OK**. In a network environment, contact your IT department for system details.

File Explorer

File Explorer  duplicates Windows Explorer from your local computer and displays *Recent Documents*, *directories*, and the *Open in SolidWorks* and *Desktop* folders.

Search

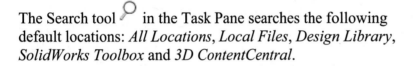

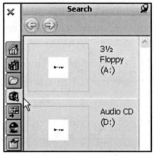

SolidWorks Search  is installed with Microsoft Windows Search and indexes the resources once before searching begins, either after installation, or when you initiate the first search.

The SolidWorks Search box is display in the upper right corner of the SolidWorks Graphics window. Enter the text or key words to search. Click the drop-down arrow to view the last 10 recent searches.

The Search tool ⌕ in the Task Pane searches the following default locations: *All Locations*, *Local Files*, *Design Library*, *SolidWorks Toolbox* and *3D ContentCentral*.

☀ Select any or all of the above locations. If you do not select a file location, all locations are searched.

View Palette

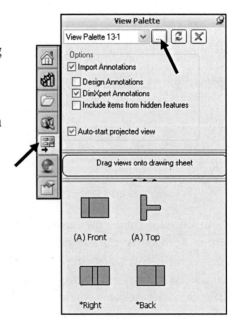

View Palette ⊞ provides the ability to insert drawing views of an active document, or click the Browse button to locate the desired document.

Click and drag the view from the View Palette into an active drawing sheet to create a drawing view.

☀ The selected model is View Palette 13-1 in the illustration. The **(A) Front** and **(A) Top** drawing views are displayed with DimXpert Annotations which were applied at the part level.

Appearances/Scenes

Appearances/Scenes  provide a simplified way to display
models in a photo-realistic setting using a library of Appearances
and Scenes.

On Appearances/Scenes compatible systems, you can select
Appearances and Scenes to display your model in the Graphics
window. Drag and drop a selected appearance onto the model or
FeatureManager. View the results in the Graphics window.

The Appearances/Scenes feature requires graphics card
support. For the latest information on graphics cards that support
Appearances/Scenes Graphics display, visit:
www.solidworks.com/pages/services/videocard
testing.html.

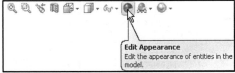

Click the Edit Appearances  icon in the
Heads-up View toolbar to edit an appearance.

Custom Properties

Custom Properties provides the ability to enter
custom and configuration specific properties directly
into SolidWorks files. See SolidWorks Help for
additional information.

Motion Study tab

Motion Studies are
graphical simulations
of motion for an
assembly. Access
MotionManager
from the Motion
Study tab. The
Motion Study tab is
located in the bottom
left corner of the
Graphics window.

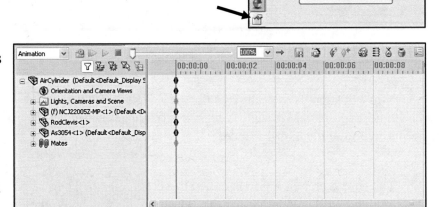

Incorporate visual properties such as lighting and camera perspective. Click the Motion
Study tab to view the MotionManager. Click the Model tab to return to the
FeatureManager design tree.

The MotionManager display a timeline-based interface, and provide the following selections from the drop-down menu as illustrated:

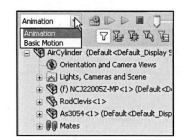

- *Animation:* Apply Animation to animate the motion of an assembly. Add a motor and insert positions of assembly components at various times using set key points. Use the Animation option to create animations for motion that do **not** require accounting for mass or gravity.

- *Basic Motion:* Apply Basic Motion for approximating the effects of motors, springs, collisions and gravity on assemblies. Basic Motion takes mass into account in calculating motion. Basic Motion computation is relatively fast, so you can use this for creating presentation animations using physics-based simulations. Use the Basic Motion option to create simulations of motion that account for mass, collisions or gravity.

If the Motion Study tab is not displayed in the Graphics window, click **View, MotionManager** from the Menu bar.

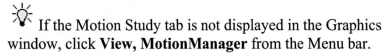
Activity: Create a New Part

A part is a 3D model which consists of features. What are features?

- Features are *geometry* building blocks.

- Features *add* or *remove* material.

- Features are created from *2D* or *3D sketched profiles* or from edges and faces of existing geometry.

- Features are *displayed* in the FeatureManager as illustrated.

You can suppress a feature as illustrated: Flat-Pattern1 in the Bent Bar FeatureManager. A suppress feature is displayed in light gray in the FeatureManager.

The first sketch of a part is called the Base Sketch. The Base sketch is the foundation for the 3D model. In this book, we focus on 2D sketches with 3D features.

There are two modes in the New
SolidWorks Document dialog
box: *Novice* and *Advanced*. The
Novice option is the default
option with three templates. The
Advanced option contains
access to more templates. In this
book, use the *Advanced* Mode.

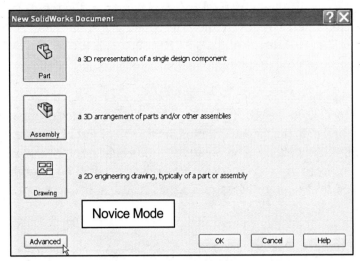

Create a New part.

6)   Click **New** ⬜ from the Menu
         bar. The New SolidWorks
         Document dialog box is
         displayed.

Select Advanced Mode.

7)   Click the **Advanced** button to
         display the New SolidWorks
         Document dialog box in
         Advance mode.

8)   The Templates tab is the
         default tab. Part is the default
         template from the New
         SolidWorks Document dialog
         box. Click **OK**.

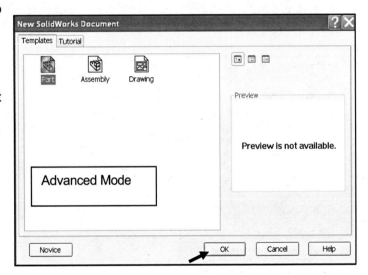

☀ SolidWorks Web Help is
active by default under Help in
the Main bar.

The Advanced mode remains selected for all new documents
in the current SolidWorks session. When you exit
SolidWorks, the Advanced mode setting is saved. The
default SolidWorks installation contains two tabs in the New
SolidWorks Document dialog box: Templates and Tutorial.
The Templates tab corresponds to the default SolidWorks
templates.

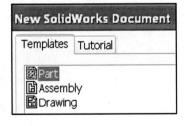

The Tutorial tab corresponds to the templates utilized in the SolidWorks Tutorials.

☀ During the initial SolidWorks installation, you are requested to select either the ISO
or ANSI drafting standard. ISO is typically a European drafting standard and uses First
Angle Projection. This book is written using the ANSI (US) overall drafting standard and
Third Angle Projection for all drawing documents.

Part1 is displayed in the FeatureManager and is the name of the document. Part1 is the default part window name. The Menu bar, CommandManager, FeatureManager, Heads-up View toolbar, SolidWorks Resources, SolidWorks Search, Task Pane, and the Origin are displayed in the Graphics window.

The Origin ⌜ is displayed in blue in the center of the Graphics window. The Origin represents the intersection of the three default reference planes: *Front Plane*, *Top Plane* and *Right Plane*. The positive X-axis is horizontal and points to the right of the Origin in the Front view. The positive Y-axis is vertical and point upward in the Front view. The FeatureManager contains a list of features, reference geometry, and settings utilized in the part.

The Tags ⌀ icon is displayed in the bottom right corner of the Graphics window. Tags are keywords you add to SolidWorks documents and features to make them easier to filter and search for.

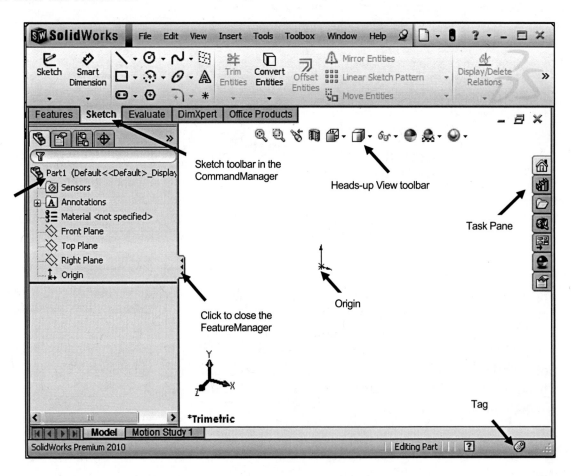

☼ In the book, Reference planes and Grid/Snaps are deactivated in the Graphics window to improve model clarity.

The CommandManager is document dependent. The tabs are located on the bottom left side of the CommandManager and display the available toolbars and features for each corresponding tab. The default tabs for a Part are: *Features, Sketch, Evaluate, DimXpert* and *Office Products*.

☼ The Features icon and Features toolbar should be selected by default in Part mode.

The CommandManager is utilized in this text. Control the CommandManager display.

Right-click in the gray area to the right of the Options ⊟ ▾ icon in the Menu bar toolbar. A complete list of toolbars is displayed. Check CommandManager if required.

☼ Another way to display a toolbar, click **View, Toolbars** from the Menu bar menu. Select the required toolbar.

Select individual toolbars from the View, Toolbars list to display in the Graphics window. Reposition toolbars by clicking and dragging.

☼ Click **View, Origins** from the Menu bar menu to display the Origin in the Graphics window.

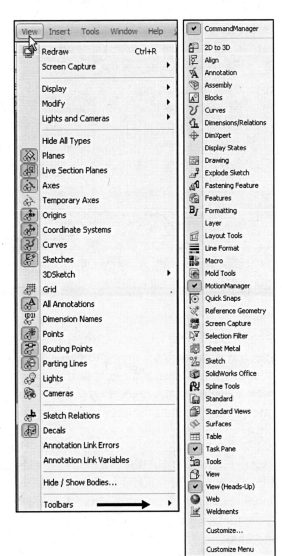

Activity: Create the AXLE Part

Set the Menu bar toolbar and Menu bar menu.

9) Click **SolidWorks** to expand the Menu bar menu.

10) **Pin** 📌 the Menu bar as illustrated. Use both the Menu bar menu and the Menu bar toolbar in this book.

The SolidWorks Help Topics contains step-by-step instructions for various commands. The Help ⑦ icon is displayed in the dialog box or in the PropertyManager for each feature.

Set the Document Properties.

11) Click **Options** 📋 from the Menu bar. The System Options General dialog box is displayed

12) Click the **Document Properties** tab.

13) Select **ANSI** from the Overall drafting standard drop-down menu. Various Detailing options are available depending on the selected standard.

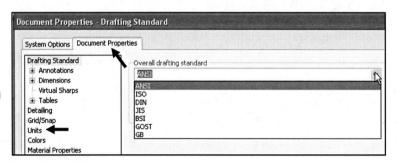

Various detailing options are available depending on the selected standard.

The Overall drafting standard determines the display of dimension text, arrows, symbols, and spacing. Units are the measurement of physical quantities. Millimeter dimensioning and decimal inch dimensioning are the two most common unit types specified for engineering parts and drawings.

The primary units in this book are provided in IPS, (inch, pound, second). The optional secondary units are provided in MMGS, (millimeters, grams, second) and are indicated in brackets [ ].

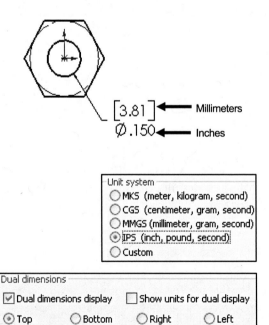

Most illustrations are provided in both inches and millimeters.

Set the document units.

14) Click **Units**.

15) Click **IPS** (inch, pound, second) [**MMGS**] for Unit system.

16) Select **.123**, **[.12]** (three decimal places) for Length basic units.

17) Select **None** for Angle decimal places.

18) Click **OK** from the Document Properties - Units dialog box. The Part FeatureManager is displayed.

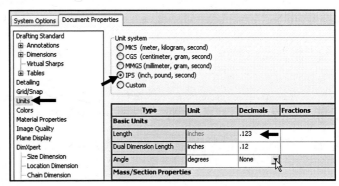

Activity: AXLE Part-Extruded Base Feature

Insert a new sketch for the Extruded Base feature.

19) Right-click **Front Plane** from the FeatureManager. This is your Sketch plane. The Context toolbar is displayed.

20) Click **Sketch** from the Context toolbar as illustrated.

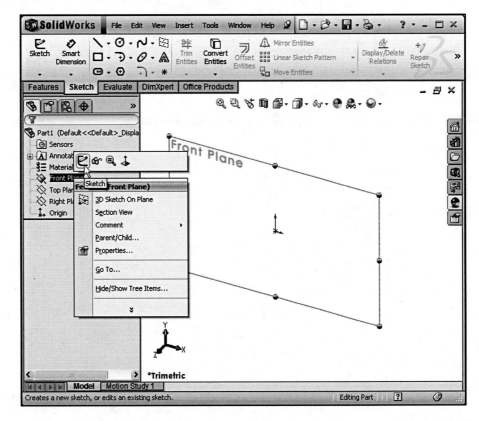

The Sketch toolbar is displayed. Front Plane is your Sketch plane. Note: the grid is deactivated for picture clarity.

You can also click the Front Plane from the FeatureManager and click the Sketch tab from the CommandManager.

21) Click the **Circle** tool from the Sketch toolbar. The Circle PropertyManager is displayed.

The Circle-based tool uses a Consolidated Circle PropertyManager. The SolidWorks application defaults to the last used tool type.

22) Drag the **mouse pointer** into the Graphics window. The cursor displays the Circle icon symbol .

23) Click the **Origin** of the circle. The cursor displays the Coincident to point feedback symbol.

24) Drag the **mouse pointer** to the right of the Origin to create the circle as illustrated. The center point of the circle is positioned at the Origin.

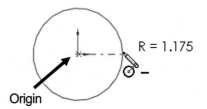

R = 1.175

Origin

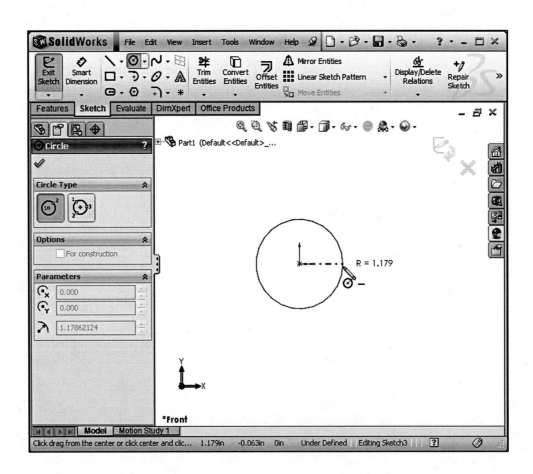

25)   Click a **position** to create the circle. The
          activated circle is displayed in blue.

Add a dimension.

26)   Click **Smart Dimension** ✏ from the Sketch
          toolbar. The cursor displays the Smart

          Dimension icon 👆.

27)   Click the **circumference** of the circle.

28)   Click a **position** diagonally above the circle in
          the Graphics window.

29)   Enter .**188**in, [**4.78**] in the Modify dialog box.

30)   Click the **Green Check mark** ✅ in the Modify
          dialog box. The diameter of the
          circle is .188 inches.

🔅 If required, click the blue arrow
head dots to toggle the direction of
the dimension arrow.

The circular sketch is centered at the Origin. The
dimension indicates the diameter of the circle.

🔅 If your sketch is not correct, select the Undo ↺ tool.

🔅 To fit your sketch to the Graphics window, press the f
key.

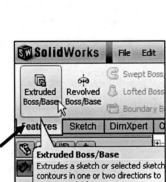

Extrude the sketch to create the Base Feature.

31)   Click the **Features** tab from the CommandManager.

32)   Click the **Extruded Boss/Base** 🗔 Features tool. The Boss-
          Extrude PropertyManager is displayed. Blind is the default
          End Condition in Direction 1.

33)   Select **Mid Plane** for End Condition in Direction 1.

34)   Enter **1.375**in, [**34.93**] for Depth in Direction 1. Accept the
          default conditions.

35)   Click **OK** ✅ from the Boss-Extrude PropertyManager.
          Boss-Extrude1 is displayed in the FeatureManager.

Fit the model to the Graphics window.
36) Press the **f** key. Note the
location of the Origin in the
model.

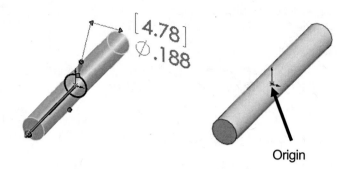

Origin

The Boss-Extrude PropertyManager displays the parameters
utilized to define the feature. The Mid Plane End Condition in
the Direction 1 box extrudes the sketch equally on both sides of
the Sketch plane. The depth defines the extrude distance.

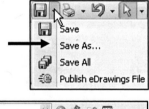

The Boss-Extrude1 feature name is displayed in the
FeatureManager. The FeatureManager lists the features, planes,
and other geometry that construct the part. Extrude features add
material. Extrude features require the following: *Sketch Plane*,
Sketch and *depth*.

The Sketch plane is the Front Plane. The Sketch is a circle with
the diameter of .188in, [4.76]. The Depth is 1.375in, [34.93].

Activity: AXLE Part-Save

Save the part.
37) Click **Save As** from the Menu bar.

38) Double-click the **MY-DOCUMENTS** file folder.

39) Click the Create New Folder 📁 icon.

40) Enter **SW-TUTORIAL-2010** for the file
folder name.

41) Double-click the **SW-TUTORIAL-2010**
file folder. SW-TUTORIAL-2010 is the
Save in file folder name.

42) Enter **AXLE** for the File name.

43) Enter **AXLE ROD** for the Description.

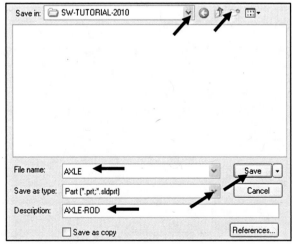

44)   Click **Save**. The AXLE FeatureManager is displayed.

💡 Organize parts into file folders. The file folder for this chapter is named: SW-TUTORIAL-2010. Save all documents in the SW-TUTORIAL-2010 file folder.

💡 Copy all files from the CD in the book to the SW-TUTORIAL-2010 folder.

Activity: AXLE Part-Edit Color

Modify the color of the part.

45)   Right-click the **AXLE**  AXLE icon at the top of the FeatureManager.

46)   Click the **Appearances** drop down arrow.

47)   Click the **Edit color** box as illustrated. The Color PropertyManager is displayed. AXLE is displayed in the Selection box.

48)   Select a **light blue** color from the Color box.

49)   Click **OK** ✔ from the Color PropertyManager. View the AXLE in the Graphics window.

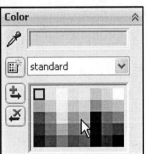

The SolidWorks FeatureManager design tree provides an indicator informing you on the status of your sketch. The sketch can either be:

1.) *(+) Over defined*. The sketch is displayed in red.

2.) *(-) Under defined*. The sketch is displayed in blue.

3.) *(?) Cannot be solved*.

4.) *No prefix*. The sketch is fully defined. This is the ideal sketch state. A fully defined sketch has complete information (manufacturing and inspection) and is displayed in **black**.

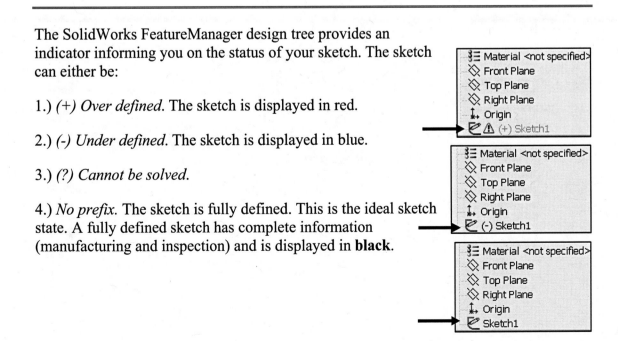

The SketchXpert PropertyManager provides the ability to diagnose an over defined sketch to create a fully defined sketch. If you have an over defined sketch, click Over Defined at the bottom of the Graphics window toolbar. The SketchXpert PropertyManager is displayed. Click the Diagnose button.

Select the desired solution and click the Accept button from the Results box.

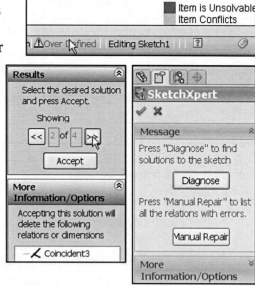

Activity: AXLE Part-View Modes

Orthographic projection is the process of projecting views onto Parallel planes with ⊥ projectors.

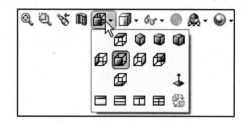

The default reference planes are the Front, Top and Right Planes.

The Isometric view displays the part in 3D with two equal projection angles.

The Heads-up View toolbar illustration may vary depending on your SolidWorks release version.

Display the various view modes using the Heads-up View toolbar.

50) Click **Front view** from the Heads-up View toolbar.

51) Click **Top view** from the Heads-up View toolbar.

52) Click **Right view** from the Heads-up View toolbar.

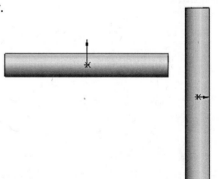

Origin

53)   Click **Isometric view** 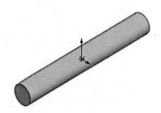 from the Heads-up View toolbar.

☀ View modes manipulate the model in the Graphics window.

Display the various View modes.
54)   Press the lower case **z** key to zoom out.

55)   Press the upper case **Z** key to zoom in.

56)   Click **Zoom to Fit** ⌕ to display the full size of the part in the current window.

57)   **Right-click** in the Graphics window. View the available view tools.

58)   Click **inside** the Graphics window.

Rotate the model.
59)   Click the **middle mouse** button and move your mouse. The model rotates. The Rotate icon ↻ is displayed.

60)   Press the **up arrow** on your key board. The arrow keys rotate the model in 15 degree increments.

☀ View modes remain active until deactivated from the View toolbar or unchecked from the pop-up menu.

☀ Utilize the center wheel of the mouse to Zoom In/Zoom Out and Rotate the model in the Graphics window.

View the various Display Styles.
61)   Click **Isometric view** 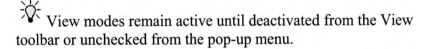 from the Heads-up View toolbar.

62)   Click the **drop down arrow** from the Display Styles box from the Heads-up Views toolbar as illustrated. SolidWorks provides five key Display Styles:

•   *Shaded* ▱. Displays a shaded view of the model with no edges.

•   *Shaded With Edges* ▱. Displays a shaded view of the model, with edges.

- *Hidden Lines Removed* 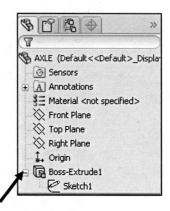 . Displays only those model edges that can be seen from the current view orientation.

- *Hidden Lines Visible* . Displays all edges of the model. Edges that are hidden from the current view are displayed in a different color or font.

- *Wireframe* . Displays all edges of the model.

Save the AXLE part.

63) Click **Save** . The AXLE part is complete.

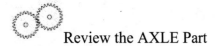 Review the AXLE Part

The AXLE part utilized the Extruded Boss/Base feature. The Extruded Boss/Base feature adds material. The Extruded feature required a Sketch Plane, sketch and depth. The AXLE Sketch plane was the Front Plane. The 2D circle was sketched centered at the Origin. A dimension defined the overall size of the sketch based on the dimensions of mating parts in the LINKAGE assembly.

The default name of the Base feature is Boss-Extrude1. Boss-Extrude1 utilized the Mid Plane End Condition. The Boss-Extrude1 feature is symmetrical about the Front Plane.

The Edit Color option modified the part color. Select the Part icon in the FeatureManager to modify the color of the part. Color and a prefix defines the sketch status. A blue sketch is under defined. A black sketch is fully defined. A red sketch is over defined.

The default Reference planes are the Front, Top, and Right Planes. Utilize the Heads-up View toolbar to display the principle views of a part. The View Orientation and Display Style tools manipulate the model in the Graphics windows.

Instant3D provides the ability to click and drag geometry and dimension manipulator points to resize features in the Graphics window, and to use on-screen rulers to measure modifications. In this book, you will primarily use the PropertyManager and dialog boxes to create and modify model dimensions. Explore Instant3D as an exercise.

SHAFT-COLLAR Part

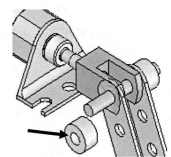

The SHAFT-COLLAR part is a hardened steel ring fastened to the AXLE part.

Two SHAFT-COLLAR parts are used to position the two FLATBAR parts on the AXLE.

Create the SHAFT-COLLAR part.

Utilize the Extruded Boss/Base feature. The Extruded Boss/Base feature requires a 2D circular profile.

Utilize symmetry. Sketch a circle on the Front Plane centered at the Origin.

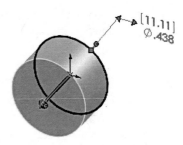

Extrude the sketch with the Mid Plane End Condition. The Extruded Boss/Base feature (Boss-Extrude1) is centered on both sides of the Front Plane.

SHAFT-COLLAR

The Extruded Cut feature removes material. Utilize an Extruded Cut feature to create a hole. The Extruded Cut feature requires a 2D circular profile. Sketch a circle on the front face centered at the Origin.

The Through All End Condition extends the Extruded Cut feature from the front face through all existing geometry.

At this time, apply the Extruded Cut feature for a Through All hole vs. using the Hole Wizard. The book is designed to expose the new user to various tools and design intents.

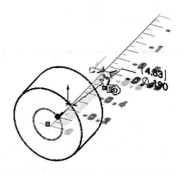

You apply the Instant3D tool or the Extruded Cut feature to create the hole.

Activity: SHAFT-COLLAR Part-Extruded Boss/Base Feature

Create a new part.

64) Click **New** ☐ from the Menu bar. The New SolidWorks Document dialog box is displayed. The Templates tab is the default tab. Part is the default template from the New SolidWorks Document dialog box.

65) Double-click **Part**. The Part FeatureManager is displayed.

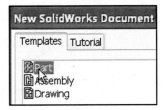

Save the part.

66) Click **Save As** from the Menu bar.

67) Enter **SHAFT-COLLAR** for File name in the SW-TUTORIAL-2010 folder.

68) Enter **SHAFT-COLLAR** for Description.

69) Click **Save**. The SHAFT-COLLAR FeatureManager is displayed.

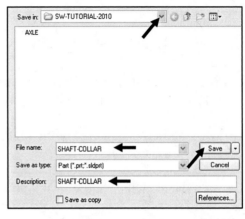

Set the Dimension standard and part units.

70) Click **Options** 📋 , **Document Properties** tab from the Menu bar.

71) Select **ANSI** from the Overall drafting standard drop-down menu.

72) Click **Units**.

73) Click **IPS** (inch, pound, second), [**MMGS**] for Unit system.

74) Select **.123**, [**.12**] (three decimal places) for Length units Decimal places.

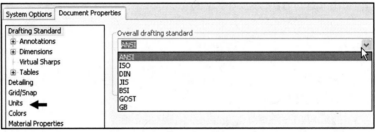

75) Select **None** for Angular units Decimal places.

76) Click **OK** from the Document Properties - Units dialog box.

🔅 To view the Origin, click **View, Origins** from the Menu bar menu.

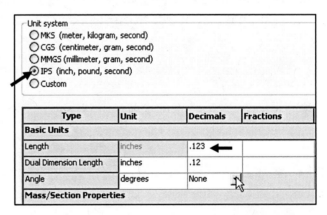

🔅 New in 2010 is the mouse gesture wheel. Right-click and drag in the Graphics area to display the wheel. You can customize the default commands for a sketch, part, assembly or drawing.

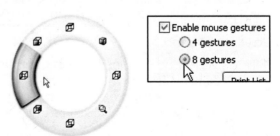

Insert a new sketch for the Extruded Base feature.

77) Right-click **Front Plane** from the FeatureManager. This is the Sketch plane. The Context toolbar is displayed.

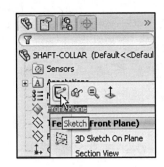

78) Click **Sketch**  from the Context toolbar as illustrated. The Sketch toolbar is displayed.

79) Click the **Circle** ◌ tool from the Sketch toolbar. The Circle PropertyManager is displayed. The cursor displays the Circle icon symbol ◌.

80) Click the **Origin** ↳. The cursor displays the Coincident to point feedback symbol.

81) Drag the **mouse pointer** to the right of the Origin as illustrated.

82) Click a **position** to create the circle.

Add a dimension.

83) Click **Smart Dimension** ✧ from the Sketch toolbar.

84) Click the **circumference** of the circle. The cursor displays the diameter feedback symbol.

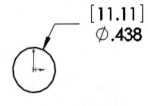

85) Click a **position** diagonally above the circle in the Graphics window.

86) Enter **.4375**in, **[11.11]** in the Modify dialog box.

87) Click the **Green Check mark** ✓ in the Modify dialog box. The black sketch is fully defined.

Note: Three decimal places are displayed. The diameter value .4375 rounds to .438.

$$[11.11]$$
$$\varnothing.438$$

Extrude the sketch to create the Base feature.

88) Click the **Features** tab from the CommandManager.

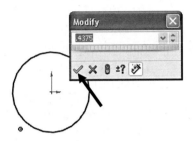

89) Click the **Extruded Boss/Base** 🗔 features tool. The Boss-Extrude PropertyManager is displayed.

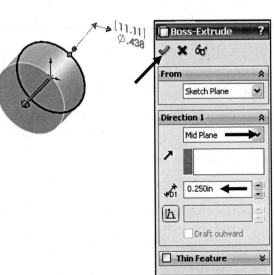

90) Select **Mid Plane** for End Condition in Direction 1.

91) Enter **.250**in, **[6.35]** for Depth. Accept the default conditions. Note the location of the Origin.

92) Click **OK** ✓ from the Boss-Extrude PropertyManager. Boss-Extrude1 is displayed in the FeatureManager.

Fit the model to the Graphics window.

93) Press the **f** key.

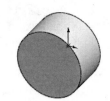

94) Click **Isometric view** 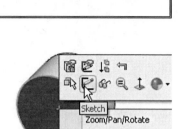 from the Heads-Up View toolbar.

Save the model.

95) Click **Save** 🖫.

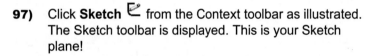
Activity: SHAFT-COLLAR Part-Extruded Cut Feature

Insert a new sketch for the Extruded Cut feature.

96) Right-click the **front circular face** of the Boss-Extrude1 feature for the Sketch plane. The mouse pointer displays the face feedback ⬜ icon.

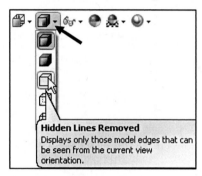

🔆 View the mouse pointer feedback icon for the correct geometry: line, face, point or vertex.

97) Click **Sketch** ✎ from the Context toolbar as illustrated. The Sketch toolbar is displayed. This is your Sketch plane!

98) Click **Hidden Lines Removed** ⬚ from the Heads-up View toolbar.

99) Click the **Circle** ⊘ tool from the Sketch toolbar. The Circle PropertyManager is displayed. The cursor displays the Circle icon symbol ⊘.

100) Click the red **Origin** ⌐. The cursor displays the Coincident to point feedback symbol.

101) Drag the **mouse pointer** to the right of the Origin.

102) Click a **position** to create the circle as illustrated.

Add a dimension.

103) Click the **Smart Dimension** ⌀ Sketch tool.

104) Click the **circumference** of the circle.

105) Click a **position** diagonally above the circle in the Graphics window.

106) Enter **.190**in, [**4.83**] in the Modify dialog box.

107) Click the **Green Check mark** ✔ in the Modify dialog box.

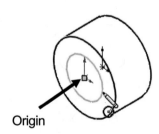

Origin

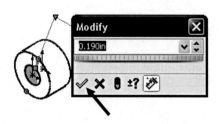

Insert an Extruded Cut feature.

108) Click the **Features** tab from the CommandManager.

109) Click **Extruded Cut** 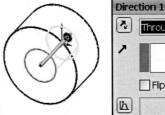 from the Features toolbar. The Cut-Extrude PropertyManager is displayed.

110) Select **Through All** for End Condition in Direction 1. The direction arrow points to the right. Accept the default conditions.

111) Click **OK** ✓ from the Cut-Extrude PropertyManager. Cut-Extrude1 is displayed in the FeatureManager,

The Extruded Cut feature is named Cut-Extrude1. The Through All End Condition removes material from the Front Plane through the Boss-Extrude1 geometry.

SolidWorks Web Help is active by default under Help in the Main bar.

Activity: SHAFT-COLLAR-Modify Dimensions and Edit Color

Modify the dimensions.

112) Click **Trimetric view** 📦 from the Heads-up View toolbar.

113) Click the **z** key a few times to Zoom in.

114) Click the **outside cylindrical face** of the SHAFT-COLLAR. The Boss-Extrude1 dimensions are displayed. Sketch dimensions are displayed in black. The Extrude depth dimensions are displayed in blue.

115) Click the .250in, [6.35] depth dimension.

116) Enter .500in, [12.70].

The Boss-Extrude1 feature and Cut-Extrude1 feature are modified.

Return to the original dimensions.

117) Click the **Undo** 🔄 tool from the Menu bar.

118) Click **Shaded With Edges** 📦 from the Heads-up View toolbar.

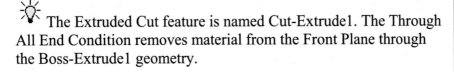

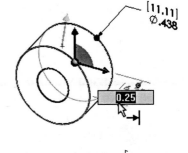

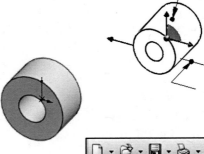

Modify the part color.

119) Right-click the **SHAFT-COLLAR Part** ◈ SHAFT-COLLAR icon at the top of the FeatureManager.

120) Click the **Appearances** drop-down arrow.

121) Click the **Edit color** box as illustrated. The Color PropertyManager is displayed. SHAFT-COLLAR is displayed in the Selection box.

122) Select a **light green** color from the Color box.

123) Click **OK** ✔ from the Color PropertyManager. View the SHAFT-COLLAR in the Graphics window.

Save the SHAFT-COLLAR part.

124) Click **Save** 🖫. The SHAFT-COLLAR part is complete. Note: The sketches are fully defined!

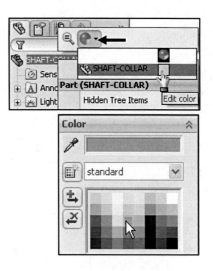

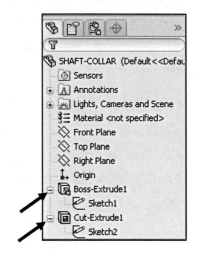

 Review the SHAFT-COLLAR Part

The SHAFT-COLLAR utilized an Extruded Boss/Base 🗟 feature. The Extruded Boss/Base feature adds material. An Extruded feature required a Sketch Plane, sketch and depth.

The Sketch plane was the Front Plane. The 2D circle was sketched centered at the Origin. A dimension fully defined the overall size of the sketch.

The default name of the feature was Boss-Extrude1. Boss-Extrude1 utilized the Mid Plane End Condition. The Boss-Extrude1 feature was symmetric about the Front Plane.

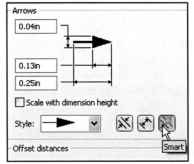

The Extruded Cut 🗎 feature removed material to create the hole. The Extruded Cut feature default named was Cut-Extrude1. The Through All End Condition option created the Cut-Extrude1 feature. Feature dimensions were modified. The Edit Color option was utilized to modify the part color.

☼ Click **Options**, **Document Properties** tab, **Dimension** and click the **Smart** box to have the dimension leader arrow head point inwards for ANSI.

The SolidWorks Help contains step-by-step instructions for various commands. The Help ✏ icon is displayed in the dialog box or in the PropertyManager for each feature.

Display Help for a rectangle.

125) Click **Help** from the Menu bar. Click **SolidWorks Help**. View the default SolidWorks Help Home Page.

126) View your options and tools.

127) Close ☒ the default SolidWorks Help Home Page dialog box.

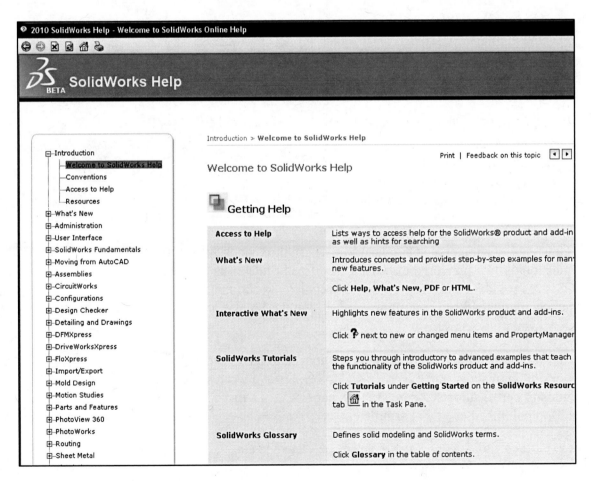

Display the SolidWorks Tutorials.

128) Click **Help** from the Menu bar.

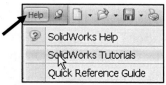

129) Click **SolidWorks Tutorials**. The SolidWorks Tutorials are displayed. The SolidWorks Tutorials are presented by category.

130) Click the **Getting Started** category. The Getting Started category provides three 30 minute lessons on parts, assemblies and drawings. This section also provides information for users who are switching from AutoCAD to SolidWorks. The tutorials also provide links to the CSWP and CSWA Certification programs and a new What's New Tutorial for 2010.

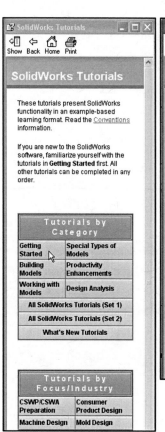

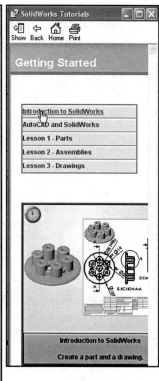

DS SolidWorks Corp. offers levels of certification representing increasing levels of expertise in 3D CAD design as it applies to engineering.

The *Certified SolidWorks Associate* CSWA certification indicates a foundation in and apprentice knowledge of 3D CAD design and engineering practices and principles.

The main requirement for obtaining the CSWA certification is to take and pass the three hour, seven question on-line proctored exam at a Certified SolidWorks CSWA Provider, "university, college, technical, vocational, or secondary educational institution" and to sign the SolidWorks Confidentiality Agreement.

Passing this exam provides students the chance to prove their working knowledge and expertise and to be part of a worldwide industry certification standard. View Chapters 7 - 11 for additional information and sample example models.

131) **Close** the ☒ Online Tutorial dialog box. Return to the SolidWorks Graphics window.

FLATBAR Part

The FLATBAR part fastens to the AXLE. The FLATBAR contains nine, ∅.190in holes spaced 0.5in apart.

The FLATBAR part is manufactured from .090inch 6061 alloy.

Create the FLATBAR part. Utilize the new Straight Slot Sketch 🔘 tool with an Extruded Boss/Base 🗔 feature.

AXLE

FLATBAR

The Extruded feature requires a 2D profile sketched on the Front Plane.

The Straight Slot Sketch tool automatically applies design symmetry, (Midpoint and Equal geometric relations). Create the 2D profile centered about the Origin.

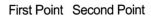

First Point Second Point

🔆 Relations control the size and position of entities with constraints.

[4.83]
∅.190

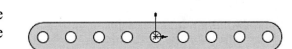

Utilize an Extruded Cut 🔲 feature to create the first hole. This is the seed feature for the Linear Pattern.

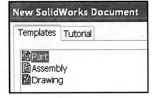

Utilize a Linear Pattern ⚏ feature to create the remaining holes. A Linear Pattern creates an array of features in a specified direction.

Activity: FLATBAR Part-Extruded Base Feature

Create a new part.

132) Click **New** ⬜ from the Menu bar. The New SolidWorks Document dialog box is displayed. The Templates tab is the default tab. Part is the default template from the New SolidWorks Document dialog box.

133) Double-click **Part**. The Part FeatureManager is displayed.

Save the part.
134) Click **Save As** from the Menu bar.

135) Enter **FLATBAR** for File name in the SW-TUTORIAL-2010 folder

136) Enter **FLAT BAR 9 HOLES** for Description.

137) Click **Save**. The FLATBAR FeatureManager is displayed.

Set the Dimension standard and part units.

138) Click **Options** , **Document Properties** tab from the Menu bar.

139) Select **ANSI** from the Overall drafting standard drop-down menu.

140) Click **Units**.

141) Click **IPS**, **[MMGS]** for Unit system.

142) Select **.123**, **[.12]** for Length units Decimal places.

143) Select **None** for Angular units Decimal places.

144) Click **OK** to set the document units.

Insert a new sketch for the Extruded Base feature.

145) Right-click **Front Plane** from the FeatureManager. This is the Sketch plane.

146) Click **Sketch** from the Context toolbar as illustrated. The Sketch toolbar is displayed.

Utilize the new Consolidated Slot Sketch toolbar. Apply the Centerpoint Straight Slot Sketch tool. The Straight Slot Sketch tool provides the ability to sketch a straight slot from a centerpoint. In this example, use the Origin as your centerpoint.

147) Click the **Centerpoint Straight Slot** tool from the Sketch toolbar. The Slot PropertyManager is displayed.

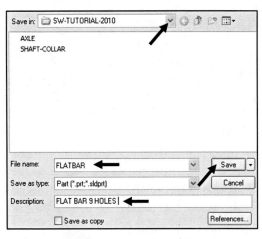

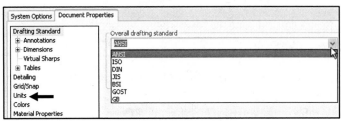

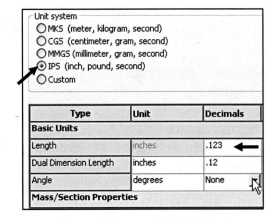

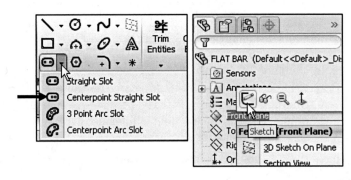

Create the Straight Slot with three points.

148) Click the **Origin**. This is your first point.

149) Click a **point** directly to the right of the Origin. This is your second point.

150) Click a **point** directly above the second point. This is your third point. The Straight Slot is displayed.

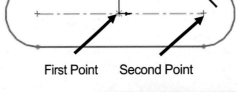

First Point   Second Point

151) Click **OK** ✅ from the Slot PropertyManager

View the Sketch relations.

152) Click **View**, **Sketch Relations** from the Menu bar menu. View the sketch relations in the Graphics window.

Deactivate the Sketch relations.

153) Click **View**; uncheck **Sketch Relations** from the Menu bar. The Straight Slot Sketch tool provides a midpoint relation with the Origin and Equal relations between the other sketch entities.

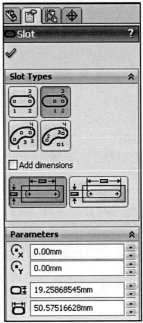

Add a dimension.

154) Click the **Smart Dimension** ✎ tool from the Sketch toolbar.

155) Click the **horizontal centerline**.

156) Click a **position** above the top horizontal line in the Graphics window.

157) Enter **4.000**in, **[101.6]** in the Modify dialog box.

158) Click the **Green Check mark** ✅ in the Modify dialog box.

159) Click the **right arc** of the FLATBAR.

160) Click a **position** diagonally to the right in the Graphics window.

161) Enter **.250**in, **[6.35]** in the Modify dialog box.

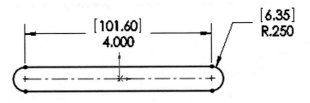

162) Click the **Green Check mark** ✅ in the Modify dialog box. The black sketch is fully defined.

☼ Origin and Tangent Edges are displayed on the models for educational purposes.

Extrude the sketch to create the Base (Boss-Extrude1) feature.

163) Click **Extruded Boss/Base** 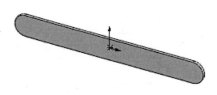 from the Features toolbar. The Boss-Extrude PropertyManager is displayed.

164) Enter .**090**in, **[2.29]** for Depth. Accept the default conditions.

165) Click **OK** ✔ from the Boss-Extrude PropertyManager. Boss-Extrude1 is displayed in the FeatureManager.

Fit the model to the Graphics window.
166) Press the **f** key.

Save the FLATBAR part.

167) Click **Save** 💾.

💡 Click **View, Origins** from the Menu bar menu to display the Origin in the Graphics window.

Activity: FLATBAR Part-Extruded Cut Feature

Insert a new sketch for the Extruded Cut Feature.
168) Right-click the **front face** of the Boss-Extrude1 feature in the Graphics window. This is the Sketch plane. Boss-Extrude1 is highlighted in the FeatureManager.

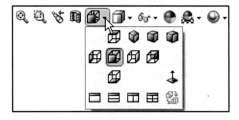

169) Click **Sketch** ✏ from the Context toolbar as illustrated. The Sketch toolbar is displayed.

Display the Front view.
170) Click **Front view** from the Heads-up View toolbar.

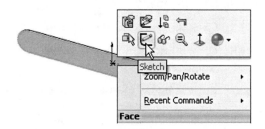

171) Click **Hidden Lines Removed** from the Heads-up View toolbar.

The process of placing the mouse pointer over an existing arc to locate its centerpoint is called "wake up".

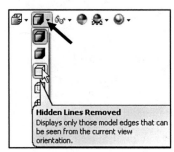

Wake up the center point.

172) Click the **Circle** ⊘ Sketch tool from the Sketch toolbar. The Circle PropertyManager is displayed.

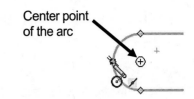

Center point of the arc

173) Place the **mouse pointer** on the left arc. Do not click. The center point of the slot arc is displayed.

174) Click the **centerpoint** of the arc.

175) Click a **position** to the right of the center point to create the circle as illustrated.

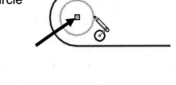

Add a dimension.

176) Click the **Smart Dimension** ✎ Sketch tool.

177) Click the **circumference** of the circle.

178) Click a **position** diagonally above and to the left of the circle in the Graphics window.

179) Enter **.190**in, **[4.83]** in the Modify box.

180) Click the **Green Check mark** ✔ in the Modify dialog box.

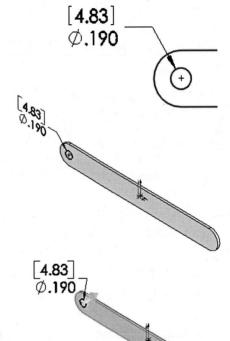

181) Click **Isometric view** ⬛ from the Heads-up View toolbar.

182) Click **Shaded With Edges** ▱ from the Heads-up View toolbar.

Insert an Extruded Cut feature.

183) Click the **Features** tab from the CommandManager.

184) Click **Extruded Cut** ▣ from the Features toolbar. The Cut- Extrude PropertyManager is displayed.

185) Select **Through All** for End Condition in Direction 1. The direction arrow points to the back. Accept the default conditions.

186) Click **OK** ✔ from the Cut-Extrude PropertyManager. The Cut-Extrude1 feature is displayed in the FeatureManager.

Save the FLATBAR part.

187) Click **Save** 💾.

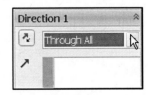

The blue Cut-Extrude1 icon indicates that the feature is selected.

Select features by clicking their icons in the FeatureManager or by selecting their geometry in the Graphics window.

Activity: FLATBAR Part-Linear Pattern Feature

Create a Linear Pattern feature.

188) Click the **Linear Pattern** tool from the Features toolbar. The Linear Pattern PropertyManager is displayed. Cut-Extrude1 is displayed in the Features to Pattern box. Note: If Cut-Extrude1 is not displayed, click inside the Features to Pattern box. Click Cut-Extrude1 from the fly-out FeatureManager.

189) Click the **top edge** of the Boss-Extrude1 feature for Direction1 in the Graphics window. Edge<1> is displayed in the Pattern Direction box.

190) Enter **0.5**in, **[12.70]** for Spacing.

191) Enter **9** for Number of Instances. Instances are the number of occurrences of a feature.

192) The Direction arrow points to the right. Click the **Reverse Direction** button if required.

193) Geometry Pattern is checked by default.

194) Click **OK** from the Linear Pattern PropertyManager. The LPattern1 feature is displayed in the FeatureManager.

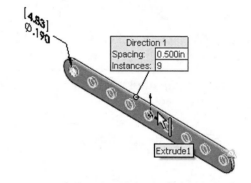

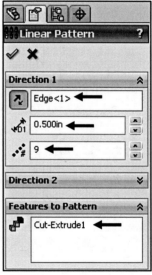

Save the FLATBAR part.

195) Click **Save** . The FLATBAR part is complete.

Close all documents.
196) Click **Windows, Close All** from the Menu bar.

To remove Tangent edges, click
Display/Selections from the Options menu;
check the **Removed** box.

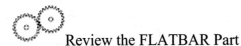 Review the FLATBAR Part

The FLATBAR part utilized an Extruded Boss/Base 🗔 feature as the first feature. The Sketch plane was the Front Plane. The 2D sketch utilized the Straight Slot Sketch tool to create the slot profile.

You added linear and radial dimensions to define your sketch. You applied the Extruded Boss/Base feature with a Blind End Condition in Direction 1. Boss-Extrude1 was created.

You created a circle sketch for the Extruded Cut feature on the front face of Boss-Extrude1. The front face was your Sketch plane for the Extruded Cut feature. The Extruded Cut 🗔 feature removed material to create the hole. The Extruded Cut feature default name was Cut-Extrude1. The Through All End Condition option in Direction 1 created the Cut-Extrude1 feature. The Cut-Extrude1 feature is the seed feature for the Linear Pattern of holes.

The Linear Pattern ⠿ feature created an array of 9 holes, equally spaced along the length of the FLATBAR part.

LINKAGE Assembly

An assembly is a document that contains two or more parts. An assembly inserted into another assembly is called a sub-assembly. A part or sub-assembly inserted into an assembly is called a component. The LINKAGE assembly consists of the following components: AXLE, SHAFT-COLLAR, FLATBAR and AirCylinder sub-assembly.

Establishing the correct component relationship in an assembly requires forethought on component interaction. Mates are geometric relationships that align and fit components in an assembly. Mates remove degrees of freedom from a component.

Mate Types

Mates reflect the physical behavior of a component in an assembly. The components in the LINKAGE assembly utilize Standard mate types. Review the *Standard*, *Advanced* and *Mechanical* mate types.

Standard Mates:

Components are assembled with various mate types. The Standard mate types are:

Coincident Mate: Locates the selected faces, edges, or planes so they use the same infinite line. A Coincident mate positions two vertices for contact

Parallel Mate: Locates the selected items to lie in the same direction and to remain a constant distance apart.

Perpendicular Mate: Locates the selected items at a 90 degree angle to each other.

Tangent Mate: Locates the selected items in a tangent mate. At least one selected item must be either a conical, cylindrical, spherical face.

Concentric Mate: Locates the selected items so they can share the same center point.

Lock Mate: Maintains the position and orientation between two components.

Distance Mate: Locates the selected items with a specified distance between them. Use the drop-down arrow box or enter the distance value directly.

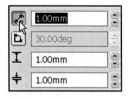

Angle Mate: Locates the selected items at the specified angle to each other. Use the drop-down arrow box or enter the angle value directly.

There are two Mate Alignment options. The Aligned option positions the components so that the normal vectors from the selected faces point in the same direction. The Anti-Aligned option positions the components so that the normal vectors from the selected faces point in opposite directions.

Mates reflect the physical behavior of a component in an assembly. In this chapter, the two most common mate types are Concentric and Coincident.

Advanced Mates:

The Advanced mate types are:

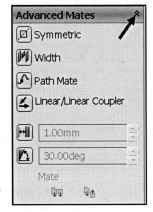

Symmetric Mate: Positions two selected entities to be symmetric about a plane or planar face. A Symmetric Mate does not create a Mirrored Component.

Width Mate: Centers a tab within the width of a groove.

Path Mate: Constrains a selected point on a component to a path.

Linear/Linear Coupler Mate: Establishes a relationship between the translation of one component and the translation of another component.

Distance Mate: Locates the selected items with a specified distance between them. Use the drop-down arrow box or enter the distance value directly.

Angle Mate: Locates the selected items at the specified angle to each other. Use the drop-down arrow box or enter the angle value directly.

Mechanical Mates:

The Mechanical mate types are:

Cam Mate: Forces a plane, cylinder, or point to be tangent or coincident to a series of tangent extruded faces.

Hinge Mate: Limits the movement between two components to one rotational degree of freedom.

Gear Mate: Forces two components to rotate relative to one another around selected axes.

Rack Pinion Mate: Provides the ability to have Linear translation of a part, rack causes circular rotation in another part, pinion, and vice versa.

Screw Mate: Constrains two components to be concentric, and adds a pitch relationship between the rotation of one component and the translation of the other.

Universal Joint Mate: The rotation of one component (the output shaft) about its axis is driven by the rotation of another component (the input shaft) about its axis.

Example: Utilize a Concentric mate between the AXLE cylindrical face and the
FLATBAR Extruded Cut feature, (hole). Utilize a Coincident mate between the SHAFT-
COLLAR back face and the FLATBAR front flat face.

The LINKAGE assembly requires the AirCylinder assembly. The
AirCylinder assembly is located on the SolidWorks Tutorial
Multi-media CD in the Pneumatic Components folder.

Activity: AirCylinder Assembly-Open and Save As option

Copy the folders and files from the CD in the book.
197) Minimize the SolidWorks Graphics window.

198) Insert the CD from the book into your computer. If required, **exit**
out of AutoPlay for the Multi-media movies.

199) Right-click your CD drive icon.

200) Click **Explore**. View the available folders.

201) Copy the folders and files from the CD to your SW-TUTORIAL-
2010 folder on the hard drive.

Return to SolidWorks. Create a new assembly.
202) Maximize the SolidWorks Graphics window.

203) Click **New** ☐ from the Menu bar. The New SolidWorks
Document dialog box is displayed. The Templates tab is the
default tab.

204) Double-click **Assembly** from the New SolidWorks Document
dialog box. The Begin Assembly PropertyManager is displayed.

205) Click the **Browse** button. Note: Open models are displayed in the
Open documents box.

206) Double-click the **AirCylinder** assembly from the SW-TUTORIAL-
2010/Pneumatic Components folder. This is an assembly that
you copied from the CD in the book. The AirCylinder assembly is
displayed in the Graphics window.

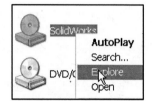

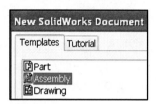

☼ If an assembly or component is loaded in a Lightweight 📦
state, right-click the **assembly name** or **component name** from
the FeatureManager. Click **Set Lightweight to Resolved**.

207) Click **OK** ✔ from the Begin Assembly PropertyManager to fix the AirCylinder assembly in the Graphics window. The (f) symbol is placed in front of the AirCylinder name in the FeatureManager.

208) If required, click **Yes** to Rebuild.

209) Click **Save As** from the Menu bar.

210) Select **SW-TUTORIAL-2010** for Save in folder.

211) Enter **LINKAGE** for file name.

212) Click the **References** button.

213) Click the **Browse** button from the Specify folder for selected items.

214) Select the **SW-TUTORIAL-2010** folder.

215) Click **OK** from the Browse For Folder dialog box.

216) Click **Save All**. The LINKAGE assembly FeatureManager is displayed.

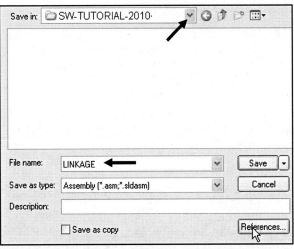

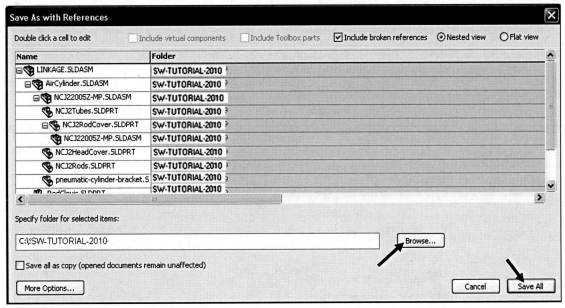

The AirCylinder assembly and its references are copied to the SW-TUTORIAL-2010 folder. Assemble the AXLE to the holes in the RodClevis.

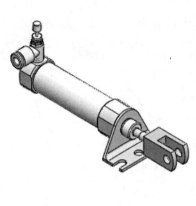

Display the RodClevis component in the FeatureManager.

217) **Expand** the AirCylinder assembly in the FeatureManager.

218) Click **RodClevis<1>** from the FeatureManager. Note: The RodClevis is displayed in blue in the Graphics window.

If required hide the Origins.

219) Click **View**; uncheck **Origins** from the Menu bar.

The AirCylinder is the first component in the LINKAGE assembly and is fixed (f) to the LINKAGE assembly Origin.

Display an Isometric view.

220) Click **Isometric view** from the Heads-up View toolbar.

Insert the AXLE part.

221) Click the **Assembly** tab in the CommandManager.

222) Click the **Insert Components** Assembly tool. The Insert Component PropertyManager is displayed.

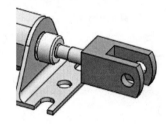

223) Click the **Browse** button. Note: If AXLE is active, double-click AXLE from the Open documents box. Skip to 226.

224) Select **All Files** from the Files of type box.

225) Double-click **AXLE** from the SW-TUTORIAL-2010 folder.

226) Click a **position** to the front of the AirCylinder assembly as illustrated.

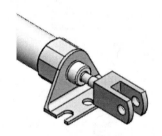

Move the AXLE component.

227) Click a **position** in front of the RODCLEVIS.

Enlarge the view.

228) **Zoom in** on the RodClevis and the AXLE.

Insert a Concentric mate.

229) Click the **Mate** tool from the Assembly toolbar. The Mate PropertyManager is displayed.

230) Click the inside **front hole face** of the RodClevis. The cursor displays the face feedback symbol.

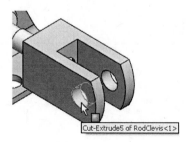

Cut-Extrude5 of RodClevis<1>

231) Click the **long cylindrical face** of the AXLE. The cursor displays the face feedback symbol. The selected faces are displayed in the Mate Selections box. Concentric mate is selected by default. The AXLE is positioned concentric to the RodClevis hole.

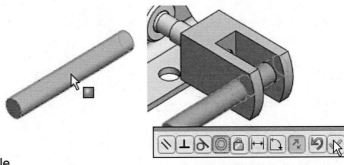

232) Click the **Green Check mark** 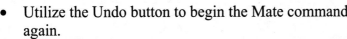 as illustrated.

Move the AXLE.

233) Click and drag the **AXLE** left to right. The AXLE translates in and out of the RodClevis holes.

The Mate Pop-up toolbar is displayed after selecting the two cylindrical faces. The Mate Pop-up toolbar minimizes the time required to create a mate.

Lock   Flip Mate Alignment

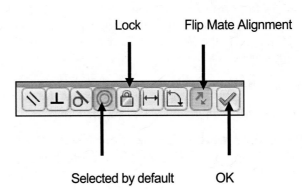

Selected by default   OK

Position the mouse pointer in the middle of the face to select the entire face. Do not position the mouse pointer near the edge of the face. If the wrong face or edge is selected, perform one of the following actions:

- Click the face or edge again to remove it from the Mate Selections box.

- Right-click in the Graphics window. Click Clear Selections to remove all geometry from the Items Selected text box.

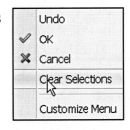

- Right-click in the Mate Selections box to either select Clear Selections or to delete a single selection.

- Utilize the Undo button to begin the Mate command again.

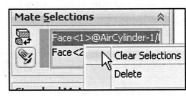

Display the Top view.

234) Click **Top view** from the Heads-up View toolbar.

Expand the LINKAGE assembly and components in the fly-out FeatureManager.

235) **Expand** the LINKAGE assembly from the fly-out FeatureManager.

236) **Expand** the AirCylinder assembly from the fly-out FeatureManager.

237) **Expand** the AXLE part from the fly-out FeatureManager.

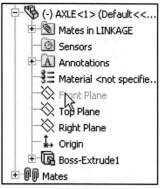

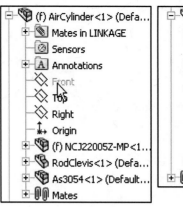

Clear all sections from the Mate Selections box.

238) If needed, right-click **Clear Selections** inside the Mate Selections box.

Insert a Coincident mate.

239) Click the **Front Plane** of the AirCylinder assembly from the fly-out FeatureManager.

240) Click the **Front Plane** of the AXLE part from the fly-out FeatureManager. The selected planes are displayed in the Mate Selections box. Coincident mate is selected by default.

241) Click the **Green Check mark** ✓.

242) Click **OK** ✓ from the Mate PropertyManager.

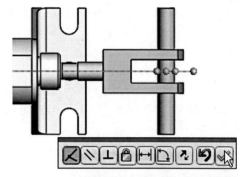

The AirCylinder Front Plane and the AXLE Front Plane are Coincident. The AXLE is centered in the RodClevis.

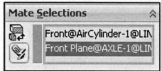

☀️ Display the Mates in the FeatureManager to check that the components and the Mate types correspond to the design intent. Note: If you delete a Mate and then recreate it, the Mate numbers will be in a different order.

Display an Isometric view.

243) Click **Isometric view** 📦 from the Heads-up View toolbar.

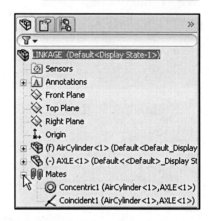

Display the Mates in the folder.

244) **Expand** the Mates folder in the FeatureManager. View the created mates.

Activity: LINKAGE Assembly-Insert FLATBAR Part

Insert the FLATBAR part.

245) Click the **Insert Components** 📦 Assembly tool. The Insert Component PropertyManager is displayed.

246) Click the **Browse** button.

247) Select **Part** for Files of type from the SW-TUTORIAL-2010 folder.

248) Double-click **FLATBAR**.

Place the component in the assembly.
249) Click a **position** in the Graphics window as illustrated. Note: Use the z key to Zoom out if required.

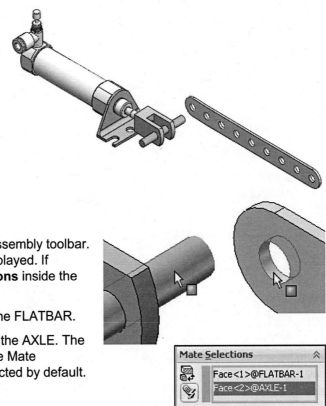

Enlarge the view.
250) **Zoom in** on the AXLE and the left side of the FLATBAR to enlarge the view.

Insert a Concentric mate.

251) Click the **Mate** ✏ tool from the Assembly toolbar. The Mate PropertyManager is displayed. If required, right-click **Clear Selections** inside the Mate Selections box.

252) Click the inside **left hole face** of the FLATBAR.

253) Click the **long cylindrical face** of the AXLE. The selected faces are displayed in the Mate Selections box. Concentric is selected by default.

254) Click the **Green Check mark** ✔ .

Fit the model to the Graphics window.
255) Press the **f** key.

Move the FLATBAR.
256) Click and drag the **FLATBAR**. The FLATBAR translates and rotates along the AXLE.

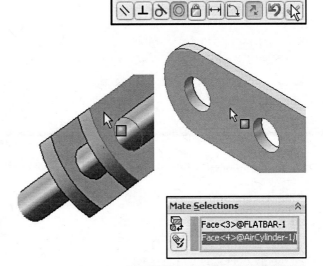

Insert a Coincident mate.
257) Click the **front face** of the FLATBAR.

258) **Rotate** the model view the back face of the RodClevis.

259) Click the **back face** of the RodClevis as illustrated. The selected faces are displayed in the Mate Selections box. Coincident is selected by default.

260) Click the **Green Check mark** .

261) Click **OK** from the Mate PropertyManager.

Display the Isometric view.

262) Click **Isometric view** from the Heads-up View toolbar.

Insert the second FLATBAR component.

263) Click the **Insert Components** Assembly tool. The Insert Component PropertyManager is displayed.

264) Click the **Browse** button.

265) Select **Part** for Files of type from the SW-TUTORIAL-2010 folder.

266) Double-click **FLATBAR**.

267) Click a **position** to the front of the AirCylinder in the Graphics window as illustrated.

Enlarge the view.
268) **Zoom in** on the second FLATBAR and the AXLE.

Insert a Concentric mate.

269) Click the **Mate** tool from the Assembly tool. The Mate PropertyManager is displayed.

270) Click the **left inside hole face** of the second FLATBAR.

271) Click the **long cylindrical face** of the AXLE. The selected faces are displayed in the Mate Selections box. Concentric is selected by default.

272) Click the **Green Check mark** .

273) Click and drag the **second FLATBAR** to the front.

Fit the model to the Graphics window.
274) Press the **f** key.

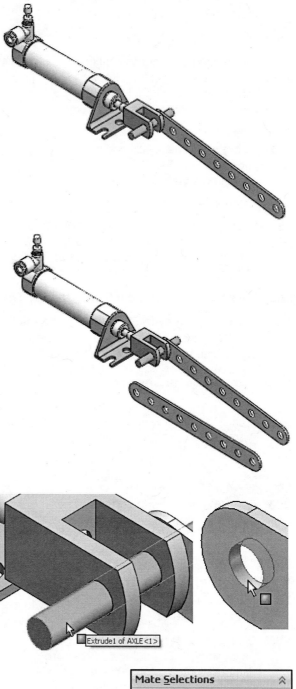

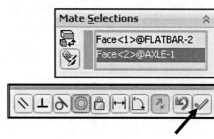

Insert a Coincident mate.

275) Press the **left arrow key** approximately 5 times to rotate the model to view the back face of the second FLATBAR.

276) Click the **back face** of the second FLATBAR.

277) Press the **right arrow key** approximately 5 times to rotate the model to view the front face of the RodClevis.

278) Click the **front face** of the RodClevis. The selected faces are displayed in the Mate Selections box. Coincident is selected by default.

279) Click the **Green Check mark** .

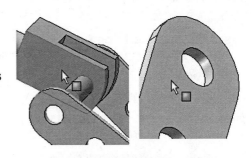

Insert a Parallel mate.

280) Press the **Shift-z** keys to Zoom in on the model.

281) Click the **top narrow face** of the first FLATBAR.

282) Click the **top narrow face** of the second FLATBAR. The selected faces are displayed in the Mate Selections box.

283) Click **Parallel** .

284) Click the **Green Check mark** .

285) Click **OK** from the Mate PropertyManager.

286) Click **Isometric view** from the Heads-up View toolbar.

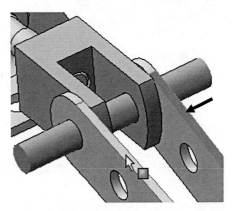

Move the two FLATBAR parts.

287) Click and drag the **second FLATBAR**. Both FLATBAR parts move together.

View the Mates folder.

288) **Expand** the Mates folder from the FeatureManager. View the created mates.

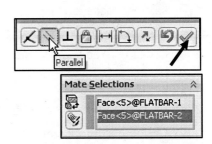

The book is designed to expose the new user to various tools and design intents.

Origins and Tangent Edges are displayed for educational purposes.

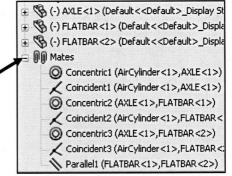

Activity: LINKAGE Assembly-Insert SHAFT-COLLAR Part

Insert the first SHAFT-COLLAR.

289) Click the **Insert Components** Assembly tool. The Insert Component PropertyManager is displayed.

290) Click the **Browse** button.

291) Select **Part** for Files of type from the SW-TUTORIAL-2010 folder.

292) Double-click **SHAFT-COLLAR**.

293) Click a **position** to the back of the AXLE as illustrated.

Enlarge the view.

294) Click the **Zoom to Area** tool.

295) **Zoom-in** on the SHAFT-COLLAR and the AXLE component.

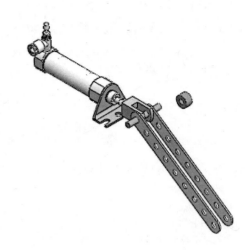

Deactivate the tool.

296) Click the **Zoom to Area** tool.

Insert a Concentric mate.

297) Click the **Mate** tool from the Assembly toolbar. The Mate PropertyManager is displayed.

298) Click the inside **hole face** of the SHAFT-COLLAR.

299) Click the **long cylindrical face** of the AXLE. The selected faces are displayed in the Mate Selections box. Concentric is selected by default.

300) Click the **Green Check mark** .

Insert a Coincident mate.
301) Press the **Shift-z** keys to Zoom in on the model.

302) Click the **front face** of the SHAFT-COLLAR as illustrated.

303) **Rotate** the model to view the back face of the first FLATBAR.

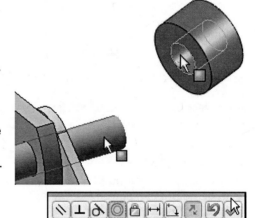

Mate Selections
Face<1>@SHAFT-COLLA
Face<2>@AXLE-1

304) Click the **back face** of the first FLATBAR. The selected faces are displayed in the Mate Selections box. Coincident is selected by default.

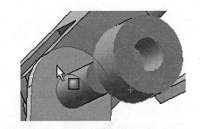

305) Click the **Green Check mark** .

306) Click **OK** from the Mate PropertyManager.

Display the Isometric view.

307) Click **Isometric view** from the Heads-up View toolbar.

Insert the second SHAFT-COLLAR.

308) Click the **Insert Components** Assembly tool. The Insert Component PropertyManager is displayed.

309) Click the **Browse** button.

310) Select **Part** for Files of type from the SW-TUTORIAL-2010 folder.

311) Double-click **SHAFT-COLLAR**.

312) Click a **position** near the AXLE as illustrated.

Enlarge the view.

313) Click the **Zoom to Area** tool.

314) **Zoom-in** on the second SHAFT-COLLAR and the AXLE to enlarge the view.

315) Click the **Zoom to Area** tool to deactivate the tool.

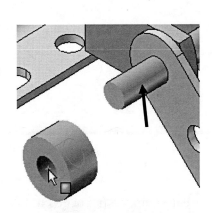

Insert a Concentric mate.

316) Click **Mate** from the Assembly toolbar. The Mate PropertyManager is displayed.

317) Click the **inside hole face** of the second SHAFT-COLLAR.

318) Click the **long cylindrical face** of the AXLE. Concentric is selected by default. The selected faces are displayed in the Mate Selections box.

319) Click the **Green Check mark** .

Insert a Coincident mate.

320) Click the **back face** of the second SHAFT-COLLAR.

321) Click the **front face** of the second FLATBAR. The selected faces are displayed in the Mate Selections box. Coincident is selected by default.

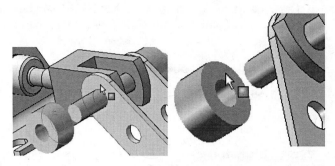

322) Click the **Green Check mark** 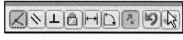.

323) Click **OK** ✓ from the Mate PropertyManager.

324) **Expand** the Mates folder. View the created mates.

Display an Isometric view.

325) Click **Isometric view** 🟦 from the Heads-up View toolbar.

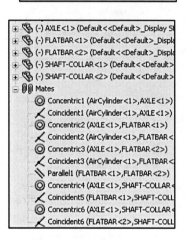

Fit the model to the Graphics window.

326) Press the **f** key.

Save the LINKAGE assembly.

327) Click **Save** 💾. The LINKAGE assembly is complete.

 Review the LINKAGE Assembly

An assembly is a document that contains two or more parts. A part or sub-assembly inserted into an assembly is called a component. You created the LINKAGE assembly. The AirCylinder sub-assembly was the first component inserted into the LINKAGE assembly. The AirCylinder assembly was obtained from the CD in the book and copied to the SW-TUTORIAL-2010 folder.

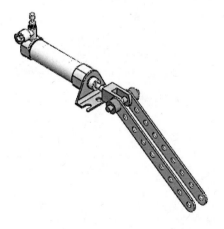

The AirCylinder assembly was fixed to the Origin. The Concentric and Coincident mates added Geometric relationships between the inserted components in the LINKAGE assembly.

The AXLE part was the second component inserted into the LINKAGE assembly. The AXLE required a Concentric mate between the two cylindrical faces and a Coincident mate between two the Front Planes.

The FLATBAR part was the third component inserted into the LINKAGE assembly. The FLATBAR required a Concentric mate between the two cylindrical faces and a Coincident mate between the two flat faces.

A second FLATBAR was inserted into the LINKAGE assembly. A Parallel mate was added between the two FLATBARs.

Two SHAFT-COLLAR parts were inserted into the LINKAGE assembly. Each SHAFT-COLLAR required a Concentric mate between the two cylindrical faces and a Coincident mate between the two flat faces.

Motion Study - Basic Motion Tool

Motion Studies are graphical simulations of motion for assembly models. You can incorporate visual properties such as lighting and camera perspective into a motion study. Motion studies do not change an assembly model or its properties. They simulate and animate the motion you prescribe for your model. Use SolidWorks mates to restrict the motion of components in an assembly when you model motion.

Create a Motion Study. Select the Basic Motion option from the MotionManager. The Basic Motion option provides the ability to approximate the effects of motors, springs, collisions and gravity on your assembly. Basic Motion takes mass into account in calculating motion. Note: The Animation option does not!

Activity: LINKAGE Assembly-Basic Motion

Insert a Rotary Motor using the Motion Study tab.

328) Click the **Motion Study 1** tab located in the bottom left corner of the Graphics window. The MotionManager is displayed.

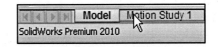

329) Select **Basic Motion** for Type of study from the MotionManager drop-down menu as illustrated.

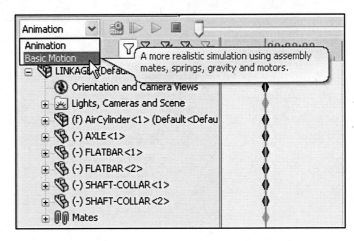

330) Click **Motor** from the MotionManager. The Motor PropertyManager is displayed.

331) Click the **Rotary Motor** box.

332) Click the **FLATBAR front face** as illustrated. A red Rotary Motor icon is displayed. The red direction arrow points counterclockwise.

333) Enter **150 RPM** for speed in the Motion box.

334) Click **OK** from the Motor PropertyManager.

Record the Simulation.

335) Click **Calculate**. The FLATBAR rotates in a counterclockwise direction for a set period of time.

336) Click **Play**. View the simulation.

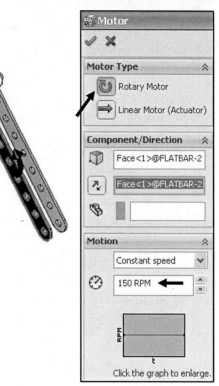

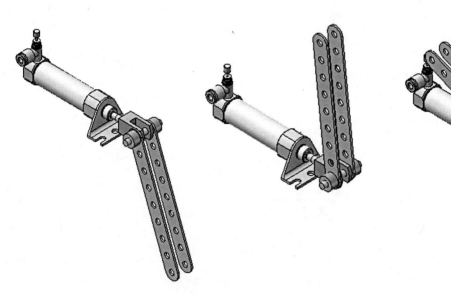

Linear Assembly Basic Simulation

Save the simulation in an AVI file to the SW-
TUTORIAL-2010 folder.

337) Click **Save Animation**.

338) Click **Save** from the Save Animation to File
dialog box. View your options.

339) Click **OK** from the Video Compression
box.

Close the Motion Study and return to
SolidWorks.

340) Click the **Model** tab location in the
bottom left corner of the Graphics
window.

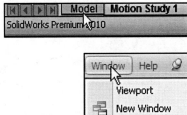

Fit the assembly to the Graphics window.

341) Press the **f** key.

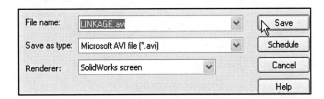

Save the LINKAGE assembly.

342) Click **Save** 💾.

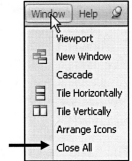

Exit SolidWorks.

343) Click **Windows**, **Close All** from the Menu bar.

The LINKAGE assembly chapter is complete.

 Review the Motion Study

The Rotary Motor Basic Motion tool combined Mates and Physical Dynamics to rotate
the FLATBAR components in the LINKAGE assembly. The Rotary Motor was applied
to the front face of the FLATBAR. You utilized the Calculate option to play the
simulation. You saved the simulation in an .AVI file.

Additional details on Motion Study, Assembly, mates, and Simulation are available
in SolidWorks Help. Keywords: Motion Study and Basic Motion.

Chapter Summary

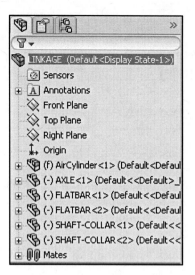

In this chapter, you created three parts (AXLE, SHAFT-COLLAR and FLATBAR), copied the AirCylinder assembly from the CD in the book and created the LINKAGE assembly.

You developed an understanding of the SolidWorks User Interface: Menus, Toolbars, Task Pane, CommandManager, FeatureManager, System feedback icons, Document Properties, Parts and Assemblies.

You created 2D sketches and addressed the three key states of a sketch: *Fully Defined*, *Over Defined* and *Under Defined*. Note: Always review your FeatureManager for the proper Sketch state.

You obtained the knowledge of the following SolidWorks features: Extruded Boss/Base, Extruded Cut, and Linear Pattern. Features are the building blocks of parts. The Extruded Boss/Base feature required a Sketch plane, sketch, and depth.

The Extruded Boss/Base feature added material to a part. The Boss-Extruded1 feature was utilized in the AXLE, SHAFT-COLLAR and FLATBAR parts.

The Extruded Cut feature removed material from the part. The Extruded Cut feature was utilized to create a hole in the SHAFT-COLLAR and FLATBAR parts. Note: Both were Through All holes. We will address the Hole Wizard later in the book.

The Linear Pattern feature was utilized to create an array of holes in the FLATBAR part.

When parts are inserted into an assembly, they are called components. You created the LINKAGE assembly by inserting the AirCylinder assembly, AXLE, SHAFT-COLLAR and FLATBAR parts.

Mates are geometric relationships that align and fit components in an assembly. Concentric, Coincident and Parallel mates were utilized to assemble the components.

You created a Motion Study. The Rotary Motor Basic Motion tool combined Mates and Physical Dynamics to rotate the FLATBAR components in the LINKAGE assembly.

During the initial SolidWorks installation, you are requested to select either the ISO or ANSI drafting standard. ISO is typically a European drafting standard and uses First Angle Projection. The book is written using the ANSI (US) overall drafting standard and Third Angle Projection for drawings.

Chapter Terminology

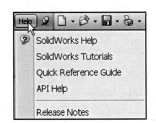

Utilize SolidWorks Help for additional information on the terms utilized in this chapter.

Assembly: An assembly is a document which contains parts, features, and other sub-assemblies. When a part is inserted into an assembly it is called a component. Components are mated together. The filename extension for a SolidWorks assembly file name is .SLDASM.

Component: A part or sub-assembly within an assembly.

Cursor Feedback: Feedback is provided by a symbol attached to the cursor arrow indicating your selection. As the cursor floats across the model, feedback is provided in the form of symbols, riding next to the cursor.

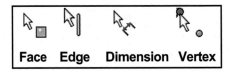

Dimension: A value indicating the size of feature geometry.

Drafting Standard: A set of drawing and detailing options developed by national and international organizations. The Dimensioning standard options are: ANSI, ISO, DIN, JIS, BSI, GOST and GB.

Features: Features are geometry building blocks. Features add or remove material. Features are created from sketched profiles or from edges and faces of existing geometry.

Instance Number: The instance number increments every time you insert the same component or mate. If you delete a component or mate and then reinsert the component or mate in the same SolidWorks session, the instance number increments by one.

Mates: A mate is a geometric relationship between components in an assembly.

Mouse Buttons: The left and right mouse buttons have distinct meanings in SolidWorks. Left mouse button is utilized to select geometry. Right-mouse button is utilized to invoke commands.

Part: A part is a single 3D object made up of features. The filename extension for a SolidWorks part file name is .SLDPRT.

Plane: To create a sketch, select a plane. Planes are flat and infinite. They are represented on the screen with visible edges. The reference plane for this project is the Front Plane.

Relation: A relation is a geometric constraint between sketch entities or between a sketch entity and a plane, axis, edge, or vertex.

Sketch: The name to describe a 2D profile is called a sketch. 2D Sketches are created on flat faces and planes within the model. Typical geometry types are lines, arcs, rectangles, circles, polygons and ellipses.

Status of a Sketch: Three states are utilized in this chapter. *Fully Defined*: has complete information (dimensions and geometric relations) displayed in Black; *Over Defined*: has duplicate information (dimensions or geometric relations) displayed in Red/Yellow; or *Under Defined*: there is inadequate definition (dimensions or geometric relations) displayed in Blue and Black.

Toolbars: The toolbar menus provide shortcuts enabling you to quickly access the most frequently used commands.

Trim Entities: Deletes selected sketched geometry. Extends a sketch segment unit it is coincident with another entity.

Units: Used in the measurement of physical quantities. Millimeter dimensioning and decimal inch dimensioning are the two types of common units specified for engineering parts and drawings.

Chapter Features

Extruded Boss/Base: An Extruded Boss/Base (Boss-Extrude1) feature is the first feature in a part. The Extruded Boss/Base feature starts with either a 2D or 3D sketch. The Extruded Boss/Base feature adds material by extrusion. Steps to create an Extruded Boss/Base Feature:

- Select the Sketch plane; Sketch the profile; Add needed dimensions and Geometric relations; Select Extruded Boss/Base from the Features toolbar; Select an End Condition and/or options; Enter a depth; Click OK from the Boss-Extrude PropertyManager.

Extruded Cut: The Extruded Cut feature removes material from a solid. The Extruded Cut feature performs the opposite function of the Extruded Boss/Base feature. The Extruded Cut feature starts with either a 2D or 3D sketch and removes material by extrusion. Steps to create an Extruded Cut Feature:

- Select the Sketch plane; Sketch the profile, Add Dimensions and Relations; Select Extruded Cut from the Features toolbar; Select an End Condition and/or options; Enter a depth; Click OK from the Cut-Extrude PropertyManager.

Linear Pattern: A Linear Pattern repeats features or geometry in an array. A Linear Patten requires the number of instances and the spacing between instances. Steps to create a Linear Pattern Feature:

- Select the features to repeat; Select Linear Pattern from the Feature toolbar; Enter Direction of the pattern; Enter Number of pattern instances in each direction; Enter Distance between pattern instances; Optional: Pattern instances to skip; Click OK from the Linear Pattern PropertyManager.

Engineering Journal

Engineers and designers utilize mathematics, science, economics and history to calculate additional information about a project. Answers to questions are written in an engineering journal.

1. Volume of a cylinder is provided by the formula, $V = \pi r^2 h$. Where:

- V is volume.

- r is the radius.

- h is the height.

a) Determine the radius of the AXLE in mm.

b) Determine the height of the AXLE in mm.

c) Calculate the Volume of the AXLE in mm^3.

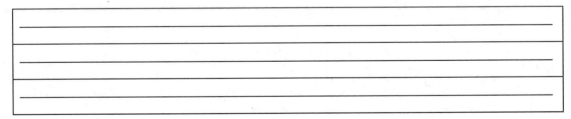

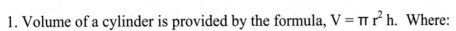

2. Density of a material is provided by the formula: $\rho = m/V$. Where:

   - ρ is density.

   - m is mass.

   - V is volume.

a) Determine the mass of the AXLE in grams if the AXLE is manufactured from hardened steel. The density of hardened steel is .007842 g/mm^3.

> _____
>
> _____

3. The material supplier catalog lists Harden Steel Rod in foot lengths.

Harden Steel Rod (Ø 3/16):		
Part Number:	Length:	Cost:
23-123-1	1 ft	$10.00
23-123-2	2 ft	$18.00
23-123-3	3 ft	$24.00

Utilize the table above to determine the following questions:

How many 1-3/8 inch AXLES can be cut from each steel rod?

Twenty AXLE parts are required for a new assembly. What length of Harden Steel Rod should be purchased?

> _____
>
> _____
>
> _____
>
> _____
>
> _____

4. Air is a gas. Boyle's Law states that with constant temperature, the pressure, P of a given mass of a gas is inversely proportional to its volume, V.

   • $P_1 / P_2 = V_2 / V_1$

   • $P_1 \times V_1 = P_2 \times V_2$

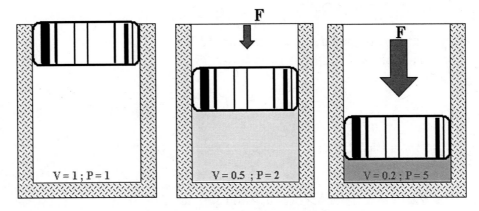

Illustration of Boyle's Law
Courtesy of SMC Corporation of America

The pressure in a closed container is doubled. How will the volume of air inside the container be modified?

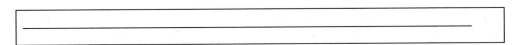

Robert Boyle (1627-1691) was an Irish born, English scientist, natural philosopher and a founder of modern chemistry. Boyle utilized experiments and the scientific method to test his theories. Along with his student, Robert Hooke (1635-1703), Boyle developed the air pump.

Research other contributions made by Robert Boyle and Robert Hooke that are utilized today.

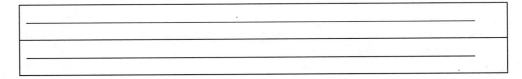

Questions

1. Explain the steps in starting a SolidWorks session.

2. Describe the procedure to begin a new 2D sketch.

3. Explain the steps required to modify part unit dimensions from inches to millimeters.

4. Describe the procedure to create a simple 3D part with an Extruded Boss/Base (Boss-Extrude1) feature.

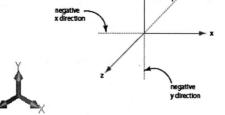

5. Identify the three default Reference planes.

6. Describe a Base feature? Provide two examples from this chapter.

7. Describe the differences between an Extruded Boss/Base feature and an Extruded Cut feature.

8. The sketch color black indicates a sketch is _____ defined.

9. The sketch color blue indicates a sketch is _____ defined.

10. The sketch color red indicates a sketch is _____ defined.

11. Describe the procedure to "wake up" a centerpoint.

12. Define a Geometric relation. Provide an example.

13. Describe the procedure to create a Linear Pattern feature.

14. Describe an assembly or sub-assembly.

15. What are mates and why are they important in assembling components?

16. In an assembly, each component has_____# degrees of freedom? Name them.

17. True or False. A fixed component cannot move in an assembly.

18. Review the Design Intent section in the book. Identify how you incorporated design intent into the parts and assembly.

Exercises

Exercise 1.1: Identify the Sketch plane for the Boss-Extrude1 (Base) feature as illustrated. Simplify the number of features!

A: Top Plane

B: Front Plane

C: Right Plane

D: Left Plane

Correct answer _____.

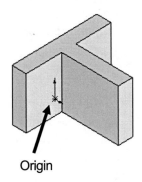

Origin

Create the part. Dimensions are arbitrary.

Exercise 1.2: Identify the Sketch plane for the Boss-Extrude1 (Base) feature as illustrated. Simplify the number of features!

A: Top Plane

B: Front Plane

C: Right Plane

D: Left Plane

Correct answer _____.

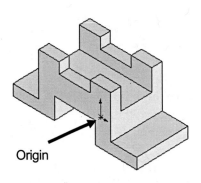

Origin

Create the part. Dimensions are arbitrary.

Exercise 1.3: Identify the Sketch plane for the Boss-Extrude1 (Base) feature as illustrated. Simplify the number of features!

A: Top Plane

B: Front Plane

C: Right Plane

D: Left Plane

Correct answer _____.

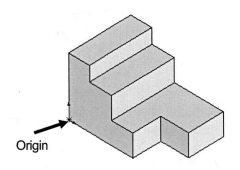

Origin

Create the part. Dimensions are arbitrary.

Exercise 1.4: FLATBAR - 3HOLE Part

Create an ANSI, IPS FLATBAR - 3HOLE part.

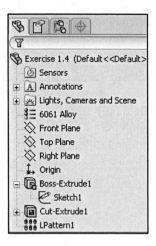

- Utilize the Front Plane for the Sketch plane. Insert an Extruded Base (Boss-Extrude1) feature. No Tangent Edges displayed.

- Create an Extruded Cut feature. This is your seed feature. Apply the Linear Pattern feature. The FLATBAR - 3HOLE part is manufactured from 0.06in., [1.5mm] 6061 Alloy.

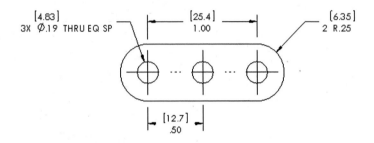

Exercise 1.5: FLATBAR - 5HOLE Part

Create an ANSI, IPS, FLATBAR - 5HOLE part as illustrated.

- Utilize the Front Plane for the Sketch plane. Insert an Extruded Base (Boss-Extrude1) feature.

- Create an Extruded Cut feature. This is your seed feature. Apply the Linear Pattern feature. The FLATBAR - 5HOLE part is manufactured from 0.06in, [1.5mm] 6061 Alloy.

- Calculate the required dimensions for the FLATBAR - 5HOLE part. Use the following information: Holes are .500in. on center, Radius is .250in., and Hole diameter is .190in.

- No Tangent Edges displayed.

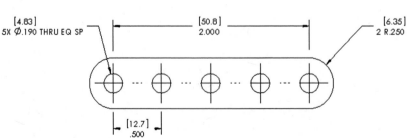

Exercise 1.6: Simple Block Part

Create the illustrated ANSI part. Note the location of the Origin in the illustration.

- Calculate the overall mass of the illustrated model.

- Apply the Mass Properties tool.

- Think about the steps that you would take to build the model.

- Review the provided information carefully.

- Units are represented in the IPS, (inch, pound, second) system.

- A = 3.50in, B = .70in

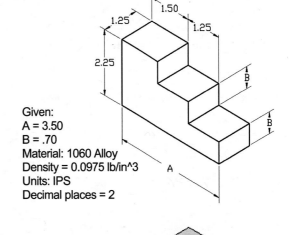

Given:
A = 3.50
B = .70
Material: 1060 Alloy
Density = 0.0975 lb/in^3
Units: IPS
Decimal places = 2

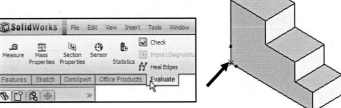

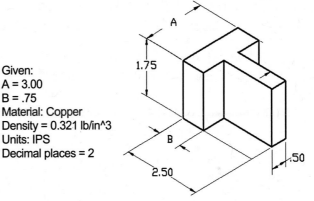

Exercise 1.7: Simple Block Part

Create the illustrated ANSI part. Note the location of the Origin in the illustration.

Create the sketch symmetric about the Front Plane. The Front Plane in this problem is **not** your Sketch Plane. Utilize the Blind End Condition in Direction 1.

Given:
A = 3.00
B = .75
Material: Copper
Density = 0.321 lb/in^3
Units: IPS
Decimal places = 2

- Calculate the overall mass of the illustrated model.

- Apply the Mass Properties tool.

- Think about the steps that you would take to build the model.

- Review the provided information carefully. Units are represented in the IPS, (inch, pound, second) system.

- A = 3.00in, B = .75in

- Note: Sketch1 is symmetrical.

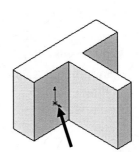

Exercise 1.8: Simple Block Part

Create an ANSI part from the illustrated model. Note the location of the Origin in the illustration.

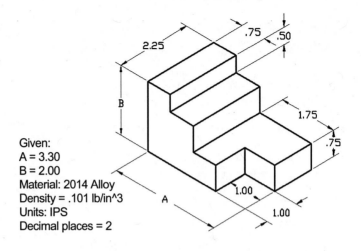

- Calculate the volume of the part and locate the Center of mass with the provided information.

  Given:
  A = 3.30
  B = 2.00
  Material: 2014 Alloy
  Density = .101 lb/in^3
  Units: IPS
  Decimal places = 2

- Apply the Mass Properties tool.

- Think about the steps that you would take to build the model.

- Review the provided information carefully.

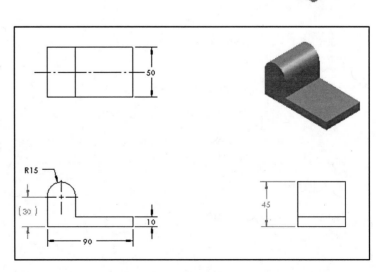

Exercise 1.9: Simple Block Part

Create an ANSI, MMGS part from the illustrated drawing: Front, Top, Right and Isometric views.

Note: The location of the Origin in the illustration. The drawing views are displayed in Third Angle Projection.

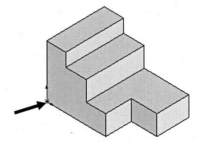

- Apply 1060 Alloy for material.

- Calculate the Volume of the part.

- Locate the Center of mass.

- Think about the steps that you would take to build the model. The part is symmetric about the Front Plane.

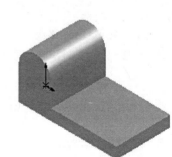

Exercise 1.10: Simple Block Part

Create the ANSI, MMGS part from the illustrated drawing: Front, Top, Right and Isometric views.

- Apply 1060 Alloy for material.

- The part is symmetric about the Front Plane.

- Calculate the Volume of the part and locate the Center of mass.

- Think about the steps that you would take to build the model.

- The drawing views are displayed in Third Angle Projection.

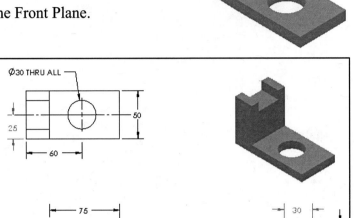

Exercise 1.11: LINKAGE-2 Assembly

Create the LINKAGE-2 assembly.

- Open the LINKAGE assembly. If required, set the LINKAGE assembly to (**Set Lightweight to Resolved**).

- Select Save As from the Menu bar.

- Check the Save as copy check box.

- Enter LINKAGE-2 for file name. LINKAGE-2 ASSEMBLY for description.

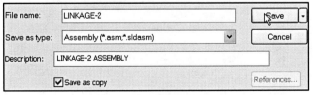

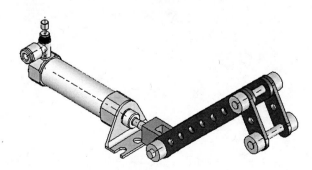

The FLATBAR-3HOLE part was created in
Exercise 1.1. Utilize two AXLE parts, four SHAFT
COLLAR parts, and two FLATBAR-3HOLE parts
to create the LINKAGE-2 assembly as illustrated.

- Insert the first AXLE part.

- Insert a Concentric mate.

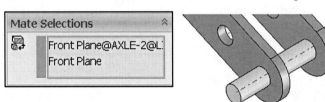

- Insert a Coincident mate.

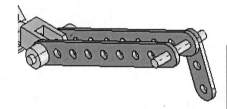

- Insert the first FLATBAR-3HOLE part.

- Insert a Concentric
  mate.

- Insert a Coincident
  mate.

- Perform the same
  procedure for the
  second FLATBAR-
  3HOLE part.

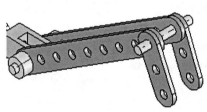

- Insert a Parallel mate
  between the 2
  FLATBAR-3HOLE
  parts. Note: The 2
  FLATBAR-3HOLE
  parts move together.

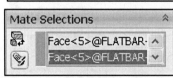

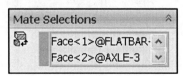

- Insert the second AXLE part.

- Insert a Concentric mate.

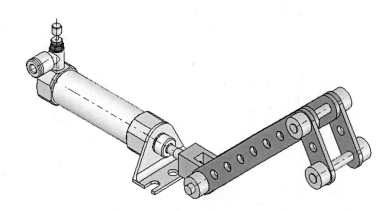

- Insert a Coincident mate.

- Insert the first SHAFT-COLLAR part.

- Insert a Concentric mate.

- Insert a Coincident mate.

- Perform the same tasks to insert the other three required SHAFT-COLLAR parts as illustrated.

Exercise 1.12: LINKAGE-2 Assembly Motion Study

Create a Motion Study using the LINKAGE-2 Assembly that was created in the previous exercise.

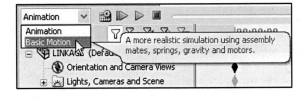

- Create a Basic Motion Study.

- Apply a Rotary Motor to the front FLATBAR-3HOLE as illustrated.

- Play and Save the Simulation.

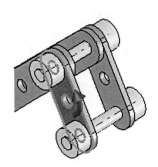

Exercise 1.13: ROCKER Assembly

Create a ROCKER assembly. The ROCKER assembly consists of two AXLE parts, two FLATBAR-5HOLE parts, and two FLATBAR-3HOLE parts.

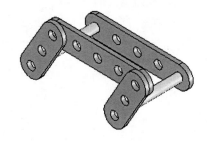

The FLATBAR-3HOLE parts are linked together with the FLATBAR-5HOLE.

The three parts rotate clockwise and counterclockwise, above the Top Plane. Create the ROCKER assembly.

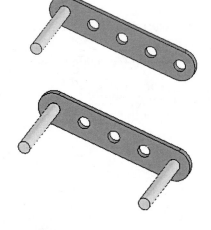

- Insert the first FLATBAR-5HOLE part. The FLATBAR-5HOLE is fixed to the Origin of the ROCKER assembly.

- Insert the first AXLE part.

- Insert a Concentric mate.

- Insert a Coincident mate.

- Insert the second AXLE part.

- Insert a Concentric mate.

- Insert a Coincident mate.

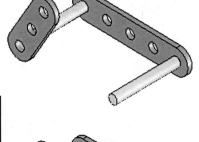

- Insert the first FLATBAR-3HOLE part.

- Insert a Concentric mate.

- Insert a Coincident mate.

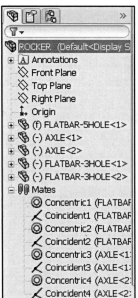

- Insert the second FLATBAR-3HOLE part.

- Insert a Concentric mate.

- Insert a Coincident mate.

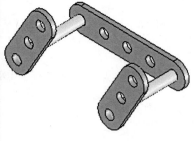

- Insert the second FLATBAR-5HOLE part.

- Insert the required mates.

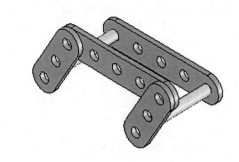

Note: The end holes of the second FLATBAR-5HOLE are concentric with the end holes of the FLATBAR-3HOLE parts.

Note: In mechanical design, the ROCKER assembly is classified as a mechanism. A Four-Bar Linkage is a common mechanism comprised of four links.

Link1 is called the Frame.

The AXLE part is Link1.

Link2 and Link4 are called the Cranks.

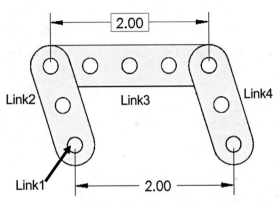

The FLATBAR-3HOLE parts are Link2 and Link4. Link3 is called the Coupler. The FLATBAR-5HOLE part is Link3.

If an assembly or component is loaded in a Lightweight state, right-click the **assembly name** or **component name** from the FeatureManager. Click **Set Lightweight to Resolved**.

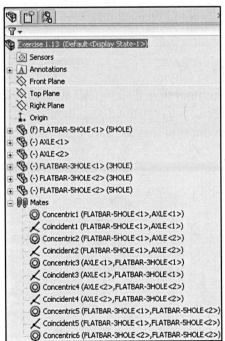

Exercise 1.14: Industry Application

Engineers and designers develop a variety of products utilizing SolidWorks.

Model information is utilized to create plastic molds for products from toys to toothbrushes.

- Utilize the World Wide Web and review the following web sites: mikejwilson.com and zxys.com.

The models obtained from these web sites are for educational purposes only.

Learn modeling techniques from others; create your own designs. A common manufacturing procedure for plastic parts is named the Injection Molding Process. Today's automobiles utilize over 50% plastic components.

Engineers and designers work with mold makers to produce plastic parts. Cost reduction drives plastic part production.

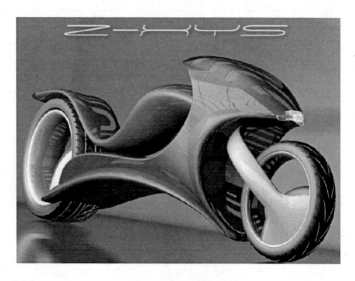

Model Courtesy of
Mike J. Wilson,
CSWP

Chapter 2

FRONT-SUPPORT Assembly

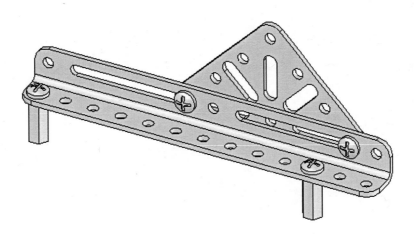

Below are the desired outcomes and usage competencies based on the completion of Chapter 2.

Desired Outcomes:	Usage Competencies:

• Create four parts:
 	
  o HEX-STANDOFF
 	
  o ANGLE-13HOLE
 	
  o TRIANGLE
 	
  o SCREW
	• Apply the following model features: Extruded Boss/Base, Extruded Thin, Extruded Cut, Revolved Boss/Base, Hole Wizard, Linear Pattern, Circular Pattern, Mirror, Fillet and Chamfer.
	
	• Apply sketch techniques with various sketch tools and Construction geometry.

• Create an assembly: o FRONT-SUPPORT assembly	• Comprehend the assembly process and insert the following Standard mate types: Concentric, Coincident, Parallel and Distance.

Notes:

Chapter 2 - FRONT-SUPPORT Assembly

Chapter Objective

Create four new parts utilizing the Top, Front and Right Planes. Determine the Sketch plane for each feature. Obtain the knowledge of the following SolidWorks features: *Extruded Boss/Base, Extruded Thin, Extruded Cut, Revolved Boss/Base, Hole Wizard, Linear Pattern, Circular Pattern, Fillet* and *Chamfer*.

Apply sketch techniques with various Sketch tools: *Line, Circle, Corner Rectangle, Centerline, Dynamic Mirror, Straight Slot, Trim Entities, Polygon, Tangent Arc, Sketch Fillet, Offset Entities* and *Convert Entities*.

Utilize centerlines as construction geometry to reference dimensions and relationships.

Create four new parts:

1. HEX-STANDOFF
2. ANGLE-13HOLE
3. TRIANGLE
4. SCREW

Create the FRONT-SUPPORT assembly.

On the completion of this chapter, you will be able to:

- Select the correct Sketch plane.
- Generate a 2D sketch.
- Insert the required dimensions and Geometric relations.
- Apply the following SolidWorks features:
    - Extruded Boss/Base
    - Extruded Cut
    - Extruded Thin
    - Revolved Base
    - Linear and Circular Pattern
    - Mirror
    - Fillet
    - Hole Wizard
    - Chamfer

Chapter Overview

The FRONT-SUPPORT assembly supports various pneumatic components and is incorporated into the PNEUMATIC-TEST-MODULE.

Create four new parts in this chapter:

1. HEX-STANDOFF

2. ANGLE-13HOLE

3. TRIANGLE

4. SCREW

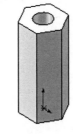

HEX-STANDOFF

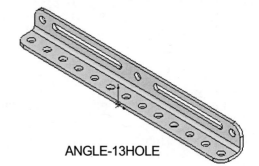

ANGLE-13HOLE

Create the FRONT-SUPPORT assembly using the four new created parts.

The FRONT-SUPPORT assembly is used in the exercises at the end of this chapter and in later chapters of the book.

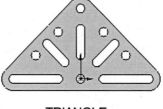

TRIANGLE

SCREW

🔅 To display the Origin, click **View**, **Origins** from the Menu bar menu.

🔅 Origin, Tangent Edges and Temporary Axis are displayed for educational purposes.

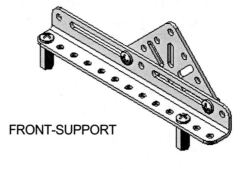

FRONT-SUPPORT

Reference Planes and Orthographic Projection

The three default ⊥ Reference planes represent infinite 2D planes in 3D space:

- Front
- Top
- Right

Planes have no thickness or mass.

Orthographic projection is the process of projecting views onto parallel planes with ⊥ projectors.

The default ⊥ datum planes are:

- Primary
- Secondary
- Tertiary

These are the planes used in manufacturing:

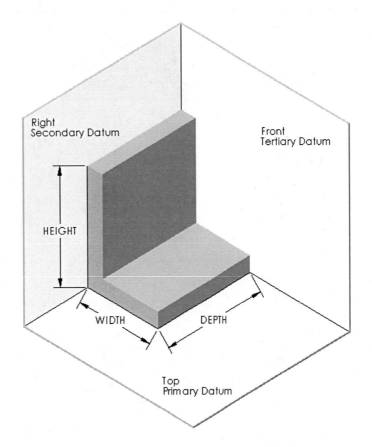

- Primary datum plane contacts the part at a minimum of three points.
- Secondary datum plane contacts the part at a minimum of two points.
- Tertiary datum plane contacts the part at a minimum of one point.

The part view orientation depends on the Base feature Sketch plane.

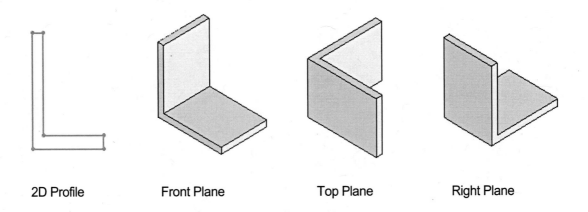

2D Profile   Front Plane   Top Plane   Right Plane

The part view orientation is dependent on the Base feature Sketch plane. Compare the available default Sketch planes in the FeatureManager: *Front Plane*, *Top Plane* and *Right Plane*.

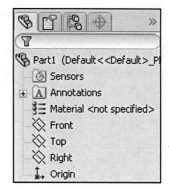

Each Boss-Extrude1 feature above was created with an L-shaped 2D Sketch profile. The six principle views of Orthographic projection listed in the ASME Y14.3M standard are:

- Top
- Front
- Right side
- Bottom
- Rear
- Left side

SolidWorks Standard view names correspond to these Orthographic projection view names.

ASME Y14.3M Principle View Name:	SolidWorks Standard View:
Front	Front
Top	Top
Right side	Right
Bottom	Bottom
Rear	Back
Left side	Left

The standard drawing views in Third Angle Orthographic projection are:

- Front
- Top
- Right
- Isometric

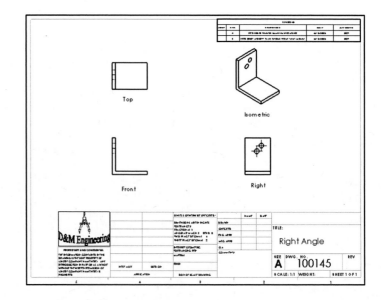

There are two Orthographic projection drawing systems. The first Orthographic projection system is called the Third Angle projection. The second Orthographic projection system is called the First Angle projection. The systems are derived from positioning a 3D object in the third or first quadrant.

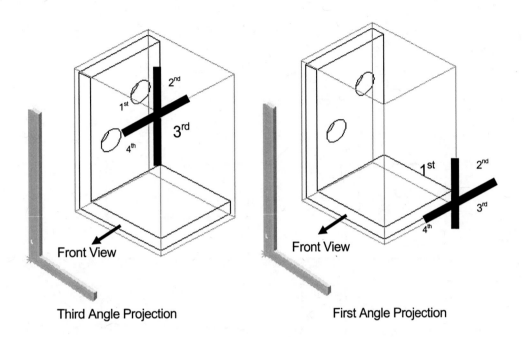

Third Angle Projection   First Angle Projection

Third Angle Projection

The part is positioned in the third quadrant in third angle projection. The 2D projection planes are located between the viewer and the part. The projected views are placed on a drawing.

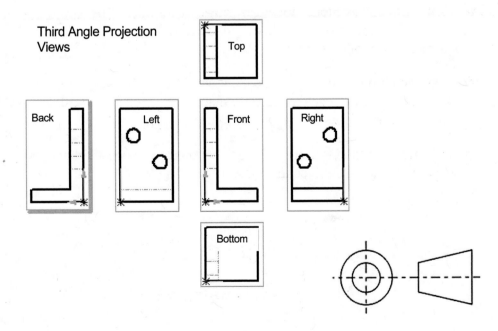

First Angle Projection

The part is positioned in the first quadrant in First Angle projection. Views are projected onto the planes located behind the part. The projected views are placed on a drawing. First Angle projection is primarily used in Europe and Asia.

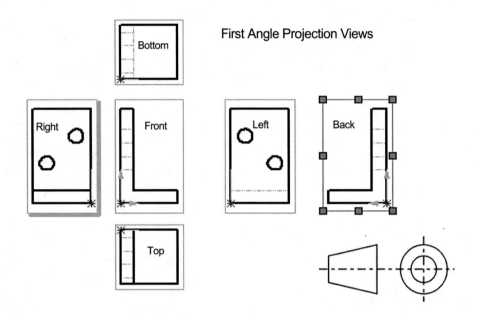

First Angle Projection Views

Third Angle projection is primarily used in the U.S. & Canada and is based on the ASME Y14.3M Multi and Sectional View Drawings standard. Designers should have knowledge and understanding of both systems.

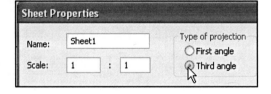

There are numerous multi-national companies.
Example: A part is designed in the U.S., manufactured in Japan and destined for a European market.

Third Angle projection is used in this text. A truncated cone symbol appears on the drawing to indicate the Projection System:

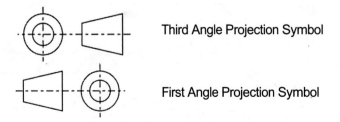

Third Angle Projection Symbol

First Angle Projection Symbol

Select the Sketch plane based on symmetry and orientation of the part in the FRONT-SUPPORT assembly. Utilize the standard views: *Front, Back, Right, Left, Top, Bottom* and *Isometric* to orient the part. Create the 2D drawings for the parts in Chapter 3.

HEX-STANDOFF Part

The HEX-STANDOFF part is a hexagonal shaped part utilized to elevate components in the FRONT-SUPPORT assembly. Machine screws are utilized to fasten components to the HEX-STANDOFF.

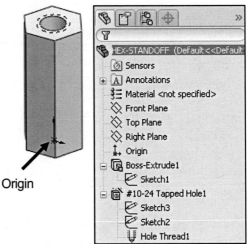

Origin

Create the HEX-STANDOFF part with the Extruded Boss/Base feature. The Sketch plane for the HEX-STANDOFF Boss-Extrude1 feature is the Top Plane.

Create the HEX-STANDOFF in the orientation utilized by the FRONT-SUPPORT assembly.

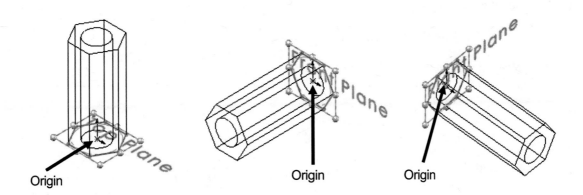

Origin   Origin   Origin

 Note the location of the Origin in the models.

 All Sketches should be fully defined in the FeatureManager.

The Boss-Extrude1 feature sketch consists of two profiles. The first sketch is a circle centered at the Origin on the Top Plane.

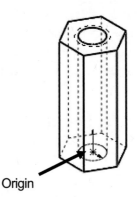

The second sketch is a polygon with 6 sides centered at the Origin. The polygon utilizes an inscribed circle to construct the geometry.

Geometric relations are constraints that control the size and position of the sketch entities. Apply a Horizontal relation in the polygon sketch.

Origin

Extrude the sketch perpendicular to the Top Plane. Utilize the Edit Sketch tool to modify the sketch.

The Hole Wizard feature creates complex and simple Hole features. Utilize the Hole Wizard feature to create a Tapped Hole.

The Tapped Hole depth and diameter are based on drill size and screw type parameters. Apply a Coincident relation to position the Tapped Hole aligned with the Origin.

Activity: HEX-STANDOFF Part-Extruded Boss/Base Feature

Create a new part.

1) Click **New** ⬜ from the Menu bar. The Templates tab is the default tab. Part is the default template from the New SolidWorks Document dialog box.

2) Double-click **Part**. The Part FeatureManager is displayed.

Set the dimensioning standard and part units.

3) Click **Options** 🖹, **Document Properties** tab from the Menu bar.

4) Select **ANSI** from the Overall drafting standard box.

Set units and decimal places.

5) Click **Units**.

6) Select **IPS**, **[MMGS]** for Unit system.

7) Select **.123**, **[.12]** for Length units Decimal places.

8) Select **None** for Angular units Decimal places.

9) Click **OK**. The Part FeatureManager is displayed.

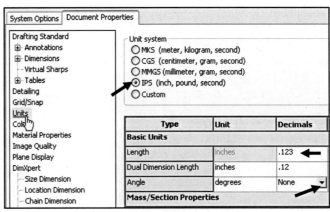
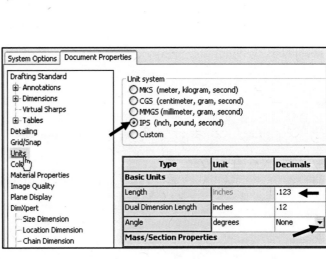

The primary units are provided in IPS, (inch, pound, seconds). The optional secondary units are provided in MMGS, (millimeter, gram, second) and are indicated in brackets [ ]. Illustrations are provided in inches and millimeters.

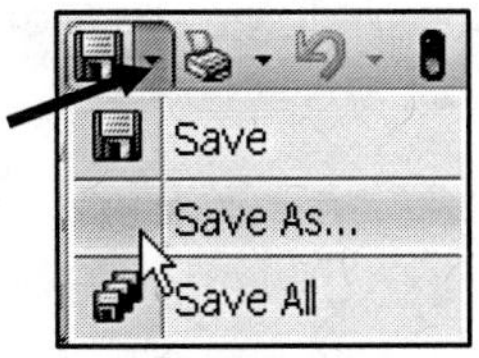

Save the part.

10) Click **Save As** from the Menu bar.

11) Select the **SW-TUTORIAL-2010** folder. Enter **HEX-STANDOFF** for File name.

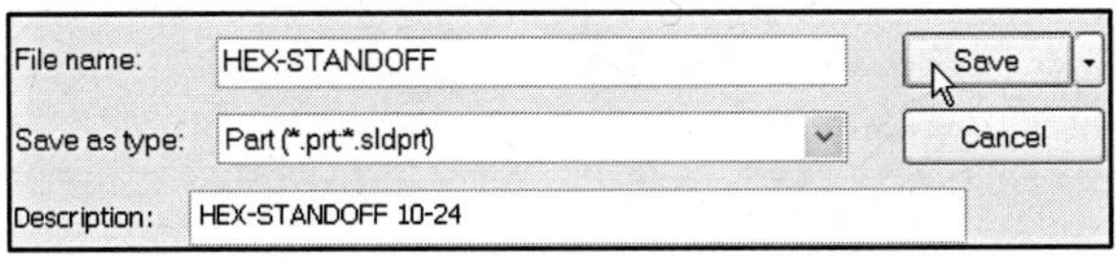

12) Enter **HEX-STANDOFF 10-24** for Description.

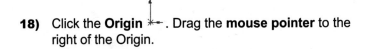

13) Click **Save**. The HEX-STANDOFF FeatureManager is displayed.

Select the Sketch plane.

14) Right-click **Top Plane** from the FeatureManager. This is the Sketch plane.

Insert a Boss-Extrude1 feature (Base feature) sketched on the Top Plane. Note: A plane is an infinite 2D area. The blue boundary is for visual reference.

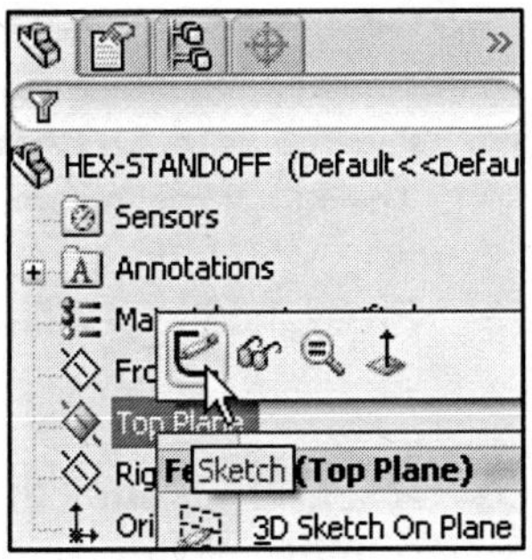

Insert a new sketch.

15) Click **Sketch** from the Context toolbar. The Sketch toolbar is displayed.

16) Click the **Circle** Sketch tool. The Circle PropertyManager is displayed.

17) Drag the **mouse pointer** into the Graphics window. The cursor displays the Circle icon.

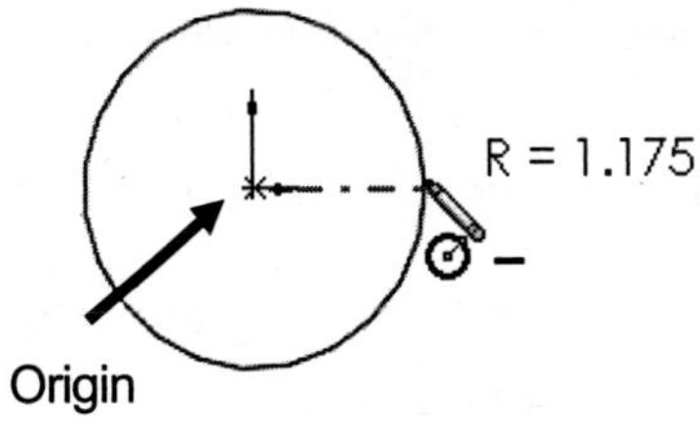

18) Click the **Origin**. Drag the **mouse pointer** to the right of the Origin.

19) Click a **position** to create the circle as illustrated.

Insert a Polygon.

20) Click the **Polygon** Sketch tool. The Polygon PropertyManager is displayed. The cursor displays the Polygon icon.

21) Click the **Origin** as illustrated.

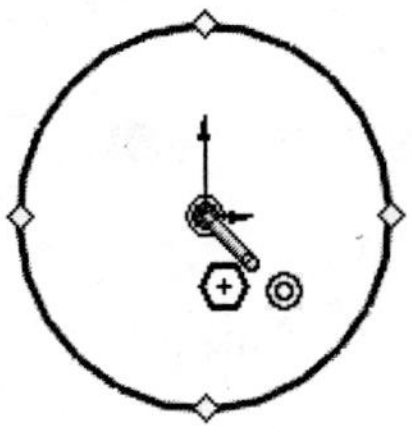

22) Drag the **mouse pointer** horizontally to the right.

23) Click a **position** to the right of the circle to create the hexagon as illustrated.

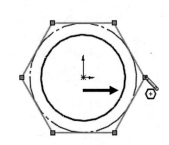

Add a dimension.

24) Click the **Smart Dimension** Sketch tool.

25) Click the **circumference** of the first circle.

26) Click a **position** diagonally above the hexagon to locate the dimension.

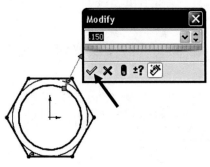

27) Enter **.150**in, **[3.81]** in the Modify box.

28) Click the **Green Check mark** in the Modify dialog box.

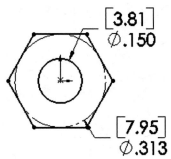

29) Click the **circumference** of the inscribed circle.

30) Click a **position** diagonally below the hexagon to locate the dimension. Enter **.313**in, **[7.95]** in the Modify box.

31) Click the **Green Check mark** in the Modify dialog box. The black sketch is fully defined.

32) Press the **f** key to fit the model to the Graphics window.

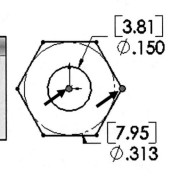

If required, click the arrow head dot to toggle the direction of the dimension arrow.

33) Click **OK** from the Dimension PropertyManager.

Add a Horizontal relation.

34) Click the **Origin** . Hold the **Ctrl** key down.

35) Click the right most **point** of the hexagon as illustrated. The Properties PropertyManager is displayed.

36) Release the **Ctrl** key. Click **Horizontal** from the Add Relations box.

37) Click **OK** from the Properties PropertyManager.

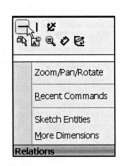

You can also right-click and click **Make Horizontal** from the Context toolbar.

Extrude the sketch.

38) Click the **Features** tab in the CommandManager.

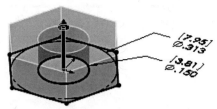

39) Click **Extruded Boss/Base** from the Features toolbar. The Boss-Extrude PropertyManager is displayed. Blind is the default End Condition in Direction1. The direction arrow points upward.

40) Enter **.735**in, **[18.67]** for Depth.

41) Click **OK** from the Boss-Extrude PropertyManager. Boss-Extrude1 is displayed in the FeatureManager.

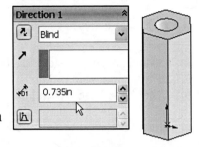

Fit the model to the Graphics window.

42) Press the **f** key.

The Boss-Extrude1 feature (Base feature) was sketched on the Top Plane. Changes occur in the design process. Edit the sketch of Boss-Extrude1. Delete the circle and close the sketch. Apply the Hole Wizard feature to create a Tapped Hole.

Edit Sketch1

43) **Expand** Boss-Extrude1 in the FeatureManager.

44) Right-click **Sketch1** in the FeatureManager.

45) Click **Edit Sketch** from the Context toolbar.

Delete the inside circle.

46) Click the **circumference** of the inside circle as illustrated. The Circle PropertyManager is displayed.

47) Press the **Delete** key.

48) Click **Yes** to the Sketcher Confirm Delete message. Both the circle geometry and its dimension are deleted.

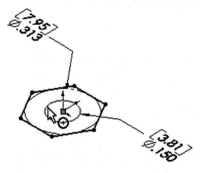

Save and close the sketch.

49) Click **Save** .

50) Click **OK** to Rebuild. The Boss-Extrude1 feature is updated. Note: Sketch1 is fully defined.

Fit the model to the Graphics window.

51) Press the **f** key.

Activity: HEX-STANDOFF Part-Hole Wizard Feature

Insert a Tapped Hole with the Hole Wizard feature tool. Create a 2D Sketch.

52) Click the **top face** of Boss-Extrude1 in the Graphics window as illustrated. Click **Hidden Lines Visible** ⬚ from the Heads-up View toolbar.

53) Click **Hole Wizard** 🔘 from the Features toolbar. The Hole Specification PropertyManager is displayed.

Note: For metric, utilize ANSI Metric and M5x0.8 for size.

54) Click **Straight Tap** for Hole Specification.

55) Select **Ansi Inch**, [**Ansi Metric**] for Standard.

56) Select **Bottoming Tapped Hole** for Type.

57) Select **#10-24**, [**Ø5**] for Size.

58) Select **Through All** for End Condition.

59) Click the **Cosmetic thread** box. Accept the default conditions.

60) Click the **Positions** tab.

The Tapped Hole is displayed in yellow. Yellow is a preview color. The Tap Hole center point is displayed in blue.

The Point ✏ Sketch tool is automatically selected. No other holes are required.

Utilize a Coincident relation to locate the center point of the Tapped Hole in the Top view. Note: the selected center point will vary depending on your original selection location on the face.

Add a Coincident relation.
61) Right-click **Select** to deselect the Point Sketch tool.

62) Click the **Origin** ⊥ as illustrated.

63) Hold the **Ctrl** key down.

64) Click the **blue center point** of the Tapped Hole. Note:This is the initial location were you clicked the top face of Boss-Extrude1. The Properties PropertyManager is displayed.

65) Release the **Ctrl** key.

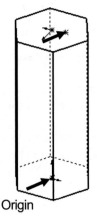

Origin

66) Click **Coincident** from the Add Relations box.

67) Click **OK** from the Properties PropertyManager.

68) Click **OK** from the Hole Position PropertyManager.

The #10-24 Tapped Hole1 feature is displayed in the
FeatureManager. Sketch3 determines the center point location
of the Tapped Hole. Sketch2 is the profile of the Tapped Hole.

Save the HEX-STANDOFF part.

69) Click **Shaded With Edges** from the
Heads-up View toolbar.

70) Click **inside** the Graphics window.

71) Click **Save** . The HEX-STANDOFF is
complete. View the Threads.

Origin

To view the thread, right-click the
Annotations folder; click Details. Check the Cosmetic thread
box and the Shaded cosmetic threads box. Click OK.

 Review the HEX-STANDOFF Part

The HEX-STANDOFF part utilized the Extruded Boss/Base feature. The Boss-Extrude1
feature required a sketch on the Top Plane. The first profile was a circle centered at the
Origin on the Top Plane. The second profile used the Polygon Sketch tool. You utilized
the Edit Sketch tool to modify the Sketch profile and to delete the circle.

The Hole Wizard feature created a Tapped Hole. The Hole Wizard feature required the
Boss-Extrude1 top face as the Sketch plane.

A Coincident relation located the center point of the Tapped Hole aligned with respect to
the Origin.

ANGLE-13HOLE Part

The ANGLE-13HOLE part is an L-shaped support
bracket. The ANGLE-13HOLE part is manufactured
from 0.090in, [2.3] aluminum.

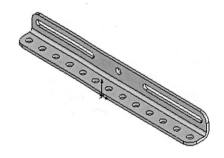

There ANGLE-13HOLE part contains fillets, holes,
and slot cuts.

Simplify the overall design into seven features.
Utilize symmetry and Linear Patterns.

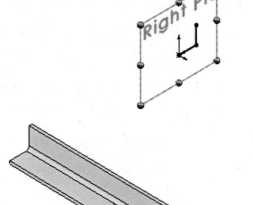

The open L-Shaped profile is sketched on the
Right Plane.

Utilize an Extruded Thin 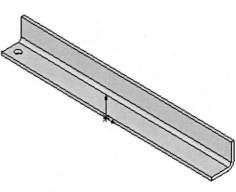 feature with the
Mid Plane option to locate the part symmetrical
to the Right Plane.

Insert the first Extruded Cut 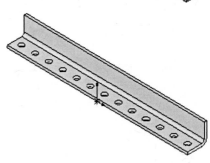 feature for the
first hole. This is the seed feature for the Linear
Pattern. The hole sketch is located on the top face
of the Extruded Thin feature.

Insert a Linear Pattern 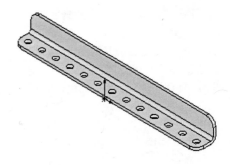 feature to create an array
of 13 holes along the bottom horizontal edge.

Insert a Fillet feature to round the four corners.

Origin, Tangent Edges and Temporary Axis are
displayed for educational purposes.

Insert the second Extruded Cut 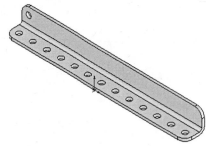 feature on the front face of the Extruded Thin feature. This is the seed feature for the second Linear Pattern.

Insert a Linear Pattern 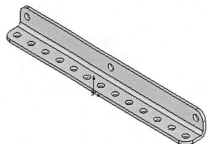 feature to create an array of 3 holes along the top horizontal edge.

Utilize the Sketch Mirror tool to create the slot profile. Use the Slot Sketch tool.

Insert the third Extruded Cut 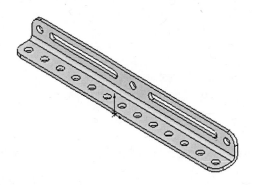 feature to create the two slots.

Select the Sketch plane for the Base feature that corresponds to the parts orientation in the assembly.

Activity: ANGLE-13HOLE Part-Documents Properties

Create a new part.

72) Click **New** ⬚ from the Menu bar. Part is the default template from the New SolidWorks Document dialog box.

73) Double-click **Part**. The Part FeatureManager is displayed.

Set the dimensioning standard and part units.

74) Click **Options** , **Document Properties** tab from the Menu bar.

75) Select **ANSI** from the Overall drafting standard drop-down menu.

76) Click **Units**.

77) Select **IPS**, [**MMGS**] for Unit system.

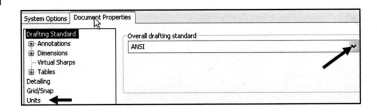

78) Select **.123**, **[.12]** for Length units Decimal places.

79) Select **None** for Angular units Decimal places.

80) Click **OK**.

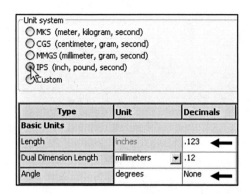

Save the part.
81) Click **Save As** from the Menu bar.

82) Select the **SW-TUTORIAL-2010** file folder.

83) Enter **ANGLE-13 HOLE** for File name. Enter **ANGLE BRACKET-13 HOLE** for Description.

84) Click **Save**. The ANGLE-13 Hole FeatureManager is displayed.

Activity: ANGLE-13HOLE Part-Extruded Thin Feature

Insert an Extruded Thin feature sketched on the Right Plane.

Select the Sketch plane.
85) Right-click **Right Plane** from the FeatureManager.

Sketch a horizontal line.
86) Click **Sketch** from the Context toolbar. The Sketch toolbar is displayed.

87) Click the **Line** Sketch tool from the Sketch toolbar.

88) Click the **Origin** as illustrated.

89) Click a **position** to the right of the Origin.

Sketch a vertical line.
90) Click a **position** directly above the right end point.

De-select the Line Sketch tool
91) Right-click **Select** in the Graphics window.

Origin

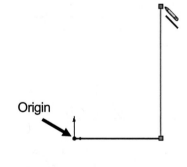

Add an Equal relation.
92) Click the **vertical** line. Hold the **Ctrl** key down.

93) Click the **horizontal line**.

94) Release the **Ctrl** key.

95) Right-click **Make Equal** from the Context toolbar.

96) Click **OK** from the Properties PropertyManager.

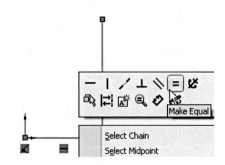

Add a dimension.

97) Click the **Smart Dimension** ✏ Sketch tool.

98) Click the **horizontal** line.

99) Click a **position** below the profile.

100) Enter .**700**in, [**17.78**] in the Modify box.

101) Click the **Green Check mark** ✔ . The black sketch is fully defined.

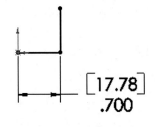

Save rebuild time. Add relations and dimensions to fully define a sketch. Fully defined sketches are displayed in black.

Extrude the sketch.

102) Click **Extruded Boss/Base** 🔲 from the Features toolbar. The Boss-Extrude PropertyManager is displayed.

103) Select **Mid Plane** for End Condition in Direction 1.

104) Enter **7.000**in, [**177.8**] for Depth. Note: Thin Feature is checked.

105) Click the **Reverse Direction Arrow** button for One-Direction. Material thickness is created above the Origin.

106) Enter .**090**in, [**2.3**] for Thickness.

107) Check the **Auto-fillet corners** box.

108) Enter .**090**in, [**2.3**] for Fillet Radius.

109) Click **OK** ✔ from the Boss-Extrude PropertyManager. Extrude-Thin1 is displayed in the FeatureManager. Sketch1 is fully defined.

Fit the model to the Graphics window.
110) Press the **f** key.

Origin

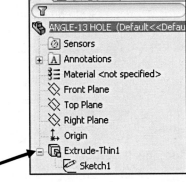

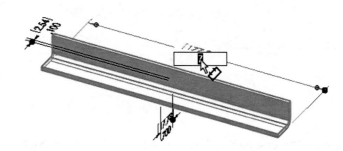

Clarify the Extrude-Thin1 feature direction and thickness options. Utilize multiple view orientations and Zoom In before selecting OK ✔ from the Boss-Extrude PropertyManager.

Modify feature dimensions.

111) Click **Extrude-Thin1** in the FeatureManager.

112) Click the **7.000**in, [**177.80**] dimension in the Graphics window.

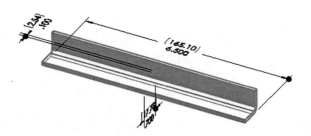

113) Enter **6.500**in, [**165.10**].

114) Click **inside** the Graphics window.

Save the model.

115) Click **Save** 💾.

Activity: ANGLE-13HOLE Part-Extruded Cut Feature

Insert a new sketch for the Extruded Cut feature.

116) Right-click the **top face** of Extrude-Thin1 as illustrated. This is the Sketch plane.

117) Click **Sketch** ✏️ from the Context toolbar. The Sketch toolbar is displayed.

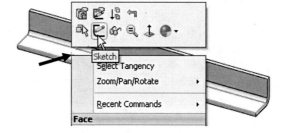

118) Click **Top view** 🔲 from the Heads-up View toolbar.

119) Click the **Circle** ⊙ Sketch tool.

120) Sketch a **circle** on the left side of the Origin as illustrated.

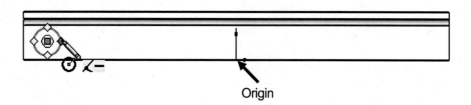

Origin

Add dimensions.

121) Click the **Smart Dimension** ⌀ Sketch tool.

122) Click the **Origin**  .

123) Click the **center point** of the circle.

124) Click a **position** below the horizontal profile line.

125) Enter **3.000**in, **[76.2]**.

126) Click the **Green Check mark**  .

127) Click the **bottom horizontal line**.

128) Click the **center point** of the circle.

129) Click a **position** to the left of the profile.

130) Enter **.250**in, **[6.35]**.

131) Click the **Green Check mark**  .

132) Create a diameter dimension. Click the **circumference** of the circle.

133) Click a **position** diagonally above the profile.

134) Enter **.190**in, **[4.83]**.

135) Click the **Green Check mark** 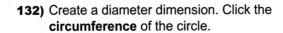 .

Insert an Extruded Cut Feature.

136) Click **Extruded Cut** 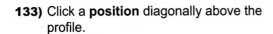 from the Features toolbar. The Cut-Extrude PropertyManager is displayed.

137) Select **Through All** for End Condition in Direction 1. Accept the default conditions.

138) Click **OK**  from the Cut-Extrude PropertyManager. Cut-Extrude1 is displayed in the FeatureManager. Cut-Extrude1 is the seed feature for the Linear Pattern feature of holes.

139) Click **Isometric view** 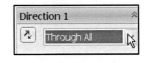 from the Heads-up View toolbar.

Save the model.

140) Click **Save**  .

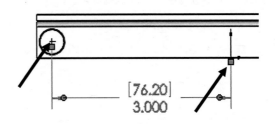

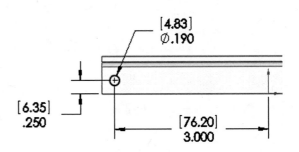

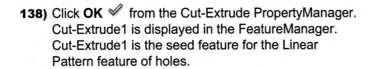

Activity: ANGLE-13HOLE Part-Linear Pattern Feature

Insert a Linear Pattern feature.

141) Click **Top View** 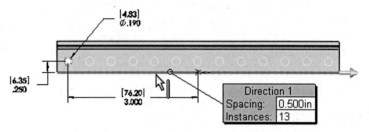 from the Heads-up View toolbar.

142) Click **Linear Pattern**
from the Features toolbar.
The Linear Pattern
PropertyManager is
displayed. Cut-Extrude1 is
displayed in the Features to
Pattern box.

143) Click the **bottom horizontal edge** of
the Extrude-Thin1 feature for
Direction1. Edge<1> is displayed in the
Pattern Direction box. The direction
arrow points to the right. If required,
click the Reverse Direction button.

144) Enter **0.5**in, [**12.70**] for Spacing.

145) Enter **13** for Number of Instances.

146) Click **OK** from the Linear Pattern
PropertyManager. LPattern1 is
displayed in the FeatureManager.

147) Click **Isometric view** from the
Heads-up View toolbar.

Save the ANGLE-13HOLE part.

148) Click **Save**. Note: All sketches
should be fully defined in the
FeatureManager.

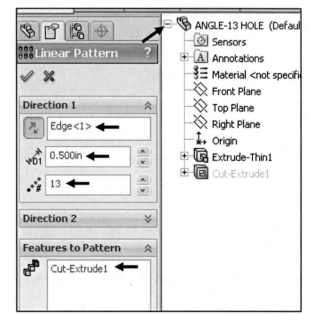

Activity: ANGLE-13HOLE Part - Fillet Feature

Insert a Fillet Feature.
149) Zoom in on the right top edge as illustrated.

150) Click the **right top edge** of the Extrude-Thin1 feature.

151) Click **Fillet** 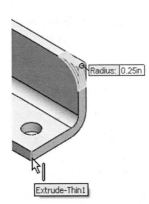 from the Features toolbar. The Fillet PropertyManager is displayed.

152) Click the **Manual** tab. Constant radius is the default Fillet Type.

153) Enter **.250 [6.35]** for Radius.

154) Click the **right bottom edge**. Edge<1> and Edge<2> are displayed in the Items To Fillet box.

155) Click **OK** ✔ from the Fillet PropertyManager. Fillet1 is displayed in the FeatureManager.

💡 Two Fillet PropertyManager tabs are available. Use the Manual tab to control features for all Fillet types. Use the FilletXpert tab when you want SolidWorks to manage the structure of the underlying features only for a Constant radius Fillet type. Click the ❓ button for additional information.

Fit the model to the Graphics window.
156) Press the **f** key.

Edit the Fillet feature.
157) Zoom in on the left side of the Extrude-Thin1 feature.

158) Right-click **Fillet1** from the FeatureManager.

159) Click **Edit Feature** from the Context toolbar. The Fillet1 PropertyManager is displayed.

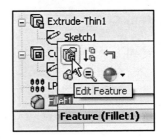

160) Click the **left top edge** and **left bottom edge**. Edge<3> and Edge <4> are added to the Items To Fillet box.

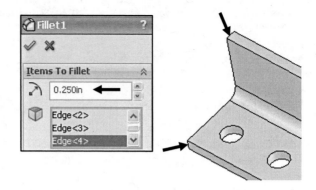

161) Click **OK** ✅ from the Fillet1 PropertyManager. The four edges have a Fillet feature with a .250in radius.

Display the Isometric view.

162) Click **Isometric view** ⬡ from the Heads-up View toolbar.

Save the ANGLE-13HOLE part.

163) Click **Save** 💾.

Activity: ANGLE-13HOLE Part-Second Extruded Cut / Linear Pattern

Insert a new sketch for the second Extruded Cut feature.

164) Right-click the **front face** of the Extrude-Thin1 feature in the Graphics window. The front face is the Sketch plane.

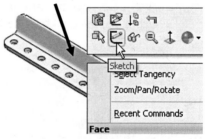

165) Click **Sketch** ✏ from the Context toolbar. The Sketch toolbar is displayed.

166) Click **Front view** ⬗ from the Heads-up View toolbar.

167) Click **Wireframe** ⬗ from the Heads-up View toolbar to display LPattern1.

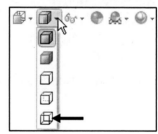

Note: Do not align the center point of the circle with the center point of the LPattern1 feature. Do not align the center point of the circle with the center point of the Fillet radius. Control the center point position with dimensions.

168) Click the **Circle** ⊙ Sketch tool. The cursor displays the Circle icon ⊘.

169) Sketch a **circle** on the left side of the Origin between the two LPattern1 holes as illustrated.

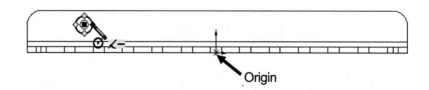

Origin

Add dimensions.

170) Click the **Smart Dimension** ✏ Sketch tool.

171) Click the **Origin** ⊥⊢ .

172) Click the **center point** of the circle.

173) Click a **position** below the horizontal profile line. Enter **3.000**in, [**76.20**].

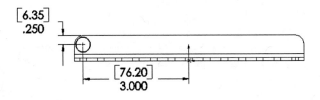

174) Click the **Green Check mark** ✓ .

175) Click the **top horizontal line**.

176) Click the **center point** of the circle.

177) Click a **position** to the left of the profile.

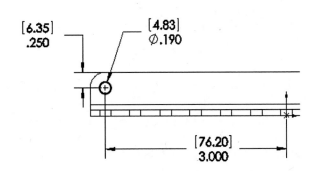

178) Enter **.250**in, [**6.35**].

179) Click the **Green Check mark** ✓ .

180) Click the **circumference** of the circle.

181) Click a **position** above the profile.

182) Enter **.190**in, [**4.83**].

183) Click the **Green Check mark** ✓ .

Insert an Extruded Cut Feature.

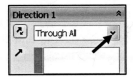

184) Click **Extruded Cut** 🔲 from the Features toolbar. The Cut-Extrude PropertyManager is displayed

185) Select **Through All** for End Condition in Direction1. Accept the default conditions.

186) Click **OK** ✓ from the Cut-Extrude PropertyManager. Cut-Extrude2 is displayed in the FeatureManager.

Create the second Linear Pattern Feature.

187) Click **Linear Pattern** ⸬ from the Features toolbar. The Linear Pattern FeatureManager is displayed. Cut-Extrude2 is displayed in the Features to Pattern box.

188) Click inside the **Pattern Direction** box.

189) Click the **top horizontal edge** of the Extrude-Thin1 feature for Direction1. Edge<1> is displayed in the Pattern Direction box. The Direction arrow points to the right. If required, click the **Reverse Direction** button

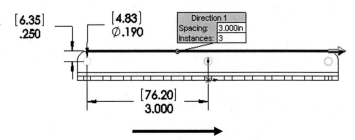

190) Enter **3.000**in, **[76.20]** for Spacing.

191) Enter **3** for Number of Instances. Note: Cut-Extude2 (Seed feature) is displayed in the Features to Pattern box.

192) Click **OK** ✔ from the Linear Pattern PropertyManager. LPattern2 is displayed in the FeatureManager.

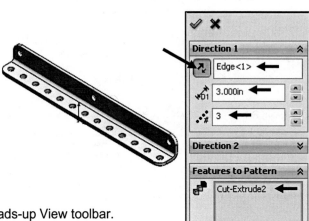

193) Click **Isometric view** ⬚ from the Heads-up View toolbar.

194) Click **Shaded With Edges** ⬚ from the Heads-up View toolbar.

Save the ANGLE-13HOLE part.
195) Click **Save** 💾 .

Activity: ANGLE-13HOLE Part-Third Extruded Cut

Insert a new sketch for the third Extruded Cut Feature.
196) Select the Sketch plane. Right-click the **front face** of Extrude-Thin1.

197) Click **Sketch** ⌐ from the Context toolbar. The Sketch toolbar is displayed.

198) Click **Front view** ⬚ from the Heads-up View toolbar.

199) Click **Hidden Lines Removed** ⬚ from the Heads-up View toolbar.

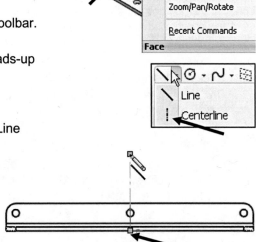

Sketch a vertical centerline.
200) Click the **Centerline** ┊ Sketch tool. The Insert Line PropertyManager is displayed.

201) Click the **Origin** ↳ .

Origin

202) Click a **vertical position** above the top horizontal line as illustrated.

203) Click **Tools**, **Sketch Tools**, **Dynamic Mirror** from the Menu bar.

204) Click the **centerline** in the Graphics window.

Sketch a rectangle.

205) Click **Wireframe** 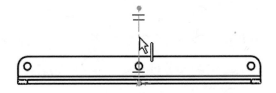 from the Heads-up View toolbar.

Apply the Straight Slot Sketch tool. Sketch a straight slot using two end points and a point for height.

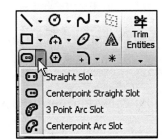

206) Click the **Straight Slot** Sketch tool from the Consolidated Slot toolbar. Do not align the rectangle first point and second point to the center points of Lpattern1.

207) Click the **first point** of the rectangle to the left of the Origin as illustrated.

208) Click the **second point** directly to the right.

209) Click the **third point** to create the slot as illustrated. View the two slots on the model.

210) Click **OK** from the Slot PropertyManager.

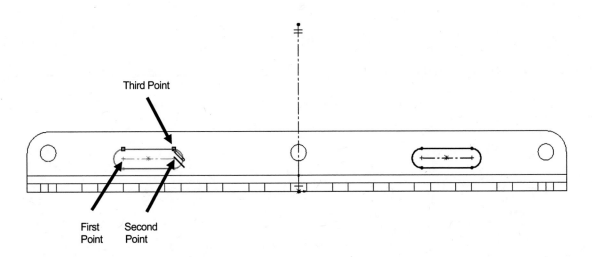

Deactivate the Dynamic Mirror tool.
211) Click **Tools, Sketch Tools, Dynamic Mirror** from the Menu bar.

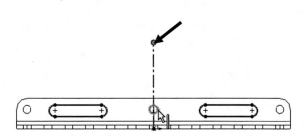

Add a Concentric relation.
212) Zoom in on the centerline.

213) Click the **top endpoint** of the centerline.

214) Hold the **Ctrl** key down.

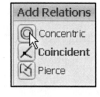

215) Click the **circumference** of the circle.

216) Release the **Ctrl** key.

217) Click **Concentric** from the Add Relations box.

The endpoint of the centerline is positioned in the center of the circle. Note: Right-click Clear Selections to remove selected entities from the Add Relations box.

Add an Equal relation.
218) Click the circumference of the **circle**.

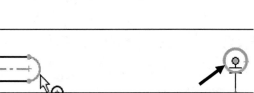

219) Hold the **Ctrl** key down.

220) Click the **left arc** of the first rectangle.

221) Release the **Ctrl** key.

222) Click **Equal** = from the Add Relations box. The arc radius is equal to the circle radius.

Add a Horizontal relation.
223) Click the **top endpoint** of the centerline as illustrated.

224) Hold the **Ctrl** key down.

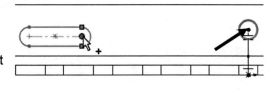

225) Click the **center point** of the left arc of the first rectangle.

226) Release the **Ctrl** key.

227) Click **Horizontal** ⎯ from the Add Relations box.

228) Click **OK** ✓ from the Properties PropertyManager.

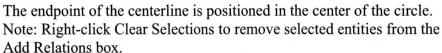

The right arc is horizontally aligned to the left arc due to symmetry from the Sketch Mirror tool.

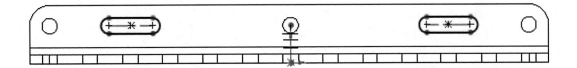

Add dimensions. Dimension the distance between the two slots.

229) Click the **Smart Dimension** ✏ Sketch tool.

230) Click the **right arc center point** of the left slot.

231) Click the **left arc center point** of the right slot.

232) Click a **position** above the top horizontal line.

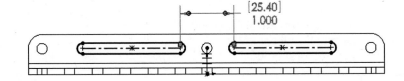

233) Enter **1.000**in, **[25.40]** in the Modify dialog box.

234) Click the **Green Check mark** ✔ .

235) Click the **left center point** of the left arc.

236) Click the **right center point** of the left arc.

237) Click a **position** above the top horizontal line.

238) Enter **2.000**in, **[50.80]** in the Modify dialog box.

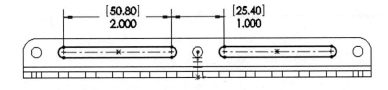

239) Click the **Green Check mark** ✔ . The black sketch is fully defined.

240) Click **Isometric view** 🔲 from the Heads-up View toolbar.

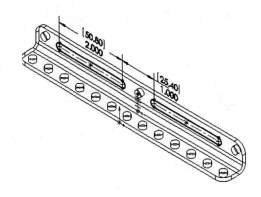

🔆 The Origin is displayed for educational purposes.

Insert an Extruded Cut Feature.

241) Click **Extruded Cut**  from the Features toolbar. The Cut-Extrude PropertyManager is displayed.

242) Select **Through All** for End Condition in Direction1. The direction arrow points to the back.

243) Click **OK** ✓ from the Extrude PropertyManager. Cut-Extrude3 is displayed in the FeatureManager.

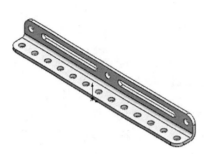

244) Click **Shaded With Edges** from the Heads-up View toolbar.

Save the ANGLE-13HOLE part.

245) Click **Save** 💾. The ANGLE-13HOLE is complete. All sketches in the FeatureManager should be fully defined.

💡 The dimension between the two slots is over-defined if the arc center points are aligned to the center points of the LPattern1 feature. An over-defined sketch is displayed in red, in the FeatureManager.

💡 The mouse pointer displays a blue dashed line when horizontal and vertical sketch references are inferred.

💡 Origin, Tangent Edges and Temporary Axis are displayed for educational purposes.

💡 Right-click and drag in the Graphics area to display the mouse gesture wheel. You can customize the default commands for a sketch, part, assembly or drawing.

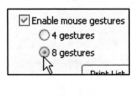

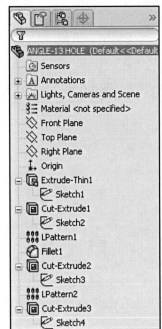

Review the ANGLE-13HOLE Part

The ANGLE-13HOLE part utilized an open L-Shaped profile sketched on the Right Plane. The Extruded Thin feature with the Mid Plane option located the part symmetrical to the Right Plane. The first Extruded Cut feature created the first hole sketched on the top face of the Extruded Thin feature.

The first Linear Pattern feature created an array of 13 holes along the bottom horizontal edge. The Fillet feature rounded the four corners. The second Extruded Cut feature created a hole on the Front face. The second Linear Pattern feature created an array of 3 holes along the top horizontal edge. The third Extruded Cut feature created two slot cuts using the Straight Slot Sketch tool.

Additional details on Extruded Base/Thin, Extruded Cut, Linear Pattern, Fillet, Mirror Entities, Add Relations, Slot, Straight Slot, Centerline, Line, Rectangle, and Smart Dimensions are available in Help. Keywords: Extruded Boss/Base - Thin, Extruded Cut, Patterns, Fillet, Sketch Entities, Sketch tools, and dimensions.

TRAINGLE Part

The TRIANGLE part is a multipurpose supporting plane.

The TRIANGLE is manufactured from .090in, [2.3] aluminum. The TRIANGLE contains numerous features.

Utilize symmetry and Sketch tools to simplify the geometry creation.

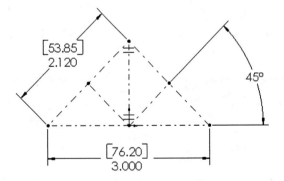

The center points of the slots and holes locate key geometry for the TRIANGLE.

Utilize sketched construction geometry to locate the center points.

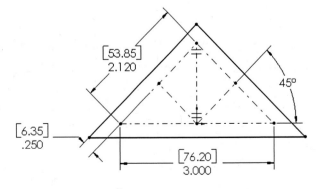

🔆 Construction geometry is not calculated in the extruded profile.

Utilize the Sketch Offset tool and Sketch Fillet to create the sketch profile for the Extruded Boss/Base ▣ (Boss-Extrude1) feature.

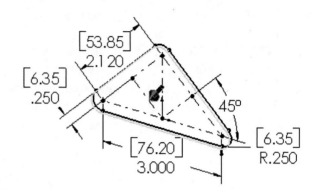

Utilize the Dynamic Mirror Sketch tool and the Circle Sketch tool to create the first Extruded Cut ▣ feature.

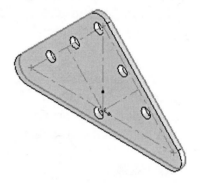

Utilize the Corner Rectangle, Trim, and the Tangent Arc Sketch tools to create the second Extruded Cut ▣ feature left bottom slot.

Note: A goal of this book is to expose the new user to different tools and methods. You can also apply the Straight Slot Sketch tool and eliminate steps.

Utilize the Mirror ▥ feature to create the right bottom slot.

Utilize the Straight Slot Sketch tool to create the third Extruded Cut ▣ feature.

Utilize the Circular Pattern 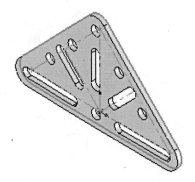 feature to create the three radial slot cuts.

Activity: TRIANGLE Part-Mirror, Offset, and Fillet Sketch Tools

Create a new part.

246) Click **New** ⬜ from the Menu bar. The Templates tab is the default tab.

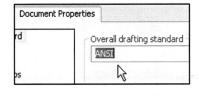

247) Double-click **Part**. The Part FeatureManager is displayed.

Save the part.
248) Click **Save As** from the Menu bar.

249) Select **SW-TUTORIAL-2010** for the Save in file folder.

250) Enter **TRIANGLE** for File name.

251) Enter **TRIANGLE** for Description.

252) Click **Save**. The TRIANGLE FeatureManager is displayed.

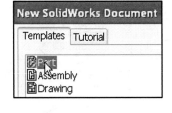

Set the dimensioning standard and part units.
253) Click **Options** 📋, **Document Properties** tab from the Menu bar.

254) Select **ANSI** from the Overall drafting standard box.

255) Click **Units**.

256) Click **IPS, [MMGS]** for Unit system.

257) Select **.123, [.12]** for Length units Decimal places.

258) Select **None** for Angular units Decimal places.

259) Click **OK** to set the document units.

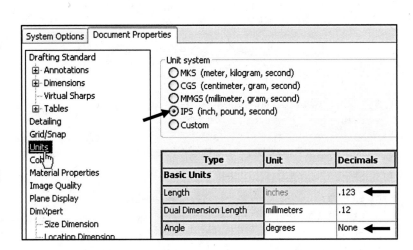

Insert a new sketch for the Extruded Base feature.
260) Right-click **Front Plane** from the FeatureManager.

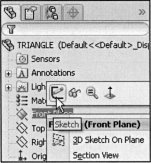

261) Click **Sketch** ⌐ from the Context toolbar. The Sketch toolbar is displayed.

Sketch a vertical centerline.
262) Click the **Centerline** ┆ Sketch tool.

263) Click the **Origin** ⊥. Click a vertical **position** above the Origin as illustrated.

Deselect the Centerline Sketch tool.
264) Right-click **Select**.

Sketch a Mirrored profile.
265) Click **Tools, Sketch Tools, Dynamic Mirror** from the Menu bar.

266) Click the **centerline** in the Graphics window.

267) Click the **Centerline** ┆ Sketch tool.

268) Click the **Origin** ⊥.

Origin

269) Click a **position** to the left of the Origin to create a horizontal line.

270) Click the **top end point** of the vertical centerline to complete the triangle as illustrated.

271) Right-click **End Chain** to end the line segment. The Centerline tool is still active.

272) Click the **Origin** ⊥.

273) Click a **position** coincident with the right-angled centerline. *Do not select the Midpoint.*

274) Right-click **End Chain** to end the line segment.

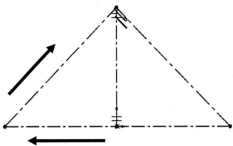

Deactivate the Dynamic Mirror Sketch tool.
275) Click **Tools, Sketch Tools, Dynamic Mirror** from the Menu bar.

Origin

Add a dimension.

276) Click **Smart Dimension** from the Sketch toolbar.

277) Click the **right horizontal** centerline.

278) Click the **inside right** centerline.

279) Click a **position** between the two lines.

280) Enter **45**deg in the Modify dialog box for the angular dimension.

281) Click the **Green Check mark** in the Modify dialog box.

282) Click the **horizontal centerline**.

283) Click a position **below** the centerline.

284) Enter **3.000**in, [76.20].

285) Click the **Green Check mark** in the Modify dialog box.

286) Click the **left angled** centerline.

287) Click **position** aligned to the left angled centerline.

288) Enter **2.120**in, [53.85].

289) Click the **Green Check mark** in the Modify dialog box.

Offset the sketch
290) Right-click **Select** in the Graphics window.

291) Hold the **Ctrl** key down.

292) Click the **three outside centerlines**; Line2, Line4, and Line5 are displayed in the Selected Entities box.

293) Release the **Ctrl** key.

294) Click the **Offset Entities** Sketch tool.

295) Enter **.250**in, [6.35] for Offset Distance. The yellow Offset direction is outward.

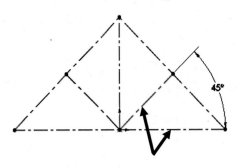

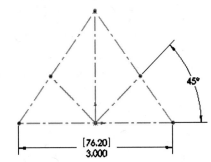

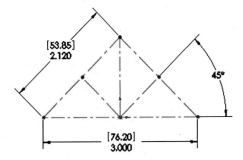

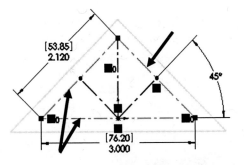

296) Click **OK** ✔ from the Offset Entities
PropertyManager.

Three profile lines are displayed. The
centerlines are on the inside.

Insert the Sketch Fillet.

297) Click **Sketch Fillet** ⌐ from the Sketch
toolbar. The Sketch Fillet
PropertyManager is displayed.

298) Enter **.250**in, **[6.35]** for Radius.

299) Click the **three outside corner points**.

300) Click **OK** ✔ from the Sketch Fillet
PropertyManager.

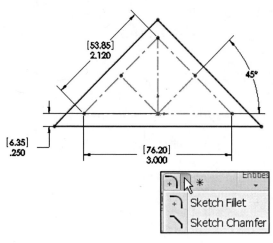

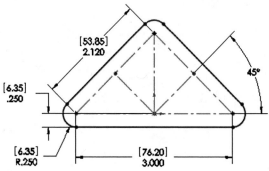

Activity: TRIANGLE Part-Extruded Boss/Base Feature

Extrude the sketch. Create the Boss-Extrude1 feature.

301) Click **Extruded Boss/Base** 📦 from the Features
toolbar. Blind is the default End Condition in
Direction1.

302) Enter **.090**in, **[2.3]** for Depth in Direction 1. The
direction arrow points to the front.

303) Click **OK** ✔ from the Boss-Extrude
PropertyManager. Boss-Extrude1 is displayed in
the FeatureManager.

Save the TRIANGLE part.

304) Click **Isometric view** 🔲 from
the Heads-up View toolbar.

305) Click **Save** 💾.

💡 Insert centerlines and add
relations to build sketches that
will be referenced by multiple
features.

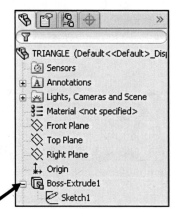

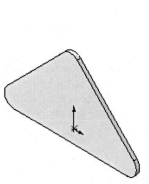

Display Sketch1.
306) Expand Boss-Extrude1 in the FeatureManager.

307) Right-click **Sketch1**.

308) Click **Show**.

Activity: TRIANGLE Part-First Extruded Cut Feature

Insert a new sketch for the first Extruded Cut.
309) Right-click the **front face** of Boss-Extrude1. This is your Sketch plane.

310) Click **Sketch** from the Context toolbar. The Sketch toolbar is displayed.

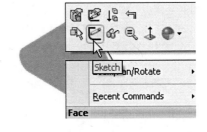

311) Click **Front view** from the Heads-up View toolbar.

312) Click the **Circle** Sketch tool. The Circle PropertyManager is displayed.

313) Sketch a **circle** centered at the Origin.

314) Sketch a **circle** centered at the endpoint of the vertical centerline as illustrated.

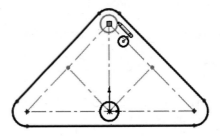

Sketch a vertical centerline.
315) Click the **Centerline** Sketch tool.

316) Click the **Origin**.

317) Click the **center point** of the top circle.

Deselect the Centerline Sketch tool.
318) Right-click **Select**.

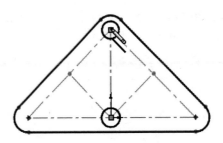

Sketch a Mirrored profile.
319) Click **Tools**, **Sketch Tools**, **Dynamic Mirror** from the Menu bar.

320) Click the **centerline** in the Graphics window.

321) Click the **Circle** Sketch tool. The Circle PropertyManager is displayed.

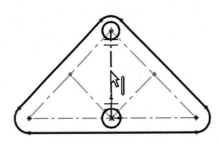

322) Sketch a **circle** on the left side of the centerline, coincident with the left centerline, in the lower half of the triangle.

323) Sketch a **circle** on the left side of the centerline, coincident with the left centerline, in the upper half of the triangle. Right-click **Select**.

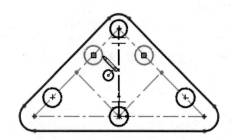

324) Deactivate the Dynamic Mirror tool. Click **Tools**, **Sketch Tools**, **Dynamic Mirror** from the Menu bar.

Add an Equal relation.
325) Click a **circle**. Hold the **Ctrl** key down. Click the five other **circles**. Release the **Ctrl** key.

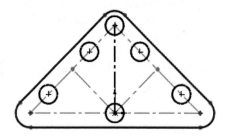

326) Click **Equal** = from the Add Relations box.

Add a dimension.
327) Click the **Smart Dimension** ✎ Sketch tool.

328) Click the circumference of the **top circle**.

329) Click a **position** off the TRIANGLE.

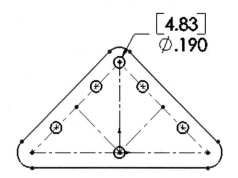

330) Enter **.190**in, **[4.83]**.

331) Click the **Green Check mark** ✔ in the Modify dialog box.

Create the aligned dimensions.
332) Click the bottom **left point**. Click the **center point** of the bottom left circle.

333) Click a **position** aligned to the angled centerline.

334) Enter **.710**in, **[18.03]**. Click the **Green Check mark** ✔ in the Modify dialog box.

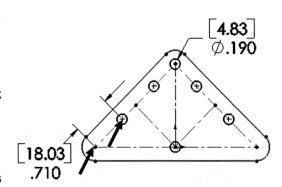

335) Click the **bottom left point**.

336) Click the **center point** of the top left circle as illustrated.

337) Click a **position** aligned to the angled centerline.

338) Enter **1.410**in, **[35.81]**.

339) Click the **Green Check mark** ✔ in the Modify dialog box.

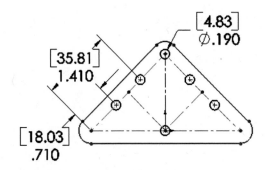

Insert an Extruded Cut Feature.

340) Click **Extruded Cut** 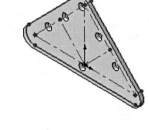 from the Features toolbar. The Cut-Extrude PropertyManager is displayed. Select **Through All** for the End Condition in Direction1.

341) Click **OK** ✔ from the Cut-Extrude PropertyManager. Cut-Extrude1 is displayed in the FeatureManager.

342) Click **Isometric view** ⬙ from the Heads-up View toolbar.

343) Click **Save** 💾 .

Activity: TRIANGLE Part-Second Extruded Cut Feature

Insert a new slot sketch for the second Extruded Cut.

344) Right-click the **front face** of Boss-Extrude1 for the Sketch plane.

345) Click **Sketch** ✏ from the Context toolbar. The Sketch toolbar is displayed.

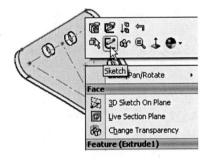

346) Click **Front view** 🔲 from the Heads-up View toolbar.

347) Click the **Corner Rectangle** ▭ tool from the Consolidated Sketch toolbar. Note: The purpose of this book is to teach you different tools and methods. You can also apply the Straight Slot Sketch tool and eliminate many of the next steps.

348) Sketch a **rectangle** to the left of the Origin as illustrated.

Trim the vertical lines.

349) Click the **Trim Entities** ✂ Sketch tool. The Trim PropertyManager is displayed.

First point

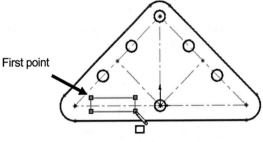

350) Click **Trim to closest** in the Options box. The Trim to closest ✂ icon is displayed.

351) Click the **left vertical** line of the rectangle.

352) Click the **right vertical** line of the rectangle.

353) Click **OK** ✔ from the Trim PropertyManager.

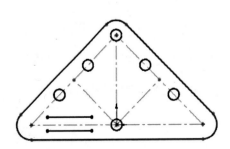

Sketch the Tangent Arcs.

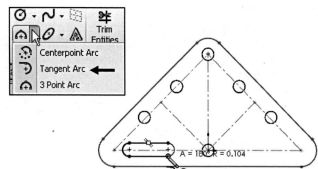

354) Click the **Tangent Arc** 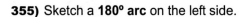 Sketch tool from the Consolidated Sketch toolbar. The Arc PropertyManager is displayed.

355) Sketch a **180° arc** on the left side.

356) Sketch a **180° arc** on the right side.

357) Click **OK** ✔ from the Arc PropertyManager.

Add an Equal relation.
358) Click the **right arc**.

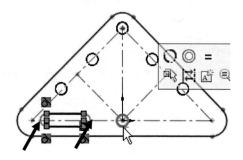

359) Hold the **Ctrl** key down.

360) Click the **bottom center circle**.

361) Release the **Ctrl** key.

362) Click **Equal** = from the Add Relations box.

363) Click **OK** ✔ from the Properties PropertyManager.

Add a Coincident relation.
364) Press the f key to fit the model to the Graphics window.

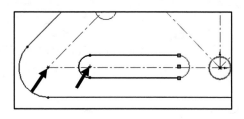

365) Click the **center point** of the left arc.

366) Hold the **Ctrl** key down.

367) Click the **left lower point** as illustrated.

368) Release the **Ctrl** key.

369) Click **Coincident** ⊀ from the Add Relations box.

Add a Tangent relation.
370) Click the **bottom horizontal** line.

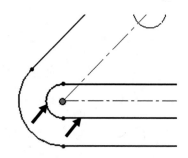

371) Hold the **Ctrl** key down.

372) Click the **first arc tangent**.

373) Release the **Ctrl** key.

374) Click **Tangent** Ȱ from the Add Relations box.

375) Click **OK** ✔ from the Properties PropertyManager.

Add a dimension.

376) Click the **Smart Dimension**  Sketch tool.

377) Click the **left center point** of the left arc.

378) Click the **right center point** of the right arc.

379) Click a **position** below the horizontal line.

380) Enter **1.000**in, **[25.40]** in the Modify dialog box.

381) Click the **Green Check mark** ✓ .

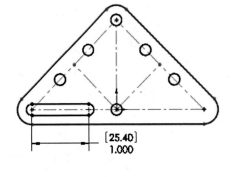

Insert an Extruded Cut feature.

382) Click **Isometric view** from the Heads-up View toolbar.

383) Click **Extruded Cut** from the Features toolbar. The Cut-Extrude PropertyManager is displayed.

384) Select **Through All** for End Condition in Direction 1.

385) Click **OK** ✓ from the Cut-Extrude PropertyManager. Cut-Extrude2 is displayed in the FeatureManager.

386) Click **Save** . Cut-Extrude2 is highlighted in the FeatureManager.

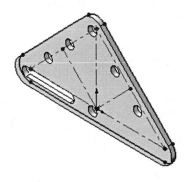

Activity: TRIANGLE Part-Mirror Feature

Mirror the Cut-Extrude2 feature.

387) Click **Mirror** from the Features toolbar. The Mirror PropertyManager is displayed. Cut-Extrude2 is displayed in the Feature to Mirror box.

388) Click **Right Plane** from the fly-out TRIANGLE FeatureManager. Right Plane is displayed in the Mirror Face/Plane box.

389) Check the **Geometry Pattern** box.

390) Click **OK** ✓ from the Mirror PropertyManager. Mirror1 is displayed in the FeatureManager.

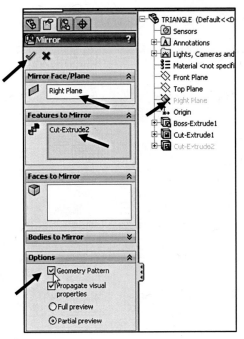

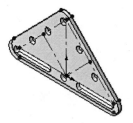

Activity: TRIANGLE Part-Third Extruded Cut Feature

Insert a new sketch for the third Extruded Cut feature.

391) Right-click the **front face** of Boss-Extrude1 for the Sketch plane.

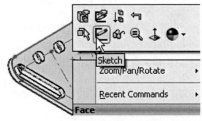

392) Click **Sketch** ⌐ from the Context toolbar. The Sketch toolbar is displayed.

393) Click **Front view** from the Heads-up View toolbar.

Sketch a Straight Slot.

394) Click the **Straight Slot** ⊂⊃ Sketch tool from the

Consolidated Rectangle toolbar. The Straight Slot icon is displayed.

395) Click a **position** coincident with the left angled centerline as illustrated.

Sketch the second point.

396) Click a **position** aligned to the centerline. A dashed blue line is displayed.

Sketch the third point.

397) Click a **position** above the inside left centerline. The Straight Slot sketch is displayed.

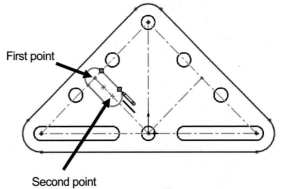

First point

Second point

Click the Question mark in the PropertyManager to obtain additional information on the tool.

398) Click **OK** ✓ from the Slot PropertyManager.

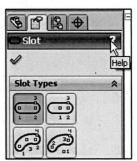

Add an Equal relation.

399) Click the **left arc**.

400) Hold the **Ctrl** key down.

401) Click the **bottom circle**.

402) Release the **Ctrl** key.

403) Click **Equal** ＝ from the Add Relations box.

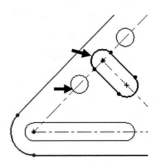

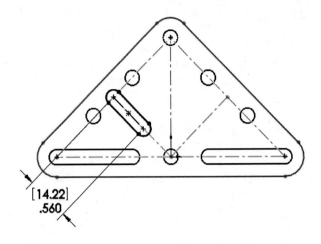

Add a dimension.

404) Click the **Smart Dimension**  Sketch tool.

405) Click the **left center point** of the left arc.

406) Click the **right center point** of the right arc.

407) Click a **position** below the horizontal line.

408) Enter **.560**in, [**14.22**] in the Modify dialog box.

409) Click the **Green Check mark** . The sketch is fully defined.

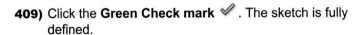

Insert an Extruded Cut Feature.

410) Click **Isometric view** from the Heads-up View toolbar.

411) Click **Extruded Cut** from the Features toolbar. The Cut-Extrude PropertyManager is displayed.

412) Select **Through All** for the End Condition in Direction 1.

413) Click **OK** from the Cut-Extrude PropertyManager. Cut-Extrude3 is displayed in the FeatureManager.

Save the model.

414) Click **Save** .

Display the Temporary Axis.

415) Click **View**; check **Temporary Axes** from the Menu bar.

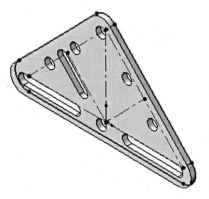

Activity: TRIANGLE Part-Circular Pattern Feature

Insert a Circular Pattern feature.

416) Click **Circular Pattern** from the Features Consolidated toolbar. The Circular Pattern PropertyManager is displayed. Cut-Extrude3 is displayed in the Features to Pattern box.

417) Click the **Temporary Axis** displayed through the center hole located at the Origin. The Temporary Axis is displayed as Axis <1> in the Pattern Axis box.

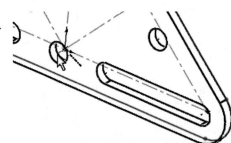

418) Enter **90**deg for Angle.

419) Enter **3** for Number of Instances.

420) Check the **Equal spacing** box. If required, click **Reverse Direction**.

421) Click **OK** from the Circular Pattern PropertyManager. CirPattern1 is displayed in the FeatureManager.

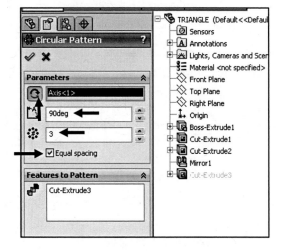

Hide Sketch1.

422) **Expand** Boss-Extrude1 from the FeatureManager.

423) Right-click **Sketch1**.

424) Click **Hide**.

Save the TRIANGLE part and deactivate the Temporary Axes.

425) Click **Isometric view** from the Heads-up View toolbar.

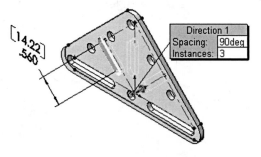

426) Click **View**; uncheck **Temporary Axes** from the Menu bar.

427) Click **Save**. The TRIANGLE part is complete.

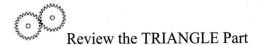 Review the TRIANGLE Part

The TRIANGLE part utilized a Boss-Extrude1 feature. A triangular shape profile was sketched on the Front Plane. Symmetry and construction geometry sketch tools located centerpoints for slots and holes.

The Sketch Fillet tool created rounded corners for the profile. The Sketch Mirror and Circle Sketch tools were utilized to create the Extruded Cut features.

The Corner Rectangle, Sketch Trim, and Tangent Arc tools were utilized to create the second Extruded Cut feature, left bottom slot. The Mirror feature was utilized to create the right bottom slot.

The Parallelogram and Tangent Arc Sketch tools were utilized to create the third Extruded Cut feature. The Circular Pattern feature created the three radial slot cuts. The following Geometric relations were utilized: *Equal*, *Parallel*, *Coincident*, and *Tangent*.

Additional details on Rectangle, Circle, Tangent Arc, Parallelogram, Mirror Entities, Sketch Fillet, Offset Entities, Extruded Boss/Base, Extruded Cut, Mirror and Circular Pattern are available in SolidWorks Help.

SCREW Part

The SCREW part is a simplified model of a 10-24 x 3/8 Machine screw. Screws, nuts and washers are classified as fasteners.

An assembly contains hundreds of fasteners. Utilize simplified versions to conserve model and rebuild time.

Machine screws are described in terms of the following:
- Nominal diameter – Size 10.
- Threads per inch – 24.
- Length – 3/8.

Screw diameter, less than ¼ inch, are represented by a size number. Size 10 refers to a diameter of .190 inch. Utilize the SCREW part to fasten components in the FRONT-SUPPORT assembly.

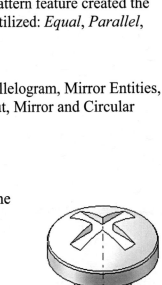

Simplified version

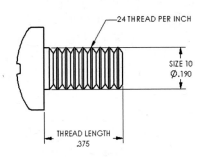

The SCREW part utilizes a Revolved Base 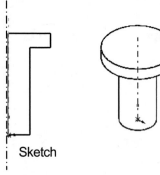 feature to add material. The Revolved Boss/Base feature requires a centerline and sketch on a Sketch plane. A Revolved feature requires an angle of revolution. The sketch is revolved around the centerline.

Sketch a centerline on the Front Sketch plane.

Sketch a closed profile.

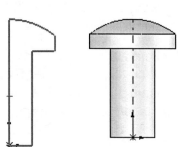

Revolve the sketch 360 degrees.

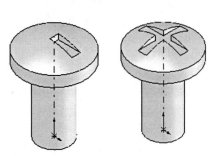

Utilize the Edit Sketch tool to modify the sketch. Utilize the Sketch Trim and Tangent Arc tool to create a new profile.

Utilize an Extruded Cut 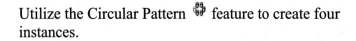 feature sketched on the Front Plane. This is the seed feature for the Circular Pattern.

Utilize the Circular Pattern feature to create four instances.

Apply the Fillet feature to round edges and faces. Utilize the Fillet feature to round the top edge.

Apply the Chamfer feature to bevel edges and faces. Utilize a Chamfer feature to bevel the bottom face.

Note: Utilize an M5 Machine screw for metric units.

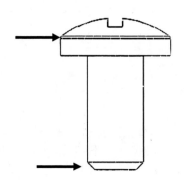

Activity: SCREW Part-Documents Properties

Create a new part.

428) Click **New** ☐ from the Menu bar. The Templates tab is the default tab. Double-click **Part**.

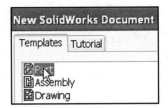

Save the part.

429) Click **Save As** from the Menu bar. Select **SW-TUTORIAL-2010** for the Save in file folder.

430) Enter **SCREW** for File name.

431) Enter **MACHINE SCREW 10-24x3/8** for Description.

432) Click **Save**. The SCREW FeatureManager is displayed.

Set the dimensioning standard and part units.

433) Click **Options** ▤, **Documents Properties** tab from the Menu bar.

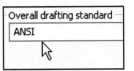

434) Select **ANSI** from the Overall drafting standard box.

435) Click **Units**. Select **IPS**, **[MMGS]** for Unit system.

436) Select **.123**, **[.12]** for Length units Decimal places.

437) Select **None** for Angular units Decimal places.

438) Click **OK**.

Activity: SCREW Part-Revolved Feature

Insert a Revolved feature sketched on the Front Plane. The Front Plane is the default Sketch plane.

Insert a new sketch.

439) Right-click **Front Plane** from the FeatureManager.

440) Click **Sketch** ⬚ from the Context toolbar. The Sketch toolbar is displayed.

441) Click the **Centerline** ┊ Sketch tool. The Insert Line PropertyManager is displayed.

Sketch a vertical centerline.

442) Click the **Origin** ↳.

443) Click a **position** directly above the Origin as illustrated.

☼ Press the **z** key to Zoom out in the Graphics window.

Origin

444) Right-click **End Chain** to end the centerline.

Add a dimension.
445) Click the **Smart Dimension** ✎ Sketch tool.

446) Click the **centerline**. Click a **position** to the left.

447) Enter **.500**in, **[12.70]**. Click the **Green Check mark** ✔ .

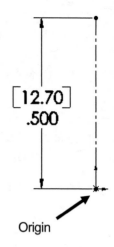

Origin

Fit the sketch to the Graphics Window.
448) Press the **f** key.

Sketch the profile.
449) Click the **Line** ＼ Sketch tool.

Sketch the first horizontal line.

450) Click the **Origin** ⌊⊷ . Click a **position** to the right of the Origin.

Sketch the first vertical line.
451) Click a position **above** the horizontal line endpoint.

452) Sketch the second **horizontal line**.

453) Sketch the second **vertical line**. The top point of the vertical line is collinear with the top point of the centerline.

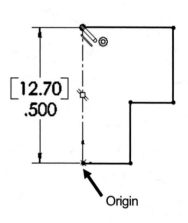

Origin

454) Sketch the third **horizontal line**. The left endpoint of the horizontal line is coincident with the top point of the centerline.

455) Right-click **Select** to deselect the Line Sketch tool.

Add a Horizontal relation.
456) Click the **top** most right point. Hold the **Ctrl** key down.

457) Click the **top** most left point. Release the **Ctrl** key.

458) Click **Horizontal** ▬ from the Add Relations box.

459) Click **OK** ✔ from the Properties PropertyManager.

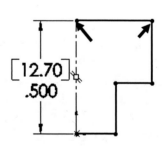

Add a dimension.
460) Click the **Smart Dimension** ✎ Sketch tool. Create the first diameter dimension.

461) Click the **centerline** in the Graphics window.

462) Click the **first vertical line**.

463) Click a **position** to the left of the Origin to create a diameter dimension.

464) Enter **.190**in, **[4.83]**.

465) Click the **Green Check mark** .

A diameter dimension for a Revolved sketch requires a centerline, profile line, and a dimension position to the left of the centerline.

A dimension position directly below the bottom horizontal line creates a radial dimension.

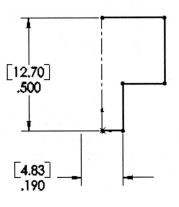

Create the second diameter dimension.
466) Click the **centerline** in the Graphics window.

467) Click the **second vertical line**.

468) Click a **position** to the left of the Origin to create a diameter dimension.

469) Enter **.373**in, **[9.47]**.

Create a vertical dimension.
470) Click the **first vertical line**.

471) Click a **position** to the right of the line.

472) Enter **.375**in, **[9.53]**.

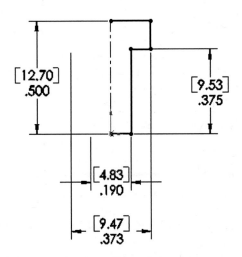

Center the dimension text.
473) Click the **.190**in, **[4.83]** dimension.

474) Drag the **text** between the two extension lines.

475) Click the **.373**in, **[9.47]** dimension.

476) Drag the **text** between the two extension lines. If required, click the **blue arrow dots** to flip the arrows inside the extension lines.

477) Right-click **Select** to deselect the Smart Dimension Sketch tool.

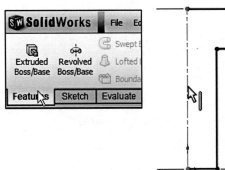

Select the Centerline for axis of revolution.
478) Click the **vertical centerline** as illustrated.

Revolve the sketch.

479) Click **Revolved Boss/Base** from the Features toolbar.

480) Click **Yes**. The Revolve PropertyManager is displayed.

The "Yes" button causes a vertical line to be automatically sketched from the top left point to the Origin. The Graphics window displays the Isometric view and a preview of the Revolved Base feature.

The Revolve PropertyManager displays 360 degrees for the Angle of Revolution.

481) Click **OK** ✅ from the Revolve PropertyManager.

The FeatureManager displays the Revolve1 name for the first feature. The Revolved Boss/Base feature requires a centerline, sketch, and an angle of revolution. A solid Revolved Boss/Base feature requires a closed sketch. Draw the sketch on one side of the centerline.

The SCREW requires a rounded profile. Edit the Revolved Base sketch. Insert a Tangent Arc.

Edit the Revolved Base sketch.
482) Right-click **Revolve1** in the FeatureManager. Click **Edit Sketch** from the Context toolbar.

483) Click **Front view** from the Heads-up View toolbar.

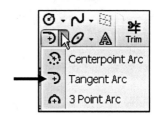

484) Click the **Tangent Arc** ⤵ Sketch tool.

485) Click the **top centerline** point as illustrated.

486) Drag the **mouse pointer** to the right and downward.

487) Click a **position** collinear with the right vertical line, below the midpoint. The arc is displayed tangent to the top horizontal line.

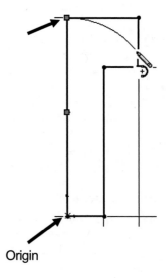

Deselect the Tangent Arc Sketch tool.
488) Right-click **Select**.

Delete unwanted geometry.
489) Click the **Trim Entities** ⯒ Sketch tool. The Trim PropertyManager is displayed.

490) Click **Trim to closest** from the Options box. The Trim to closest icon is displayed.

Origin

491) Click the **right top vertical line** as illustrated.

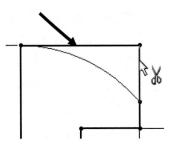

492) Click the **top horizontal line** as illustrated. The two lines are removed.

493) Click **OK** ✔ from the Trim PropertyManager. Note: You may still view lines until you exit the sketch.

Add a dimension.
494) Click the **Smart Dimension** ⬦ Sketch tool.

495) Click the **arc**.

496) Click a **position** above the profile.

497) Enter .304in, **[7.72]**.

498) Click the **Green Check mark** ✔. The sketch should be fully defined, if not add a .05 inch dimension as illustrated.

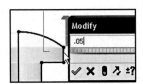

499) Click **Exit Sketch** from the Sketch toolbar.

500) Click **Save** 🖫.

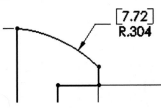

The SCREW requires an Extruded Cut feature on the Front Plane. Utilize the Convert Entities Sketch tool to extract the Revolved Base top arc edge for the profile of the Extruded Cut.

Activity: SCREW Part-Extruded Cut Feature

Insert a new sketch for the Extruded Cut feature.
501) Right-click **Front Plane** from the FeatureManager.

502) Click **Sketch** ⬡ from the Context toolbar. The Sketch toolbar is displayed.

503) Click the **top arc** as illustrated. The mouse pointer displays the silhouette edge icon for feedback.

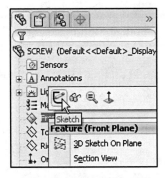

504) Click the **Convert Entities** 🗗 Sketch tool.

505) Click **OK** ✔ from the Convert Entities PropertyManager.

506) Click the **Line** ╲ Sketch tool.

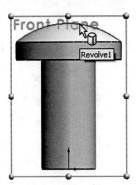

507) Sketch a **vertical line**. The top endpoint of the line is coincident with the arc, vertically aligned to the Origin.

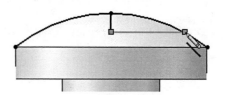

508) Sketch a **horizontal line**. The right end point of the line is coincident with the arc. Do not select the arc midpoint. Right-click **Select**.

509) Click **Isometric view** from the Heads-up View toolbar.

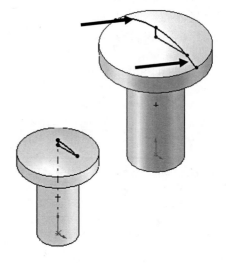

510) Click the **Trim Entities** Sketch tool. The Trim PropertyManager is displayed.

511) Click **Power trim** from the Options box.

512) Click a position to the **left** side of the arc.

513) Drag the mouse pointer to **intersect** the left arc line.

514) Click a position to the **right** side of the right arc.

515) Drag the mouse pointer to **intersect** the right arc line.

516) Click **OK** from the Trim PropertyManager.

Add a dimension.
517) Click the **Smart Dimension** Sketch tool.

518) Click the **vertical line**.

519) Click a **position** to the right of the profile.

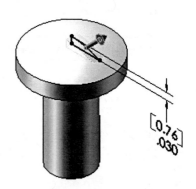

520) Enter **.030**in, **[0.76]**.

521) Click the **Green Check mark** .

Insert an Extruded Cut Feature.
522) Click **Isometric view** from the Heads-up View toolbar.

523) Click **Extruded Cut** from the Features toolbar. The Cut-Extrude PropertyManager is displayed.

524) Select **Mid Plane** for the End Condition in Direction 1.

525) Enter **.050**in, **[1.27]** for Depth.

526) Click **OK** from the Cut-Extrude PropertyManager. Cut-Extrude1 is displayed in the FeatureManager.

Activity: SCREW Part-Circular Pattern Feature

Insert the Circular Pattern feature.

527) Click **View**; check **Temporary Axes** from the Menu bar. The Temporary Axis is required for the Circular Pattern feature.

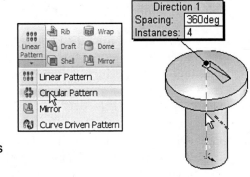

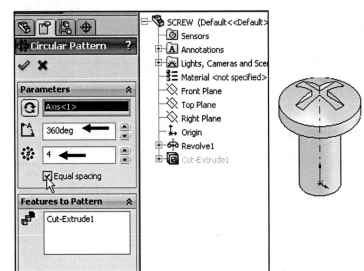

528) Click **Circular Pattern** from the Features Consolidated toolbar. Cut-Extrude1 is displayed in the Features to Pattern box.

529) Click the **Temporary Axis** in the Graphics window. Axis<1> is displayed in the Pattern Axis box.

530) Enter **360**deg for Angle.

531) Enter **4** for Number of Instances.

532) Check the **Equal spacing** box.

533) Click **OK** from the Circular Pattern PropertyManager. CirPattern1 is displayed in the FeatureManager.

Save the model.

534) Click **Save** .

Activity: SCREW Part-Fillet Feature

Insert the Fillet feature.

535) Click the **top circular edge** as illustrated.

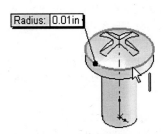

536) Click **Fillet** from the Features toolbar. The Fillet PropertyManager is displayed.

537) Click the **Manual** tab. Edge<1> is displayed in the Items to Fillet box.

538) Enter **.010**in, **[.25]** for Radius.

539) Click **OK** from the Fillet PropertyManager. Fillet1 is displayed in the FeatureManager.

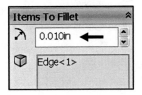

Activity: SCREW Part-Chamfer Feature

Insert the Chamfer feature.
540) Click the **bottom circular edge**.

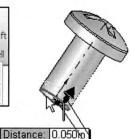

541) Click **Chamfer**  from the Features Consolidated toolbar. Edge<1> is displayed in the Items to Chamfer box.

542) Enter **.050**in, [**1.27**] for Distance.

543) Click **OK** ✓ from the Chamfer PropertyManager. Chamfer1 is displayed in the FeatureManager.

🔆 Simplify the part. Save rebuild time. Suppress features that are not required in the assembly.

A suppressed feature is not displayed in the Graphics window. A suppressed feature is removed from any rebuild calculations.

Suppress the Fillet and Chamfer feature.
544) Hold the **Ctrl** key down.

545) Click **Fillet1** and **Chamfer1** from the FeatureManager.

546) Release the **Ctrl** key.

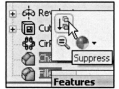

547) Right-click **Suppress** ⬇ Suppress from the Context toolbar. Note: Suppressed features are displayed in light gray in the FeatureManager.

Deactivate the Temporary Axes in the Graphics window.
548) Click **View**; uncheck **Temporary Axes** from the Menu bar.

Save the SCREW part.
549) Click **Isometric view** 🔲 from the Heads-up View toolbar.

550) Click **Save** 💾.

Close all open documents.
551) Click **Window**, **Close All** from the Menu bar.

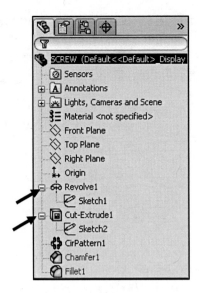

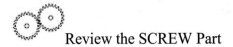 Review the SCREW Part

The Revolved Boss/Base feature was utilized to create the SCREW part. The Revolved Boss/Base feature required a centerline sketched on the Front Sketch plane and a closed profile. The sketch was revolved 360 degrees to create the Base feature for the SCREW part.

Edit Sketch was utilized to modify the sketch. The Sketch Trim and Tangent Arc tools created a new profile.

The Extruded Cut feature was sketched on the Front Plane.

The Circular Pattern feature created four instances.

The Fillet feature rounded the top edges.

The Chamfer feature beveled the bottom edge. The Fillet and Chamfer are suppressed to save rebuild time in the assembly. Note: Suppressed features are displayed in light gray in the FeatureManager.

Additional details on Convert Entities, Silhouette Edge, Revolved Boss/Base, Circular Pattern, Fillet, and Chamfer are available in SolidWorks Help. Keywords: Sketch tools, silhouette, features, Pattern, Revolve, Fillet and Chamfer.

Origin and Tangent Edges are displayed for educational purposes.

FRONT-SUPPORT Assembly

The FRONT-SUPPORT assembly consists of the following parts:

- ANGLE-13HOLE part

- TRIANGLE part

- HEX-STANDOFF part

- SCREW part

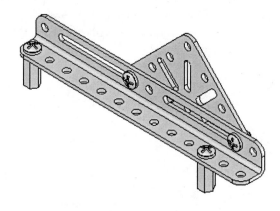

Create the FRONT-SUPPORT assembly. Insert the ANGLE-13HOLE part. The ANGLE-13HOLE part is fixed to the FRONT-SUPPORT Origin. Insert the first HEX-STANDOFF part.

Utilize Concentric and Coincident mates to assemble the HEX-STANDOFF to the left hole of the ANGLE-13HOLE part. Insert the second HEX-STANDOFF part.

Utilize Concentric and Coincident mates to assemble the HEX-STANDOFF to the third hole from the right side. Insert the TRIANGLE part. Utilize Concentric, Distance, and Parallel mates to assemble the TRIANGLE. Utilize Concentric/Coincident SmartMates to assemble the four SCREWS.

Activity: FRONT-SUPPORT Assembly-Insert ANGLE-13HOLE

Create a new assembly.

552) Click **New** ⬚ from the Menu bar.

553) Double-click **Assembly** from the Templates tab. The Begin Assembly PropertyManager is displayed. Note: The Begin Assembly PropertyManager is displayed if the Start command when creating new assembly box is checked.

554) Click the **Browse** button.

555) Select **Part** from the Files of type in the SW-TUTORIAL-2010 folder.

556) Double-click the **ANGLE-13HOLE** part.

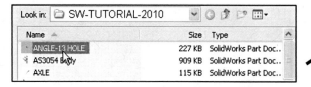

Fix the first component to the Origin.

557) Click **OK** ✔ from the Begin Assembly
PropertyManager. The first component is fixed to the
Origin (f).

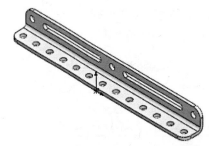

Save the assembly.
558) Click **Save As** from the Menu bar.

559) Select **SW-TUTORIAL-2010** for the Save in file folder.

560) Enter **FRONT-SUPPORT** for File name.

561) Enter **FRONT SUPPORT ASSEMBLY** for Description.

562) Click **Save**. The FRONT-SUPPORT assembly FeatureManager
is displayed.

Set the dimensioning standard and assembly units.
563) Click **Options** 📋, **Document Properties** tab from the Menu
bar.

564) Select **ANSI** from the Overall drafting standard box.

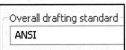

Set the units.
565) Click **Units**.

566) Select **IPS**, **[MMGS]** for Unit
system.

567) Select **.123**, **[.12]** for Length units
Decimal places.

568) Select **None** for Angular units
Decimal places.

569) Click **OK**.

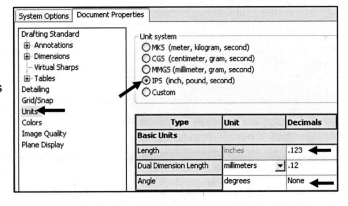

The ANGLE-13HOLE name in the
FeatureManager displays an (f) symbol. The (f) symbol
indicates that the ANGLE-13HOLE component is fixed
to the FRONT-SUPPORT assembly Origin. The
component cannot move or rotate.

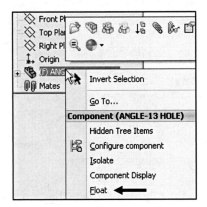

💡 To remove the fixed state, Right-click a component
name in the FeatureManager. Click **Float**. The
component is free to move.

Display the Isometric view.

570) Click **Isometric view** 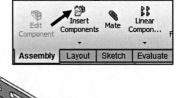 from the Heads-up View toolbar.

Save the assembly.

571) Click **Save** 💾 .

Activity: FRONT-SUPPORT Assembly-Inset HEX-STANDOFF

Insert the HEX-STANDOFF part.

572) Click the **Insert Components** 🗒 Assembly tool. The Insert Component PropertyManager is displayed.

573) Click the **Browse** button.

574) Select **Part** from the Files of type box.

575) Double-click **HEX-STANDOFF** from the SW-TUTORIAL 2010 folder.

576) Click a **position** near the left top hole as illustrated.

Enlarge the view.
577) **Zoom in** on the front left side of the assembly.

Move the component.
578) Click and drag the **HEX-STANDOFF** component below the ANGLE-13HOLE left hole.

The HEX-STANDOFF name in the FeatureManager displays a (-) minus sign. The minus sign indicates that the HEX-STANDOFF part is free to move.

Insert a Concentric mate.
579) Click the **Mate** 🗒 Assembly tool. The Mate PropertyManager is displayed.

580) Click the **left inside cylindrical hole face** of the ANGLE-13HOLE component.

581) Click inside the **cylindrical hole face** of the HEX-STANDOFF component. The selected faces are displayed in the Mate Selections box. Concentric is selected by default.

582) Click the **Green Check mark** ✔ .

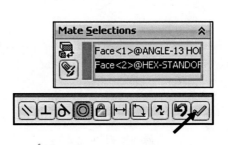

583) Click and drag the **HEX-STANDOFF** component below the ANGLE-13HOLE component until the top face is displayed.

Insert a Coincident mate.
584) Click the **HEX-STANDOFF top face**.

585) Press the **Up Arrow key** approximately 5 times to view the bottom face of the ANGLE-13HOLE component.

586) Click the **ANGLE-13HOLE bottom face**. The selected faces are displayed in the Mate Selections box. Coincident Mate is selected by default.

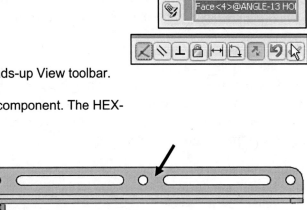

587) Click the **Green Check mark** ✓ .

588) Click **Isometric view** ⬒ from the Heads-up View toolbar.

589) Click and drag the **HEX-STANDOFF** component. The HEX-STANDOFF rotates about its axis.

Insert a Parallel mate.
590) Click **Front view** ⬚ from the Heads-up View toolbar.

591) Click the **HEX-STANDOFF front face**.

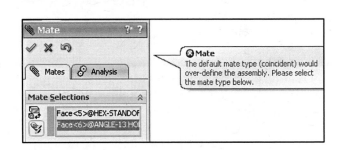

592) Click the **ANGLE-13HOLE front face**. The selected faces are displayed in the Mate Selections box. A Mate message is displayed.

593) Click **Parallel** ⟍ .

594) Click the **Green Check mark** ✓ .

595) Click **OK** ✓ from the Mate PropertyManager.

Display the created mates.
596) Expand the Mates folder in the FRONT-SUPPORT FeatureManager. Three mates are displayed between the ANGLE-13HOLE component and the HEX-STANDOFF component. The HEX-STANDOFF component is fully defined.

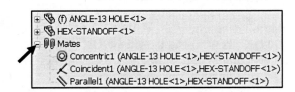

Save the FRONT-SUPPORT assembly.
597) Click **Save** 💾 .

Insert the second HEX-STANDOFF part.
598) Hold the **Ctrl** key down.

599) Click and drag the **HEX-STANDOFF<1>**
⊞ 🐾 (f) ANGLE-13 HOLE<1> name from the FeatureManager into
the FRONT-SUPPORT assembly Graphics window.

600) Release the **mouse pointer** below the far right hole of the
ANGLE-13HOLE component.

601) Release the **Ctrl** key. HEX-STANDOFF<2> is displayed in the
Graphics window and listed in the FeatureManager.

☀️ The number <2> indicates the second instance or copy of
the same component. The instance number increments every time
you insert the same component. If you delete a component and
then reinsert the component in the same SolidWorks session, the
instance number increments by one.

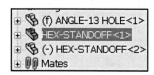

Enlarge the view.
602) **Zoom in** on the right
side of the assembly.

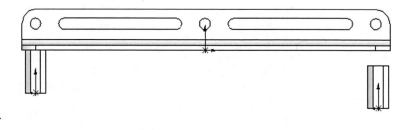

Insert a Concentric mate.
603) Click the **Mate** 📎
Assembly tool. The
Mate PropertyManager
is displayed.

604) Click the **third hole cylindrical face**
from the right ANGLE-13HOLE
component.

605) Click inside the **cylindrical hole face** of
the second HEX-STANDOFF
component. Concentric is selected by
default.

606) Click the **Green Check mark** ✔️ .

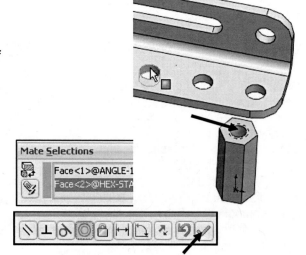

Move the second HEX-STANDOFF part.
607) Click and drag the **HEX-STANDOFF**
component below the ANGLE-13HOLE
component until its top face is
displayed.

Insert a Coincident mate.
608) Click the **second HEX-STANDOFF** top face.

609) Press the **up arrow key** approximately 5 times to view the bottom face of the ANGLE-13HOLE component.

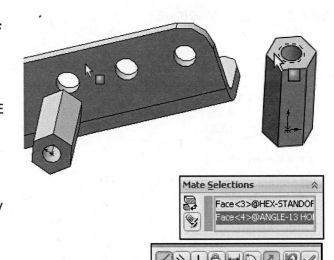

610) Click the **ANGLE-13HOLE bottom face**. The selected faces are displayed in the Mate Selections box. Coincident Mate is selected by default.

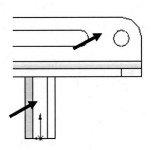

611) Click the **Green Check mark** ✓.

Insert a Parallel mate.
612) Click **Front view** 🔲 Heads-up View toolbar.

613) Click the **front face** of the second HEX-STANDOFF.

614) Click the **front face** of the ANGLE-13HOLE. A Mate message is displayed.

615) Click **Parallel** ⬈.

616) Click the **Green Check mark** ✓.

617) Click **OK** ✓ from the Mate PropertyManager.

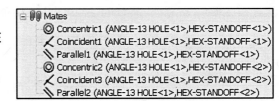

Display the created mates.
618) **Expand** the Mates folder in the FRONT-SUPPORT FeatureManager. Three mates are displayed between the ANGLE-13HOLE component and the second HEX-STANDOFF component. The second HEX-STANDOFF is fully defined.

```
⊟ 🔗 Mates
    ◎ Concentric1 (ANGLE-13 HOLE<1>,HEX-STANDOFF<1>)
    ⟨ Coincident1 (ANGLE-13 HOLE<1>,HEX-STANDOFF<1>)
    ⬈ Parallel1 (ANGLE-13 HOLE<1>,HEX-STANDOFF<1>)
    ◎ Concentric2 (ANGLE-13 HOLE<1>,HEX-STANDOFF<2>)
    ⟨ Coincident3 (ANGLE-13 HOLE<1>,HEX-STANDOFF<2>)
    ⬈ Parallel2 (ANGLE-13 HOLE<1>,HEX-STANDOFF<2>)
```

Activity: FRONT-SUPPORT Assembly-Insert TRIANGLE

Insert the TRIANGLE part.
619) Click **Isometric view** 🔲 from the Heads-up View toolbar.

620) Click the **Insert Components** 🗂 Assembly tool. The Insert Component PropertyManager is displayed.

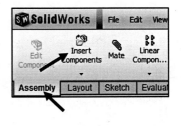

621) Click the **Browse** button.

622) Select **Part** from the Files of type box.

623) Double-click **TRIANGLE**.

624) Click a **position** in back of the ANGLE-13HOLE
component as illustrated.

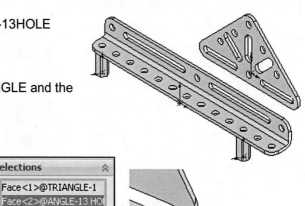

Enlarge the view.
625) Zoom in on the right side of the TRIANGLE and the
ANGLE-13HOLE.

Insert a Concentric mate.
626) Click the **Mate** Assembly
tool. The Mate
PropertyManager is
displayed.

627) Click the **inside right
arc face** of the
TRAINGLE.

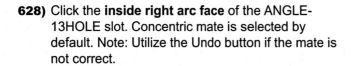

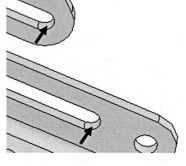

628) Click the **inside right arc face** of the ANGLE-
13HOLE slot. Concentric mate is selected by
default. Note: Utilize the Undo button if the mate is
not correct.

629) Click the **Green Check mark** .

Fit the model to the Graphics window.
630) Press the **f** key.

Insert a Distance mate.
631) Click the **front face** of the TRIANGLE.

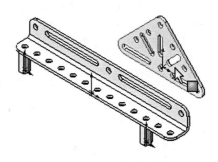

632) Press the **left Arrow key** approximately 5 times to view
the back face of the ANGLE-13HOLE component.

633) Click the **back face** of the ANGLE-13HOLE component.

634) Click **Distance** from the Mate dialog box.

635) Enter **0**.

636) Click the **Green Check mark** .

A Distance Mate of 0
provides additional flexibility
compared to a Coincident mate. A
Distance mate value can be
modified.

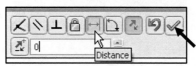

Insert a Parallel mate.

637) Click **Bottom view**  from the Heads-up View toolbar.

638) Click the **narrow bottom face** of the TRIANGLE.

639) Click the **bottom face** of the ANGLE-13HOLE. The selected faces are displayed in the Mate Selections box. A Mate message is displayed.

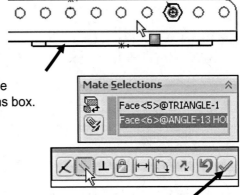

640) Click **Parallel** ⟍.

641) Click the **Green Check mark** ✔ .

642) Click **OK** ✔ from the Mate PropertyManager.

Display the Isometric view.
643) Click **Isometric view** 🔲 from the Heads-up View toolbar.

View the created mates.
644) Expand the Mates folder. View the created mates.

Save the FRONT-SUPPORT assembly.

645) Click **Save** 💾 .

Mates
◎ Concentric1 (ANGLE-13 HOLE<1>,HEX-STANDOFF<1>)
⟋ Coincident1 (ANGLE-13 HOLE<1>,HEX-STANDOFF<1>)
⟍ Parallel1 (ANGLE-13 HOLE<1>,HEX-STANDOFF<1>)
◎ Concentric2 (ANGLE-13 HOLE<1>,HEX-STANDOFF<2>)
⟋ Coincident3 (ANGLE-13 HOLE<1>,HEX-STANDOFF<2>)
⟍ Parallel2 (ANGLE-13 HOLE<1>,HEX-STANDOFF<2>)
◎ Concentric3 (ANGLE-13 HOLE<1>,TRIANGLE<1>)
⊢⊣ Distance1 (TRIANGLE<1>,ANGLE-13 HOLE<1>)
⟍ Parallel3 (ANGLE-13 HOLE<1>,TRIANGLE<1>)

Assemble the four SCREW parts with SmartMates.

A SmartMate is a mate that automatically occurs when a component is placed into an assembly.

The mouse pointer displays a SmartMate feedback symbol when common geometry and relationships exist between the component and the assembly.

SmartMates are Concentric, Coincident, or Concentric and Coincident.

A Concentric SmartMate assumes that the geometry on the component has the same center as the geometry on an assembled reference.

Mating entities	Type of mate	Pointer
2 linear edges	Coincident	
2 planar faces	Coincident	
2 vertices	Coincident	
2 conical faces, or 2 temporary axes, or 1 conical face and 1 temporary axis	Concentric	
2 circular edges (peg-in-hole SmartMates). The edges do not have to be complete circles.	Concentric (conical faces) - and - Coincident (adjacent planar faces)	
2 circular patterns on flanges (flange SmartMates).	Concentric and coincident	

As the component is dragged into place, the mouse pointer provides various feedback icons.

The SCREW utilizes a Concentric and Coincident SmartMate. Assemble the first SCREW. The circular edge of the SCREW mates Concentric and Coincident with the circular edge of the right slot of the TRIANGLE.

Activity: FRONT-SUPPORT Assembly-Inset SCREW

Insert the SCREW part.

646) Click **Open** from the Menu bar.

647) Double-click **SCREW** from the SW-TUTORIAL-2010 folder. The SCREW PropertyManager is displayed.

Display the SCREW part and the FRONT-SUPPORT assembly.
648) Click **Window, Tile Horizontally** from the Menu bar.

649) **Zoom in** on the right side of the FRONT-SUPPORT assembly. Note: Work between the two tile windows.

Insert the first SCREW.
650) Click and drag the **circular edge** of the SCREW part into the FRONT-SUPPORT assembly Graphic window.

651) Release the mouse pointer on the **top 3rd circular hole edge** of the ANGLE-13HOLE. The mouse pointer displays the Coincident / Concentric circular edges icon.

Origins and Tangent Edges are displayed for educational purposes.

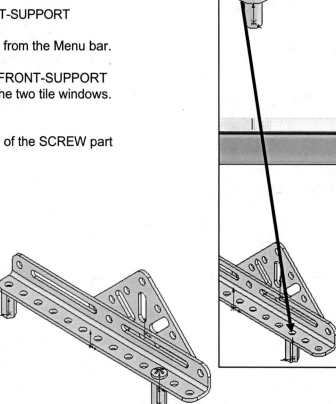

Insert the second SCREW.
652) Zoom in on the right side of the FRONT-SUPPORT assembly.

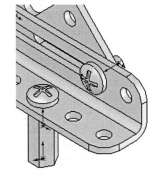

653) Click and drag the **circular edge** of the SCREW part into the FRONT-SUPPORT assembly Graphic window.

654) Release the mouse pointer on the **right arc edge** of the ANGLE-13HOLE. The mouse pointer displays the 🖰 Coincident/ Concentric circular edges icon.

Insert the third SCREW part.
655) Zoom in on the left side of the FRONT-SUPPORT assembly

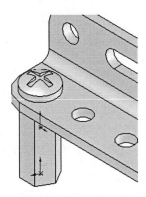

656) Click and drag the **circular edge** of the SCREW part into the FRONT-SUPPORT Assembly Graphic window.

657) Release the mouse pointer on the **left arc edge** of the ANGLE-13HOLE. The mouse pointer displays the 🖰 Coincident/ Concentric circular edges icon.

Insert the forth SCREW part.
658) Zoom in on the bottom circular edge of the ANGLE-13HOLE.

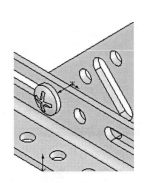

659) Click and drag the **circular edge** of the SCREW part into the FRONT-SUPPORT Assembly Graphic window.

660) Release the mouse pointer on the **bottom circular edge** of the ANGLE-13HOLE. The mouse pointer displays the 🖰 Coincident/Concentric circular edges icon.

661) Close the SCREW part window.

662) Maximize the FRONT-SUPPORT assembly window.

Display the Isometric view.
663) Click **Isometric view** 🧊 from the Heads-up View toolbar.

Deactivate the Origins.
664) Click **View**; uncheck **Origins** from the Menu bar menu.

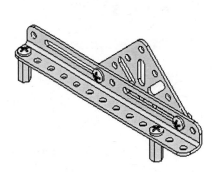

Save the FRONT-SUPPORT assembly.

665) Click **Save** .

🔆 Select the Ctrl-Tab keys to quickly alternate between open SolidWorks documents.

Close all open parts and assemblies.
666) Click **Windows**, **Close All** from the Menu bar.

The FRONT-SUPPORT assembly is complete.

🔆 Display the Mates in the FeatureManager to check that the components and the mate types correspond to the design intent. Utilize the Edit Feature command to modify mate references.

🔆 If an assembly or component is loaded in a Lightweight
🪶 state, right-click the **assembly name** or **component name** from the FeatureManager. Click **Set Lightweight to Resolved**.

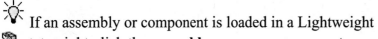 Review the FRONT-SUPPORT Assembly.

The ANGLE-13HOLE part was the first part inserted into the FRONT-SUPPORT assembly. The ANGLE-13HOLE part was fixed to the FRONT-SUPPORT Origin.

Concentric, Coincident, and Parallel mates were utilized to assemble the HEX-STANDOFF to the ANGLE-13HOLE. *Concentric*, *Distance* and *Parallel* mates were utilized to assemble the TRIANGLE to the ANGLE-13HOLE. The *Concentric/ Coincident* SmartMate was utilized to mate the four SCREW parts to the FRONT-SUPPORT assembly.

Chapter Summary

In this chapter you created four parts; HEX-STANDOFF, ANGLE-13HOLE, TRIANGLE and SCREW utilizing the Top, Front, Right Planes and the FRONT-SUPPORT assembly.

You obtained the knowledge of the following SolidWorks features: Extruded Boss/Base, Extruded Thin, Extruded Cut, Revolved Boss/Base, Hole Wizard, Linear Pattern, Circular Pattern, Fillet, and Chamfer. You also applied sketch techniques with various Sketch tools: Line, Circle, Corner Rectangle, Centerline, Dynamic Mirror, Straight Slot, Trim Entities, Polygon, Tangent Arc, Sketch Fillet, Offset Entities and Convert Entities.

You utilized centerlines as construction geometry to reference dimensions and relationships. You incorporated the four new parts to create the FRONT-SUPPORT assembly. Concentric, Distance, and Parallel mates were utilized to assemble the TRIANGLE to the ANGLE-13HOLE. The Concentric/Coincident SmartMate was utilized to mate the four SCREW parts to the FRONT-SUPPORT assembly.

During the initial SolidWorks installation, you were requested to select either the ISO or ANSI drafting standard. ISO is typically a European drafting standard and uses First Angle Projection. The book is written using the ANSI (US) overall drafting standard and Third Angle Projection for drawings.

Chapter Terminology

Utilize SolidWorks Help for additional information on the terms utilized in this project.

Assembly: An assembly is a document which contains components, features, and other sub-assemblies. When a part is inserted into an assembly it is called a component. Components are mated together. The filename extension for a SolidWorks assembly file name is .SLDASM.

Component: A part or sub-assembly within an assembly.

Convert Entities: Converts model entities or sketch entities into sketch segments on the current sketch plane.

Features: Features are geometry building blocks. Features add or remove material. Features are created from sketched profiles or from edges and faces of existing geometry.

Instance Number: The instance number increments every time you insert the same component or mate. If you delete a component or mate and then reinsert the component or mate in the same SolidWorks session, the instance number increments by one.

Mates: A mate is a Geometric relation between components in an assembly.

Mirror Entities: Sketch tool that mirrors sketch geometry to the opposite side of a sketched centerline

Offset Entities: Insert sketch entities by offsetting faces, edges, curves, construction geometry by a specified distance on the current sketch plane.

Orthographic Projection: Orthographic projection is the process of projecting views onto parallel planes with $\perp$ projectors. The default reference planes are the Front, Top and Right Planes.

Part: A part is a single 3D object made up of features. The filename extension for a SolidWorks part file name is .SLDPRT.

Plane: To create a sketch, choose a plane. Planes are flat and infinite. They are represented on the screen with visible edges. The Front, Top and Right Planes were utilized as Sketch planes for parts in this project.

Relation: A relation is a geometric constraint between sketch entities or between a sketch entity and a plane, axis, edge or vertex.

Sketch: The name to describe a 2D or 3D profile is called a sketch. 2D Sketches are created on flat faces and planes within the model. Typical geometry types are lines, arcs, rectangles, circles and ellipses.

SmartMates: A SmartMate is a mate that automatically occurs when a component is placed into an assembly and references geometry between that component and the assembly.

Standard Views: Front, Back, Right, Left, Top, Bottom and Isometric are Standard views utilized to orient the model. Note: Third Angle Projection is used in this book.

Suppress features: A suppress feature is not displayed in the Graphics window. A suppress feature is removed from any rebuild calculations.

Trim Entities: Sketch tool that removes highlighted geometry.

Chapter Features

Chamfer: A Chamfer feature creates bevels on selected edges and faces.

Circular Pattern: A Circular Pattern feature repeats features or faces about an axis in a circular array. A Circular Pattern requires and axis, number of instances, and the angle of revolution.

Extruded Boss/Base: A Boss-Extrude1 feature is the first feature in a part. The Extruded Boss/Base feature starts with either a 2D or 3D sketch. An Extruded Boss feature (Boss-Extrude2) occurs after the Extruded Base (Boss-Extrude1) feature. The Extruded Boss/Base feature adds material by extrusion. Steps to create an Extruded Boss/Base Feature:

- Select the Sketch plane; Sketch the profile 2D or 3D; Add dimensions and Geometric relations; Select Extruded Boss/Base from the Features toolbar; Select an End Condition and/or options; Enter a depth; Click OK from the Boss-Extrude PropertyManager.

Extruded Cut: The Extruded Cut feature removes material from a solid. The Extruded Cut feature performs the opposite function of the Extruded Boss/Base feature. The Extruded Cut feature starts with either a 2D or 3D sketch and removes material by extrusion. Steps to create an Extruded Cut Feature:

- Select the Sketch plane; Sketch the profile, 2D or 3D; Add dimensions and Geometric relations; Select Extruded Cut from the Features toolbar; Select an End Condition and/or options; Enter a depth; Click OK from the Cut-Extrude PropertyManager.

Extruded Thin: The Extruded Thin feature adds material of constant thickness. The Extruded Thin feature requires an open profile.

Fillet: The Fillet feature creates a rounded internal or external face on a part. You can fillet all edges of a face, selected sets of faces, selected edges or edge loops.

Hole Wizard: The Hole Wizard feature provides the ability to determine the capabilities, available selections, and graphic previews for various hole types. First select a hole type, then determine the appropriate fastener. The fastener dynamically updates the appropriate parameters.

Linear Pattern: A Linear Pattern repeats features or geometry in an array. A Linear Patten requires the number of instances and the spacing between instances. Steps to create a Linear Pattern Feature:

- Select the feature/s to repeat (Seed feature); Select Linear Pattern from the Feature toolbar; Enter Direction of the pattern; Enter Number of pattern instances in each direction; Enter Distance between pattern instances; Optional: Pattern instances to skip; Click OK from the Linear Pattern PropertyManager.

Mirror: The Mirror feature mirrors features or faces about a selected plane. Select the features to copy and a plane about which to mirror them. If you select a planar face on the model, you mirror the entire model about the selected face.

Revolved Boss/Base: The Revolved Boss/Base feature adds material by revolving one or more profiles around a centerline. Create Revolved boss/bases, Revolved cuts, or Revolved surfaces. The Revolve feature can be a solid, a thin feature, or a surface.

Engineering Journal

Engineers and designers research their customer's requirements and criteria. They utilize mathematics, science, economics and history to calculate additional information about a project.

Engineers adhere to federal regulations and standards to design parts that are safe and reliable. Record the answers to the questions in an engineering journal.

1. Estimation. The volume of the golf ball is approximated with the model of a sphere. A sphere is a revolved feature. What is the volume of the sphere?

Volume of a sphere is provided by the formula; $V = 4/3 \, \pi \, r^3$. Where:

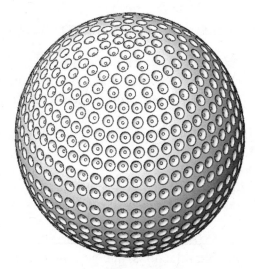

Model Courtesy of
Scott Baugh, CSWP
www.scottjbaugh.com

- V is volume.

- r is the radius.

a.) Determine the radius of the sphere in mm and inches.

b.) Calculate the Volume of the sphere in mm^3 and in^3.

c.) The actual volume of the golf ball model is $1.001 \, in^3$. Why does the volume value differ from the calculated volume of the sphere?

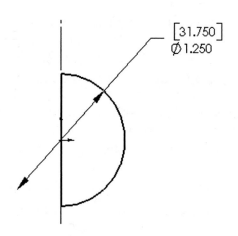

[31.750]
Ø1.250

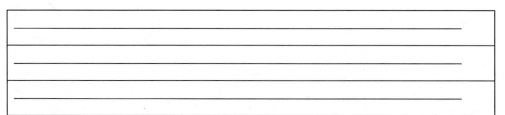

2. Sketching.

- Sketch the top view of a Flat-Plate. The overall dimensions of the Flat-Plate are: 8.688in x 5.688in x 0.090in.

The four corners of the Flat-Plate are rounded with a .25in Radius.

A two dimensional array of Ø.190in holes is spaced .500in apart.

The holes are .344in from all four sides.

- Determine the size of the two dimensional array of holes. Determine the total number of holes contained on the Flat-Plate. (Note: Sketch Not to Scale).

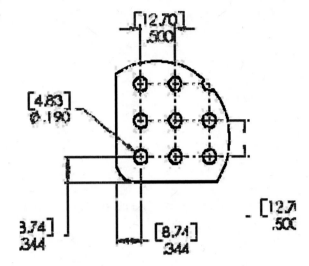

3. Sketching on Planes.

a) Label the Front, Top, and Right Planes. Sketch an L-shaped profile on the Front Plane.

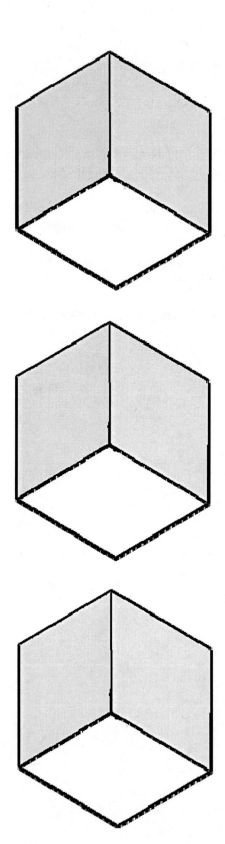

b) Sketch an L-shaped profile on the Top Plane. Label the Primary Datum plane.

c) Sketch an L-shaped profile on the Right Plane. Label the Secondary Datum plane.

4. Industry Application

Calculating material volume is important when designing parts.

Volume = Width x Height x Depth.

The Extruded Base feature of the container is 45cm x 20cm x 30cm.

- Estimate the approximate volume of the container in cm^3.

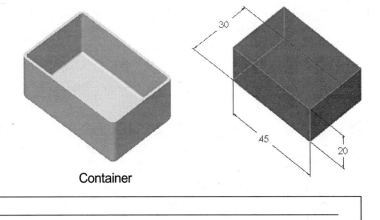

Container

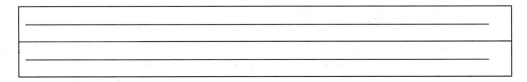

Volume for food containers is commonly provided in liters or gallons.

Examples: 2-liter soda bottle or a gallon of milk.

- Calculate the volume of the container in liters and in gallons.

Given: 1 liter = 1000 cm^3

       1 gallon = 3.785 liters.

- Approximately how many liters would the container hold? How many gallons?

The actual volume of the Container is 23 liters. Explain why this value does not equal your first estimated volume.

Questions

1. Identify the three default Reference planes used in SolidWorks.

2. True or False. Sketches are created only on the Front Plane.

3. Identify the sketch tool required to create a hexagon.

4. Describe the profile required for an Extruded Thin feature.

5. Mirror Entities, Offset Entities, Sketch Fillet, and Trim Entities are located in the _____ toolbar.

6. List the six principle views in a drawing _____, _____, _____, _____, _____, _____,

7. Identify the type of Geometric relations that can be added to a sketch.

8. Describe the difference between a Circular Pattern feature and a Linear Pattern feature.

9. Describe the difference between a Fillet feature and a Chamfer feature.

10. Identify the function of the Hole Wizard feature.

11. Four 10-24X3/8 Machine Screws are required in the FRONT-SUPPORT assembly. The diameter is _____. The threads per inch are _____. The length is _____.

12. Describe the difference between a Distance mate and a Coincident mate.

13. True or False. A fixed component cannot move in an assembly.

14. Describe the procedure to remove the fix state, (f) of a component in an assembly.

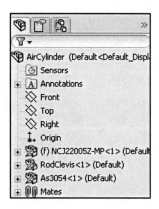

15. Determine the procedure to rotate a component in an assembly.

16. Describe the procedure to resolve a Lightweight component in an assembly.

17. Describe the procedure to resolve a Lightweight assembly.

Exercises

Exercise 2.1: HEX-NUT Part

Create an ANSI, IPS HEX-NUT Part. Apply 6061 Alloy material. Apply the following dimensions:

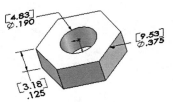

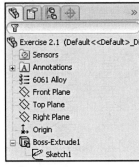

- Depth: .125 in, [3.18].

- Inside hole diameter: .190in, [4.83].

- Outside diameter: .375in, [9.53].

Use the Top Plane as the Sketch plane.

Exercise 2.2: FRONT-SUPPORT-2 Assembly

Create an ANSI, IPS FRONT-SUPPORT-2 assembly.

- Name the new assembly FRONT-SUPPORT-2.

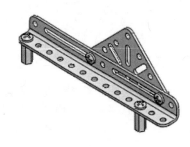

- Insert the FRONT-SUPPORT assembly. The FRONT-SUPPORT assembly was created in this Chapter. Note: The FRONT-SUPPORT assembly is provided in the Chapter 2 Homework folder on the CD. Copy all parts to your folder on the computer. Do not work from the CD.

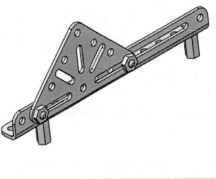

- Fix the FRONT-SUPPORT assembly to the Origin.

- Insert the first HEX-NUT (Exercise 2.1) into the FRONT-SUPPORT-2 assembly.

- Insert a Concentric mate.

- Insert a Coincident mate.

- Insert the second HEX-NUT part.

- Insert a Concentric mate.

- Insert a Coincident mate.

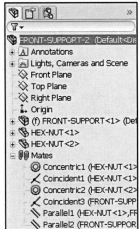

Note: You can also insert a Parallel mate between the HEX-NUT parts and the FRONT-SUPPORT assembly.

Exercise 2.3: BALL Part

Create an ANSI, IPS Ball part. Utilize the
Revolved Base feature. Note: This is just
ONE way to create the model.

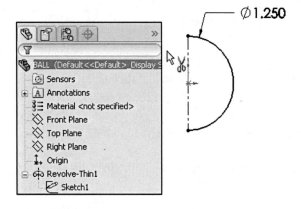

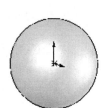

- Create a new part named BALL.

- Use the Front Plane as the Sketch
  plane. Sketch a circle with a diameter
  of 1.250in, [31.75].

- Sketch a vertical centerline Coincident with the Origin.

- Use Power Trim to trim the left half of the ball to create an
  arc.

- Utilize the Revolved Base feature to create the Revolve-Thin1
  feature as illustrated in the FeatureManager.

Exercise 2.4: Weight-Hook Assembly

Create an ANSI, IPS Weight-Hook assembly. The Weight-Hook
assembly has two components: WEIGHT and HOOK.

- Create a new assembly document. Copy and insert the
  WEIGHT part from the Chapter 2 Homework folder in the
  book CD. Note: Do not use the component directly from the
  folder on the CD. Copy all parts to your computer.

- Fix the WEIGHT to the Origin as illustrated in the Assem1
  FeatureManager.

- Insert the HOOK part from the Chapter2 - Homework
  folder into the assembly.

- Insert a Concentric mate between the inside top
  cylindrical face of the WEIGHT and the cylindrical face
  of the thread. Concentric is the default mate.

- Insert the first Coincident mate between the top edge of
  the circular hole of the WEIGHT and the top circular
  edge of Sweep1, above the thread.

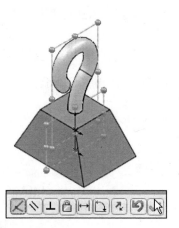

- Coincident is the default mate. The HOOK can rotate in the WEIGHT.

- Fix the position of the HOOK. Insert the second Coincident mate between the Right Plane of the WEIGHT and the Right Plane of the HOOK. Coincident is the default mate.

- Expand the Mates folder and view the created mates.

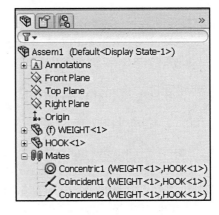

Exercise 2.5: Weight-Link Assembly

Create an ANSI, IPS Weight-Link assembly. The Weight-Link assembly has two components and a sub-assembly: Axle component, FLATBAR component, and the Weight-Hook sub-assembly that you created in Exercise 2.4.

- Create a new assembly document. Copy and insert the Axle part from the Chapter 2 Homework folder in the book CD. Note: Do not use the part/component directly from the folder on the CD. Copy all parts and components to your computer from the CD

- Fix the Axle component to the Origin.

- Copy and insert the FLATBAR part from the Chapter2 - Homework folder in the book CD. Note: Do not use the part/component directly from the folder on the CD. Copy all parts and components to your computer from the CD.

- Insert a Concentric mate between the Axle cylindrical face and the FLATBAR inside face of the top circle.

☼ If an assembly or component is loaded in a Lightweight 🔖 state, right-click the **assembly name or component name** from the FeatureManager. Click **Set Lightweight to Resolved**.

- Insert a Coincident mate between the Front Plane of the Axle and the Front Plane of the FLATBAR.

- Insert a Coincident mate between the Right Plane of the Axle and the Top Plane of the FLATBAR. Position the FLATBAR as illustrated.

- Insert the Weight-Hook sub-assembly that you created in exercise 2.4.

- Insert a Tangent mate between the inside bottom cylindrical face of the FLATBAR and the top circular face of the HOOK, in the Weight-Hook assembly. Tangent mate is selected by default.

- Insert a Coincident mate between the Front Plane of the FLATBAR and the Front Plane of the Weight-Hook sub-assembly. Coincident mate is selected by default. The Weight-Hook sub-assembly is free to move in the bottom circular hole of the FLATBAR.

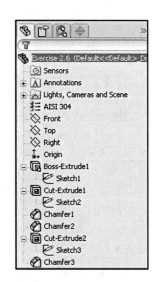

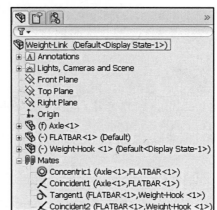

Exercise 2.6: Mounting-Nut Part

Create a Mounting-Nut Part using the features displayed in the illustrated FeatureManager.

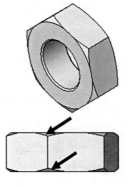

Exercise 2.7: Slider Part

Create the part from the illustrated ANSI - MMGS Third Angle Projection drawing: Front, Top, Right and Isometric views.

Note: The location of the Origin.

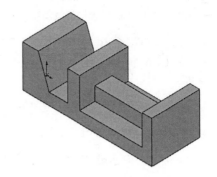

- Apply Cast Alloy steel for material.

- The part is symmetric about the Front Plane.

- Calculate the Volume of the part and locate the Center of mass.

Think about the steps that you would take to build the model. Do you need the Right view for manufacturing? Does it add any information?

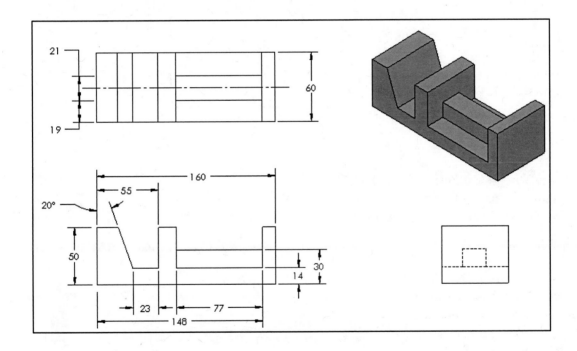

Exercise 2.8: Cosmetic Thread Part

Apply a Cosmetic thread: 1/4-20x2 UNC. A cosmetic thread represents the inner diameter of a thread on a boss or the outer diameter of a thread.

Open the **Cosmetic thread** part model from the Chapter 2 Homework folder on the CD. Note: Do not use the part/component directly from the folder on the CD. Copy all parts and components to your computer from the CD.

Create a Cosmetic thread. Produce the geometry of the thread. Click the bottom edge of the part as illustrated.

Click Insert, Annotations, Cosmetic Thread from the Menu bar menu. View the Cosmetic Thread PropertyManager. Edge<1> is displayed.

Select Blind for End Condition.

Enter 1.00 for depth.

Enter .200 for min diameter.

Enter ¼-20-2 UNC 2A in the Thread Callout box.

Click OK ✔ from the Cosmetic Thread FeatureManager.

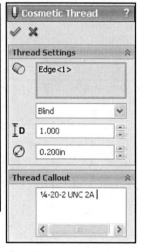

Expand the FeatureManager. View the Cosmetic Thread feature.

If needed, right-click the Annotations folder; click Details.

Check the Cosmetic threads and Shaded cosmetic threads box.

Click OK. View the cosmetic thread on the model.

☼ The Thread Callout: ¼-20-2UNC 2A is automatically inserted into a drawing document if the drawing document is in the ANSI drafting standard.

☼ ¼-20-2 UNC 2A - ¼ inch drill diameter. The annotation means - 20 threads / inch, Unified National Coarse thread series, Class 2, External threads

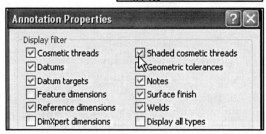

Exercise 2.9: Hole - Block

Create the Hole - Block (Hole Wizard feature) part as illustrated. Create the Part document: ANSI drafting standard, IPS unit system and set precision. Display the Origin and Sketch relations. Create the Hole - Block part on the Front Plane. Note: All sketches should be fully defined.

Create a rectangular prism 2 inches wide by 5 inches long by 2 inches high. On the top surface of the prism, place four holes, 1 inch apart:

- Hole #1: Simple hole Type: Fractional Drill Size, 7/16 diameter, End Condition: Blind, 0.75 inch deep.
- Hole #2: Counterbore hole Type: for 3/8 inch diameter Hex bolt, End Condition: Through All.
- Hole #3: Countersink hole Type: for 3/8 inch diameter Flat head screw, 1.5 inch deep.
- Hole #4: Tapped hole Type, Size ¼-20, End Condition: Blind, 1.0 inch deep.

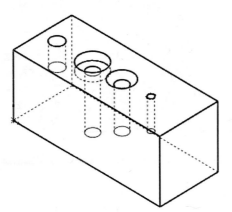
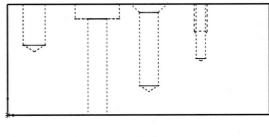

Exercise 2.10: Hole Wizard Part

Apply the 3D sketch placement method as illustrated in the FeatureManager. Insert and dimension a hole on a cylindrical face.

Open Hole Wizard 2-10 from the Chapter 2 Homework folder on the CD. Note: Do not use the part/component directly from the folder on the CD. Copy it first to your folder.

Click the Hole Wizard 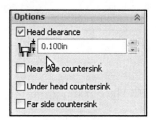 Features tool. The Hole Specification PropertyManager is displayed.

Select the Counterbore Hole Type.

Select ANSI Inch for Standard.

Select Socket Head Cap Screw for fastener Type.

Select 1/4 for Size. Select Normal for Fit.

Select Through All for End Condition.

Enter .100 for Head clearance in the Options box.

Click the Positions Tab. The Hole Position PropertyManager is displayed. SolidWorks

displays a 3D interface with the Point 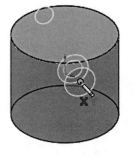 tool active.

When the Point tool is active, wherever you click, you will create a point.

Click the cylindrical face of the model as illustrated. The selected face is displayed in orange. This indicates that an OnSurface sketch relation will be created between the sketch point and the cylindrical face. The hole is displayed in the model.

Insert a dimension between the top face and the Sketch point.

Click the Smart Dimension 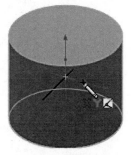 Sketch tool.

Click the top flat face of the model and the sketch point.

Enter .25in.

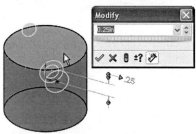

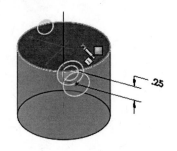

Locate the point angularly around the cylinder. Apply construction geometry.

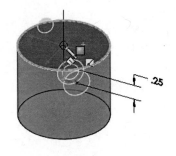

Activate the Temporary Axes. Click View; check the Temporary Axes box from the Menu bar toolbar.

Click the Line ✎ Sketch tool. Note: 3D sketch is still activated.

Ctrl+click the top flat face of the model. This moves the red space handle origin to the selected face. This also constrains any new sketch entities to the top flat face. Note the mouse

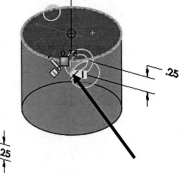

pointer ✎ ⎿ icon.

Move the mouse pointer near the center of the activated top flat face as illustrated. View the small black circle. The circle indicates that the end point of the line will pick up a Coincident relation.

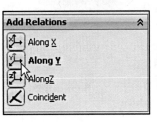

Click the centerpoint of the circle.

Sketch a line so it picks up the **AlongZ sketch relation**. The cursor displays the relation to be applied. **This is a very important step!**

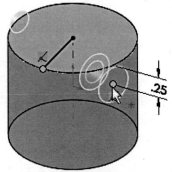

Add Relations ⌃

⬈	Along X
⬈	**Along Y**
⬈	AlongZ
⤡	Coincident

Create an AlongY sketch relation between the centerpoint of the hole on the cylindrical face and the endpoint of the sketched line as illustrated.

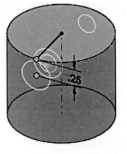

Click OK ✔ from the Properties PropertyManager.

Click OK ✔ from the Hole Position PropertyManager.

Expand the FeatureManager and view the results. The two sketches are fully defined.

Close the model.

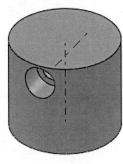

You can create a second sketched line and insert an angle dimension between the two lines. This process is used to control the position of the centerpoint of the hole on the cylindrical face as illustrated. Insert an AlongY sketch relation between the centerpoint of the hole on the cylindrical face and the end point of the second control line. Control the hole position with the angular dimension.

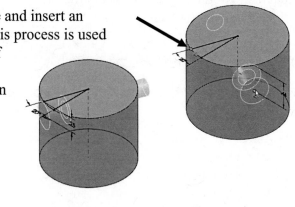

Exercise 2.11: DFMXpress

Apply the DFMXpress Wizard. DFMXpress is an analysis tool that validates the manufacturability of SolidWorks parts. Use DFMXpress to identify design areas that may cause problems in fabrication or increase the costs of production.

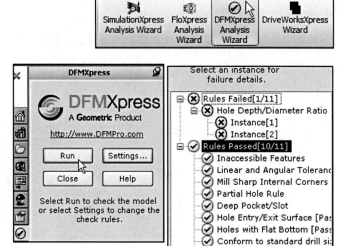

- Open the ROD Part from the Chapter 2 Homework folder on the CD. Note: Do not use the part/component directly from the folder on the CD. Copy all parts and components to your computer from the CD.

- Click the Evaluate tab in the CommandManager.

- Click DFMXpress Analysis Wizard.

- Click the RUN button.

- Expand each folder. View the results.

- Make any needed changes and save the ROD. Use other models that you created and apply DFMXpress Wizard.

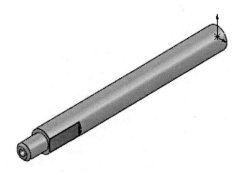

Exercise 2.12: Counter Weight Assembly

Create the Counter Weight assembly as illustrated from the Assembly FeatureManager. All components and sub-assemblies are supplied in the Chapter 2 – Homework/ Counter-Weight folder on the CD.

Copy all components and sub-assemblies to your working folder.

The Counter Weight consists of the following items:

- Weight-Hook sub-assembly.
- Axle component (f). Fixed to the origin!
- Flat component.
- Flat Washer Type A from the SolidWorks Toolbox.
- Pan Cross Head Screw from the SolidWorks Toolbox.
- Flat Washer Type A from the SolidWorks toolbox.
- Machine Screw Nut Hex from the SolidWorks Toolbox.

Note: The symbol (f) represents a fixed component. A fixed component cannot move and is locked to the assembly Origin. To fix the first component to the Origin, click OK ✔ from the Begin Assembly PropertyManager or click the Origin in the Graphics window.

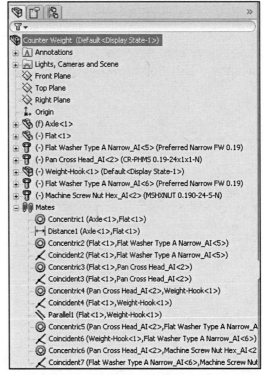

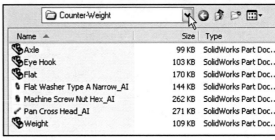

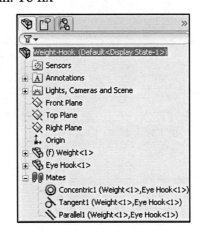

Exercise 2.13: **AIR RESERVOIR SUPPORT AND PLATE Assembly**

The project team developed a concept sketch of the PNEUMATIC TEST MODULE assembly. Develop the AIR RESERVOIR SUPPORT AND PLATE assembly.

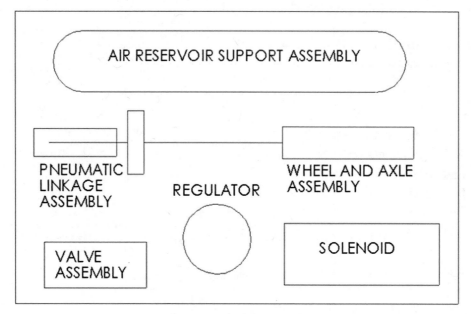

PNEUMATIC TEST MODULE Assembly Layout

Create three new parts:

- FLAT-PLATE

- IM15-MOUNT

- ANGLE-BRACKET

The Reservoir is a purchased part. The assembly file is available from the CD in the book.

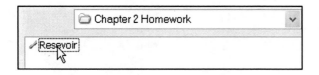

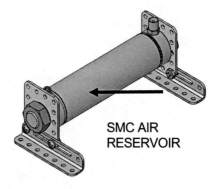

SMC AIR
RESERVOIR

AIR RESERVOIR SUPPORT Assembly
Courtesy of Gears Educational Systems & SMC
Corporation of America

- Create a new assembly named AIR RESERVOIR SUPPORT AND PLATE.

- Two M15-MOUNT parts and two ANGLE-BRACKET parts hold the SMC AIR RESERVOIR.

- The ANGLE-BRACKET parts are fastened to the FLAT-PLATE.

Exercise 2.13a: FLAT-PLATE Part

Create the FLAT-PLATE Part on the Top Plane. The FLAT-PLATE is machined from .090, [2.3] 6061 Alloy flat stock. The default units are inches.

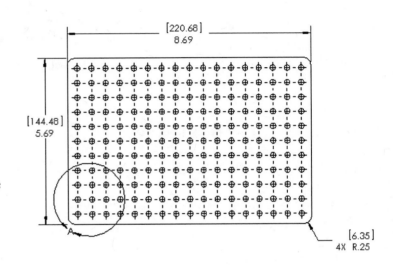

Utilize the Top Plane for the Sketch plane.

Locate the Origin at the Midpoint of the left vertical line.

The 8.690, [220.68mm] x 5.688, [144.48mm] FLAT PLATE contains a Linear Pattern of ∅.190, [4.83mm] Thru holes.

The Holes are equally spaced, .500, [12.7mm] apart.

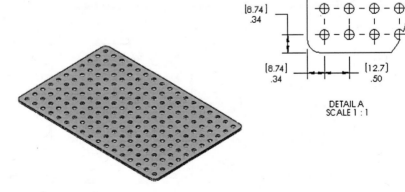

DETAIL A
SCALE 1 : 1

Determine the maximum number of holes contained in the FLAT-PLATE.

Maximum # of holes_____.

- Utilize a Linear Pattern in two Directions to create the holes.

- Utilize the Geometric Pattern Option.

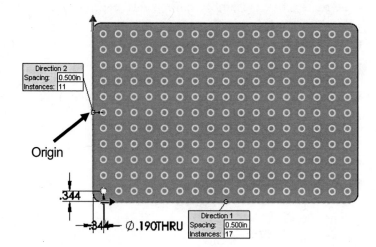

Exercise 2.13b: IM15-MOUNT Part

- Create the IM15-MOUNT part on the Right plane.

- Center the part on the Origin. Utilize the features in the FeatureManager.

- The IM15-MOUNT Part is machined from 0.060, [1.5mm] 6061 Alloy flat stock. The default units are inches.

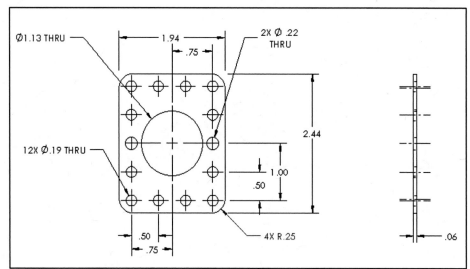

Exercise 2.13c: ANGLE BRACKET Part

- Create the ANGLE BRACKET part.

- The Extruded Base (Boss-Extrude1) feature is sketched with an L-Shaped profile on the Right Plane. The ANGLE BRACKET Part is machined from 0.060, [1.5mm] 6061 Alloy flat stock. The default units are inches.

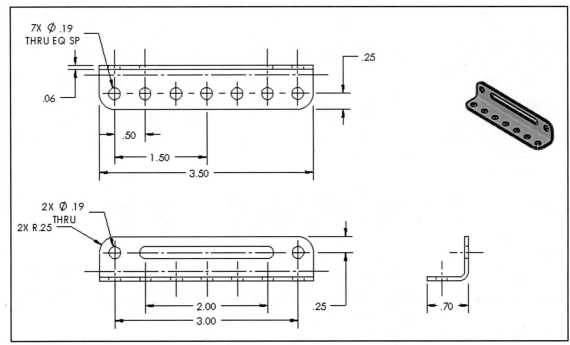

Exercise 2.13d: Reservoir Assembly

The Reservoir stores compressed air. Air is
pumped through a Schrader Valve into the
Reservoir.

Schrader Valve

A Quick Connect Straight Fitting is utilized to
supply air to the Pneumatic Test Module
Assembly. Quick Connect Fittings allow air
tubing to be assembled and disassembled without
removing the fitting.

Quick Connect
Straight Fitting

Copy the Pneumatic Components folder from the
CD in the book to the SW-TUTORIAL folder.

Reservoir and Fittings
Courtesy of SMC Corporation of America and
Gears Educational Systems

Open the part, Reservoir from the Pneumatics
Components folder or from the Chapter 2
Homework folder. The Reservoir default units are in millimeters (MMGS).

Engineers and designers work in metric and english units. Always verify your units for
parts and other engineering data. In pneumatic systems, common units for volume,
pressure and temperature are defined in the below table.

Magnitude	Metric Unit (m)	English (e)
Mass	kg	pound
	g	ounce
Length	m	foot
	m	yard
	mm	inch
Temperature	°C	°F
Area, Section	m ^{2}	sq.ft
	cm ^{2}	sq.inch
Volume	m ^{3}	cu.yard
	cm ^{3}	cu.inch
	dm ^{3}	cu.ft.
Volume Flow	m ^{3}n / min	scfm
	dm ^{3}n /min (ℓ/min)	scfm
Force	N	pound force (ℓbf.)
Pressure	bar	ℓbf./sq.inch (psi)

Common Metric and English Units

The ISO unit of pressure is the Pa (Pascal). 1Pa = 1N/m.

Exercise 2.13e: AIR RESERVOIR SUPPORT AND PLATE Assembly

Create the AIR RESERVOIR SUPPORT AND PLATE assembly. Note: There is more than one solution for the mate types illustrated below.

The FLAT-PLATE is the first component in the AIR RESERVOIR SUPPORT AND PLATE assembly. Insert the FLAT-PLATE. The FLAT-PLATE is fixed to the Origin.

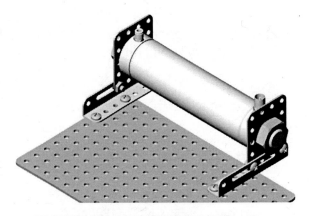

AIR RESERVOIR SUPPORT AND PLATE Assembly
Courtesy of SMC Corporation of America

- Insert the ANGLE BRACKET.

- Mate the ANGLE BRACKET to the FLAT-PLATE. The bottom flat face of the ANGLE BRACKET is coincident to the top face of the FLAT-PLATE.

- The center hole of the ANGLE BRACKET is concentric to the upper left hole of the FLAT-PLATE.

- The first hole of the ANGLE bracket is concentric with the hole in the 8th row, 1st column of the FLAT-PLATE.

- Insert the IM15-MOUNT.

- Mate the IM15-MOUNT. The IM15-MOUNT flat back face is coincident to the flat inside front face of the ANGLE BRACKET.

- The bottom right hole of the IM15-MOUNT is concentric with the right hole of the ANGLE BRACKET.

- The bottom edge of the IM15-MOUNT is parallel to bottom edge of the ANGLE BRACKET.

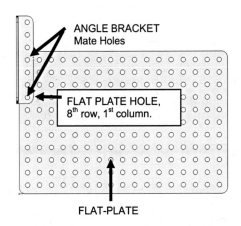

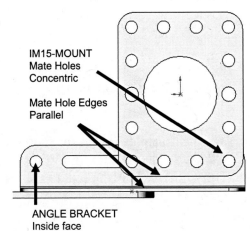

- Insert the Reservoir Assembly.

- Mate the Reservoir Assembly. The conical face of the Reservoir is concentric to the IM15-MOUNT center hole.

- The left end cap of the Reservoir Assembly is coincident to the front face of the IM15-MOUNT.

- The Hex Nut flat face is parallel to the top face of the FLAT-PLATE.

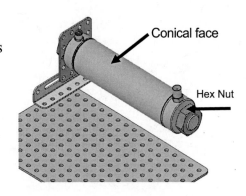

Conical face

Hex Nut

- Insert the second ANGLE BRACKET.

- Mate the ANGLE BRACKET to the FLAT-PLATE. The bottom flat face of the ANGLE BRACKET is coincident to the top face of the FLAT-PLATE.

- The center hole of the ANGLE BRACKET is concentric with the hole in the 11th row, 13th column of the FLAT-PLATE.

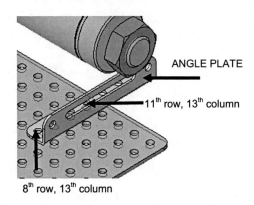

ANGLE PLATE

11th row, 13th column

8th row, 13th column

- The first hole of the ANGLE bracket is concentric with the hole in the 8th row, 13th column of the FLAT-PLATE.

- Insert the second IM15-MOUNT.

- Mate the IM15-MOUNT to the outside face of the ANGLE BRACKET. The bottom right hole of the IM15-MOUNT is concentric with the right hole of the ANGLE BRACKET.

- The top edge of the IM15-MOUNT is parallel to the top edge of the ANGLE BRACKET.

- Save the assembly. Insert the required SCREWS. The AIR RESERVOIR SUPPORT AND PLATE assembly is complete.

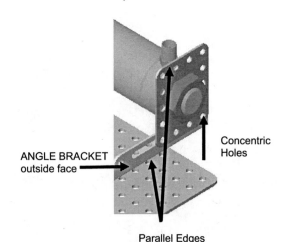

ANGLE BRACKET outside face

Concentric Holes

Parallel Edges

Chapter 3

Fundamentals of Drawing

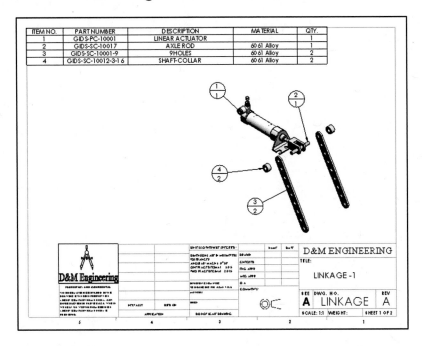

ITEM NO.	PART NUMBER	DESCRIPTION	MATERIAL	QTY.
1	GIDS-PC-10001	LINEAR ACTUATOR		1
2	GIDS-SC-10017	AXLE ROD	6061 Alloy	1
3	GIDS-SC-10001-9	9HOLES	6061 Alloy	2
4	GIDS-SC-10012-3-16	SHAFT-COLLAR	6061 Alloy	2

Below are the desired outcomes and usage competencies based on the completion of Chapter 3.

Desired Outcomes:	Usage Competencies:
• CUSTOM-A Sheet Format. • A-ANSI-MM Drawing Template.	• Ability to create a Custom Sheet Format, Drawing Template, Company logo and Title block.
• FLATBAR configurations. • FLATBAR part drawing. • LINKAGE assembly drawing. • FLATBAR-SHAFTCOLLAR assembly.	• Understand Standard, Isometric, Detail, Section and Exploded views. • Knowledge of the View Palette. • Ability to incorporate a Bill of Materials with Custom Properties
	• Proficiency to create and edit drawing dimensions and annotations. • Aptitude to create a Design Table.

Notes:

Chapter 3 - Fundamentals of Drawing

Chapter Objective

Create a FLATBAR drawing with a customized Sheet Format and a Drawing Template containing a Company logo and Title block.

Obtain an understanding to display the following views with the ability to insert, add and edit dimensions and annotations:

- Standard: Top, Front and Right

- Isometric, Detail and Section

- Exploded

Create a LINKAGE assembly drawing with a Bill of Materials. Obtain knowledge to develop and incorporate a Bill of Materials with Custom Properties. Create a FLATBAR-SHAFTCOLLAR assembly.

On the completion of this chapter, you will be able to:

- Create a customized Sheet Format.

- Generate a custom Drawing Template.

- Produce a Bill of Materials with Custom Properties.

- Develop various drawing views.

- Reposition views on a drawing.

- Move dimensions in the same view.

- Apply Edit Sheet Format mode and Edit Sheet mode.

- Modify the dimension scheme.

- Create a Parametric drawing note.

- Link notes in the Title block to SolidWorks properties.

- Generate an Exploded view.

- Create and edit a Design Table.

Chapter Overview

Generate two drawings in this chapter:

- FLATBAR part drawing and a LINKAGE assembly drawing.

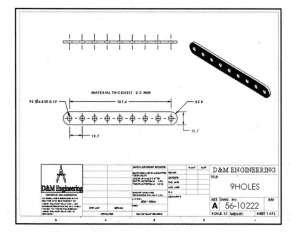

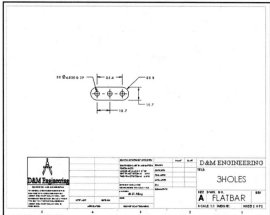

The FLATBAR drawing utilizes a custom Drawing Template and a custom Sheet Format. The FLATBAR drawing contains two sheets:

- Sheet1 contains a Front, Top and Isometric view with dimensions and a linked Parametric note.

- Sheet2 contains the 3HOLE configuration of the FLATBAR. Configurations are created with a Design Table.

The LINKAGE assembly drawing contains two sheets:

- Sheet1 contains the LINKAGE assembly in an Exploded view with a Bill of Materials.

- Sheet2 contains the AirCylinder assembly with a Section view, Detail view, and a Scale view.

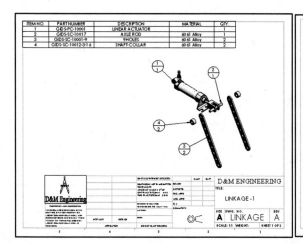

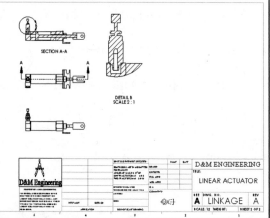

Create the FLATBAR-SHAFTCOLLAR assembly.
Utilize a Design Table to create four new
configurations of the assembly.

☀ Tangent Edges are displayed for educational
purposes.

There are two major design modes used to develop
a drawing:

- *Edit Sheet Format*

- *Edit Sheet*

The *Edit Sheet Format* mode provides the ability to:

- Change the Title block size and text headings.

- Incorporate a Company logo.

- Add Custom Properties and text.

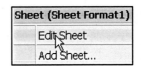

The *Edit Sheet* mode provides the ability to:

- Add or modify views

- Add or modify dimensions

- Add or modify notes

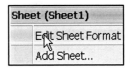

Drawing Template and Sheet Format

The foundation of a SolidWorks drawing is the Drawing Template.
Drawing size, drawing standards, company information,
manufacturing and or assembly requirements, units and other
properties are defined in the Drawing Template.

The Sheet Format is incorporated into the Drawing Template. The
Sheet Format contains the border, Title block information, Revision
block information, Company name and or Logo information,
Custom Properties, and SolidWorks Properties.

Custom Properties and SolidWorks Properties are shared values
between documents. Utilize an A-size Drawing Template with Sheet
format for the FLATBAR drawing and LINKAGE assembly
drawing.

During the initial SolidWorks installation, you are requested to select either the ISO or ANSI drafting standard. ISO is typically a European drafting standard and uses First Angle Projection. The book is written using the ANSI (US) overall drafting standard and Third Angle Projection for drawings.

Views from the part or assembly are inserted into the SolidWorks drawing.

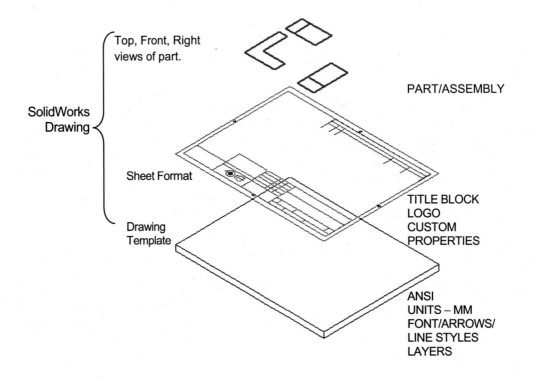

Create Sheet Formats for different parts types. Example: sheet metal parts, plastic parts, and high precision machined parts.

Create Sheet Formats for each category of parts that are manufactured with unique sets of title block notes.

Note: The Third Angle Projection scheme is illustrated in this chapter.

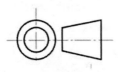

Third Angle
Projection icon

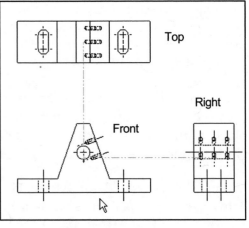

Third Angle Projection

For non-ANSI dimension standards, the dimensioning techniques are the same, even if the displayed arrows and text size are different. For printers supporting millimeter paper sizes, select A4 (ANSI) Landscape (297mm × 210mm).

The default Drawing Templates contain predefined Title block Notes linked to Custom Properties and SolidWorks Properties.

Activity: New Drawing

Create a new drawing. Close all parts and drawings.

1) Click **Windows**, **Close All** from the Menu bar.

2) Click **New** ⬚ from the Menu bar.

3) Double-click **Drawing** from the Templates tab.

4) Select **A (ANSI) Landscape**.

5) Click **OK** from the Sheet Format/Size box.

6) If required, click **Cancel** ✖ from the Model View PropertyManager. The Draw FeatureManager is displayed.

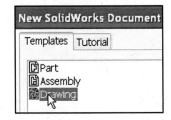

🔆 A new drawing invokes the Model View PropertyManager if the Start Command When Creating New Drawing option is checked.

The A (ANSI) Landscape paper is displayed in a new Graphics window. The sheet border defines the drawing size, $11'' \times 8.5''$ or ($279.4mm \times 215.9mm$).

🔆 To view the sheet properties, right-click Properties in the drawing sheet. View the Sheet Properties dialog box. Click OK to return to the drawing sheet.

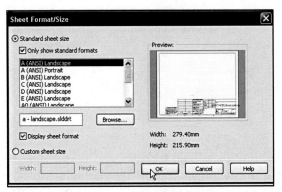

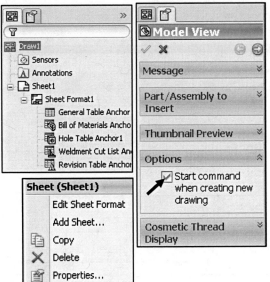

Draw1 is the default drawing name. Sheet1 is the default first Sheet name. For an active drawing document, the *View Layout*, *Annotation*, *Sketch*, *Evaluate* and *Office Products* tabs are displayed in the CommandManager.

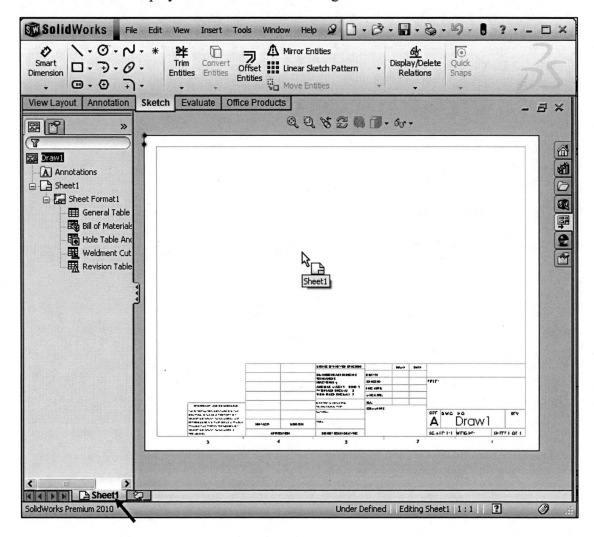

Utilize the CommandManager tabs or individual toolbars to access the needed features in this chapter.

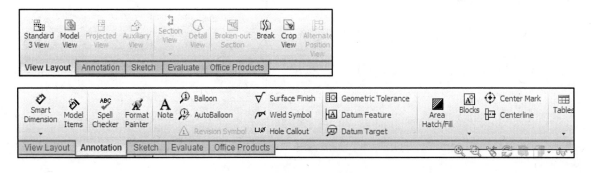

Set the Sheet Properties.

7) Right-click in the **Graphics window**.

8) Click **Properties**. The Sheet Properties are displayed.

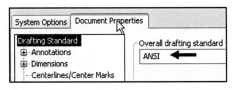

9) Enter Sheet Scale **1:1**.

10) Check the **Third angle** box for Type of projection.

11) Click **OK** from the Sheet Properties dialog box.

Activity: Drawing-Document Properties

Set the drawing document properties.

12) Click **Options** 🗒 , **Document Properties** tab from the Menu bar.

13) Select **ANSI** for Overall drafting standard from the drop-down menu.

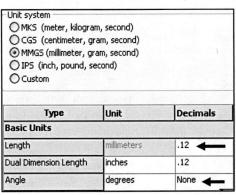

14) Click **Units**.

15) Click **MMGS** (millimeter, gram, second) for Unit system.

16) Select **.12** for Length units Decimal places.

17) Select **None** for Angular units Decimal places.

View the available Document Properties options. Click each folder under the Document Properties tab.

🔅 Available Document Properties are document dependent.

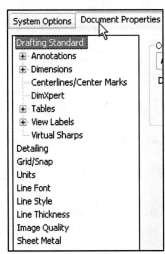

Companies develop drawing format standards and use specific text height for Metric and English drawings. Numerous engineering drawings use the following format:

- *Font*: Century Gothic - All capitals.

- *Text height*: 3mm for drawings up to B Size, 17in. × 22in.

- *Text height*: 5mm for drawings larger than B Size, 17in × 22in.

- *Arrow heads*: Solid filled with a 1:3 ratio of arrow width to arrow height.

Set the dimension font.
18) Click **Annotations** folder as illustrated.

19) Click the **Font** button. The Choose Font dialog box is displayed.

Set the dimension text height.
20) Click the **Units** box from the Choose Font dialog box.

21) Enter **3.0**mm for Height.

22) Click **OK** from the Choose Font dialog box.

Set the arrow size.
23) Click the **Dimensions** folder as illustrated.

24) Enter **1**mm for arrow Height.

25) Enter **3**mm for arrow Width.

26) Enter **6**mm for arrow Length.

27) Click **OK** from the Document Properties dialog box.

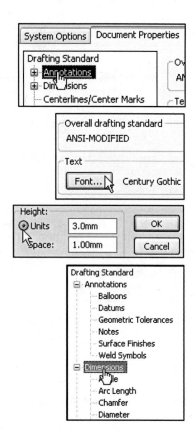

There are three dimension style type buttons: Outside, Inside, and Smart. Smart is the default option.

Check the Dual dimensions display box to display dual dimensions for your model or drawing.

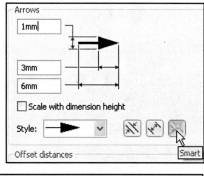

Title Block

The Title block contains text fields linked to System Properties and Custom Properties. System Properties are determined from the SolidWorks documents. Custom Property values are assigned to named variables.

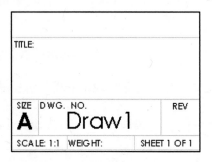

Save time. Utilize System Properties and define Custom Properties in your Sheet Formats.

System Properties Linked to fields in default Sheet Formats:	Custom Properties of drawings linked to fields in default Sheet Formats:		Custom Properties of parts and assemblies linked to fields in default Sheet Formats:
SW-File Name (in DWG. NO. field):	CompanyName:	EngineeringApproval:	Description (in TITLE field):
SW-Sheet Scale:	CheckedBy:	EngAppDate:	Weight:
SW-Current Sheet:	CheckedDate:	ManufacturingApproval:	Material:
SW-Total Sheets:	DrawnBy:	MfgAppDate:	Finish:
	DrawnDate:	QAApproval:	Revision:
	EngineeringApproval:	QAAppDate:	

The Title block is located in the lower right hand corner of Sheet1.

The Drawing contains two modes:

1. *Edit Sheet Format*

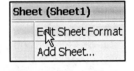

2. *Edit Sheet*

Insert views and dimensions in the Edit Sheet mode. Modify the Sheet Format text, lines or title block information in the Edit Sheet Format mode.

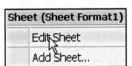

The CompanyName Custom Property is located in the title block above the TITLE box. There is no value defined for CompanyName. A small text box indicates an empty field.

Define a value for the Custom Property CompanyName. Example: D&M ENGINEERING.

Activity: Title Block

Activate the Edit Sheet Format Mode.
28)   Right-click in **Sheet1**.

29)   Click **Edit Sheet Format**. The Title block lines turn blue.

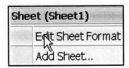

View the right side of the Title block.

30)   Click the **Zoom to Area** tool from the Heads-up View toolbar.

31)   **Zoom in** on the Title block.

32) Click the **Zoom to Area** tool to deactivate.

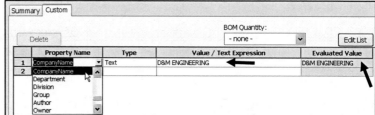

Define CompanyName Custom Property.
33) Position the **mouse pointer** in the middle of the box above the TITLE box as illustrated.

34) Click **File**, **Properties** from the Menu bar. The Summary Information dialog box is displayed.

35) Click the **Custom** tab.

36) Click inside the **Property Name box**.

37) Click the **drop down arrow** in the Property Name box.

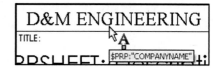

38) Select **CompanyName** from the Property menu.

39) Enter **D&M ENGINEERING** (or your company name) in the Value/Text Expression box.

40) Click inside the **Evaluated Value** box. The CompanyName is displayed in the Evaluated Value box.

41) Click **OK** from the dialog box.

42) Move your **mouse pointer** in the center of the block as illustrated. The Custom Property, $PRP: "COMPANYNAME", is displayed in the Title block.

Modify the font size.
43) Double-click the **D&M ENGINEERING** text. The Formatting dialog box is displayed.

44) Click the **drop down arrows** to set the Text Font and Height from the Formatting toolbar.

45) Click the **Style buttons** and **Justification buttons** to modify the selected text.

46) **Close** the Formatting dialog box.

47) Click **OK** from the Note PropertyManager.

Click a position outside the selected text box to save and exit the text.

The Tolerance block is located in the Title block. The Tolerance block provides information to the manufacturer on the minimum and maximum variation for each dimension on the drawing. If a specific tolerance or note is provided on the drawing, the specific tolerance or note will override the information in the Tolerance block.

General tolerance values are based on the design requirements and the manufacturing process.

Create Sheet Formats for different part types; examples: sheet metal parts, plastic parts, and high precision machined parts. Create Sheet Formats for each category of parts that are manufactured with unique sets of Title block notes.

Modify the Tolerance block in the Sheet Format for ASME Y14.5 machined, millimeter parts. Delete unnecessary text. The FRACTIONAL text refers to inches. The BEND text refers to sheet metal parts. The Three Decimal Place text is not required for this millimeter part in the chapter.

Modify the Tolerance Note.

48) Double-click the text **INTERPRET GEOMETRIC TOLERANCING PER:**

49) Enter **ASME Y14.5**.

50) Click **OK** ✔ from the Note PropertyManager.

51) Double-click inside the **Tolerance block** text. The Formatting dialog box and the Note PropertyManager is displayed.

52) Delete the text **INCHES**.

53) Enter **MILLIMETERS**.

54) Delete the line **FRACTIONAL ±**.

55) Delete the text **BEND ±**.

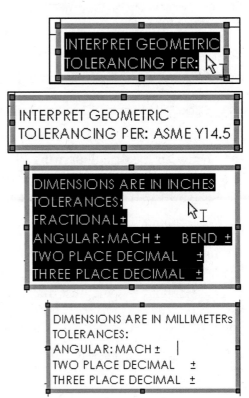

56) Click a **position** at the end of the ANGULAR: MACH ± line.

57) Enter **0**. Click the **Add Symbol** button from the Text Format box. The Symbols dialog box is displayed.

58) Select **Degree** from the Symbols dialog box.

59) Click **OK** from the Symbols dialog box.

60) Enter **30'** for minutes of a degree.

Modify the TWO and THREE PLACE DECIMAL LINES.
61) Delete the **TWO** and **THREE PLACE DECIMAL lines**.

62) Enter **ONE PLACE DECIMAL ± 0.5**.

63) Enter **TWO PLACE DECIMAL ± 0.15**.

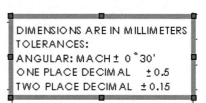

64) Click **OK** from the Note PropertyManager.

Fit the drawing to the Graphics window.
65) Press the **f** key.

Save Draw1.
66) Click **Save**. Accept the default name.

67) Click **Save** from the Save As box.

Draw1 is the default drawing file name. This name is temporary. In the next activity, invoke Microsoft Word. Always save before selecting another software application.

Various symbols are available through the Symbol dialog box. The ± symbol is located in the Modify Symbols list. The ± symbol is sometimes displayed as <MOD-PM>. The degree symbol ° is sometimes displayed as <MOD-DEG>.

Interpretation of tolerances is as follows:

• The angular dimension 110° is machined between 109.5° and 110.5°.

• The dimension 2.5 is machined between 2.0 and 3.0.

• The dimension 2.05 is machined between 1.90 and 2.20.

Company Logo

A Company logo is normally located in the Title block. Create a Company logo. Copy a picture file from Microsoft ClipArt using Microsoft Word. Paste the logo into the SolidWorks drawing. Note: The following logo example was created in Microsoft Word 2003 using the COMPASS.wmf file. You can utilize any ClipArt picture, scanned image, or bitmap for a logo in this activity.

The Compass logo clipart and finished Compass logo for the drawing is located on the CD enclosed in the book. Click **Insert**, **Picture** and **browse** to the Logo folder. Click the **Logo** Logo file. **Move** and **resize** the finished logo in the drawing.

Activity: Drawing Logo

Create a New Microsoft Word Document. In the next step, MS Office Word 2003 is used.

68)   Click **Start** from the Microsoft desktop.

69)   Click **All Programs**. Click **Microsoft Office Word 2003**.

70)   Click **File**, **New** from the Standard toolbar in MS Word.

71)   Click **Insert, Picture, ClipArt** from the Main menu. The Insert Clip Art menu is displayed.

72)   In the Search text enter **compass**. Note: Enter any name for Clip Art to Search For. If you do not have the Clip Art loaded on your system, click **Clips Online** to obtain additional Clip Art. Follow the provided directions to select and download.

The Compass logo clipart is located in the Logo folder provided on the CD enclosed in the book.

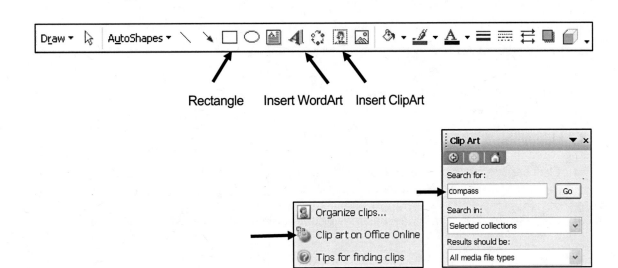

Rectangle   Insert WordArt   Insert ClipArt

Locate the picture file.
73) Click **Go**. Locate the **Compass.wmf** file. **Double-click** the file. The picture is displayed in the Word document. Note: You can use any picture file. The Compass Logo file is also located on the CD enclosed in the book.

Redefine the picture layout.
74) Click the **picture**. Right-click **Format Picture**. The Format Picture dialog box is displayed.

Display the drag handles.
75) Click the **Layout** tab. Click **Square**.

76) Click **OK** from the Format Picture dialog box.

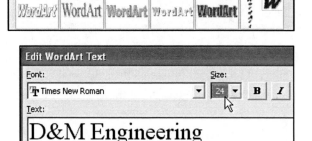

Add text to the logo picture.
77) Click the **picture**. Click **Insert WordArt** ◀ from the Draw toolbar. The WordArt Gallery dialog box is displayed.

78) Click a **WordArt** style. Click **OK**.

79) Enter **D&M Engineering** in the text box.

80) Click **24** from the Size drop down list.

81) Click **OK** from the Edit WordArt Text dialog box.

82) Click the **Word Art text**. A WordArt toolbar is displayed.

83) Click **Text Wrapping** . Click **Square**.

84) Click and drag the **Word Art text** under the Compass picture.

85) Size the **Word Art text** by dragging the picture handles.

Group the Word Art text and the picture to create the logo.
86) Click on the **Word Art text**.

87) Hold the **Ctrl** key down.

88) Click the **compass** picture. Release the **Ctrl** key. Right-click and select **Grouping**.

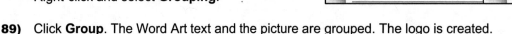

89) Click **Group**. The Word Art text and the picture are grouped. The logo is created.

Copy the new logo.
90) Click the **logo**.

91) Click **Edit**, **Copy** from the Main menu.

92) The logo is placed into the Clipboard. **Minimize** the Microsoft Word Graphics window.

Return to the SolidWorks Title block.
93) Click a **position** on the left side of the Title block in the SolidWorks Graphics window. **Zoom out** if required.

Paste the logo.
94) Click **Edit**, **Paste** from the Menu bar.

95) **Move** and **Size** the logo to the SolidWorks Title block by dragging the picture handles.

Return to the Edit Sheet mode.
96) Right-click in the **Graphics window**.

97) Click **Edit Sheet**. The Title block is displayed in black/gray.

Fit the Sheet Format to the Graphics window.
98) Press the **f** key.

Draw1 displays Editing Sheet1 in the Status bar. The Title block is displayed in black when in Edit Sheet mode.

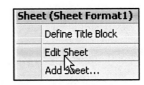

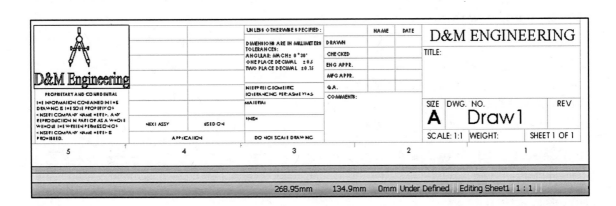

Save Sheet Format and Save As Drawing Template

Save the drawing document in the Graphics window in two forms: Sheet Format and Drawing Template. Save the Sheet Format as a custom Sheet Format named CUSTOM-A. Use the CUSTOM-A Sheet Format for the drawings in this project. The Sheet Format file extension is .slddrt.

The Drawing Template can be displayed with or without the Sheet Format. Combine the Sheet Format with the Drawing Template to create a custom Drawing Template named A-ANSI-MM. Utilize the Save As option to save a Drawing Template. The Drawing Template file extension is .drwdot.

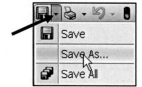

Always select the Save as type option first, then select the Save in folder to avoid saving in default SolidWorks installation directories.

The System Options, File Locations, Document Templates option is only valid for the current session of SolidWorks in some network locations. Set the File Locations option in order to view the SW-TUTORIAL-2010 tab in the New Document dialog box.

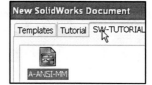

Activity: Save Sheet Format and Save As Drawing Template

Save the Sheet Format.

99) Click **File, Save Sheet Format** from the Menu bar. The Save Sheet Format dialog box appears.

100) Click **drop down arrow** from the Save Sheet Format dialog box.

The default Sheet Format folder is called SolidWorks 2010 on a new installation. Do not select this folder. The file extension for Sheet Format is .slddrt.

101) Select **SW-TUTORIAL-2010** for the Save in folder.

102) Enter **CUSTOM-A** for File name.

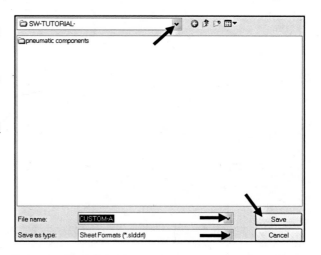

103) Click **Save** from the Save Sheet Format dialog box.

Save the Drawing Template.
104) Click **Save As** from the Menu bar.

105) Click **Drawing Templates (*.drwdot)** from the Save as
type box.

106) Select **SW-TUTORIAL-2010** for
the Save in folder.

107) Enter **A-ANSI-MM** for File name.

108) Click **Save**.

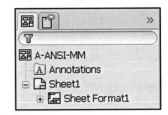

The A-ANSI-MM.drwdot drawing template is displayed in
the Graphics window. Add the SW-TUTORIAL-2010
folder to the File Locations Document Template System
Option.

Set System Options - File Locations.
109) Click **Options** ▤ , **File Locations** from the Menu bar.

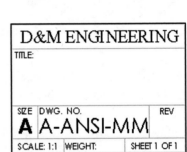

110) Click **Add**.

111) Select the **SW-TUTORIAL-2010** folder.

112) Click **OK** from the Browse for Folder menu.

113) Click **OK** to exit System Options.

114) Click **Yes**.

Close all files.
115) Click **Windows, Close All**
from the Menu bar.

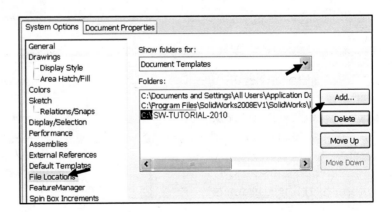

Open a new drawing.

116) Click **New** ⬜ from the Menu bar.

117) Select the **SW-TUTORIAL-2010** tab.

118) Double-click the **A-ANSI-MM** Drawing Template.

119) If required, click **Cancel** ✖ from the Model View PropertyManager. Draw2 is displayed in the Graphics window.

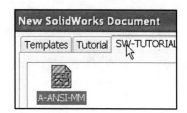

🔆 The Draw2-Sheet1 drawing is displayed in the Graphics window. You have successfully created a new drawing Template with a Custom sheet format.

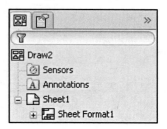

Close all files.
120) Click **Windows**, **Close All** from the Menu bar.

🔆 Combine customize Drawing Templates and Sheet Formats to match your company's drawing standards. Save the empty Drawing Template and Sheet Format separately to reuse information.

🔍 Additional details on Drawing Templates, Sheet Format and Custom Properties are available in SolidWorks Help Topics. Keywords: Documents (templates, properties) Sheet Formats (new, new drawings, note text), Properties (drawing sheets), Customize Drawing Sheet Formats.

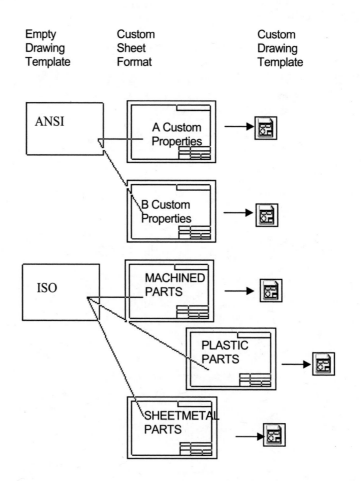

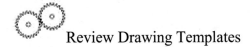
Review Drawing Templates

The Custom Drawing Template was created from the default Drawing Template. You modified Sheet Properties and Document Properties to control the Sheet size, Scale, Annotations and Dimensions.

The Sheet Format contained a Title block and Custom Property information. You inserted a Company Logo and modified the Title block.

The Save Sheet Format option was utilized to save the CUSTOM-A.slddrt Sheet Format. The Save As option was utilized to save the A-ANSI-MM.drwdot template.

The Sheet Format and Drawing Template were saved in the SW-TUTORIAL-2010 folder.

FLATBAR Drawing

A drawing contains part views, geometric dimensioning and tolerances, notes and other related design information. When a part is modified, the drawing automatically updates. When a dimension in the drawing is modified, the part is automatically updated.

Create the FLATBAR drawing from the FLATBAR part. Display the Front, Top, Right, and Isometric views. Utilize the Model View tool from the View Layout toolbar.

Insert dimensions from the part. Utilize the Insert Model Items tool from the Annotation toolbar. Insert and modify dimensions and notes.

Insert a Parametric note that links the dimension text to the part depth. Utilize a user defined Part Number. Define the part material with the Material Editor. Add Custom Properties for Material and Number.

Activity: FLATBAR Drawing-Open the FLATBAR Part

Open the FLATBAR part. Note: The FLATBAR part was created in Chapter 1.

121) Click **Open** from the Menu bar.

122) Select the **SW-TUTORIAL-2010** folder.

123) Select **Part** for Files of type.

124) Double-click **FLATBAR**. The FLATBAR FeatureManager is displayed.

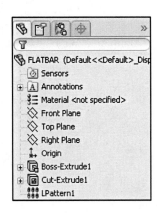

Create a new drawing.

125) Click **New** ⬜ from the Menu bar.

126) Select the **SW-TUTORIAL-2010** tab.

127) Double-click **A-ANSI-MM**.

The Model View PropertyManager is displayed if the Start command when creating new drawing box is checked. If the Model View PropertyManager is not displayed, click the Model View tool from the View Layout toolbar.

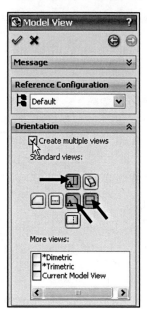

The FLATBAR part icon is displayed in the Open documents box. Drawing view names are based on the part view orientation. The Front view is the first view inserted into the drawing. The Top view and Right view are projected from the Front view.

Insert the Front, Top and Right view.

128) Click **Next** ↪ from the Model View PropertyManager.

129) Check the **Create multiple views** box.

130) De-activate the Isometric view. Click the ***Isometric** icon from the Standard views box.

131) Click ***Front**, ***Top** and ***Right** view from the Standard views box.

132) Click **OK** ✔ from the Model View PropertyManager. Click **Yes**. The three views are displayed on Sheet1.

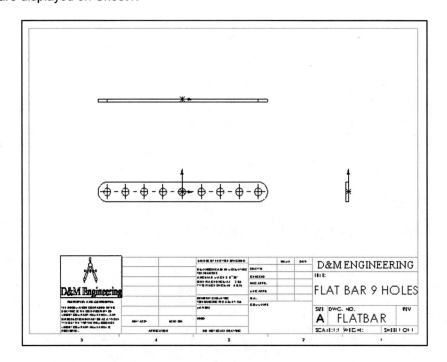

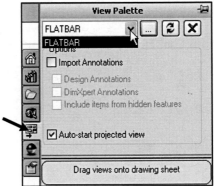

🔆 A part cannot be inserted into a drawing when the *Edit Sheet Format* is selected. You are required to be in the *Edit Sheet* mode.

Insert an Isometric view using the View Palette.

133) Click the **View Palette** tab on the right side of the Graphics window.

134) Select **FLATBAR** from the View Palette drop-down menu as illustrated. View the available views.

135) Click and drag the **Isometric view** in the top right corner as illustrated.

136) Click **OK** ✔ from the Drawing View PropertyManager.

🔆 Click the View Palette tab in the Task Pane. Click the drop-down arrow to view any active documents or click the Browse button to locate a document. Click and drag the desired view/views into the active drawing sheet.

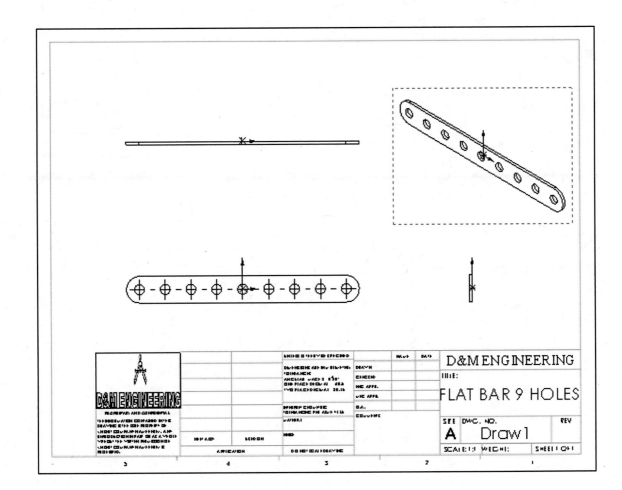

Modify the Sheet Scale.
137) Right-click a **position** inside the Sheet1 boundary.

138) Click **Properties**. The Sheet Properties dialog box is displayed.

139) Enter **1:1** for Sheet Scale.

140) Click **OK** from the Sheet Properties dialog box.

If needed, hide the Origins.
141) Click **View**; uncheck **Origins** from the Menu bar.

Save the drawing.
142) Click **Save As** from the Menu bar.

143) Enter **FLATBAR** in the SW-
TUTORIAL-2010 folder.

144) Click **Save**.

145) Click **Save** .

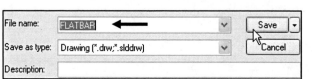

Text in the Title block is linked to the Filename and
Description created in the part. The DWG. NO. text box utilizes
the Property, $PRP:"SW-File Name" passed from the
FLATBAR part to the FLATBAR drawing.

The Title text box utilizes the Property, $PRPSHEET:
"Description".

The filename FLATBAR is displayed in the DWG. NO. box.
The Description FLATBAR 9 HOLE is displayed in the Title
box. The FLATBAR drawing contains three Principle views
(Standard views): Front, Top, Right and an Isometric view.

Insert drawing views as follows:

*   Utilize the Model View tool.

    o   Drag a part into the drawing to create three Standard
        views.

    o   Predefine views in a custom Drawing Template.

    o   Drag a hyperlink through Internet Explorer.

- Drag an active part view from the View Palette. The View Palette is located in the Task Pane. With an open part, drag the selected view into the active drawing sheet.

The View Palette populates when you:

- Click Make Drawing from Part/Assembly.

- Browse to a document from the View Palette.

- Select from a list of open documents in the View Palette.

Move Views and Properties of the Sheet

Move Views on Sheet1 to create space for additional Drawing View placement.

The mouse pointer provides feedback in both the Drawing Sheet

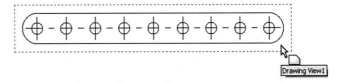

and Drawing View modes.

The mouse pointer displays the Drawing Sheet icon when the Sheet properties and commands are executed.

The mouse pointer displays the Drawing View icon when the View properties and commands are executed.

View the mouse pointer icon for feedback to select Sheet, View, and Component and Edge properties in the Drawing.

Sheet Properties

- Sheet Properties display properties of the selected sheet.

  Right-click in the sheet boundary to view the available commands.

View Properties

- View Properties display properties of the selected view.

  Right-click inside the view boundary. Modify the View Properties in the Display Style box or the View Toolbar.

Component Properties

- Component Properties display properties of the selected component. Right-click to on the face of the component. View the available options.

Edge Properties

- Edge Properties display properties of the selected geometry. Right-click on an edge inside the view boundary. View the available options.

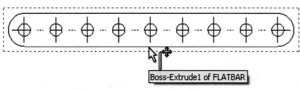

Boss-Extrude1 of FLATBAR

Reposition the views on the drawing. Provide approximately 25mm - 50mm between each view for dimension placement.

Activity: FLATBAR Drawing-Position Views

Position the views.

146) Click inside the view boundary of **Drawing View1** (Front). The mouse pointer displays the Drawing View

icon.

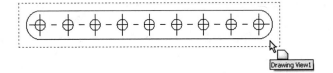

147) Position the **mouse pointer** on the edge of the view boundary until the

Drawing View   icon is displayed.

148) Drag **Drawing View1** in an upward vertical direction. The Top and Right views move aligned to Drawing View1 (Front).

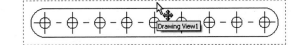

149) Press **Shift + Z** key to Zoom in on Sheet1.

150) Click the **Right view** boundary.

151) Position the **mouse pointer** on the edge of the view until the Drawing Move View

icon is displayed.

152) Drag the **Right view** in a right to left direction towards the Front view.

Tangent Edges are displayed for educational purposes.

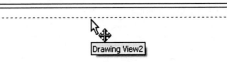

Move the Top view in a downward vertical direction.
153) Click the **Top view**, "Drawing View3" boundary.

154) Drag the **Top view** in a downward direction towards Drawing View1.

Fit Sheet1 to the Graphics window.
155) Press the **f** key.

Detail Drawing

The design intent of this project is to work with dimensions inserted from parts and to incorporate them into the drawings. Explore methods to move, hide and recreate dimensions to adhere to a drawing standard.

There are other solutions to the dimensioning schemes illustrated in this project. Detail drawings require dimensions, annotations, tolerance, materials, Engineering Change Orders, authorization, etc. to release the part to manufacturing and other notes prior to production.

Review a hypothetical "worse case" drawing situation. You just inserted dimensions from a part into a drawing. The dimensions, extensions lines and arrows are not in the correct locations. How can you address the position of these details? Answer: Dimension to an ASME Y14.5M standard.

No.	Situation:
1	Extension line crosses dimension line. Dimensions not evenly spaced.
2	Largest dimension placed closest to profile.
3	Leader lines overlapping.
4	Extension line crossing arrowhead.
5	Arrow gap too large.
6	Dimension pointing to feature in another view. Missing dimension – inserted into Detail view (not shown).
7	Dimension text over centerline, too close to profile.
8	Dimension from other view – leader line too long.
9	Dimension inside section lines.
10	No visible gap.
11	Arrows overlapping text.
12	Incorrect decimal display with whole number (millimeter), no specified tolerance.

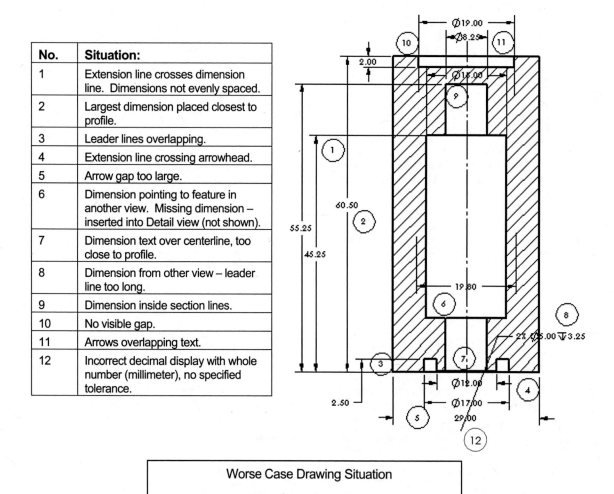

Worse Case Drawing Situation

The ASME Y14.5M standard defines an engineering drawing standard.

Review the twelve changes made to the drawing to meet the standard.

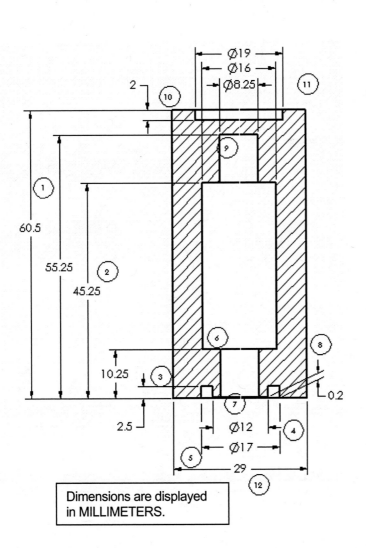

Dimensions are displayed in MILLIMETERS.

No.	Preferred Application of the Dimensions:
1	Extension lines do not cross unless situation is unavoidable. Stagger dimension text.
2	Largest dimension placed farthest from profile. Dimensions are evenly spaced and grouped.
3	Arrow heads do not overlap.
4	Break extension lines that cross close to arrowhead.
5	Flip arrows to the inside.
6	Move dimensions to the view that displays the outline of the feature. Insure that all dimensions are accounted for.
7	Move text off of reference geometry (centerline).
8	Drag dimensions into their correct view boundary. Create reference dimensions if required. Slant extension lines to clearly illustrate feature.
9	Locate dimensions outside off section lines.
10	Create a visible gap between extension lines and profile lines.
11	Arrows do not overlap the text.
12	Whole numbers displayed with no zero and no decimal point (millimeter).

Apply these dimension practices to the FLATBAR and other drawings in this project.

A Detailed drawing is used to manufacture a part. A mistake on a drawing can cost your company substantial loss in revenue. The mistake could result in a customer liability lawsuit.

Dimension and annotate your parts clearly to avoid common problems and mistakes.

Dimensions and Annotations

Dimensions and annotations are inserted from the part. The annotations are not in the correct location. Additional dimensions and annotations are required.

Dimensions and annotations are inserted by selecting individual features, views or the entire sheet. Select the entire sheet. Insert Model Items command from the Annotations toolbar.

Activity: FLATBAR Drawing-Dimensions and Annotations

Insert dimensions.

156) Click **Sheet1** in the center of the drawing. The mouse pointer

displays the Sheet icon.

157) Click the **Annotation** tab from the CommandManager.

158) Click the **Model Items** tool from the Annotation toolbar. The Model Items PropertyManager is displayed. The Import items into all views option is checked.

159) Select **Entire model** from the Source box.

160) Click **OK** from the Model Items PropertyManager. Dimensions are inserted into the drawing.

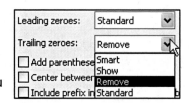

Remove Trailing zeroes.

161) Click **Options** , **Document Properties** tab from the Menu bar.

162) Click the **Dimensions** folder.

163) Select **Remove** for the Trailing zeroes drop-down menu.

164) Click **OK** from the Document Properties – Dimensions dialog box.

Dimensions are inserted into the drawing. The dimensions *MAY NOT BE* in the correct location with respect to the profile lines. Move them later in the chapter and address extension line gaps.

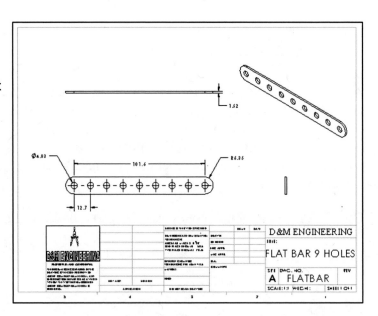

The dimensions and text in the next section have been enlarged for visibility. Drawing dimension location is dependent on: *Feature dimension creation* and *Selected drawing views.*

Move dimensions within the same view. Use the mouse pointer to drag dimensions and leader lines to a new location. Leader lines reference the size of the profile. A gap must exist between the profile lines and the leader lines. Shorten the leader lines to maintain a drawing standard. Use the blue Arrow buttons to flip the dimension arrows.

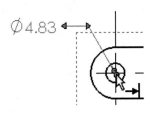

Plan ahead for general drawing notes. Notes provide relative part or assembly information. Example: Material type, material finish, special manufacturing procedure or considerations, preferred supplier, etc.

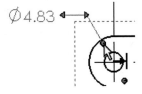

Below are a few helpful guidelines to create general drawing notes:

- *Use capitol letters.*

- *Use left text justification.*

- *Font size should be the same as the dimension text.*

Create Parametric notes by selecting dimensions in the drawing. Example: Specify the material thickness of the FLATBAR as a note in the drawing. If the thickness is modified, the corresponding note is also modified.

Hide superfluous feature dimensions. Do not delete feature dimensions. Recall hidden dimension with the View, Show Annotations command. Move redundant, dependent views outside the sheet boundary.

Move the linear dimensions in Drawing View1, (Front).
165) Click the vertical dimension text **101.6**. The dimension text turns blue.

166) Drag the **dimension text** downward.

167) Click the horizontal dimension **12.7**.

168) Drag the **text** approximately 10mm's from the profile. The smallest linear dimensions are closest to the profile.

169) Click the radial dimension **R6.35**.

170) Drag the **text** diagonally off the profile if required.

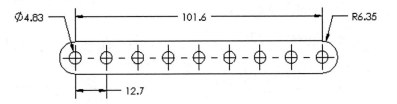

Modify dimension text.
171) Click the diameter dimension **4.83**. It turns blue. The Dimension PropertyManager is displayed.

172) Click inside the **Dimension Text** box.

173) Enter **9X** before <MOD-DIAM>. Enter **EQ SP** after <DIM>.

174) Click **OK** ✔ from the Dimension PropertyManager.

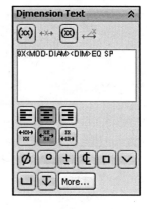

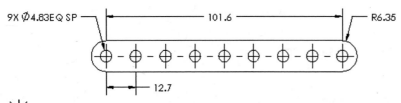

Inserted dimensions can be moved from one drawing view to another. Hold the Shift key down. Click and drag the dimension text from one view into the other view boundary. Release the Shift key.

Modify the precision of the material thickness.
175) Click the depth dimension text **1.52** in the Top view.

176) Select **.1** from the Tolerance/Precision box.

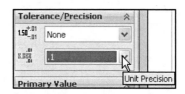

177) Click **OK** ✔ from the Dimension PropertyManager. The text displays 1.5.

Insert a Parametric note.
178) Click the **Annotation** tab from the CommandManager.

179) Click the **Note** A tool from the Annotation toolbar. The Note icon is displayed.

180) Click a **position** above Front view.

181) Enter **MATERIAL THICKNESS**.

182) Click the depth dimension text **1.5** in the Top view. The variable name for the dimension is displayed in the text box.

183) Enter **MM**.

184) Click **OK** ✔ from the Note PropertyManager.

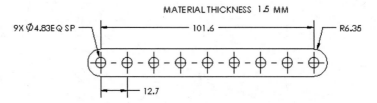

Hide superfluous dimensions.
185) Right-click the **1.5** dimension text in the Top view.

186) Click **Hide**.

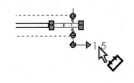

Hide the Right view.
187) Right-click the **Right view** boundary.

188) Click **Hide**. Note: If required, expand the drop-down menu. The Right view is not displayed in the Graphics window.

189) Click **OK** ✔ from the Drawing View PropertyManager.

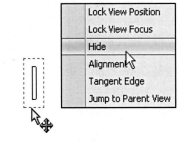

Fit the model to the drawing and address all needed extension line gaps.
190) Press the **f** key.

Save the drawing.
191) Click **Save** 💾.

Locate the Top view off of Sheet1.
192) Click and drag the **Top view boundary** off of the Sheet1 boundary as illustrated.

Views and notes outside the sheet boundary do not print. The Parametric note is controlled through the FLATBAR part Boss-Extrude1 depth. Modify the depth to update the note.

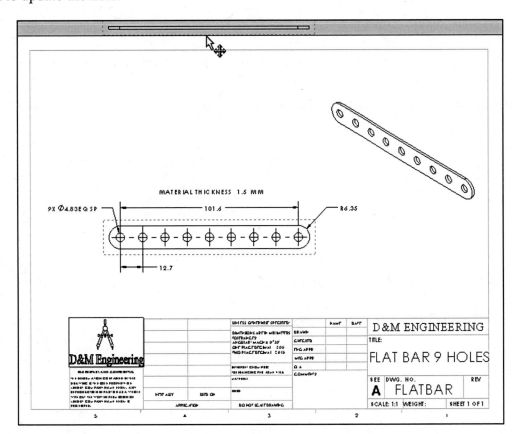

Open the FLATBAR part.
193) Right-click inside the **Front view** boundary.

194) Click **Open Part**. The FLATBAR part is displayed.

Modify the Boss-Extrude1 depth dimension.
195) Click **Boss-Extrude1** from the FeatureManager.

196) Click **.060**in, [1.52].

197) Enter **2.3MM** as illustrated. Note: You need to enter MM.

198) Click **inside** the Graphics window.

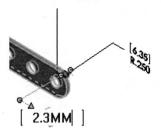

199) Click **Save** 💾.

Return to the drawing.
200) Click **Window**, **FLATBAR –Sheet1** from the Menu bar. The Parametric note is updated to reflect the dimension change in the part.

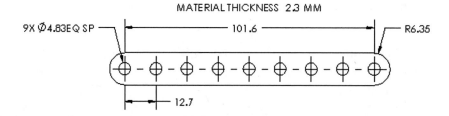

The FLATBAR drawing references the FLATBAR part. Do not delete the part or move the part location. Work between multiple documents:

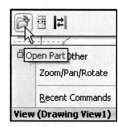

- Press Ctrl-Tab to toggle between open SolidWorks documents.

- Right-click inside the Drawing view boundary. Select Open Part.

- Right-click the part icon in the FeatureManager. Select Open Drawing.

🔆 Commands are accessed through the toolbars and drop-down menus. Commands are also accessed with a right-click in the Graphics window and FeatureManager.

A majority of FLATBAR drawing dimensions are inserted from the FLATBAR part. An overall dimension is required to dimension the slot shape profile. Add a dimension in the drawing.

Add a dimension to Drawing View1.

201) Click the **Smart Dimension** 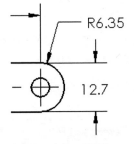 tool from the Annotation toolbar. The Autodimension tab is selected by default.

202) Click the **Smart dimensioning** box.

203) Click the **top horizontal line** of the FLATBAR.

204) Click the **bottom horizontal line** of the FLATBAR.

205) Click a **position** to the right of the Front view as illustrated.

Modify the Radius text.
206) Click the **R6.36** dimension text.

207) Delete **R<DIM>** in the Dimension Text box.

208) Click **Yes** to confirm dimension override.

209) Enter **2X R** for Dimension text. Do not enter the radius value.

210) Click **OK** 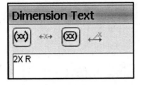 from the Dimension PropertyManager.

211) Add any **extension line gaps (5mm)** if needed.

Save the FLATBAR drawing.

212) Click **Save** 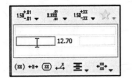 . Note: Click Options, Document Properties, Dimensions from the Menu bar. Uncheck the Add parentheses by default box. View the results in the Graphics window.

Note the new dialog pop-up for 2010. This saves mouse travel to the Dimension PropertyManager.

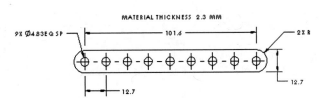

Part Number and Document Properties

Engineers manage the parts they create and modify. Each part requires a Part Number and Part Name. A part number is a numeric representation of the part. Each part has a unique number. Each drawing has a unique number. Drawings incorporate numerous part numbers or assembly numbers.

There are software applications that incorporate unique part numbers to create and perform:

- Bill of Materials

- Manufacturing procedures

- Cost analysis

- Inventory control / Just in Time, JIT

You are required to procure the part and drawing numbers from the documentation control manager. Utilize the following prefix codes to categorize created parts and drawings. The part name, part number and drawing numbers are as follows:

Category:	Prefix:	Part Name:	Part Number:	Drawing Number:
Machined Parts	56-	FLATEPLATE	GIDS-SC-10001-9	56-10222
		AXLE	GIDS-SC-10017	56-10223
		SHAFT-COLLAR	GIDS-SC-10012-3-16	56-10224
Purchased Parts	99-	AIRCYLINDER	99-FBM8x1.25	999-101-8
Assemblies	10-	LINKAGE ASM	GIDS-SC-1000	10-10123

Link notes in the Title block to SolidWorks Properties. Properties are variables shared between documents and applications.

The machined parts are manufactured from Aluminum. Specify the Material Property in the part. Link the Material Property to the drawing title block. Create a part number that is utilized in the Bill of Materials. Create additional notes in the title block to complete the drawing.

Activity: FLATBAR Drawing-Part Number and Document Properties

Return to the FLATEBAR part.
213) Right-click in the **Front view** boundary.

214) Click **Open Part**.

215) Right-click **Material** in the FLATBAR FeatureManager.

216) Click **Edit Material**. The Material dialog box is displayed.

217) **Expand** the Aluminum Alloys folder.

218) Select **2014 Alloy**. View the material properties.

219) Click the **Apply** button.

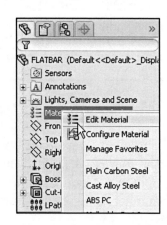

220) Click **Close**. The 2014 Alloy is displayed in the FeatureManager.

Save the FLATBAR.
221) Click **Save** 🖫.

Define the part number property for the BOM.
222) Click the FLATBAR **ConfigurationManager** 🖻 tab.

223) Right-click **Default**.

224) Click **Properties**. The Configuration Properties PropertyManager is displayed.

225) Click **User Specified Name** from the drop-down box under Document Name.

226) Enter **GIDS-SC-10001-9** in the Part number text box.

Define a material property.
227) Click the **Custom Properties** button.

228) Click inside the **Property Name** box.

229) Click the **down arrow**.

230) Select **Material** from the Property Name list.

231) Click inside the **Value / Text Expression** box.

232) Click the **down arrow**.

233) Select **Material**.

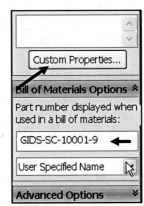

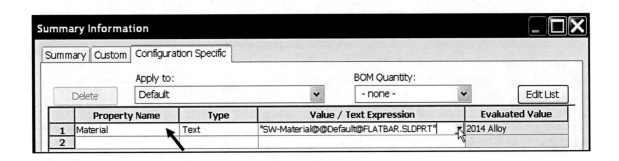

	Property Name	Type	Value / Text Expression	Evaluated Value
1	Material	Text	"SW-Material@@Default@FLATBAR.SLDPRT"	2014 Alloy
2				

Define the Number Property.
234) Click inside the **second Property Name** box.

235) Click the **down arrow**.

236) Select **Number** from the Name list.

237) Click inside the **Value / Text Expression** box.

238) Enter **56-10222** for Drawing Number.

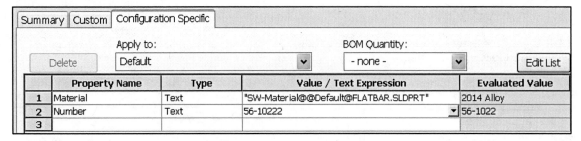

	Property Name	Type	Value / Text Expression	Evaluated Value
1	Material	Text	"SW-Material@@Default@FLATBAR.SLDPRT"	2014 Alloy
2	Number	Text	56-10222	56-1022
3				

239) Click **OK** from the Summary Information dialog box.

240) Click **OK** ✓ from the Configuration Properties PropertyManager.

Return to the FeatureManager.
241) Click the FLATBAR **FeatureManager** 🔖 tab.

Save the FLATBAR part.
242) Click **Save** 🖫.

Return to the drawing.
243) Click **Windows, FLATBAR - Sheet1** from the
      Main menu.

The Material Property is inserted into the Title
block.

INTERPRET GEOMETRIC
TOLERANCING PER: ASME Y14.5

MATERIAL
2014 Alloy

Activity: FLATBAR Drawing-Linked Note

Create a Linked Note.
244) Right-click in **Sheet1**.

245) Click **Edit Sheet Format**.

246) **Zoom in** on the lower right corner of the drawing.

247) Double-click on the DWG. NO. text **FLATBAR**. The Note
      PropertyManager is displayed.

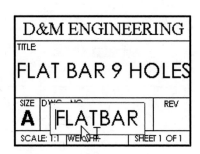

D&M ENGINEERING

TITLE

FLAT BAR 9 HOLES

SIZE | DWG. NO. | REV
A | FLATBAR |
SCALE: 1:1 | WEIGHT: | SHEET 1 OF 1

248) Click **Link to Property** 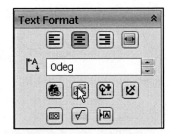 from the Text Format box.

249) Select **Model in view specified in sheet properties**.

250) Select **Number** from the Link to Property drop-down menu.

251) Click **OK** from the Link to Property box.

252) Click **OK** ✔ from the Note PropertyManager.

Return to the drawing sheet.
253) Right-click a **position** in the Graphics window.

254) Click **Edit Sheet**.

255) If needed, **remove all Tangent Edges** from the Top and Isometric view.

256) Address **all extension line gaps (5mm)** as illustrated below

Save the FLATBAR drawing.
257) Click **Save** 💾.

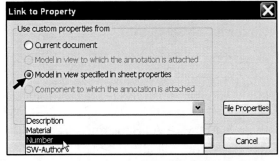

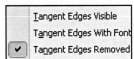

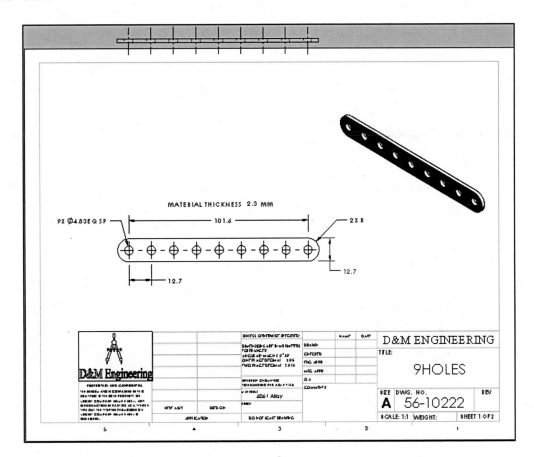

Custom Properties such as Revision and Drawn By are created in the chapter exercises.

Additional details on Drawing Views, New Drawing, Details, Dimensions, Dimensions and Annotations are available in SolidWorks Help.

Keywords: Drawing Views (overview), Drawing Views (model), Move (drawing views), Dimensions (circles, extension lines, inserting into drawings, move, parenthesis), Annotations (Note, Hole Callout, Centerline, Centermark), Notes (linked to properties, in sheet formats, parametric).

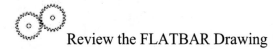 Review the FLATBAR Drawing

You created the FLATBAR drawing with the A-ANSI-MM Drawing Template. The FLATBAR drawing utilized the FLATBAR part with the Model View tool and the View Palette tool.

The Model View PropertyManager provided the ability to insert new views of a document. You selected the Front, Top and Right views. You applied the View Palette to insert an Isometric view.

You moved the views by dragging the blue view boundary. You inserted part dimensions and annotations into the drawing with the Insert Model Items tool. Dimensions were moved to new positions. Leader lines and dimension text were repositioned. Annotations were edited to reflect the dimension standard.

You created a Parametric note that referenced part dimensions in the drawing text. Aluminum 2014 was assigned in the FLATBAR part. The Material Custom Property and Number Custom Property were assigned in the FLATBAR part and referenced in the drawing Title block.

Know inch/mm decimal display. The ASME Y14.5 standard states:

- *For millimeter dimensions < 1, display the leading zero. Remove trailing zeros.*

- *For inch dimensions < 1, delete the leading zero. The dimension is displayed with the same number of decimal places as its tolerance.*

Note: The FLATBAR drawing linked Title block notes to Custom Properties in the drawing and in the part. The additional drawings in this project utilize drawing numbers linked to the model file name. The Title of the drawing utilizes a Note.

LINKAGE Assembly Drawing - Sheet1

The LINKAGE assembly drawing Sheet 1 utilizes the LINKAGE assembly. Add an Exploded view and a Bill of Materials to the drawing.

Create an Exploded view in the LINKAGE assembly. The Bill of Materials reflects the components of the LINKAGE assembly. Create a drawing with a Bill of Materials. Perform the following steps:

- Create a new drawing with the custom A-ANSI-MM size Drawing Template with the CUSTOM-A sheet format.

- Create and display the Exploded view of the LINKAGE assembly.

- Insert the Exploded view of the assembly into the drawing.

- Insert a Bill of Materials.

- Label each component with Balloon text.

Activity: LINKAGE Assembly Drawing-Sheet1

Close all parts and drawings.
258) Click **Windows**, **Close All** from the Menu bar.

Create a new drawing.
259) Click **New** ⬜ from the Menu bar.

260) Double-click **A-ANSI-MM** from the SW-TUTORIAL-2010 folder. The Model View PropertyManager is displayed.

Open the LINKAGE assembly.
261) Click the **Browse** button.

262) Select **Assembly** for Files of type in the SW-TUTORIAL-2010 folder.

263) Double-click **LINKAGE**. Note: Single view is selected by default.

264) Click **Isometric view** from the Standard views box.

265) Select **Shaded With Edges** 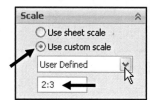 from the Display Style box.

266) Check the **Use custom scale** box.

267) Select **User Defined** from the drop down menu.

268) Enter **2:3** for Scale.

269) Click a **position** on the right side of Sheet1 as illustrated.

270) Click **OK** ✓ from the Drawing View1 PropertyManager.

Deactivate the Origins if needed.
271) Click **View**; uncheck **Origin** from the Menu bar.

Save the LINKAGE assembly drawing.

272) Click **Save** 🖫. Accept the default file name.

273) Click **Save**.

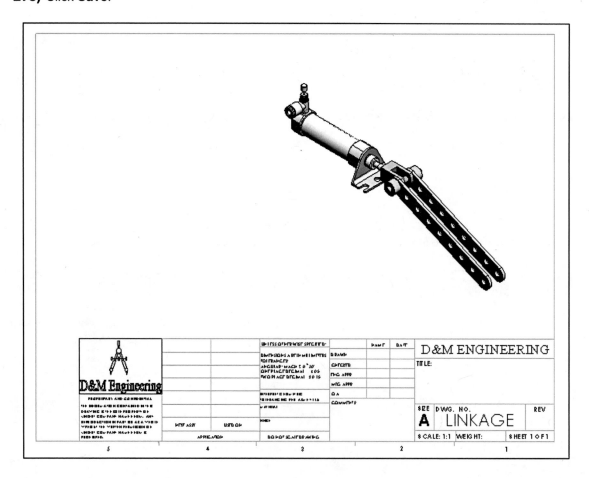

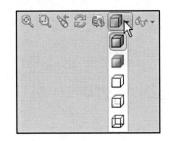

Display modes for a Drawing view are similar to a part document. The 3D Drawing View 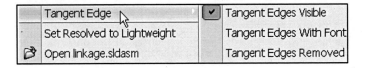 tool provides the ability to manipulate the model view in 3D, to select a difficult face, edge, or point.

Wireframe and Shaded Display modes provide the best graphic performance. Mechanical details require Hidden Lines Visible display and Hidden Lines Removed display. Select Shaded/Hidden Lines Removed to display Auxiliary Views to avoid confusion.

Tangent Edges Visible provides clarity for the start of a Fillet edge. Tangent Edges Removed provides the best graphic performance.

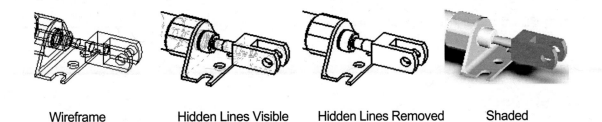

Right-click in the view boundary to access the Tangent Edge options.

Utilize the Lightweight Drawing option to improve performance for large assemblies.

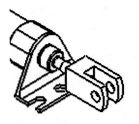

Wireframe

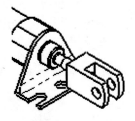

Hidden Lines Visible   Hidden Lines Removed

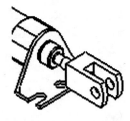

Shaded

Tangent Edges Visible   Tangent Edges With Font   Tangent Edges Removed

To address Tangent lines views:

- Right-click in a Drawing view.

- Click Tangent Edge.

- Click a Tangent Edge view option.

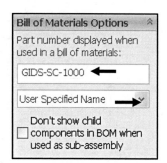

Return to the LINKAGE assembly.

274) Right-click inside the **Isometric view** boundary.

275) Click **Open linkage.sldasm**. The LINKAGE assembly is displayed.

276) Click the **ConfigurationManager** tab.

277) Right-click **Default [LINKAGE]**.

278) Click **Properties**. The Configuration Properties PropertyManager is displayed.

279) Select **User Specified Name** from the Part number displayed when used in Bill of Materials.

280) Enter **GIDS-SC-1000** in the Part number text box.

281) Click **OK** ✓ from the Configuration Properties PropertyManager.

282) Click the LINKAGE **FeatureManager** tab.

283) Click **Save** .

Exploded View

The Exploded View illustrates how to assemble the components in an assembly. Create an Exploded View with four steps. Click and drag components in the Graphics window.

The Manipulator icon ⤢ indicates the direction to explode. Select an alternate component edge for the Explode direction. Drag the component in the Graphics window or enter an exact value in the Explode distance box.

Manipulate the top-level components in the assembly. Access the Explode view option as follows:

- Right-click the configuration name in the ConfigurationManager.

- Select the Exploded View tool in the Assembly toolbar.

- Select Insert, Exploded View from the Menu bar.

Activity: LINKAGE Assembly Drawing-Exploded View

Insert an Exploded view.

284) Click the **ConfigurationManager** tab.

285) Right-click **Default [GIDS-SC-1000]**.

286) Click **New Exploded view**  New Exploded View.... The Explode PropertyManager is displayed.

Create Explode Step 1. Use the distance box option.
287) Click the back **SHAFT-COLLAR** as illustrated.

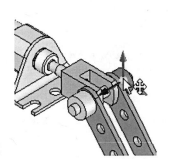

288) Enter **50**mm in the Explode distance box.

289) Click **Apply**. The SHAFT-COLLAR moves 50mms to the back of the model. If required, click the **Reverse direction** button.

290) Click **Done**. Explode Step1 is created.

Create Explode Step 2. Use the Manipulator icon.
291) Click the front **SHAFT-COLLAR** in the Graphics window as illustrated.

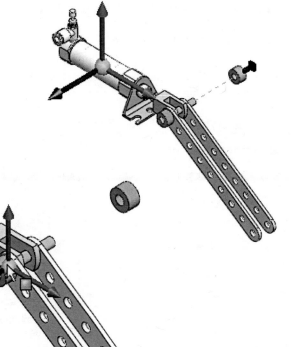

292) Drag the blue/orange **Manipulator icon** 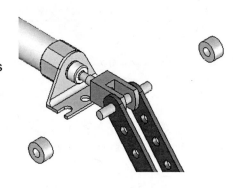 to the front of the assembly approximately 50mms.

293) Click **inside** the Graphics window. Explode Step2 is created.

Create Explode Step 3.
294) Click the **back FLATBAR** in the Graphics window as illustrated.

295) Drag the blue/orange **Manipulator icon** to the back of the assembly. Explode Step3 is created.

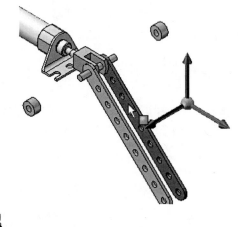

Create Explode Step 4.
296) Click the front **FLATBAR** in the Graphics window.

297) Drag the blue/orange **Manipulator icon** to the front of the assembly. Explode Step4 is created.

298) Click **inside** the Graphics window.

299) Expand each Explode Step to review.

300) Click **OK** from the Explode PropertyManager.

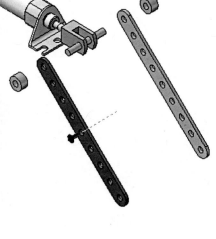

Save the LINKAGE part in the Exploded State.
301) Click **Save**.

Activity: LINKAGE Assembly Drawing-Animation

Animate the Exploded view.
302) Expand Default [GIDS-SC-1000].

303) Right-click **ExplView1** in the ConfigurationManager.

304) Click **Animate collapse** to play the animation. View the Animation.

Return the Exploded view in its collapsed state.

305) Close ☒ the Animation Controller dialog box.

Return to the Assembly FeatureManager
306) Click the LINKAGE **FeatureManager** 🗗 tab.

307) Click **Save** 🖫.

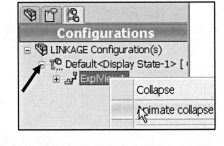

Open the LINKAGE drawing.
308) Click **Window, LINKAGE – SHEET1** from the Menu bar.

Display the Exploded view in the drawing.
309) Right-click inside the **Isometric view**.

310) Click **Properties**.

311) Check the **Show in exploded state** box.

312) Click **OK** from the Drawing Views Properties box.

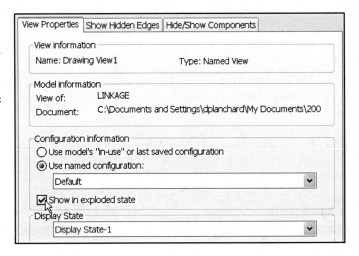

313) Click **OK** ✔ from the Drawing View1 PropertyManager. View the exploded state in the drawing on Sheet1.

314) Rebuild 🗲 the model.

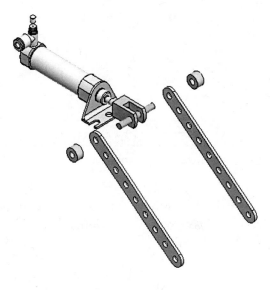

Bill of Materials

A Bill of Materials (BOM) is a table inserted into a drawing to keep a record of the parts used in an assembly. The default BOM template contains the Item Number, Quantity, Part No. and Description. The default Item number is determined by the order in which the component is inserted into the assembly. Quantity is the number of instances of a part or assembly.

Part No. is determined by the following: file name, default and the User Defined option, Part number used by the Bill of Materials. Description is determined by the description entered when the document is saved.

Activity: LINKAGE Assembly Drawing-Bill of Materials

Create a Bill of Materials.

315) Click inside the **Isometric view** boundary.

316) Click the **Annotation** tab from the CommandManager.

317) Click the **Bill of Materials** tool from the Consolidated Tables toolbar. The Bill of Materials PropertyManager is displayed.

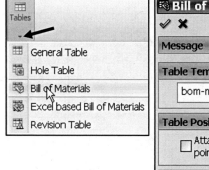
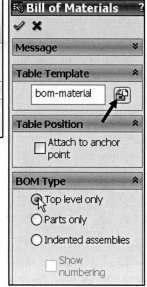

318) Select **bom-material** for Table Template.

319) Select **Top Level only** for BOM Type.

320) Click **OK** from the Bill of Materials PropertyManager.

321) Double-click a position in the **upper left corner** of the Sheet1.

322) Click a **position** in Sheet1.

ITEM NO.	PART NUMBER	DESCRIPTION	MATERIAL	QTY.
1	GIDS-PC-10001	LINEAR ACTUATOR		1
2	AXLE	AXLE ROD		1
3	GIDS-SC-10001-9	FLAT BAR 9 HOLES	2014 Alloy	2
4	SHAFT-COLLAR	SHAFT-COLLAR		2

The Bill of Materials requires some editing. The AXLE and SHAFT-COLLAR PART NUMBER values are not defined. The current part file name determines the PART NUMBER value.

The current part description determines the DESCRIPTION values. Redefine the PART NUMBER for the Bill of Materials. Note: You will also scale the LINKAGE assembly.

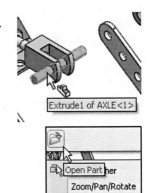

Modify the AXLE Part number.
323) Right-click the **AXLE** part in the LINKAGE drawing. Click **Open Part**. The AXLE FeatureManager is displayed.

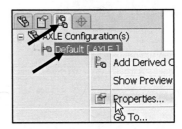

324) Click the AXLE **ConfigurationManager** tab.

325) Right-click **Default [AXLE]** in the ConfigurationManager.

326) Click **Properties**.

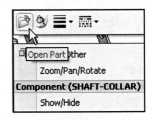

327) Select **User Specified Name** from the Configuration Properties dialog box.

328) Enter **GIDS-SC-10017** for the Part Number to be utilized in the Bill of Materials.

329) Click **OK** from the Configuration Properties PropertyManager.

330) **Return** to the FeatureManager.

331) Click **Save**.

Return to the LINKAGE drawing.
332) Click **Window**, **LINKAGE - Sheet1** from the Menu bar.

Modify the SHAFT-COLLAR PART NUMBER.
333) Right-click the left **SHAFT-COLLAR** part in the LINKAGE drawing.

334) Click **Open Part**. The SHAFT-COLLAR FeatureManager is displayed.

335) Click the SHAFT-COLLAR **ConfigurationManager** tab.

336) Right-click **Default [SHAFT-COLLAR]** from the ConfigurationManager.

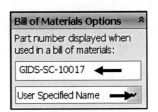

337) Click **Properties**. Select the **User Specified Name** from the Configuration Properties box.

338) Enter **GIDS-SC-10012-3-16** for the Part Number in the Bill of Materials. Click **OK** from the Configuration Properties PropertyManager.

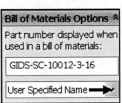

339) **Return** to the FeatureManager.

340) Click **Save**.

Return to the LINKAGE assembly drawing.
341) Click **Window, LINKAGE - Sheet1** from the Menu bar.

342) Rebuild the drawing and update the BOM.

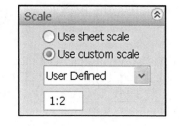

Modify the LINKAGE assembly scale.
343) Click inside the **Isometric view** boundary.

344) Enter **1:2** for Scale.

345) Click **OK** ✔ from the Drawing View1 PropertyManager.

346) Click **Save** 🖫.

ITEM NO.	PART NUMBER	DESCRIPTION	MATERIAL	QTY.
1	GIDS-PC-10001	LINEAR ACTUATOR		1
2	GIDS-SC-10017	AXLE ROD		1
3	GIDS-SC-10001-9	FLAT BAR 9 HOLES	2014 Alloy	2
4	GIDS-SC-10012-3-16	SHAFT-COLLAR		2

Note: As an exercise, complete the Bill of Materials. Label each component with a unique item number. The item number is placed inside a circle. The circle is called Balloon text. List each item in a Bill of Materials table. Utilize Auto Balloon to apply Balloon text to all BOM components.

The Circle Split Line option contains the Item Number and Quantity. Item number is determined by the order listed in the assembly FeatureManager. Quantity lists the number of instances in the assembly.

Activity: LINKAGE Assembly Drawing-Automatic Balloons

Insert the Automatic Balloons.
347) Click inside the **Isometric view** boundary of the LINKAGE.

348) Click the **Auto Balloons** 🖉 tool from the Annotation toolbar. The Auto Balloon PropertyManager is displayed. Accept the Square default Balloon Layout.

349) Click **OK** ✔ from the Auto Balloon PropertyManager.

Reposition the Balloon text.
350) Click and drag each **Balloon** to the desired position.

351) Click and drag the **Balloon arrowhead** to reposition the arrow on a component edge.

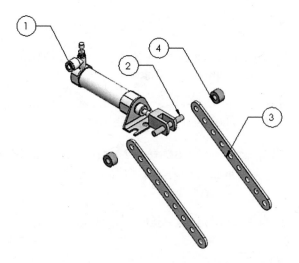

352) Click **OK** ✔ from the Balloon PropertyManager.

Display Item Number/Quantity.
353) Ctrl-Select the **four Balloon text** in the Graphics window. The
Balloon PropertyManager is displayed.

354) Select **Circular Split Line** for Style.

355) Click **OK** ✔ from the Balloon
PropertyManager.

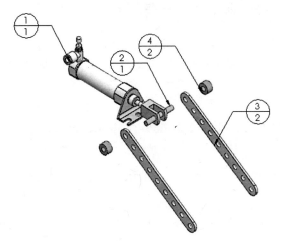

Save the LINKAGE assembly drawing.
356) Click **Save** 🖫 .

🔅 Select the BOM table in the drawing
and Right-click Properties to modify entries
and display table parameters.

LINKAGE Assembly Drawing - Sheet2

A drawing consists of one or more sheets. Utilize the Model View tool in the View
Layout toolbar to insert the AirCylinder assembly. The LINKAGE drawing Sheet2
displays the Front view and Top view of the AirCylinder assembly.

Insert a Section View to display the internal features of the AirCylinder. Insert a Detail
View to display an enlarged area of the AirCylinder.

Activity: LINKAGE Assembly Drawing-Sheet2

Add Sheet2.
357) **Right-click** in the Graphics window.

358) Click **Add Sheet**. Sheet2 is displayed. **Right-click** in Sheet2.

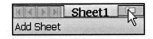

🔅 You can also add a sheet by clicking the Add
Sheet icon in the lower left corner of the Graphics
window.

359) Click **Properties**.

360) Enter **1:2** for Scale.

Select the CUSTOM-A Sheet Format.
361) Click **Browse** from the Sheet Properties box.

362) Select **SW-TUTORIAL-2010** for Look in folder.

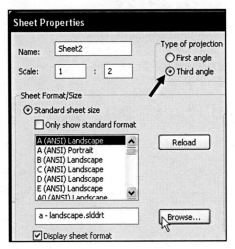

363) Double-click **CUSTOM-A**.

364) Click **OK** from the Sheet Properties box. Sheet 2 of 2 is displayed in the Graphics window.

Insert the AirCylinder assembly.
365) Click the **View Layout** tab from the CommandManager.

366) Click the **Model View** 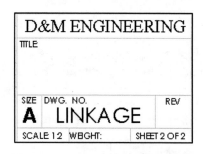 tool from the View Layout toolbar. The Model View PropertyManager is displayed.

367) Click the **Browse** button.

368) Double-click the **AirCylinder** assembly from the SW-TUTORIAL-2010 folder.

369) Check the **Create multiple views** box.

370) Click **Top view** as illustrated in the Standard views box. Note: Front view is selected by default. Both views should be active.

371) Click **OK** ✓ from the Model View PropertyManager.

Save Sheet2.
372) Click **Save** 💾.

Modify the Title Name font size.
373) **Right-click** in the Graphics window.

374) Click **Edit Sheet Format**.

375) Double-click on the Title: **LINEAR ACTUATOR**.

376) Resize the text to the Title block. Enter **5**mm for text height.

377) Click inside the **Graphics window**.

378) **Right-click** in the Graphics window.

379) Click **Edit Sheet**.

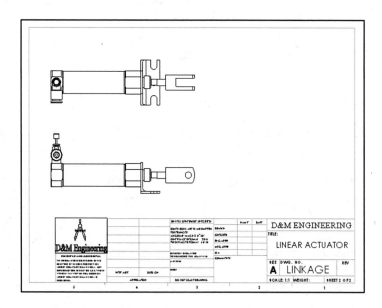

Section views display the interior features. Define a cutting plane with a sketched line in a view perpendicular to the Section view. Create a full Section view by sketching a section line in the Top view. Detailed views enlarge an area of an existing view. Specify location, shape and scale. Create a Detail view from a Section view at a 2:1 scale.

Activity: LINKAGE Assembly Drawing-Sheet2 Section view

Add a Section View to the drawing.
380) Click the **Drawing View3** boundary.

381) Click the **Section View** ⇶ tool from the View Layout toolbar. The Section View PropertyManager is displayed. The Sketch line ✎ icon is displayed.

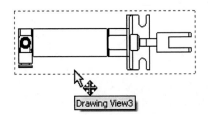

382) Sketch a section line through the **midpoints** of the view boundary.

383) Click the **end point**. The Section line extends beyond the left and right profile lines. The Section View dialog box is displayed.

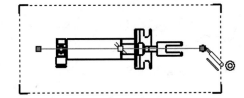

Position Section View A-A.
384) Click **OK** from the Section View dialog box.

385) Click a **location** above the Top view. The section arrows points downward.

386) Check the **Flip direction** box.

387) Click **OK** ✔ from the Section View PropertyManager.

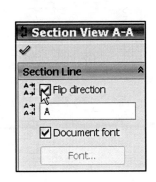

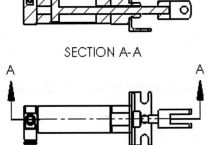

SECTION A-A

Fit the views to the drawing.
388) Press the **f** key.

Activity: LINKAGE Assembly Drawing-Sheet2 Detail view

Add a Detail view to the drawing.
389) Click inside the **Section View** boundary. The Section View A-A PropertyManager is displayed.

390) **Zoom in** to enlarge the view.

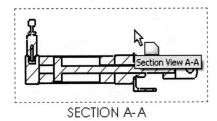

SECTION A-A

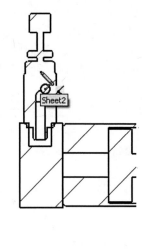

391) Click the **Detail View** 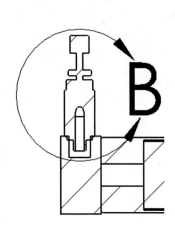 tool from the View Layout toolbar. The Circle Sketch tool is selected.

392) Click the **center** of the air fitting on the left side in the Section View as illustrated.

393) Sketch a **Circle** to encompass the air fitting.

394) If required, enter **B** for Detail View Name in the Label text box.

Position Detail View B.
395) Press the **f** key.

396) Click a **location** on Sheet2 to the right of the SECTION View.

397) Enter **2:1** for Scale.

398) Click **OK** ✅ from the Detail View B PropertyManager.

💡 Select a view boundary before creating Projected Views, Section Views or Detail Views.

Move views if required.
399) Click and drag the **view boundary** to allow for approximately 1 inch, [25mm] spacing between views.

Save the LINKAGE assembly drawing.
400) Click **Save** 💾.

Close all parts and assemblies.
401) Click **Window**, **Close All** from the Menu bar.

🔍 Additional details on Exploded View, Notes, Properties, Bill of Materials, Balloons, Section View and Detail View are available in SolidWorks Help. Keywords: Exploded, Notes, Properties (configurations), Bill of Materials, Balloons, Auto Balloon, Section and Detail.

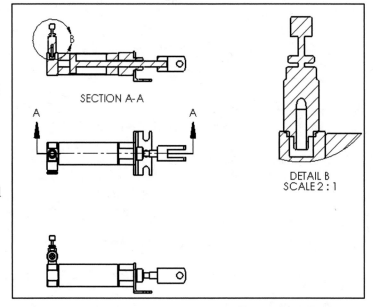

SECTION A-A

DETAIL B
SCALE 2 : 1

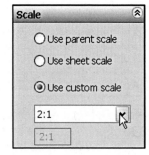

 Review the LINKAGE Assembly Drawing

The LINKAGE Assembly drawing consisted of two sheets. Sheet1 contained an Exploded view. The Exploded view was created in the LINKAGE assembly.

The Bill of Materials listed the Item Number, Part Number, Description, Material and Quantity of components in the assembly. Balloons were inserted to label top level components in the LINKAGE assembly. You developed Custom Properties in the part and utilized the Properties in the drawing and Bill of Materials.

Sheet2 contained the Front view, Top view, Section view and Detail view of the AirCylinder assembly.

Design Tables

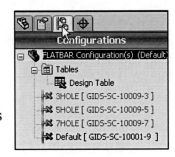

A Design Table is a spreadsheet used to create multiple configurations in a part or assembly. The Design Table controls the dimensions and parameters in the part. Utilize the Design Table to modify the overall length and number of holes in each FLATBAR.

Create three configurations of the FLATBAR:

- 3HOLE

- 5HOLE

- 7HOLE

Utilize the Design Table to control the Part Number and Description in the Bill of Materials. Insert the custom parameter $PRP@DESCRIPTION into the Design Table. Insert the system parameter $PARTNUMBER into the Design Table.

Activity: FLATBAR Part-Design Table

Open the FLATBAR part.
402) Click **Open** from the Menu bar.

403) Double-click the **FLATBAR** part from the SW-TUTORIAL-2010 folder. The FLATBAR FeatureManager is displayed.

Insert a Design Table.
404) Click **Insert**, **Tables**, **Design Table** from the Menu bar. The Auto-create option is selected. Accept the default settings.

405) Click **OK** from the Design Table PropertyManager.

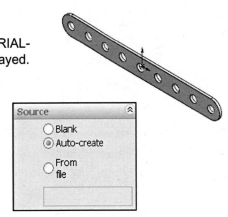

Select the input dimension.
406) Hold the **Ctrl key** down.

407) Click the **D1@Sketch1, D2@Sketch1, D1@Boss-Extude1, D1@Sketch2, D3@LPattern1** and **D1@LPattern1** from the Dimensions box.

408) Release the **Ctrl key**.

409) Click **OK** from the Dimensions dialog box.

 The illustrated dimension variable names in the Dimensions dialog box will be different if sketches or features were deleted when creating the FLATBAR part.

The input dimension names and default values are automatically entered into the Design Table. The Design Table displays the Primary Units of the Part. Example: Inches. The value Default is entered in Cell A3.

The values for the FLATBAR are entered in Cells B3 through G9. The FLATBAR length is controlled in Column B. The Number of Holes is controlled in Column G.

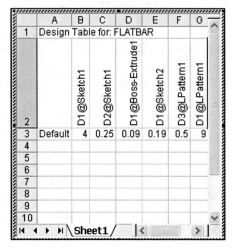

Enter the three configuration names.
410) Click **Cell A4**.

411) Enter **3HOLE**.

412) Click **Cell A5**.

413) Enter **5HOLE**.

414) Click **Cell A6**.

415) Enter **7HOLE**.

416) Click Cell **D3**.

417) If needed, enter **0.09** to round off the Thickness value.

Enter the dimension values for the 3HOLE configuration.
418) Click **Cell B4**. Enter **1**.

419) Click **Cell G4**. Enter **3**.

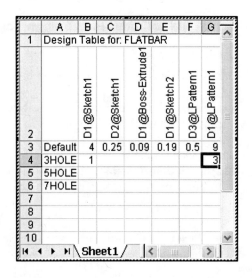

Enter the dimension values for the 5HOLE configuration.
420) Click **Cell B5**.

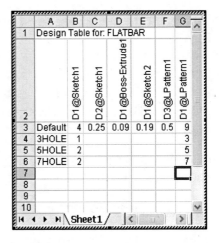

421) Enter **2**.

422) Click **Cell G5**.

423) Enter **5**.

Enter the dimension values for the 7HOLE configuration.
424) Click **Cell B6**.

425) Enter **3**.

426) Click **Cell G6**.

427) Enter **7**.

Build the three configurations.
428) Click a **position** outside the EXCEL Design Table in the Graphics window.

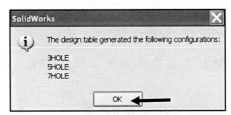

429) Click **OK** to generate the configurations. The Design Table icon is displayed in the FLATBAR FeatureManager.

Display the configurations.
430) Double-click **3HOLE**.

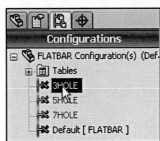

431) Double-click **5HOLE**.

432) Double-click **7HOLE**.

433) Double-click **Default**.

434) Click **Save** 🖫 .

Edit the Design Table.
435) Right-click **Design Table** in the ConfigurationManager.

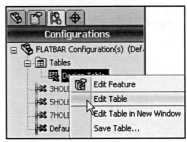

436) Click **Edit Table**. The Add Rows and Columns dialog box is displayed.

437) Click **Cancel** from the Add Rows and Columns dialog box.

Columns C through F are filled with the default FLATBAR values.

Enter parameters for DESCRIPTION and PARTNUMBER. Custom Properties begin with the prefix, "$PRP@". SolidWorks Properties begin with the prefix, "$".

Enter DESCRIPTION custom Property.
438) Double-click **Cell H2**.

439) Enter **$PRP@DESCRIPTION**.

440) Click **Cell H3**. Enter **9HOLES**.

441) Click **Cell H4**. Enter **3HOLES**.

442) Click **Cell H5**. Enter **5HOLES**.

443) Click **Cell H6**. Enter **7HOLES**.

Enter the PARTNUMBER Property.
444) Double-click **Cell I2**.

445) Enter **$PARTNUMBER**.

446) Click **Cell I3**.

447) Enter **GIDS-SC-10009-9**.

448) Click **Cell I4**.

449) Enter **GIDS-SC-10009-3**.

450) Click **Cell I5**.

451) Enter **GIDS-SC-10009-5**.

452) Click **Cell I6**.

453) Enter **GIDS-SC-10009-7**.

454) Click a **position** in the Graphics window to update the Design Table.

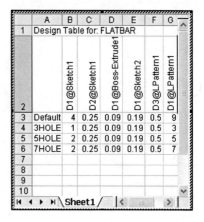

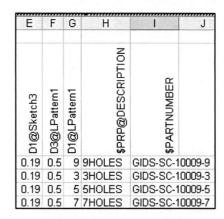

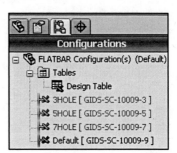

Activity: FLATBAR Drawing - Sheet2

Select configurations in the drawing. The Properties option in the Drawing view displays a list of configuration names.

Open the FLATBAR drawing.

455) Click **Open** 📄 from the Menu bar.

456) Select Files of type: **Drawing (*drw,*slddrw)**.

457) Double-click **FLATBAR** from the SW-TUTORIAL-2010 folder. The FLATBAR drawing is displayed. The dimensions tied to the Design table are displayed in a different color. The dimension color is controlled from the System Options, Colors section.

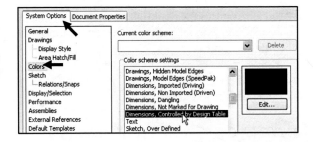

Copy the Front view.

458) Click inside the FLATBAR **Front view** boundary. Press **Ctrl C**.

459) **Right-click** in the Graphics window.

460) Click **Add Sheet**. Sheet2 is displayed.

461) Right-click **Properties**.

462) Click **Browse** from the Sheet Properties dialog box.

463) Double-click **CUSTOM-A** Sheet Format from the SW-TUTORIAL-2010 folder.

464) Click **OK** from the Sheet Properties box.

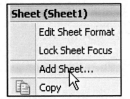

Paste the Front view from Sheet1.

465) Click a **position** inside the Sheet2 boundary.

466) Press **Ctrl V**. The Front view is displayed.

Display the 3HOLE FLATBAR configuration on Sheet2.

467) Right-click inside the **Front view** boundary.

468) Click **Properties**.

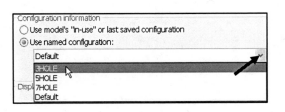

469) Select **3HOLE** from the Use named configuration list.

470) Click **OK** from the Drawing View Properties dialog box. The 3HOLE FLATBAR configuration is displayed.

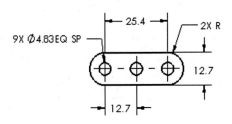

471) Right-click inside the **Drawing View** boundary.

472) Click **Open Part**.

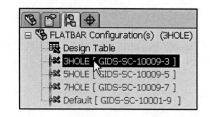

473) Double-click the **3HOLE** configuration from the ConfigurationManager tab.

Return to the FLATBAR Drawing Sheet2.
474) Click **Window**, **FLATBAR - Sheet2** from the Menu bar.

475) Click on the **9X** dimension text in the Graphics window. The Dimension PropertyManager is displayed.

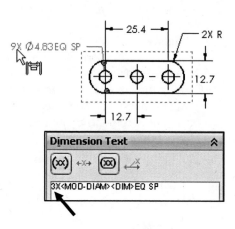

476) Replace the 9X dimension text with **3X** in the Dimension Text box as illustrated..

477) Click **OK** ✓ from the Dimension PropertyManager.

478) **Align** all dimension text as illustrated below.

479) Address **all extension line gaps**.

Save the FLATBAR Sheet2 drawing.

480) Click **Save** 💾 .

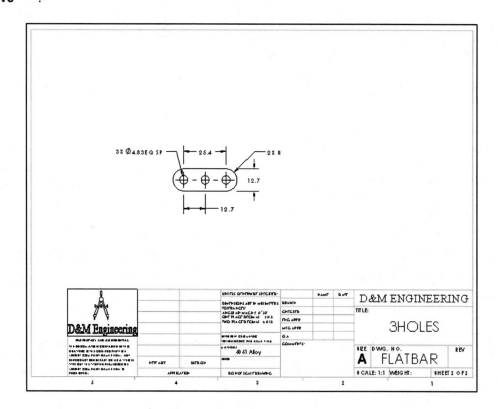

The 5HOLE and 7HOLE configurations are explored as an exercise. Combine the FLATBAR configurations with the SHAFT-COLLAR part to create three different assemblies. Select configuration in the assembly. The Properties in the FeatureManager option displays a list of configuration names.

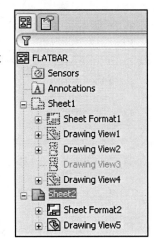

The FLATBAR-SHAFTCOLLAR assembly contains a FLATBAR fixed to the assembly Origin and a SHAFTCOLLAR mated to the FLATBAR left hole. The default configuration utilizes the FLATBAR-9HOLE part.

Design Tables exist in the assembly. Utilize a Design Table to control part configurations, 3HOLE, 5HOLE and 7HOLE. Utilize the Design Table to Control Suppress/Resolve state of a component in an assembly. Insert the parameter $STATE into the Design Table.

Activity: FLATBAR-SHAFTCOLLAR Assembly

Return to the Default FLATBAR configuration.
481) Right-click in the **3HOLE FLATBAR** view boundary.

482) Click **Open Part**.

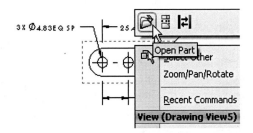

483) Click the **ConfigurationManager** tab.

484) Double-click the **Default** configuration.

485) Click the **FeatureManager** tab. The FLATBAR (Default) FeatureManager is displayed.

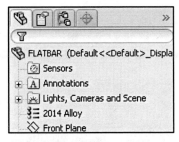

486) Click **Save**.

Create the FLATBAR-SHAFTCOLLAR assembly.
487) Click **New** from the Menu bar.

488) Double-click **Assembly** from the Templates tab. The Begin Assembly PropertyManager is displayed. FLATBAR is an active document. FLATBAR is displayed in the Open documents box.

489) Click **FLATBAR** from the Open documents box.

490) Click **OK** from the Begin Assembly PropertyManager. The FLATBAR is fixed to the Origin.

Save the FLATBAR-SHAFTCOLLAR assembly.

491) Click **Save** 🖫.

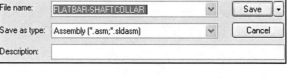

492) Enter **FLATBAR-SHAFTCOLLAR** for Assembly name.

493) Click **Save**.

Insert the SHAFTCOLLAR part.

494) Click the **Insert Components** tool from the Assembly toolbar. The Insert Component PropertyManager is displayed.

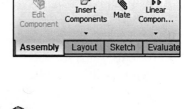

495) Click **BROWSE**. Double-click the **SHAFT-COLLAR** part.

496) Click a **position** to the front left of the FLATBAR as illustrated in the Graphics window.

Fit the model to the Graphics window.
497) Press the **f** key.

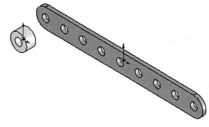

498) Click **Save** 🖫.

Mate the SHAFTCOLLAR.

499) Click the **Mate** tool from the Assembly toolbar. The Mate PropertyManager is displayed.

Insert a Concentric mate.
500) Click the **left hole face** of the FLATBAR.

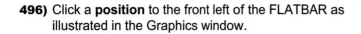

501) Click the outside **cylindrical face** of the SHAFT-COLLAR. The selected faces are displayed in the Mate Selections box. Concentric is selected by default.

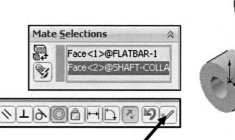

502) Click the **Green Check mark** ✓.

Insert a Coincident mate.
503) Click the **back flat face** of the SHAFT-COLLAR.

504) Click the **front face** of the FLATBAR as illustrated. Coincident ∠ is selected by default.

505) Click the **Green Check mark** ✓.

506) Click **OK** ✓ from the Mate PropertyManager.

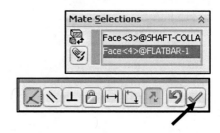

Insert and mate the second SHAFT-COLLAR to the right hole.

507) Click the **Insert Components** 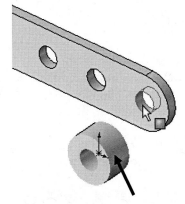 tool from the Assembly toolbar. The Insert Component PropertyManager is displayed.

508) Click the **Browse** button.

509) Double-click the **SHAFT-COLLAR** part.

510) Click a **position** to the front right of the FLATBAR as illustrated.

Mate the second SHAFTCOLLAR.

511) Click the **Mate** tool from the Assembly toolbar. The Mate PropertyManager is displayed.

Insert a Concentric mate.
512) Click the **right hole face** of the FLATBAR.

513) Click the outside **cylindrical face** of the SHAFT-COLLAR. Concentric is selected by default.

514) Click the **Green Check mark** .

Insert a Coincident mate.
515) Click the **back flat face** of the SHAFT-COLLAR.

516) Click the **front face** of the FLATBAR. Coincident is selected by default.

517) Click the **Green Check mark** .

518) Click **OK** from the Mate PropertyManager.

Save the FLATBAR-SHAFTCOLLAR assembly.

519) Click **Save** .

The FLATBAR-SHAFTCOLLAR FeatureManager displays the Default configuration of the FLATBAR in parenthesis, FLATBAR<1> (Default).

The instance number, <1> indicates the first instance of the FLATBAR. Note: Your instance number will be different, if you delete the FLATBAR and then reinsert into the assembly. The exact instance number is required for the Design Table.

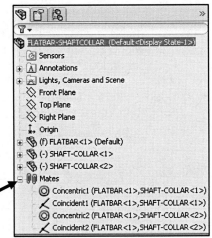

Create a Design Table that contains three new configurations. Each configuration utilizes a different FLATBAR configuration. Control the Suppress/Resolve State of the second SHAFT-COLLAR.

Insert a Design Table.

520) Click **Insert**, **Tables**, **Design Table** from the Menu bar. The Auto-create option is selected by default.

521) Click **OK** ✔ from the Design Table PropertyManager.

Enter the Design Table values.

522) Default is displayed in Cell A3. Click **Cell A4**.

523) Enter **NO SHAFT-COLLAR**.

524) Double-click **CELL B2**.

525) Enter **$STATE@SHAFT-COLLAR<2>**.

526) Click **Cell B3**.

527) Enter **R** for Resolved.

528) Click **Cell B4**.

529) Enter **S** for Suppressed.

530) Click a **position** outside the Design Table in the Graphics window.

531) Click **OK** to display the NO SHAFT-COLLAR configuration.

Display the configurations.

532) Click the **ConfigurationManager** ⧉ tab.

533) Double-click the **NO SHAFT-COLLAR** configuration. The second SHAFT-COLLAR is suppressed in the Graphics window.

534) Double-click the **Default** configuration. The second SHAFT-COLLAR is resolved. Both SHAFT-COLLARs are displayed in the Graphics window.

💡 Tangent Edges are displayed for educational purposes.

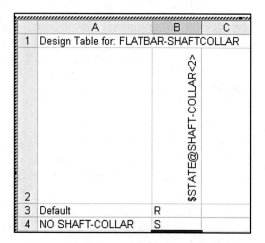

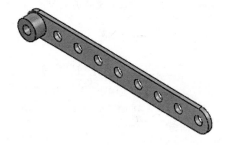

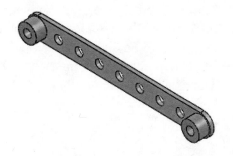

Insert FLATBAR configurations.
535) Right-click **Design Table**.

536) Click **Edit Table**.

537) Click **Cancel** from the Add Rows and Columns dialog box.

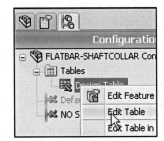

Enter Configuration names.
538) Click **Cell A5**. Enter **3HOLE FLATBAR**.

539) Click **Cell A6**. Enter **5HOLE FLATBAR**.

540) Click **Cell A7**. Enter **7HOLE FLATBAR**.

Enter STATE values.
541) Click **Cell B5**. Enter **S** for Suppress.

542) Click Cell **B6**. Enter **S**.

543) Click Cell **B7**. Enter **S**.

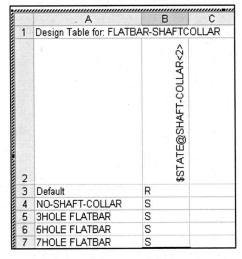

Enter Design Table values.
544) Double-click **Cell C2**.

545) Enter **$CONFIGURATION@FLATBAR<1>**.

546) Click **Cell C5**.

547) Enter **3HOLE**.

548) Click **Cell C6**.

549) Enter **5HOLE**.

550) Click **Cell C7**.

551) Enter **7HOLE**.

552) Click a **position** in the Graphics window to exit.

553) Click **OK** to create the three configurations.

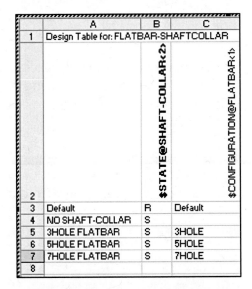

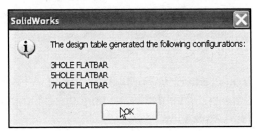

Display the configurations.
554) Double-click the **3HOLE FLATBAR** configuration.

555) Double-click the **5HOLE FLATBAR** configuration.

556) Double-click the **7HOLE FLATBAR** configuration.

557) Double-click the **Default** configuration.

558) Click the **Assembly FeatureManager** tab.

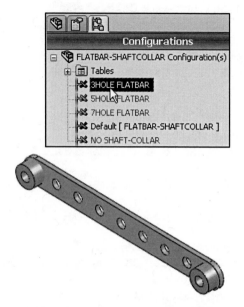

Save the FLATBAR-SHAFTCOLLAR assembly.
559) Click **Isometric view** from the Heads-up View
toolbar.

560) Click **Save** .

Close all documents.
561) Click **Windows**, **Close All** from the Menu bar.

Always return to the Default configuration in the
assembly. Control the individual configuration
through properties of a view in a drawing and
properties of a component in the assembly.

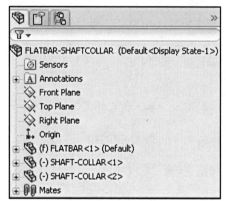

To modify configuration specific notes or
dimensions in an assembly drawing, the configuration
in the assembly must be the active configuration.

If an assembly or component is loaded in a
Lightweight state, right-click the **assembly name**
or **component name** from the FeatureManager. Click **Set Lightweight to Resolved**.

Additional details on Design Tables and Configurations are available in SolidWorks
Help.

Chapter Summary

You created two drawings: the FLATBAR drawing and the LINKAGE assembly
drawing. The drawings contained Standard views, a Detail view, a Section view and an
Isometric view.

The drawings utilized a Custom Sheet Format and a Custom Drawing Template. The Sheet Format contained the Company logo and Title block information.

The FLATBAR drawing consisted of two Sheets: Sheet1 and Sheet2. You obtained an understanding of displaying views with the ability to insert, add, and modify dimensions. You used two major design modes in the drawings: Edit Sheet Format and Edit Sheet.

The LINKAGE assembly drawing contained two sheets. Sheet1 contained an Exploded view and a Bill of Materials. The Properties for the Bill of Materials were developed in each part and assembly. Sheet2 utilized a Detail view and a Section view of the AirCylinder assembly.

You created three configurations of the FLATBAR part with a Design Table. The Design Table controlled parameters and dimensions of the FLATBAR part. You utilized these three configurations in the FLATBAR-SHAFTCOLLAR assembly.

Drawings are an integral part of the design process. Part, assemblies and drawings all work together. From your initial design concepts, you created parts and drawings that fulfilled the design requirements of your customer.

Additional SolidWorks examples are provided in the text **Drawing and Detailing with SolidWorks**, Planchard & Planchard, SDC Publications.

Chapter Terminology

Bill of Materials (BOM): A BOM is an EXCEL table in a drawing that lists the item, quantity, part number and description of the components in an assembly. Balloon labels are placed on items in the drawing that correspond to the number in the table. A BOM template controls additional information such as Material or Cost.

Center marks: Represents two perpendicular intersecting centerlines.

Design Table: A Design Table is a spreadsheet used to create multiple configurations in a part or assembly. The Design Table controls the dimensions and parameters in the part.

Detailed view: Detailed views enlarge an area of an existing view. Specify location, shape, and scale.

Drawing file name: Drawing file names end with a .slddrw suffix.

Drawing Layers: Contain dimensions, annotations and geometry.

Drawing Template: The foundation of a SolidWorks drawing is the Drawing Template. Drawing size, drawing standards, company information, manufacturing and or assembly requirements, units and other properties are defined in the Drawing Template. In this chapter, the Drawing Template contained the drawing Size and Document Properties.

Edit Sheet Format Mode: Provides the ability to:

- Change the Title block size and text headings.

- Incorporate a Company logo.

- Add a drawing, design or company text.

Remember: A part cannot be inserted into a drawing when the Edit Sheet Format mode is selected.

Edit Sheet Mode: Provides the ability to:

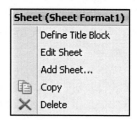

- Add or modify views.

- Add or modify dimensions.

- Add or modify text.

General Notes: Below are a few helpful guidelines to create general drawing notes:

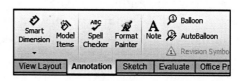

- Use capitol letters.

- Use left text justification.

- Font size should be the same as the dimension text.

Hole Callout: The Hole Callout function creates additional notes required to dimension the holes.

Hole Centerlines: Are composed of alternating long and short dash lines. The lines identify the center of a circle, axes or other cylindrical geometry.

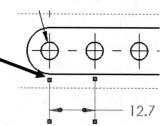

Insert Model Items: The tool utilized to insert part dimensions and annotations into drawing views. The Insert Model Items tool is located in the Annotate toolbar.

Leader lines: Reference the size of the profile. A gap must exist between the profile lines and the leader lines.

Model View: The tool utilized to insert named views into a drawing. The Model View tool is located in the Layout View toolbar.

Notes: Notes can be used to add text with leaders or as a stand-alone text string. If an edge, face or vertex is selected prior to adding the note, a leader is created to that location.

Part file name: Part file names end with a .sldprt suffix. Note: A drawing or part file can have the same prefix. A drawing or part file cannot have the same suffix. Example: Drawing file name: FLATBAR.slddrw. Part file name: FLATBAR.sldprt

Section view: Section views display the interior features. Define a cutting plane with a sketched line in a view perpendicular to the Section view.

Sheet Format: The Sheet Format is incorporated into the Drawing Template. The Sheet Format contains the border, title block information, revision block information, company name and or logo information, Custom Properties and SolidWorks Properties. In this chapter the Sheet Format contained the title block information.

Title block: Contains vital part or assembly information. Each company can have a unique version of a title block.

View Appearance: There are two important factors that affect the appearance of views:

1. Whether the view is shown wireframe, hidden lines removed, or hidden lines visible.

2. How tangent edges on entities such as fillets are displayed.

Questions

1. Describe a Bill of Materials and its contents.

2. Name the two major design modes used to develop a drawing in SolidWorks.

3. True or False. Units, Dimensioning Standards, Arrow size, Font size are modified in the Options, Document Properties section.

4. How do you save a Sheet Format?

5. Identify seven components that are commonly found in a title block.

6. Describe the procedure to insert an Isometric view to the drawing?

7. In SolidWorks, drawing file names end with a _____ suffix. Part file names end with a _____ suffix.

8. True or False. In SolidWorks, if a part is modified, the drawing is updated with a Rebuild command.

9. True or False. In SolidWorks, when a dimension in the drawing is modified, the part is updated with a Rebuild command.

10. Name three guidelines to create General Notes on a drawing.

11. True or False. Most engineering drawings use the following font: Times New Roman – All small letters.

12. What are Leader lines? Provide an example.

13. Describe the key differences between a Detail view and a Section view on a drawing.

14. Identify the procedure to create an Exploded view.

15. Describe the purpose of a Design Table in a part and in an assembly.

16. Review the Design Intent section in the Introduction. Identify how you incorporated design intent into the drawing.

17. Identify how you incorporate design intent into configurations with a Design Table.

18. Review the Keyboard Short Cut keys in the Appendix. Identify the Short Cut keys you incorporated into this chapter.

19. Discuss why a part designed in inch units would utilize a drawing detailed in millimeter units.

Exercises

Exercise 3.1: FLATBAR - 3 HOLE Drawing

Note: Dimensions are enlarged for clarity. Utilize inch, millimeter, or dual dimensioning.

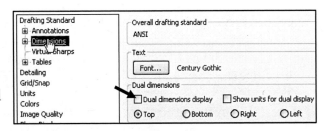

- Create the ANSI-IPS Third Angle Projection FLATBAR - 3HOLE drawing. First create the part from the drawing - then create the drawing. Use the default A-Landscape Sheet Format/Size.

- Insert a Shaded Isometric view. No Tangent Edges displayed.

- Insert a Front and Top view. Insert dimensions. Insert 3X – EQ. SP. Insert the Company and Third Angle Projection icon. Add a Parametric Linked Note for MATERIAL THICKNESS.

- Hide the Thickness dimension in the Top view. Insert needed Centerlines.

- Insert Custom Properties for Material (2014 Alloy), DRAWNBY, DRAWNDATE, COMPANYNAME, etc.

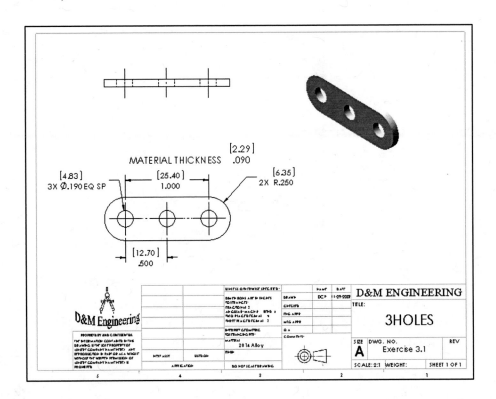

Exercise 3.2: CYLINDER Drawing

Create the ANSI - IPS - Third Angle CYLINDER drawing.

- First create the part from the drawing - then create the drawing. Use the default A-Landscape Sheet Format/Size.

- Insert the Front and Right views as illustrated. Insert dimensions. Think about the proper view for your dimensions!

- Insert Company and Third Angle projection icons. The icons are available in the homework folder.

- Insert needed Centerlines and Center Marks.

- Insert Custom Properties: Material, Description, DrawnBy, DrawnDate, CompanyName, etc. Note: Material is AISI 1020.

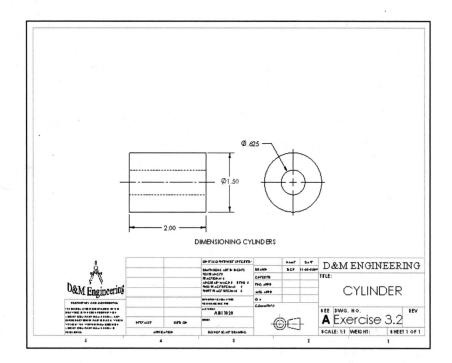

- Utilize the Mass Properties tool from the Evaluate toolbar to calculate the volume and mass of the CYLINDER part. Set decimal places to 4.

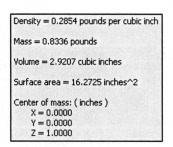

Density = 0.2854 pounds per cubic inch

Mass = 0.8336 pounds

Volume = 2.9207 cubic inches

Surface area = 16.2725 inches^2

Center of mass: (inches)
    X = 0.0000
    Y = 0.0000
    Z = 1.0000

Exercise 3.3: PRESSURE PLATE Drawing

Create the ANSI - IPS - Third Angle PRESSURE PLATE drawing.

- First create the part from the drawing - then create the drawing. Use the default A-Landscape Sheet Format/Size.

- Insert the Front and Right views as illustrated. Insert dimensions. Think about the proper view for your dimensions!

- Insert Company and Third Angle projection icons. The icons are available in the homework folder.

- Insert needed Centerlines and Center Marks.

- Insert Custom Properties: Material, Description, DrawnBy, DrawnDate, CompanyName, etc. Note: Material is 1060 Alloy.

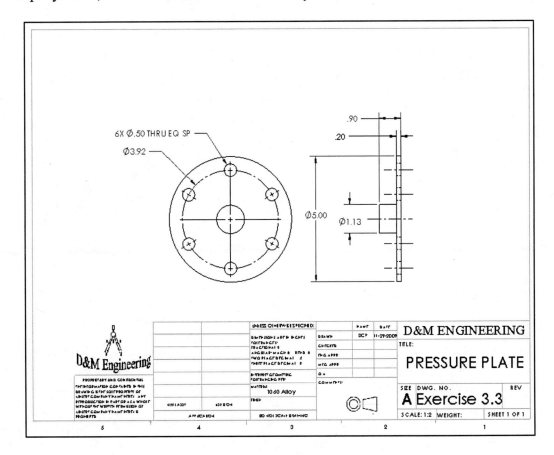

Exercise 3.4: LINKS Assembly Drawing

- Create the LINK assembly. Utilize three different FLATBAR configurations and a SHAFT-COLLAR.

- Create the LINK assembly drawing as illustrated. Use the default A-Landscape Sheet Format/Size.

- Insert Company and Third Angle projection icons. The icons are available in the homework folder. Remove all Tangent Edges.

- Insert Custom Properties: Description, DrawnBy, DrawnDate, CompanyName, etc.

- Insert a Bill of Materials as illustrated with Balloons.

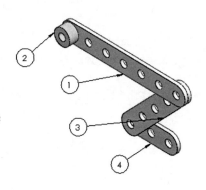

ITEM NO.	PART NUMBER	DESCRIPTION	QTY.
1	GIDS-SC-10009-7	7HOLES	1
2	GIDS-SC-10012-3-16	SHAFT-COLLAR	1
3	GIDS-SC-10009-5	5HOLES	1
4	GIDS-SC-10009-3	3HOLES	1

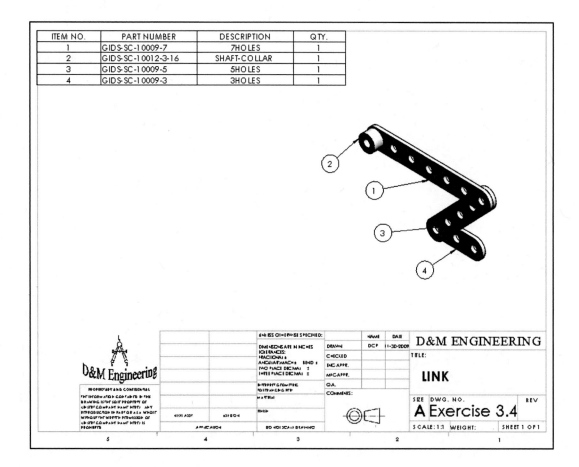

Exercise 3.5: PLATE-1 Drawing

Create the ANSI - MMGS - Third Angle PLATE-1 drawing.

- First create the part from the drawing - then create the drawing. Use the default A-Landscape Sheet Format/Size.

- Insert the Front and Right views as illustrated. Insert dimensions. Think about the proper view for your dimensions!

- Insert Company and Third Angle projection icons. The icons are available in the homework folder.

- Insert needed Centerlines and Center Marks.

- Insert Custom Properties: Material, Description, DrawnBy, DrawnDate, CompanyName, etc. Note: Material is 1060 Alloy.

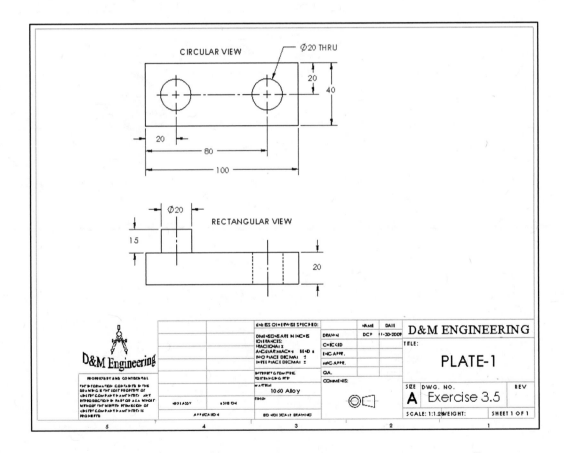

Exercise 3.6: FLATE-PLATE Drawing

Create the ANSI - IPS - Third Angle PLATE-1 drawing.

- First create the part from the drawing - then create the drawing. Use the default A-Landscape Sheet Format/Size. Remove all Tangent Edges.

- Insert the Front, Top, Right and Isometric views as illustrated. Insert dimensions. Think about the proper view for your dimensions!

- Insert Company and Third Angle projection icons. The icons are available in the homework folder.

- Insert needed Centerlines and Center Marks.

- Insert Custom Properties: Material, Description, DrawnBy, DrawnDate, CompanyName, Hole Annotation, etc. Note: Material is 1060 Alloy

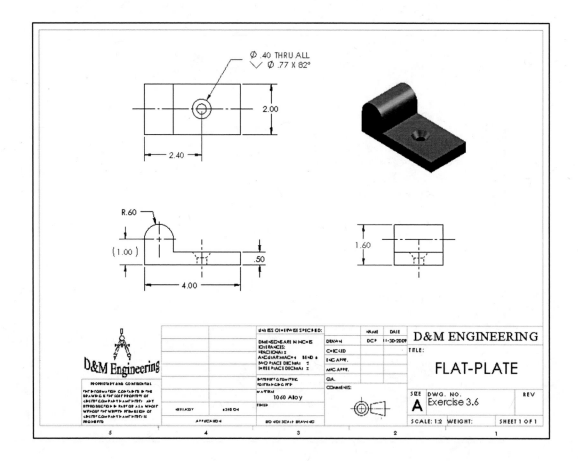

Exercise 3.7: LINKAGE-2 Drawing

- Create a new drawing named, LINKAGE-2.

- Insert an Isometric view, shaded view of the LINKAGE-2 Assembly created in the Chapter 1 exercises.

- Define the PART NO. Property and the DESCRIPTION Property for the AXLE, FLATBAR- 9HOLE, FLATBAR - 3HOLE and SHAFT COLLAR.

- Save the LINKAGE-2 assembly to update the properties. Return to the LINKAGE-2 Drawing. Insert a Bill of Materials with Auto Balloons as illustrated.

- Insert the Company and Third Angle Projection icon. Insert Custom Properties for DRAWNBY, DRAWNDATE and COMPANYNAME

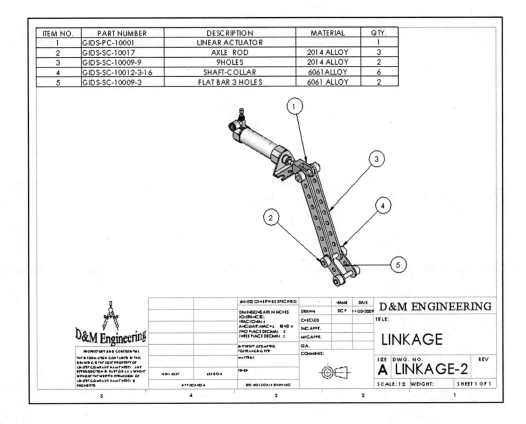

ITEM NO.	PART NUMBER	DESCRIPTION	MATERIAL	QTY.
1	GIDS-PC-10001	LINEAR ACTUATOR		1
2	GIDS-SC-10017	AXLE ROD	2014 ALLOY	3
3	GIDS-SC-10009-9	9HOLES	2014 ALLOY	2
4	GIDS-SC-10012-3-16	SHAFT-COLLAR	6061 ALLOY	6
5	GIDS-SC-10009-3	FLAT BAR 3 HOLES	6061 ALLOY	2

Exercise 3.8: **eDrawing**

Create an eDrawing of the LINKAGE-2 drawing. A SolidWorks eDrawing is a compressed document that does not require the corresponding part or assembly. SolidWorks eDrawing is animated to display multiple views and dimensions. Review the eDrawing On-line Help for additional functionality.

- Click Publish eDrawing File from the Menu bar menu.

- Click the Play button.

- Click the Stop button.

- Save the LINKAGE-2 eDrawing.

- Return to the LINKAGE2 drawing.

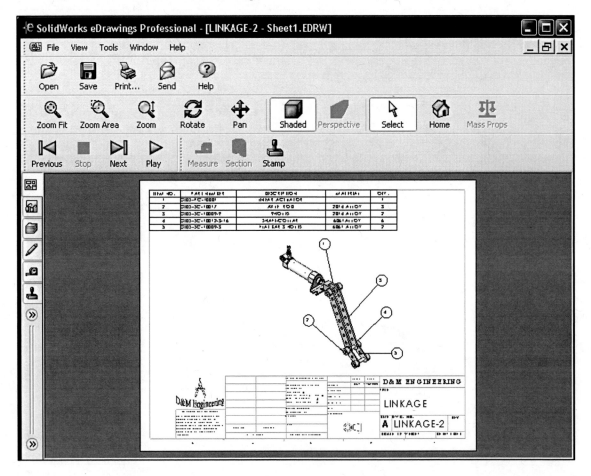

Chapter 4

Advanced Features

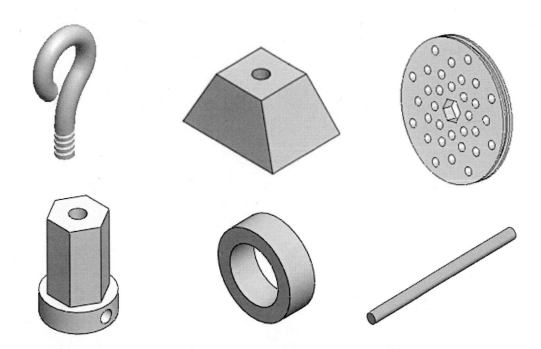

Below are the desired outcomes and usage competencies based on the completion of Chapter 4.

Desired Outcomes:	**Usage Competencies**:

• Six parts for the PNEUMATIC-TEST-MODULE assembly:
   o WEIGHT
   o HOOK
   o WHEEL
   o HEX-ADAPTER
   o AXLE-3000
   o SHAFTCOLLAR-500
	• Apply the following Advanced modeling features: Plane, Lofted Base, Extruded Cut, Swept Base, Dome, Helix and Spiral, Swept Cut, Extruded Boss/Base, Revolved Cut, Extruded Cut, Circular Pattern, Axis, Instant3D and Hole Wizard.
	
	• Reuse geometry.
	
	• Modify existing parts to create new parts with the Save as copy command.

Notes:

Chapter 4 - Advanced Features

Chapter Objective

Obtain an understanding to create parts for the configuration of the PNEUMATIC-TEST-MODULE assembly. Attain the ability to reuse geometry by modifying existing parts and to create new parts. Knowledge of the following SolidWorks features: *Extruded Boss/Base, Extruded Cut, Dome, Plane, Axis, Lofted Boss/Base, Swept Boss/Base, Helix and Spiral Swept Cut, Revolved Cut, Hole Wizard, Instant3D* and *Circular Pattern*.

Create six individual parts:

- *WEIGHT*

- *HOOK*

- *WHEEL*

- *HEX-ADAPTER*

- *AXLE-3000*

- *SHAFTCOLLAR-500*

In Chapter 5, develop a working understanding with multiple documents in an assembly. Build on sound assembly modeling techniques that utilize symmetry, component patterns, and mirrored components.

Create five assemblies:

- 3HOLE-SHAFTCOLLAR assembly

- 5HOLE-SHAFTCOLLAR assembly

- WHEEL-FLATBAR assembly

- WHEEL-AND-AXLE assembly

- PNEUMATIC-TEST-MODULE assembly

On the completion of this chapter, you will be able to:

- Create new parts and copy parts with the Save As command to reuse similar geometry.

- Utilize Construction geometry in a sketch.

- Apply the following SolidWorks features:

    o Extruded Boss/Base

    o Extruded Cut

    o Dome

    o Plane

    o Lofted Boss/Base

    o Swept Boss/Base

    o Swept Cut

    o Revolved Cut

    o Hole Wizard

    o Helix and Spiral

    o Axis

    o Circular Pattern

    o Instant3D

Chapter Overview

Six additional parts are required for the final
PNEUMATIC-TEST-MODULE assembly. Each
part explores various modeling techniques.

Create three new parts in this chapter:

- WEIGHT

- HOOK

- WHEEL

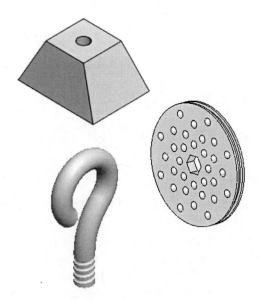

The WEIGHT and HOOK parts were applied
in the Chapter 2 exercises. See Chapter 2
Homework folder on the CD in the book.

Utilize the Save As command and modify existing parts that were created in the previous chapters to create three additional parts for the PNEUMATIC-TEST-MODULE assembly.

- HEX-ADAPTER

- AXLE-3000

- SHAFTCOLLAR-500

The HEX-ADAPTER part utilizes modified geometry from the HEX-STANDOFF part.

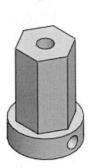

HEX-STANDOFF

The AXLE-3000 part utilizes modified geometry from the AXLE part.

The SHAFTCOLLAR-500 part utilizes modified geometry from the SHAFT-COLLAR part.

HEX-
ADAPTER

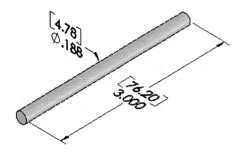

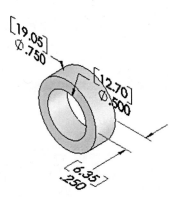

Press the **g** key to activate the Magnifying glass tool. Use the Magnifying glass tool to inspect a model and make selections without changing the overall view of your model in the Graphics window.

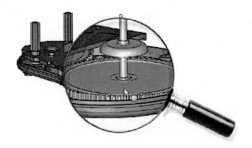

WEIGHT Part

The WEIGHT part is a machined part. Utilize the Loft 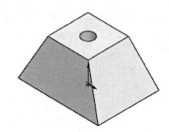 feature. Create a Loft by blending two or more profiles. Each profile is sketched on a separate plane.

🔅 Model Origin is displayed for educational purpose.

Create Plane1. Offset Plane1 from the Top Plane.

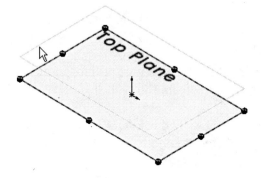

Sketch a rectangle for the first profile on the Top Plane.

Sketch a square for the second profile on Plane1.

Select the corner of each profile to create the Loft feature.

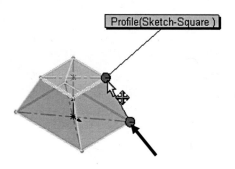

Utilize the Instant3D tool to create an Extruded Cut 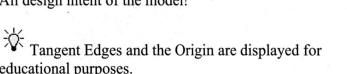 feature to create a Though All hole centered on the top face of the Loft feature.

🔅 When using the Instant3D tool, you lose the Through All design intent of the model!

🔅 Tangent Edges and the Origin are displayed for educational purposes.

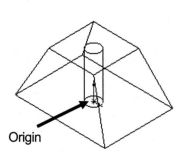

All parts in this chapter utilize a custom part template. Create the custom part template from the default part template. Save the Custom Part template in the SW-TUTORIAL-2010 folder.

Activity: Create the WEIGHT Part

Create a new part template.

1)   Click **New** ⬚ from the Menu bar.

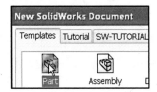

2)   Double-click **Part** from the Templates tab. The Part FeatureManager is displayed.

Set the Dimensioning standard.

3)   Click **Options** ▤, **Document Properties** tab from the Menu bar.

4)   Select **ANSI** from the Overall drafting standard drop-down menu.

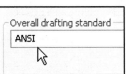

Set units.

5)   Click **Units**.

6)   Select **IPS**, [**MMGS**] for Unit system.

7)   Select **.123**, [**.12**] for Linear units Decimal places.

8)   Select **None** for Angular units Decimal places.

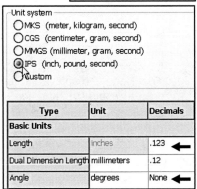

Set Leader arrow direction.

9)   Click **Dimensions**.

10)   Check the **Smart** box as illustrated.

11)   Click **OK** from the Document Properties - Detailing - Dimensions dialog box.

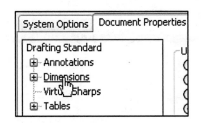

Save the part template.

12)   Click **Save As** from the Menu bar.

13)   Select **Part Templates (*.prtdot)** for Save as type.

14)   Select **SW-TUTORIAL-2010** for Save in folder.

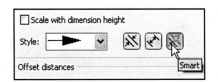

15)   Enter **PART-ANSI-IN**, [PART-ANSI-MM] for File name.

16)   Click **Save**.

17)   Click **File**, **Close** from the Menu bar.

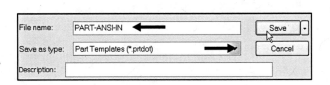

Create a new part.

18)   Click **New** ⬜ from the Menu bar.

19)   Click the **SW-TUTORIAL-2010** tab.

20)   Double-click **PART-ANSI-IN**, [PART-ANSI-MM]. The Part FeatureManager is displayed.

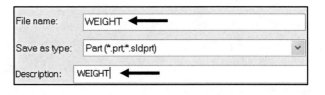

Save the part.
21)   Click **Save As** from the Menu bar.

22)   Select the **SW-TUTORIAL-2010** folder.

23)   Enter **WEIGHT** for File name.

24)   Enter **WEIGHT** for Description.

25)   Click **Save**.

Insert Plane1.
26)   Right-click **Top Plane** from the FeatureManager. Click **Show**. The Top Plane is displayed in the Graphics window. Note: In a new installation, Planes and Origins may be displayed by default.

27)   Hold the **Ctrl** key down.

28)   Click the **boundary** of the Top Plane as illustrated.

29)   Drag the **mouse pointer** upward.

30)   Release the **mouse pointer**.

31)   Release the **Ctrl** key. The Plane PropertyManager is displayed. Top Plane is displayed in the First Reference box.

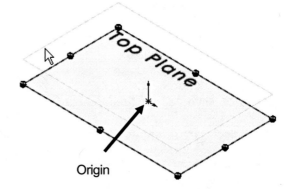

Origin

🔅 To display the Origin, click **View**, **Origins** from the Menu bar menu.

🔅 SolidWorks 2010 has a new Plane PropertyManager.

32) Enter **.500**in, **[12.70]** for Distance.

33) Click **OK** ✓ from the Plane PropertyManager.

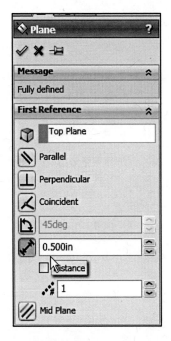

Plane1 is displayed in the Graphics window and is listed in the FeatureManager. Plane1 is offset from the Top Plane.

A Loft feature requires two sketches. The first sketch, Sketch1 is a rectangle sketched on the Top Plane centered about the Origin ⌞. The second sketch, Sketch2 is a square sketched on Plane1 centered about the Origin.

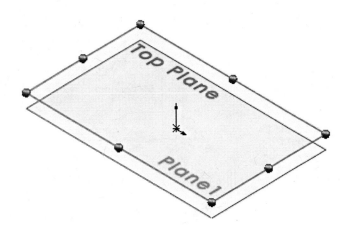

Create Sketch1.
34) Right-click **Top Plane** from the FeatureManager.

35) Click **Sketch** ✑ from the Context toolbar. The Sketch toolbar is displayed.

36) Click **Center Rectangle** ⊡ from the Consolidated Sketch tool. The Center Rectangle ⊡ icon is displayed.

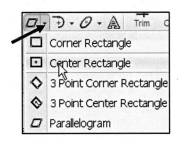

37) Click the **Origin** ⌞ as illustrated.

38) Click a **position** to the top right.

💡 The Center Rectangle tool provides the ability to sketch a rectangle located at a center point, in this case the Origin. This eliminates the need for centerlines to the Origin with a Midpoint geometric relation.

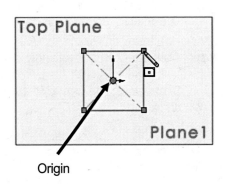

Origin

Add dimensions.

39) Click the **Smart Dimension** 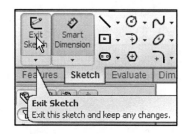 Sketch tool.

40) Click the **top horizontal** line. Click a **position** above the line.

41) Enter **1.000**in, [25.40].

42) Click the **Green Check mark** .

43) Click the **right vertical** line.

44) Click a **position** to the right.

45) Enter **.750**in, [19.05].

46) Click the **Green Check mark** .

Close Sketch1.

47) Click **Exit Sketch** from the Sketch toolbar. The sketch is fully defined and is displayed in black.

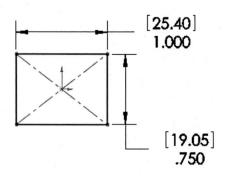

Rename Sketch1.

48) Click **Sketch1** from the FeatureManager.

49) Enter **Sketch-Rectangle** for name.

Save the part

50) Click **Save** .

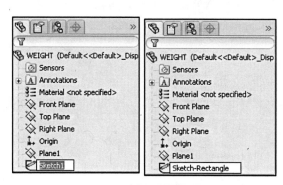

Display an Isometric view.

51) Click **Isometric view** from the Heads-up View toolbar.

Create Sketch2.

52) Right-click **Plane1** from the FeatureManager. Plane1 is your Sketch plane.

53) Click **Sketch** from the Context toolbar. The Sketch toolbar is displayed.

54) Click the **Center Rectangle** Consolidated Sketch tool. The Center Rectangle icon is displayed.

55) Click the **red Origin** as illustrated.

56)   Click a **position** as illustrated.

57)   Right-click **Select** to de-select the Center Rectangle tool.

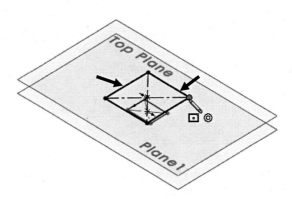

Add an Equal relation between the left vertical line and the top horizontal line.

58)   Click the **left vertical line** of the rectangle.

59)   Hold the **Ctrl** key down.

60)   Click the **top horizontal line** of the rectangle.

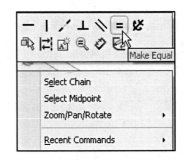

61)   Release the **Ctrl** key.

62)   Right-click **Make Equal** = from the Context toolbar.

63)   Click **OK** ✅ from the Properties PropertyManager.

Add a dimension.

64)   Click the **Smart Dimension** ⬦ Sketch tool.

65)   Click the **top horizontal** line.

66)   Click a **position** above the line.

67)   Enter .500in, [12.70].

68)   Click the **Green Check mark** ✅ .

Close Sketch2.

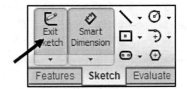

69)   Click **Exit Sketch** ⬏ from the Sketch toolbar. Sketch2 is fully defined and is displayed in black.

☀ If you did not select the Origin, insert a Coincident relation between the rectangle and the Origin to fully define Sketch2.

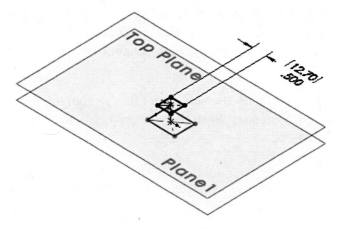

Rename Sketch2.

70) Click **Sketch2** from the FeatureManager.

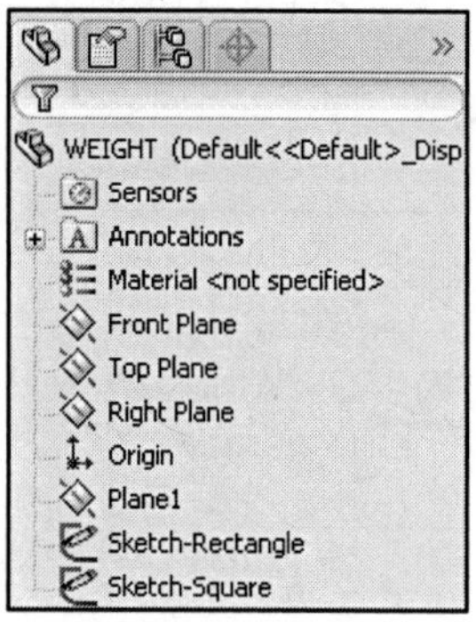

71) Enter **Sketch-Square** for name.

Save the WEIGHT part.

72) Click **Save**.

Loft features are comprised of multiple sketches. Name sketches for clarity.

Activity: WEIGHT Part-Loft Feature

Insert a Loft feature.

73) Click the **Features** tab from the CommandManager.

74) Click the **Lofted Boss/Base** Feature tool. The Loft PropertyManager is displayed.

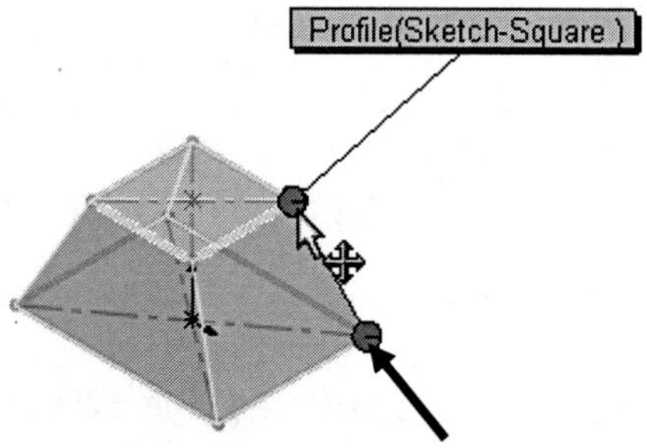

75) Clear the **Profiles** box.

76) Click the **back right corner** of Sketch-Rectangle as illustrated.

77) Click the **back right corner** of Sketch-Square. Sketch-Rectangle and Sketch-Square are displayed in the Profiles box.

78) Click **OK** from the Loft PropertyManager. Loft1 is displayed in the FeatureManager.

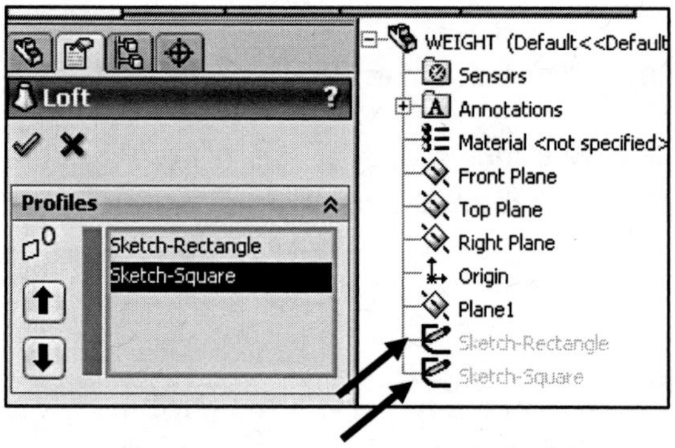

A Loft feature creates transitions between profiles. A Loft feature can be a Base, Boss, Cut, or Surface. Create a Loft feature by using two or more profiles. Only the first and last profiles can be points.

To display the Selection Filter toolbar, click **View**, **Toolbars**, **Selection Filter**. The Selection Filter is displayed.

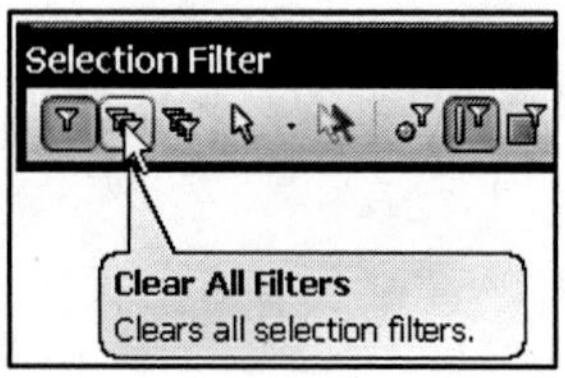

To clear a Filter icon, click **Clear All Filters** from the Selection Filter toolbar.

79)   Expand Loft1 in the FeatureManager. Sketch-Rectangle and Sketch-Square are the two sketches that contain the Loft feature.

80)   Zoom in on the Loft1 feature.

Activity: WEIGHT Part-Instant3D - Extruded Cut Feature

Insert a new sketch for the Extruded Cut feature.

81)   Right-click the **top square face** of the Loft1 feature for the Sketch plane.

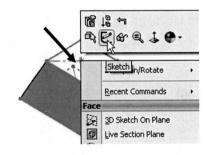

82)   Click Sketch from the Context toolbar. The Sketch toolbar is displayed.

83)   Click the **Circle** Sketch tool. The circle icon is displayed.

84)   Click the **Origin** as illustrated.

85)   Click a **position** to the right of the Origin as illustrated.

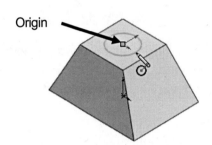

Origin

Add a dimension.

86)   Click the **Smart Dimension** Sketch tool.

87)   Click the **circumference** of the circle.

88)   Click a **position** in the Graphics window above the circle to locate the dimension.

89)   Enter .150in, **[3.81]** in the Modify box.

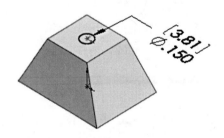

[3.81]
Ø.150

Insert an Extruded Cut feature using the Instant3D tool.

90)   Exit the Sketch. By default, Instant3D is activated.

91)   Click the **diameter** of the circle, Sketch3, as illustrated. A green arrow is displayed.

92)   Click the **arrowhead** and drag it below the model.

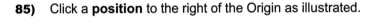

93)   Click a **position** on the Instant3D ruler. Cut-Extrude1 is displayed in the FeatureManager.

94)   Click Wireframe from the Heads-up View toolbar. View the Cut-Extrude1 feature.

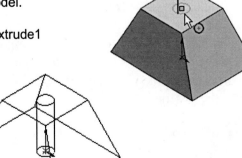

Rename the Cut-Extrude1 feature.
95) Click **Cut-Extrude1** from the FeatureManager.

96) Enter **Hole-for-Hook** for name.

Save the WEIGHT part.
97) Click **Isometric view**  from the Heads-up View toolbar.

98) Click **Shaded With Edges** from the Heads-up View toolbar.

99) If needed, **Hide** all Planes.

100) Click **Save** . The WEIGHT part is complete.

 Review the WEIGHT Part

The WEIGHT part was created with the Loft feature. The Loft feature required two planes: Top Plane and Plane1. Profiles were sketched on each plane. Profiles were selected to create the Loft feature.

An Extruded Cut feature was created using the Instant3D tool to create a Through All center hole in the WEIGHT.

When using the Instant3D tool, you lose the Through All design intent of the model.

HOOK Part

The HOOK part fastens to the WEIGHT part. The HOOK is created with a Swept Boss/Base feature.

The Swept Boss/Base feature adds material by moving a profile along a path. A simple Swept feature requires two sketches. The first sketch is called the path. The second sketch is called the profile.

The profile and path are sketched on perpendicular planes.

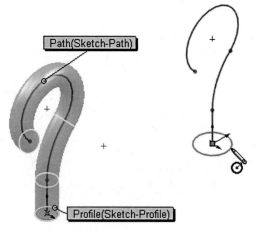

Create the HOOK part with a Swept Base feature.

The Swept Base feature uses:

- A path sketched on the Right Plane.

- A profile sketched on the Top Plane.

Utilize the Dome feature 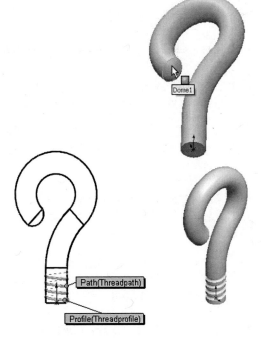 tool to create a spherical feature on a circular face.

Utilize the Swept Cut feature tool to create the thread for the HOOK part as illustrated. The Swept Cut feature removes material.

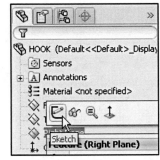

Activity: Create the HOOK Part

Create the new part.

101) Click **New** ☐ from the Menu bar.

102) Select the **SW-TUTORIAL-2010** tab.

103) Double-click **PART-ANSI-IN**, [PART-ANSI-MM].

Save the part.

104) Click **Save** 🖫.

105) Select the **SW-TUTORIAL-2010** folder.

106) Enter **HOOK** for File name.

107) Enter **HOOK** for Description.

108) Click **Save**. The HOOK FeatureManager is displayed.

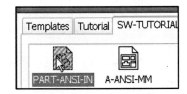

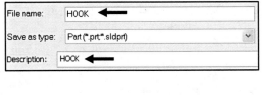

The Swept feature requires two sketches.
Sketch1 is the Sweep Path sketched on the Right Plane.
Sketch2 is the Sweep Profile sketched on the Top Plane.

Sketch the Sweep Path.
109) Right-click **Right Plane** from the FeatureManager.

110) Click **Sketch** from the Context toolbar.

111) Click the **Line** Sketch tool. The Insert Line
PropertyManager is displayed.

112) Sketch a **vertical line** from the Origin as illustrated.

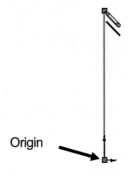

Origin

Add a dimension.
113) Click the **Smart Dimension** Sketch tool.

114) Click the **vertical line**.

115) Click a **position** to the right.

116) Enter **.250**in, **[6.35]**.

117) Click the **Green Check mark** .

Fit the model to the Graphics window.
118) Press the **f** key.

Create the Centerpoint arc.
119) Click the **Centerpoint Arc** Sketch
tool from the Consolidated Sketch

toolbar. The Centerpoint Arc icon is
displayed.

120) Click the **arc center point**
vertically aligned to the Origin.

121) Click the **arc start point** as
illustrated.

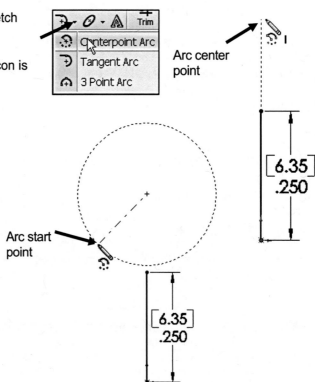

Arc center
point

Arc start
point

122) Move the **mouse pointer** clockwise approximately 260°.

123) Click a point **horizontally aligned** to the arc start point.

124) Click the **3 Point Arc** Sketch tool from the Consolidated Sketch toolbar. The Arc PropertyManager is displayed.

125) Click the **vertical line endpoint**.

126) Click the **Centerpoint arc endpoint**.

127) Drag and pull the center of the **3 Point Arc downwards**.

128) Click the center of the **Centerpoint arc line** as illustrated.

129) Click **OK** ✅ from the Arc PropertyManager.

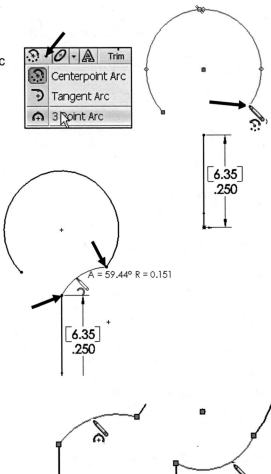

🔆 It is important to draw the correct shape with the 3 Point Arc tool as illustrated.

Add a Vertical relation between the Origin and the center point of the arc.

130) Click the **Origin** ⌐.

131) Hold the **Ctrl** key down.

132) Click the **centerpoint** of the Centerpoint arc.

133) Release the **Ctrl** key.

134) Click **Vertical** ❙ from the Add Relations box.

Correct shape   **Incorrect shape**

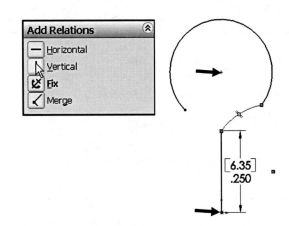

Add a Horizontal relation.
135) Click the **start point** of the Center point arc.

136) Hold the **Ctrl** key down.

137) Click the **end point** of the Center point arc.

138) Release the **Ctrl** key.

139) Click **Horizontal** ▬ from the Add Relations box.

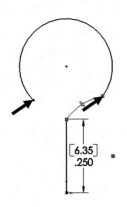

Add a Tangent relation.
140) Click the **vertical line**.

141) Hold the **Ctrl** key down.

142) Click the **3 Point Arc**.

143) Release the **Ctrl** key.

144) Click **Tangent** ⟋ from the Add Relations box.

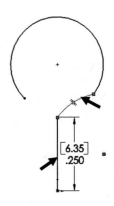

Add a second Tangent relation.

145) Click the **3 Point Arc**.

146) Hold the **Ctrl** key down.

147) Click the **Center point arc**.

148) Release the **Ctrl** key.

149) Click **Tangent** ⟋ from the Add Relations box.

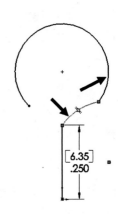

Add dimensions.
150) Click the **Smart Dimension** ⟋ Sketch tool.

151) Click the **3 Point Arc**.

152) Click a **position** to the left.

153) Enter .500in, [12.70].

154) Click the **Green Check mark** ✔ .

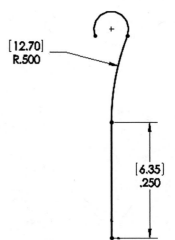

Dimension the overall length of the sketch.
155) Click the **top of the arc**.

156) Click the **Origin** ⌊➛.

157) Click a **position** to the right of the profile.
Accept the default dimension.

158) Click the **Green Check mark** ✓.

159) Click the **Leaders** tab in the Dimension
PropertyManager.

Modify the Arc condition.
160) Click the **First arc condition: Max**.

161) Click **OK** ✓ from the Dimension PropertyManager.

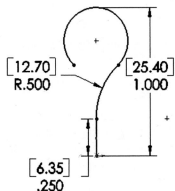

Modify the overall length.
162) Double-click the default **dimension**.

163) Enter **1.000**in, **[25.40]**.

164) Click the **Green Check mark** ✓.

Fit the model to the Graphics window.
165) Press the **f** key.

166) Move the **dimensions** to the correct location.

By default, the Dimension tool utilizes the center point of
an arc or circle. Select the
circle profile during
dimensioning. Utilize the
Leaders tab in the Dimension
PropertyManager to modify
the arc condition to Minimum
or Maximum.

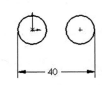

Center point | Minimum | Maximum
Arc Conditions

Close the sketch.

167) Click **Exit Sketch** ⤶ from
the Sketch toolbar.

168) Rename **Sketch1** to **Sketch-Path**.

Save the HOOK.

169) Click **Save** 💾.

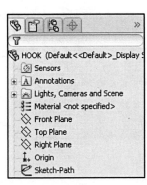

Activity: HOOK Part-Sweep Profile

Create the Sweep profile (cross section).

170) Click **Isometric view** 🔲. Right-click **Top Plane** from the FeatureManager.

171) Click **Sketch** ✏ from the Context toolbar.

172) Click the **Circle** ⊘ Sketch tool. The Circle PropertyManager is displayed.

173) Click the **Origin** ↳. Click a **position** to the right of the Origin.

Add a dimension.

174) Click the **Smart Dimension** ✏ Sketch tool.

175) Click the **circumference** of the small circle.

176) Click a **position** diagonally to the right.

177) Enter **.150**in, **[3.81]**.

178) Click the **Green Check mark** ✅ .

179) Click **OK** ✅ from the Dimension PropertyManager.

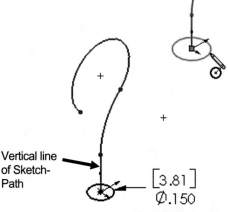

Vertical line of Sketch-Path

$\begin{bmatrix}3.81\end{bmatrix}$
∅.150

A Pierce Geometric relation positions the center of the cross section on the sketched path. The center point of the small circle pierces the sketch-path, (vertical line).

Add a Pierce relation.

180) Click the **Origin** ↳.

181) Hold the **Ctrl** key down.

182) Click the **vertical line** of the Sketch-Path.

183) Release the **Ctrl** key.

184) Click **Pierce** 🗹 from the Add Relations box.

185) Click **OK** ✅ from the Properties PropertyManager

Close the sketch.

186) Click **Exit Sketch** ✏ from the Sketch toolbar.

187) Rename **Sketch2** to **Sketch-Profile**.

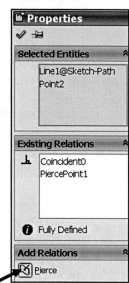

Save the part.

188) Click **Save** 🖫.

Activity: HOOK Part-Swept Base Feature

Insert a Swept feature.
189) Click **Sketch-Profile** in the FeatureManager.

190) Click the **Swept Boss/Base** ⌾ Features tool. The Sweep PropertyManager is displayed. Sketch-Profile is displayed in the Profile box.

191) **Expand** HOOK from the fly-out FeatureManager.

192) Click inside the **Path** box.

193) Click **Sketch-Path** from the fly-out FeatureManager. Sketch-Path is displayed in the Path box.

194) Click **OK** ✔ from the Sweep PropertyManager. Sweep1 is displayed in the FeatureManager.

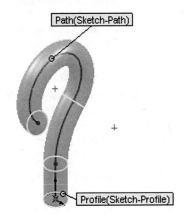

Save the HOOK part.

195) Click **Save** 🖫.

🔅 Sketch the path, then sketch the profile or cross section for the Swept Base feature. Pierce the profile at the start of the path trajectory.

Activity: HOOK Part-Dome Feature

Insert a Dome feature.
196) **Rotate** the model with the middle mouse button.

197) Click the **flat face** of the Sweep1 feature in the Graphics window as illustrated.

198) Click the **Dome** ⌓ Features tool. The Dome PropertyManager is displayed. Face<1> is displayed in the Parameters box.

199) Enter .050in, [1.27] for Distance.

200) Click **OK** ✔ from the Dome PropertyManager. Dome1 is displayed in the FeatureManager.

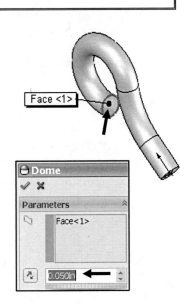

The HOOK requires threads. Use the Swept Cut feature to create the required threads. The thread requires a spiral path. The path is called the Threadpath. The thread requires a sketched profile. The circular cross section is called the Threadprofile.

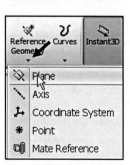

There are numerous steps required to create a thread. The thread is not flush with the bottom face. Use an offset plane to start the thread. Create a new offset Sketch plane, ThreadPlane.

Use the below steps to create the thread: Note: Steps on threads for plastic parts, springs, and coils. **1.)** *Create a new plane for the thread.* **2.)** *Create the spiral path.* **3.)** *Create a large cross section circular profile to improve visibility.* **4.)** *Pierce the cross section circular profile to the spiral path.* **5.)** *Dimension the circular profile.* **6.)** *Create the Swept feature.*

Activity: HOOK Part-Threads with Swept Cut Feature

Create the Offset Reference Plane.
201) Rotate the model with the middle mouse button.

202) Click the **bottom circular** face of Sweep1. Do not click the Origin.

203) Click **Insert, Reference Geometry, Plane** from the Menu bar. The Plane PropertyManager is displayed. Face<1> is displayed in the Selections box.

204) Enter **.020in, [0.51]** for Distance.

205) Check the **Flip** box. Plane1 is located above the Top Plane.

206) Click **OK** ✓ from the Plane PropertyManager. Plane1 is displayed in the FeatureManager.

207) Rename **Plane1** to **Threadplane**.

208) Rebuild the model.

☼ You can also access the Plane PropertyManager by using the Consolidated Reference Geometry drop-down menu from the Features toolbar.

Display the Isometric view.

209) Click **Isometric view** 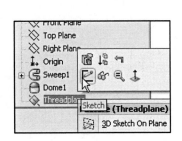 from the Heads-up View toolbar.

210) Click **Hidden Lines Removed** from the Heads-up View toolbar.

Create the Thread path.
211) Rotate and **Zoom in** on the bottom of Sweep1.

212) Right-click **Threadplane** from the FeatureManager.

213) Click **Sketch** from the Context toolbar.

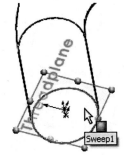

214) Click the **bottom** of Sweep1 as illustrated.

215) Click the **Convert Entities** Sketch tool. Click **OK** from the PropertyManager.

Create the Thread Path.
216) Click **Insert**, **Curve**, **Helix/Spiral** from the Menu bar. The Helix/Spiral PropertyManager is displayed.

217) Enter **.050**in, [**1.27**] for Pitch.

218) Check the **Reverse direction** box.

219) Enter **4** for Revolutions.

220) Enter **0**deg for the Start angle.

221) Click the **Clockwise** box.

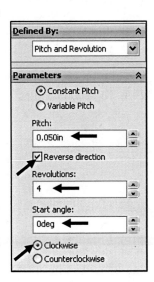

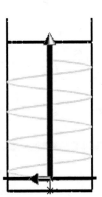

222) Click **OK** from the Helix/Spiral PropertyManager. Helix/Spiral1 is displayed in the FeatureManager.

223) Rename **Helix/Spiral1** to **Threadpath**.

224) Click **Isometric view** from the Heads-up View toolbar.

225) Click **Save**.

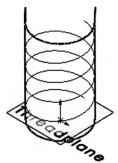

You can also access the Helix/Spiral PropertyManager through the Consolidated Curves drop-down menu from the Features toolbar.

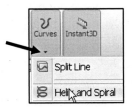

Create the Thread Profile, (cross section).
226) Right-click **Right Plane** from the FeatureManager.

227) Click **Sketch** from the Context toolbar. The Sketch toolbar is displayed.

228) Click **Right view** from the Heads-up View toolbar.

229) Right-click **Threadplane** from the FeatureManager.

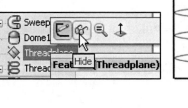

230) Click **Hide** from the Context toolbar.

231) Click the **Circle** Sketch tool. The Circle PropertyManager is displayed.

232) Sketch a **circle** to the right of the profile as illustrated.

De-select the Circle Sketch tool.
233) Right-click **Select**.

Add a Pierce relation.
234) Click the **Threadpath** at the start of the helical curve as illustrated.

235) Hold the **Ctrl** key down.

236) Click the **center point** of the circle.

237) Release the **Ctrl** key. The Properties PropertyManager is displayed. The selected sketch entities are displayed in the Properties box.

238) Click **Pierce** from the Add Relations box.

239) Click **OK** from the Properties PropertyManager. View the results.

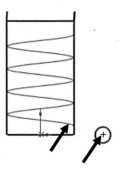

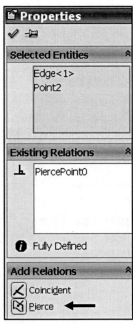

Add a dimension.

240) Click the **Smart Dimension** 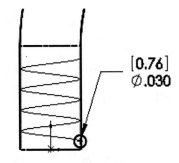 Sketch tool.

241) Click the **circumference**.

242) Click a **position** off the profile.

243) Enter .030in, [0.76].

244) Click the **Green Check mark** ✅ .

Close the sketch.
245) Click **Exit Sketch** from the Sketch toolbar.

246) Click **Isometric view** 🔲 from the Heads-up View toolbar.

247) Rename **Sketch3** to **Threadprofile**.

248) Click **Threadprofile** in the FeatureManager.

Insert the Swept Cut feature.

249) Click **Swept Cut** 🔲 from the Features toolbar. The Cut-Sweep PropertyManager is displayed. Threadprofile is displayed in the Profile box.

250) Click inside the **Path** box.

251) Click **Threadpath** from the fly-out FeatureManager. Threadpath is displayed in the Path box.

252) Click **OK** ✅ from the Cut-Sweep PropertyManager. Cut-Sweep1 is displayed in the FeatureManager.

253) Rename **Cut-Sweep1** to **Thread**.

🔆 Tangent Edges and the Origin are displayed for educational purposes.

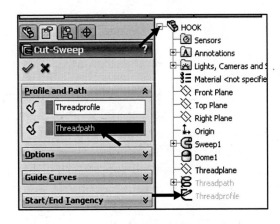

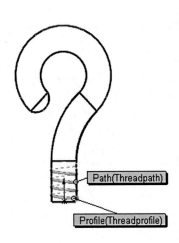

Save the HOOK part.

254) Click **Shaded** from the Heads-up View toolbar.

255) Click **Save** . The HOOK part is complete.

Utilize Insert, Feature from the Menu bar to select other Feature tools which are not located on the Features tab in the CommandManager.

Utilize Tools, Customize, Command, Features to modify the Features toolbar.

Review the HOOK Part

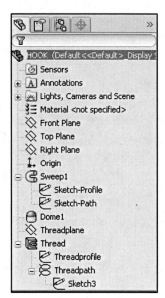

The HOOK part was created with two Swept features. A Swept Base feature added material by moving a profile along a path. The Swept feature required two sketches. The first sketch was called the path. The path was sketched on the Right Plane. The second sketch was called profile. The profile was sketched on the Top Plane. The path and profile were sketched on perpendicular planes. The path was sweep along the profile to create the Swept Base feature.

The Dome feature created a spherical face on the end of the Swept Base feature.

A Swept Cut feature removed material to create the thread. The thread required a spiral path and a circular profile. The path was created on a reference plane, parallel to the Top Plane. The path utilized a Helical Curve. The thread required a sketched profile. This circular cross section was sketched perpendicular to the Front Plane. The thread profile was pierced to the thread path.

Additional details on Loft, Swept, Swept Cut, Helix and Spiral, Relations, Pierce and Reference planes are available in SolidWorks Help.

WHEEL Part

The WHEEL part is a machined part.

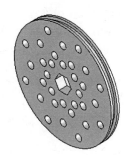

Create the WHEEL part with the Extruded Boss/Base feature  tool. Utilize the Mid Plane option to center the WHEEL on the Front Plane.

Utilize the Revolved Cut feature 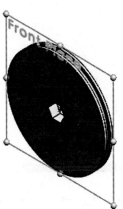 tool to remove material from the WHEEL and to create a groove for a belt.

The WHEEL contains a complex pattern of holes. Apply the Extruded Cut feature 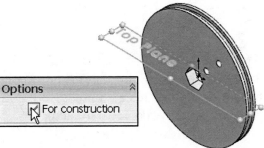 tool.

Simplify the geometry by dividing the four holes into two Extruded Cut features.

The first Extruded Cut feature contains two small circles sketched on two bolt circles. The bolt circles utilize Construction geometry.

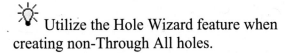

☼ Utilize the Hole Wizard feature when creating non-Through All holes.

The second Extruded Cut feature  utilizes two small circles sketched on two bolt circles. The bolt circles utilize Construction geometry.

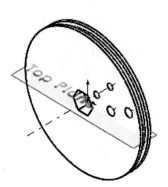

Utilize the Circular Pattern Feature tool. The two Extruded Cut features are contained in the Circular Pattern. Revolve the Extruded Cut features about the Temporary Axis located at the center of the Hexagon.

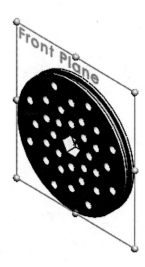

Create a Reference Axis. The Reference Axis is utilized in the WHEEL-AXLE assembly.

💡 Construction geometry is used only to assist in creating the sketch entities and geometry that are ultimately incorporated into the part. Construction geometry is ignored when the sketch is used to create a feature. Construction geometry uses the same line style as centerlines.

💡 You can utilize the Hole Wizard feature tool instead of the Cut-Extrude feature tool, or use the Instant3D tool to create a Through All hole for any part. See SolidWorks Help for additional information.

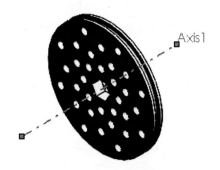

Activity: WHEEL Part

Create the new part.

256) Click **New** ☐ from the Menu bar.

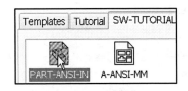

257) Click the **SW-TUTORIAL-2010** tab.

258) Double-click **PART-ANSI-IN**, [PART-ANSI-MM].

Save the part.

259) Click **Save** 💾.

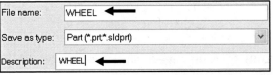

260) Select the **SW-TUTORIAL-2010** folder.

261) Enter **WHEEL** for File name.

262) Enter **WHEEL** for Description.

263) Click **Save**. The WHEEL FeatureManager is displayed.

Insert the sketch for the Extruded Base feature.

264) Right-click **Front Plane** from the FeatureManager.

265) Click **Sketch** ✏ from the Context toolbar. The Sketch toolbar is displayed.

266) Click the **Circle** ⊘ Sketch tool. The Circle PropertyManager is displayed.

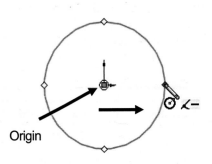

267) Click the **Origin** ⌐ as illustrated.

268) Click a **position** to the right of the Origin.

Origin

Insert a polygon.

269) Click the **Polygon** ⊕ Sketch tool. The Polygon PropertyManager is displayed.

270) Click the **Origin** ⌐.

271) Drag and click the **mouse pointer** horizontally to the right of the Origin to create the hexagon as illustrated.

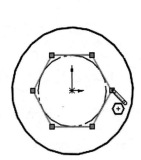

272) Click **OK** ✔ from the Polygon PropertyManager.

De-select the Polygon Sketch tool.

273) Right-click **Select**.

Add a Horizontal relation.

274) Click the **Origin** ⌊.

275) Hold the **Ctrl** key down.

276) Click the **right point** of the hexagon.

277) Release the **Ctrl** key.

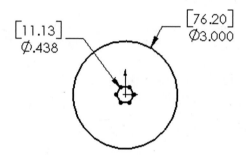

278) Right-click **Make Horizontal** ▬ from the Context toolbar.

279) Click **OK** ✓ from the Properties PropertyManager.

Add dimensions.

280) Click the **Smart Dimension** ◇ Sketch tool.

281) Click the **circumference** of the large circle.

282) Click a **position** above the circle.

283) Enter **3.000**in, **[76.20]**.

284) Click the **Green Check mark** ✓.

285) Click the **circumference** of the inscribed circle for the Hexagon.

286) Click a **position** above the Hexagon.

287) Enter **.438**in, **[11.13]**.

288) Click the **Green Check mark** ✓.

Activity: WHEEL Part-Extruded Boss/Base Feature

Insert an Extruded Boss/Base feature.

289) Click **Extruded Boss/Base** 🗔 from the Features toolbar. The Boss-Extrude PropertyManager is displayed.

290) Select **Mid Plane** for End Condition in Direction 1.

291) Enter **.250**in, **[6.35]** for Depth.

292) Click **OK** ✓ from the Boss-Extrude PropertyManager. Boss-Extrude1 is displayed in the FeatureManager.

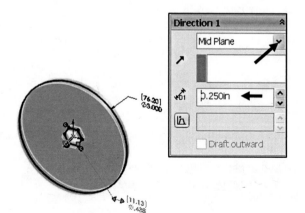

Fit the model to the Graphics window.
293) Press the **f** key.

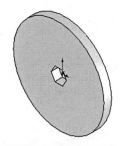

Save the WHEEL part.
294) Click **Save** 🖫.

Activity: WHEEL Part-First Revolved Cut Feature

Insert a new sketch for the Revolved Cut feature.
295) Right-click **Right Plane** from the FeatureManager.

296) Click **Sketch** ✍ from the Context toolbar. The Sketch toolbar is displayed.

297) Click **Right view** 🔲 from the Heads-up View toolbar.

Sketch the axis of revolution.
298) Click the **Centerline** ┊ Sketch tool from the Consolidated Sketch toolbar. The Insert Line PropertyManager is displayed.

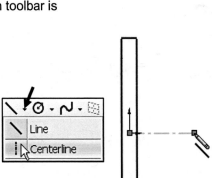

299) Click the **Origin** ⌐.

300) Click a **position** horizontally to the right of the Origin.

De-select the sketch tool.
301) Right-click **Select**.

302) **Zoom in** on the top edge.

Sketch the profile.
303) Click the **Line** ＼ Sketch tool.

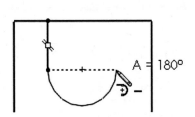

304) Sketch the **first vertical line** as illustrated.

305) Click the **Tangent Arc** ᗡ Sketch tool. The Arc PropertyManager is displayed.

306) Click the **end point** of the vertical line.

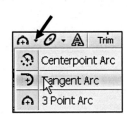

307) Sketch a **180° arc** as illustrated.

De-select the sketch tool.
308) Right-click **Select** in the Graphics window.

309) Click the **Line** \ Sketch tool.

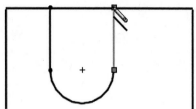

310) Sketch the **second vertical line** as illustrated. The end point of the line is Coincident with the top horizontal edge of Extrude1.

311) Sketch a **horizontal line** collinear with the top edge to close the profile.

Add a Vertical relation.
312) Right-click **Select** in the Graphics window.

313) Click the **Origin** L from the FeatureManager.

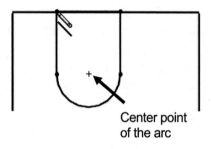

314) Hold the **Ctrl** key down.

315) Click the **center point** of the arc.

Center point
of the arc

316) Release the **Ctrl** key.

317) Click **Vertical** | from the Add Relations box.

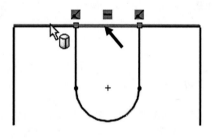

If needed, add a Collinear relation.
318) Click the **horizontal line**. Hold the **Ctrl** key down.

319) Click the **horizontal silhouette edge** as illustrated.

320) Release the **Ctrl** key.

321) Click **Collinear** / from the Add Relations box.

Add an Equal relation.
322) Click the **left vertical** line. Hold the **Ctrl** key down.

323) Click the **right vertical** line.

324) Release the **Ctrl** key.

325) Click **Equal** from the Add Relations box.

Add dimensions.
326) Click the **Smart Dimension** ◇ Sketch tool.

327) Click the **arc**.

328) Click a position to the **left** of the profile.

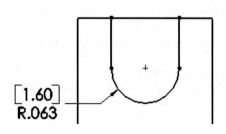

329) Enter .063in, [1.6].

[1.60]
R.063

330) Click the **Green Check mark** ✓ .

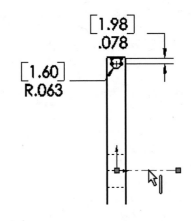

331) Click the **right vertical line**.

332) Click a position to the **right** of the profile.

333) Enter .078in, [**1.98**].

334) Click the **Green Check mark** ✓ .

Fit the model to the Graphics window.
335) Press the **f** key.

De-select the sketch tool.
336) Right-click **Select** in the Graphics window.

Activity: WHEEL Part-Second Revolved Cut Feature

Insert a Revolved Cut feature.
337) Select the axis of revolution. Click the **centerline** in the Graphics window as illustrated.

338) Click **Revolved Cut** 🔯 from the Features toolbar. The Cut-Revolve PropertyManager is displayed. The Cut-Revolve PropertyManager displays 360 degrees for the Angle of Revolution.

339) Click **OK** ✓ from the Cut-Revolve PropertyManager. Cut-Revolve1 is displayed in the FeatureManager.

Save the WHEEL part.
340) Click **Save** 💾 .

Four bolt circles, spaced 0.5in, [12.7] apart locate the 8 - Ø.190, [4.83] holes. Simplify the situation. Utilize two Extruded Cut features on each bolt circle.

Position the first Extruded Cut feature hole on the first bolt circle and third bolt circle.

Position the second Extruded Cut feature hole on the second bolt circle and forth bolt circle.

Activity: WHEEL Part- First Extruded Cut Feature

Display the Top Plane.
341) Right-click **Top Plane** from the FeatureManager.

342) Click **Show** 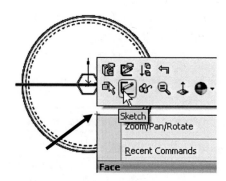 from the Context toolbar.

343) Click **Front view** from the Heads-up View toolbar.

344) Click **Hidden Lines Visible** from the Heads-up View toolbar.

Insert a new sketch for the first Extruded Cut feature.
345) Right-click the **Boss-Extrude1 front face** as illustrated.

346) Click **Sketch** from the Context toolbar. The Sketch toolbar is displayed.

Create the first construction bolt circle.
347) Click the **Circle** Sketch tool. The Circle PropertyManager is displayed.

348) Click the **Origin**.

349) Click a **position** to the right of the hexagon as illustrated.

350) Check the **For construction** box.

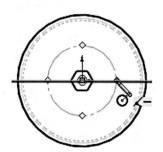

Create the second construction bolt circle.
351) Click the **Origin**.

352) Click a **position** to the right of the first construction bolt circle as illustrated.

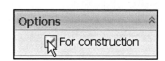

353) Check the **For construction** box. The two bolt circles are displayed with Construction style lines.

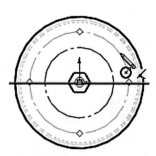

Construction geometry is used only to assist in creating the sketch entities and geometry that are ultimately incorporated into the part. Construction geometry is ignored when the sketch is used to create a feature. Construction geometry uses the same line style as centerlines.

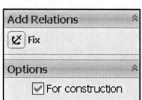

De-select the circle Sketch tool.
354) Right-click **Select**.

Insert a centerline.

355) Click the **Centerline** ⋮ Sketch tool. The Insert Line PropertyManager is displayed.

356) Sketch a **45° centerline** (approximately) from the Origin to the second bolt circle as illustrated.

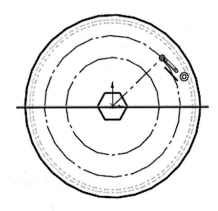

Sketch the two circle profiles.

357) Click the **Circle** ⵔ Sketch tool. The Circle PropertyManager is displayed.

358) Sketch a **circle** at the intersection of the centerline and the first bolt circle.

359) Sketch a **circle** at the intersection of the centerline and the second bolt circle.

De-select the Circle Sketch tool.
360) Right-click **Select** in the Graphics window.

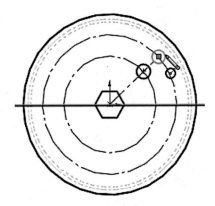

Note: An Intersection relation is created between three entities: the center point of the small circle, the centerline, and the bolt circle.

Add an Equal relation.
361) Click the **first circle**.

362) Hold the **Ctrl** key down.

363) Click the **second circle**.

364) Release the **Ctrl** key.

365) Right-click **Make Equal** = from the Context toolbar.

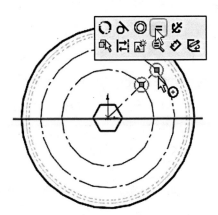

Add dimensions.
366) Click the **Smart Dimension** ✧ Sketch tool.

367) Click the **first construction circle**.

368) Click a **position** above the profile.

369) Enter **1.000**in, **[25.4]**.

370) Click the **Green Check mark** ✓ .

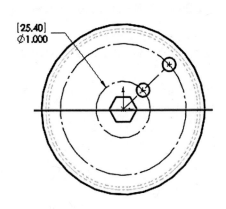

371) Click the **second construction circle**.

372) Click a **position** above the profile.

373) Enter **2.000**in, [50.80].

374) Click the **Green Check mark** ✓ .

375) Click the **second small circle**.

376) Click a **position** above the profile.

377) Enter **.190**in, [4.83].

378) Click the **Green Check mark** ✓ .

379) Click **Top Plane** from the fly-out FeatureManager.

380) Click the **45° centerline**.

381) Click a **position** between the two lines.

382) Enter **45**deg for angle.

383) Click the **Green Check mark** ✓ .

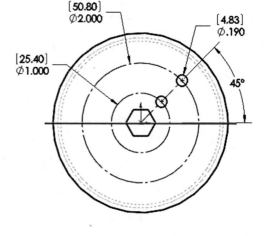

Note: If the sketch is not fully defined, you may need to add an Intersection relation between the center point of the small circle, the centerline, and the bolt circle.

Insert an Extruded Cut feature.
384) Click **Extruded Cut** 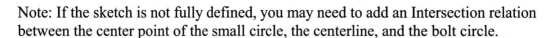 from the Features toolbar. The Cut-Extrude PropertyManager is displayed.

385) Select **Through All** for the End Condition in Direction 1.

386) Click **OK** ✓ from the Cut-Extrude PropertyManager. Cut-Extrude1 is displayed in the FeatureManager.

Activity: WHEEL Part- Second Extruded Cut Feature

Insert a new sketch for the second Extruded Cut feature.
387) Right-click the **Boss-Extrude1** front face.

388) Click **Sketch** ⌐ from the Context toolbar.

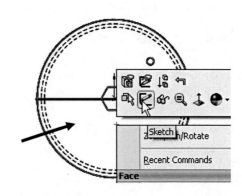

Sketch two additional Construction line bolt circles, 1.500in,
[38.1] and 2.500in, [63.5]. Create the first Construction bolt
circle.

389) Click the **Circle** ⊘ Sketch tool. The Circle PropertyManager is
displayed.

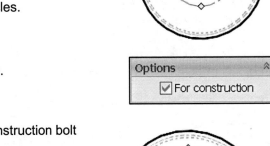

390) Click the **Origin** ⌞►.

391) Click a **position** between the two small circles.

392) Check the **For construction** box.

Create the second additional construction bolt circle.

393) Click the **Origin** ⌞►.

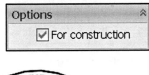

394) Click a **position** to the right of the large construction bolt
circle as illustrated.

395) Check the **For construction** box from the Circle
PropertyManager. The two bolt circles are displayed with
the two construction lines.

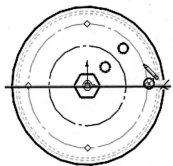

Insert a centerline.

396) Click the **Centerline** ┆ Sketch tool. The Insert Line
PropertyManager is displayed.

397) Sketch a **22.5° centerline** to the right from the
Origin to the second bolt circle as illustrated.

398) Select **.1** from the Primary
Unit Precision box.

399) Click **Hidden Lines
Removed** ⬜ from the
Heads-up View toolbar.

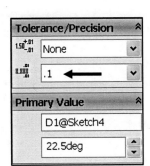

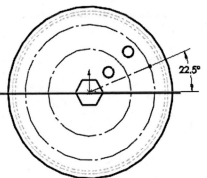

Sketch the two circle profiles.

400) Click the **Circle** ⊘ Sketch tool. The Circle PropertyManager is displayed

401) Sketch a **circle** at the intersection of the centerline and the first bolt circle.

402) Sketch a **circle** at the intersection of the centerline and the second bolt circle.

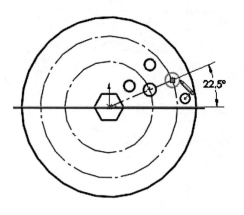

De-select the Circle Sketch tool.
403) Right-click **Select**.

Add an Equal relation.
404) Click the **first circle**.

405) Hold the **Ctrl** key down.

406) Click the **second circle**. Release the **Ctrl** key.

407) Right-click **Make Equal** ＝ from the shortcut toolbar.

Add dimensions.
408) Click the **Smart Dimension** ✧ Sketch tool. The Smart Dimension ⌖ icon is displayed.

409) Click the **first construction circle**.

410) Click a **position** above the profile.

411) Enter **1.500**in, [**38.1**].

412) Click the **second construction circle**.

413) Click a **position** above the profile.

414) Enter **2.500**in, [**63.5**].

415) Click the **small circle** as illustrated.

416) Click a **position** above the profile.

417) Enter **.190**in, [**4.83**].

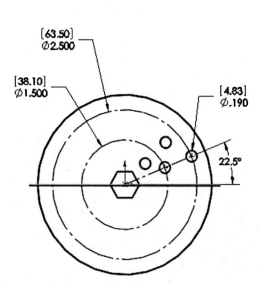

☼ If the sketch is not fully defined, you may need to add an Intersection relation between the center point of the small circle, the centerline, and the bolt circle.

Insert an Extruded Cut feature.

418) Click **Extruded Cut** 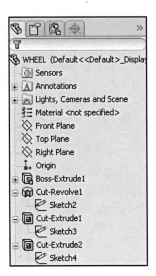 from the Features toolbar. The Cut-Extrude PropertyManager is displayed.

419) Select **Through All** for End Condition in Direction 1.

420) Click **OK** ✔ from the Cut-Extrude PropertyManager. Cut-Exturde2 is displayed in the FeatureManager.

421) Click **Save** 💾.

View the Temporary Axes.
422) Click **View**; check **Temporary Axes** from the Menu bar.

Activity: WHEEL Part-Circular Pattern Feature

Insert a Circular Pattern.

423) Click **Isometric view** ⬜ from the Heads-up View toolbar.

424) Click **Circular Pattern** ⬚ from the Consolidated Features toolbar. The Circular Pattern PropertyManager is displayed.

425) Click **inside** the Pattern Axis box.

426) Click the **Temporary Axis** in the Graphics window at the center of the Hexagon. Axis<1> is displayed in the Pattern Axis box.

427) Enter **360**deg for Angle.

428) Enter **8** for Number of Instances.

429) Click inside the **Features to Pattern** box.

430) Click **Cut-Extrude1** and **Cut-Extrude2** from the fly-out FeatureManager. Cut-Extrude1 and Cut-Extrude2 are displayed in the Features to Pattern box.

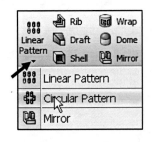
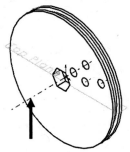
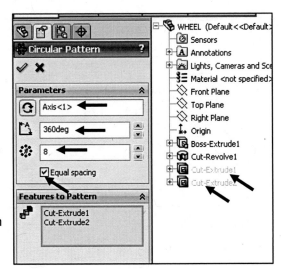

431) Check the **Geometry pattern** box.

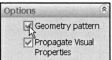

432) Click **OK** ✓ from the Circular Pattern PropertyManager. CirPattern1 is displayed in the FeatureManager.

Save the WHEEL part.

433) Click **Save** 💾.

Utilize a Reference Axis to locate the WHEEL in the PNEUMATIC-TEST-MODULE assembly. The Reference Axis is located in the FeatureManager and Graphics window. The Reference Axis is a construction axis defined between two planes.

Insert a Reference axis.

434) Click the **Axis** ⟍ tool from the Reference Geometry Consolidated Features toolbar. The Axis PropertyManager is displayed.

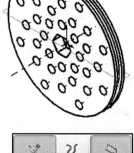

435) Click **Top Plane** from the fly-out FeatureManager.

436) Click **Right Plane** from the fly-out FeatureManager. The selected planes are displayed in the Selections box.

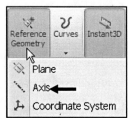

437) Click **OK** ✓ from the Axis PropertyManager. Axis1 is displayed in the FeatureManager.

Axis1 is positioned through the Hex

Cut centered at the Origin .

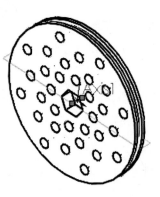

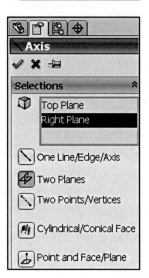

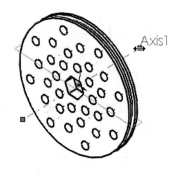

438) Click and drag the **Axis1 handles** outward to extend the
length on both sides as illustrated.

Save the WHEEL part.
439) Click **Isometric view** .

440) Click **View**; uncheck **Temporary Axes** from the Menu bar.

441) **Hide** all Planes.

442) Click **Shaded With Edges** from the Heads-up View toolbar.

443) Click **Save** .

The Geometry pattern option in the Circular Pattern PropertyManager and the Linear Pattern PropertyManager saves rebuild time. The End Conditions are not recalculated. For extruded parts, utilize the Geometry pattern option.

Sketched lines, arcs or circles are modified from profile geometry to construction geometry. Select the geometry in the sketch. Check the For construction box option.

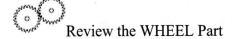 Review the WHEEL Part

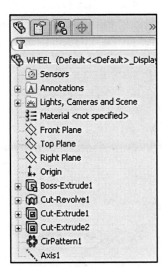

The WHEEL part was created with the Extruded Boss/Base feature. You sketched a circular sketch on the Front Plane and extruded the sketch with the Mid Plane option.

A Revolved Cut feature removed material from the WHEEL and created the groove. The Revolved Cut feature utilized an arc sketched on the Right Plane. A sketched centerline was required to create the Revolved Cut feature.

The WHEEL contained a complex pattern of holes. The first Extruded Cut feature contained two small circles sketched on two bolt circles. The bolt circles utilized construction geometry. Geometric relationships and dimensions were used in the sketch. The second Extruded Cut feature utilized two small circles sketched on two bolt circles.

The two Extruded Cut features were contained in one Circular Pattern and revolved about the Temporary Axis. The Reference Axis was created with two perpendicular planes. Utilize the Reference Axis, Axis1 in the WHEEL-AXLE assembly.

Modify a Part

Conserve design time and cost. Modify existing parts
and assemblies to create new parts and assemblies.
Utilize the Save as copy tool to avoid updating the
existing assemblies with new file names.

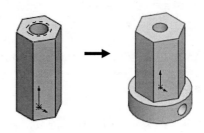

The HEX-STANDOFF part was created in Chapter 2.
The HEX-ADAPTER is required to fasten the WHEEL
to the AXLE. Start with the HEX-STANDOFF part.

Utilize the Save As command and enter the HEX-ADAPTER for the new file name.
Important: Check the Save as copy check box. The HEX-ADAPTER is the new part
name. Open the HEX-ADAPTER. Modify the dimensions of the Extruded Base feature.

Utilize Edit Definition to modify the Hole Wizard Tap Hole to a Standard Hole. Insert an
Extruded Boss/Base feature to create the head of the HEX-ADAPTER.

Insert an Extruded Cut feature. Sketch a circle on the Right Plane. Extrude the circle in
Direction1 and Direction2 with the Through All End Condition option. Note: You can
use the Hole Wizard feature with a 3D Sketch.

Feature order determines the internal geometry of the Hole. If the Hole feature is created
before the Extrude2-Head feature, the Through All End Condition will extend through
the Boss-Extrude1 feature.

If the Hole feature is created after the Extrude2-Head feature, the Through All End
Condition will extend through the Boss-Extrude1 feature and the Extrude2-Head feature.

Modify feature order by dragging feature names in the FeatureManager. Utilize the Save
As command to create the AXLE3000 part from the AXLE part.

Utilize the Save As command to create the SHAFTCOLLAR-500 part from the SHAFT-
COLLAR part. Save the HEX-STANDOFF as the HEX-ADAPTER part.

Activity: HEX-ADAPTER Part

Create the HEX-ADAPTER.

444) Click **Open** 📂 from the Menu bar.

445) Select **Part** for Files of type from the SW-TUTORIAL-2010 folder.

446) Double-click **HEX-STANDOFF**. The HEX-STANDOFF FeatureManager is displayed.

447) Click **Save As** from the Menu bar.

448) Select the **SW-TUTORIAL-2010** folder.

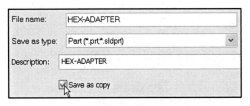

449) Enter **HEX-ADAPTER** for File name.

450) Enter **HEX-ADAPTER** for Description.

451) Check the **Save as copy** box.

452) Click **Save**.

453) Click **File**, **Close** from the Menu bar.

Open the HEX-ADAPTER.
454) Click **Open** 📂 from the Menu bar.

455) Double-click **HEX-ADAPTER** from the SW-TUTORIAL-2010 folder. The HEX-ADAPTER FeatureManager is displayed.

Modify the Boss-Extrude1 dimensions.
456) Double-click **Boss-Extrude1** from the FeatureManager.

457) Click **.735**in, [**18.67**].

458) Enter **.700**in, [**17.78**] for depth.

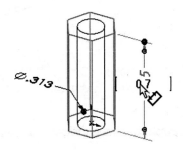

459) Click **.313**in, [**7.95**].

460) Enter **.438**in, [**11.13**] for diameter.

Modify the #10-24 Tapped Hole1 feature.
461) Right-click **#10-24 Tapped Hole1** from the FeatureManager.

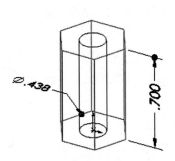

462) Click **Edit Feature** 🗔 from the Context toolbar. The Hole Specification PropertyManager is displayed.

The Hole Specification PropertyManager is part of the Hole Wizard tool located in the Features toolbar.

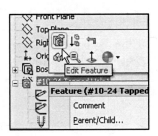

The Type tab is selected by default. Select the **Hole** tab from the Hole Specification box.

463) Select **Ansi Inch** for Standard.

464) Select **Tap Drills** for Type.

465) Select **#10-24** for Size.

466) Select **Through All** for End Condition.

467) Click **OK** ✓ from the Hole Specification PropertyManager. The Tap Hole is modified.

Insert a sketch for the Extruded Boss feature.
468) Press the **Up Arrow key** approximately four times.

469) Right-click the **bottom hexagonal face** of the Boss-Extrude1 feature as illustrated. Note: The face icon feedback symbol.

470) Click **Sketch** ⌐ from the Context toolbar.

471) Click **Bottom view** ⊞ from the Heads-up View toolbar.

472) Click the **Circle** ⊘ Sketch tool. The Circle PropertyManager is displayed.

473) Click the **Origin** ⌐↑ as illustrated.

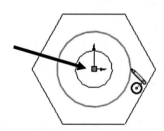

474) Click a **position** in the Graphics window to the right of the Origin.

Add a dimension.
475) Click the **Smart Dimension** ⌀ Sketch tool.

476) Click the **circumference** of the circle.

477) Click a **position** above the circle to locate the dimension.

478) Enter **.625**in, **[15.88]** in the Modify dialog box.

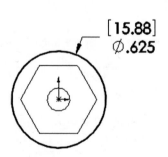

[15.88]
⌀.625

Fit the model to the Graphics window.
479) Press the **f** key.

Activity: HEX-ADAPTER Part-Extruded Boss/Base Feature

Extrude the sketch to create the Extruded Boss/Base feature.

480) Click **Isometric view** 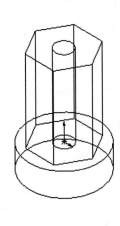 from the Heads-up View toolbar.

481) Click **Extruded Boss/Base** from the Features toolbar. The Boss-Extrude PropertyManager is displayed.

482) Enter **.200**in, **[6.35]** for Depth. The Direction arrow points downward. Flip the **Direction arrow** if required.

483) Click **OK** from the Boss-Extrude PropertyManager. Boss-Extrude2 is displayed in the FeatureManager.

484) Rename **Boss-Extrude2** to **Extrude2-Head**.

485) Click **Save** .

Activity: HEX-ADAPTER Part-Extruded Cut Feature

Insert a new sketch for the Extruded Cut on the Right Plane.

486) Right-click **Right Plane** from the FeatureManager.

487) Click **Sketch** from the Context toolbar.

488) Click **Right view** from the Heads-up View toolbar. Note the location of the Origin.

489) Click the **Circle** Sketch tool. The Circle PropertyManager is displayed.

490) Sketch a **circle** below the Origin . The centerpoint is vertically aligned to the Origin as illustrated. If required, add a Vertical relation between the centerpoint of the circle and the Origin.

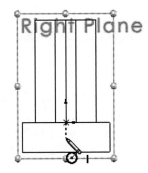

Origin

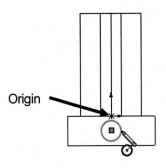

Add dimensions.

491) Click the **Smart Dimension** 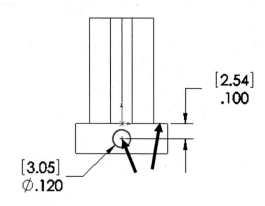 Sketch tool.

492) Click the **middle horizontal edge**.

493) Click the **center point** of the circle.

494) Click a **position** to the right of the profile.

495) Enter **.100**in, **[2.54]**.

496) Click the **Green Check mark** .

497) Click the **circumference** of the circle.

498) Click a **position** below the profile.

499) Enter .**120**in, **[3.95]**.

500) Click the **Green Check mark** .

Insert an Extruded Cut feature.

501) Click **Extruded Cut** from the Features toolbar. The Cut-Extrude PropertyManager is displayed.

502) Select **Through All** for End Condition in Direction 1.

503) Check the **Direction 2** box.

504) Select **Through All** for End Condition in Direction 2.

505) Click **OK** from the Cut-Extrude PropertyManager.

506) Click **Isometric view** from the Heads-up View toolbar.

507) Rename the feature to **Extrude3-SetScrew**.

Save the HEX-ADAPTER part.

508) Click **Save** .

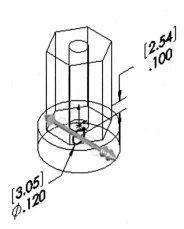

The Through All End Condition is required to penetrate both the Boss-Extrude1 and Extrude2 features. Reorder features in the FeatureManager. Position the Extrude2 feature before the Tap Drill for # 10 Tap 1 feature in the FeatureManager.

Reorder the Features.
509) Click and drag **Extrude2-Head** from the FeatureManager upward as illustrated.

510) Click a **position** below Boss-Extrude1. The Through All End Condition option for the Tap Drill for # 10 Tap 1 feature creates a hole through both Boss-Extrude1 and Extrude2.

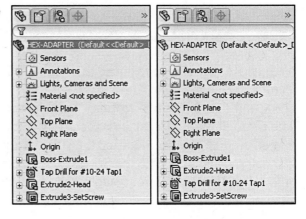

Display a Section view.
511) Click **Front Plane** from the FeatureManager.

512) Click **Section view**  from the Heads-up View toolbar in the Graphics window. The Section View PropertyManager is displayed. View the results.

513) Click **OK** ✔ from the Section View PropertyManager.

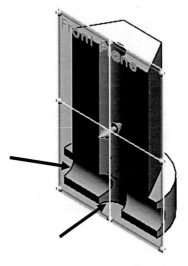

Display the full view.
514) Click **Section view** from the Heads-up View toolbar in the Graphics window.

515) Click **Shaded With Edges** ⬚ from the Heads-up View toolbar.

Save the HEX-ADAPTER.
516) Click **Save** 🖫. Note the location of the Origin in the model.

Close all documents.
517) Click **Windows**, **Close All** from the Menu bar.

🔅 Utilize the Save As command and work on the copied version of the document before making any changes to the original. Keep the original document in tact.

Origin

🔅 Tangent Edges and the Origin are displayed for educational purposes in this book.

 Review the HEX-ADAPTER Part

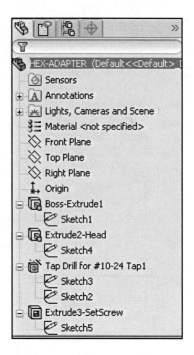

The HEX-ADAPTER part was created by utilizing the Save As, and the Save as copy command with the HEX-STANDOFF part. The Boss-Extrude1 feature dimensions were modified. Edit Definition was utilized to modify the Hole type from the Hole Wizard feature.

An Extruded Boss feature added material. An Extruded Cut feature, sketched on the Right Plane with the Through All End Condition for both Direction1 and Direction2, created a hole through the Extruded Boss feature. Reordering features in the FeatureManager modified the Hole. Utilizing existing geometry saved time with the Save as copy command. The original part and its references to other assemblies are not affected with the Save as copy command.

You require additional work before completing the PNEUMATIC-TEST-MODULE assembly. The AXLE and SHAFT-COLLAR were created in Chapter 1. Utilize the Save as copy command to save the parts.

Additional details on Save (Save as copy), Reorder (features), Section View PropertyManager are available in SolidWorks Help.

Utilize Design Table configurations for the AXLE part and SHAFT-COLLAR part developed in the previous chapter.

Note: The AXLE-3000 part and SHAFT-COLLAR-500 part utilize the Save as copy option in the next section. Utilize the Save as copy components or the configurations developed with Design Tables in Chapter 3 for the WHEEL-AXLE assembly.

Activity: AXLE-3000 Part

Create the AXLE-3000 part from the AXLE part.

518) Click **Open** from the Menu bar.

519) Double-click **AXLE** from the SW-TUTORIAL-2010 folder. The AXLE FeatureManager is displayed.

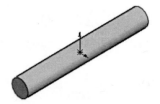

520) Click **Save As** from the Menu bar.

521) Select the **SW-TUTORIAL-2010** folder.

522) Enter **AXLE-3000** for File name.

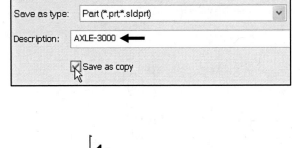

523) Enter **AXLE-3000** for Description.

524) Click **Save as copy** check box.

525) Click **Save**.

Close the AXLE part
526) Click **File**, **Close** from the Menu bar.

Open AXLE-3000 part.
527) Click **Open** from the Menu bar.

528) Double-click **AXLE-3000** from the SW-TUTORIAL-2010 folder. The AXLE-3000 FeatureManager is displayed.

Modify the depth dimension.
529) Double-click the **cylindrical face** in the Graphics window. Dimensions are displayed.

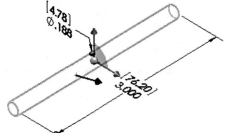

530) Click **1.375**in, [**34.93**].

531) Enter **3.000**in, [**76.20**].

Fit the model to the Graphics window.
532) Press the **f** key.

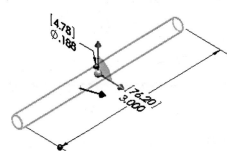

Save the AXLE-3000 part.
533) Click **Save** 🖫.

534) Click **inside** the Graphics window.

Activity: SHAFTCOLLAR-500 Part

Create the SHAFTCOLLAR-500 part.
535) Click **Open** from the Menu bar.

536) Double-click **SHAFT-COLLAR** from the SW-TUTORIAL-2010 folder.

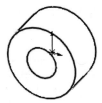

537) Click **Save As** from the Menu bar.

538) Enter **SHAFT-COLLAR-500** for File name.

539) Enter **SHAFT-COLLAR-500** for Description.

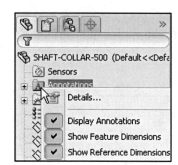

540) Click **Save as copy** check box.

541) Click **Save**.

Close the SHAFT-COLLAR part.
542) Click **File**, **Close** from the Menu bar.

Open the SHAFT-COLLAR-500 part.
543) Click **Open** 🖑 from the Menu bar.

544) Double-click **SHAFT-COLLAR-500** from the SW-TUTORIAL-2010 folder. SHAFT-COLLAR-500 is displayed in the Graphics window.

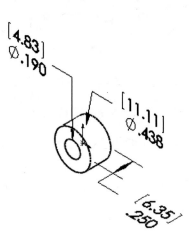

Modify the diameter dimensions.
545) Right-click **Annotations** in the FeatureManager.

546) Check the **Show Feature Dimensions** box.

547) Press the **f** key to fit the model to the graphics area.

548) Click **.438**in, **[11.11]**.

549) Enter **.750**in, **[19.05]** for outside diameter.

550) Click **.190**in, **[4.83]**.

551) Enter **.500**in, **[12.70]** for inside diameter. View the results.

552) Right-click **Annotations** in the FeatureManager.

553) Uncheck the **Show Feature Dimensions** box.

554) **Rebuild** the model.

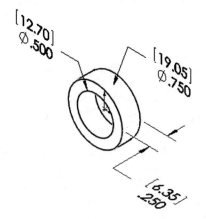

Fit the model to the Graphics window.
555) Press the **f** key.

Save the SHAFT-COLLAR-500 part.
556) Click **Save** .

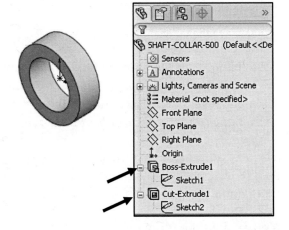

Close all documents.
557) Click **Windows**, **Close All** from the Menu
bar.

☀ Press the **s** key in the Graphics window.
A Context Pop-up features toolbar is
displayed. The features toolbar displays the
last few feature tools applied.

☀ The Origin is displayed for educational
purposes.

☀ You can select the types of Annotations that
you want to display and set text scale and other
Annotations options. In the FeatureManager design
tree, right-click the **Annotations** folder, and click
details. View the options from the Annotation
Properties dialog box.

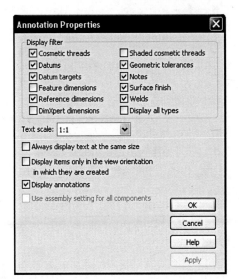

Chapter Summary

In this chapter, you created six parts. The WEIGHT part utilized the Plane feature, Lofted Base feature and the Extruded Cut (Instant3D tool) feature. The HOOK part utilized the *Swept Base feature, Dome feature, Plane feature, Helix and Spiral feature* and *Swept Cut* feature. The WHEEL part utilized the *Extruded Base feature, Revolved Cut feature, Extruded Cut feature, Circular Pattern feature* and *Axis* feature.

The second three parts utilized existing parts created in early chapter. The HEX-ADAPTER part, AXLE-3000 part and the SHAFTCOLLAR-500 part utilized existing part geometry along with the Hole Wizard feature.

You applied the following Sketch tools in this chapter: *Circle, Line, Centerline, Tangent Arc, Polygon, Smart Dimension, Center Rectangle, Centerpoint Arc, 3 Point Arc* and *Convert Entities*.

Chapter Terminology

Circular Pattern: A Circular Pattern repeats features or geometry in a polar array. A Circular Patten requires an axis of revolution, the number of instances and an angle.

ConfigurationManager: The ConfigurationManager on the left side of the Graphics window is utilized to create, select, and view the configurations of parts and assemblies.

Dome: A Dome feature creates a spherical or elliptical feature from a selected face.

Loft: A Loft feature blends two or more profiles. Each profile is sketched on a separate plane.

Mirror Component: A mirror component creates a mirrored or copied part or assembly. A mirrored component is sometimes called a "right-hand" version of the original "left hand" version.

Replace: The Replace command substitutes one or more open instances of a component in an assembly with a different component.

Revolved Cut: A Revolved Cut removes material. A sketched profile is revolved around a centerline. The Revolved Cut requires a direction and an angle of revolution.

Swept Boss/Base: A Swept Boss/Base feature adds material by moving a profile along a path. A basic Swept feature requires two sketches. The first sketch is called the path. The second sketch is called profile. The profile and path are sketched on perpendicular planes.

Swept Cut: A Swept Cut feature removes material by moving a profile along a path. A basic Swept feature requires two sketches. The first sketch is called the path. The second sketch is called profile. The profile and path are sketched on perpendicular planes.

1. Sketch various FLATBAR Parts.

Sketch the front view of the FLATBAR configurations that contain 11, 13, 15, and 17 holes. Determine the center-to-center distance between the first hole and the last hole for each FLATBAR configuration.

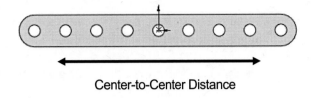

Center-to-Center Distance

FLATBAR-11HOLE.

FLATBAR-13HOLE.

FLATBAR-15HOLE.

FLATBAR-17HOLE.

Questions

1. What is the minimum number of profiles and planes required for a Loft feature?

2. A Swept Boss/Base feature requires a _____ and a _____.

3. Describe the differences between a Loft feature and a Swept feature.

4. Identify the three default reference planes in an assembly.

5. True of False. A Revolved-Cut feature (Cut-Revolve1) requires an axis of revolution.

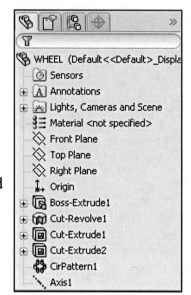

6. True or False. A Circular Pattern contains only one feature to pattern.

7. Describe the difference between a Swept Boss/Base feature and a Swept Cut feature.

8. Identify the type of Geometric relations that can be added to a sketch.

9. What function does the Save as copy check box perform when saving a part under a new name?

10. True or False. Never reuse geometry from one part to create another part.

Exercises

Exercise 4.1: Advance Part

Build the illustrated model. Calculate the volume of the part and locate the Center of mass with the provided information. Insert three features: Extruded Base, Extruded Boss, and Mirror. Three holes are displayed with an Ø1.00in. Set the document properties for the model.

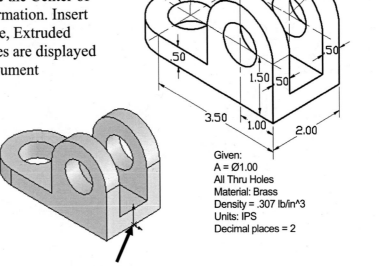

🔆 Tangent Edges and the Origin are displayed for educational purposes.

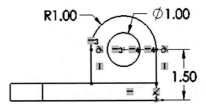

Given:
A = Ø1.00
All Thru Holes
Material: Brass
Density = .307 lb/in^3
Units: IPS
Decimal places = 2

Exercise 4.2: Advanced Part

Build the illustrated model. Calculate the overall mass of the part and locate the Center of mass with the provided information. Insert a Revolved Base feature and Extruded Cut feature to build this part.

Note: Select the Front Plane as the Sketch plane. Apply the Centerline Sketch tool for the Revolve1 feature. Insert the required geometric relations and dimensions. Sketch1 is the profile for the Revolve1 feature.

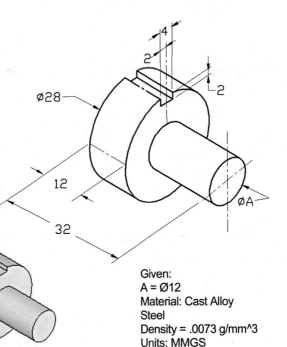

Given:
A = Ø12
Material: Cast Alloy
Steel
Density = .0073 g/mm^3
Units: MMGS

Exercise 4.3: Advance Part

Build the illustrated model. Calculate the overall mass of the part and locate the Center of mass with the provided information.

Note: Insert two features: Extruded Base and Revolved Boss.

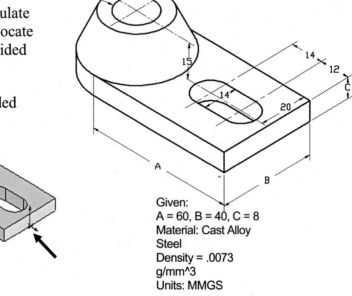

Given:
A = 60, B = 40, C = 8
Material: Cast Alloy Steel
Density = .0073 g/mm^3
Units: MMGS

Exercise 4.4: Advance Part

Build the illustrated model. Calculate the overall mass of the part and locate the Center of mass with the provided information.

Think about the various features that create the model. Insert seven features to build this model: Extruded Base, Extruded Cut, Extruded Boss, Fillet, second Extruded Cut, Mirror and a second Fillet. Apply symmetry. Create the left half of the model first, and then apply the Mirror feature.

Tangent Edges and the Origin are displayed for educational purposes.

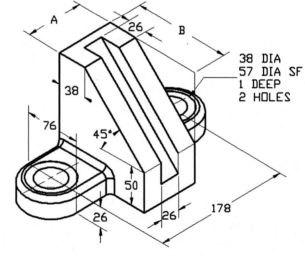

38 DIA
57 DIA SF
1 DEEP
2 HOLES

Given:
A = 76, B = 127
Material: 2014 Alloy
Density: .0028 g/mm^3
Units: MMGS
ALL ROUNDS EQUAL 6MM

Exercise 4.5: Advance Part

Build the illustrated model. Calculate the overall mass of the part and locate the Center of mass with the provided information.

Think about the various features that create the part. Insert seven features to build this part: Extruded-Thin, Extruded Boss, two Extruded Cuts, and three Fillets. Apply reference construction planes to build the circular features.

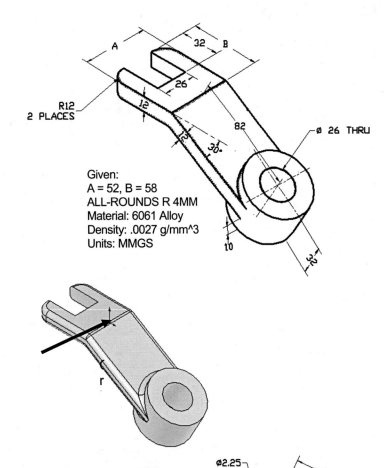

Given:
A = 52, B = 58
ALL-ROUNDS R 4MM
Material: 6061 Alloy
Density: .0027 g/mm^3
Units: MMGS

Exercise 4.6: Advance Part

Build the illustrated model.
Build this model. Calculate the volume of the part and locate the Center of mass with the provided information.

Think about the various features that create this model. Insert five features to build this part: Extruded Base, two Extruded Bosses, Extruded Cut and a Rib. Insert a reference plane to create the Extrude feature.

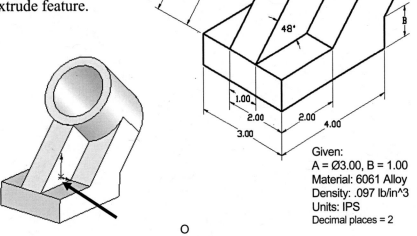

Given:
A = Ø3.00, B = 1.00
Material: 6061 Alloy
Density: .097 lb/in^3
Units: IPS
Decimal places = 2

Exercise 4.7: Advance Part

Build the illustrated model.

Calculate the overall mass and locate the Center of mass of the illustrated model.

Insert seven features: Extruded Base, two Extruded Bosses, two Extruded Cuts, Chamfer and a Fillet.

Think about the steps that you would take to build the illustrated part.

Identify the location of the part Origin. Start with the back base flange. Review the provided dimensions and annotations in the part illustration.

☀ Tangent Edges and the Origin are displayed for educational purposes.

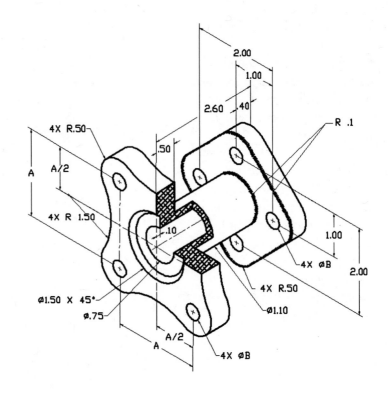

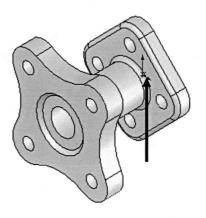

Given:
A = 2.00, B = Ø.35
Material: 1060 Alloy
Density: 0.097 lb/in^3
Units: IPS
Decimal places = 2

Chapter 5

PNEUMATIC-TEST-MODULE and Final ROBOT Assembly

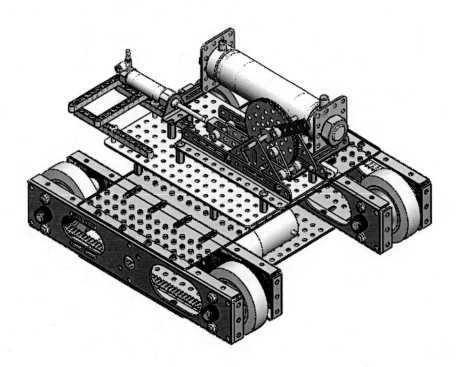

Below are the desired outcomes and usage competencies based on the completion of Chapter 5.

Desired Outcomes:	**Usage Competencies**:
<ul><li>Create five sub-assemblies:<ul><li>WHEEL-AND-AXLE</li><li>WHEEL-FLATBAR</li><li>3HOLE-SHAFTCOLLAR</li><li>5HOLE-SHAFTCOLLAR</li><li>PNEUMATIC-TEST-MODULE</li></ul></li><li>Create the final ROBOT assembly</li></ul>	<ul><li>Reuse geometry.</li><li>Apply Standard Mate types.</li><li>Modify existing assemblies to create new assemblies.</li><li>Utilize the following Assembly tools: Mate, Linear Component Pattern, Feature Driven Component Pattern, Mirror Components, Replace Components, and AssemblyXpert.</li><li>Work with multiple documents in an assembly.</li></ul>

Notes:

Chapter 5 - PNEUMATIC-TEST-MODULE and ROBOT Assembly

Chapter Objective

Develop a working understanding with multiple documents in an assembly. Build on sound assembly modeling techniques that utilize symmetry, component patterns and mirrored components.

Create five sub-assemblies and the final ROBOT assembly:

- 3HOLE-SHAFTCOLLAR sub-assembly

- 5HOLE-SHAFTCOLLAR sub-assembly

- WHEEL-FLATBAR sub-assembly

- WHEEL-AND-AXLE sub-assembly

- PNEUMATIC-TEST-MODULE sub-assembly

- ROBOT final assembly

On the completion of this chapter, you will be able to:

- Utilize various Assembly techniques

- Suppress and hide components

- Create new assemblies and copy assemblies to reuse similar parts

- Use the following Assembly tools:

    o Insert Component

    o Standard Mates: Concentric, Coincident and Parallel

    o Linear Component Pattern

    o Feature Driven Component Pattern

    o Circular Component Pattern

    o Mirror Components

    o Replace Components

    o AssemblyXpert

Chapter Overview

Create the 3HOLE-SHAFTCOLLAR sub-assembly.

Utilize the 3HOLE-SHAFTCOLLAR sub-assembly to create the 5HOLE-SHAFTCOLLAR sub-assembly.

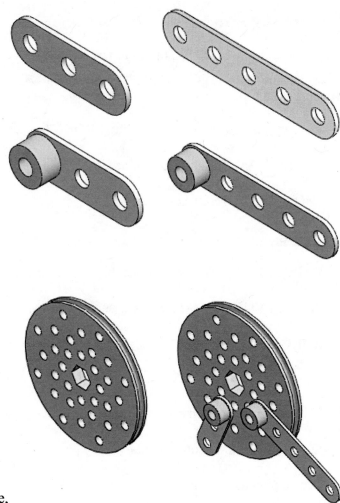

The WHEEL-FLATBAR sub-assembly contains the following items:

- 3HOLE-SHAFTCOLLAR assembly

- 5HOLE-SHAFTCOLLAR assembly

- WHEEL part

⚡ If an assembly or component is loaded in a Lightweight 🔷 state, right-click the **assembly name** or **component name** from the FeatureManager. Click **Set Lightweight to Resolved**.

⚡ To remove Tangent edges, click **Display/Selections** from the Options menu; check the **Removed** box.

Relations/Snaps	☐ Allow selection in HLR and shaded r
Display/Selection	Part/Assembly tangent edge display
Performance	○ As visible
Assemblies	○ As phantom
External References	⦿ Removed
Default Templates	

The WHEEL-AND-AXLE assembly contains the following items:

- WHEEL-FLATBAR assembly

- AXLE-3000 part

- SHAFTCOLLAR-500 part

- HEX-ADAPTER part

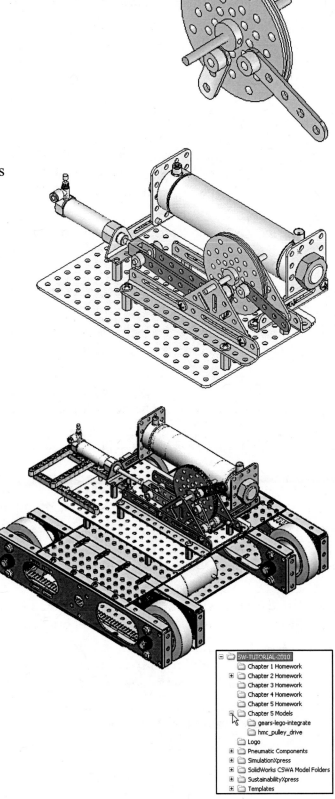

Combine the created new assemblies and parts to develop the PNEUMATIC-TEST-MODULE assembly.

Create the final ROBOT assembly. Insert the Robot-platform assembly, PNEUMATIC-TEST-MODULE assembly, basic_integration assembly and the HEX-STANDOFF components. All assemblies and components for the final ROBOT assembly are located on the CD under the Chapter 5 Models folder.

🔆 Add additional Pneumatic components in the chapter exercises.

Assembly Techniques

Assembly modeling requires practice and time. Below are a few helpful techniques to address Standard Mates. These techniques are utilized throughout the development of all assemblies.

Mating Techniques:
• Plan your assembly and sub-assemblies in an assembly layout diagram. Group components together to form smaller sub-assemblies.
• Utilize symmetry in an assembly. Utilize Mirror Component and Component Pattern to create multiple instances (copies) of components. Reuse similar components with Save as copy and configurations.
• Use the Zoom and Rotate commands to select the geometry in the Mate process. Zoom to select the correct face.
• Apply various colors to features and components to improve display.
• Activate Temporary Axes and Show Planes when required for Mates, otherwise Hide All Types from the View menu.
• Select Reference planes from the FeatureManager for complex components. Expand the FeatureManager to view the correct plane.
• Remove display complexity. Hide components when visibility is not required.
• Suppress components when Mates are not required. Group fasteners at the bottom of the FeatureManager. Suppress fasteners and their assembly patterns to save rebuild time and file size.
• Utilize Section views to select internal geometry.
• Use the Move Component and Rotate Component commands before Mating. Position the component in the correct orientation.
• Create additional flexibility in a Mate. Distance Mates are modified in configurations and animations. Rename Mates in the FeatureManager.
• Verify the position of the components. Use Top, Front, Right and Section views.

PNEUMATIC TEST MODULE Layout

The PNEUMATIC TEST MODULE assembly is comprised of four major sub-assemblies:

- LINKAGE assembly

- RESERVOIR assembly

- FRONT-SUPPORT assembly

- WHEEL-AND-AXLE assembly

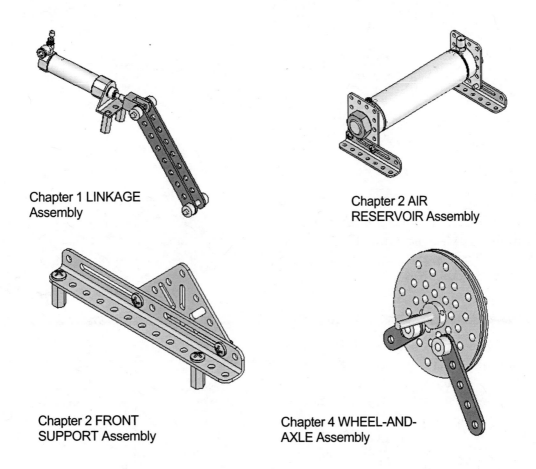

Chapter 1 LINKAGE
Assembly

Chapter 2 AIR
RESERVOIR Assembly

Chapter 2 FRONT
SUPPORT Assembly

Chapter 4 WHEEL-AND-
AXLE Assembly

There are over one hundred components in the PNEUMATIC TEST MODULE assembly. Complex assemblies require planning. The Assembly Layout diagram provides organization for a complex assembly by listing sub-assemblies and parts.

Review the Assembly Layout diagram for the PNEUMATIC TEST MODULE assembly.

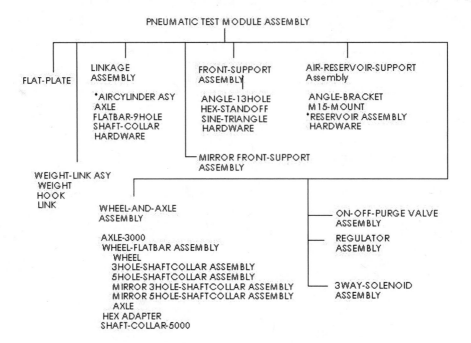

Physical space on the FLAT-PLATE is at a premium. Determine the requirements for hardware and placement after the mechanical components are assembled to the FLAT-PLATE part.

The FLAT-PLATE was created in the Chapter 2 exercises. The FLAT-PLATE is available on the enclosed CD in the book under the Chapter 5 models folder. If needed, copy the FLAT-PLATE from the CD to your working SW-TUTORIAL-2010 folder. View the available models in this folder. The LINKAGE assembly, FRONT-SUPPORT assembly and the AIR-RESERVOIR SUPPORT assembly were created in Chapters 1 and 2.

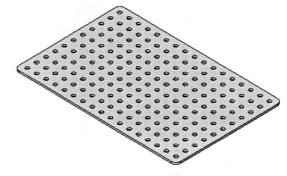

The ON-OFF-PURGE VALVE assembly, REGULATOR assembly and the 3WAY SOLENOID VALVE assembly require additional hardware and are addressed in the chapter exercises.

The WHEEL-FLATBAR assembly consists of the following:

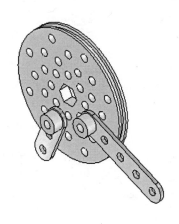

- WHEEL part

- 3HOLE-SHAFTCOLLAR assembly

- 5HOLE-SHAFTCOLLAR assembly

FLATBAR Sub-assemblies

There are two similar sub-assemblies contained in the WHEEL-FLATBAR assembly:

- 3HOLE-SHAFTCOLLAR assembly

- 5HOLE-SHAFTCOLLAR assembly

Create the 3HOLE-SHAFTCOLLAR assembly. Utilize parts and mating techniques developed in Chapter 1.

Utilize the Save as copy command and create the 5HOLE-SHAFTCOLLAR assembly.

Combine the 3HOLE-SHAFTCOLLAR assembly, 5HOLE-SHAFTCOLLAR assembly and the WHEEL part to create the WHEEL-FLATBAR assembly.

The FLATBAR-3HOLE and FLATBAR 5HOLE parts were created in the Chapter 1 exercises. If needed, copy the models from the Chapter 5 models folder on the CD to your working SW-TUTORIAL-2010 folder.

| Activity: 3HOLE-SHAFTCOLLAR Assembly |

Create the 3HOLE-SHAFTCOLLAR assembly.

1)   Click **New** ☐ from the Menu bar.

2)   Double-click **Assembly** from the Templates tab. The Begin Assembly PropertyManager is displayed.

3)   Click the **Browse** button.

4)   Select **Part** for Files of type in the SW-TUTORIAL-2010 folder.

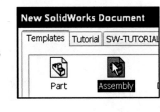

5)   Double-click **FLATBAR-3HOLE**. The
FLATBAR-3HOLE part was created in the
Chapter 1 exercises. If you did not create this
part, follow the below procedures; otherwise,
skip the next few steps.

6)   Click **Open** from the Menu bar.

7)   Double-click **FLATBAR** from the SW-
TUTORIAL-2010 folder.

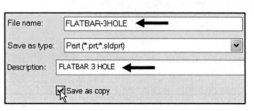

8)   Click **Save As** from the Menu bar.

9)   Select the **SW-TUTORIAL-2010** folder.

10) Enter **FLATBAR-3HOLE** for File name.

11) Enter **FLATBAR-3HOLE** for Description.

12) Check the **Save as copy** box.

13) Click **Save**.

14) **Close** the FLATBAR model.

15) Click **Open** from the Menu bar.

16) Double-click **FLATBAR-3HOLE** from the SW-
TUTORIAL-2010 folder.

17) Right-click **LPATTERN1** from the FeatureManager.

18) Click **Edit Feature**
from the Context
toolbar. The
LPattern1
PropertyManager is
displayed.

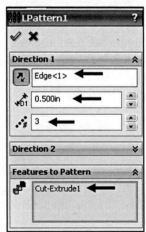

19) Enter **3** in the
Number of Instances.

20) Click **OK** from the
LPattern1
PropertyManager.
Note: If needed,
delete the Design
Table in the CommandManager.

21) Click Boss-**Extrude1** from the FeatureManager. View the dimensions in the Graphics window.

22) Click the **4.000**in, **[101.60]** dimension.

23) Enter **1.000**in, **[25.4]**.

24) Click **Cut-Extrude1** from the FeatureManager. View the dimensions in the Graphics window.

25) Click the **9X** dimension text in the Graphics window. The Dimension PropertyManager is displayed.

26) Delete the **9X** text in the Dimension Text box.

27) Enter **3X** in the Dimension Text box.

28) Click **OK** ✔ from the Dimension PropertyManager.

29) Click **Save** 💾.

30) Click **New** ☐ from the Main menu.

31) Double-click **Assembly** from the Templates tab. The Begin Assembly PropertyManager is displayed.

32) Double-click **FLATBAR-3HOLE.**

33) Click **OK** ✔ from the Begin Assembly PropertyManager. The FLATBAR-3HOLE is fixed to the Origin.

Save the assembly.
34) Click **Save As** from the Menu bar.

🔅 Tangent Edges and Origin is displayed for educational purpose.

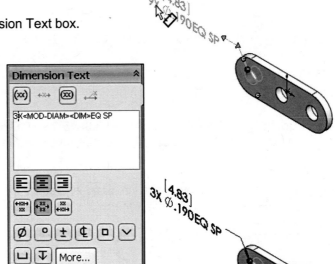

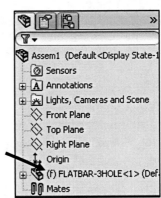

35) Enter **3HOLE-SHAFTCOLLAR** for File
name.

36) Enter **3HOLE-SHAFTCOLLAR** for
Description.

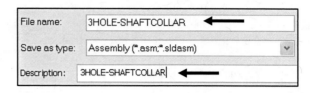

37) Click **Save**.

Save the 3HOLE-SHAFTCOLLAR assembly.

38) Click **Save** 💾.

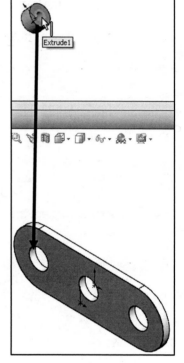

Utilize a Concentric/Coincident 🖱️ SmartMate between the
SHAFT-COLLAR and the FLATBAR-3HOLE.

Open the **SHAFT-COLLAR** part.

39) Click **Open** 📂 from the Menu bar.

40) Double-click **SHAFT-COLLAR** from the SW-TUTORIAL-
2010 folder. SHAFT-COLLAR is the current document
name.

41) Press the **Left Arrow** key approximately 5 times to rotate
the SHAFT-COLLAR to view the back circular edge.

42) Click **Window**, **Tile Horizontally** from the Menu bar.

43) Drag the **back circular edge** of the SHAFT-COLLAR to the
left circular hole edge of the FLATBAR-3HOLE in the
Assembly Graphics window as illustrated. The mouse
pointer displays the Concentric/Coincident 🖱️ icon.

44) **Release** the mouse button. Note: Select the back circular
edge of the SHAFT-COLLAR, not the face.

Save the 3HOLE-SHAFTCOLLAR assembly.

45) **Close** ✕ the SHAFT-COLLAR window.

46) **Maximize** 🗖 the 3HOLE-SHAFTCOLLAR assembly.

Fit the model to the Graphics window.

47) Press the **f** key.

48) Click **Save** 💾.

Create the 5HOLE-SHAFTCOLLAR assembly. Utilize the Save
As command with the Save as copy option. Recover from Mate
errors.

Save the 3HOLE-SHAFTCOLLAR assembly as the 5HOLE-
SHAFTCOLLAR assembly.

49)   Click **Save As** from the Menu bar.

50)   Check **Save as copy**.

51)   Enter **5HOLE-SHAFTCOLLAR** for
       File name.

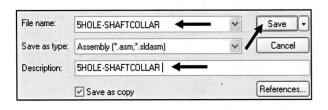

52)   Enter **5HOLE-SHAFTCOLLAR** for
       Description.

53)   Click **Save**.

Close the model.

54)   Click **File**, **Close** from the Menu bar.

Open the new assembly.

55)   Click **Open** from the Menu bar.

56)   Select **Assembly** for Files of type.

57)   Double-click **5HOLE-SHAFTCOLLAR**. The 5HOLE-
       SHAFTCOLLAR FeatureManager is displayed.

58)   Right-click **FLATBAR-3HOLE** from the FeatureManager.
       Expand the Pop-up menu if needed.

59)   Click **Replace Components**. The Replace PropertyManager
       is displayed.

60)   Click the **Browse** button.

61)   Double-click **FLATBAR-5HOLE**. Note:The FLATBAR-5HOLE
       part was created in the Chapter 1 exercises.

62)   Check the **Re-attach mates** box.

63)   Click **OK**  from the Replace PropertyManager. The Mate
       Entities PropertyManager and the Wants Wrong dialog box is
       displayed. There are two red Mate error marks displayed in the
       Mate Entities box.

64)　　The What's Wrong dialog box is displayed. Recover from the Mate errors. Click **Close** from the What's Wrong dialog box.

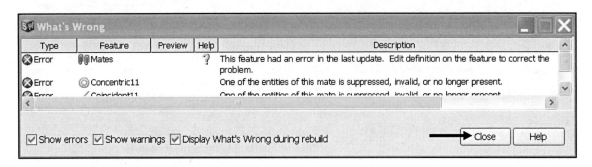

65)　　Click **OK** ✓ from the Mated Entities PropertyManager.

66)　　Click **Close** from the What's Wrong dialog box. View the location of the SHAFT-COLLAR in the Graphics window.

Recover from the Mate errors.

67)　　**Expand** the Mates folder from the FeatureManager.

68)　　Right-click the first mate, **Concentric #** from the Mates folder.

69)　　Click **Edit Feature** from the Context toolbar. The Mate PropertyManager is displayed.

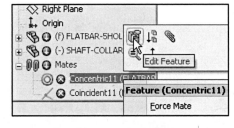

70)　　Right-click the **Mate Face error** in the Mate Selections box as illustrated.

71)　　Click **Delete**.

72)　　Click the **inside face** of the left hole of the FLATBAR as illustrated. Concentric is selected by default.

73)　　Click the **Green Check mark** ✓ .

74)　　Click **OK** ✓ from the Mate PropertyManager.

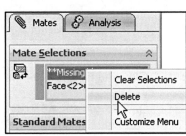

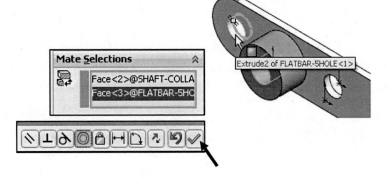

75) Right-click the second mate, **Coincident #** from the Mates folder.

76) Click **Edit Feature** from the Context toolbar. The Mate PropertyManager is displayed.

77) Right-click the **Mate Face error** in the Mate Selections box as illustrated.

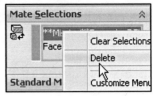

78) Click **Delete** as illustrated.

79) Click the **front face** of the FLATBAR as illustrated. The selected faces are displayed in the Mate Selections box. Coincident is selected by default.

80) Click the **Green Check mark** ✓ .

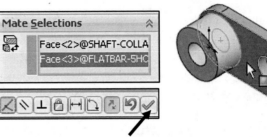

81) Click **OK** ✓ from the Mate PropertyManager.

82) **Expand** the Mate folder from the FeatureManager. View the corrected mates.

 The Mate Entities box will list red X's if the faces, edges or planes are not valid. Expand the Mate Entities and select new references in the Graphics window to redefine the mates.

The FLATBAR-3HOLE is replaced with the FLATBAR-5HOLE part. The Mates are updated.

Fit the model to the Graphics window.
83) Press the **f** key.

Save the 5HOLE-SHAFTCOLLAR assembly.
84) Click **Isometric view** from the Heads-up View toolbar.

85) Click **Save** .

Incorporate symmetry into the assembly. Divide large assemblies into smaller sub-assemblies.

 The Multimedia CD illustrates the FLATBAR configurations created in Chapter 2 to create the FLATBAR-3HOLE and FLATBAR-5HOLE assemblies.

Utilize Design Tables to create multiple configurations of assemblies.

WHEEL-FLATBAR Assembly

The WHEEL-FLATBAR assembly consists of the following components:

- 3HOLE-SHAFTCOLLAR assembly

- 5HOLE-SHAFTCOLLAR assembly

- WHEEL part

Create the WHEEL-FLATBAR assembly. Mate the 3HOLE-SHAFTCOLLAR assembly 67.5 degrees counterclockwise from the Top Plane.

The 3HOLE-SHAFTCOLLAR assembly is concentric with holes on the second and forth bolt circle.

Mate the 5HOLE-SHAFTCOLLAR assembly 22.5 degrees clockwise from the Top Plane.

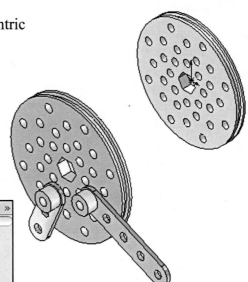

The 5HOLE-SHAFTCOLLAR assembly is concentric with holes on the second and forth bolt circle.

⚞ Tangent Edges and model Origins are displayed for educational purpose.

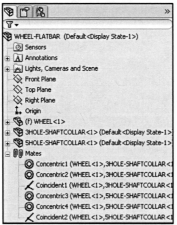

Activity: WHEEL-FLATBAR Assembly

Create the WHEEL-FLATBAR assembly.

86)   Click **New** ☐ the Menu bar.

87)   Double-click **Assembly** from the Templates tab. The Begin Assembly PropertyManager is displayed.

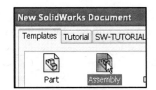

Insert the WHEEL.

88)   Click the **Browse** button.

89)   Select **Part** for Files of type from the SW-TUTORIAL-2010 folder.

90)   Double-click **WHEEL**.

91)   Click **OK** ✔ from the Begin Assembly PropertyManager. The WHEEL part is fixed to the assembly Origin. If needed, click View, Origins from the Menu bar menu to displayed the Origin in the Graphics window.

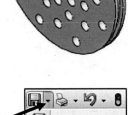

Save the assembly.

92)   Click **Save As** from the Menu bar.

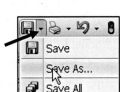

93)   Select the **SW-TUTORIAL-2010** folder.

94)   Enter **WHEEL-FLATBAR** for File name.

95)   Enter **WHEEL-FLATBAR** for Description.

96)   Click **Save**.

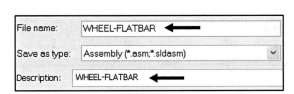

Display the Top Plane in the Front view.

97)   Click **Front view** ⊞ from the Heads-up View toolbar. View the WHEEL part.

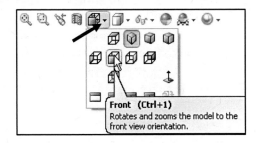

Locate the first set of holes from the Right
plane (-Y-axis). Left Hole1 and Left Hole2
are positioned on the second and forth bolt
circle, 22.5° from the Right plane. Select
Left Hole1. The x, y, z coordinates, -.287,
-.693, .125 are displayed.

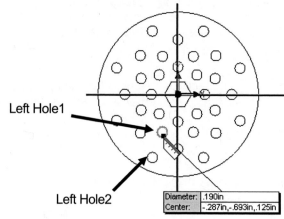

Tan^{-1} (-.287/.693) = 22.5°

As an exercise, utilize the Measure tool to
determine the center-to-center distance
between the Left Hole1 and Left Hole2. The center-to-
center distance is .500in.

Insert two Concentric mates between Left Hole1 and Left
Hole2 and the 3HOLE-SHAFTCOLLAR assembly holes.
The FLATBAR-3HOLE center-to-center distance is also
.500in.

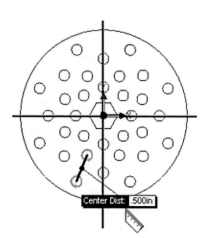

To determine tolerance issues, utilize two Concentric
mates between components with mating cylindrical
geometry. If the mating components center-to-center
distance is not exact, a Mate error is displayed on the
second Concentric mate.

Insert a Coincident mate between the back face of the
3HOLE-SHAFTCOLLAR assembly and
the front face of the WHEEL.

Right Hole1 and Right Hole2 are 22.5°
from the Top Plane.

Insert two Concentric mates between
Right Hole1 and Right Hole2 and the
5HOLE-SHAFTCOLLAR assembly
holes.

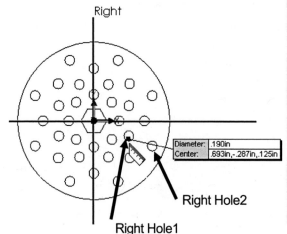

Insert a Coincident mate between the
back face of the 5HOLE-
SHAFTCOLLAR assembly and the front
face of the WHEEL.

Activity: WHEEL-FLATBAR Assembly-Insert 3HOLE-SHAFTCOLLAR Assembly

---

Insert the 3HOLE-SHAFTCOLLAR assembly.

98) Click **Isometric view** 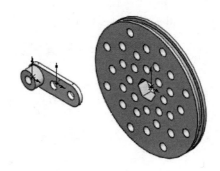 from the Heads-up View
toolbar.

99) Click **Insert Components** from the Assembly
toolbar. The Insert Components PropertyManager is
displayed.

100) Click the **Browse** button.

101) Select **Assembly** for Files of type from the
SW-TUTORIAL-2010 folder.

102) Double-click the **3HOLE-SHAFTCOLLAR** assembly.

103) Click a **position** to the left of the WHEEL as illustrated.

Move and rotate the 3HOLE-SHAFTCOLLAR component.
104) Click the front face of the **3HOLE-
SHAFTCOLLAR**.

105) Right-click **Move with Triad**.

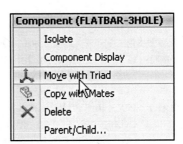

106) Hold the **left mouse button** down on the X-
axis (red).

107) Drag the **component** to the left.

108) Hold the **right mouse button** down on the Z-
axis (blue).

109) Drag the **component** and rotate it about the
Z-axis.

110) **Position** the component until the SHAFT-
COLLAR part is approximately in front of the
WHEEL Left Hole1.

111) Release the **right mouse** button.

112) Click a **position** in the Graphics window to
deselect the face.

Insert the required mates.

113) Click the **Mate** 🖉 tool from the Assembly
toolbar. The Mate PropertyManager is
displayed.

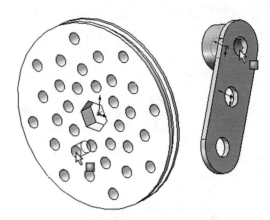

Insert a Concentric mate.
114) Click the **back top inside cylindrical face** of
the SHAFT-COLLAR.

115) Click the **WHEEL Left Hole1** cylindrical face
as illustrated. Concentric is selected by
default. The selected faces are displayed in
the Mate Selections box.

116) Click the **Green Check mark** ✅.

Insert the second Concentric mate.
117) Click the **back middle inside cylindrical
face** of the FLATBAR.

118) Click the **WHEEL Left Hole2** inside
cylindrical face as illustrated. Concentric is
selected by default. The selected faces are
displayed in the Mate Selections box.

119) Click the **Green Check mark** ✅.

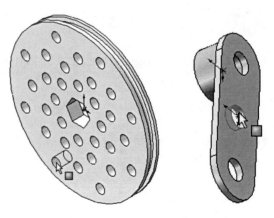

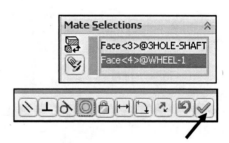

Insert a Coincident mate.
120)　Click the **FLATBAR-3HOLE back** face.

121)　Click the front face of the **WHEEL**. Coincident is selected by default.

122)　Click the **Green Check mark** ✓.

123)　Click **OK** ✓ from the Mate PropertyManager.

124)　Click **Front view** 🗗 from the Heads-up View toolbar.

Save the WHEEL-FLATBAR assembly.

125)　Click **Save** 💾.

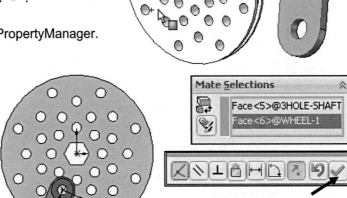

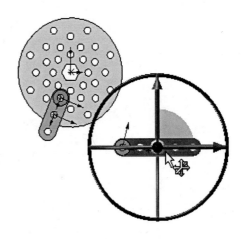

Activity: WHEEL-FLATBAR Assembly-Insert 5HOLE-SHAFTCOLLAR Assembly

Insert the 5HOLE-SHAFTCOLLAR assembly.
126)　Click **Insert Components** 🗗 from the Assembly toolbar. The Insert Components PropertyManager is displayed.

127)　Click the **Browse** button.

128)　Double-click the **5HOLE-SHAFTCOLLAR** assembly from the SW-TUTORIAL-2010 folder.

129)　Click a **position** to the right of the WHEEL.

Move the 5HOLE-SHAFTCOLLAR component.
130)　Click the **5HOLE-SHAFTCOLLAR** front face.

131)　Right-click **Move with Triad**.

132)　Hold the **left mouse button** down on the X-axis (red). Drag the **component** to the right. View the results.

133)　Click **Isometric view** 🗐 from the Heads-up View toolbar.

134)　Click **inside** the Graphics window.

Mate the 5HOLE-SHAFTCOLLAR assembly.

135)   Click the **Mate** ✎ tool from the Assembly toolbar. The Mate PropertyManager is displayed.

Insert a Concentric mate.

136)   Click the **back inside cylindrical face** of the first hole on the FLATBAR-5HOLE assembly.

137)   Click the **WHEEL Right Hole1** cylindrical face. Concentric is selected by default.

138)   Click the **Green Check mark** ✅.

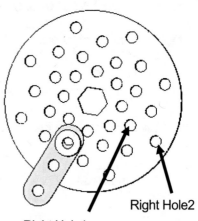

Right Hole2

Right Hole1

Insert a Concentric mate.

139)   **Move** the 5HOLE-SHAFTCOLLAR to view the back side.

140)   Click the **back inside cylindrical** face of the second hole on the FLATBAR-5HOLE assembly.

141)   Click the **WHEEL Right Hole2** cylindrical face. Concentric is selected by default.

142)   Click the **Green Check mark** ✅.

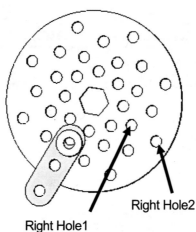

Right Hole2

Right Hole1

Insert a Coincident mate.

143) Click the **back face** of the FLATBAR-5HOLE.

144) Click the **front face** of the WHEEL. Coincident is the selected by default.

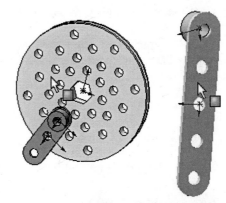

145) Click the **Green Check mark** ✓.

146) Click **OK** ✓ from the Mate PropertyManager.

De-activate the Origins.

147) Click **View**; uncheck **Origin** from the Menu bar.

Measure the angle between the 3HOLE-SHAFTCOLLAR assembly and the 5HOLE-SHAFTCOLLAR assembly.

148) Click **Front view** from the Heads-up View toolbar.

149) Click the **Measure** Measure... tool from the Evaluate tab in the CommandManager. The Measure dialog box is displayed.

150) Select the **two inside edges** of the FLATBAR assemblies. View the results.

151) If required, click the **Show XYZ Measurements button**. The items are perpendicular.

🔆 The Measure tool provides the ability to display dual units. Click the **Units/Precision** $\overset{in}{mm}$ icon from the Measure dialog box. Set the desired units.

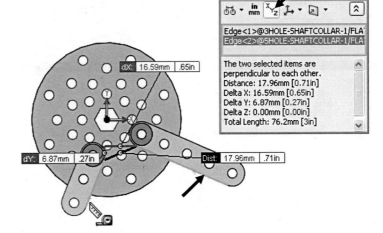

152) **Close** ✖ the Measure dialog box.

Apply the AssemblyXpert tool. The AssemblyXpert tool displays statistics and checks the health of the current assembly.

153) Click the **AssemblyXpert** ⊞ tool in the Evaluate toolbar. The AssemblyXpert dialog box is displayed. Review the Status and description for the assembly.

154) Click **OK** from the AssemblyXpert dialog box.

Fit the model to the Graphics window.
155) Press the **f** key.

156) Click **Isometric view** 🔲 from the Heads-up View toolbar.

Save the WHEEL-FLATBAR assembly.

157) Click **Save** 💾.

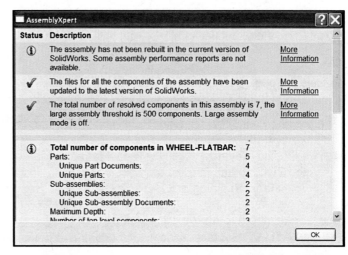

WHEEL-AND-AXLE Assembly

The WHEEL-AND-AXLE assembly contains the following items:

- WHEEL-FLATBAR assembly

- AXLE-3000 part

- SHAFTCOLLAR-500 part

- HEX-ADAPTER part

Create the WHEEL-AND-AXLE assembly. The AXLE-3000 part is the first component in the assembly. A part or assembly inserted into a new assembly is called a component. The WHEEL-FLATBAR assembly rotates about the AXLE part.

Combine the created new assemblies and parts to develop the PNEUMATIC-TEST-MODULE assembly.

Activity: WHEEL-AND-AXLE Assembly

Create the WHEEL-AND-AXLE assembly.

158) Click **New** ☐ from the Menu bar.

159) Double-click **Assembly** from the Templates tab. The Begin Assembly PropertyManager is displayed.

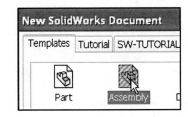

Insert the AXLE-3000 part.
160) Click the **Browse** button.

161) Select **Part** for Files of type from the SW-TUTORIAL-2010 folder.

162) Double-click **AXLE-3000**. Note: AXLE-3000 was created in the homework problems.

163) Click **OK** ✓ from the Begin Assembly PropertyManager. The AXLE-3000 part is fixed to the assembly Origin.

Save the assembly.
164) Click **Save As** from the Menu bar.

165) Enter **WHEEL-AND-AXLE** for File name in the SW-TUTORIAL-2010 folder.

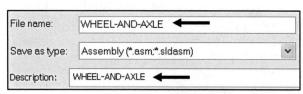

166) Enter **WHEEL-AND-AXLE** for Description.

167) Click **Save**.

Insert a Coincident mate between the Axis of the AXLE-3000 and the Axis of the WHEEL. Insert a Coincident mate between the Front Plane of the AXLE-3000 and the Front Plane of the WHEEL. The WHEEL-FLATBAR assembly rotates about the AXLE-3000 axis.

Display the Temporary Axes.
168) Click **View**; check **Temporary Axes** from the Menu bar.

Insert the WHEEL-FLATBAR assembly.

169) Click **Insert Components** from the Assembly toolbar. The Insert Components PropertyManager is displayed.

170) Click the **Browse** button.

171) Double-click the **WHEEL-FLATBAR** assembly from the SW-TUTORIAL-2010 folder.

172) Click a **position** to the right of AXLE-3000.

View the Reference WHEEL Axis.
173) Click **View**; check **Axes** from the Menu bar.

174) Click **View**; uncheck **Origins** from the Menu bar.

Reference geometry defines the shape or form of a surface or a solid. Reference geometry includes planes, axes, coordinate systems, and points.

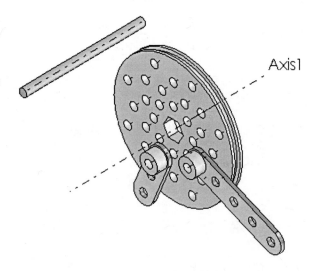

Insert a Coincident mate.

175) Click the **Mate** ✎ tool from the Assembly toolbar. The Mate PropertyManager is displayed.

176) Click **Axis1** in the Graphics window.

177) Click the **AXLE-3000 Temporary Axis**. Coincident is selected by default.

178) Click the **Green Check mark** ✓ .

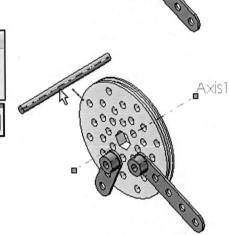

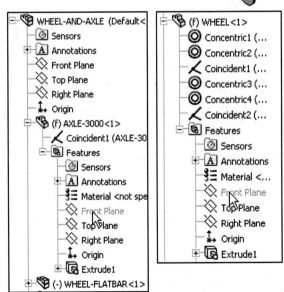

Insert a Coincident mate.

179) **Expand** WHEEL-AND-AXLE from the fly-out FeatureManager.

180) **Expand** AXLE-3000 from the fly-out FeatureManager.

181) **Expand** the Features folder.

182) Click **Front Plane** of AXLE-3000<1>.

183) **Expand** WHEEL from the fly-out FeatureManager.

184) **Expand** the Features folder.

185) Click **Front Plane** of the WHEEL. Coincident is selected by default.

186) Click the **Green Check mark** ✓ .

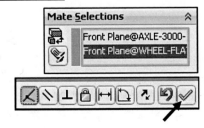

187)   Click **OK** ✔ from the Mate PropertyManager.

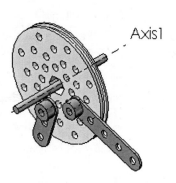

Rotate the WHEEL-FLATBAR assembly about AXLE-3000.
188)   Click and drag the **WHEEL** around AXLE-3000.

Save the WHEEL-AND-AXLE assembly.

189)   Click **Save** 🖫.

Activity: WHEEL-AND-AXLE Assembly-Insert the HEX-ADAPTER Part

Insert the HEX-ADAPTER part.

190)   Click the **Insert Components** 🖼 tool from the
Assembly toolbar. The Insert Component
PropertyManager is displayed.

191)   Click the **Browse** button.

192)   Select **Part** for Files of type in the SW-TUTORIAL-
2010 folder.

193)   Double-click **HEX-ADAPTER**.

194)   Click a **position** to the left of the WHEEL as
illustrated. The HEX-ADAPTER is displayed in
the FeatureManager.

195)   **Expand** the Mates folder. View the created
mates for the assembly. View the inserted
components: AXLE-3000, WHEEL-FLATBAR
and HEX-ADAPTER.

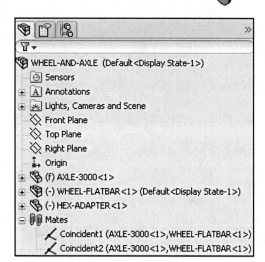

Insert a Concentric mate. Mate the HEX-ADAPTER.

196) Click the **Mate** 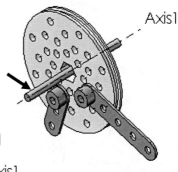 tool from the Assembly toolbar. The Mate PropertyManager is displayed.

197) Click the **HEX-ADAPTER** cylindrical face as illustrated.

198) Click the **AXLE-3000** cylindrical face as illustrated. Concentric is selected by default. The selected faces are displayed in the Mate Selections box.

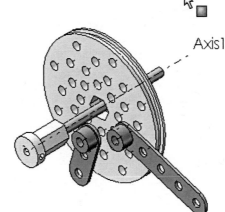

199) Click **Aligned**  from the Concentric1 PropertyManager to flip the HEX-ADAPTER, if required.

200) Click **OK** ✔ from the Concentric PropertyManager.

Insert a Coincident mate.

201) Click the **front face** of the WHEEL.

202) Press the **left arrow key** to rotate the model.

203) Click the **flat back circular face** of the HEX-ADAPTER as illustrated. Coincident is selected by default.

204) Click the **Green Check mark** ✔.

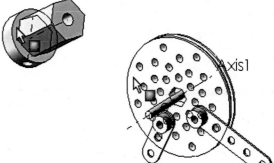

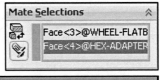

Insert a Parallel mate.

205)   **Rotate** the WHEEL-AND-AXLE assembly to view the back bottom edge of the HEX-ADAPTER.

206)   **Zoom in** on the back bottom edge of the HEX-ADAPTER.

207)   Click the **back bottom edge** of the WHEEL. Note: Do not select the midpoint.

208)   Click the **top edge** of the HEX-ADAPTER. Do not select the midpoint. The selected edges are displayed in the Mate Selections box.

209)   Click **Parallel** ⟍ as illustrated.

210)   Click the **Green Check mark** ✓.

211)   Click **OK** ✓ from the Mate PropertyManager.

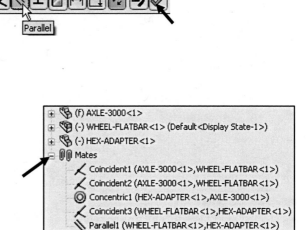

Fit the model to the Graphics window.

212)   Press the **f** key.

213)   Click **Isometric view** 🔲 from the Heads-up View toolbar.

View the created mates.

214)   **Expand** the Mates folder.

Save the WHEEL-AND-AXLE assembly.

215)   Click **Save** 💾.

Activity: WHEEL-AND-AXLE Assembly-Insert SHAFTCOLLAR-500 Part

Insert the SHAFTCOLLAR-500 part.

216)   Click the **Insert Components** 🖱 tool from the Assembly toolbar. The Insert Component PropertyManager is displayed.

217)   Click the **Browse** button.

218)   Select **Part** for Files of type from the SW-TUTORIAL-2010 folder.

219)   Double-click **SHAFTCOLLAR-500**.

220)   Click a **position** behind the WHEEL-AND-AXLE assembly as illustrated.

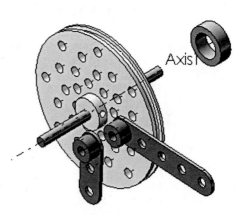

Insert a Concentric mate.

221)　Click **View**; uncheck **Temporary Axes** from the Menu bar.

222)　Click **View**; uncheck **Axes** from the Menu bar.

223)　Click the **Mate** ✎ tool from the Assembly toolbar. The Mate PropertyManager is displayed.

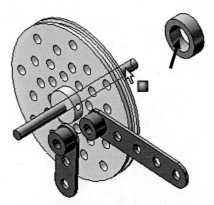

224)　Click the **front inside cylindrical face** of the SHAFTCOLLAR-500 part.

225)　Click the **cylindrical face** of the AXLE-3000 part. Concentric is selected by default.

226)　Click the **Green Check mark** ✓.

Insert a Coincident mate.

227)　Click the **front face** of the SHAFTCOLLAR-500 part.

228)　Click the **back face** of the WHEEL. Coincident is selected by default.

229)　Click the **Green Check mark** ✓.

230)　Click **OK** ✓ from the Mate PropertyManager.

Display an Isometric view.

231)　Click **Isometric view** ⬠ from the Heads-up View toolbar.

View the created Mates.

232)　**Expand** the Mates folder. View the created mates.

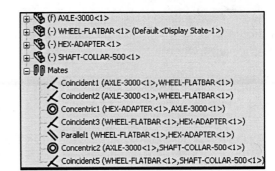

Save the WHEEL-AND-AXLE assembly.

233)　Click **Save** 💾.

Close all files.

234)　Click **Windows**, **Close All** from the Menu bar.

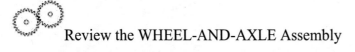 Determine the static and dynamic behavior of mates in each sub-assembly before creating the top level assembly.

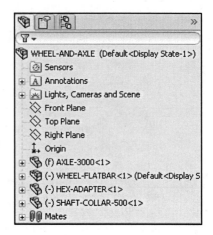

Review the WHEEL-AND-AXLE Assembly

You combined the WHEEL-FLATBAR sub assembly, the AXLE-3000 part, the HEX-ADAPTER part and the SHAFTCOLLAR-500 part to create the WHEEL-AND-AXLE assembly.

The WHEEL-FLATBAR sub-assembly rotated about the AXLE-3000 part. The WHEEL-FLATBAR assembly combined the 3HOLE-SHAFTCOLLAR assembly and the 5HOLE-SHAFTCOLLAR assembly. The 5HOLE-SHAFTCOLLAR assembly was created from the 3HOLE-SHAFTCOLLAR assembly by replacing the FLATBAR component and recovering from two Mate errors. Additional components are added to the WHEEL-AND-AXLE assembly in the chapter exercises.

PNEUMATIC-TEST-MODULE Assembly

Create the PNEUMATIC-TEST-MODULE assembly. The first component is the FLAT-PLATE. The FLAT-PLATE is fixed to the Origin ⌞. The FLAT-PLATE part was created in the Chapter 2 exercises: and is located on the enclosed CD and supports the other components.

Modify the LINKAGE assembly. Insert the HEX-STANDOFF part. Insert the LINKAGE assembly into the PNEUMATIC-TEST-MODULE assembly.

Insert the AIR-RESERVOIR-SUPPORT assembly. Utilize the Linear Component Pattern, and Feature Driven Component Pattern tools. Insert the FRONT-SUPPORT assembly. Utilize the Mirror Components tool to create a mirrored version of the FRONT-SUPPORT assembly.

Insert the WHEEL-AND-AXLE assembly. Utilize Component Properties and create a Flexible State. Utilize the ConfigurationManager to select the Flexible configuration for the AirCylinder assembly.

Work between multiple part and sub-assembly documents to create the final assembly. Illustrations indicate the active document.

Activity: PNEUMATIC-TEST-MODULE Assembly

Create the PNEUMATIC-TEST-MODULE assembly.

235)   Click **New** ⬚ from the Menu bar.

236)   Double-click **Assembly** from the
Templates tab. The Begin Assembly
PropertyManager is displayed.

Insert the FLAT-PLATE part.
237)   Click the **Browse** button.

238)   Select **Part** for Files of type from the
SW-TUTORIAL-2010 folder.

239)   Double-click **FLAT-PLATE**. Note:
FLAT-PLATE was created in a
Chapter 2 exercise.

240)   Click **OK** ✓ from the Begin Assembly
PropertyManager. FLAT-PLATE is fixed to the Origin.

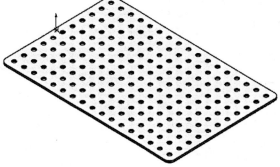

Save the assembly.
241)   Click **Save As** from the Menu bar.

242)   Enter **PNEUMATIC-TEST-MODULE** for File name.

243)   Enter **PNEUMATIC-TEST-MODULE** for
Description.

244)   Click **Save**.

🔆 Click **View, Origins** from the Menu bar
menu to display the Origin in the Graphics
window.

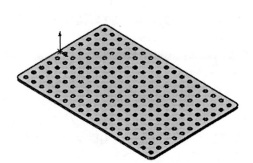

Activity: Modify the LINKAGE Assembly

Modify the LINKAGE assembly created in Chapter 1.

245)   Click **Open** 📂 from the Menu bar.

246)   Select **Assembly** for Files of type from the SW-TUTORIAL-2010 folder.

247)   Double-click **LINKAGE**. The LINKAGE assembly is displayed.

Insert the HEX-STANDOFF part into the LINKAGE assembly.

248)   Click the **Insert Components** tool from the Assembly toolbar. The Insert Component PropertyManager is displayed.

249)   Click the **Browse** button.

250)   Select **Parts** for Files of type from the SW-TUTORIAL-2010 folder.

251)   Double-click **HEX-STANDOFF**.

252)   Click a **position** to the front of the half Slot Cut as illustrated.

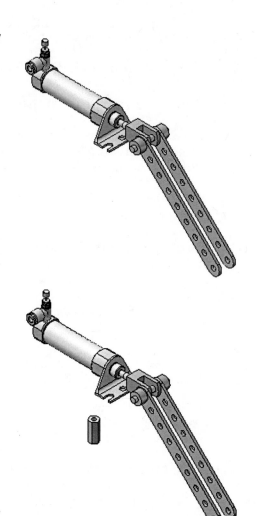

View the Temporary Axes.

253)   Click **View**; check **Temporary Axes** from the Menu bar.

254)   Click **View**; check **Axes** from the Menu bar.

Insert a Coincident mate.

255)   Click the **Mate** tool from the Assembly toolbar. The Mate PropertyManager is displayed.

256)   Click the **HEX-STANDOFF** tapped hole Temporary Axis.

257)   Click the **half Slot Cut Axis1**. The selected entities are displayed in the Mate Selections box. Coincident is selected by default.

258)   Click the **Green Check mark** .

If an assembly or component is loaded in a Lightweight state, right-click the **assembly name** or **component name** from the FeatureManager. Click **Set Lightweight to Resolved**.

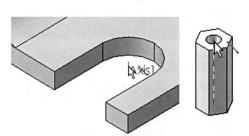

Insert a Coincident mate.
259)   Click the **HEX-STANDOFF** top face.

260)   Click the **BRACKET bottom face**.
          Coincident is selected by default.
          The selected faces are displayed in
          the Mate Selections box.

261)   Click the **Green Check mark** .

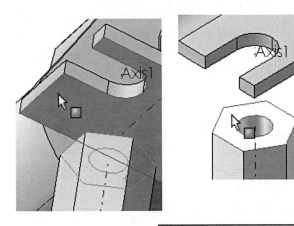

Insert a Parallel mate.
262)   Click the **HEX-STANDOFF** front
          face.

263)   Click the **BRACKET front face**. The
          selected faces are displayed in the
          Mate Selections box.

264)   Click **Parallel** as illustrated.

265)   Click the **Green Check mark** .

266)   Click **OK** from the Mate
          PropertyManager.

Fit the model to the Graphics window.
267)   Press the **f** key.

268)   Click **Isometric view**
          from the Heads-up View
          toolbar.

269)   Click **Save** .

View the created Mates.
270)   **Expand** the Mates folder.
          View the created mates.

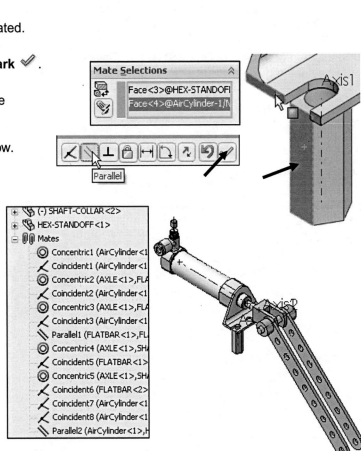

Insert the second HEX-STANDOFF.

271) Click the **Insert Components**  tool from the Assembly toolbar. The Insert Component PropertyManager is displayed.

272) Click the **Browse** button.

273) Select **Parts** for Files of type from the SW-TUTORIAL-2010 folder.

274) Double-click **HEX-STANDOFF**.

275) Click a **position** to the back right of the back half Slot Cut as illustrated.

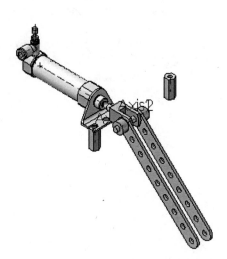

Insert a Concentric mate.

276) Click the **Mate** tool from the Assembly toolbar. The Mate PropertyManager is displayed.

277) Click the **second HEX-STANDOFF** Tapped Hole Temporary Axis.

278) Click the **back half Slot Cut Axis2**. Coincident is selected by default.

279) Click the **Green Check mark**.

Insert a Coincident mate.
280) Click the **second HEX-STANDOFF top** face.

281) Click the **BRACKET bottom face**. Coincident is selected by default.

282) Click the **Green Check mark**.

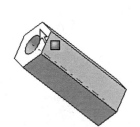

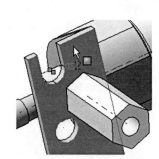

Insert a Parallel mate.

283) Click the **second HEX-STANDOFF** face as illustrated.

284) Click the **BRACKET back right** face.

285) Click **Parallel** ⟍ as illustrated.

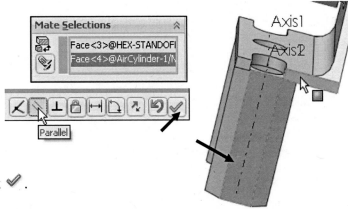

286) Click the **Green Check mark** ✅ .

287) Click **OK** ✅ from the Mate PropertyManager.

💡 Use Selection Filter toolbar to select the correct face, edge, Axis, etc.

Fit the model to the Graphics window.

288) Press the **f** key. Click **Isometric view** 🔲 from the Heads-up View toolbar.

289) Click **Save** 💾 .

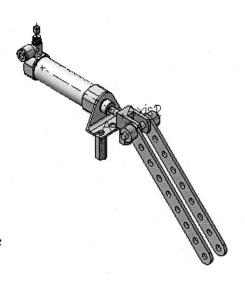

In the Chapter 1 exercises, you created the LINKAGE-2 assembly. Insert the second AXLE. Insert the two SHAFT-COLLAR parts as an exercise at the end of this chapter.

Insert the second AXLE.

290) Click the **Insert Components** 📦 tool from the Assembly toolbar.

291) Click the **Browse** button.

292) Select **Parts** for Files of type from the SW-TUTORIAL-2010 folder.

293) Double-click **AXLE**.

294) Click a **position** to the front bottom of the FLATBAR as illustrated.

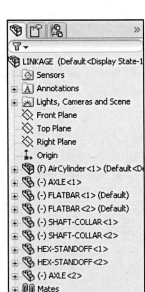

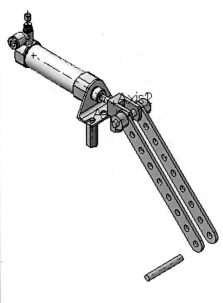

Insert a Concentric mate.

295) Click the **Mate** <span></span> Assembly tool. The Mate PropertyManager is displayed.

296) Click the **second AXLE cylindrical** face.

297) Click the **FLATBAR bottom hole** face as illustrated. Concentric is selected by default.

298) Click the **Green Check mark** <span></span>.

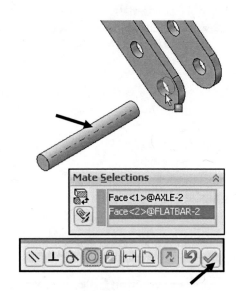

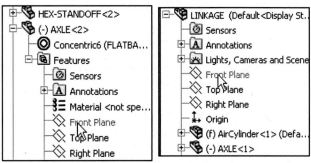

Insert a Coincident mate.

299) Click the second **AXLE Front Plane** from the fly-out FeatureManager.

300) Click the **LINKAGE assembly Front Plane** from the fly-out FeatureManager. Coincident is selected by default. The selected Front Planes are displayed in the Mate Selections box.

301) Click the **Green Check mark** <span></span>.

302) Click **OK** <span></span> from the Mate PropertyManager.

Fit the model to the Graphics window.

303) Press the **f** key.

304) Click **Isometric view** <span></span> from the Heads-up View toolbar.

Save the LINKAGE assembly.

305) Click **Save** <span></span>.

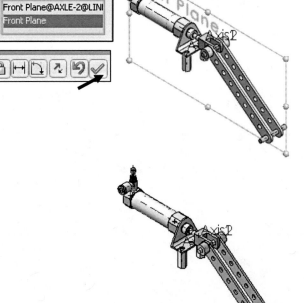

Insert the first SHAFT-COLLAR on the second AXIS.

306)   Click the **Insert Components** 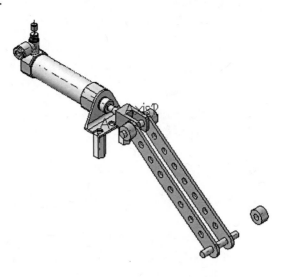 Assembly tool.

307)   Click the **Browse** button.

308)   Select **Part** type from the SW-TUTORIAL-2010 folder.

309)   Double-click **SHAFT-COLLAR.**

310)   Click a **position** to the back of the second AXLE as illustrated.

Enlarge the view.
311)   Zoom-in on the **SHAFT-COLLAR** and the **AXLE** to enlarge the view.

Insert a Concentric mate.
312)   Click the **Mate** Assembly tool. The Mate PropertyManager is displayed.

313)   Click the inside **hole face** of the SHAFT-COLLAR.

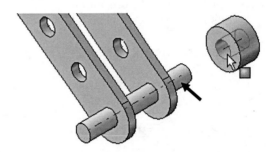

314)   Click the **long cylindrical face** of the AXLE. Concentric is selected by default. The selected faces are displayed in the Mate Selections box.

315)   Click the **Green Check mark** .

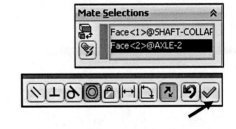

Insert a Coincident mate.
316)   Click the **front face** of the SHAFT-COLLAR.

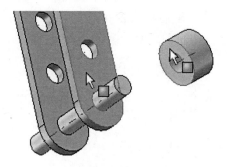

317)   Press the **left arrow key** approximately 5 times to rotate the model to view the back face of the first FLATBAR.

318)   Click the **back face** of the FLATBAR. Coincident is selected by default.

319)   Click the **Green Check mark** ✅ .

320)   Click **OK** ✅ from the Mate PropertyManager.

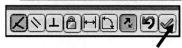

Display the Isometric view.
321)   Click **Isometric view** 🔲 from the Heads-up View toolbar.

Insert the second SHAFT-COLLAR.
322)   Click the **Insert Components** 🔧 Assembly tool. The Insert Component PropertyManager is displayed.

323)   Click the **Browse** button.

324)   Select **Part** for Files of type from the SW-TUTORIAL-2010 folder.

325)   Double-click **SHAFT-COLLAR**.

326)   Click a **position** to the front of the AXLE as illustrated.

Enlarge the view.
327)   **Zoom in** on the second SHAFT-COLLAR and the AXLE to enlarge the view.

Insert a Concentric mate.
328)   Click the **Mate** ✏️ Assembly tool. The Mate PropertyManager is displayed.

329)   Click the inside **hole face** of the second SHAFT-COLLAR. Note: The icon face feedback symbol.

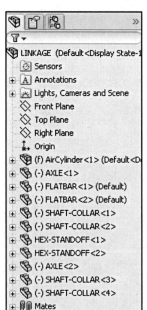

330) Click the **long cylindrical face** of the AXLE. Concentric is selected by default.

331) Click the **Green Check mark** ✓ .

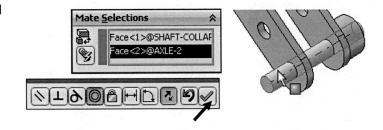

Insert a Coincident mate.
332) Press the **f** key to fit the model to the Graphics window.

333) Zoom in on the front face of the second FLATBAR.

334) Click the **front face** of the second FLATBAR.

335) Click the **back face** of the second SHAFT-COLLAR. Coincident is selected by default.

336) Click the **Green Check mark** ✓ .

337) Click **OK** ✓ from the Mate PropertyManager.

Display the Isometric view.
338) Click **Isometric view** ⬦ from the Heads-up View toolbar.

Save the LINKAGE assembly.
339) Rebuild the model.

340) Click **View**; uncheck **Axis** from the Menu bar.

341) Click **View**; uncheck **Temporary Axis** from Menu bar.

342) Click **Save** 🖫. Note: As an exercise, insert SCREWs between the AirCylinder assembly and the two HEX-STANDOFFs as illustrated.

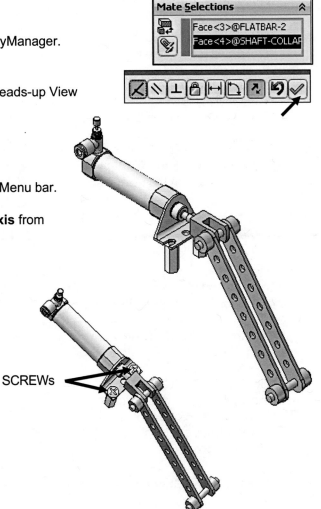

SCREWs

Activity: PNEUMATIC-TEST-MODULE-Insert LINKAGE Assembly

Insert the LINKAGE assembly into the PNEUMATIC-TEST-MODULE assembly.

343) Click **Window**, **Tile Horizontally** from the Menu bar. Note: The PNEUMATIC-TEST-MODULE assembly should be open.

344) Rotate the two **FLATBARs** approximately 45°.

345) Click and drag the **LINKAGE** 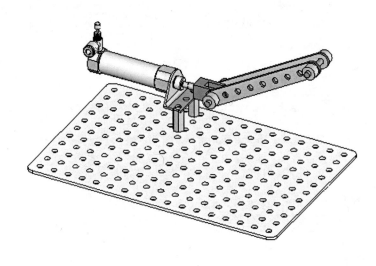 LINKAGE assembly icon into the PNEUMATIC-TEST-MODULE assembly.

346) Click a **position** above the FLAT-PLATE as illustrated.

347) **Maximize** the PNEUMATIC-TEST-MODULE Graphics window.

348) Click **View**; uncheck **Origins** from the Menu bar. If required, click View; un-check Planes from the Menu bar.

349) Click **Trimetric view** from the Heads-up View toolbar.

Insert a Concentric mate.

350) Click the **Mate** Assembly tool. The Mate PropertyManager is displayed.

351) Click the **Front HEX-STANDOFF Tapped** Hole face as illustrated.

352) Click the **FLAT-PLATE Hole** face in the 5th row, 4th column as illustrated. Concentric is selected by default. The selected faces are displayed in the Mate Selections box.

353) Click the **Green Check mark** .

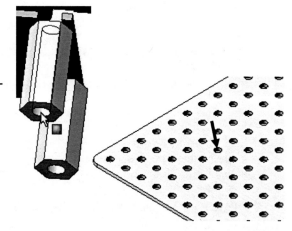

Insert a Parallel mate.

354) Click the **PNEUMATIC-TEST-MODULE Front Plane** from the fly-out FeatureManager.

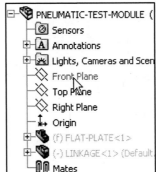

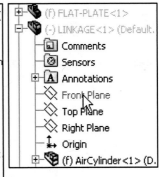

355) Click the **LINKAGE assembly Front Plane** from the fly-out FeatureManager.

356) Click **Parallel**.

357) Click the **Green Check mark** ✔.

Insert a Coincident mate.

358) Click the **Front HEX-STANDOFF** bottom face.

359) Click the **FLAT-PLATE top face**. Coincident is selected by default.

360) Click the **Green Check mark** ✔.

361) Click **OK** ✔ from the Mate PropertyManager.

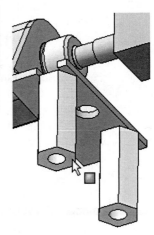

Display the Isometric view.

362) Click **Isometric view** from the Heads-up View toolbar.

Save the PNEUMATIC-TEST-MODULE assembly.

363) Click **Save** 💾.

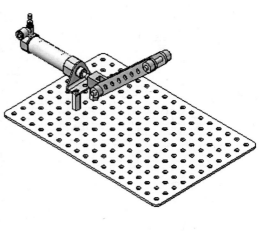

The LINKAGE assembly is fully defined, and located on the FLAT-PLATE part. Insert the AIR-RESERVOIR-SUPPORT assembly. The AIR-RESERVOIR-SUPPORT assembly was created in the Chapter 2 exercises. Note: The AIR-RESERVOIR SUPPORT is also located in the book's CD.

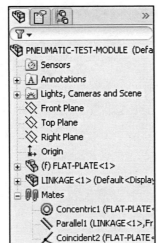

Activity: PNEUMATIC-TEST-MODULE Insert AIR-RESERVOIR-SUPPORT

Insert the AIR-RESERVOIR-SUPPORT assembly.

364) Click the **Insert Components** Assembly tool. The Insert Component PropertyManager is displayed.

365) Click the **Browse** button.

366) Select **Assembly** for Files of type from the SW-TUTORIAL-2010 folder.

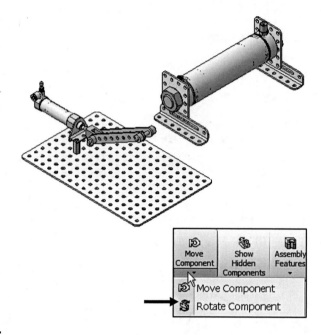

367) Double-click the **AIR-RESERVOIR-SUPPORT** assembly. Note: The AIR-RESERVOIR SUPPORT assembly is supplied on the CD in the book: Chapter 5 models folder.

368) Click a **position** above the FLAT-PLATE as illustrated.

369) Click the **Rotate Component** Assembly tool. The Rotate Component PropertyManager is displayed. The Rotate icon is displayed in the Graphics window.

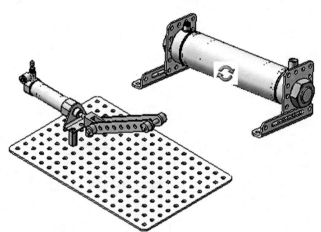

370) Click and drag the **AIR-RESERVOIR-SUPPORT** until the tank is parallel with the AirCylinder assembly as illustrated.

371) Click **OK** from the Rotate Component PropertyManager.

Insert a Concentric mate.

372)   Click the **Mate** ✎ Assembly tool. The Mate PropertyManager is displayed.

373)   Click the **FLAT-PLATE back left** inside hole face as illustrated.

374)   Click the fourth **ANGLE-BRACKET** inside hole face. Concentric is selected by default.

375)   Click the **Green Check mark** ✓ .

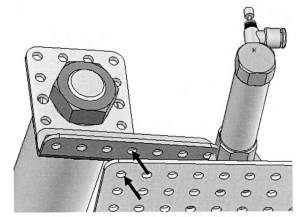

Insert a Coincident mate.

376)   Click the **ANGLE-BRACKET bottom face**.

377)   Click the **FLAT-PLATE top face**. Coincident is selected by default.

378)   Click the **Green Check mark** ✓ .

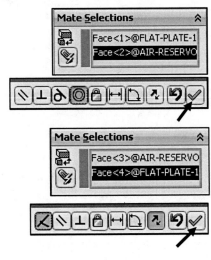

Insert a Parallel mate.

379)   Click **Left view** ⬒ from the Heads-up View toolbar.

380)   Click the **ANGLE-BRACKET** narrow face.

381)   Click the **FLAT-PLATE narrow face**.

382)   Click **Parallel** ╲ .

383)   Click the **Green Check mark** ✓ .

384)   Click **OK** ✓ from the Mate PropertyManager.

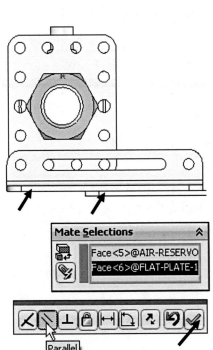

Display the Isometric view.

385) Click **Isometric view** 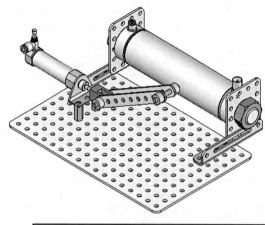 from the Heads-up View toolbar.

Save the PNEUMATIC-TEST-MODULE assembly.

386) Click **Save** .

Component Patterns in the Assembly

There are three methods to define a pattern in an assembly.

- Linear

- Circular

- Feature Driven

A Feature Driven Component Pattern utilizes an existing feature pattern.

A Linear / Circular Component pattern utilizes geometry in the assembly to arrange instances in a Linear or Circular pattern.

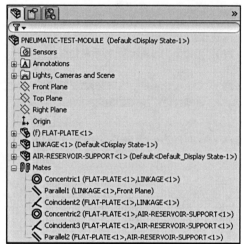

The SCREW part fastens the ANGLE-BRACKET part to the FLAT-PLATE part. Mate one SCREW to the first instance on the ANGLE-BRACKET Linear Pattern.

Utilize the Feature Driven Component Pattern tool to create instances of the SCREW. Suppress the instances.

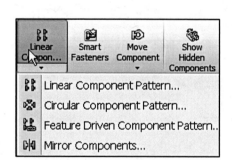

Utilize the Linear Component Pattern tool to copy the Feature Driven Pattern of SCREWS to the second ANGLE-BRACKET part.

Drag the part by specific geometry to create a mate.

Activity: PNEUMATIC-TEST-MODULE-Component Pattern

Open the SCREW part.

387) Click **Open** ☐ from the Menu bar.

388) Double-click **SCREW** from the SW-TUTORIAL-2010 folder.

389) Un-suppress the **Fillet1** and **Chamfer1** feature.

390) Click **Window**, **Tile Horizontally** to display the SCREW and the PNEUMATIC-TEST-MODULE assembly.

Insert and mate the SCREW.

391) Click the **bottom circular edge** of the SCREW.

392) Drag the **SCREW** into the PNEUMATIC-TEST-MODULE assembly window. Note: Zoom in on the top circular edge of the ANGLE-BRACKET left hole.

393) Release the mouse pointer on the **top circular edge** of the ANGLE-BRACKET left hole. The mouse pointer displays the ⬚ Coincident/Concentric feedback symbol.

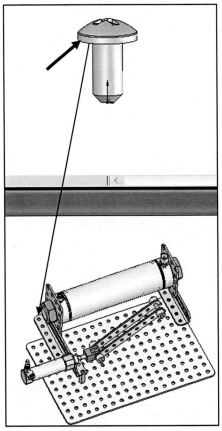

394) **Return** to the PNEUMATIC-TEST-MODULE assembly window. Click **Left view** ⬚ from the Heads-up View toolbar.

The SCREW part is position in the left hole with a Coincident/Concentric mate.

Create a Feature Driven Component Pattern.

395) Click the **Feature Driven Component Pattern** ⬚ tool from the Consolidate Assembly toolbar. The Feature Driven PropertyManager is displayed.

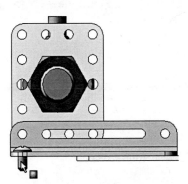

396) Click the **SCREW** component in the Graphics window. SCREW<1> is displayed in the Components to Pattern box.

397) Click inside the **Driving Feature** box. **Expand** the AIR-RESERVOIR-SUPPORT assembly in the PNEUMATIC-TEST-MODULE fly-out FeatureManager.

398) **Expand** ANGLE-BRACKET <1>. **Expand** the Features folder.

399) Click **LPattern1** in the fly-out FeatureManager. Note: The SCREW is the seed feature.

400) Click **OK** ✔ from the Feature Driven PropertyManager. Six instances are displayed in the Graphics window. DerivedLPattern1 is displayed in the FeatureManager.

401) Click **SCREW<1>** from the FeatureManager.

402) Hold the **Ctrl** key down.

403) **Expand** DerivedLPattern1 from the FeatureManager.

404) Click the first two entries: **SCREW<2>** and **SCREW<3>**.

405) Release the **Ctrl** key.

406) Right-click **Suppress**. The first three SCREWs are not displayed.

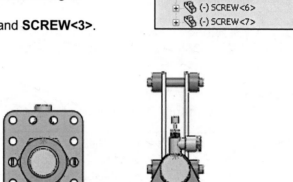

🔅 The Feature Driven PropertyManager contains an option to skip instances of a feature component in a pattern.

Activity: PNEUMATIC-TEST-MODULE-Linear Component Pattern

Create a Linear Component Pattern.

407) Click **Front view** 📦 from the Heads-up View toolbar.

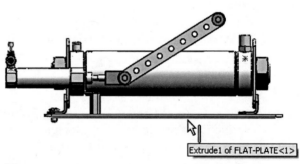

408) Click the **Linear Component Pattern** ⬚ tool from the Assembly toolbar. The Linear Pattern PropertyManager is displayed.

409) Click inside the **Pattern Direction** box for Direction 1.

410) Click the long front edge of the **FRONT-PLATE** as illustrated. Edge<1> is displayed in the Pattern Direction box. The direction arrow points to the right.

411) Enter **177.80**mm, [7in] for Spacing.

412) Enter **2** for Instances.

413) Click inside the **Components to Pattern** box.

414) Click **DerivedLPattern1** from the fly-out FeatureManager.

415) Click **OK** ✓ from the Linear Pattern PropertyManager.

416) Click **Top view** ⊞ from the Heads-up View toolbar. View the results.

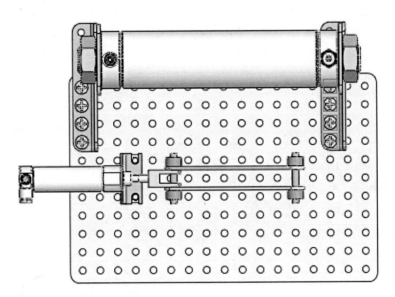

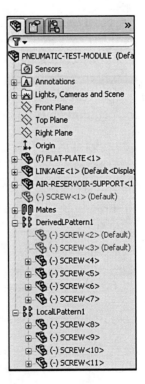

The Linear Component Pattern feature is displayed in the second ANGLE-BRACKET part. LocalLPattern1 is displayed in the FeatureManager.

Save the PNEUMATIC TEST MODULE assembly.

417) Click **Isometric view** ⬦ from the Heads-up View toolbar. View the FeatureManager and the created features in their states.

418) Click **Save** 🖫.

Hide the AIR-RESERVOIR-SUPPORT
assembly.

419)   Right-click **AIR-RESERVOIR-
SUPPORT<1>** in the
FeatureManager.

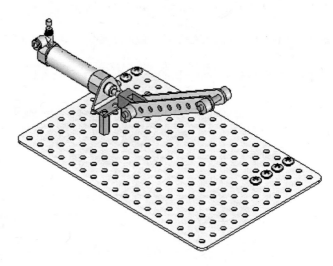

420)   Click **Hide components** 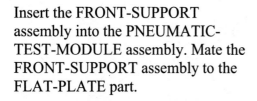.
Note: Utilize the Show
components tool to display a
component that has been hidden.

Hide the LINKAGE assembly.

421)   Right-click **LINKAGE<1>** in the
FeatureManager.

422)   Click **Hide components** 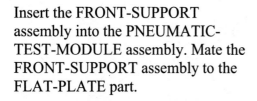.

Insert the FRONT-SUPPORT
assembly into the PNEUMATIC-
TEST-MODULE assembly. Mate the
FRONT-SUPPORT assembly to the
FLAT-PLATE part.

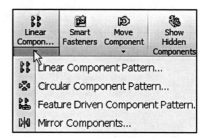

Utilize the Mirror Components tool to
create a mirrored copy of the
FRONT-SUPPORT assembly.

🔆 You can create new components
by mirroring existing part or sub-
assembly components. The new components can either be
a copy or a mirror of the original components. A mirrored
component is sometimes called a "right-hand" version of
the original "left-hand" version.

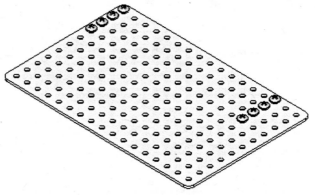

🔆 Access the Mirror Components tool from the
Consolidated Linear Component Pattern drop-down menu.

Activity: PNEUMATIC-TEST-MODULE-Insert FRONT-SUPPORT Assembly

---

Insert and mate the FRONT-SUPPORT assembly.

423)   Click the **Insert Components** 🗐 tool from the Assembly toolbar. The Insert Component
PropertyManager is displayed.

424)   Click the **Browse** button. Select **Assembly** for Files of type.

425)   Double-click **FRONT-SUPPORT**.

Hide the SCREWs in the FRONT-SUPPORT.
426) Click a **position** above the FLAT-PLATE as illustrated.

427) Right-click **FRONT-SUPPORT** in the FeatureManager.

428) Click **Open Assembly**.

429) **Hide** the SCREW parts and HEX-NUTS if required in the assembly.

430) Click **Save** 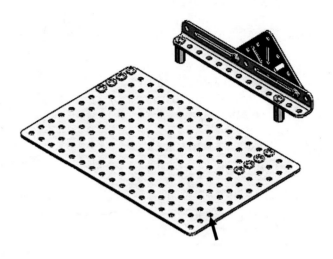.

Return to the PNEUMATIC-TEST-MODULE assembly.
431) Press **Ctrl Tab**.

432) Select the **PNEUMATIC-TEST-MODULE** document.

433) Click **Save** .

434) Click **Yes** to the Message, "Save the document and referenced models now?"

The PNEUMATIC-TEST-MODULE is displayed. The SCREW and HEX-NUT components are hidden in the FRONT-SUPPORT assembly.

Insert a Concentric mate.
435) Click the **Mate** 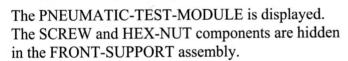 Assembly tool. The Mate PropertyManager is displayed.

436) Click the **FLAT-PLATE hole face** in the 3rd row, right most column (17th column).

437) Click the **HEX-STANDOFF Tapped Hole as** illustrated. Concentric is selected by default.

438) Click the **Green Check mark** .

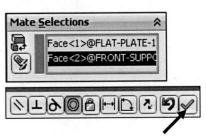

Insert a Coincident mate.

439) Click the bottom face of the **HEX-STANDOFF** part.

440) Click the top face of the **FLAT-PLATE**. The selected faces are displayed in the Mate Selections box. Coincident is selected by default.

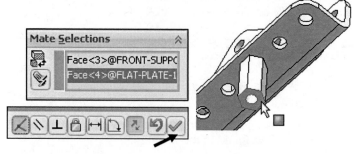

441) Click the **Green Check mark** .

Insert a Parallel mate.

442) Click the **FRONT-SUPPORT Front Plane** from the fly-out FeatureManager.

443) **Show** the LINKAGE assembly.

444) Click the **LINKAGE Front Plane** from the fly-out FeatureManager.

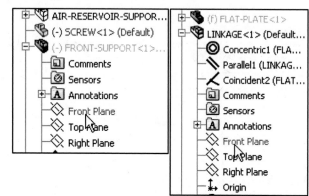

445) Click **Parallel** .

446) Click the **Green Check mark** .

447) Click **OK** from the Mate PropertyManager.

448) **Hide** the LINKAGE assembly.

Save the PNEUMATIC-TEST-MODULE assembly.

449) Click **Save** .

Mirrored Components

Create new components by mirroring existing parts or sub-assemblies. New components are created as copied geometry or mirrored geometry.

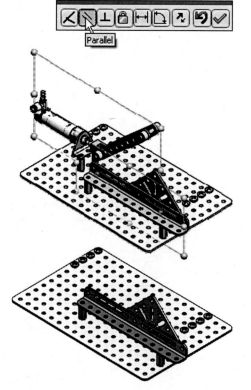

A mirrored component is sometimes called a "right-hand" version of the original "left hand" version.

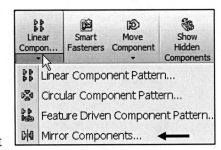

The copied or mirrored component changes, when the original component is modified.

A mirrored component creates a new document. The default document prefix is mirror. A copied component does not create a new document.

Suppressed components in the original sub-assembly are not mirrored or copied. The SCREW parts in the FRONT-SUPPORT assembly are not copied.

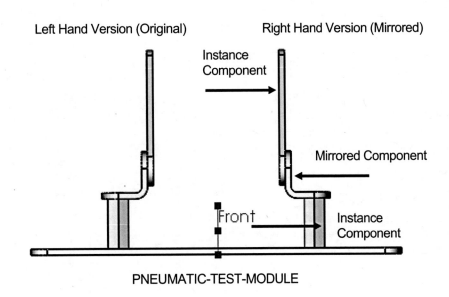

Left Hand Version (Original)   Right Hand Version (Mirrored)

Instance Component

Mirrored Component

Front

Instance Component

PNEUMATIC-TEST-MODULE

Activity: PNEUMATIC-TEST-MODULE Assembly: Mirrored Component

Insert a Mirrored Component.

450) Click the **Mirror Components** 🔲 tool from the Consolidated Assembly toolbar. The Mirror Components PropertyManager is displayed.

Step 1: The Selections box is displayed. The first Step requires the mirrored plane, the components to mirror, and the components to copy.

451) **Expand** the PNEUMATIC-TEST-MODULE fly-out FeatureManager.

452) Click the **FLAT-PLATE Front Plane**. The Front Plane is displayed in the Mirror plane box.

453) Click the **FRONT-SUPPORT** assembly from the fly-out FeatureManager. The FRONT-SUPPORT assembly is displayed in the Components to Mirror box.

454) **Expand** the FRONT-SUPPORT entry in the Components to Mirror box.

455) Check the **FRONT-SUPPORT-1** box.

456) Check the **Recreate mates to new components** box.

457) Click **Next**.

Step 2: The Filenames box is displayed. "Mirror" is the default prefix utilized in the mirror part and assembly. MirrorFRONT-SUPPORT is the new assembly name.

458) Accept Mirror as the default prefix. Click **Next**.

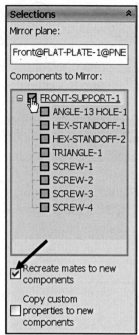

Step 3: The Orientation box is displayed. The instanced components check box is automatically selected. A preview of the mirrored TRIANGLE and HEX-STANDOFF components are displayed.

459) Check the **Preview mirrored components** box. The ANGLE-13HOLE part is displayed in a preview in the Graphics window.

460) Click **OK** ✔ from the Mirror Components PropertyManager.

461) Click **OK** from the New SolidWorks Document dialog box.

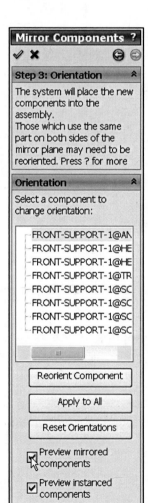

🔆 Select suppressed components and their mates to be mirrored in the Components to Mirror box.

The MirrorFRONT-SUPPORT, TRIANGLE, ANGLE-13HOLE, and SCREW components are mated.

Utilize the Fix option to mate the MirrorFRONT-SUPPORT to its current location in the PNEUMATIC-TEST-MODULE. No other mates are required.

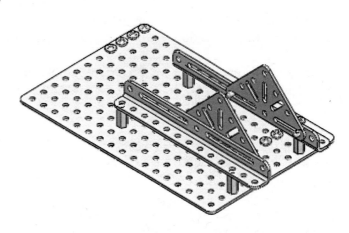

Activity: PNEUMATIC-TEST-MODULE-Fix the MIRRORFRONT-SUPPORT

Fix the MirrorFRONT-SUPPORT.
462) Right-click **MirrorFRONT-SUPPORT** from the FeatureManager.

463) Click **Fix**. The MirrorFRONT assembly is fixed in the PNEUMATIC-TEST-MODULE assembly. The MirrorFRONT-SUPPORT does not move or rotate.

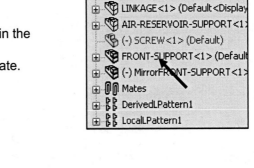

Display the LINKAGE assembly.
464) Right-click **LINKAGE** in the FeatureManager.

465) Click **Show components**.

Save the PNEUMATIC-TEST-MODULE assembly.

466) Click **Save** 💾.

🔆 Reuse geometry in the assembly. Utilize the Mirror Component tool to create a left and right version of parts and assemblies.

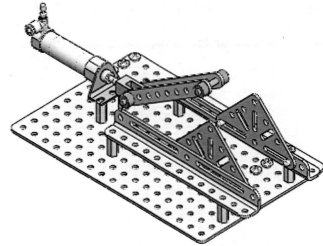

Component Properties

Component Properties control the flexibility of the sub-assembly when inserted into an assembly. Components do not translate or rotate after insertion into the assembly.

The FLATBAR parts in the LINKAGE assembly do not rotate after insertion into the PNEUMATIC TEST MODULE assembly. The LINKAGE assembly is in the Rigid State.

Insert the WHEEL-AND-AXLE assembly into the PNEUMATIC-TEST-MODULE assembly. Modify the Mate state of the LINKAGE assembly from the Rigid State to the Flexible State. The LINKAGE assembly is free to rotate.

Modify the Mate State of the AirCylinder assembly from the Rigid State to the Flexible State. The AirCylinder assembly is free to translate.

By default, when you create a sub-assembly, it is rigid. Within the parent assembly, the sub-assembly acts as a single unit and its components do not move relative to each other.

Activity: PNEUMATIC-TEST-MODULE Assembly-Insert WHEEL-AND-AXLE Assembly

Insert the WHEEL-AND-AXLE assembly.

467) Click the **Insert Components** tool from the Assembly toolbar. The Insert Component PropertyManager is displayed.

468) Click the **Browse** button.

469) Select **Assembly** for Files of type.

470) Double-click the **WHEEL-AND-AXLE** assembly from the SW-TUTORIAL-2010 folder.

471) Click a **position** above the FLAT-PLATE part as illustrated.

Insert a Concentric mate.

472) Click the **Mate**  tool from the Assembly toolbar.

473) Click the **AXLE-3000 cylindrical** face.

474) Click the inside **TRIANGLE top hole** face. The selected faces are displayed in the Mate Selections box. Concentric is selected by default.

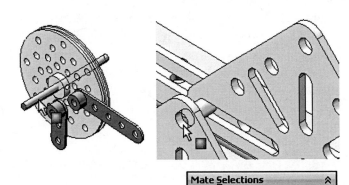

475) Click the **Green Check mark** .

Insert a Coincident mate.

476) Click the **WHEEL-AND-AXLE Front Plane** from the fly-out FeatureManager.

477) Click the **LINKAGE Front Plane** from the fly-out FeatureManager. Coincident is selected by default.

478) Click the **Green Check mark** .

479) Click **OK** from the Mate PropertyManager.

A Concentric mate is required between the left hole of the FLATBAR-3HOLE and right AXLE of the LINKAGE assembly.

DO NOT INSERT A CONCENTRIC MATE AT THIS TIME!

A Concentric mate will result in Mate errors.

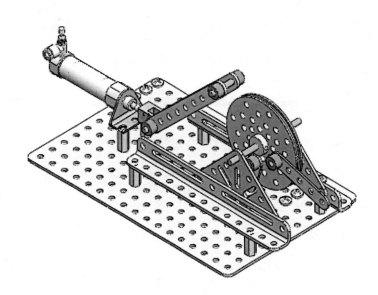

The WHEEL-AND-AXLE is free to rotate in the PNEUMATIC-TEST-MODULE assembly. The LINKAGE assembly interferes with the WHEEL-AND-AXLE. The LINKAGE assembly is not free to rotate or translate. Mate errors will occur.

Sub-assemblies within the LINKAGE assembly are in a Rigid Mate state when inserted into the PNEUMATIC-TEST-MODULE assembly. Remove the Rigid Mate state and insert a Concentric mate between the LINKAGE assembly and the WHEEL-AND-AXLE.

Activity: PNEUMATIC-TEST-MODULE Assembly-Remove Rigid state

Remove the Rigid State.

480) Right-click the **LINKAGE** assembly from the FeatureManager.

481) Click **Component Properties** from the Context toolbar. The Component Properties dialog box is displayed.

482) Check **Flexible** in the Solve as box.

483) Click **OK** from the Component Properties dialog box. Note the icon next to the LINKAGE assembly in the FeatureManager.

484) Right-click the **AirCylinder** assembly from the FeatureManager.

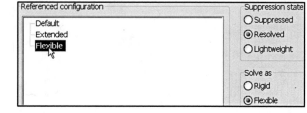

485) Click **Component Properties**.

486) Check **Flexible** in the Solve as box.

487) Click **Flexible** in the Referenced configuration box.

488) Click **OK** from the Component Properties dialog box.

Hide the FRONT-SUPPORT assembly.

489) Right-click **FRONT-SUPPORT** from the FeatureManager.

490) Click **Hide components**.

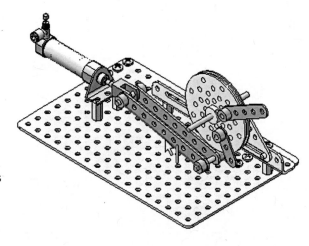

Move the LINKAGE assembly.

491) Click and drag the **front FLATBAR-9HOLE** downward. The FLATBAR-9HOLE rotates about the left AXLE.

492) Click a **position** below the WHEEL-AND-AXLE. Click **inside** the Graphics window to deselect.

Insert a Concentric mate.

493) Click the **Mate** 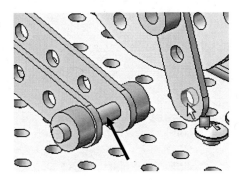 tool from the Assembly toolbar.

494) Click the second bottom **AXLE** face of the LINKAGE assembly.

495) Click the **bottom hole** of the FLATBAR-3HOLE as illustrated. Concentric is the default.

496) Click the **Green Check mark** ✓ .

497) Click **OK** ✓ from the Mate PropertyManager.

Save the PNEUMATIC-TEST-MODULE assembly.

498) Click **Isometric view** 🔲 from the Heads-up View toolbar.

499) Click **Save** 💾.

The AirCylinder assembly is inserted in a Rigid state by default. The AirCylinder contains three configurations:

- Default

- Extended

- Flexible

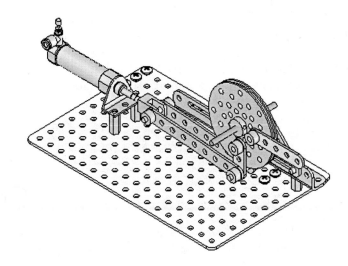

Open the AirCylinder assembly. Modify the configuration to Flexible.

Open the LINKAGE assembly. Modify the AirCylinder Component Properties from Default to Flexible.

Activity: PNEUMATIC-TEST-MODULE Assembly - Review AirCylinder Configurations

Review the AirCylinder configurations.

500) Right-click **LINKAGE** from the PNEUMATIC-TEST-MODULE FeatureManager.

501) Click **Open Assembly** from the Context toolbar.

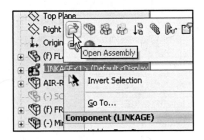

502) Right-click **AirCylinder** in the LINKAGE FeatureManager.

503) Click **Open Assembly**.

504) Click the **Configuration Manager** tab at the top of the AirCylinder FeatureManager. Three configurations are displayed: *Default*, *Extended* and *Flexible*. The current Default configuration sets the Piston Rod at 0 mm.

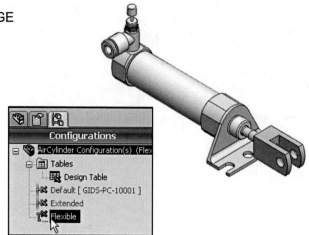

Display the Extended Configuration.
505) Double-click **Extended**. The Piston Rod of the AirCylinder extends 25mm.

Display the Flexible Configuration.
506) Double-click **Flexible**.

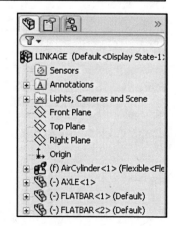

507) Click the **Rod-Clevis** in the Graphics window.

508) Click and drag the **Piston Rod** from left to right.

509) Click a **position** near its original location. The AirCylinder remains in the Flexible configuration for the rest of this project.

Update the LINKAGE assembly.
510) Click **Window**, **LINKAGE** from the Menu bar. The current configuration of the AirCylinder part in the LINKAGE assembly is Default. Modify the configuration.

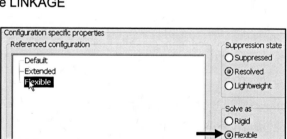

511) Right-click **AirCylinder** from the LINKAGE assembly FeatureManager.

512) Click **Component Properties**.

513) Click **Flexible** for Solve as. Click **Flexible** for Referenced configuration.

514) Click **OK**. The AirCylinder displays the Flexible configuration next to its name in the FeatureManager.

☼ A Rebuild 🐝 icon is displayed in the Assembly FeatureManager and a flexible rebuild 📇 icon at the sub-assembly level when the AirCylinder assembly is in the Flexible state.

Update the PNEUMATIC-TEST-MODULE.
515) Click **Window**, **PNEUMATIC-TEST-MODULE** assembly from the Menu bar.

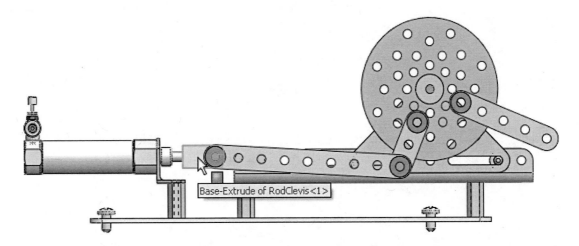

Move the ROD-CLEVIS.
516) Click and drag the **ROD-CLEVIS** to the right. The WHEEL rotates in a counterclockwise direction.

517) Click and drag the **ROD-CLEVIS** to the left. The WHEEL rotates in a clockwise direction.

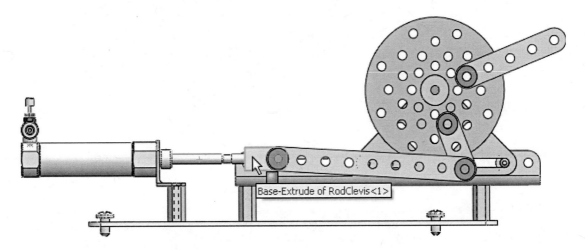

Display the AIR-RESERVOIR-SUPPORT assembly.
518) Right-click **AIR-RESERVOIR-SUPPORT** in the FeatureManager.

519) Click **Show components**.

Display the second FRONT-SUPPORT assembly.
520) Right-click **FRONT-SUPPORT** in the FeatureManager.

521) Click **Show components**.

522) **Display** the SCREWs in the FRONT-SUPPORT.

Save the PNEUMATIC-TEST-MODULE.
523)   Click **Isometric view** from the Heads-up View toolbar.

524)   Click **Save**.

525)   Click **Yes** to update referenced documents.

Close all documents.
526)   Click **Windows**, **Close All** from the Menu bar.

Explore additional parts and assemblies at the end of this project. Add the WEIGHT, HOOK and FLATBAR parts.

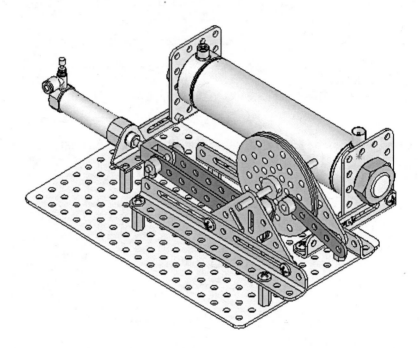

A Rebuild icon is displayed in the Assembly FeatureManager and a flexible rebuild icon at the sub-assembly level when the AirCylinder assembly is in the Flexible state.

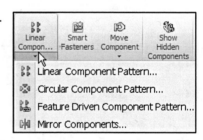

Additional details on Show components, Hide components, Linear Component Pattern, Circular Component Pattern, Feature Driven Component Pattern, Mirror Components, Configurations, Configuration Manager are available in SolidWorks Help. Select Help, SolidWorks Help topics.

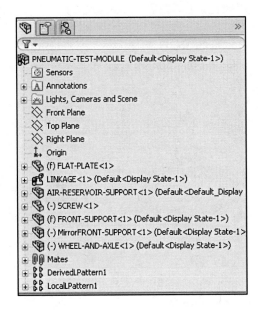

Review the PNEUMATIC-TEST-MODULE Assembly

The PNEUMATIC TEST MODULE assembly was created by combining five major mechanical sub-assemblies.

The PNEUMATIC TEST MODULE assembly utilized the FLAT-PLATE as the first component. The LINKAGE assembly, AIR-RESERVOIR-SUPPORT assembly, FRONT-SUPPORT assembly, MirrorFRONT-SUPPORT assembly and the WHEEL-AND-AXLE assembly were mated to the FLAT-PLATE part.

Work at the lowest assembly level. The LINKAGE assembly required two HEX-STANDOFF parts. The HEX-STANDOFF components were inserted into the LINKAGE assembly. The LINKAGE assembly was inserted into the PNEUMATIC-TEST-MODULE assembly.

The AIR-RESERVOIR-SUPPORT assembly was inserted into the PNEUMATIC-TEST-MODULE assembly. The SCREW component utilized a Feature Driven Component Pattern tool and the Linear Component Pattern tool to create multiple copies.

The FRONT-SUPPORT assembly was inserted into the PNEUMATIC-TEST-MODULE assembly. The Mirror Components tool created a mirrored version of the FRONT-SUPPORT assembly.

The WHEEL-AND-AXLE assembly was inserted into the PNEUMATIC-TEST-MODULE assembly. Component Properties created a Flexible state mate.

The LINKAGE assembly, "AirCylinder" is in a Flexible state.

In the section, create the final ROBOT assembly. Either use your created assemblies and components, or use the created assemblies and components provided in the Chapter 5 Models folder on the enclosed CD.

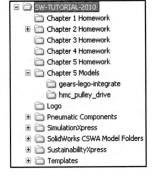

Work from your hard drive. Copy the folders from the CD to your hard drive.

Final ROBOT Assembly

The final ROBOT assembly is comprised of three major sub-assemblies and the HEX-STANDOFF component:

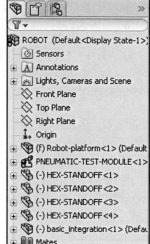

- Robot Platform assembly

- PNEUMATIC-TEST-MODULE assembly

- Basic_integration assembly

- 4 – HEX-STANDOFF components

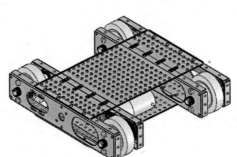

 The LINKAGE assembly is in a Flexible state.

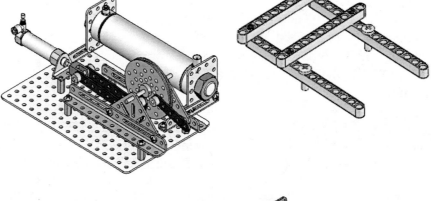

A Rebuild icon is displayed in the final ROBOT Assembly FeatureManager and a flexible rebuild icon at the sub-assembly level when the AirCylinder assembly is in the Flexible state.

All assemblies and components for the final ROBOT assembly are provided in the Chapter 5 models folder on the enclosed CD.

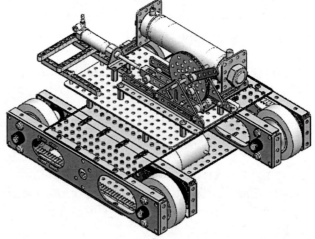

The Robot-platform assembly was provided by **GEARS Educational Systems** (www.gearseds.com).

Combine the created new assemblies and components to develop the final ROBOT assembly. In this next section, work from the Chapter 5 models folder located on the CD in the book. If needed, copy all models from the CD to your hard drive. Create the SW-TUTORIAL-2010/Chapter 5 models folder.

Note: Step-by-step instructions are not provided in this section for the mates.

Activity: Create the ROBOT Assembly

Create the final ROBOT assembly.

527) Click **New** ⬚ from the Menu bar.

528) Double-click **Assembly** from the Templates tab. The Begin Assembly PropertyManager is displayed.

Insert the Robot-platform assembly.
529) Click the **Browse** button.

530) Select **Assembly** for Files of type from the SW-TUTORIAL-2010/Chapter 5 Models folder. Note: The Chapter 5 models folder is located on the CD in the book.

531) Double-click **Robot-platform**.

532) Click **OK** ✔ from the Begin Assembly PropertyManager. The Robot-platform is fixed to the assembly Origin.

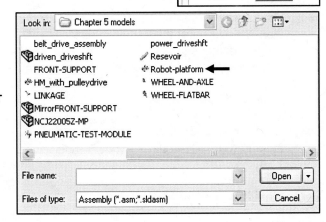

Save the Assembly.
533) Click **Save As** from the Menu bar.

534) Enter **ROBOT** for File name in the SW-TUTORIAL-2010/Chapter 5 models folder.

535) Enter **Final ROBOT Assembly** for Description.

536) Click **Save**.

Insert the PNEUMATIC-TEST-MODULE assembly.

537) Click **Insert Components** 🖫 from the Assembly toolbar. The Insert Components PropertyManager is displayed.

538) Click the **Browse** button.

539) Double-click the **PNEUMATIC-TEST-MODULE** assembly from the SW-TUTORIAL-2010/Chapter 5 models folder.

540) Click a **position** above the Robot-platform.

If an assembly or component is loaded in a Lightweight state, right-click the **assembly name** or **component name** from the FeatureManager. Click **Set Lightweight to Resolved**.

Insert 4 HEX-STANDOFF components.

541) Click **Insert Components** from the Assembly toolbar. The Insert Components PropertyManager is displayed.

542) Click the **Browse** button.

543) Select **Part** for Files of type from the SW-TUTORIAL-2010/Chapter 5 models folder.

544) Double-click **HEX-STANDOFF**.

545) **Pin** the Insert Components PropertyManager.

546) Click **four positions** as illustrated for the four HEX-STANDOFF components.

547) **Un-Pin** the Insert Components PropertyManager.

548) Click **OK** from the Insert Components PropertyManager.

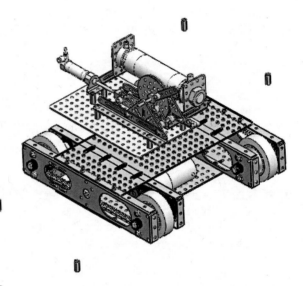

Insert Coincident and Concentric mates between the four HEX-STANDOFF components and the PNEUMATIC-TEST-MODULE and the Robot-platform as illustrated. View the location of the HEX-STANDOFF components on the PNEUMATIC-TEST-MODULE assembly.

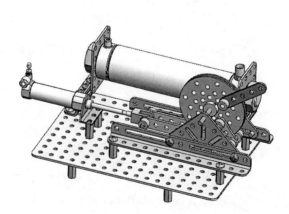

View the location of the HEX-STANDOFF
components on the Robot-platform as
illustrated.

549)   **Expand** the Mates folder. View the
created mates.

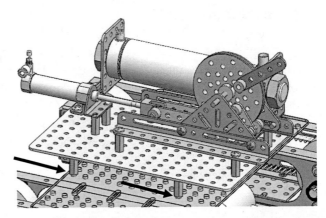

Insert the basic_integration assembly.

550)   Click the **Browse** button.

551)   Select **Assembly** for Files of type from the
SW-TUTORIAL-2010/Chapter 5 models
folder.

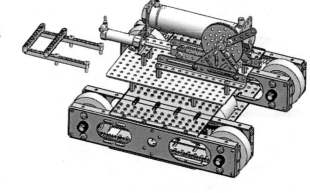

552)   Double-click **basic_integration**.

553)   Click a position to the **left** of the
assembly as illustrated.

Insert Coincident and Concentric mates
between the two screws in the
basic_integration assembly and the
PNEUMATIC-TEST-MODULE
assembly.

554)   **Expand** the Mates folder. View the
created mates.

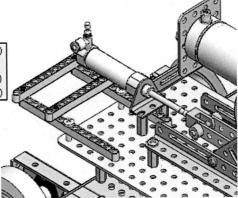

Save the ROBOT assembly.

555)   Click **Save** 🖫. You are finished with the final
ROBOT assembly.

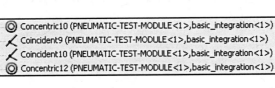

Chapter Summary

In this chapter, you created and worked with multiple documents in sub-assemblies and assemblies. You developed sound assembly modeling techniques that utilized Standard mates, fixed components, symmetry, component patterns and mirrored components.

The WHEEL-AND-AXLE assembly combined the WHEEL-FLATBAR assembly with the AXLE-3000 part, SHAFTCOLLAR-500 part and HEX-ADAPTER part.

The WHEEL-FLATBAR assembly combined the 3HOLE-SHAFTCOLLAR assembly and 5HOLE-SHAFTCOLLAR assembly.

The PNEUMATIC-TEST-MODULE assembly combined four major mechanical sub-assemblies. The final ROBOT assembly was comprised of three major sub-assemblies and the HEX-STANDOFF component.

Organize your assemblies. For an exercise, create an assembly Layout Diagram of the final ROBOT assembly to determine the grouping of components and assemblies.

Chapter Terminology

Mates: A mate is a Geometric relationship between components in an assembly.

Circular Pattern: A Circular Pattern repeats features or geometry in a polar array. A Circular Patten requires an axis of revolution, the number of instances and an angle.

Component Pattern: There are two methods to define a component pattern in an assembly. A Derive Component Pattern utilizes an existing feature pattern. A Local Component pattern utilizes geometry in the assembly to arrange instances in a Linear or Circular pattern.

Component Properties: The properties of a component, part or assembly are controlled through Component Properties. The Rigid/Flexible Mate State property and Configuration property were explored in this project. Component Properties are used to define visibility and color.

ConfigurationManager: The ConfigurationManager on the left side of the Graphics window is utilized to create, select, and view the configurations of parts and assemblies.

Dome: A Dome feature creates a spherical or elliptical feature from a selected face.

Loft: A Loft feature blends two or more profiles. Each profile is sketched on a separate plane.

Mirror Component: A mirror component creates a mirrored or copied part or assembly. A mirrored component is sometimes called a "right-hand" version of the original "left hand" version.

Replace: The Replace command substitutes one or more open instances of a component in an assembly with a different component.

Revolved Cut: A Revolved Cut removes material. A sketched profile is revolved around a centerline. The Revolved Cut requires a direction and an angle of revolution.

Swept: A Swept feature adds/removes material by moving a profile along a path. A basic Swept feature requires two sketches. The first sketch is called the path. The second sketch is called profile. The profile and path are sketched on perpendicular planes.

Engineering Journal

1. Engineers research, specify and test the components utilized in their designs. The PNEUMATIC TEST MODULE assembly was partially completed in this chapter. Additional pneumatic components are required.

The Regulator utilizes a plastic knob to control the pressure from the Air Reservoir.

Knob

Regulator Assembly
Courtesy of SMC
Corporation of America

The Knob controls the Pressure at P2 by adjusting the screw loading on the setting Spring. The Main valve is held open, allowing flow from the inlet, P1 to the outlet, P2. When the air consumption rate drops, the force at P2 increases. This increase in force causes the Diaphragm to drop maintaining the constant pressure through the valve.

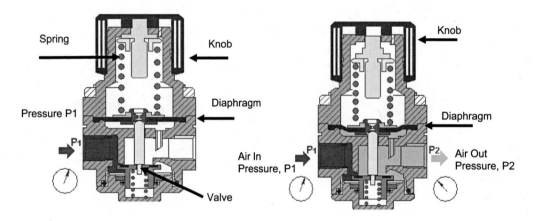

Images Courtesy of SMC Corporation of America

Utilize the internet to research different types of Air Regulators. What design parameters are required for the Regulator before placing an order to purchase one?

_____

_____

_____

2. Pneumatic Applications

Plastic components are utilized in a variety of applications. The ON/OFF/PURGE value utilizes plastic components for the Knob and Inlet and Outlet ports.

The ON/OFF/PURGE valve controls the airflow from the Regulator. The valve knob indiates the direction of flow. The valve is Off when the knob is perpendicular to the direction of flow.

ON/OFF/PURGE Valve
Courtesy of SMC
Corporation of America

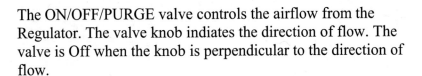
Knob

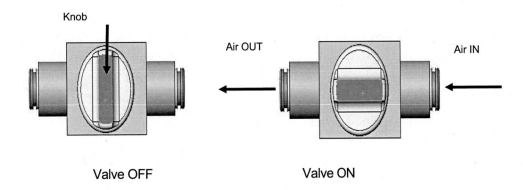
Air OUT   Air IN

Valve OFF   Valve ON

The valve is On when the knob is parallel to the direction of flow.

Write a 2 step operating procedure to instruct your customer how to operate the valve. Indicate the position of the value and the state of the air in each step.

Valve Operating Procedure

1
2

Questions

1. What function does the Save as copy check box perform when saving a part under a new name?

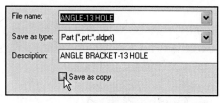

2. True or False. Never reuse geometry from one part to create another part.

3. Describe 5 Assembly techniques utilized in this project.

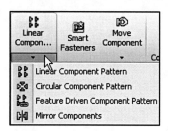

4. True or False. A fixed (f) component cannot move and is locked to the Origin.

5. Describe the purpose of an Assembly Layout diagram.

6. Describe the difference between a Feature Driven Component Pattern and a Linear Component Pattern.

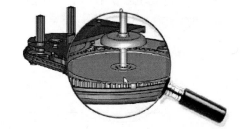

7. Describe the difference between copied geometry and mirrored geometry utilizing the Mirror Components tool.

8. True of False. An assembly contains one or more configurations.

9. Review the Design Intent section in the Introduction. Identify how you incorporated design intent into the assembly.

10. Review the Keyboard Short Cut keys in the Appendix. Identify the Short Cut keys you incorporated into this chapter. What is the g key used for?

Exercises

Exercise 5.1: Regulator-Standoff Assembly

The Regulator assembly is a pneumatic component. The Regulator assembly is available in the pneumtatic component folder or from the Chapter 5 Homework folder which are on the CD in the book.

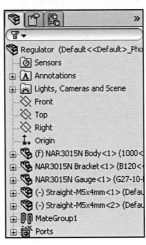

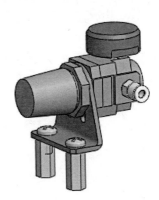

The Regulator assembly cannot be directly fastened to the PNEUMATIC-TEST-MODULE assembly. The slotted holes in the bracket do not fit directly onto the FLAT-PLATE.

- Insert two HEX-STANDOFF parts. Note: Use the View, Temporary Axis option.

- Insert two SCREWs as illustrated.

Exercise 5.2: VALVE-BRACKET Assembly

The ON-OFF-PURGE-VALVE assembly cannot be directly fastened to the FLAT-PLATE.

- Create the Servo-Bracket part on the Top Plane.

The VALVE-BRACKET assembly consists of the ON-OFF-PURGE-VALVE assembly, the Servo-Bracket and two HEX-STANDOFF parts.

The ON-OFF-PURGE VALVE assembly is available in the pneumtatic component folder and the Chapter 5 Homework folder on the Multi-media CD.

- The Servo Bracket Part is machined from 0.09in, [2.7mm] Stainless Steel flat stock.

- The Ø4.2mm, [.165in] Mounting Holes fasten to the back Slot Cuts of the Servo Bracket.

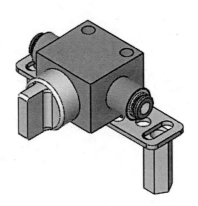

- The Servo-Bracket default units are inches. The Purge-Valve Assembly default units are millimeters.

- Engineers and designers work with components in multiple units such as inches and millimeters. Utilize Tools, Options, Document Properties, Units to check default units and precision.

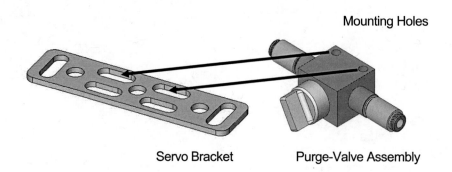

Servo Bracket   Purge-Valve Assembly

The Servo-Bracket Part illustration represents part dimensions, only.

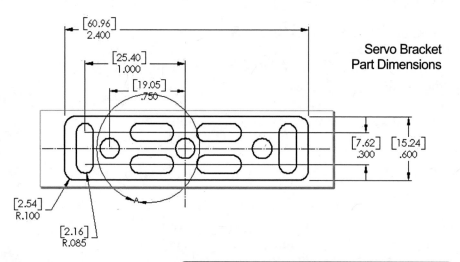

Servo Bracket
Part Dimensions

- Locate the center circle at the part Origin.

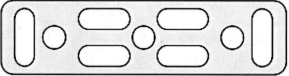

- Utilize a Mirror Feature.

- Utilize a Distance
  Mate to align the
  Mounting Holes
  of the ON-OFF-
  PURGE-VALVE
  Valve to the Slot
  Cuts of the Servo
  Bracket.

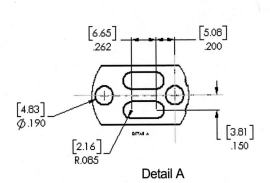

Detail A

The valve knob
indicates the
direction of flow.
The valve is off when the knob is perpendicular to the direction of
flow.

The valve is on when the knob is parallel to the direction of flow.

Review the ON-OFF-PURGE-VALVE Configurations and Mates.
The Angle Mate controls the orientation of the Knob.

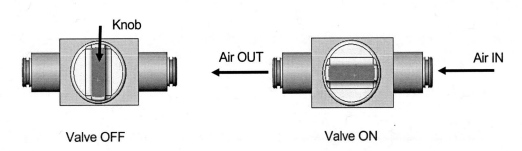

Valve OFF   Valve ON

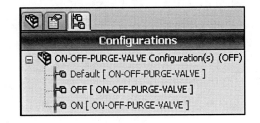

Exercise 5.3: FLATBAR Design Table

Create FLATBAR configurations with a Design Table.

The configurations contain 11, 13, 15, and 17 holes. Note the 0.09in dimension.

	A	B	C	D	E	F	G
1	Design Table for: FLATBAR						
2		D1@Sketch1	D2@Sketch1	D1@Extrude1	D1@Sketch3	D3@LPattern1	D1@LPattern1
3	Default	4.000	0.25	0.09	0.19	0.5	9
4	11HOLE	5.000	0.25	0.09	0.19	0.5	11
5	13HOLE	6.000	0.25	0.09	0.19	0.5	13
6	15HOLE	7.000	0.25	0.09	0.19	0.5	15
7	17HOLE	8.000	0.25	0.09	0.19	0.5	17
8							
9							
10							

Sheet1

Exercise 5.4: SOLENOID-VALVE Assembly and PNEUMATIC-TEST-MODULE Assembly

The 3Way SOLENOID-VALVE utilizes a plastic housing to protect the internal electronic components. The 3Way Solenoid value controls the electrical operation of to the AirCylinder.

The Solenoid acts like a switch. The SOLENOID-VALVE is assembled to the PNEUMATIC-TEST-MODULE with cable ties.

Insert the following components into PNEUMATIC TEST MODULE assembly:

- SOLENOID-VALVE assembly.

- VALVE-BRACKET assembly.

- REGULATOR-STANDOFF assembly.

- WEIGHT-AND-LINK assembly.

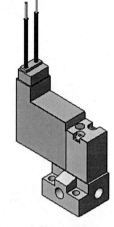

3WAY SOLENOID VALVE
Courtesy of SMC Corporation of America

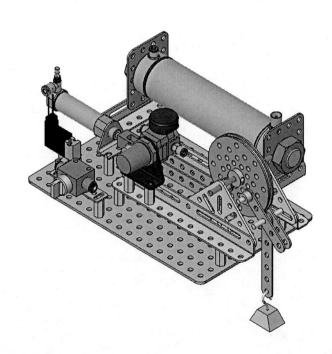

Exercise 5.5: Drive Motor Mount Assembly

Create the Drive Motor Mount Assembly. The Drive Motor
Mount assembly is utilized on a MARS Rover Training
Robot (courtesy of Gears Educational Systems).

Create the Drive Motor Mount assembly from the
components located on the enclosed CD in the book.

Create an Exploded view that represents how the components
would be assembled in manufacturing.

ITEM NO.	PART NUMBER	QTY.
1	4-40_5-8_socket_capsc	8
2	4-40_nut	8
3	90_deg_semi_tube	1
4	4_40_washer	8
5	chamf-1-25_tube	1
6	semi-tube_master4	1
7	pittmam_motor	1
8	hex_axle_adapter	1
9	solid_swivell_arm2	1
10	wheel assembly	1
11	hex_nut	1
12	#10_1.5_cap screw	2
13	#10_nut	2

Exercise 5.6: GEAR-DRIVE Assembly

Create the GEAR-DRIVE assembly.

The DC Motor shaft drives the
36TOOTH-GEAR. The TIRE, WHEEL,
60TOOTH-GEAR parts are all located
on the same axle rod and rotate at the
same angular velocity.

GEAR-DRIVE Assembly
Courtesy of Gears Educational Systems, LLC

The TIRE, 60TOOTH-GEAR,
36TOOTH-GEAR and SHAFT -
PLATE2 parts and BearingPlate-
Bushing assembly are located on the CD
contained with the text.

Copy these components to the SW-
TUTORIAL file folder.

You created the other components in the
projects and exercises.

Design unknowns:

- The AXLE-ROD length required to mount the WHEEL, TIRE and 60TOOTH-GEAR.

- Clearance distance between the 60TOOTH-GEAR and the WHEEL-TIRE assembly.
  Stack multiple LARGE-WASHER parts for the clearance distance.

- Mating Distance between the 36TOOTH-GEAR and the 60TOOTH-GEAR.

Utilize your skills to create the following documents:

- Draw an assembly layout listing all parts, sub-assemblies and assemblies on paper.

- In SolidWorks create a top level assembly and sub-assemblies.

- In SolidWorks create a top level assembly drawing and sub-assembly drawings with
  Bill of Materials.

- In SolidWorks create individual part drawings for machined parts.

- In SolidWorks create exploded view and animation of the GEAR-DRIVE.

Note: Balloons have been enlarged. Actual GearsEds (www.gearseds.com) purchased parts may vary from the model file.

- The IM15-MOUNT PLATE was created in the Chapter 2 exercises.

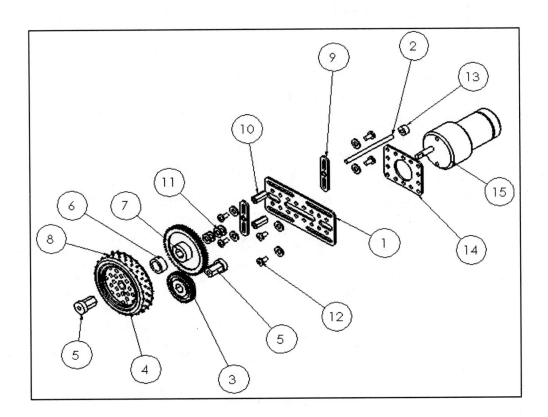

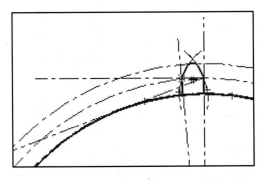

The gears in the assembly utilize imported geometry.

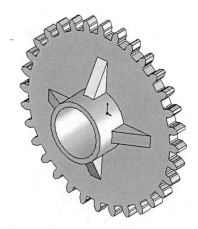

Parts List for GEAR-DRIVE assembly:

ITEM NO.	PART NUMBER:	DESCRIPTION:	QTY:
1	GIDS-SC-10003	SHAFT-PLATE2	1
2	GIDS-SC-10017	AXLE-ROD	1
3	GIDS-SC-60036	36-TOOTH, 24-PITCH GEAR	1
4	GIDS-SC-10014	WHEEL	1
5	GIDS-SC-10013	HEX-ADAPTER	2
6	GIDS-SC-10012-3-16	LARGE-WASHERS	?
7	GIDS-SC-60060	60-TOOTH, 24-PITCH GEAR	1
8	GIDS-SC-10004	TIRE-RUBBER	1
9	GIDS-SC-10010	BEARING PLATE-BUSHING ASM	1
10	GIDS-SC-10015	HEX-STANDOFF	2
11	GIDS-SC-10016-SW	SMALL WASHER ¼ IN	8
12	GIDS-SC-10016-MS	MACHINE SCREW 10-24X3/8	6
13	GIDS-SC-10012-3-16	SMALL SHAFT-COLLAR	1
14	GIDS-SC-10009	IM15-MOUNT PLATE	1
15	GIDS-MC-11515	MOTOR DC	1

Answers will vary. Simplify a large design problem. Create multiple sub-assemblies.

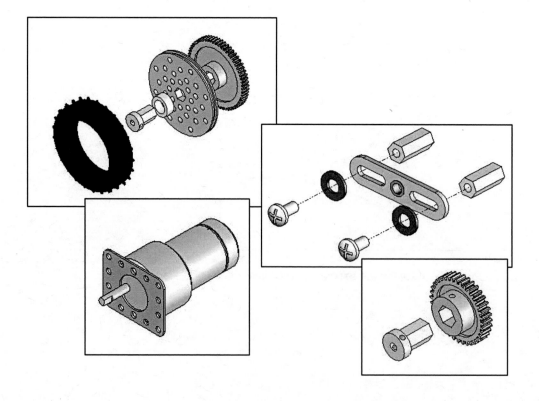

Chapter 6

SolidWorks SimulationXpress, Sustainability and DFMXpress

Below are the desired outcomes and usage competencies based on the completion of Chapter 6.

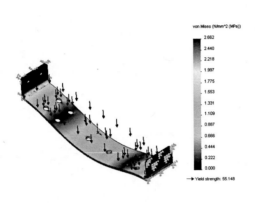

Desired Outcomes:	Usage Competencies:
• Understand and navigate SolidWorks SimulationXpress analysis. • Awareness of SolidWorks SustainabilityXpress. • Knowledge SolidWorks DFMXpress	• Utilize SolidWorks SimulationXpress Wizard. • Apply SolidWorks SimulationXpress to a simple part. • Use SolidWorks SustainabilityXpress. • Display and understand the four environmental impact factors. • Generate a customer report and find suitable alternative materials. • Utilize SolidWorks DFMXpress Wizard.

Notes:

Chapter 6 - SimulationXpress, Sustainabilty and DFMXpress

Chapter Objective

Execute a SolidWorks SimulationXpress analysis on a simple part. Determine if the part can support an applied load under a static load condition.

Perform a SustainabilityXpress analysis on a part. View the environmental impact calculated in four key areas: *Carbon Footprint, Energy Consumption, Air Acidification* and *Water Eutrophication*. Material and Manufacturing process region and Usage region are used as input variables. Compare similar materials and environmental impacts.

Implement DFMXpress on a part. DFMXpress is an analysis tool that validates the manufacturability of SolidWorks parts. Use DFMXpress to identify design areas that may cause problems in fabrication or increase the costs of production.

On the completion of this chapter, you will be able to:

- Implement a SolidWorks SimulationXpress analysis on a simple part.

- Apply SustainabilityXpress to a part.

- View the four key environmental impact areas:
    - o Carbon Emissions
    - o Total Energy Consumed
    - o Air Acidification
    - o Water Eutrophication

- Generate a customer sustainability report and locate suitable alternative materials

- Perform a DFMXpress analysis on a simple part

SolidWorks SimulationXpress

SimulationXpress is a Finite Element Analysis (FEA) tool incorporated into SolidWorks. SimulationXpress calculates the displacement and stress in a part based on material, restraints and static loads.

When loads are applied to a part, the part tries to absorb its effects by developing internal forces. Stress is the intensity of these internal forces. Stress is defined in terms of Force per unit Area: $Stress = \dfrac{f}{A}$.

Different materials have different stress property levels. Mathematical equations derived from Elasticity theory and Strength of Materials are utilized to solve for displacement and stress. These analytical equations solve for displacement and stress for simple cross sections.

Example: Bar or Beam. In complicated parts, a computer based numerical method such as Finite Element Analysis is used.

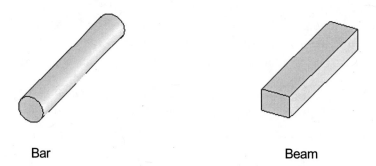

Bar   Beam

SimulationXpress utilizes linear static analysis based on the Finite Element Method. The Finite Element Method is a numerical technique used to analyze engineering designs. FEM divides a large complex model into numerous smaller models. A model is divided into numerous smaller segments called elements.

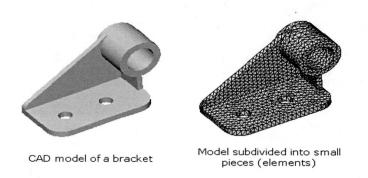

CAD model of a bracket   Model subdivided into small
                                pieces (elements)

SimulationXpress utilizes a tetrahedral element containing 10 nodes. Each node contains a series of equations. SimulationXpress develops the equations governing the behavior of each element. The equations relate displacement to material properties, restraints, "boundary conditions" and applied loads.

SimulationXpress organizes a large set of simultaneous algebraic equations.

The Finite Element Analysis (FEA) equation is:

$[K]\{U\} = \{F\}$ where:

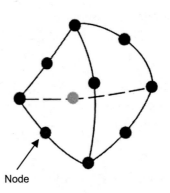

1. [K] is the structural stiffness matrix.

2. {U} is the vector of unknown nodal displacements.

3. {F} is the vector of nodal loads.

Node

SimulationXpress determines the X, Y and Z displacement at each node. This displacement is utilized to calculate strain.

Tetrahedral Element

Strain is defined as the ratio of the change in length, δL to the original length, L.

Stress is proportional to strain in a Linear Elastic Material.

The Elastic Modulus (Young's Modulus) is defined as stress divided by strain.

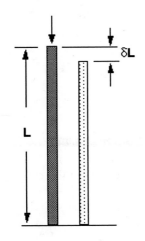

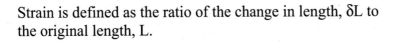

Strain = δ L / L

Compression Force Applied
Original Length L
Change in Length δL

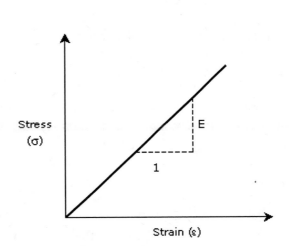

Elastic Modulus is the ratio of Stress to Strain for Linear Elastic Materials.

SimulationXpress determines the stress for each element based on the Elastic Modulus of the material and the calculated strain.

The Stress versus Strain Plot for a Linearly Elastic Material provides information about a material.

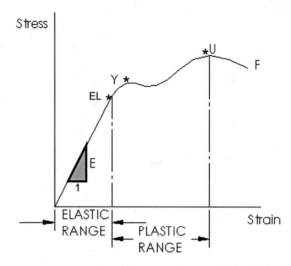

The Elastic Modulus, E is the stress required to cause one unit of strain. The material behaves linearly in the Elastic Range.

The material remains in the Elastic Range until it reaches the elastic limit.

The point EL is the elastic limit. The material begins Plastic deformation.

Stresss versus Strain Plot
Linearly Elastic Material

The point Y is called the Yield Point. The material begins to deform at a faster rate. The material behaves non-linearly in the Plastic Range. The point U is called the ultimate tensile strength. Point U is the maximum value of the non-linear curve. Point U represents the maximum tensile stress a material can handle before a facture or failure. Point F represents where the material will fracture.

Designers utilize maximum and minimum stress calculations to determine if a part is safe. SimulationXpress reports a recommended Factor of Safety during the analysis.

The SimulationXpress Factor of Safety is a ratio between the material strength and the calculated stress.

The von Mises stress is a measure of the stress intensity required for a material to yield. The SimulationXpress Results plot displays von Mises stress.

A Newton is defined as the force acting on a mass of one kilogram at a location where the acceleration due to gravity is 1m/s^2. Weight equals mass * gravity. Weight is a Force.

$$1\ newton = \frac{1\,kg - m}{s^2}$$

The SimulationXpress wizard (located in the Task Pane) steps you through various screens. The screen tabs are:

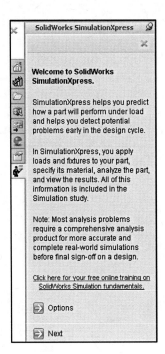

- *Welcome tab*: Informs the user about SolidWorks SimulationXpress. Provides the ability to set units and a save in folder location for the results.

- *Fixtures tab*: Provides the ability to apply fixtures to selected entities of the part. This keeps the part from moving when loads are applied. Faces with fixtures are treated as rigid. This may cause unrealistic results when the fixture is in the vicinity of: Fixed Holes, Fixed vs. Supported and Fixed vs. Attached Parts.

- *Loads tab*: Provides the ability to apply either a force or pressure to the selected entity of the part. Loads are assumed to be uniform and constant when using SimulationXpress.

- *Material tab*: Provides the ability to assign material to the part. SimulationXpress requires that part's material to predict how it will respond to loads. SimulationXpress assumes that the material deforms in a linear fashion with increasing load.

- *Run tab*: Provides the ability to run the simulation and to mesh the study. The results are based on the specified study criterion.

- *Result tab*: Examine the animation of the part's response to verify that the correct loads and fixtures were applied. The Results folder in the SimulationXpress Study displays the following:

  - Stress (-vonMises-)

  - Displacment (-Res disp-)

  - Deformation (-Displacement-)

  - Factor of Safety (-Max von Mises Stress-)

- *Optimize tab*: SimulationXpress can identify the optimal dimension for most features in your SolidWorks model based on your simulation results. This is an optional step.

Run the SimulationXpress wizard: Analyzes the **Bent Bar** part.

Note: Use the model from the SimulationXpress folder located on the CD in the book.

The book is designed to expose the new user to many tools, techniques and procedures. It may not always use the most direct tool or process.

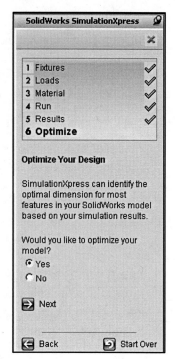

Activity: SolidWorks SimulationXpress - Analyze the Bent Bar

Start a SolidWorks SimulationXpress session.

1) Open the **Bent Bar** part from the SolidWorks 2010/SimulationXpress folder.

2) Click **SimulationXpress Analysis Wizard** from the Evaluate tab. The Welcome box is displayed.

3) Click the **Options** button to select the system units and to specify a save in folder.

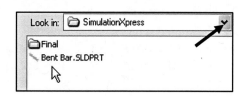

4) Select **SI (MMGS)** for unit system.

5) Select the **Results location** - your file folder.

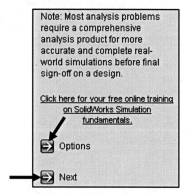

6)   Click **OK** from the SimulationXpress Options dialog box.

Add a Fixture. Fix the part to apply a load.

7)   Click **Next**. Apply fixtures to keep the part from moving.

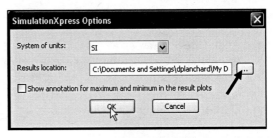

8)   Click **Add a fixture**. The Fixture PropertyManager is displayed.

☀ You can specify multiple sets of fixtures (restraints) for a part. Each set of fixtures can have multiple faces.

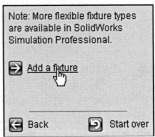

9)   Select the **two illustrated end faces** of the Bent Bar as illustrated. Face1 and Face2 are displayed.

10) Click **OK** ✓ from the Fixture PropertyManager. Fixed-1 is displayed in the Study tree.

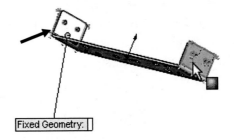

Add a Load (force) to the part.

11) Click **Next**.

12) Click **Add a force**. The Force PropertyManager is displayed.

13) Click **SI** for units.

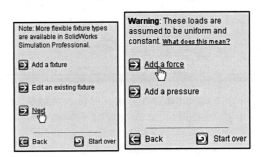

14) Click the **top flat face** of the Bent Bar as illustrated. Note: The edges of the Bent Bar are fixed.

15) The direction of the applied force is displayed. The direction is downward and is normal to the selected face. Enter **5N** for Force Value.

16) Click **OK** ✓ from the Force PropertyManager. Force-1 is displayed in the Study tree. View your options to edit, go back, etc.

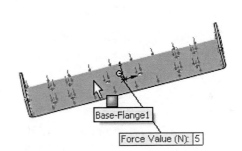

Apply material to the part.

17) Click **Next**.

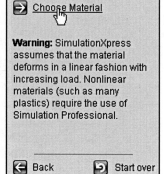

18) Click **Choose Material**. View the Material dialog box. This is the same information available when adding material to a part in SolidWorks.

19) **Expand** the Aluminum Alloys folder.

20) Select **6061 Alloy**. View the available material information.

21) Click **Apply**.

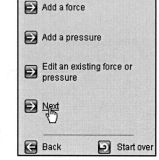

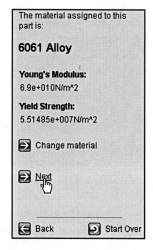

22) Click **Close**. A green check mark is displayed in the Study tree. This indicates that material is applied.

🔆 Brittle materials do not have a specific yield point and hence it is not recommended to use the yield strength to define the limit stress for the criterion.

🔆 You can apply multiple pressures to a single face or to multiple faces. SimulationXpress applies pressure loads normal to each face.

Run the analysis.

23) Click **Next**. View your options. Click **Change settings**. This option provides the ability to modify the element size and element tolerance during the mesh period to analyze the part. The larger the element size and element tolerance, the longer it will take to calculate. Accept the default conditions.

🔆 Specifying a smaller mesh element size provides a more accurate result.

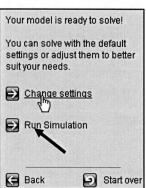

24) Click **Back**.

25) Click **Run Simulation**. View the animation in the Graphics window and the SimulationXpress Study tree. The Results folder displays: *Stress, Displacement, Deformation* and *Factor of Safety*.

26) Click **Stop animation**.

27) **Double-click each folder** (Stress, Displacement, Deformation, and Factor of Safety) in the Results section of the Study tree to view the graph. Explore your options. End viewing the Factor of Safety graph.

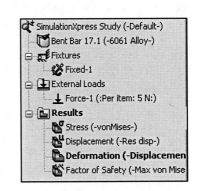

28) Click the **Yes, continue** button. The result is displayed. The Factor of safety for the specified parameters is approximately 20. What does this mean? This indicates that the current design is safe or maybe overdesigned.

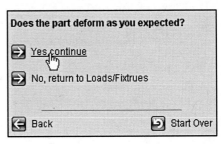

💡 The FOS plot displays in red, where the FOS is less than 1. The plot displays in blue, where the FOS is greater than one.

💡 The Factor of Safety is a ratio between the material strength and the calculated stress.

Interpretation of factor of safety values:

- A factor of safety less than 1.0 at a location indicates that the material at that location has yielded and that the design is not safe.

- A factor of safety of 1.0 at a location indicates that the material at that location has just started to yield.

- A factor of safety greater than 1.0 at a location indicates that the material at that location has not yielded.

- The material at a location will start to yield if you apply new loads equal to the current loads multiplied by the resulting factor of safety.

View the area of the model with a FOS of 3 or below.
29) Enter **3**.

30) Click the **Show where factor of safety (FOS) is below**. View the results. Note: The color red indicates areas below 3.

31) Click **Done Viewing results**.

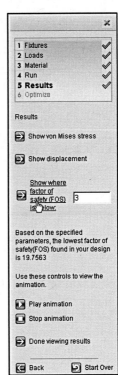

32) There are two kinds of reports that you can generate. As an exercise, generate a report. Click **Next**.

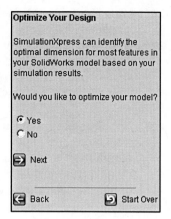

Optimize the model.
33) Check the **Yes** box. Click **Next**. The Add Parameters dialog box and Optimization table is displayed.

Select a Dimension.
34) **Rotate the part** and click the Sheet metal part thickness of **2.5mm** as illustrated.

35) Click **OK** from the Add Parameters dialog. View the updated Optimization table. Accept the Min (1.25mm) and Max (3.75mm) default values.

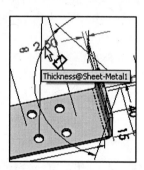

Optimize the model using the Factor of Safety.
36) Click **Next**. View the dialog box.

37) Click **Next**. Set the Constraint in the next step.

38) Click **Specify the constraint**.

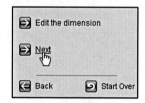

39) Select **Factor of Safety** from the Constraints drop-down menu as illustrated.

40) Accept the default: Is greater than. Enter **6** in the for Min of Factor of Safety box.

41) Click **Next**.

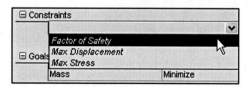

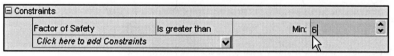

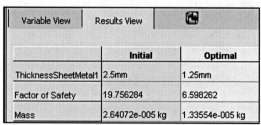

	Initial	Optimal
ThicknessSheetMetal1	2.5mm	1.25mm
Factor of Safety	19.756284	6.598262
Mass	2.64072e-005 kg	1.33554e-005 kg

42) Click **Run the optimization**. Note: This may take 2-3 minutes. View the results. To optimize the value of 1.25mm, the Factor of Safety would be approximately 6. You have the option to select the Initial Value, or to select the Optimal Value.

43) Check the **Optimal Value** box.

44) Click **Next**. The results are now out of date because study parameters have changed. You must rerun the study to update the plot results.

45) Click **Run** in the Wizard window.

46) Re-run the Simulation. Click **Run Simulation**.

The SolidWorks SimulationXpress Wizard window is updated. Generate a HTML report.

47) Click **Generate HTML report**.

48) View your options. **Fill out** the needed fields.

49) **Close** the report.

50) **Save** the part.

51) Click **Sheet-Metal1** in the FeatureManager. View the new updated thickness.

52) **Close** the model.

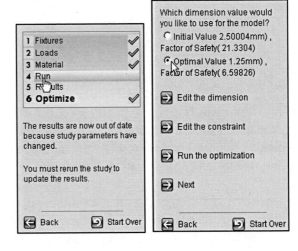

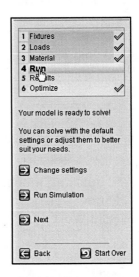

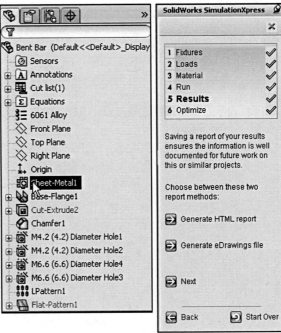

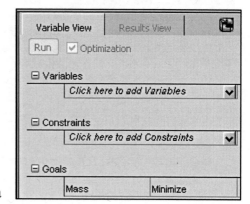

Use the Study Optimization table to select Variables, Constraints and Goals when performing the Optimize procedure in SimuationXpress.

Here are a few tips in performing the analysis. Remember you are dealing with thousands or millions of equations. These tips are a starting point. Every analysis situation is unique.

- Utilize symmetry. If a part is symmetric about a plane, utilize one half of the model for analysis. If a part is symmetric about two planes, utilize one fourth of the model for analysis.

- Suppress small fillets and detailed features in the part.

- Avoid parts that have aspect ratios over 100.

- Utilize consistent units.

- Estimate an intuitive solution based on the fundamentals of stress analysis techniques.

- Factor of Safety is a guideline for the designer. The designer is responsible for the safety of the part.

Additional information on SolidWorks SimulationXpress is located in SolidWorks Help. Additional analysis tools for static, dynamic, thermal and fluid analysis are also available in SolidWorks.

 Review of SolidWorks SimulationXpress

SolidWorks SimulationXpress is a Finite Element tool that calculates stress, displacement and FOS based on Fixtures, Loads, and material on a part. You utilized SolidWorks SimulationXpress to analysis the stress, displacement and FOS on a part.

You assigned the Material to be Aluminum, added fixtures and applied a force of 5Ns. Based on the inputs, the results provided visual representation of displacement and von Mises stress. See SolidWorks Help for additional information.

SolidWorks SustainabilityXpress

Every license of SolidWorks 2010 contains a copy of
SolidWorks SustainabilityXpress. SustainabilityXpress
calculates environmental impact on a model in four key areas:
Carbon Footprint, Energy Consumption, Air Acidification and
Water Eutrophication.

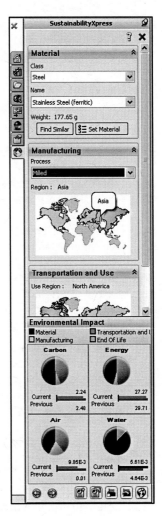

Material and Manufacturing process region and Transportation
Usage region are used as input variables. Two SolidWorks
Sustainability products are available:

- **SolidWorks SustainabilityXpress**: Handles part documents
  and is included in the core software.

- **SolidWorks Sustainability**: Handles parts and assemblies,
  available as a separate product. Other functionality includes
  configuration support, expanded reporting and expanded
  environmental impact options.

SolidWorks Sustainability provides real-time feedback on key
impact factors in the Environmental Impact Dashboard, which
updates dynamically with any changes by the user. You can
generate customize reports to share the results.

Run SustainabilityXpress and analyzes a simple part. Display
the four environmental impact factors, view suitable alternative
materials, compare their environmental impact factors and
generate a customer report.

Activity: SolidWorks SustainabilityXpress - Analyze the CLAMP Part

Close all documents.
53)   Click **Window**, **Close All** from the Menu bar.

Open the CLAMP part.
54)   Open the CLAMP part from the **SolidWorks 2010\
SustainabilityXpress** folder. The CLAMP FeatureManager is
displayed. Note: The folder is located on the CD in the book.
Copy all models to your local hard drive.

Activate SustainabilityXpress.

55) Click **Tools**, **SustainabilityXpress** from the Main menu. SustainabilityXpress is displayed in the Task Pane area.

Select Material Class.

56) Select **Steel** from the drop-down menu.

Select Material Name.

57) Select **Stainless Steel (ferritic)** from the drop-down menu.

Select Manufacturing Process.

58) Select **Milled** from the drop-down menu.

Select the Manufacturing Region.

59) Accept the default setting: **Asia**.

Select the Transportation and Usage region.

60) Accept the default setting: **North America**.

Set the Baseline for your design.

61) Click the **Set Baseline** tool from the bottom of the Environmental Impact screen. The Environmental Impact of this part is displayed. The Environmental Impact is calculated in four key areas: *Carbon Footprint, Energy Consumption, Air Acidification* and *Water Eutrophication*.

62) Click inside the **Carbon** box to display a Baseline bar chart of the Carbon Footprint.

63) Click the **right arrow** to move to the next (Energy Consumption) impact screen to display a Baseline bar chart.

64) Click the **right arrow** to move to the next (Air Acidification) impact screen to display a Baseline bar chart.

65) Click the **right arrow** to move to the next (Water Eutrophication) impact screen to display a Baseline bar chart.

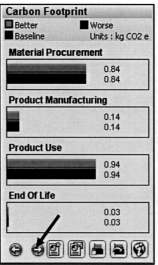

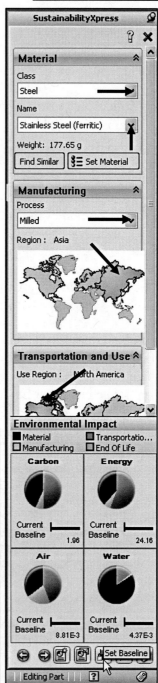

Return to the Baseline screen.
66) Click the **right arrow** to move to back to the original impact screen.

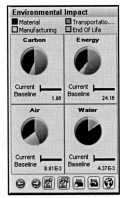

In the next section, compare the baseline design to a different design so you can determine if you can make a meaningful design change. Let's compare the present material Stainless Steel (ferritic) to Nylon 6/10.

Select a new Material Class.
67) Select **Plastic** from the drop-down menu.

Select a new Material Name.
68) Select **Nylon 6/10** from the drop-down menu.

Select new Manufacturing Process.
69) Select Injection Molded.

Select the Manufacturing Region.
70) Accept the default setting: **Asia**.

Select the Transportation and Usage region.
71) Accept the default setting: **United States**.

View the results. Changing the material from Stainless Steel to Nylon 6/10 and the manufacturing process from milled to injection molded had a positive environmental impact in all four categories, but a further material change may provide a better results!

72) Click **inside each** of the environmental categories to view the results. Return to the default Baseline Impact screen.

Fine a similar material and compare the Environmental Impact to Nylon 6/10.
73) Click the **Find Similar Material** button as illustrated. The Find Similar Material dialog box is displayed.

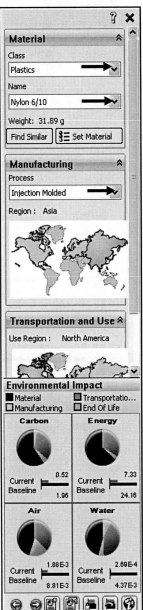

74) Click the **Value (-any-)** drop-down arrow.

75) Select **Plastic.** At this time, you can perform a general search or customize your search on physical properties of the material.

76) Click the **Find Similar** button as illustrated. SolidWorks provides a full list of comparable materials that you can further refine.

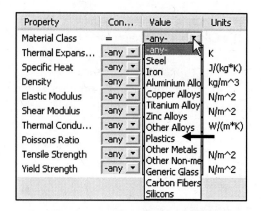

Select a Similar Material from the provided list.
77) Check the **ABS PC** box.

78) Check the **Nylon 101** box.

79) Check the **PE High Density** box.

80) Click **inside the top left box** as illustrated. The selected materials are displayed.

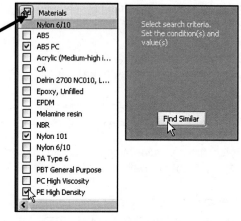

View the Environment Impact for the alternative materials.
81) Click the **ABS PC** material row as illustrated. View the results. The material is lower in Carbon Footprint, Energy Consumption, and Water Eutrophication, but higher in Air Acidification.

82) Click the **Nylon 101** material row. View the results. The material is lower in Carbon Footprint, Air Acidification and Water Eutrophication, but higher in Energy Consumption.

83) Click the **PE High Density** material row. View the results. The material is lower in Carbon Footprint, Energy Consumption, and Water Eutrophication, but is higher in Air Acidification. You decide to stay with Nylon 6/10.

84) Click the **Cancel** button from the Find Similar Material dialog box.

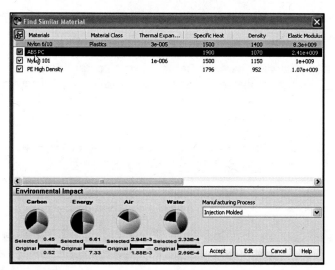

Run a Report.

85) Click the **Generate Report** button as illustrated. SolidWorks provides the ability to communicate this report information throughout your organization. SustainabilityXpress generates a report that will compare designs (material, regions) and explain each category of Environmental Impact and show how each design compares.

86) **Review** the Generated report.

Inside the generated report, access the Sustainability calculator by clicking the link at the bottom of page 2. Your results will be presented in the savings to the environment.

87) **Close** the report. **Close** the CLAMP part.

Review of SolidWorks SustainabilityXpress

Every license of SolidWorks 2010 contains a copy of SolidWorks SustainabilityXpress. SustainabilityXpress calculates environmental impact on a model in four key areas: *Carbon Footprint*, *Energy Consumption*, *Air Acidification* and *Water Eutrophication*.

Material and Manufacturing process region and Transportation Usage region are used as input variables.

You ran a SolidWorks SustainabilityXpress analysis on a simple part. You applied material, manufacturing process and selected the manufacturing process region and the part transportation and usage region.

You then viewed the environmental impact of your design. You viewed suitable alternative materials, re-ran the environmental impact study and compared their environmental impact factors in all four categories. A customer report was generated.

SolidWorks DFMXpress

DFMXpress is an analysis tool that validates the manufacturability of SolidWorks parts. Use DFMXpress to identify design areas that may cause problems in fabrication or increase the costs of production.

The DFMXpress tool uses a Wizard. Run the DFMXpress Wizard. Analysis a simple part. View the results.

Activity: SolidWorks DFMXpress - Analyze the AXLE and ROD Part

Close all documents.
88) Click **Window**, **Close All** from the Menu bar.

Open the AXLE part.
89) Open the AXLE part from the **ENGDESIGN-W-SOLIDWORKS\DFMXpress** folder. The AXLE FeatureManager is displayed. Note: The folder is located on the CD in the book. Copy all models to your local hard drive.

Activate DFMXpress.
90) Click **Tools**, **DFMXpress**. View the DFMXpress wizard in the Task Pane location.

91) Click the **Settings** button. View the optional settings in DFMXpress.

92) Click the **Back** button to return to the Main menu.

Run the DFMXpress wizard on the AXLE part.
93) Click the **Run** button.

94) **Expand** each folder. View the results.

95) Click on each **red check mark**. The hole in the AXLE was created with an Extruded Cut feature (failed due to flat bottom). Use the Hole Wizard to create holes for Manufacturing. Use caution for depth to diameter ratio.

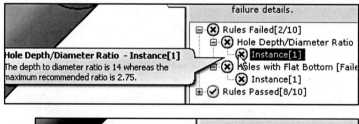

96) Click on each **green check mark**. Review the information. This is a very useful tool to use for manufacturing guidelines.

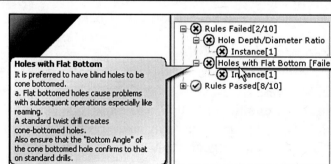

Close the DFMXpress Wizard.
97) Click the **Close** button.

Open the ROD part.

98) Open the ROD part from the **ENGDESIGN-W-SOLIDWORKS\DFMXpress** folder. The ROD FeatureManager is displayed. Note: The folder is located on the CD in the book. Copy all models to your local hard drive.

Activate DFMXpress.

99) Click **Tools**, **DFMXpress**. View the DFMXpress wizard in the Task Pane location.

Run the DFMXpress wizard on the AXLE part.

100) Click the **Run** button.

101) Expand each folder. View the results.

102) Click on each **red check mark**. The hole in the ROD was created using the Hole Wizard feature. Use caution for depth to diameter ratio.

103) Click on each **green check mark**. Review the information. This is a very useful tool to use for manufacturing guidelines.

Close the DFMXpress Wizard.

104) Click the **Close** button.

105) Close all models.

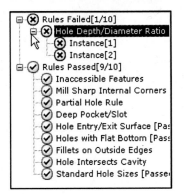

 Review the DFMXpress Wizard

DFMXpress is an analysis tool that validates the manufacturability of SolidWorks parts. Use DFMXpress to identify design areas that may cause problems in fabrication or increase the costs of production.

The DFMXpress tool uses a Wizard. Run the DFMXpress Wizard. Analysis a simple part. View the results.

Chapter Summary

You performed a SolidWorks SimulationXpress analysis on a simple part with a Force load. You applied material, set loads and fixtures. Run the optimization tool as an exercise.

You then applied SolidWorks SustainabiityXpress to a simple part. Every license of SolidWorks 2010 contains a copy of SolidWorks SustainabilityXpress.

SustainabilityXpress calculates environmental impact on a model in four key areas: *Carbon Footprint*, *Energy Consumption*, *Air Acidification* and *Water Eutrophication*.

Material and Manufacturing process region and Transportation Usage region are used as input variables.

You applied material, manufacturing process and selected the manufacturing process region and the part transportation and usage region. You then viewed the environmental impact of your design.

You viewed suitable alternative materials, re-ran the environmental impact study and compared their environmental impact factors in all four categories. A customer report was generated.

You used DFMXpress to identify design areas that may cause problems in fabrication or increase the costs of production. The DFMXpress tool uses a Wizard.

Chapter 7
Basic Theory and Drawing Theory

Introduction

SolidWorks Corporation offers various levels of certification representing increasing levels of expertise in 3D CAD design as it applies to engineering: Certified SolidWorks Associate CSWA and the Certified SolidWorks Professional CSWP along with specialty fields in Sheet Metal, Surfacing and FEA.

The CSWA certification indicates a foundation in and apprentice knowledge of 3D CAD design and engineering practices and principles. The main requirement for obtaining the CSWA certification is to take and pass the three hour, seven question on-line proctored exam at a Certified SolidWorks CSWA Provider and to sign the SolidWorks Confidentiality Agreement. Passing this exam provides students the chance to prove their knowledge and expertise and to be part of a worldwide industry certification standard!

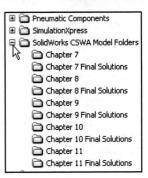

FeatureManager names were changed from 2009 to 2010. Example: Extrude1 vs. Boss-Extrude1. These changes will not affect the models or answers in this book.

Goals

The primary goal of the next five chapters is not only to help you pass the CSWA exam, but also to ensure that you understand and comprehend the concepts and implementation details of the CSWA process.

The second goal is to provide the most comprehensive coverage of CSWA exam related topics available, without too much coverage of topics not on the exam.

The third and ultimate goal is to get you from where you are today to the point that you can confidently pass the CSWA exam.

Objectives

Drawing Theory is one of the five categories on the CSWA exam. This chapter covers the general concepts, symbols and terminology (Basic Theory) and then the core element (Drawing Theory) which is aligned to the CSWA exam.

There are two questions on the CSWA exam in the Drawing Theory category. Each question is worth five (5) points. The two questions are in a multiple choice single answer format.

In the Drawing Theory category of the exam, you are not required to perform an analysis on a part, assembly, or drawing but you are required to have general drawing knowledge and understanding of drawing view methods.

On the completion of the chapter, you will be able to:

- Recognize 3D modeling techniques:

- Identify and understand the procedure for the following:

  - Assign and edit material to a part, Apply the Measure tool to a part or an assembly, Locate the Center of mass, and Principal moments of inertia relative to the default coordinate location, and Origin.

- Calculate the overall mass and volume of a part

- Identify the process of creating a simple drawing from a part or an assembly

- Identify the procedure to create a named drawing view

- Specify Document Properties: Select Unit System, and Set Precision

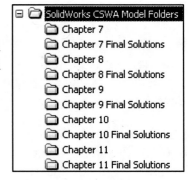

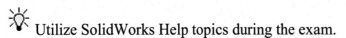 In Simple Part Modeling, Advanced Part Modeling and Assembly Modeling categories, you are required to read and interpret all types of drawing views.

Utilize SolidWorks Help topics during the exam.

Identify the correct reference planes: Top, Right and Front

Most SolidWorks features start with a 2D sketch. Sketches are the foundation for creating features. SolidWorks provides the ability to create either 2D or 3D sketches.

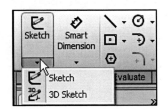

A 2D sketch is limited to a flat 2D Sketch plane. A 3D sketch can include 3D elements. As you create a 3D sketch, the entities in the sketch exist in 3D space. They are not related to a specific Sketch plane as they are in a 2D sketch.

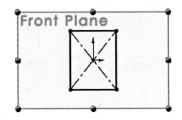

🔆 You may need to create a 3D sketch on the exam. The illustrated model displays a 3D sketch, using the Sketch Line tool for an Extruded Cut feature. You will create a 3D sketch in Chapter 3.

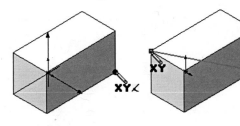
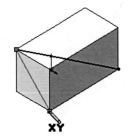
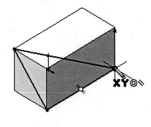

Does it matter where you start sketching a 2D sketch? Yes! When you create a new part or assembly, the three default planes (Front, Right and Top) are aligned with specific views.

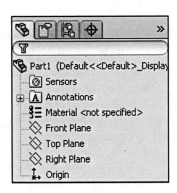

The plane you select for your first sketch determines the orientation of the part. Selecting the correct plane is very important.

🔆 When you create a new part or assembly, the three default planes (Front, Right and Top) are aligned with specific views. The plane you select for the Base sketch determines the orientation of the part.

Identify material, measure, and mass properties

Understand the process and procedure of the following:

- Assign and edit material to a part

- Apply the Measure tool to a part or assembly

- Locate the Center of mass, and Principal moments of inertia relative to the default coordinate location, Origin.

- Calculate the overall mass and volume of a part

Assign and edit material

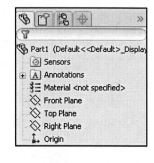

Use the Material dialog box to assign or edit material in a part. Material is required to calculate the correct Mass Properties of a part or an assembly. You will need this knowledge in the exam.

The Material icon $\xi\equiv$ is displayed in the FeatureManager regardless of whether a material is applied. Right-click the icon to view a list of the ten most recently used materials.

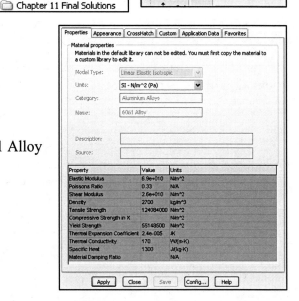

Tutorial: Assign and edit material 7-1

Assign material to the Machine Screw part.

1. **Open** the Machine Screw part from the SolidWorks CSWA Model Folders\Chapter 7 location.

2. **Assign** 6061 Alloy to the part.

3. **View** the available materials.

4. **View** the physical properties of the 6061 Alloy in the Physical Properties box.

5. **Close** the model.

Know the available default materials and their location.

Question 1: Identify the material category for 6061 Alloy.

- A: Steel

- B: Iron

- C: Aluminum Alloys

- D: Other Alloys

- E: None of the provided

The correct answer is C.

Tutorial: Assign and edit material 7-2

Edit the material for the Hook-1 part.

1. **Open** the Hook-1 part from the SolidWorks CSWA Model Folders\Chapter 7 location.

2. **Edit** the material from 2014 Alloy to 6061 Alloy.

3. **Close** the model.

Measure tool

The Measure tool measures distance, angle, radius, and size of and between lines, points, surfaces, and planes in sketches, 3D models, assemblies, or drawings.

When you measure the distance between two entities, the delta X, Y and Z distances can be displayed. When you select a vertex or sketch point, the X, Y and Z coordinates are displayed.

Activate the Measure tool from the Evaluate tab in the CommandManager or click **Tools**, **Measure** from the Menu bar menu.

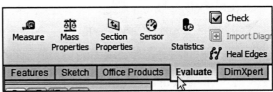

Select the Units/Precision option to specify custom measurement units and precision for your model.

Tutorial: Measure tool 7-1

1. **Open** the Gear-Holder-1 part from the SolidWorks CSWA Model Folders\Chapter 7 location.

Activate the Measure dialog box.

2. Click the **Measure** tool from the Evaluate tab. The Measure dialog box is displayed.

3. **Measure** the overall length of the Holder. Select the two edges as illustrated.

4. **Close** the Measure dialog box.

5. **Close** the model.

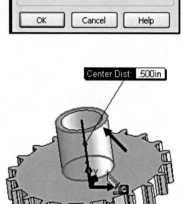

Tutorial: Measure tool 7-2

1. **Open** the Collar part from the SolidWorks CSWA Model Folders\Chapter 7 location.

Activate the Measure dialog box.

2. Click the **Measure** tool from the Evaluate tab. The Measure dialog box is displayed.

3. **Measure** the inside diameter of the Collar. Select the inside circular edge as illustrated. The inside diameter = .650in. Length = 2.042in.

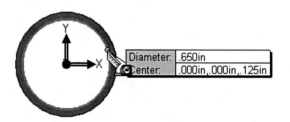

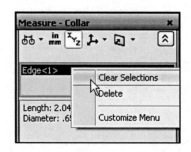

4. **Clear** all selections in the Measure - Collar dialog box.

Measure the inside area, perimeter, and diameter of the Collar.

5. Click the **inside face** as illustrated. View the results.

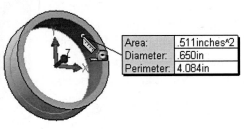

Area: .511 inches^2
Perimeter: 4.084in
Diameter: .650in

Area:	.511inches^2
Diameter:	.650in
Perimeter:	4.084in

6. **Clear** all selections.

7. **Close** the Measure dialog box.

8. **Close** the model.

Locate the Center of mass, and Principal moments of inertia relative to the default coordinate location

The Mass Properties tool displays the mass properties of a part or assembly model, or the section properties of faces or sketches.

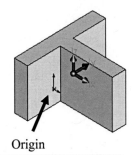

Origin

The results are displayed in the Mass Properties dialog box. The principal axes and Center of mass are displayed graphically on the model in the Graphics window.

On the CSWA exam, you may see the word centroid. What is a centroid? Let's view a simple example of a triangle. In the plane of any triangle ABC, let:

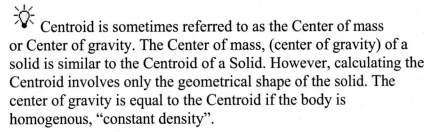

- D = midpoint of side BC
- E = midpoint of side CA
- F = midpoint of side AB

From the sketch, the lines AD, BE, CF come together to a single point. This point is called the centroid of the triangle ABC. There are many other points that are called triangle centers, but unlike most of them, "centroid" works on arbitrary shapes.

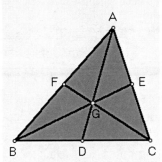

Centroid is sometimes referred to as the Center of mass or Center of gravity. The Center of mass, (center of gravity) of a solid is similar to the Centroid of a Solid. However, calculating the Centroid involves only the geometrical shape of the solid. The center of gravity is equal to the Centroid if the body is homogenous, "constant density".

Tutorial: Mass Properties 7-1

Use the Mass Properties tool to calculate the density, mass, volume, surface area, and Center of mass for a part relative to the default coordinate location.

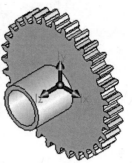

1. **Open** the Gear-Mass part from the SolidWorks CSWA Model Folders\Chapter 7 location. 6061 Alloy is the applied material.

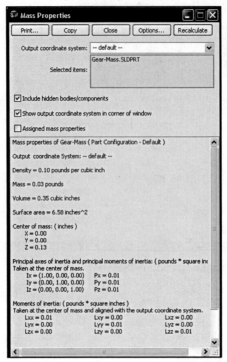

Activate the Mass Properties dialog box.

2. Click the **Mass Properties** tool from the Evaluate tab in the CommandManager. The Mass Properties dialog box is displayed. View the various Mass Properties of the Gear-Mass part.

3. **Close** the Mass Properties dialog box.

4. **Close** the model.

By default, the Centroid is relative to the part or assembly default coordinate location.

View the Center of mass based on the default part Origin location. The density, mass, volume, surface area, Center of mass, Principal axes of inertia and principal moments of inertia, and Moments of inertia are displayed.

To evaluate components or solid bodies in an assembly or multi-body part documents, click the **component** or **body**, and click **Recalculate**. If no component or solid body is selected, the mass properties for the entire assembly or multi-body part are reported.

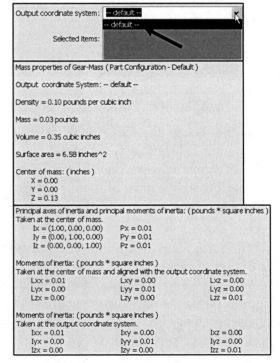

Tutorial: Mass Properties 7-2

Calculate the density, overall mass, volume, surface area, and Center of mass for an assembly relative to the default coordinate location.

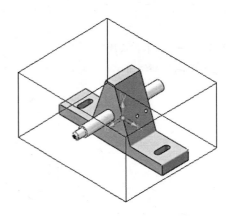

1. **Open** the Wedge-Tube-Mass assembly from the SolidWorks CSWA Model Folders\Chapter 7 location.

Activate the Mass Properties dialog box.

2. Click the **Mass Properties** tool from the Evaluate tab. The Mass Properties dialog box is displayed. The Centroid is displayed relative to default assembly Origin. The density, volume, surface area, moments of inertia, etc. are displayed in the Mass Properties dialog box.

Obtain the Mass Properties of the Tube component in the Wedge-Tube-Mass assembly.

3. **Clear** all selected items.

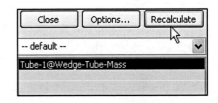

4. Click **Tube** from the FeatureManager. Tube-1 is displayed in the Selected items box.

5. Click **Recalculate** from the Mass Properties dialog box.

6. **View** the Tube properties. The Centroid location is relative to Tube part Origin.

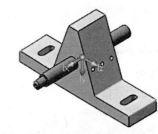

7. **Close** the Mass Properties dialog box.

8. **Close** the model.

You will require this knowledge in the Assembly Modeling category of the CSWA exam.

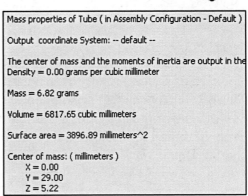

Mass properties of Tube (in Assembly Configuration - Default)

Output coordinate System: -- default --

The center of mass and the moments of inertia are output in the
Density = 0.00 grams per cubic millimeter

Mass = 6.82 grams

Volume = 6817.65 cubic millimeters

Surface area = 3896.89 millimeters^2

Center of mass: (millimeters)
    X = 0.00
    Y = 29.00
    Z = 5.22

Procedure to create a Named Drawing view

You need the ability to identify the procedure to create a named drawing view: *Standard 3 View, Model View, Projected View, Auxiliary View, Section View, Aligned Section View, Detail View, Broken-out Section, Break, Crop View and Alternate Position View.*

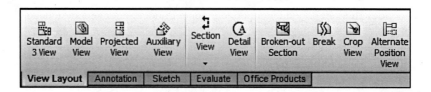

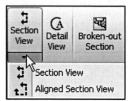

Create a Section view in a drawing by cutting the parent view with a section line. The section view can be a straight cut section or an offset section defined by a stepped section line. The section line can also include concentric arcs.

Create an Aligned section view in a drawing through a model, or portion of a model, that is aligned with a selected section line segment. The Aligned Section view is similar to a Section View, but the section line for an aligned section comprises two or more lines connected at an angle.

Create a Detail view in a drawing to show a portion of a view, usually at an enlarged scale. This detail may be of an orthographic view, a non-planar (isometric) view, a section view, a crop view, an exploded assembly view, or another detail view.

Crop any drawing view except a Detail view, a view from which a Detail view has been created, or an Exploded view. To create a Crop view, sketch a closed profile such as a circle or spline. The view outside the closed profile disappears as illustrated.

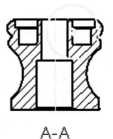

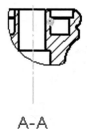

Create a Detail view in a drawing to display a portion of a view, usually at an enlarged scale. This detail may be of an orthographic view, a non-planar (isometric) view, a Section view, a Crop view, an Exploded assembly view, or another Detail view.

A-A

A-A

Tutorial: Drawing Named Procedure 7-1

Identify the drawing name view and understand the procedure to create the name view.

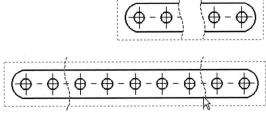

1. **View** the illustrated drawing views. The top drawing view is a Break view. The Break view is created by adding a break line to a selected view.

☀ Broken views make it possible to display the drawing view in a larger scale on a smaller size drawing sheet. Reference dimensions and model dimensions associated with the broken area reflect the actual model values.

☀ In views with multiple breaks, the Break line style must be the same.

Tutorial: Drawing Named Procedure 7-2

Identify the drawing name view and understand the procedure to create the name view.

1. **View** the illustrated drawing views. The right drawing view is a Section View. The Section view is created by cutting the parent view with a cutting section line.

☀ Create a Section view in a drawing by cutting the parent view with a section line. The section view can be a straight cut section or an offset section defined by a stepped section line. The section line can also include Concentric arcs.

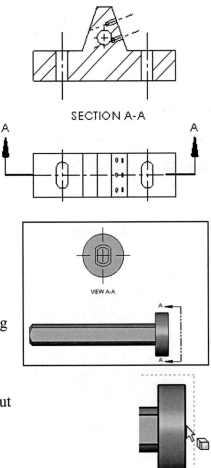

Tutorial: Drawing Named Procedure 7-3

Identify the drawing name view and understand the procedure to create the name view.

1. **View** the illustrated drawing views. The Top drawing view is an Auxilary view of the Front view. Select a reference edge to create an Auxiliary view.

☀ An Auxiliary view is similar to a Projected view, but it is unfolded normal to a reference edge in an existing view.

Tutorial: Drawing Named Procedure 7-4

Identify the drawing name view and understand the procedure to create the name view.

1. **View** the illustrated drawing views. The right drawing view is an Aligned Section view of the bottom view. The Section view is created by using two lines connected at an angle. Create an Aligned Section view in a drawing through a model, or portion of a model, that is aligned with a selected section line segment.

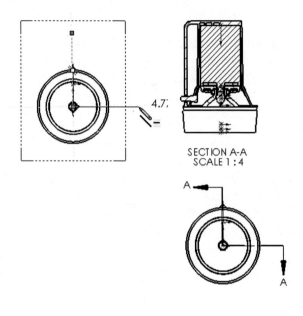

SECTION A-A
SCALE 1 : 4

🔆 The Aligned Section view is very similar to a Section View, with the exception that the section line for an aligned section comprises of two or more lines connected at an angle.

Tutorial: Drawing Named Procedure 7-5

Identify the drawing name view and understand the procedure to create the name view.

1. **View** the illustrated drawing views. The left drawing view is a Detail view of the Section view. The Detail view is created by sketching a circle with the Circle Sketch tool. Click and drag for the location.

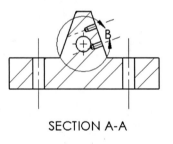

SECTION A-A

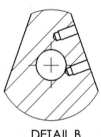

DETAIL B
SCALE 1 : 1

🔆 The Detail view Ⓐ tool provides the ability to add a Detail view to display a portion of a view, usually at an enlarged scale.

🔆 To create a profile other than a circle, sketch the profile before clicking the Detail view tool. Using a sketch entity tool, create a closed profile around the area to be detailed.

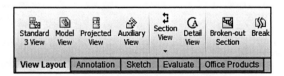

Tutorial: Drawing Named Procedure 7-6

Identify the drawing name view and understand the procedure to create the name view.

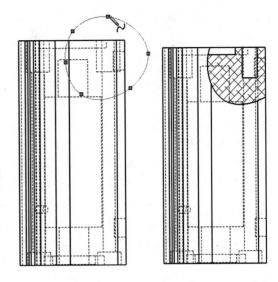

1. **View** the illustrated drawing views. The right drawing view is a Broken-out Section view. The Broken-out Section View is part of an existing drawing view, not a separate view. Create the Broken-out Section view with a closed profile, usually by using the Spline Sketch tool. Material is remove to a specified depth to expose inner details.

Tutorial: Drawing Named Procedure 7-7

Identify the drawing name view and understand the procedure to create the name view.

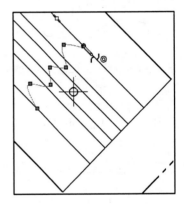

1. **View** the illustrated drawing view. The top drawing view is a Crop view. The Crop view is created by a closed sketch profile such as a circle, or spline as illustrated.

The Crop View provides the ability to crop an existing drawing view. You can not use the Crop tool on a Detail view, a view from which a Detail view has been created, or an Exploded view.

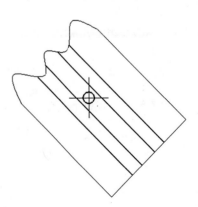

☼ Use the Crop tool to save steps. Example: instead of creating a Section View and then a Detail view, then hiding the unnecessary Section view, use the Crop tool to crop the Section view directly.

Tutorial: Drawing Named Procedure 7-8

Identify the drawing name view and understand the procedure to create the name view.

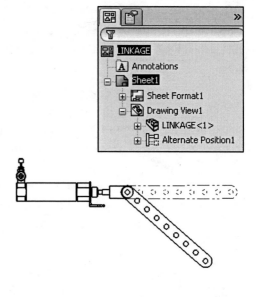

1. **View** the illustrated drawing view. The drawing view is an Alternate Position View.

   The Alternate Position view tool ⊞ provides the ability to superimpose an existing drawing view precisely on another. The alternate position is displayed with phantom lines.

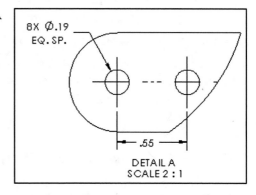

☀ Use the Alternate Position view is display the range of motion of an assembly. You can dimension between the primary view and the Alternate Position view. You can not use the Alternate Position view tool with Broken, Section, or Detail views.

Engineering Documentation Practices

A 2D drawing view is displayed in the Advanced Part and Assembly modeling section of the CSWA exam to clarify dimensions and details.

The ability to interpret the 2D drawing views is required.

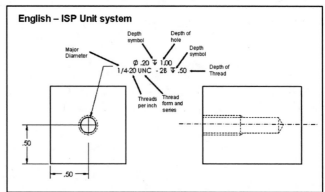

- Example 1: The provided 2D detail drawing view illustrates that eight holes are required. The hole diameters are .19. The equal spacing between the holes is .55. Note: units are provided in the CSWA exam problem.

- Example 2: Hole Wizard hole callout annotation. Note: the symbol for depth.

- Example 3: Hole Wizard hole
  callout annotation. Note: The
  symbol for C Bore.

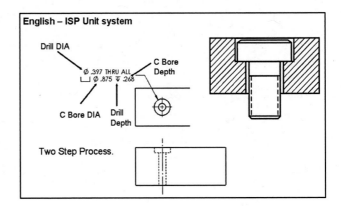

Document Properties

You need the ability to identify the
procedure to select system units and
precision of a SolidWorks model using
the Document Properties section.
Access the Document Properties tab
from the Options tool located in the
Menu bar toolbar.

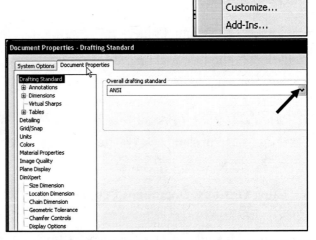

You are required to set the
precision for the selected unit system
and to set the Tolerance / Precision
using the Dimension PropertyManager
or the Document Properties dialog
box.

Document properties apply to the current
document. The Document Properties tab is
only available when a document is open.

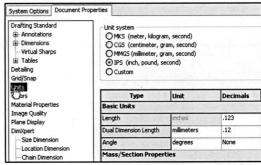

New documents get their document settings
(such as Units, Image Quality, etc.) from the
document properties of the template used to
create the document.

Know how to set the Unit system, and Tolerance/Precision option in a document for the CSWA exam.

Tutorial: Document Properties 7-1

Set dimensioning (drafting) standard, system units, and precision.

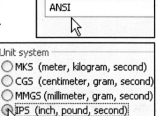

1. **Create** a New part in SolidWorks.

2. Click **Options**, **Document Properties** tab from the Menu bar toolbar.

3. Select **ANSI** for Dimensioning (drafting) overall standard.

4. Click **Units**.

5. Select **IPS** for Unit system.

6. Select **.123** Decimal places for Length units.

7. Select **None** Decimal places for Angular units.

8. **Close** the part.

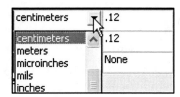

Type	Unit	Decimals
Basic Units		
Length	inches	.123
Dual Dimension Length	inches	.12
Angle	degrees	None

Tutorial: Document Properties 7-2

Set dimensioning standard, system units, and precision.

1. **Create** a New part in SolidWorks.

2. Click **Options**, **Document Properties** tab from the Menu bar menu.

3. Select **ANSI** for Dimensioning (drafting) standard.

4. Select **Units**.

5. Click **Custom** for Unit system.

6. Select **centimeters** from the length units drop down box.

7. Select **.12** Decimal places for Length units.

8. Select **None** Decimal places for Angular units.

9. **Close** the part.

Chapter Summary

Drawing Theory is one of the five categories on the CSWA exam. In this chapter, you covered general concepts, symbols, and terminology and then the core element (Drawing Theory) that is aligned to the CSWA exam.

There are two questions on the CSWA exam in this category. Each question is worth five (5) points. The two questions are in a multiple choice single answer format.

Spend no more than 10 minutes on each question in this category. This is a timed exam. Manage your time.

Simple Part Modeling is the next chapter in this book. This chapter covers the knowledge to identify the part Origin, design intent, and key features to create a simple part from a detailed dimensioned illustration.

The complexity of the models along with the features progressively increases throughout the chapter to simulate the final types of parts that could be provided on the CSWA exam.

There is one question on the CSWA exam in the Simple Part Modeling category. The question is worth thirty (30) points. You are required to create a model, with six or more features and to answer a question either on the overall mass, volume or the location of the Center of mass relative to part Origin.

☼ No PhotoWorks, Motion Study, Display Pane, or assembly configuration questions on the CSWA exam as this time.

☼ View sample screen shots from an older CSWA exam for a Drawing Theory question at the end of the Homework section in this chapter.

Questions

1. Identify the following Drawing view icon .

- A: Projected view
- B: Trim view
- C: Cut view
- D: Crop view

2. Identify the following Drawing View icon **t.¹**.

- A: Section view
- B: Broken view
- C: Break view
- D: Aligned Section view

3. Identify the following Drawing view icon .

- A: Projected view
- B: Standard 3 view
- C: Break view
- D: Aligned Section view

4. Identify the illustrated Drawing view.

- A: Projected view
- B: Alternative Position view
- C: Extended view
- D: Aligned Section view

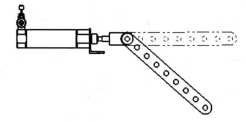

5. Identify the illustrated Drawing view.

- A: Crop view
- B: Break view
- C: Broken-out Section view
- D: Aligned Section view

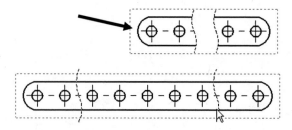

6. Identify the illustrated Drawing view.

- A: Section view

- B: Crop view

- C: Broken-out Section view

- D: Aligned Section view

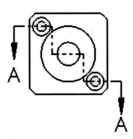

7. Identify the view procedure. To create the following view, you need to insert a:

- A: Rectangle Sketch tool

- B: Closed Profile: Spline

- C: Open Profile: Circle

- D: None of the above

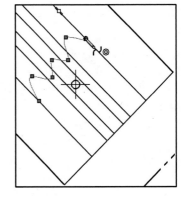

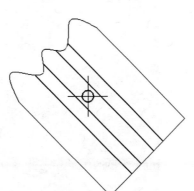

8. Identify the view procedure. To create the following view, you need to insert a:

- A: Open Spline

- B: Closed Spline

- C: 3 Point Arc

- D: None of the above

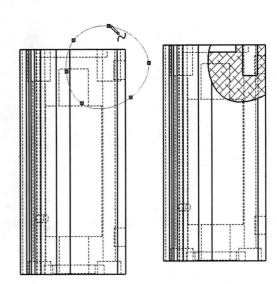

9. Identify the illustrated view type.

- A: Crop view

- B: Section view

- C: Projected view

- D: None of the above

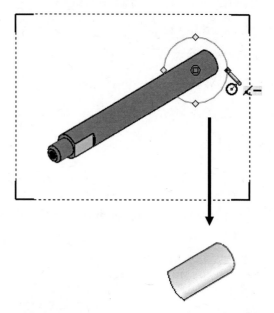

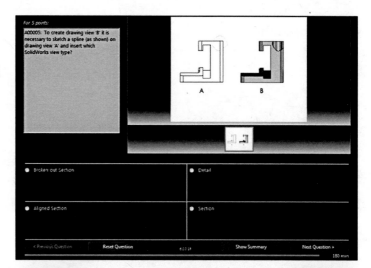

Sample screen shots from an older CSWA exam for the Drawing Theory category. Read each question carefully. Use SolidWorks help if needed.

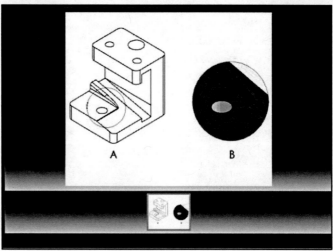

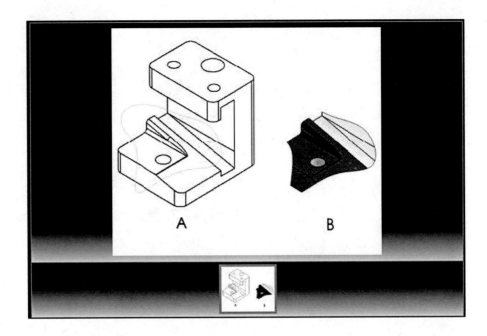

☼ Zoom in on the part or view if needed.

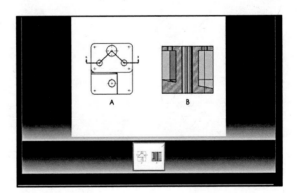

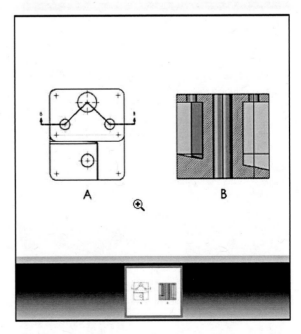

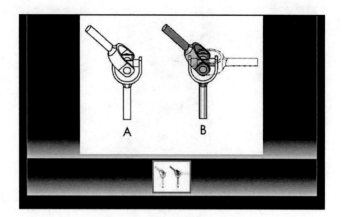

Chapter 8
Simple Part Modeling

Objectives

Simple Part Modeling is one of the five categories on the CSWA exam. This chapter covers the knowledge to identify the part Origin, design intent and key features to build a simple part from a detailed dimensioned illustration for the Part Modeling category of the exam.

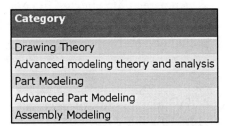

Category
Drawing Theory
Advanced modeling theory and analysis
Part Modeling
Advanced Part Modeling
Assembly Modeling

There is one question on the CSWA exam in this category. The question is in a multiple choice single answer format. The question is worth thirty (30) points. You are required to build a model, with six or more features and to answer a question either on the overall mass, volume, or the location the Center of mass for the created part relative to the default part Origin location.

☀ The complexity of the models along with the features progressively increases throughout this chapter to simulate the final types of parts that would be provided on the CSWA exam.

☀ The main difference between the Simple Part Modeling category and the Advanced Part Modeling category is the complexity of the sketches and the number of dimensions and geometric relations along with an increase in the number of features.

On the completion of the chapter, you will be able to:

- Read and understand an Engineering document used in the CSWA exam:

  - Identify the Sketch plane, part Origin location, part dimensions, geometric relations, and design intent of the sketch and feature.

- Build a part from a detailed dimensioned illustration using the following SolidWorks tools and features:

  - 2D & 3D sketch tools, Extruded Boss/Base, Extruded Cut, Fillet, Mirror, Revolved Base, Chamfer, Reference geometry, Plane, Axis, Calculate the overall mass and volume of the created part, and Locate the Center of mass for the created part relative to the Origin.

☀ FeatureManager names were changed in 2010. Example: Extrude1 vs. Boss-Extrude1. These changes do not affect the models or answers in this book.

Read and understand an Engineering document

What is an Engineering document? In a SolidWorks application, each part, assembly, and drawing is referred to as a document. Each document is displayed in the Graphics window.

🔆 An asterisk (*) beside the document name in the title bar indicates that the document has changed since it was last saved.

🔆 All SW models (initial and final) are provided on the CD in the book. Copy the folders and model files to your local hard drive. Do not work off the CD.

Build a simple part from a detailed illustration

Tutorial: Volume / Center of mass 8-1

Build this model. Calculate the volume of the part and locate the Center of mass with the provided information.

1. **Create** a New part in SolidWorks.

2. **Build** the illustrated dimensioned model. The model displays all edges on perpendicular planes. Think about the steps to build the model. Insert two features: Extruded Base (Boss-Extrude1) and Extruded Cut (Cut-Extrude1). The part Origin is located in the front left corner of the model. Think about your Base Sketch plane. Keep your Base Sketch simple.

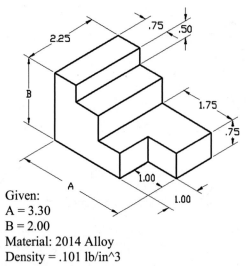

Given:
A = 3.30
B = 2.00
Material: 2014 Alloy
Density = .101 lb/in^3
Units: IPS
Decimal places = 2

3. **Set** the document properties for the model.

4. Create **Sketch1**. Select the Front Plane as the Sketch plane. Sketch1 is the Base sketch. Sketch1 is the profile for the Extruded Base (Boss-Extrude1) feature. Insert the required geometric relations and dimensions.

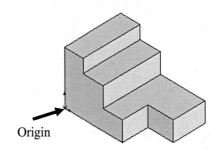

Origin

5. Create the **Extruded Base** feature. Boss-Extrude1 is the Base feature. Blind is the default End Condition in Direction 1. Depth = 2.25in. Identify the extrude direction to maintain the location of the Origin.

6. Create **Sketch2**. Select the Top right face as the Sketch plane for the second feature. Sketch a square. Sketch2 is the profile for the Extruded Cut feature. Insert the required geometric relations and dimensions.

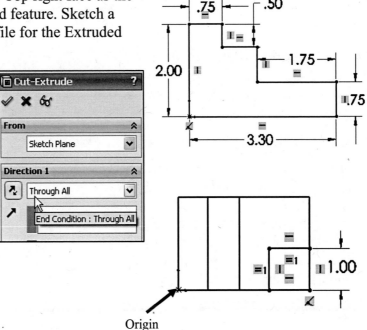

7. Create the **Extruded Cut** feature. Select Through All for End Condition in Direction 1.

There are numerous ways to create the models in this and other chapters.

8. **Assign** 2014 Alloy material to the part. Material is required to locate the Center of mass.

Origin

9. **Calculate** the volume. The volume = 8.28 cubic inches.

Mass = 0.84 pounds

Volume = 8.28 cubic inches

Surface area = 29.88 inches^2

Center of mass: (inches)
    X = 1.14
    Y = 0.75
    Z = -1.18

There are numerous ways to build the models in this chapter. The goal for this chapter is to display different design intents and techniques.

10. **Locate** the Center of mass. The location of the Center of mass is derived from the part Origin.

- X: 1.14 inches

- Y: 0.75 inches

- Z: -1.18 inches

11. **Save** the part and name it Volume-Center of mass 8-1.

12. **Close** the model.

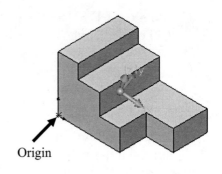
Origin

The principal axes and Center of mass are displayed graphically on the model in the Graphics window.

Tutorial: Volume / Center of mass 8-2

Build this model. Calculate the volume of the part and locate the Center of mass with the provided information.

1. **Create** a New part in SolidWorks.

2. **Build** the illustrated dimensioned model. The model displays all edges on perpendicular planes. Think about the steps that are required to build this model. Remember, there are numerous ways to build the models in this chapter. The goal is to display different design intents and techniques.

Given:
A = 100
B = 40
Material: Brass
Density = .0085 g/mm^3
Units: MMGS

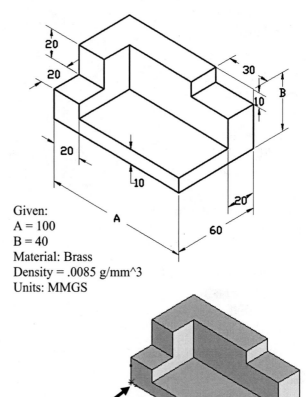
Origin

The CSWA is a three hour timed exam. Work efficiently.

View the provided Part FeatureManagers. Both FeatureManagers create the same illustrated model. In Option1, there are four sketches and four features (Extruded Base and three Extruded Cuts) that are used to build the model.

In Option2, there are three sketches and three features (Extruded Boss/Base) that are used to build the model. Which FeatureManager is better? In a timed exam, optimize your time and use the least amount of features through mirror, pattern, symmetry, etc.

Use Centerlines to create symmetrical sketch elements and revolved features, or as construction geometry.

Create the model using the Option2 Part FeatureManager.

3. **Set** the document properties for the model.

4. Create **Sketch1**. Select the Top Plane as the Sketch plane. Sketch a rectangle. Insert the required dimensions.

5. Create the **Extruded Base** feature. Boss-Extrude1 is the Base feature. Blind is the default End Condition in Direction 1. Depth = 10mm.

6. Create **Sketch2**. Select the back face of Boss-Extrude1. Select **Normal To** view. Sketch2 is the profile for the second Extruded Boss/Base feature. Insert the required geometric relations and dimensions as illustrated.

7. Create the second Extruded Boss/Base feature (**Boss-Extrude2**). Blind is the default End Condition in Direction 1. Depth = 20mm. Note the direction of the extrude, towards the front of the model.

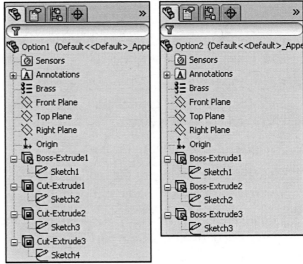

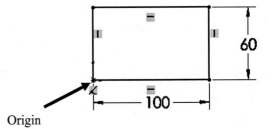

Origin

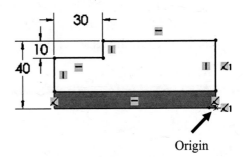

Origin

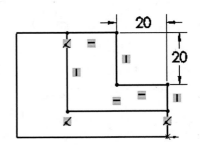

8. Create **Sketch3**. Select the left face of Boss-Extrude1 as the Sketch plane. Sketch3 is the profile for the third Extrude feature. Insert the required geometric relations and dimensions.

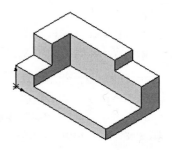

9. Create the third Extruded Boss/Base feature (**Boss-Extrude3**). Blind is the default End Condition in Direction 1. Depth = 20mm.

10. **Assign** Brass material to the part.

11. **Calculate** the volume of the model. The volume = 130,000.00 cubic millimeters.

12. **Locate** the Center of mass. The location of the Center of mass is derived from the part Origin.

Mass = 1105.00 grams

Volume = 130000.00 cubic millimeters

Surface area = 23400.00 millimeters^2

Center of mass: (millimeters)
   X = 43.46
   Y = 15.00
   Z = -37.69

- X: 43.36 millimeters

- Y: 15.00 millimeters

- Z: -37.69 millimeters

13. **Save** the part and name it Volume-Center of mass 8-2.

14. **Calculate** the volume of the model using the IPS unit system. The volume = 7.93 cubic inches.

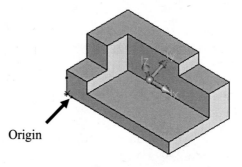

Origin

15. **Locate** the Center of mass using the IPS unit system. The location of the Center of mass is derived from the part Origin.

- X: 1.71 inches

- Y: 0.59 inches

- Z: -1.48 inches

16. **Save** the part and name it Volume-Center of mass 8-2-IPS.

17. **Close** the model.

Mass = 2.44 pounds

Volume = 7.93 cubic inches

Surface area = 36.27 inches^2

Center of mass: (inches)
   X = 1.71
   Y = 0.59
   Z = -1.48

☼ There are numerous ways to create the models in this chapter. The goal is to display different design intents and techniques.

Tutorial: Mass-Volume 8-3

Build this model. Calculate the overall mass of the illustrated model with the provided information.

1. **Create** a New part in SolidWorks.

2. **Build** the illustrated model. The model displays all edges on perpendicular planes. Think about the steps required to build the model. Apply the Mirror Sketch tool to the Base sketch. Insert an Extruded Base (Boss-Extrude1) and Extruded-Cut (Cut-Extrude1) feature.

3. **Set** the document properties for the model.

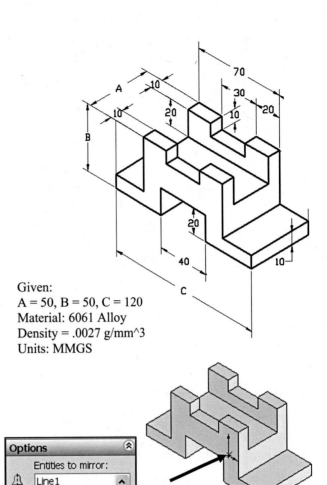

Given:
A = 50, B = 50, C = 120
Material: 6061 Alloy
Density = .0027 g/mm^3
Units: MMGS

To activate the Mirror Sketch tool, click **Tools**, **Sketch Tools**, **Mirror** from the Menu bar menu. The Mirror PropertyManager is displayed.

4. Create **Sketch1**. Select the Front Plane as the Sketch plane. Apply the Mirror Sketch tool. Select the construction geometry to mirror about as illustrated. Select the Entities to mirror. Insert the required geometric relations and dimensions.

Construction geometry is ignored when the sketch is used to create a feature. Construction geometry uses the same line style as centerlines.

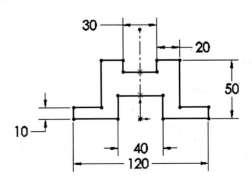

5. Create the **Boss-Extrude1** feature. Boss-Extrude1 is the Base feature. Apply the Mid Plane End Condition in Direction 1 for symmetry. Depth = 50mm.

6. Create **Sketch2**. Select the right face for the Sketch plane. Sketch2 is the profile for the Extruded Cut feature. Insert the required geometric relations and dimensions. Apply construction geometry.

7. Create the **Extruded Cut** feature. Through All is the selected End Condition in Direction 1.

8. **Assign** 6061 Alloy material to the part.

9. **Calculate** the overall mass. The overall mass = 302.40 grams.

10. **Save** the part and name it Mass-Volume 8-3.

11. **Close** the model.

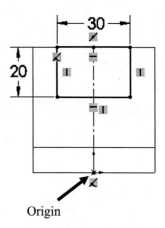

Origin

Mass = 302.40 grams

Volume = 112000.00 cubic millimeters

Surface area = 26200.00 millimeters^2

Center of mass: (millimeters)
  X = 0.00
  Y = 19.20
  Z = 0.00

Tutorial: Mass-Volume 8-4

Build this model. Calculate the volume of the part and locate the Center of mass with the provided information.

1. **Create** a New part in SolidWorks.

2. **Build** the illustrated model. The model displays all edges on perpendicular planes.

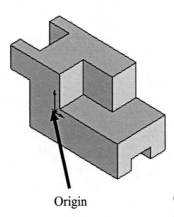

Origin

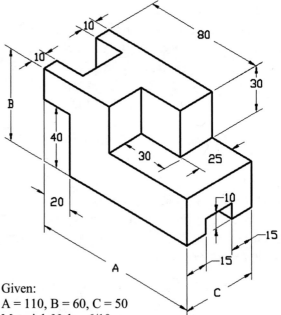

Given:
A = 110, B = 60, C = 50
Material: Nylon 6/10
Density = .0014 g/mm^3
Units: MMGS

View the provided Part FeatureManagers. Both FeatureManagers create the same model. In Option4, there are three sketches and three features that are used to build the model.

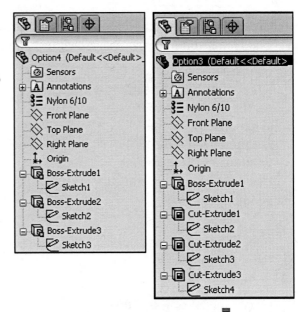

In Option3, there are four sketches and four features that are used to build the model. Which FeatureManager is better? In a timed exam, optimize your design time and use the least amount of features. Use the Option4 FeatureManager in this tutorial. As an exercise, build the model using the Option3 FeatureManager.

3. **Set** the document properties for the model.

4. Create **Sketch1**. Select the Right Plane as the Sketch plane. Sketch1 is the Base sketch. Apply the Mirror Entities Sketch tool. Select the construction geometry to mirror about as illustrated. Select the Entities to mirror. Insert the required geometric relations and dimensions.

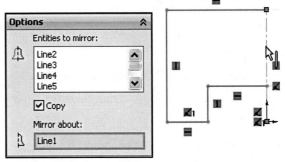

5. Create the **Boss-Extrude1** feature. Boss-Extrude1 is the Base feature. Blind is the default End Condition in Direction 1. Depth = (A - 20mm) = 90mm. Note the direction of the extrude.

6. Create **Sketch2**. Select the Top face of Boss-Extrude1 for the Sketch plane. Sketch2 is the profile for the second Extruded Boss/Base feature (Boss-Extrude2). Insert the required geometric relations and dimensions.

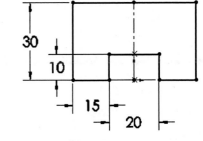

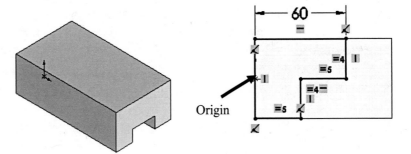

Origin

7. Create the **Boss-Extrude2** feature. Blind is the default End Condition in Direction 1. Depth = 30mm.

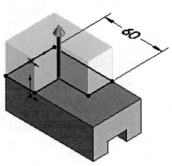

8. Create **Sketch3**. Select the left face of Boss-Extrude1 for the Sketch plane. Apply symmetry. Insert the required geometric relations and dimensions. Use construction reference geometry.

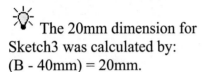

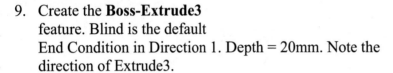

The 20mm dimension for Sketch3 was calculated by: (B - 40mm) = 20mm.

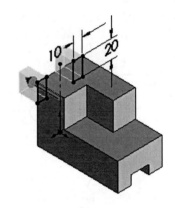

9. Create the **Boss-Extrude3** feature. Blind is the default End Condition in Direction 1. Depth = 20mm. Note the direction of Extrude3.

10. **Assign** Nylon 6/10 material to the part.

11. **Calculate** the volume. The volume = 192,500.00 cubic millimeters.

12. **Locate** the Center of mass. The location of the Center of mass is derived from the part Origin.

- X: 35.70 millimeters
- Y: 27.91 millimeters
- Z: -1.46 millimeters

13. **Save** the part and name it Mass-Volume 8-4.

14. **Close** the model.

```
Mass = 269.50 grams
Volume = 192500.00 cubic millimeters
Surface area = 27800.00 millimeters^2
Center of mass: ( millimeters )
    X = 35.70
    Y = 27.91
    Z = -1.46
```

In the previous section, all of the models that you created displayed all edges on Perpendicular planes and used the Extruded Base, Extruded Boss, or the Extruded Cut feature from the Features toolbar.

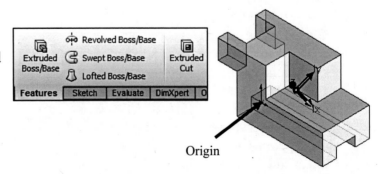

Origin

In the next section, build models where all edges are not located on Perpendicular planes.

First, let's review a simple 2D Sketch for a Extruded Cut feature.

Tutorial: Simple Cut 8-1

1. **Create** a New part in SolidWorks.

2. **Build** the illustrated model. Start with a 60mm x 60mm x 100mm block. System units = MMGS. Decimal places = 2. Note the location of the part Origin.

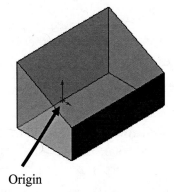

Origin

3. Create **Sketch1**. Select the Front Plane as the Sketch plane. Sketch a square as illustrated. Insert the required dimension. The part Origin is located in the bottom left corner of the model.

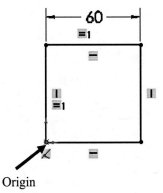

4. Create the **Extruded Base (Boss-Extrude1)** feature. Apply the Mid Plane End Condition in Direction 1. Depth = 100mm.

Origin

5. Create **Sketch2**. Select the front face as the Sketch plane. Apply the Line Sketch tool. Sketch a diagonal line. Select the front right vertical midpoint as illustrated.

6. Create the **Extruded Cut (Cut-Extrude1)** feature. Through All for End Condition in Direction 1 and Direction 2 is selected by default.

7. **Save** the part and name it Simple-Cut 8-1. View the FeatureManager.

8. **Close** the model.

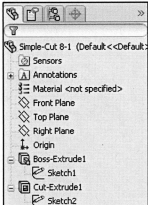

Tutorial: Mass-Volume 8-5

Build this model. Calculate the overall mass of the part and locate the Center of mass with the provided information.

1. **Create** a New part in SolidWorks.

2. **Build** the illustrated model. All edges of the model are not located on Perpendicular planes. Insert an Extruded Base (Boss-Extrude1) feature and three Extruded Cut features to build the model.

3. **Set** the document properties for the model.

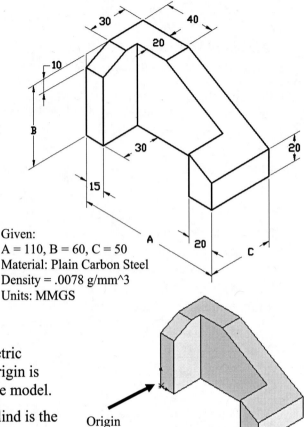

Given:
A = 110, B = 60, C = 50
Material: Plain Carbon Steel
Density = .0078 g/mm^3
Units: MMGS

4. Create **Sketch1**. Select the Front Plane as the Sketch plane. Sketch a rectangle. Insert the required geometric relations and dimensions. The part Origin is located in the left bottom corner of the model.

5. Create the **Extruded Base** feature. Blind is the default End Condition in Direction 1. Depth = 50mm. Note the direction of Extrude1.

Origin

6. Create **Sketch2**. Select the top face of Boss-Extrude1 for the Sketch plane. Sketch2 is the profile for the first Extruded Cut feature. Insert the required relations and dimensions.

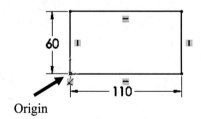

Origin

7. Create the **Extruded Cut** feature. Select Through All for End Condition in Direction 1.

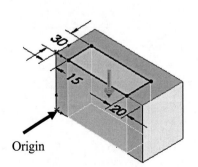

Origin

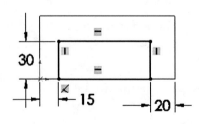

8. Create **Sketch3**. Select the back face of Boss-Extrude1 as the Sketch plane. Sketch a diagonal line. Insert the required geometric relations and dimensions.

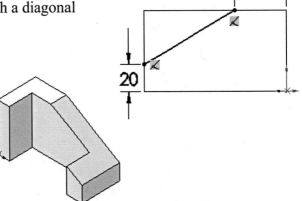

9. Create the second **Extruded Cut** feature. Through All for End Condition in Direction 1 and Direction 2 is selected by default. Note the direction of the extrude feature.

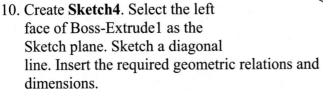

10. Create **Sketch4**. Select the left face of Boss-Extrude1 as the Sketch plane. Sketch a diagonal line. Insert the required geometric relations and dimensions.

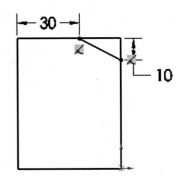

11. Create the third **Extruded Cut** feature. Through All for End Condition in Direction 1 and Direction 2 is selected by default.

12. **Assign** Plain Carbon Steel material to the part.

13. **Calculate** the overall mass. The overall mass = 1130.44 grams.

14. **Locate** the Center of mass. The location of the Center of mass is derived from the part Origin.

- X: 45.24 millimeters

- Y: 24.70 millimeters

- Z: -33.03 millimeters

Density = 0.01 grams per cubic millimeter

Mass = 1130.44 grams

Volume = 144928.57 cubic millimeters

Surface area = 23631.77 millimeters^2

Center of mass: (millimeters)
  X = 45.24
  Y = 24.70
  Z = -33.03

In this category, Part Modeling an exam question could read: Build this model. Locate the Center of mass with respect to the part Origin.

- A: X = 45.24 millimeters, Y = 24.70 millimeters, Z = -33.03 millimeters

- B: X = 54.24 millimeters, Y = 42.70 millimeters, Z = 33.03 millimeters

- C: X = 49.24 millimeters, Y = -37.70 millimeters, Z = 38.03 millimeters

- D: X = 44.44 millimeters, Y = -24.70 millimeters, Z = -39.03 millimeters

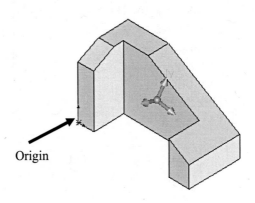

Origin

The correct answer is A.

💡 The principal axes and Center of mass are displayed graphically on the model in the Graphics window.

15. **Save** the part and name it Mass-Volume 8-5.

16. **Close** the model.

Tutorial: Mass-Volume 8-6

Build this model. Calculate the overall mass of the part and locate the Center of mass with the provided information.

1. **Create** a New part in SolidWorks.

2. **Build** the illustrated model. All edges of the model are not located on Perpendicular planes. Think about the steps required to build the model. Insert two features: Extruded Base (Boss-Extrude1) and Extruded Cut (Cut-Extrude1).

3. **Set** the document properties for the model.

4. Create **Sketch1**. Select the Right Plane as the Sketch plane. Apply construction geometry. Insert the required geometric relations and dimensions.

5. Create the **Extruded Base** feature. Boss-Extrude1 is the Base feature. Apply symmetry. Select Mid Plane as the End Condition in Direction 1. Depth = 3.00in.

Given:
A = 3.00, B = 1.00
Material: 6061 Alloy
Density = .097 lb/in^3
Units: IPS
Decimal places = 2

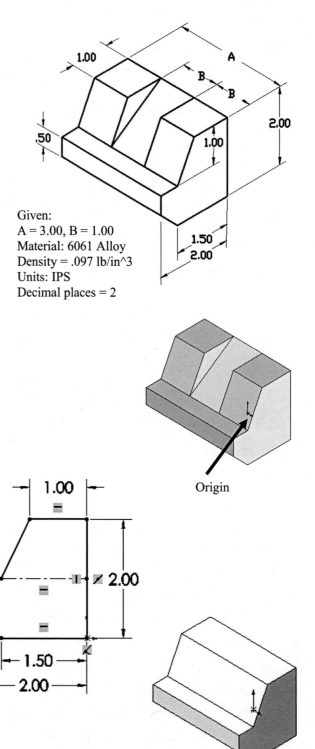

Origin

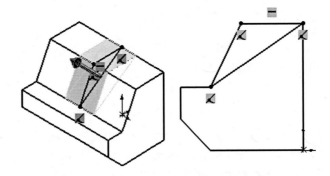

6. Create **Sketch2**. Select the Right Plane as the Sketch plane. Select the Line Sketch tool. Insert the required geometric relations. Sketch2 is the profile for the Extruded Cut feature.

7. Create the **Extruded Cut (Cut-Extrude1)** feature. Apply symmetry. Select Mid Plane as the End Condition in Direction 1. Depth = 1.00in.

8. **Assign** 6061 Alloy material to the part.

```
Mass = 0.87 pounds

Volume = 8.88 cubic inches

Surface area = 28.91 inches^2

Center of mass: ( inches )
    X = 0.00
    Y = 0.86
    Z = 0.82
```

9. **Calculate** overall mass. The overall mass = 0.87 pounds.

10. **Locate** the Center of mass. The location of the Center of mass is derived from the part Origin.

- X: 0.00 inches

- Y: 0.86 inches

- Z: 0.82 inches

In this category, Part Modeling an exam question could read: Build this model. Locate the Center of mass with respect to the part Origin.

- A: X = 0.10 inches, Y = -0.86 inches, Z = -0.82 inches

- B: X = 0.00 inches, Y = 0.86 inches, Z = 0.82 inches

- C: X = 0.15 inches, Y = -0.96 inches, Z = -0.02 inches

- D: X = 1.00 inches, Y = -0.89 inches, Z = -1.82 inches

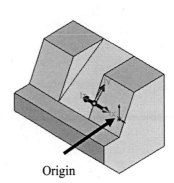

Origin

The correct answer is B.

11. **Save** the part and name it Mass-Volume 8-6.

12. **Close** the model.

As an exercise, modify the Mass-Volume 8-6 part using the MMGS unit system. Assign Nickel as the material. Calculate the overall mass. The overall mass of the part = 1236.20 grams. Save the part and name it Mass-Volume 8-6-MMGS.

Tutorial: Mass-Volume 8-7

Build this model. Calculate the overall mass of the part and locate the Center of mass with the provided information.

1. **Create** a New part in SolidWorks.

2. **Build** the illustrated model. All edges of the model are not located on Perpendicular planes. Think about the steps required to build the model. Insert two features: Extruded Base (Boss-Extrude1) and Extruded Cut (Cut-Extrude1).

3. **Set** the document properties for the model.

4. Create **Sketch1**. Select the Right Plane as the Sketch plane. Apply the Line Sketch tool. Insert the required geometric relations and dimension. The location of the Origin is in the left lower corner of the sketch.

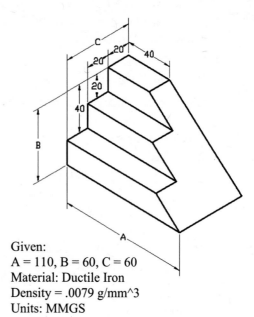

Given:
A = 110, B = 60, C = 60
Material: Ductile Iron
Density = .0079 g/mm^3
Units: MMGS

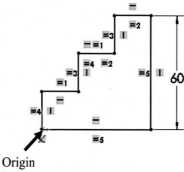

Origin

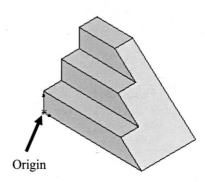

Origin

5. Create the **Extruded Base** feature. Boss-Extrude1 is the Base feature. Blind is the default End Condition in Direction 1. Depth = 110mm.

6. Create **Sketch2**. Select the Front Plane as the Sketch plane. Sketch a diagonal line. Complete the sketch. Sketch2 is the profile for the Extruded Cut feature.

7. Create the **Extruded Cut** feature. Through All for End Condition in Direction 1 and Direction 2 is selected by default.

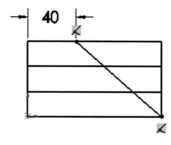

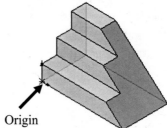

Origin

8. **Assign** Ductile Iron material to the part.

9. **Calculate** overall mass. The mass = 1569.47 grams.

10. **Locate** the Center of mass. The location of the Center of mass is derived from the part Origin.

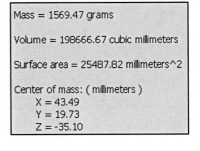

Mass = 1569.47 grams

Volume = 198666.67 cubic millimeters

Surface area = 25487.82 millimeters^2

Center of mass: (millimeters)
  X = 43.49
  Y = 19.73
  Z = -35.10

- X: 43.49 millimeters

- Y: 19.73 millimeters

- Z: -35.10 millimeters

11. **Save** the part and name it Mass-Volume 8-7.

12. **Close** the model.

In this category, Part Modeling an exam question could read: Build this model. Locate the Center of mass with respect to the part Origin.

- A: X = -43.99 millimeters, Y = 29.73 millimeters, Z = -38.10 millimeters

- B: X = -44.49 millimeters, Y = -19.73 millimeters, Z = 35.10 millimeters

- C: X = 43.49 millimeters, Y = 19.73 millimeters, Z = -35.10 millimeters

- D: X = -1.00 millimeters, Y = 49.73 millimeters, Z = -35.10 millimeters

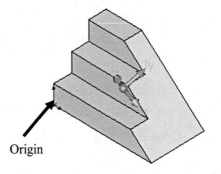

Origin

The correct answer is C.

As an exercise, locate the Center of mass using the IPS unit system, and re-assign copper material. Re-calculate the Center of mass location, with respect to the part Origin. Save the part and name it Mass-Volume 8-7-IPS.

- X: 1.71 inches

- Y: 0.78 inches

- Z: -1.38 inches

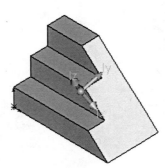

Mass = 3.90 pounds

Volume = 12.12 cubic inches

Surface area = 39.51 inches^2

Center of mass: (inches)
  X = 1.71
  Y = 0.78
  Z = -1.38

2D vs. 3D Sketching

Up to this point, the models that you created in this chapter started with a 2D sketch. Sketches are the foundation for creating features. SolidWorks provides the ability to create either 2D or 3D sketches. A 2D sketch is limited to a flat 2D Sketch plane. A 3D sketch can include 3D elements.

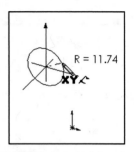

☀ As you create a 3D sketch, the entities in the sketch exist in 3D space. They are not related to a specific Sketch plane as they are in a 2D sketch.

You may need to apply a 3D sketch in the CSWA exam. Below is an example of a 3D sketch to create a Cut-Extrude feature.

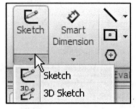

☀ The complexity of the models increases throughout this chapter to simulate the types of models that are provided on the CSWA exam.

Tutorial 3DSketch 8-1

1. **Create** a New part in SolidWorks.

2. **Build** the illustrated model. Insert two features: Extruded Base and Extruded Cut. Apply the 3D Sketch tool to create the Extruded Cut feature. System units = MMGS. Decimal places = 2.

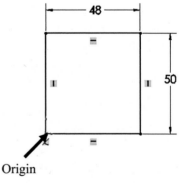

Origin

3. **Set** the document properties for the model.

4. Create **Sketch1**. Select the Front Plane as the Sketch plane. Sketch a rectangle. The part Origin is located in the bottom left corner of the sketch. Insert the illustrated geometric relations and dimensions.

5. Create the **Extruded Base (Boss-Extrude1)** feature. Apply symmetry. Select the Mid Plane End Condition in Direction 1. Depth = 100.00mm.

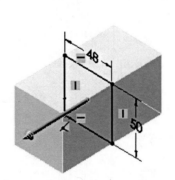

Origin

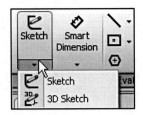

☼ Click **3D Sketch** from the Sketch toolbar. Select the proper Sketch tool.

6. Create **3DSketch1**. Use the Line Sketch tool. 3DSketch1 is a four point sketch as illustrated. 3DSketch1 is the profile for Extruded Cut feature.

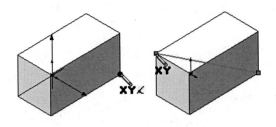 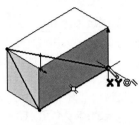 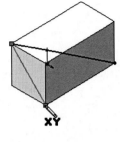 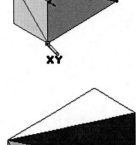

7. Create the **Extruded Cut) Cut-Extrude1)** feature. Select the front right vertical edge as illustrated to remove the material. Edge<1> is displayed in the Direction of Extrusion box.

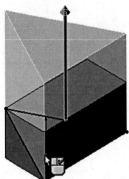 

8. **Save** the part and name it 3DSketch 8-1.

9. **Close** the model.

☼ You can either select the front right vertical edge or the Top face to remove the require material in this tutorial.

You can use any of the following tools to create 3D sketches: Lines, Circles, Rectangles, Arcs, Splines and Points.

Most relations that are available in 2D sketching are available in 3D sketching. The exceptions are:

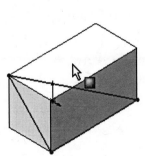

- Symmetry

- Patterns

- Offset

Tutorial: Mass-Volume 8-8

Build this model. Calculate the volume of the part and locate the Center of mass with the provided information.

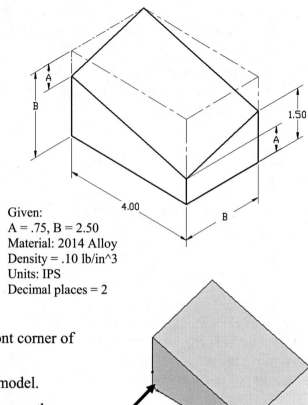

1. **Create** a New part in SolidWorks.

2. **Build** the illustrated model. All edges of the model - are not located on Perpendicular planes. Insert two features: Extruded Base (Boss-Extrude1) and Extruded Cut (Cut-Extrude1). Apply a closed four point 3D sketch as the profile for the Extruded Cut feature. The part Origin is located in the lower left front corner of the model.

Given:
A = .75, B = 2.50
Material: 2014 Alloy
Density = .10 lb/in^3
Units: IPS
Decimal places = 2

3. **Set** the document properties for the model.

4. Create **Sketch1**. Select the Right Plane as the Sketch plane. Sketch a square. Insert the required geometric relations and dimension.

Origin

5. Create the **Extruded Base** feature. Boss-Extrude1 is the Base feature. Blind is the default End Condition in Direction 1. Depth = 4.00in.

6. Create **3DSketch1**. Apply the Line Sketch tool. Create a closed five point 3D sketch as illustrated. 3DSketch1 is the profile for the Extruded Cut feature. Insert the required dimensions.

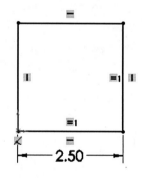

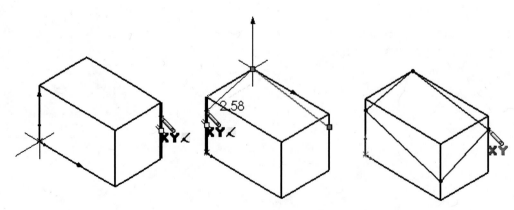

7. Create the **Extruded Cut** feature. Select the front right vertical edge as illustrated. Select Through All for End Condition in Direction 1. Note the direction of the extrude feature.

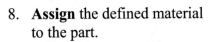
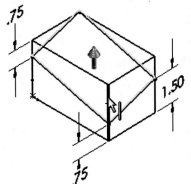
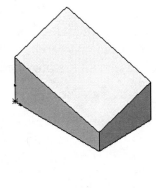

8. **Assign** the defined material to the part.

9. **Calculate** the volume. The volume = 16.25 cubic inches.

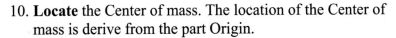

```
Mass = 1.64 pounds

Volume = 16.25 cubic inches

Surface area = 41.86 inches^2

Center of mass: ( inches )
     X = 1.79
     Y = 0.85
     Z = -1.35
```

10. **Locate** the Center of mass. The location of the Center of mass is derive from the part Origin.

- X = 1.76 inches

- Y = 0.85 inches

- Z = -1.35 inches

In this category, Part Modeling an exam question could read: Build this model. What is the volume of the part?

- A: 18.88 cubic inches

- B: 19.55 cubic inches

- C: 17.99 cubic inches

- D: 16.25 cubic inches

The correct answer is D.

View the triad location of the Center of mass for the part.

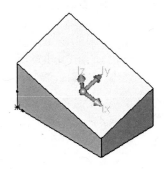

11. **Save** the part and name it Mass-Volume 8-8.

12. **Close** the model.

As an exercise, calculate the overall mass of the part using the MMGS unit system, and re-assign Nickel as the material. The overall mass of the part = 2263.46 grams. Save the part and name it Mass-Volume 8-8-MMGS.

```
Mass = 2263.46 grams

Volume = 266289.79 cubic millimeters

Surface area = 27006.69 millimeters^2

Center of mass: ( millimeters )
     X = 45.59
     Y = 21.66
     Z = -34.19
```

Tutorial: Mass-Volume 8-9

Build this model. Calculate the overall mass of the part and locate the Center of mass with the provided information.

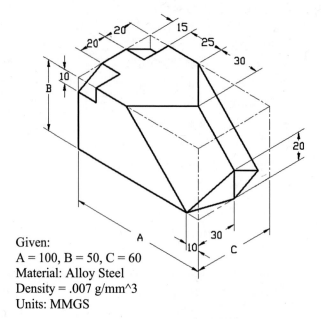

1. **Create** a New part in SolidWorks.

2. **Build** the illustrated model. Insert five sketches and five features to build the model: Extruded Base, three Extruded Cut features and a Mirror feature.

There are numerous ways to build the models in this chapter. The goal is to display different design intents and techniques.

Given:
A = 100, B = 50, C = 60
Material: Alloy Steel
Density = .007 g/mm^3
Units: MMGS

3. **Set** the document properties for the model.

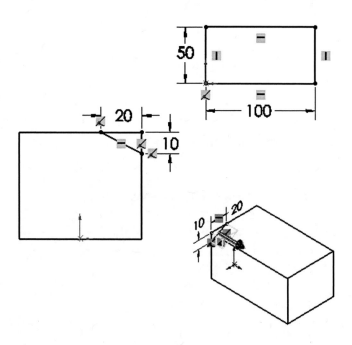

Origin

4. Create **Sketch1**. Select the Front Plane as the Sketch plane. Sketch a rectangle. Insert the required dimensions. The part Origin is located in the lower left corner of the sketch.

5. Create the **Extruded Base (Boss-Extrude1)** feature. Apply symmetry. Select the Mid Plane End Condition for Direction 1. Depth = 60mm.

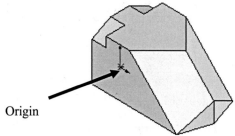

6. Create **Sketch2**. Select the left face of Boss-Extrude1 as the Sketch plane. Insert the required geometric relations and dimensions.

7. Create the first **Extruded Cut** feature. Blind is the default End Condition in Direction 1. Depth = 15mm. Note the direction of the extrude feature.

8. Create **Sketch3**. Select the bottom face of Boss-Extrude1 for the Sketch plane. Insert the required geometric relations and dimension.

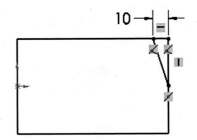

9. Create the second **Extruded Cut** feature. Blind is the default End Condition in Direction 1. Depth = 20mm.

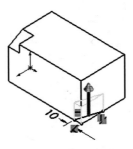

10. Create **Sketch4**. Select Front Plane as the Sketch plane. Sketch a diagonal line. Sketch4 is the direction of extrusion for the third Extruded Cut feature. Insert the required dimension.

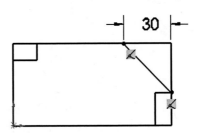

11. Create **Sketch5**. Select the top face of Boss-Extrude1 as the Sketch plane. Sketch5 is the sketch profile for the third Extruded Cut feature. Apply construction geometry. Insert the required geometric relations and dimensions.

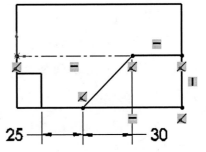

12. Create the third **Extruded Cut** feature. Select Through All for End Condition in Direction 1.

13. Select Sketch4 in the Graphics window for Direction of Extrusion. Line1@Sketch4 is displayed in the Cut-Extrude PropertyManager.

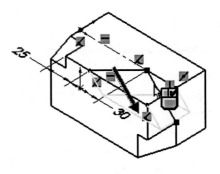

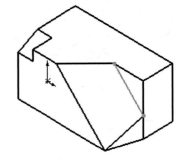

14. Create the **Mirror** feature. Mirror the three Extruded Cut features about the Front Plane. Use the fly-out FeatureManager.

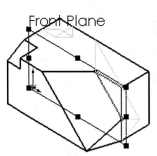

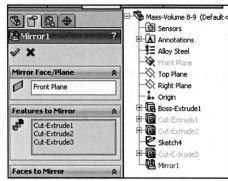

15. **Assign** Alloy Steel material to the part.

16. **Calculate** the overall mass. The overall mass = 1794.10 grams.

17. **Locate** the Center of mass. The location of the Center of mass is derived from the part Origin.

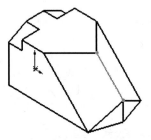

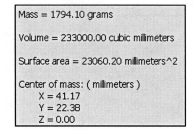

- X = 41.17 millimeters

- Y = 22.38 millimeters

- Z = 0.00 millimeters

View the triad location of the Center of mass for the part.

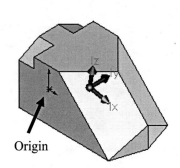

18. **Save** the part and name it Mass-Volume 8-9.

19. **Close** the model.

Origin

☼ You can set document precision from the Document Properties dialog box or from the Dimension PropertyManager. You can also address: Callout value, Tolerance type, and Dimension Text symbols in the Dimension PropertyManager.

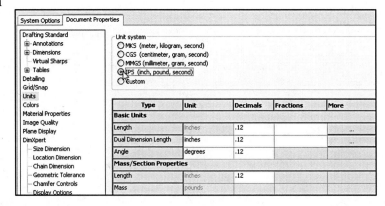

Callout value

A Callout value is a value that you select in a
SolidWorks document. Click a dimension in
the Graphics window, the selected dimension
is displayed in blue and the Dimension
PropertyManager is displayed.

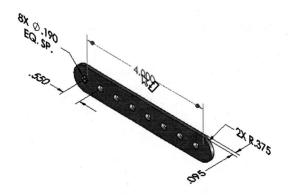

A Callout value is available for
dimensions with multiple values in the
callout.

Tolerance type

A Tolerance type is selected from the available drop down list in the Dimension
PropertyManager. The list is dynamic. A few examples of Tolerance type display are
listed below:

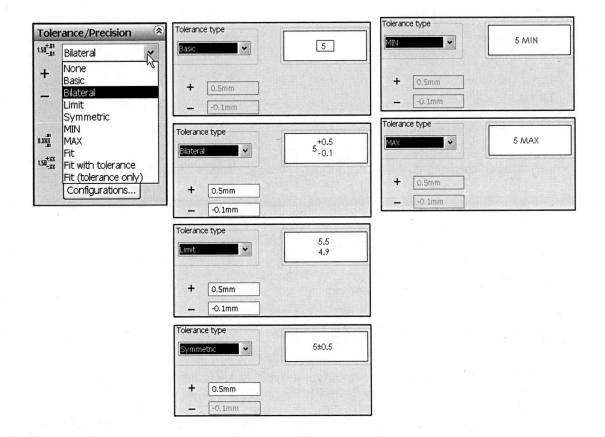

Tutorial: Dimension text 8-1

1. **View** the illustrated model.

2. **Review** the Tolerance, Precision, and Dimension Text.

   a. 2X Ø.190 - Two holes with a diameter of .190. Precision is set to three decimal places.

   b. 2X R.250 - Two corners with a radius of .250. Precision is set to three decimal places.

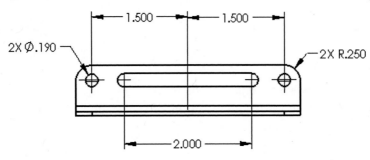

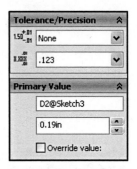

Tutorial: Dimension text 8-2

1. **View** the illustrated model.

2. **Review** the Tolerance, Precision, and Dimension text.

   a. Ø **22±0.25** - The primary diameter value of the hole = 22.0mm. Tolerance type: Symmetric. Maximum Variation 0.25mm. Tolerance / Precision is set to two decimal place.

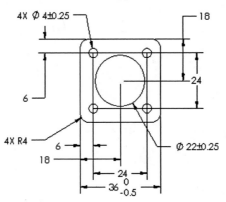

For a Chamfer feature, a second Tolerance/Precision is available.

   b. 36 $^{0}_{-0.5}$ - The primary diameter value of the hole = 36mm. Tolerance type: Bilateral. Maximum Variation is 0.0mm. Minimum Variation = -0.5mm. Precision is set to two decimal place. Tolerance is set to one decimal place.

Trailing zeros are removed according to the ANSI standard.

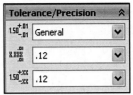

c. **24** - The primary value = 24mm. Tolerance type: General. Tolerance / Precision is set to two decimal place.

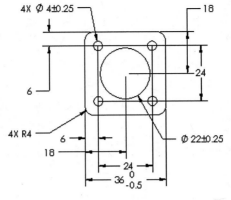

d. **4X ⌀ 4±0.25** - Four holes with a primary diameter value = 4mm. Tolerance type: Symmetric. Maximum Variation = 0.25mm. Precision / Tolerance is set to two decimal place.

Tutorial: Dimension text 8-3

1. **View** the illustrated model.

2. **Review** the Tolerance, and Precision.

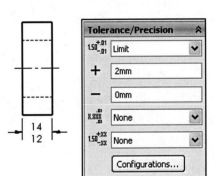

a. $^{14}_{12}$ - The primary value = 12mm. Tolerance type: Limit. Maximum Variation = 2mm. Minimum Variation = 0mm. Tolerance / Precision is set to none.

Dimension text symbols

Dimension Text symbols are displayed in the Dimension PropertyManager. The Dimension Text box provides eight commonly used symbols and a more button to access the Symbol Library. The eight displayed symbols in the Dimension Text box from left to right are: Diameter, Degree, Plus/Minus, Centerline, Square, Countersink, Counterbore and Depth/Deep.

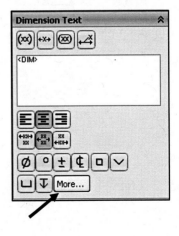

Review each symbol in the Dimension Text box and in the Symbol library. You are required to understand the meaning of these symbols in a SolidWorks document.

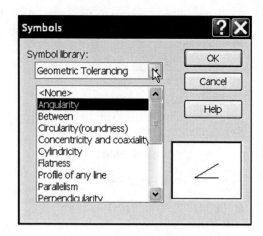

Tutorial: Dimension text symbols 8-1

1. **View** the illustrated model.

2. **Review** the Dimension Text and document symbols.

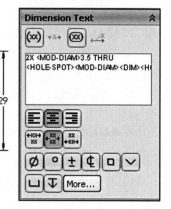

   a. 2X ⌀3.5 THRU
   ⌴ ⌀6.5⍌3.5
   - Two holes with a primary diameter value = 3.5mm, Cbore ⌀6.5 with a depth 3.5.

Tutorial: Dimension text symbols 8-2

1. **View** the illustrated model.

2. **Review** the Dimension Text and document symbols.

   a. 2X ⌴ ⌀5.5 ⍌ 8.8 - Two Cbores with a primary diameter value = 5.5mm with a depth 8.8.

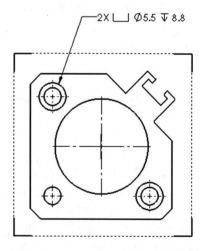

Build additional simple parts

Tutorial: Mass-Volume 8-10

Build this model. Calculate the overall mass of the part and locate the Center of mass with the provided information.

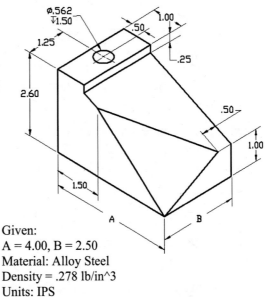

1. **Create** a New part in SolidWorks.

2. **Build** the illustrated model. Note the Depth/Deep ⟱ symbol with a 1.50 dimension associated with the hole. The hole Ø.562 has a three decimal place precision. Insert three features: Extruded Base (Boss-Extrude1) and two Extruded Cuts. Insert a 3D sketch for the first Extruded Cut feature.

Given:
A = 4.00, B = 2.50
Material: Alloy Steel
Density = .278 lb/in^3
Units: IPS
Decimal places = 2

☀ There are numerous ways to build the models in this chapter. The goal is to display different design intents and techniques.

3. **Set** the document properties for the model.

4. Create **Sketch1**. Select the Front Plane as the Sketch plane. The part Origin is located in the lower left corner of the sketch. Insert the required geometric relations and dimensions.

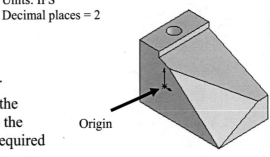

Origin

5. Create the **Extruded Base (Boss-Extrude1)** feature. Apply symmetry. Select the Mid Plane End Condition in Direction 1. Depth = 2.50in.

6. Create **3DSketch1**. Apply the Line Sketch tool. Create a closed four point 3D sketch. 3DSketch1 is the profile for the first Extruded Cut feature. Insert the required dimensions.

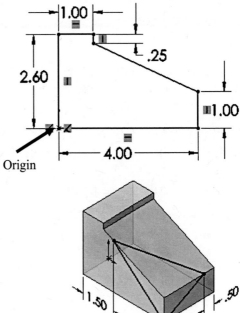

7. Create the first **Extruded Cut** feature. Blind is the default End Conditions. Select the top face as illustrated to be removed. Note the direction of the extrude.

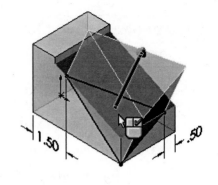

8. Create **Sketch2**. Select the top flat face of Boss-Extrude1. Sketch a circle. Insert the required geometric relations and dimensions. The hole diameter Ø.562 has a three decimal place precision.

9. Create the second **Extruded Cut** feature. Blind is the default End Condition. Depth = 1.50in. Note: For the exam, you do not need to insert the Depth/Deep ⏚ symbol or note.

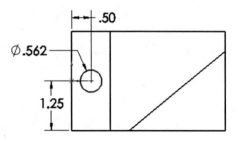

10. **Assign** Alloy Steel material to the part.

11. **Calculate** the overall mass. The overall mass = 4.97 pounds.

12. **Locate** the Center of mass. The location of the Center of mass is derived from the part Origin.

- X: 1.63 inches

- Y: 1.01 inches

- Z: -0.04 inches

View the triad location of the Center of mass for the part.

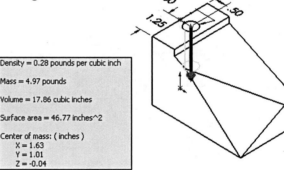

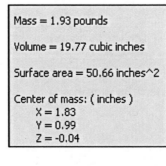

Density = 0.28 pounds per cubic inch

Mass = 4.97 pounds

Volume = 17.86 cubic inches

Surface area = 46.77 inches^2

Center of mass: (inches)
   X = 1.63
   Y = 1.01
   Z = -0.04

13. **Save** the part and name it Mass-Volume 8-10.

14. **Close** the model.

As an exercise, calculate the overall mass of the part using 6061 Alloy.

Modify the A dimension from 4.00 to 4.50. Modify the hole dimension from Ø.562 to Ø.575. The overall mass of the part = 1.93 pounds.

Save the part and name it Mass-Volume 8-10A.

Mass = 1.93 pounds

Volume = 19.77 cubic inches

Surface area = 50.66 inches^2

Center of mass: (inches)
   X = 1.83
   Y = 0.99
   Z = -0.04

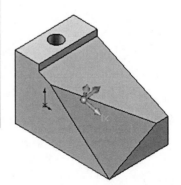

Tutorial: Mass-Volume 8-11

Build this model. Calculate the overall mass of the part and locate the Center of mass with the provided information.

1. **Create** a New part in SolidWorks.

2. **Build** the illustrated model. Think about the required steps to build this part. Insert four features: Extruded Base, two Extruded Cuts, and a Fillet.

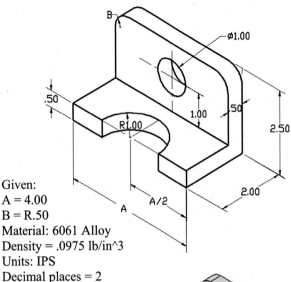

There are numerous ways to build the models in this chapter. The goal is to display different design intents and techniques.

Given:
A = 4.00
B = R.50
Material: 6061 Alloy
Density = .0975 lb/in^3
Units: IPS
Decimal places = 2

3. **Set** the document properties for the model.

4. Create **Sketch1**. Select the Right Plane as the Sketch plane. The part Origin is located in the lower left corner of the sketch. Insert the required geometric relations and dimensions.

5. Create the **Extruded Base (Boss-Extrude1)** feature. Apply symmetry. Select the Mid Plane End Condition for Direction 1. Depth = 4.00in.

6. Create **Sketch2**. Select the top flat face of Boss-Extrude1 as the Sketch plane. Sketch a circle. The center of the circle is located at the part Origin. Insert the required dimension.

7. Create the first **Extruded Cut** feature. Select Through All for End Condition in Direction 1.

8. Create **Sketch3**. Select the front vertical face of Extrude1 as the Sketch plane. Sketch a circle. Insert the required geometric relations and dimensions.

9. Create the second **Extruded Cut** feature. Select Through All for End Condition in Direction 1.

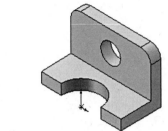

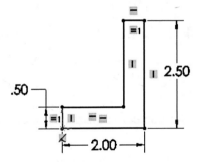

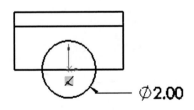

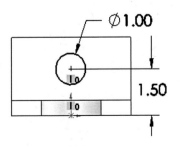

10. Create the **Fillet** feature. Constant radius is selected by
    default. Fillet the top two edges as illustrated.
    Radius = .50in.

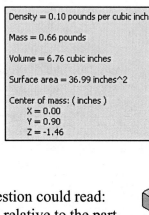

Radius: 0.5in

A Fillet feature removes material. Selecting the correct
radius value is important to obtain the correct mass and
volume answer in the exam.

11. **Assign** the defined material to the part.

12. **Calculate** the overall mass. The
    overall mass = 0.66 pounds.

13. **Locate** the Center of mass. The
    location of the Center of mass is
    derived from the part Origin.

Density = 0.10 pounds per cubic inch

Mass = 0.66 pounds

Volume = 6.76 cubic inches

Surface area = 36.99 inches^2

Center of mass: (inches)
   X = 0.00
   Y = 0.90
   Z = -1.46

- X: 0.00 inches

- Y: 0.90 inches

- Z: -1.46 inches

In this category, Part Modeling an exam question could read:
Build this model. Locate the Center of mass relative to the part
Origin.

- A: X = -2.63 inches, Y = 4.01 inches, Z = -0.04 inches

- B: X = 4.00 inches, Y = 1.90 inches, Z = -1.64 inches

- C: X = 0.00 inches, Y = 0.90 inches, Z = -1.46 inches

- D: X = -1.69 inches, Y = 1.00 inches, Z = 0.10 inches

The correct answer is C. Note: Tangent Edges are displayed
for educational purposes.

14. **Save** the part and name it Mass-Volume 8-11.

15. **Close** the model.

As an exercise, calculate the overall mass of the part using
the MMGS unit system, and assign 2014 Alloy material to
the part.

The overall mass of the part = 310.17 grams. Save the part
and name it Mass-Volume 8-11-MMGS.

Mass = 310.17 grams

Volume = 110774.26 cubic millimeters

Surface area = 23865.83 millimeters^2

Center of mass: (millimeters)
   X = 0.00
   Y = 22.83
   Z = -37.11

Tutorial: Mass-Volume 8-12

Build this model. Calculate the overall mass of the part and locate the Center of mass with the provided information.

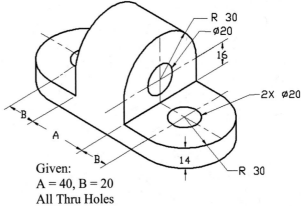

1. **Create** a New part in SolidWorks.

2. **Build** the illustrated model. Insert two features: Extruded Base (Boss-Extrude1) and Extruded Boss (Boss-Extrude2).

3. **Set** the document properties for the model.

Given:
A = 40, B = 20
All Thru Holes
Material: Copper
Density = .0089 g/mm^3
Units: MMGS

4. Create **Sketch1**. Select the Top Plane as the Sketch plane. Apply the Centerline Sketch tool. Locate the part Origin at the center of the sketch. Insert the required geometric relations and dimensions. Note: This is a good case to use the Slot Sketch tool!

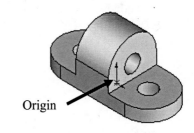

Origin

5. Create the **Extruded Base (Boss-Extrude1)** feature. Blind is the default End Condition. Depth = 14mm.

6. Create **Sketch2**. Select the Right Plane as the Sketch plane. Insert the required geometric relations and dimensions.

7. Create the **Extruded Boss (Boss-Extrude2)** feature. Apply symmetry. Select the Mid Plane End Condition. Depth = 40mm.

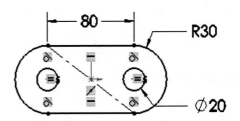

8. **Assign** the defined material to the part.

9. **Calculate** the overall mass. The overall mass = 1605.29 grams.

10. **Locate** the Center of mass. The location of the Center of mass is derived from the part Origin.

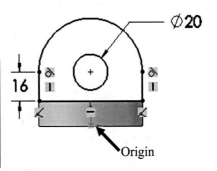

- X: 0.00 millimeters

- Y: 19.79 millimeters

- Z: 0.00 millimeters

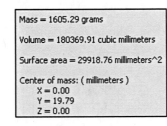

Mass = 1605.29 grams

Volume = 180369.91 cubic millimeters

Surface area = 29918.76 millimeters^2

Center of mass: (millimeters)
X = 0.00
Y = 19.79
Z = 0.00

11. **Save** the part and name it Mass-Volume 8-12.

12. **Close** the model.

☀ There are numerous ways to build the
models in this chapter. Optimize your time.
The CSWA is a timed exam.

Tutorial: Mass-Volume 8-13

Build this model. Calculate the volume of
the part and locate the Center of mass with
the provided information.

1. **Create** a New part in SolidWorks.

2. **Build** the illustrated model. Insert three
   features: Extruded Base (Boss-
   Extrude1), Extruded Boss (Boss-
   Extrude2) and Mirror. Three holes are
   displayed with an Ø1.00in.

3. **Set** the document properties for the
   model.

4. Create **Sketch1**. Select the Top Plane as
   the Sketch plane. Apply the Tangent Arc and
   Line Sketch tool. Insert the required geometric
   relations and dimensions. Note the location of
   the Origin.

5. Create the **Extruded Base (Boss-Extrude1)**
   feature. Blind is the default End Condition.
   Depth = .50in.

6. Create **Sketch2**. Select the front vertical face of
   Extrude1 as the Sketch plane. Insert the
   required geometric relations and dimensions.

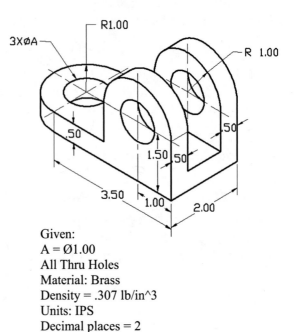

Given:
A = Ø1.00
All Thru Holes
Material: Brass
Density = .307 lb/in^3
Units: IPS
Decimal places = 2

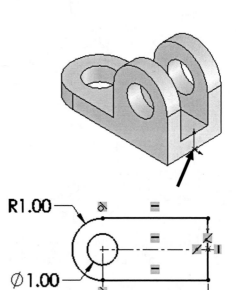

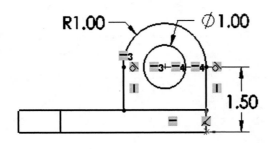

7. Create the **Extruded Boss (Boss-Extrude2)** feature. Blind is the default End Condition in Direction 1. Depth = .50in. Note the direction of the extrude.

8. Create the **Mirror** feature. Apply Symmetry. Mirror Boss-Extrude2 about the Front Plane.

9. **Assign** the defined material to the part.

10. **Calculate** the volume. The volume = 6.68 cubic inches.

11. **Locate** the Center of mass. The location of the Center of mass is derived from the part Origin.

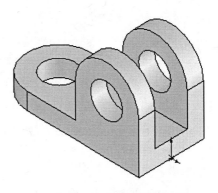

- X: -1.59 inches

- Y: 0.72 inches

- Z: 0.00 inches

In this category, Part Modeling an exam question could read: Build this model. What is the volume of the model?

- A = 6.19 cubic inches

- B = 7.79 cubic inches

- C = 7.87 cubic inches

- D = 6.68 cubic inches

```
Mass = 2.05 pounds

Volume = 6.68 cubic inches

Surface area = 40.64 inches^2

Center of mass: ( inches )
     X = -1.59
     Y = 0.72
     Z = 0.00
```

The correct answer is D.

View the triad location of the Center of mass for the part. Note: Tangent Edges are displayed for educational purposes.

12. **Save** the part and name it Mass-Volume 8-13.

13. **Close** the model.

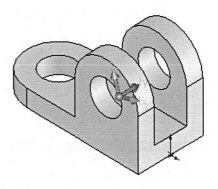

As an exercise, calculate the overall mass of the part using the IPS unit system, and assign Copper material to the part. Modify the hole diameters from 1.00in to 1.125in.

The overall mass of the part = 2.05 pounds. Save the part and name it Mass-Volume 8-13A.

```
Mass = 2.05 pounds

Volume = 6.37 cubic inches

Surface area = 39.97 inches^2

Center of mass: ( inches )
     X = -1.58
     Y = 0.70
     Z = 0.00
```

Tutorial: Mass-Volume 8-14

Build this model. Calculate the overall mass of the part and locate the Center of mass with the provided information.

1. **Create** a New part in SolidWorks.

2. **Build** the illustrated model. Insert a Revolved Base feature and Extruded Cut feature to build this part.

3. **Set** the document properties for the model.

4. Create **Sketch1**. Select the Front Plane as the Sketch plane. Apply the Centerline Sketch tool for the Revolve1 feature. Insert the required geometric relations and dimensions. Sketch1 is the profile for the Revolve1 feature.

5. Create the **Revolved Base** feature. The default angle is 360deg. Select the centerline for the Axis of Revolution.

🔅 A Revolve feature adds or removes material by revolving one or more profiles around a centerline.

6. Create **Sketch2**. Select the right large circular face of Revolve1 as the Sketch plane. Apply reference construction geometry. Use the Convert Entities and Trim Sketch tools. Insert the required geometric relations and dimensions.

🔅 You could also use the 3 Point Arc Sketch tool instead of the Convert Entities and Trim Sketch tools to create Sketch2.

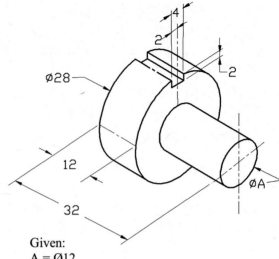

Given:
A = Ø12
Material: Cast Alloy Steel
Density = .0073 g/mm^3
Units: MMGS

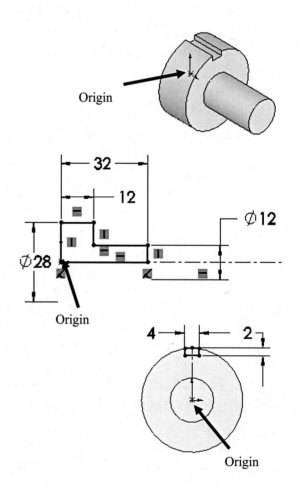

7. Create the **Extruded Cut** feature. Select Through All for End Condition in Direction 1.

8. **Assign** the defined material to the part.

9. **Calculate** the overall mass. The overall mass = 69.77 grams.

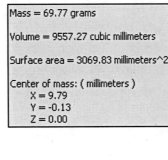
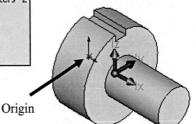

Origin

10. **Locate** the Center of mass. The location of the Center of mass is derived from the part Origin.

Mass = 69.77 grams

Volume = 9557.27 cubic millimeters

Surface area = 3069.83 millimeters^2

Center of mass: (millimeters)
   X = 9.79
   Y = -0.13
   Z = 0.00

- X = 9.79 millimeters

- Y = -0.13 millimeters

- Z = 0.00 millimeters

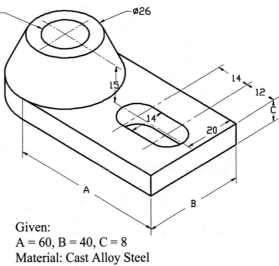

Origin

11. **Save** the part and name it Mass-Volume 8-14.

12. **Close** the model.

Tutorial: Mass-Volume 8-15

Build this model. Calculate the overall mass of the part and locate the Center of mass with the provided information.

1. **Create** a New part in SolidWorks.

2. **Build** the illustrated model. Insert two features: Extruded Base (Boss-Extrude1) and Revolved Boss.

3. **Set** the document properties for the model.

Ø16   Ø26

15
14
12
14
20
A
B
C

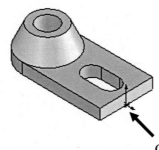

Tangent Edges are displayed for educational purposes.

Given:
A = 60, B = 40, C = 8
Material: Cast Alloy Steel
Density = .0073 g/mm^3
Units: MMGS

Origin

4. Create **Sketch1**. Select the Top Plane as the Sketch plane. Apply construction geometry. Apply the Tangent Arc and Line Sketch tool. Insert the required geometric relations and dimensions.

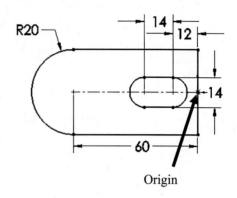

5. Create the **Extruded Base** feature. Blind is the default End Condition. Depth = 8mm.

6. Create **Sketch2**. Select the Front Plane as the Sketch plane. Apply construction geometry for the Revolved Boss feature. Insert the required geometric relations and dimension.

7. Create the **Revolved Boss** feature. The default angle is 360deg. Select the centerline for Axis of Revolution.

Origin

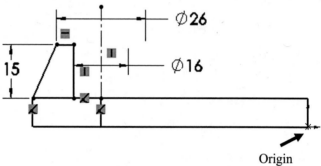

Origin

8. **Assign** the defined material to the part. **Calculate** the overall mass. The overall mass = 229.46 grams.

9. **Locate** the Center of mass. The location of the Center of mass is derived from the part Origin.

- X = -46.68 millimeters

- Y = 7.23 millimeters

- Z = 0.00 millimeters

Mass = 229.46 grams

Volume = 31433.02 cubic millimeters

Surface area = 9459.63 millimeters^2

Center of mass: (millimeters)
  X = -46.68
  Y = 7.23
  Z = 0.00

In this category, Part Modeling an exam question could read: Build this model. What is the overall mass of the part?

- A: 229.46 grams

- B: 249.50 grams

- C: 240.33 grams

- D: 120.34 grams

The correct answer is A.

10. **Save** the part and name it Mass-Volume 8-15.

11. **Close** the model.

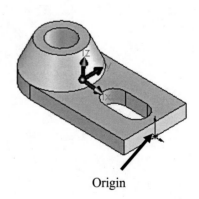

Origin

Tutorial: Mass-Volume 8-16

Build this model. Calculate the overall mass of the part and locate the Center of mass with the provided information.

1. **Create** a New part in SolidWorks.

2. **Build** the illustrated model. Insert three features: Extruded Base, Extruded Cut and Circular Pattern. There are eight holes Ø14mm equally spaces on an Ø56mm bolt circle. The center hole = Ø22mm.

3. **Set** the document properties for the model.

4. Create **Sketch1**. Select the Front Plane as the Sketch plane. Sketch two circles. The part Origin is located in the center of the sketch. Insert the required geometric relations and dimensions.

5. Create the **Extruded Base (Boss-Extrude1)** feature. Blind is the default End Condition. Depth = 20mm.

6. Create **Sketch2**. Select the front face as the Sketch plane. Apply construction geometry to locate the seed feature for the Circular Pattern. Insert the required geometric relations and dimensions.

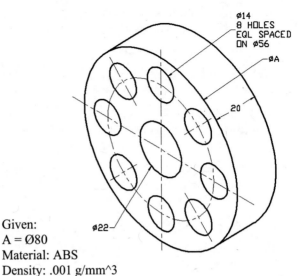

Ø14
8 HOLES
EQL SPACED
ON ø56

øA

20

ø22

Given:
A = Ø80
Material: ABS
Density: .001 g/mm^3
Units: MMGS

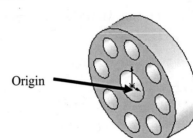

Origin

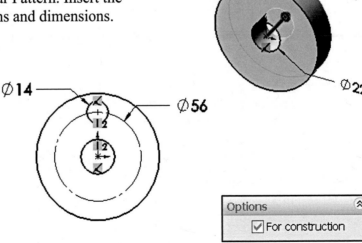

☼ Apply construction reference geometry to assist in creating the sketch entities and geometry that are incorporated into the part. Construction reference geometry is ignored when the sketch is used to create a feature. Construction reference geometry uses the same line style as centerlines.

Ø14

Ø56

Ø80

Ø22

Options   ⊗
☑ For construction

7. Create the **Extruded Cut** feature. Select Through All for End Condition in Direction 1.

8. Create the **Circular Pattern** feature. Create a Circular Pattern of the Cut-Extrude1 feature. Use the View, Temporary Axes command to select the Pattern Axis for the CirPattern1 feature. Instances = 8. Equal spacing is selected by default.

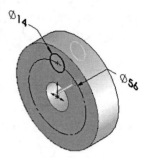

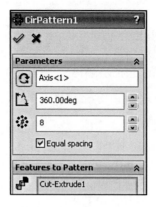

Apply a circular pattern feature to create multiple instances of one or more features that you can space uniformly about an axis.

9. **Assign** the defined material to the part.

10. **Calculate** the overall mass. The overall mass = 69.66 grams.

11. **Locate** the Center of mass. The location of the Center of mass is derived from the part Origin.

- X = 0.00 millimeters

- Y = 0.00 millimeters

- Z = -10.00 millimeters

12. **Save** the part and name it Mass-Volume 8-16.

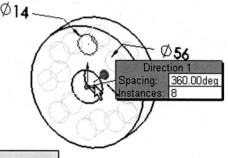

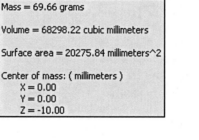

Mass = 69.66 grams

Volume = 68298.22 cubic millimeters

Surface area = 20275.84 millimeters^2

Center of mass: (millimeters)
    X = 0.00
    Y = 0.00
    Z = -10.00

13. **Close** the model.

As an exercise, select the Top Plane for the Sketch plane to create Sketch1. Recalculate the location of the Center of mass with respect to the part Origin: X = 0.00 millimeters, Y = -10.00 millimeters and Z = 0.00 millimeters. Save the part and name it Mass-Volume 8-16-TopPlane.

Mass = 69.66 grams

Volume = 68298.22 cubic millimeters

Surface area = 20275.84 millimeters^2

Center of mass: (millimeters)
    X = 0.00
    Y = -10.00
    Z = 0.00

Origin

The complexity of the models along with the features increases throughout this chapter to simulate the final types of parts that would be provided on the CSWA exam. In the next section, the parts represent the feature types and complexity that you would see in the Part Modeling category of the CSWA exam.

Tutorial: Basic-part 8-1

Build this model. Calculate the overall mass of the part and locate the Center of mass with the provided information.

1. **Create** a New part in SolidWorks.

2. **Build** the illustrated model. Think about the various features that create the model. Insert seven features to build this model: Extruded Base, Extruded Cut, Extruded Boss, Fillet, second Extruded Cut, Mirror and a second Fillet. Apply symmetry. Create the left half of the model first, and then apply the Mirror feature.

☀ There are numerous ways to build the models in this chapter. The goal is to display different design intents and techniques.

3. **Set** the document properties for the model.

4. Create **Sketch1**. Select the Front Plane as the Sketch plane. Create the main body of the part. The part Origin is located in the bottom left corner of the sketch. Insert the required geometric relations and dimensions.

5. Create the **Extruded Base** feature. Boss-Extrude1 is the Base feature. Select Mid Plane for End Condition in Direction 1. Depth = 76mm.

6. Create **Sketch2**. Select the top flat face of Extrude1 as the Sketch plane. Create the top cut on the Base feature. Apply construction geometry. Insert the required geometric relations and dimensions.

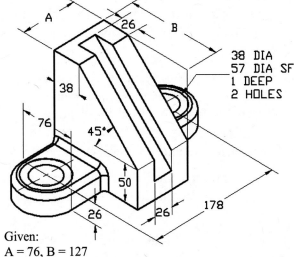

Given:
A = 76, B = 127
Material: 2014 Alloy
Density: .0028 g/mm^3
Units: MMGS
ALL ROUNDS EQUAL 6MM

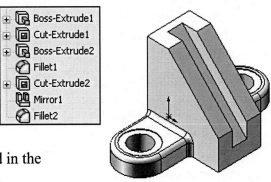

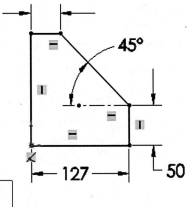

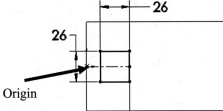

Origin

7. Create the first **Extruded Cut** feature. Select Through All for End Condition in Direction 1. Select the illustrated angled edge for the Direction of Extrusion.

8. Create **Sketch3**. Select the bottom face of Boss-Extrude1 as the Sketch plane. Sketch the first tab with a single hole as illustrated. Insert the required geometric relations and dimensions.

9. Create the **Extruded Boss** feature. Blind is the default End Condition in Direction 1. Depth = 26mm.

10. Create the first **Fillet** feature. Fillet the top edge of the left tab. Radius = 6mm. Constant radius is selected by default.

11. Create **Sketch4**. Select the top face of Extrude3 as the Sketch plane. Sketch a circle. Insert the required dimension.

12. Create the second **Extruded Cut** feature. Blind is the default End Condition in Direction 1. Depth = 1mm. The model displayed an Ø57mm Spot Face hole with a 1mm depth.

13. Create the **Mirror** feature. Mirror about the Front Plane. Mirror the Cut-Extrude2, Fillet1, and Boss-Extrude2 feature.

14. Create the second **Fillet** feature. Fillet the top inside edge of the left tab and the top inside edge of the right tab. Radius = 6mm.

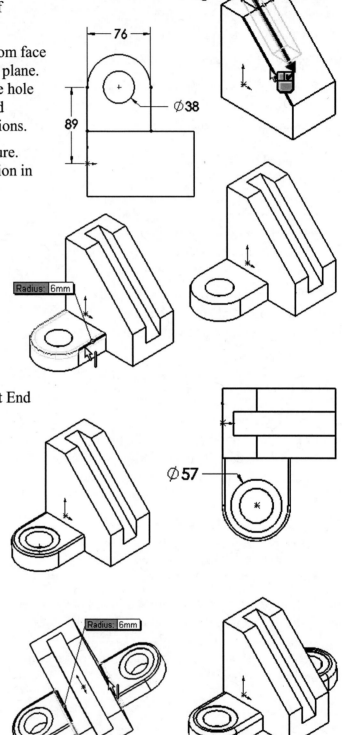

15. **Assign** the defined material to the part.

16. **Calculate** the overall mass of the part. The overall mass = 3437.29 grams.

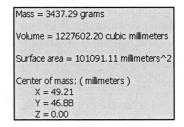

17. **Locate** the Center of mass. The location of the Center of mass is derived from the part Origin.

- X = 49.21 millimeters

- Y = 46.88 millimeters

- Z = 0.00 millimeters

18. **Save** the part and name it Part-Modeling 8-1.

19. **Close** the model.

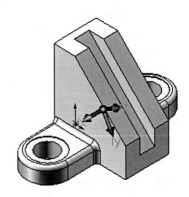

In this category, Part Modeling an exam question could read: Build this model. What is the overall mass of the part?

- A: 3944.44 grams

- B: 4334.29 grams

- C: 3437.29 grams

- D: 2345.69 grams

The correct answer is C.

As an exercise, modify all ALL ROUNDS from 6MM to 8MM. Modify the material from 2014 Alloy to 6061 Alloy.

Modify the Sketch1 angle from 45deg to 30deg. Modify the Extrude3 depth from 26mm to 36mm. Recalculate the location of the Center of mass with respect to the part Origin.

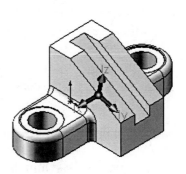

- X = 49.76 millimeters

- Y = 34.28 millimeters

- Z = 0.00 millimeters

20. **Save** the part and name it Part-Modeling 8-1-Modify.

☼ Tangent Edges are displayed for educational purposes.

☼ There are numerous ways to create the models in this chapter. The goal is to display different design intents and techniques.

Tutorial: Basic-part 8-2

Build this model. Calculate the overall mass of the part and locate the Center of mass with the provided information.

1. **Create** a New part in SolidWorks.

2. **Build** the illustrated model. Think about the various features that create the part. Insert seven features and a plane to build this part: Extruded-Thin1, Boss-Extrude1, Cut-Extrude1, Cut-Extrude2 and three Fillets. Apply reference construction planes to build the circular features.

3. **Set** the document properties for the model.

4. Create **Sketch1**. Select the Front Plane as the Sketch plane. Apply construction geometry as the reference line for the 30deg angle. Insert the required geometric relations and dimensions. Note the location of the Origin.

5. Create the **Extrude-Thin1** feature. This is the Base feature. Apply symmetry. Select Mid Plane for End Condition in Direction 1 to maintain the location of the Origin. Depth = 52mm. Thickness = 12mm.

Use the Thin Feature option to control the extrude thickness, not the Depth.

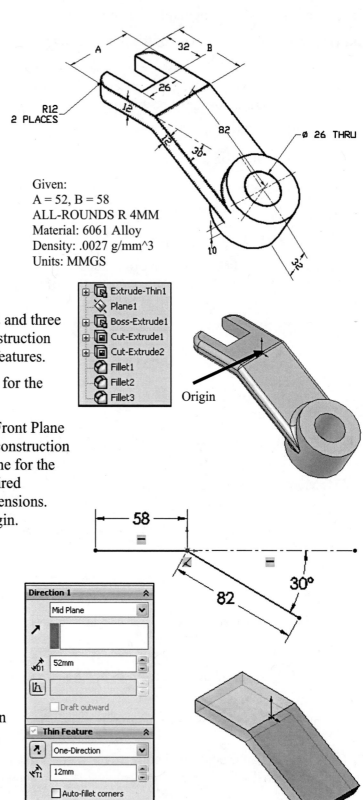

Given:
A = 52, B = 58
ALL-ROUNDS R 4MM
Material: 6061 Alloy
Density: .0027 g/mm^3
Units: MMGS

6. Create **Plane1**. Plane1 is the Sketch plane for the Extruded Boss (Boss-Extrude1) feature. Select the midpoint and the top face as illustrated. Plane1 is located in the middle of the top and bottom faces. Select Parallel Plane at Point for option.

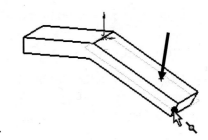

☀ Create Plane1 to use the Depth dimension of 32mm.

7. Create **Sketch2**. Select Plane1 as the Sketch plane. Use the Normal To view tool. Sketch a circle to create the Extruded Boss feature. Insert the required geometric relations.

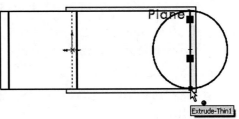

☀ The Normal To view tool rotates and zooms the model to the view orientation normal to the selected plane, planar face, or feature.

8. Create the **Extruded Boss** feature. Apply Symmetry. Select Mid Plane for End Condition in Direction 1. Depth = 32mm.

9. Create **Sketch3**. Select the top circular face of Boss-Extrude1 as the Sketch plane. Sketch a circle. Insert the required geometric relation and dimension.

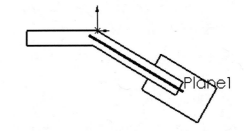

☀ There are numerous ways to create the models in this chapter. The goal is to display different design intents and techniques.

10. Create the first **Extruded Cut** feature. Select Through All for End Condition in Direction 1.

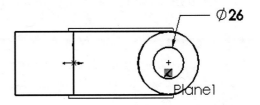

11. Create **Sketch4**. Select the top face of Extrude-Thin1 as the Sketch plane. Apply construction geometry. Insert the required geometric relations and dimensions.

12. Create the second **Extruded Cut** feature. Select Through All for End Condition in Direction 1.

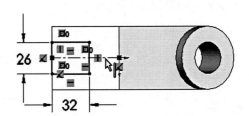

13. Create the **Fillet1** feature. Fillet the left and right edges of Extrude-Thin1 as illustrated. Radius = 12mm.

14. Create the **Fillet2** feature. Fillet the top and bottom edges of Extrude-Thin1 as illustrated. Radius = 4mm.

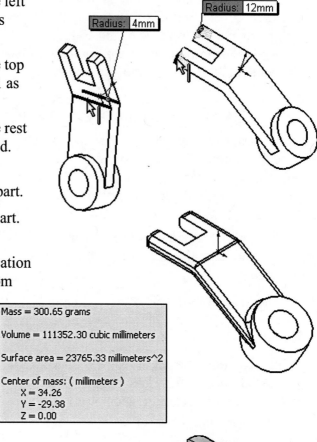

15. Create the **Fillet3** feature. Fillet the rest of the model; six edges as illustrated. Radius = 4mm.

16. **Assign** the defined material to the part.

17. **Calculate** the overall mass of the part. The overall mass = 300.65 grams.

18. **Locate** the Center of mass. The location of the Center of mass is derived from the part Origin.

- X: 34.26 millimeters

- Y: -29.38 millimeters

- Z: 0.00 millimeters

```
Mass = 300.65 grams

Volume = 111352.30 cubic millimeters

Surface area = 23765.33 millimeters^2

Center of mass: ( millimeters )
       X = 34.26
       Y = -29.38
       Z = 0.00
```

19. **Save** the part and name it Part-Modeling 8-2.

20. **Close** the model.

As an exercise, modify the Fillet2 and Fillet3 radius from 4mm to 2mm. Modify the Fillet1 radius from 12m to 10mm. Modify the material from 6061 Alloy to ABS.

Modify the Sketch1 angle from 30deg to 45deg. Modify the Extrude1 depth from 32mm to 38mm. Recalculate the location of the Center of mass with respect to the part Origin.

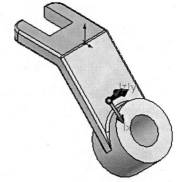

- X = 27.62 millimeters

- Y = -40.44 millimeters

- Z = 0.00 millimeters

21. **Save** the part and name it Part-Modeling 8-2-Modify.

```
Mass = 123.60 grams

Volume = 121173.81 cubic millimeters

Surface area = 25622.46 millimeters^2

Center of mass: ( millimeters )
       X = 27.62
       Y = -40.44
       Z = 0.00
```

Tutorial: Basic-part 8-3

Build this model. Calculate the volume of the part and locate the Center of mass with the provided information.

1. **Create** a New part in SolidWorks.

2. **Build** the illustrated model. Think about the various features that create this model. Insert five features and a plane to build this part: Extruded Base, two Extruded Bosses, Extruded Cut and a Rib. Insert a reference plane to create the Boss-Extrude2 feature.

3. **Set** the document properties for the model.

4. Create **Sketch1**. Select the Top Plane as the Sketch plane. Sketch a rectangle. Apply two construction lines for an Intersection relation. Use the horizontal construction line as the Plane1 reference. Insert the required relations and dimensions.

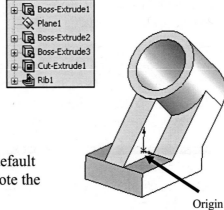

Given:
A = Ø3.00, B = 1.00
Material: 6061 Alloy
Density: .097 lb/in^3
Units: IPS
Decimal places = 2

Boss-Extrude1
Plane1
Boss-Extrude2
Boss-Extrude3
Cut-Extrude1
Rib1

5. Create the **Extruded Base** feature. Blind is the default End Condition in Direction 1. Depth = 1.00in. Note the extrude direction is downward.

Origin

You can create planes in part or assembly documents. You can use planes to sketch, to create a section view of a model, for a neutral plane in a draft feature, and so on.

The created plane is displayed 5% larger than the geometry on which the plane is created, or 5% larger than the bounding box. This helps reduce selection problems when planes are created directly on faces or from orthogonal geometry.

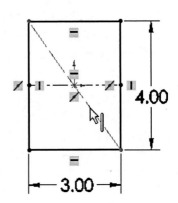

6. Create **Plane1**. Plane1 is the Sketch plane for the Extruded Boss feature. Show Sketch1. Select the horizontal construction line in Sketch1 and the top face of Boss-Extrude1. Angle = 48deg.

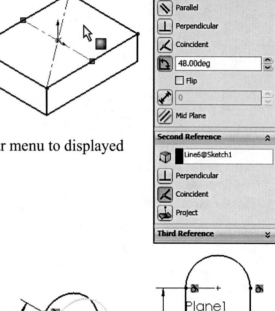

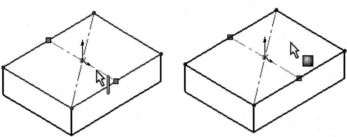

Click **View**, **Sketches** from the Menu bar menu to displayed sketches in the Graphics window.

7. Create **Sketch2**. Select Plane1 as the Sketch plane. Create the Extruded Boss profile. Insert the

   required geometric relations and dimension. Note: Dimension to the front top edge of Boss-Extrude1 as illustrated.

8. Create the first **Extruded Boss** feature. Select the Up To Vertex End Condition in Direction 1. Select the back top right vertex point as illustrated.

9. Create **Sketch3**. Select the back angled face of Boss-Extrude2 as the Sketch plane. Sketch a circle. Insert the required geometric relations.

10. Create the third **Extruded Boss** feature. Blind is the default End Condition in Direction 1.   Depth = 3.00in.

11. Create **Sketch4**. Select the front face of Boss-Extrude3 as the Sketch plane. Sketch a circle. Sketch4 is the profile for the Extruded Cut feature. Insert the required geometric relation and dimension.

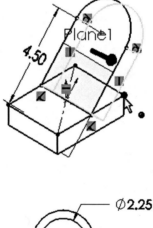
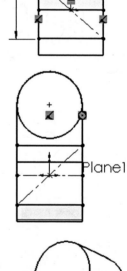
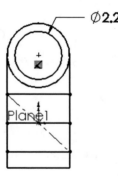
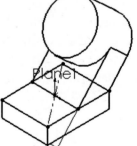

The part Origin is displayed in blue.

12. Create the **Extruded Cut** feature. Select Through All for End Condition in Direction 1.

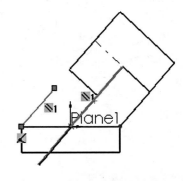

13. Create **Sketch5**. Select the Right Plane as the Sketch plane. Insert a Parallel relation to partially define Sketch5. Sketch5 is the profile for the Rib feature. Sketch5 does not need to be fully defined. Sketch5 locates the end conditions based on existing geometry.

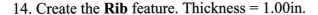
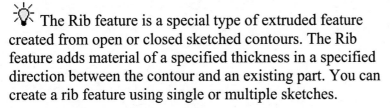

14. Create the **Rib** feature. Thickness = 1.00in.

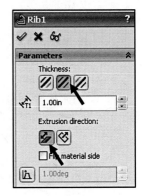

☀ The Rib feature is a special type of extruded feature created from open or closed sketched contours. The Rib feature adds material of a specified thickness in a specified direction between the contour and an existing part. You can create a rib feature using single or multiple sketches.

15. **Assign** 6061 Alloy material to the part.

16. **Calculate** the volume. The volume = 30.65 cubic inches.

17. **Locate** the Center of mass. The location of the Center of mass is derived from the part Origin.

Mass = 2.99 pounds

Volume = 30.65 cubic inches

Surface area = 100.96 inches^2

Center of mass: (inches)
 X = 0.00
 Y = 0.73
 Z = -0.86

- X: 0.00 inches

- Y: 0.73 inches

- Z: -0.86 inches

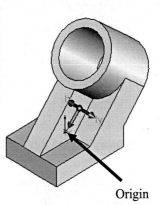

Origin

18. **Save** the part and name it Part-Modeling 8-3.

19. **Close** the model.

As an exercise, modify the Rib1 feature from 1.00in to 1.25in. Modify the Extrude3 depth from 3.00in to 3.25in. Modify the material from 6061 Alloy to Copper.

Modify the Plane1 angle from 48deg to 30deg. Recalculate the volume of the part. The new volume = 26.94 cubic inches.

Volume = 26.94 cubic inches

Surface area = 98.18 inches^2

Center of mass: (inches)
 X = 0.00
 Y = 0.58
 Z = -0.85

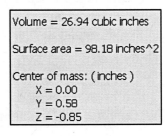

20. **Save** the part and name it Part-Modeling 8-3-Modify.

Tutorial: Basic-part 8-4

Build this model.
Calculate the volume
of the part and locate
the Center of mass
with the provided
information.

1. **Create** a New part
    in SolidWorks.

2. **Build** the
    illustrated model.
    Apply symmetry.
    Think about the
    various features
    that create the part.
    Insert six features: Extruded Base, two Extruded
    Cuts, Mirror, Extruded Boss, and a third Extruded
    Cut.

Given:
A = 6.00, B = 4.50
Material: 2014 Alloy
Plate thickness = .50
Units: IPS
Decimal places = 2

3. **Set** the document properties for the model.

4. Create **Sketch1**. Select the Top Plane as the Sketch
    plane. Apply symmetry. The part
    Origin is located in the center of
    the rectangle. Insert the required
    relations and dimensions.

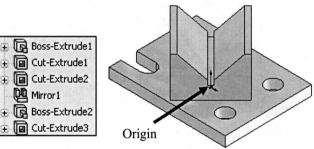

Origin

5. Create the **Extruded Base** (Boss-
    Extrude1) feature. Blind is the
    default End Condition in
    Direction 1. Depth = .50in.

6. Create **Sketch2**. Select
    the top face of Boss-
    Extrude1 for the Sketch
    plane. Sketch a circle.
    Insert the required
    relations and dimensions.

7. Create the first **Extruded
    Cut** feature. Select
    Through All as End
    Condition in Direction1.

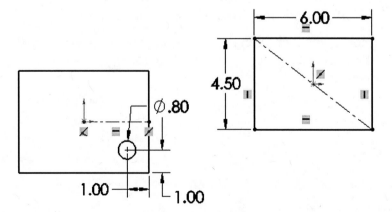

8. Create **Sketch3**. Select the top face of Boss-Extrude1 for the Sketch plane. Insert the required geometric relations and dimensions.

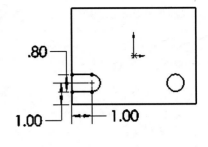

 Click **View, Temporary** axes to view the part temporary axes in the Graphics window.

9. Create the second **Extruded Cut** feature. Select Through All as End Condition in Direction1.

10. Create the **Mirror** feature. Mirror the two Extruded Cut features about the Front Plane.

11. Create **Sketch4**. Select the top face of Boss-Extrude1 as the Sketch plane. Apply construction geometry to center the sketch. Insert the required relations and dimensions.

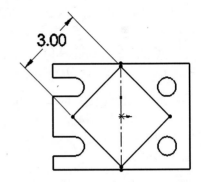

12. Create the **Extruded Boss** feature. Blind is the default End Condition in Direction 1. Depth = 2.00in.

13. Create **Sketch5**. Select the front face of Boss-Extrude as illustrated for the Sketch plane. Sketch5 is the profile for the third Extruded Cut feature. Apply construction geometry. Insert the required dimensions and relations.

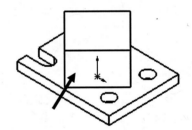

14. Create the third **Extruded Cut** feature. Through All is selected for End Condition in Direction 1 and Direction 2.

15. **Assign** 2014 Alloy material to the part.

16. **Calculate** the volume of the part. The volume = 25.12 cubic inches.

17. **Locate** the Center of mass. The location of the Center of mass is derived from the part Origin.

- X: 0.06 inches

- Y: 0.80 inches

- Z: 0.00 inches

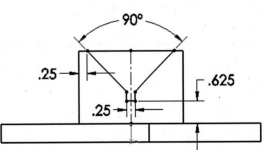

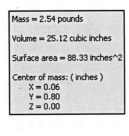

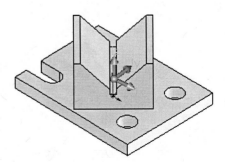

18. **Save** the part and name it Part-Modeling 8-4.

19. **Close** the model.

Summary

Simple Part Modeling is one of the five categories on the CSWA exam. There is one question on the CSWA exam in this category. The question is in a multiple choice single answer format. The question is worth thirty (30) points. You are required to build a model, with six or more features and to answer a question - either on the overall mass, volume or the location the Center of mass for the created part relative to the default part Origin location.

In this chapter, you covered the knowledge to identify the part Origin, design intent and key features to create a simple part from a detailed dimensioned illustration.

The complexity of the models along with the features increased throughout this chapter to simulate the final types of parts that would be provided on the CSWA exam. Spend no more than 40 minutes on the question in this category. This is a timed exam. Manage your time.

At this time, there are no modeling questions on the exam that requires you to use Sheet Metal, Loft, Swept or Shell features.

Advanced Part Modeling is the next chapter in this book. There is one question on the CSWA exam in the Advanced Part Modeling category. The question is worth twenty (20) points.

The main difference between the Part Modeling category and the Advanced Part Modeling category is the complexity of the sketches and the number of dimensions and geometric relations along with an increase in the number of features.

View sample screen shots from an older CSWA exam for a simple part at the end of the Homework section in this chapter.

Questions

1: In Tutorial: Volume / Center of mass 8-2 you built the model using the FeatureManager that had three features vs. four features in the FeatureManager.

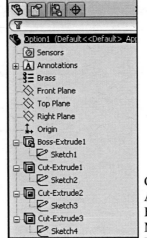

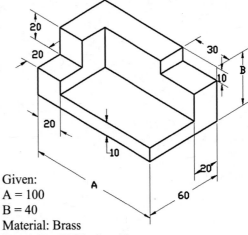

Given:
A = 100
B = 40
Material: Brass
Density = .0085 g/mm^3
Units: MMGS

Calculate the overall mass of the part, volume, and locate the Center of mass with the provided information using the Option1 FeatureManager.

2. In Tutorial: Mass / Volume 8-4 you built the model using the FeatureManager that had three features vs. four features.

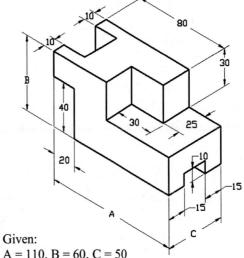

Calculate the overall mass of the part, volume, and locate the Center of mass with the provided information using the Option3 FeatureManager.

Given:
A = 110, B = 60, C = 50
Material: Nylon 6/10
Density = .0014 g/mm^3
Units: MMGS

3. In Tutorial: Base Part 8-4 you built the illustrated model. Modify the plate thickness from .50in to .25in. Modify the Sketch5 angle from 90deg to 75deg.   Re-assign the material from 2014 Alloy to 6061 Alloy.

Calculate the overall mass of the part, volume, and locate the Center of mass with the provided information.

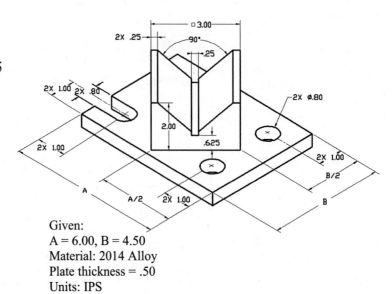

Given:
A = 6.00, B = 4.50
Material: 2014 Alloy
Plate thickness = .50
Units: IPS
Decimal places = 2

4. Build this model: Set document properties, identify the correct Sketch planes, apply the correct Sketch and Feature tools and apply material.

Calculate the overall mass of the part, volume, and locate the Center of mass with the provided illustrated information.

- Material: 6061 Alloy

- Units: MMGS

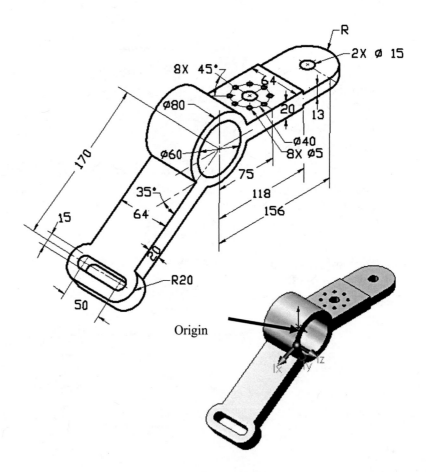

Origin

5. Build this model. Set document properties and identify the correct Sketch planes. Apply the correct Sketch and Feature tools, and apply material.

Calculate the overall mass of the part, volume, and locate the Center of mass with the provided information.

- Material: 6061 Alloy

- Units: MMGS

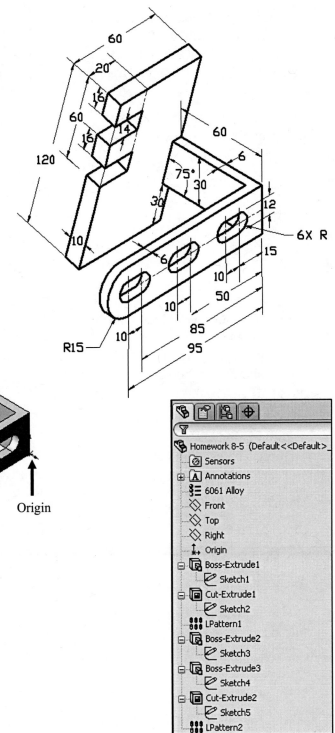

Origin

6. Build this model. Set document properties and identify the correct Sketch planes. Apply the correct Sketch and Feature tools, and apply material.

Calculate the overall mass of the part with the provided information. Note: The Origin is arbitrary.

- Material: Copper
- Units: MMGS
- A = 100
- B = 80

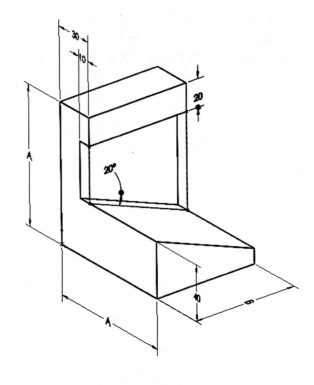

7. Build this model. Set document properties and identify the correct Sketch planes. Apply the correct Sketch and Feature tools, and apply material.

Calculate the overall mass of the part with the provided information. The location of the Origin is arbitrary.

- Material: 6061
- Units: MMGS
- A = 16
- B = 40
- Side A is perpendicular to side B.
- C = 16

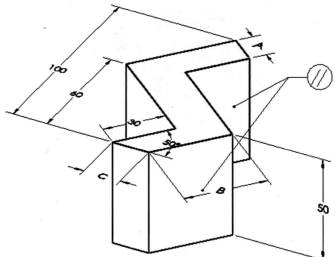

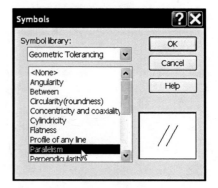

8. Build this model. Set document properties and identify the correct Sketch planes. Apply the correct Sketch and Feature tools, and apply material.

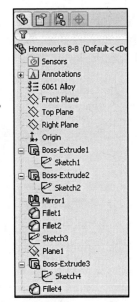

Calculate the overall mass of the part, volume, and locate the Center of mass with the provided information.

- Material: 6061

- Units: IPS

- View the provided drawing views for details.

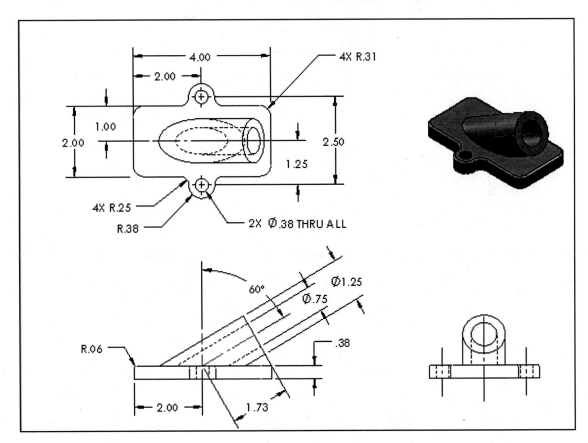

9. Build this model. Set document properties and identify the correct Sketch planes. Apply the correct Sketch and Feature tools, and apply material.

Calculate the overall mass of the part, volume, and locate the Center of mass with the provided information.

*   Material: 6061

*   Units: IPS

*   View the provided drawing views for details.

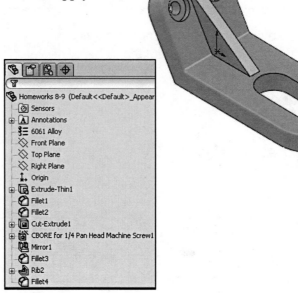

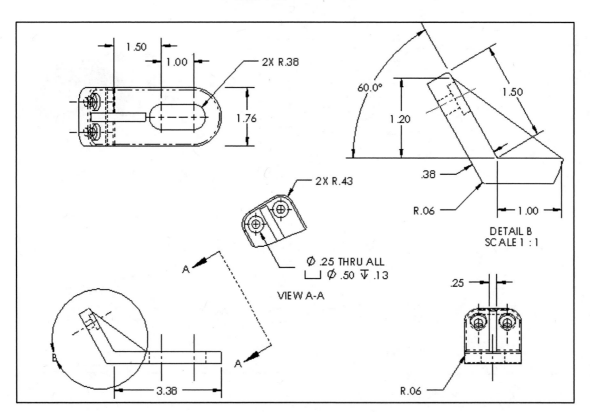

Sample screen shots from an older CSWA exam for a simple part. Click on the additional views to understand the part and to provide information. Read each question carefully. Understand the dimensions, center of mass and units. Apply needed materials.

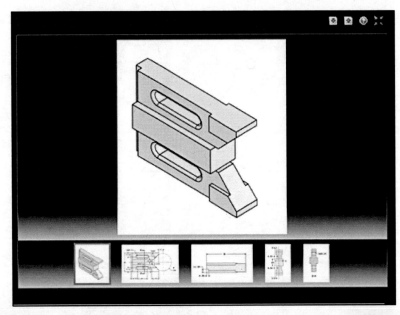

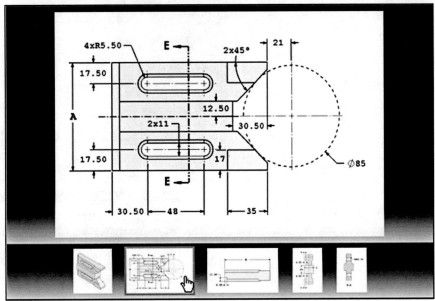

☀ Zoom in on the part or view if needed.

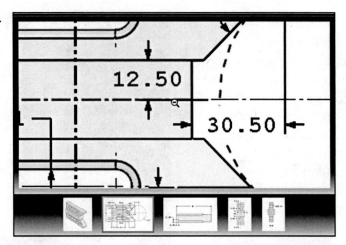

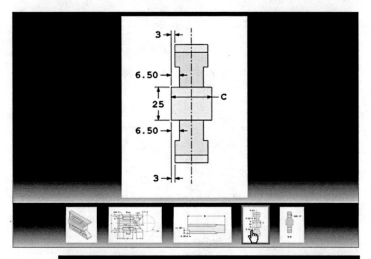

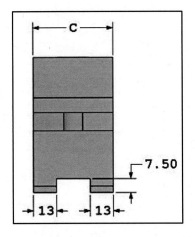

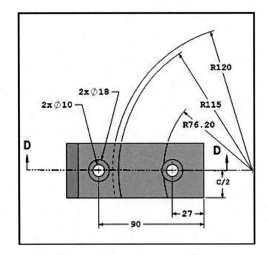

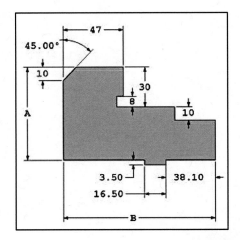

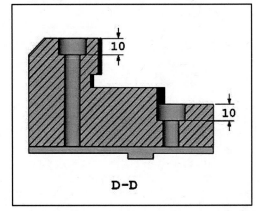

D-D

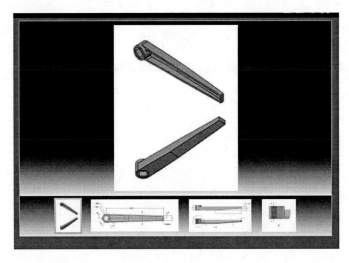

Notes:

Chapter 9
Advanced Part Modeling

Objectives

Advanced Part Modeling is one of the five categories on the CSWA exam. The main difference between the Advanced Part Modeling and the Simple Part Modeling category is the complexity of the sketches and the number of dimensions and geometric relations along with an increase number of features.

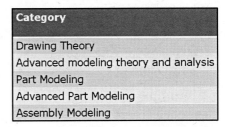

Category
Drawing Theory
Advanced modeling theory and analysis
Part Modeling
Advanced Part Modeling
Assembly Modeling

There is one question on the CSWA exam in this category. The question is worth twenty (20) points and is in a multiple choice single answer format. The question is either on the location of the Center of mass relative to the default part Origin or to a new created coordinate system and all of the mass properties located in the Mass Properties dialog box: total overall mass, volume, etc.

There are numerous ways to create the models in this chapter. The goal is to display different design intents and techniques.

On the completion of the chapter, you will be able to:

- Specify Document Properties
- Interpret engineering terminology:
  - Create and manipulate a coordinate system
- Build an advanced part from a detailed dimensioned illustration using the following tools and features:
  - 2D & 3D Sketch tools, Extruded Boss/Base, Extruded Cut, Fillet, Mirror, Revolved Boss/Base, Linear & Circular Pattern, Chamfer and Revolved Cut
- Locate the Center of mass relative to the part Origin
- Create a coordinate system location
- Locate the Center of mass relative to a created coordinate system

In the Simple Part Modeling, Advanced Part Modeling and Assembly Modeling categories, you are required to read and interpret all types of drawing views.

Build an Advanced part from a detailed dimensioned illustration

Tutorial: Advanced Part   9-1

An exam question in this category could read: Build this part. Calculate the overall mass and locate the Center of mass of the illustrated model.

1. **Create** a New part in SolidWorks.

2. **Build** the illustrated model. Insert seven features: Extruded Base, two Extruded Bosses, two Extruded Cuts, a Chamfer and a Fillet.

Think about the steps that you would take to build the illustrated part. Identify the location of the part Origin. Start with the back base flange. Review the provided dimensions and annotations in the part illustration.

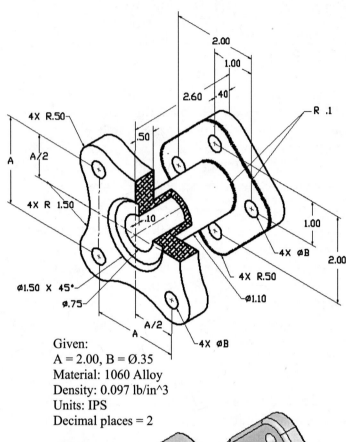

Given:
A = 2.00, B = Ø.35
Material: 1060 Alloy
Density: 0.097 lb/in^3
Units: IPS
Decimal places = 2

🔅 The key difference between the Advanced Part Modeling and the Part Modeling category is the complexity of the sketches and the number of features, dimensions and geometric relations.

🔅 Final solutions and homework solutions are located on the CD in the book!

🔅 There are numerous ways to build the models in this chapter. The goal is to display different design intents and techniques.

Boss-Extrude1
Boss-Extrude2
Boss-Extrude3
Cut-Extrude1
Cut-Extrude2
Chamfer1
Fillet1

Origin

SolidWorks CSWA Model Folders
Chapter 7
Chapter 7 Final Solutions
Chapter 8
Chapter 8 Final Solutions
Chapter 9
Chapter 9 Final Solutions
Chapter 10
Chapter 10 Final Solutions
Chapter 11
Chapter 11 Final Solutions

3. **Set** the document properties for the model.

4. Create **Sketch1**. Sketch1 is the Base sketch. Select the Front Plane as the Sketch plane. Apply construction geometry. Sketch a horizontal and vertical centerline. Sketch four circles. Insert an Equal relation. Insert a Symmetric relation about the vertical and horizontal centerlines. Sketch two top angled lines and a tangent arc. Apply the Mirror Sketch tool. Complete the sketch. Insert the required geometric relations and dimensions.

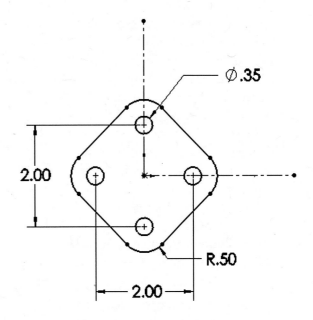

In a Symmetric relation, the selected items remain equidistant from the centerline, on a line perpendicular to the centerline. Sketch entities to select: a centerline and two points, lines, arcs or ellipses.

The Sketch Fillet tool rounds the selected corner at the intersection of two sketch entities, creating a tangent arc.

5. Create the **Extruded Base** feature. Boss-Extrude1 is the Base feature. Blind is the default End Condition in Direction 1. Depth = .40in.

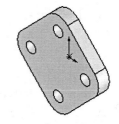

6. Create **Sketch2**. Select the front face of Boss-Extrude1 as the Sketch plane. Sketch a circle. Insert the required geometric relation and dimension.

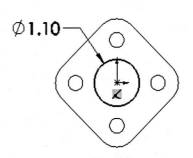

7. Create the first **Extruded Boss** feature. Blind is the default End Condition in Direction 1. The Extrude feature is the tube between the two flanges. Depth = 1.70in. Note: 1.70in = 2.60in - (.50in + .40in).

The complexity of the models along with the features progressively increases throughout this chapter to simulate the final types of parts that could be provided on the CSWA exam.

Tangent Edges are displayed for educational purposes.

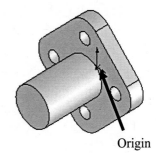

Origin

8. Create **Sketch3**. Select the front circular face of Boss-Extrude2 as the Sketch plane. Sketch a horizontal and vertical centerline. Sketch the top two circles. Insert an Equal and Symmetric relation between the two circles. Mirror the top two circles about the horizontal centerline. Insert dimensions to locate the circles from the Origin. Apply either the 3 Point Arc or the Centerpoint Arc Sketch tool. The center point of the Tangent Arc is aligned with a Vertical relation to the Origin. Complete the sketch.

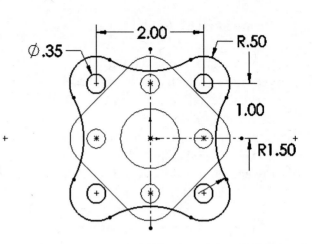

🔆 There are numerous ways to create the models in this chapter. The goal is to display different design intents and techniques

🔆 Use the Centerpoint Arc Sketch tool to create an arc from a: centerpoint, a start point, and an end point.

🔆 Apply the Tangent Arc Sketch tool to create an arc, tangent to a sketch entity.

🔆 The Arc PropertyManager controls the properties of a sketched Centerpoint Arc, Tangent Arc, and 3 Point Arc.

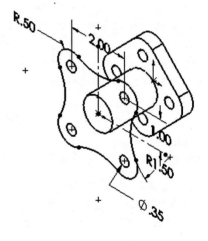

9. Create the second **Extruded Boss** feature. Blind is the default End Condition in Direction 1.
    Depth = .50in.

10. Create **Sketch4**. Select the front face of the Extrude feature as the Sketch plane. Sketch a circle. Insert the required geometric relation and dimension.

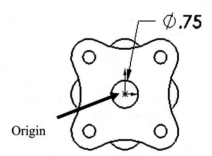

Origin

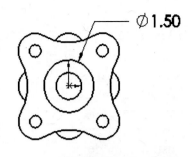

11. Create the first **Extruded Cut** feature. Select the Through All End Condition for Direction 1.

12. Create **Sketch5**. Select the front face of the Extrude feature as the Sketch plane. Sketch a circle. Insert the required geometric relation and dimension.

13. Create the second **Extruded Cut** feature. Blind is the default End Condition for Direction1. Depth = .10in.

14. Create the **Chamfer** feature. In order to have the outside circle 1.50in, select the inside edge of the sketched circle. Create an Angle distance chamfer. Distance = .10in. Angle = 45deg.

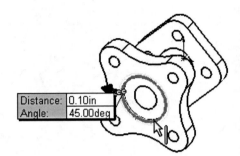

🔆 The Chamfer feature creates a beveled feature on selected edges, faces or a vertex.

15. Create the **Fillet** feature. Fillet the two edges as illustrated. Radius = .10in.

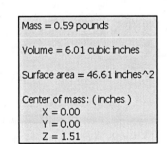

16. **Assign** 1060 Alloy material to the part. Material is required to calculate the overall mass of the part.

17. **Calculate** the overall mass. The overall mass = 0.59 pounds.

18. **Locate** the Center of mass. The location of the Center of mass is relative to the part Origin.

- X: 0.00

- Y: 0.00

- Z: 1.51

19. **Save** the part and name it Advanced Part 9-1.

20. **Close** the model.

Mass = 0.59 pounds

Volume = 6.01 cubic inches

Surface area = 46.61 inches^2

Center of mass: (inches)
    X = 0.00
    Y = 0.00
    Z = 1.51

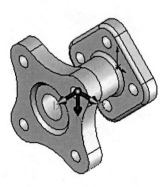

Tutorial: Advanced Part 9-2

An exam question in this category could read: Build this part. Calculate the overall mass and locate the Center of mass of the illustrated model.

1. **Create** a New part in SolidWorks.

2. **Build** the illustrated dimensioned model. Insert eight features: Extruded Base, Extruded Cut, Circular Pattern, two Extruded Bosses, Extruded Cut, Chamfer and Fillet.

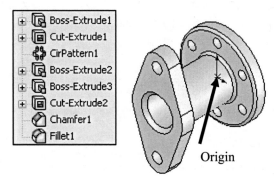

Given:
A = 70, B = 76
Material: 6061 Alloy
Density: .0027 g/mm^3
Units: MMGS

Think about the steps that you would take to build the illustrated part. Review the provided information. Start with the six hole flange.

🔅 Tangent Edges are displayed for educational purposes.

3. **Set** the document properties for the model.

4. Create **Sketch1**. Sketch1 is the Base sketch. Select the Front Plane as the Sketch plane. Sketch two circles. Insert the required geometric relations and dimensions.

5. Create the **Extruded Base** feature. Blind is the default End Condition in Direction 1. Depth = 10mm. Note the direction of the extrude feature to maintain the Origin location.

6. Create **Sketch2**. Select the front face of Boss-Extrude1 as the Sketch plane. Sketch2 is the profile for first Extruded Cut feature. The Extruded Cut feature is the seed feature for the Circular Pattern. Apply construction reference geometry. Insert the required geometric relations and dimensions.

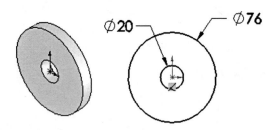

Origin

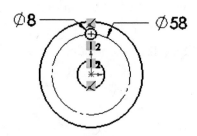

7. Create the **Extruded Cut** feature. Cut-Extrude1 is the first bolt hole. Select Through All for End Condition in Direction 1.

8. Create the **Circular Pattern** feature. Default Angle = 360deg. Number of instances = 6. Select the center axis for the Pattern Axis box.

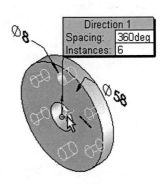

☼ The Circular Pattern PropertyManager is displayed when you pattern one or more features about an axis.

9. Create **Sketch3**. Select the front face of the Extrude feature as the Sketch plane. Sketch two circles. Insert a Coradial relation on the inside circle. The two circles share the same centerpoint and radius. Insert the required dimension.

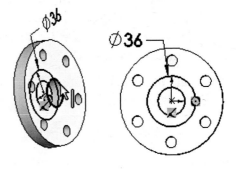

10. Create the first **Extruded Boss (Boss-Extrude2)** feature. The Boss-Extrude2 feature is the connecting tube between the two flanges. Blind is the default End Condition in Direction 1. Depth = 48mm.

11. Create **Sketch4**. Select the front circular face of Extrude3 as the Sketch plane. Sketch a horizontal and vertical centerline from the Origin. Sketch the top and bottom circles symmetric about the horizontal centerline. Dimension the distance between the two circles and their diameter. Create the top centerpoint arc with the centerpoint Coincident to the top circle. The start point and the end point of the arc are horizontal. Sketch the two top angled lines symmetric about the vertical centerline. Apply symmetry. Mirror the two lines and the centerpoint arc about the horizontal centerline. Insert the left and right tangent arcs with a centerpoint Coincident with the Origin. Complete the sketch.

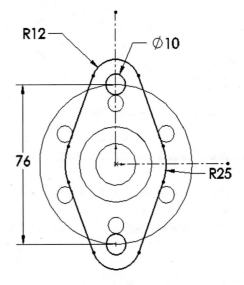

12. Create the second **Extruded Boss** (Boss-Extrude3) feature. Blind is the default End Condition in Direction 1. Depth = 12mm.

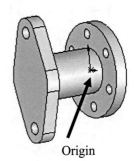

Origin

13. Create **Sketch5**. Select the front face of the Extrude feature as the Sketch plane. Sketch a circle. The part Origin is located in the center of the model. Insert the required dimension.

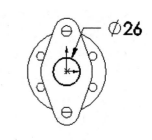

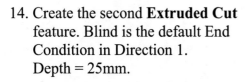

14. Create the second **Extruded Cut** feature. Blind is the default End Condition in Direction 1. Depth = 25mm.

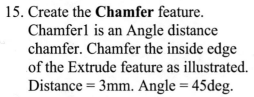

15. Create the **Chamfer** feature. Chamfer1 is an Angle distance chamfer. Chamfer the inside edge of the Extrude feature as illustrated. Distance = 3mm. Angle = 45deg.

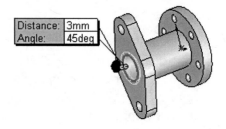

16. Create the **Fillet** feature. Fillet the two edges of Extrude1. Radius = 2mm.

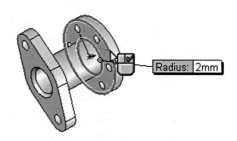

17. **Assign** 6061 Alloy material to the part.

18. **Calculate** the overall mass of the part. The overall mass = 276.97 grams.

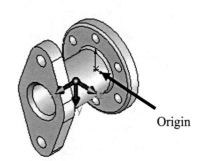

19. **Locate** the Center of mass. The location of the Center of mass is relative to the part Origin.

- X: 0.00 millimeters

- Y: 0.00 millimeters

- Z: 21.95 millimeters

20. **Save** the part and name it Advanced Part 9-2.

21. **Close** the model.

In the Advanced Part Modeling category, an exam question could read: Build this model. Locate the Center of mass with respect to the part Origin.

- A: X = 0.00 millimeters, Y = 0.00 millimeters, Z = 21.95 millimeters

- B: X = 21.95 millimeters, Y = 10.00 millimeters, Z = 0.00 millimeters

- C: X = 0.00 millimeters, Y = 0.00 millimeters, Z = -27.02 millimeters

- D: X= 1.00 millimeters, Y = -1.01 millimeters, Z = -0.04 millimeters

The correct answer is A.

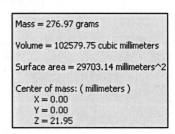

Origin

Mass = 276.97 grams

Volume = 102579.75 cubic millimeters

Surface area = 29703.14 millimeters^2

Center of mass: (millimeters)
X = 0.00
Y = 0.00
Z = 21.95

Tutorial: Advanced Part 9-3

An exam question in this category could read: Build this part. Calculate the volume and locate the Center of mass of the illustrated model.

1. **Create** a New part in SolidWorks.

2. **Build** the illustrated dimensioned model. Insert five sketches, five features and a Reference plane: Extruded Base, Plane1, Extruded Boss, Extruded Cut, Fillet and Extruded Cut.

Think about the steps that you would take to build the illustrated part. Insert a Reference plane to create the Extruded Boss feature. Create Sketch2 for Plane1. Plane1 is the Sketch plane for Sketch3. Sketch3 is the profile for Boss-Extrude2.

3. **Set** the document properties for the model.

4. Create **Sketch1**. Sketch1 is the Base sketch. Select the Top Plane as the Sketch plane. Sketch a rectangle. Insert the required geometric relations and dimensions.

5. Create the **Extruded Base (Boss-Extrude1)** feature. Blind is the default End Condition in Direction 1. Depth = .700in.

6. Create **Sketch2**. Select the top face of Boss-Extrude1 as the Sketch plane. Sketch a diagonal line as illustrated. Plane1 is the Sketch plane for Sketch3. Sketch3 is the sketch profile for Boss-Extrude2. The Origin is located in the bottom left corner of the sketch. Complete the sketch.

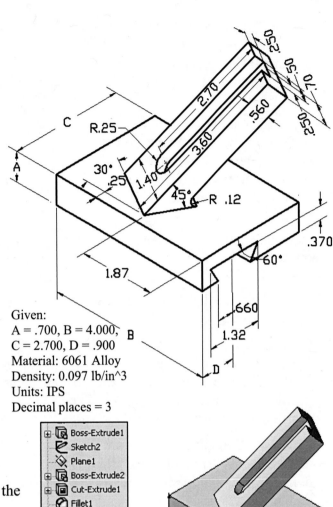

Given:
A = .700, B = 4.000,
C = 2.700, D = .900
Material: 6061 Alloy
Density: 0.097 lb/in^3
Units: IPS
Decimal places = 3

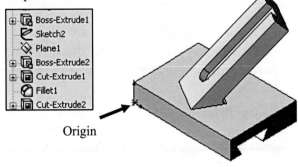

Origin

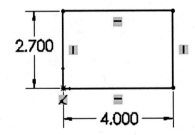

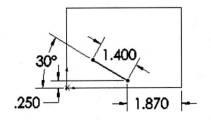

7. Create **Plane1**. Show Sketch2. Select the top face of Boss-Extrude1 and Sketch2. Sketch2 and face<1> are the Reference Entities. Angle = 45 deg.

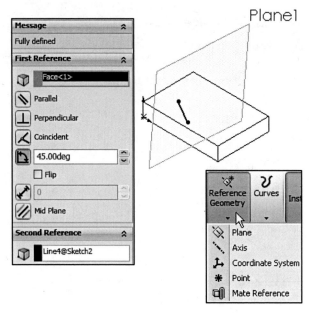

Plane1

💡 Activate the Plane PropertyManager. Click **Plane** from the Reference Geometry Consolidated toolbar, or click **Insert, Reference Geometry, Plane** from the Menu bar.

💡 View Sketch2. Click **View, Sketches** from the Menu bar.

💡 View Plane1. Click **View, Planes** from the Menu bar.

8. Create **Sketch3**. Select Plane1 as the Sketch plane. Select the Line Sketch tool. Use Sketch2 as a reference for the width dimension of the rectangle. Insert the required geometric relations and dimension. Sketch3 is the sketch profile for Boss-Extrude2.

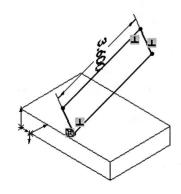

9. Create the **Extruded Boss** feature. Boss-Extrude2 is located on Plane1. Blind is the default End Condition in Direction 1. Depth = .560in.

10. Create **Sketch4**. Select the top angle face of Boss-Extrude2 as the Sketch plane. Sketch4 is the profile for the first Extruded Cut feature. Apply a Mid point relation with the Centerline Sketch tool. Insert a Parallel, Symmetric, Perpendicular, and Tangent relation. Insert the required dimensions.

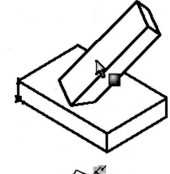

11. Create the first **Extruded Cut** feature. Blind is the default End Condition. Depth = .250in.

💡 There are numerous ways to build the models in this chapter. The goal is to display different design intents and techniques.

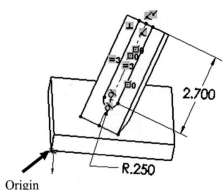

2.700

R.250

Origin

12. Create the **Fillet** feature. Fillet the illustrated edge. Edge<1> is displayed in the Items To Fillet box. Radius = .12in.

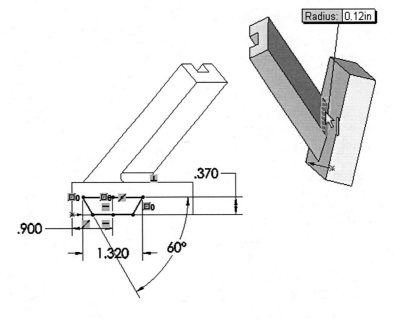

13. Create **Sketch5**. Select the right face of Boss-Extrude1 as the Sketch plane. Insert the required relations and dimensions.

14. Create the second **Extruded Cut** feature. Select Through All as the End Condition in Direction 1.

15. **Assign** 6061 Alloy material to the part.

16. **Calculate** the volume of the part. The volume = 8.19 cubic inches.

17. **Locate** the Center of mass. The location of the Center of mass is relative to the part Origin.

- X: 2.08 inches

- Y: 0.79 inches

- Z: -1.60 inches

Mass = 0.80 pounds

Volume = 8.19 cubic inches

Surface area = 49.02 inches^2

Center of mass: (inches)
  X = 2.08
  Y = 0.79
  Z = -1.60

18. **Save** the part and name it Advanced Part 9-3.

19. **Close** the model.

As an exercise, apply the MMGS unit system to the part. Modify the material from 6061 Alloy to ABS. Modify the Plane1 angle from 45deg to 30deg.

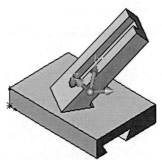

Calculate the total mass of the part and the location of the Center of mass relative to the part Origin. Save the part and name it Advanced Part 9-3 MMGS System.

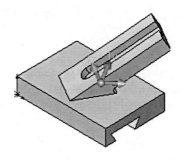

Mass = 134.58 grams

Volume = 131941.14 cubic millimeters

Surface area = 30575.45 millimeters^2

Center of mass: (millimeters)
  X = 53.89
  Y = 16.98
  Z = -42.47

Tutorial: Advanced Part 9-4

An exam question in this category could read: Build this part. Calculate the volume and locate the Center of mass of the illustrated model.

1. **Create** a New part in SolidWorks.

2. **Build** the illustrated dimensioned model. Create the part with eleven sketches, eleven features and a Reference plane: Extruded Base, Plane1, two Extruded Bosses, two Extruded Cuts, Extruded Boss, Extruded Cut, Extruded-Thin, Mirror, Extruded Cut and Extruded Boss.

Think about the steps that you would take to build the illustrated part. Create the rectangular Base feature. Create Sketch2 for Plane1. Insert Plane1 to create the Extruded Boss feature: Boss-Extrude2. Plane1 is the Sketch plane for Sketch3. Sketch3 is the sketch profile for Boss-Extrude2.

3. **Set** the document properties for the model.

4. Create **Sketch1**. Sketch1 is the Base sketch. Select the Top Plane as the Sketch plane. Sketch a rectangle. Insert the required geometric relations and dimensions. Note the location of the Origin.

5. Create the **Extruded Base (Boss-Extrude1)** feature. Blind is the default End Condition in Direction 1. Depth = .500in.

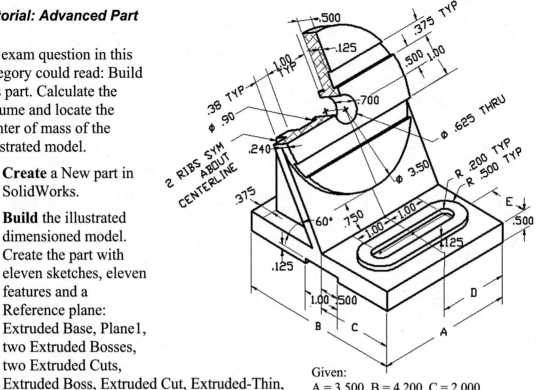

Given:
A = 3.500, B = 4.200, C = 2.000,
D =1.750, E = 1.000
Material: 6061 Alloy
Density: 0.097 lb/in^3
Units: IPS
Decimal places = 3

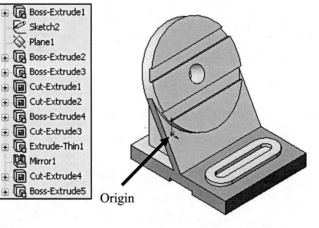

- Boss-Extrude1
- Sketch2
- Plane1
- Boss-Extrude2
- Boss-Extrude3
- Cut-Extrude1
- Cut-Extrude2
- Boss-Extrude4
- Cut-Extrude3
- Extrude-Thin1
- Mirror1
- Cut-Extrude4
- Boss-Extrude5

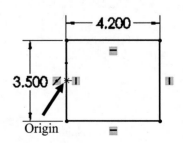

Origin

6. Create **Sketch2**. Sketch2 is the sketch profile for Plane1. Select the top face of Extrude1 as the Sketch plane. Sketch a centerline. Show Sketch2.

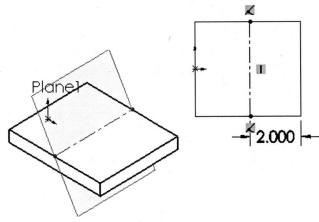

7. Create **Plane1**. Select the top face of Boss-Extrude1 and Sketch2. Face<1> and Line1@Sketch2 are displayed in the Selections box. Angle = 60deg.

8. Create **Sketch3**. Select Plane1 as the Sketch plane. Sketch3 is the sketch profile for the Extrude feature. Utilize the Convert Entities Sketch tool to convert the Sketch2 line to Plane1. Sketch two equal vertical lines Collinear with the left and right edges. Sketch a construction circle with a diameter Coincident to the left and right vertical lines. Create an 180deg tangent arc between the two vertical lines. Insert the required geometric relations and dimensions. Complete the sketch. Utilize the First arc condition from the Leaders tab in the Dimension PropertyManager to minimum the dimension to the bottom of the circle, Sketch2.

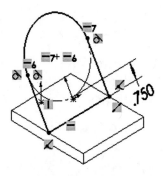

🔆 Insert a construction circle when dimensions are reference to a minimum or maximum arc condition.

9. Create the **Extruded Boss** (Boss-Extrude2) feature. Blind is the default End Condition. Depth = .260in. Note: .260in = (.500in - .240in). The extrude direction is towards the back.

10. Create **Sketch4**. Select the right angled face of the Extrude feature as the Sketch plane. Wake-up the center point of the tangent Arc. Sketch a circle. The circle is Coincident and Coradial to the Extrude feature.

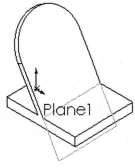

11. Create the second **Extruded Boss** (Boss-Extrude3) feature. Blind is the default End Condition in Direction 1. Depth = .240in.

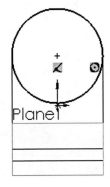

12. Create **Sketch5**. Sketch5 is the profile for the Extruded Cut feature. Select the right angle face of the Extrude feature as the Sketch plane. Apply the Convert Entities and Trim Sketch tools. Insert the required geometric relations and dimensions.

13. Create the first **Extruded Cut** feature. Blind is the default End Condition. Depth = .125in.

14. Create **Sketch6**. Select the right angle face of Boss-Extrude3 as the Sketch plane. Apply the Convert Entities and Trim Sketch tools. Insert the required geometric relations and dimensions.

15. Create the second **Extruded Cut** feature. Blind is the default End Condition. Depth = .125in.

16. Create **Sketch7**. Select the left angled face of Boss-Extrude2 as the Sketch plane. Sketch a circle. Insert the required geometric relation and dimension.

17. Create the third **Extruded Boss (Boss-Extrude4)** feature. Blind is the default End Condition. Depth = .200in. Note: .200in = (.700in - .500in).

18. Create **Sketch8**. Select the flat circular face of the Extrude feature as illustrated as the Sketch plane. Sketch a circle. Insert the required dimension.

19. Create the third **Extruded Cut** feature. Select Through All for End Condition in Direction 1.

20. Create **Sketch9**. Select the left flat top face of Extrude1 as the Sketch Plane. Sketch a line parallel to the front edge as illustrated. Insert the required geometric relations and dimensions.

There are numerous ways to build the models in this chapter. The goal is to display different design intents and techniques.

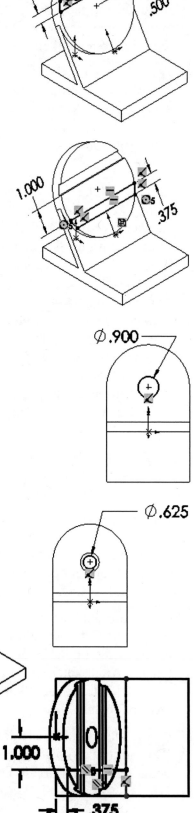

21. Create the **Extrude-Thin1** feature. Extrude-Thin1 is the left support feature. Select Up To Surface for End Condition in Direction 1. Select face<1> for direction as illustrated. Thickness = .38in. Select One-Direction.

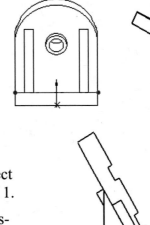

22. Create the **Mirror** feature. Mirror the Extrude-Thin1 feature about the Front Plane.

23. Create **Sketch10**. Select the bottom front flat face of Boss-Extrude1 as the Sketch plane. Sketch10 is the profile for the forth Extruded Cut feature. Insert the required geometric relations and dimensions.

24. Create the forth **Extruded Cut** feature. Select Through All for End Condition in Direction 1.

25. Create **Sketch11**. Select the top face of Boss-Extrude1 as the Sketch plane. Apply construction geometry. Sketch11 is the profile for the Boss-Extrude5 feature. Insert the required geometric relations and dimensions.

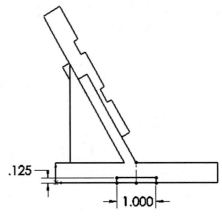

26. Create the **Extruded Boss** feature. Blind is the default End Condition in Direction 1. Depth = .125in.

There are numerous ways to build the models in this chapter. The goal is to display different design intents and techniques.

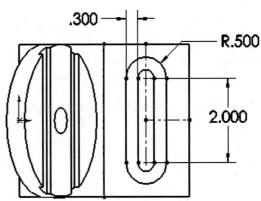

27. **Assign** 6061 Alloy material to the part.

28. **Calculate** the volume of the part. The volume = 14.05 cubic inches.

29. **Locate** the Center of mass. The location of the Center of mass is relative to the part Origin.

- X: 1.59 inches
- Y: 1.19 inches
- Z: 0.00 inches

30. **Save** the part and name it Advanced Part 9-4.

31. **Close** the model.

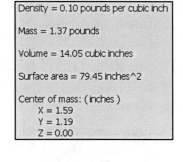

In the Advanced Part Modeling category, an exam question could read: Build this model. Calculate the volume of the part.

- A: 14.05 cubic inches
- B: 15.66 cubic inches
- C: 13.44 cubic inches
- D: 12.71 cubic inches

The correct answer is A.

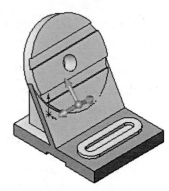

As an exercise, modify A from 3.500in to 3.600in. Modify B from 4.200in to 4.100in. Modify the Plane1 angle from 60deg to 45deg. Modify the system units from IPS to MMGS.

Calculate the mass and locate the Center of mass. The mass = 597.09 grams.

- X: 34.27 millimeters
- Y: 26.70 millimeters
- Z: 0.00 millimeters

32. **Save** the part and name it Advanced Part 9-4 Modified.

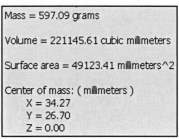

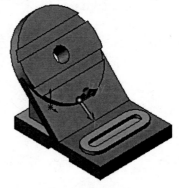

Calculate the Center of mass relative to a created coordinate system location

In the Simple Part Modeling chapter, you located the Center of mass relative to the default part Origin. In the Advanced Part Modeling category, you may need to locate the Center of mass relative to a created coordinate system location. The exam model may display a created coordinate system location. Example:

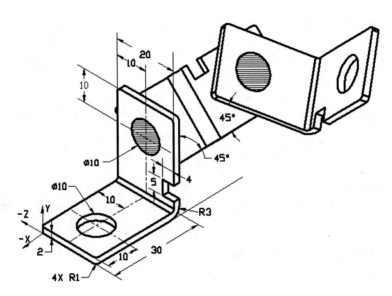

The SolidWorks software displays positive values for (X, Y, Z) coordinates for a reference coordinate system. The CSWA exam displays either a positive or negative sign in front of the (X, Y, Z) coordinates to indicate direction as illustrated, (-X, +Y, -Z).

The following section reviews creating a coordinate system location for a part.

Tutorial: Coordinate location 9-1

Use the Mass Properties tool to calculate the Center of mass for a part located at a new coordinate location through a point.

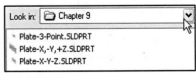

1. **Open** the Plate-3-Point part from the SolidWorks CSWA Folders\Chapter 9 location. View the location of the part Origin.

2. **Locate** the Center of mass. The location of the Center of mass is relative to the part Origin.

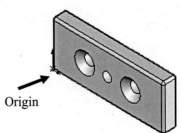

Origin

- X = 28 millimeters

- Y = 11 millimeters

- Z = -3 millimeters

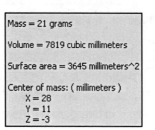

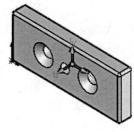

Mass = 21 grams

Volume = 7819 cubic millimeters

Surface area = 3645 millimeters^2

Center of mass: (millimeters)
  X = 28
  Y = 11
  Z = -3

Create a new coordinate system location.
Locate the new coordinate system location
at the center of the center hole as
illustrated.

3. Right-click the **front face** of Base-Extrude.

4. Click **Sketch** from the Context toolbar.

5. Click the **edge** of the center hole as illustrated.

6. Click **Convert Entities** from the Sketch
   toolbar. The center point for the new
   coordinate location is displayed.

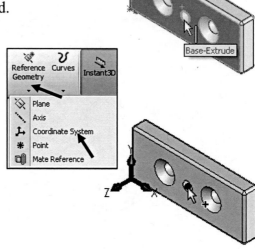

7. **Exit** the sketch. Sketch4 is displayed.

8. Click the **Coordinate System** tool from the
   Consolidated Reference Geometry toolbar.
   The Coordinate System PropertyManager is
   displayed.

9. Click the **center point** of the center hole in
   the Graphics window. Point2@Sketch4 is
   displayed in the Selections box as the
   Origin.

10. Click **OK** from the Coordinate System
    PropertyManager. Coordinate System1 is
    displayed.

11. **View** the new coordinate location at
    the center of the center hole.

View the Mass Properties of the part with
the new coordinate location.

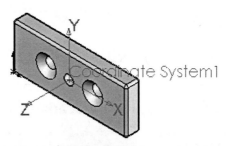

12. Click the **Mass Properties** tool from
    the Evaluate tab.

13. Select **Coordinate System1** from the
    Output box. The Center of mass
    relative to the new location is located
    at the following coordinates: X = 0
    millimeters, Y = 0 millimeters,
    Z = -3 millimeters

Output coordinate system: Coordinate System 1
-- default --
Coordinate System 1
Selected items:

Center of mass: (millimeters)
  X = 0
  Y = 0
  Z = -3

14. **Reverse** the direction of the axes as illustrated. On the CSWA exam, the coordinate system axes could be represented by: (+X, -Y, -Z).

15. **Close** the model.

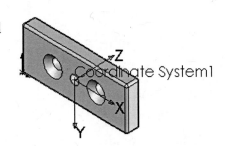

To reverse the direction of an axis, click its **Reverse Axis Direction** button in the Coordinate System PropertyManager.

Tutorial: Coordinate location 9-2

Create a new coordinate system location. Locate the new coordinate system at the top back point as illustrated.

1. **Open** the Plate-X-Y-Z part from the SolidWorks CSWA Folders\Chapter 9 location.

2. **View** the location of the part Origin.

3. Drag the **Rollback bar** under the Base-Extrude feature in the FeatureManager.

4. Click the **Coordinate System** tool from the Consolidated Reference Geometry toolbar. The Coordinate System PropertyManager is displayed.

5. Click the **back left vertex** as illustrated.

6. Click the **top back horizontal** edge as illustrated. Do not select the midpoint.

7. Click the **back left vertical** edge as illustrated.

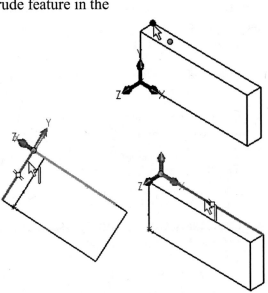

8. Click **OK** from the Coordinate System PropertyManager. Coordinate System1 is displayed in the FeatureManager and in the Graphics window.

9. Drag the **Rollback bar** to the bottom of the FeatureManager.

10. **Calculate** the Center of mass relative to the new coordinate system.

11. Select **Coordinate System1**. The Center of mass relative to the new location is located at the following coordinates:

- X = -28 millimeters

- Y = -11 millimeters

- Z = -4 millimeters

12. **Reverse** the direction of the axes as illustrated.

13. **Close** the model.

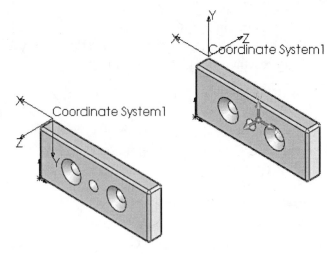

🔆 You can define a coordinate system for a part or assembly. Use the coordinate system with the Measure and Mass Properties tools.

Tutorial: Advanced part 9-5

An exam question in this category could read: Build this part. Calculate the overall mass and locate the Center of mass of the illustrated model.

1. **Create** a New part in SolidWorks.

2. **Build** the illustrated dimensioned model. Insert thirteen features: Extrude-Thin1, Fillet, two Extruded Cuts, Circular Pattern, two Extruded Cuts, Mirror, Chamfer, Extruded Cut, Mirror, Extruded Cut and Mirror.

Think about the steps that you would take to build the illustrated part. Review the provided information. The depth of the left side is 50mm. The depth of the right side is 60mm.

🔆 There are numerous ways to build the models in this chapter. The goal is to display different design intents and techniques.

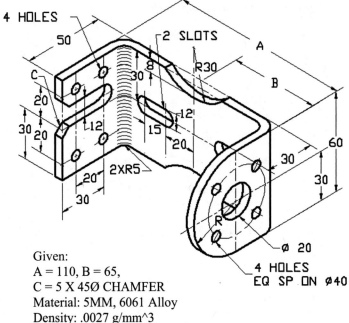

Given:
A = 110, B = 65,
C = 5 X 45∅ CHAMFER
Material: 5MM, 6061 Alloy
Density: .0027 g/mm^3
Units: MMGS
ALL HOLES 6MM

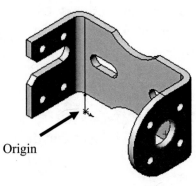

Origin

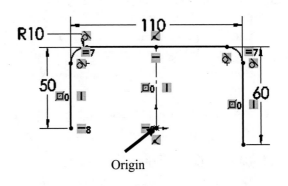

💡 If the inside radius = 5mm and the material thickness = 5mm, then the outside radius = 10mm.

3. **Set** the document properties for the model.

4. Create **Sketch1**. Sketch1 is the Base sketch. Select the Top Plane as the Sketch plane. Apply the Line and Sketch Fillet Sketch tools. Apply construction geometry. Insert the required geometric relations and dimensions.

5. Create the **Extrude-Thin1** feature. Extrude-Thin1 is the Base feature. Apply symmetry in Direction 1. Depth = 60mm. Thickness = 5mm. Check the Auto-fillet corners box. Radius = 5mm.

💡 The Auto-fillet corners option creates a round at each edge where lines meet at an angle.

6. Create the **Fillet** feature. Fillet1 is a full round fillet. Fillet the three illustrated faces: top, front and bottom.

7. Create **Sketch2**. Select the right face as the Sketch plane. Wake-up the centerpoint. Sketch a circle. Insert the required relation and dimension.

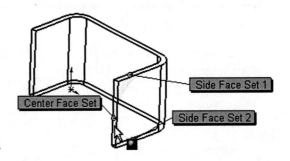

8. Create the first **Extruded Cut** feature. Select Up To Next for the End Condition in Direction 1.

💡 The Up To Next End Condition extends the feature from the sketch plane to the next surface that intercepts the entire profile. The intercepting surface must be on the same part.

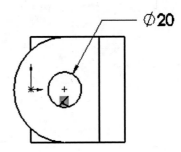

9. Create **Sketch3**. Select the right face as the Sketch plane. Create the profile for the second Extruded Cut feature. This is the seed feature for CirPattern1. Apply construction geometry to locate the center point of Sketch3. Insert the required relations and dimensions.

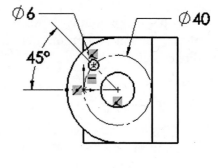

10. Create the second **Extruded Cut** feature. Select Up To Next for the End Condition in Direction 1.

11. Create the **Circular Pattern** feature. Number of Instances = 4. Default angle = 360deg.

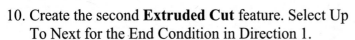

12. Create **Sketch4**. Select the left outside face of Extrude-Thin1 as the Sketch plane. Apply the Line and Tangent Arc Sketch tool to create Sketch4. Insert the required geometric relations and dimensions.

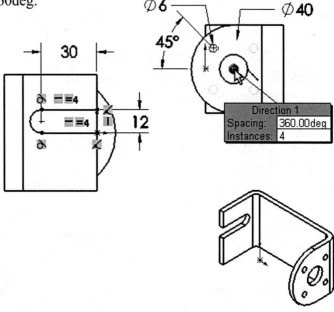

13. Create the third **Extruded Cut** feature. Select Up To Next for End Condition in Direction 1. The Slot on the left side of Extrude-Thin1 is created.

14. Create **Sketch5**. Select the left outside face of Extrude-Thin1 as the Sketch plane. Sketch two circles. Insert the required geometric relations and dimensions.

15. Create the forth **Extruded Cut** feature. Select Up To Next for End Condition in Direction 1.

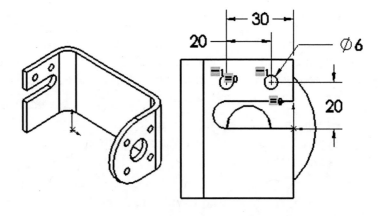

There are numerous ways to create the models in this chapter. The goal is to display different design intents and techniques

16. Create the first **Mirror** feature. Mirror the top two holes about the Top Plane.

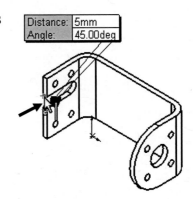

17. Create the **Chamfer** feature. Create an Angle distance chamfer. Chamfer the selected edges as illustrated. Distance = 5mm. Angle = 45deg.

18. Create **Sketch6**. Select the front face of Extrude-Thin1 as the Sketch plane. Insert the required geometric relations and dimensions.

19. Create the fifth **Extruded Cut** feature. Select Thought All for End Condition in Direction 1.

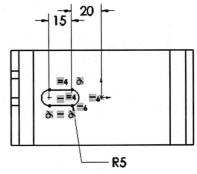

20. Create the second **Mirror** feature. Mirror Extrude5 about the Right Plane.

21. Create **Sketch7**. Select the front face of Extrude-Thin1 as the Sketch plane. Apply the 3 Point Arc Sketch tool. Apply the min First Arc Condition option. Insert the required geometric relations and dimensions.

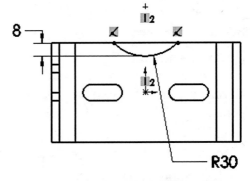

22. Create the last **Extruded Cut** feature. Through All is the End Condition in Direction 1 and Direction 2.

23. Create the third **Mirror** feature. Mirror the Extrude feature about the Top Plane as illustrated.

24. **Assign** the material to the part.

25. **Calculate** the overall mass of the part. The overall mass = 134.19 grams.

26. **Locate** the Center of mass relative to the part Origin:

- X: 1.80 millimeters

- Y: -0.27 millimeters

- Z: -35.54 millimeters

Mass = 134.19 grams

Volume = 49701.13 cubic millimeters

Surface area = 24415.20 millimeters^2

Center of mass: (millimeters)
   X = 1.80
   Y = -0.27
   Z = -35.54

27. **Save** the part and name it Advanced Part 9-5.

28. **Close** the model.

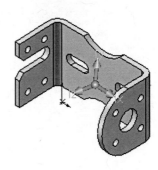

All questions on the exam are in a multiple choice single answer or fill in the blank format. In the Advanced Part Modeling category, an exam question could read: Build this model. Calculate the overall mass of the part with the provided information.

- A: 139.34 grams
- B: 155.19 grams
- C: 134.19 grams
- D: 143.91 grams

The correct answer is C.

Use the Options button in the Mass Properties dialog box to apply custom settings to units.

Tutorial: Advanced part 9-5A

An exam question in this category could read: Build this part. Locate the Center of mass. Note the coordinate system location of the model as illustrated.

Where do you start? Build the model as you did in the Tutorial: Advanced Part 9-5. Create Coordinate System1 to locate the Center of mass.

1. **Open** Advanced Part 9-5 from your SolidWorks folder.

Create the illustrated coordinate system location.

2. Show **Sketch2** from the FeatureManager design tree.

3. Click the **center point** of Sketch2 in the Graphics window as illustrated.

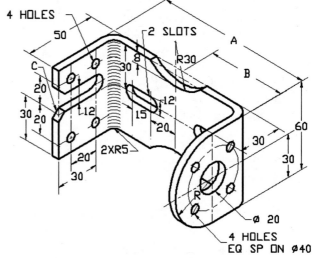

A = 110, B = 65, C = 5 X 45Ø CHAMFER
Material: 5MM, 6061 Alloy
Density: .0027 g/mm^3
Units: MMGS
ALL HOLES 6MM

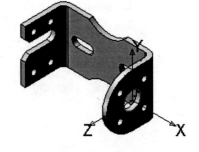

Coordinate system: +X, +Y, +Z

4. Click the **Coordinate System** tool from the Consolidated Reference Geometry toolbar. The Coordinate System PropertyManager is displayed. Point2@Sketch2 is displayed in the Origin box.

5. Click **OK** from the Coordinate System PropertyManager. Coordinate System1 is displayed

6. **Locate** the Center of mass based on the location of the illustrated coordinate system. Select Coordinate System1.

- X: -53.20 millimeters

- Y: -0.27 millimeters

- Z: -15.54 millimeters

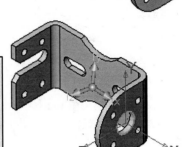

Mass = 134.19 grams

Volume = 49701.13 cubic millimeters

Surface area = 24415.20 millimeters^2

Center of mass: (millimeters)
     X = -53.20
     Y = -0.27
     Z = -15.54

7. **Save** the part and name it Advanced Part 9-5A.

8. **Close** the model.

Tutorial: Advanced part 9-5B

Build this part. Locate the Center of mass. View the location of the coordinate system. The coordinate system is located at the left front point of the model.

Build the illustrated model as you did in the Tutorial: Advanced Part 9-5. Create Coordinate System1 to locate the Center of mass for the model.

1. **Open** Advance Part 9-5 from your SolidWorks folder.

Create the illustrated coordinate system.

2. Click the **vertex** as illustrated for the Origin location.

☀ To reverse the direction of an axis, click its **Reverse Axis Direction** button in the Coordinate System PropertyManager.

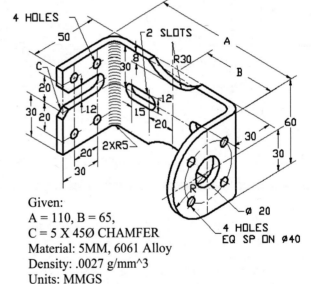

Given:
A = 110, B = 65,
C = 5 X 45Ø CHAMFER
Material: 5MM, 6061 Alloy
Density: .0027 g/mm^3
Units: MMGS
ALL HOLES 6MM

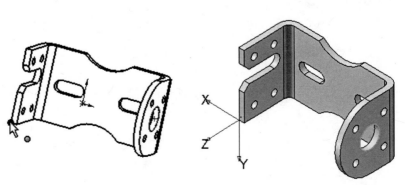

3. Click the **Coordinate System** tool from the Consolidated Reference Geometry toolbar. The Coordinate System PropertyManager is displayed. Vertex<1> is displayed in the Origin box.

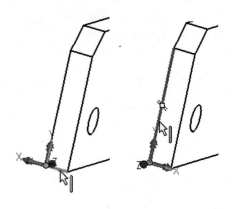

4. Click the **bottom horizontal edge** as illustrated. Edge<1> is displayed in the X Axis Direction box.

5. Click the **left back vertical edge** as illustrated. Edge<2> is displayed in the Y Axis Direction box.

6. Click **OK** from the Coordinate System PropertyManager. Coordinate System1 is displayed.

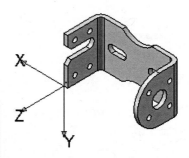

7. **Locate** the Center of mass based on the location of the illustrated coordinate system. Select Coordinate System1.

- X: -56.80 millimeters

- Y: -29.73 millimeters

- Z: -35.54 millimeters

Mass = 134.19 grams

Volume = 49701.13 cubic millimeters

Surface area = 24415.20 millimeters^2

Center of mass: (millimeters)
  X = -56.80
  Y = -29.73
  Z = -35.54

8. **Save** the part and name it Advanced Part 9-5B.

9. **Close** the model.

In the Advanced Part Modeling category, an exam question could read: Build this model. Locate the Center of mass.

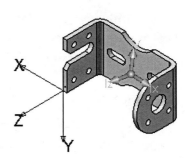

- A: X = -56.80 millimeters, Y = -29.73 millimeters, Z = -35.54 millimeters

- B: X = 1.80 millimeters, Y = -0.27 millimeters, Z = -35.54 millimeters

- C: X = -59.20 millimeters, Y = -0.27 millimeters, Z = -15.54 millimeters

- D: X= -1.80 millimeters, Y = 1.05 millimeters, Z = -0.14 millimeters

The correct answer is A.

Tutorial: Advanced part 9-6

An exam question in this category could read: Build this part. Calculate the overall mass and locate the Center of mass of the illustrated model.

1. **Create** a New part in SolidWorks.

2. **Build** the illustrated dimensioned model. Insert twelve features and a Reference plane: Extrude-Thin1, two Extruded Bosses, Extruded Cut, Extruded Boss, Extruded Cut, Plane1, Mirror and five Extruded Cuts.

Think about the steps that you would take to build the illustrated part. Create an Extrude-Thin1 feature as the Base feature.

3. **Set** the document properties for the model. Review the given information.

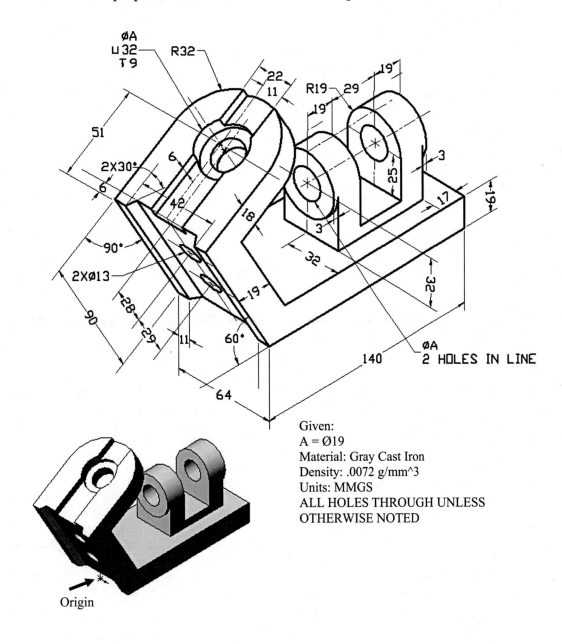

Given:
A = Ø19
Material: Gray Cast Iron
Density: .0072 g/mm^3
Units: MMGS
ALL HOLES THROUGH UNLESS
OTHERWISE NOTED

Origin

4. Create **Sketch1**. Sketch1 is the Base sketch. Select the Right Plane as the Sketch plane. Apply construction geometry. Insert the required geometric relations and dimensions. Sketch1 is the profile for Extrude-Thin1. Note the location of the Origin.

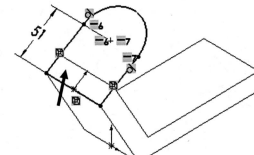

5. Create the **Extrude-Thin1** feature. Apply symmetry. Select Mid Plane as the End Condition in Direction 1. Depth = 64mm. Thickness = 19mm.

6. Create **Sketch2**. Select the top narrow face of Extrude-Thin1 as the Sketch plane. Sketch three lines: two vertical and one horizontal and a tangent arc. Insert the required geometric relations and dimensions.

7. Create the **Boss-Extrude1** feature. Blind is the default End Condition in Direction 1. Depth = 18mm.

8. Create **Sketch3**. Select the Right Plane as the Sketch plane. Sketch a rectangle. Insert the required geometric relations and dimensions.
Note: 61mm = (19mm - 3mm) x 2 + 29mm.

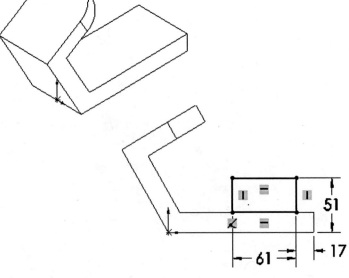

9. Create the **Boss-Extrude2** feature. Select Mid Plane for End Condition in Direction 1. Depth = 38mm. Note: 2 x R19.

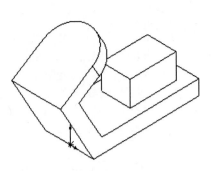

10. Create **Sketch4**. Select the Right Plane as the Sketch plane. Sketch a vertical centerline from the top midpoint of the sketch. The centerline is required for Plane1. Plane1 is a Reference plane. Sketch a rectangle symmetric about the centerline. Insert the required relations and dimensions. Sketch4 is the profile for Extrude3.

11. Create the first **Extruded Cut** feature. Extrude in both directions. Select Through All for End Condition in Direction 1 and Direction 2.

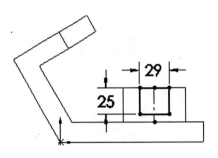

12. Create **Sketch5**. Select the inside face of the Extrude feature for the Sketch plane. Sketch a circle from the top midpoint. Sketch a construction circle. Construction geometry is required for future features. Complete the sketch.

13. Create the **Extruded Boss** (Boss-Extrude3) feature. Blind is the default End Condition. Depth = 19mm.

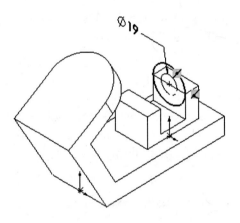

14. Create **Sketch6**. Select the inside face for the Sketch plane. Show Sketch5. Select the construction circle in Sketch5. Apply the Convert Entities Sketch tool.

15. Create the second **Extruded Cut** feature. Select the Up To Next End Condition in Direction 1.

🔆 There are numerous ways to create the models in this chapter. The goal is to display different design intents and techniques

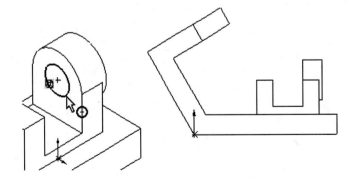

16. Create **Plane1**. Apply symmetry. Create Plane1 to mirror Cut-Extrude2 and Boss-Extrude3. Create a Parallel Plane at Point. Select the midpoint of Sketch4, and Face<1> as illustrated. Point1@Sketch4 and Face<1> is displayed in the Selections box.

17. Create the **Mirror** feature. Mirror Cut-Extrude2 and Boss-Extrude3 about Plane1.

The Mirror feature creates a copy of a feature, (or multiple features), mirrored about a face or a plane. You can select the feature or you can select the faces that comprise the feature.

18. Create **Sketch7**. Select the top front angled face of Extrude-Thin1 as the Sketch plane. Apply the Centerline Sketch tool. Insert the required geometric relations and dimensions.

19. Create the third **Extruded Cut** feature. Select Through All for End Condition in Direction 1. Select the angle edge for the vector to extrude as illustrated.

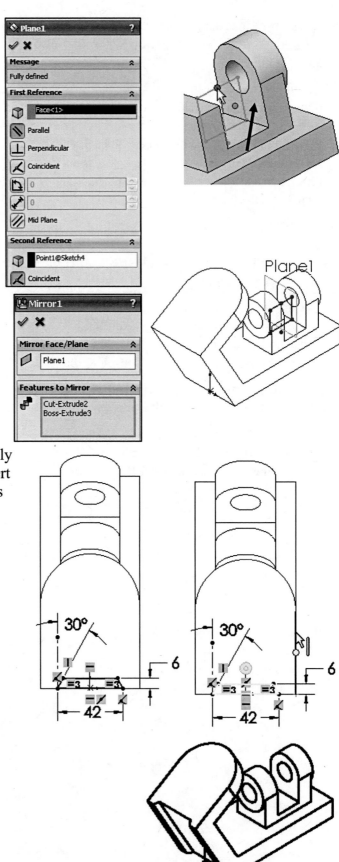

20. Create **Sketch8**. Select the top front angled face of Extrude-Thin1 as the Sketch plane. Sketch a centerline. Sketch two vertical lines and a horizontal line. Select the top arc edge. Apply the Convert Entities Sketch tool. Apply the Trim Sketch tool to remove the unwanted arc geometry. Insert the required geometric relations and dimension.

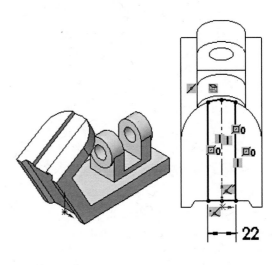

21. Create the forth **Extruded Cut** feature. Blind is the default End Condition in Direction 1. Depth = 6mm.

22. Create **Sketch9**. Create a Cbore with Sketch9 and Sketch10. Select the top front angled face of Extrude-Thin1 as illustrated for the Sketch plane. Extrude8 is the center hole in the Extrude-Thin1 feature. Sketch a circle. Insert the required geometric relations and dimension.

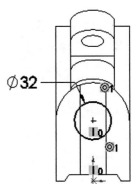

23. Create the fifth **Extrude Cut** feature. Blind is the default End Condition. Depth = 9mm. Note: This is the first feature for the Cbore.

24. Create **Sketch10**. Select the top front angled face of Extrude-Thin1 as the Sketch plane. Sketch a circle. Insert the required geometric relation and dimension. Note: A = Ø19.

25. Create the sixth **Extruded Cut** feature. Select the Up To Next End Condition in Direction 1. The Cbore is complete.

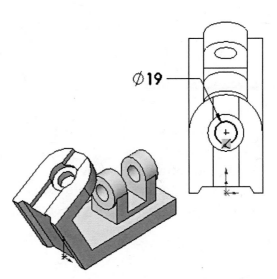

There are numerous ways to create the models. The goal is to display different design intents and techniques

26. Create **Sketch11**. Select the front angle face of the Extrude feature for the Sketch plane. Sketch two circles. Insert the required geometric relations and dimensions.

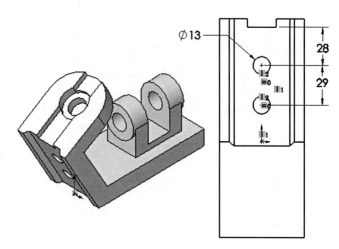

27. Create the last **Extruded Cut** feature. Select the Up To Next End Condition in Direction 1.

The FilletXpert manages, organizes, and reorders constant radius fillets.

The FilletXpert automatically calls the FeatureXpert when it has trouble placing a fillet on the specified geometry.

28. **Assign** the material to the part.

29. **Calculate** the overall mass of the part. The overall mass = 2536.59 grams.

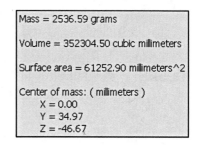

Mass = 2536.59 grams

Volume = 352304.50 cubic millimeters

Surface area = 61252.90 millimeters^2

Center of mass: (millimeters)
  X = 0.00
  Y = 34.97
  Z = -46.67

30. **Locate** the Center of mass relative to the part Origin:

- X: 0.00 millimeters

- Y: 34.97 millimeters

- Z: -46.67 millimeters

31. **Save** the part and name it Advanced Part 9-6.

Due to software rounding, you may view a negative -0.00 coordinate location in the Mass Properties dialog box.

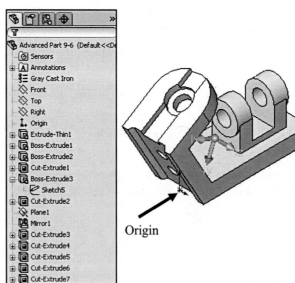

Origin

Tutorial: Advanced part 9-6A

An exam question in this category could read:
Build this part. Locate the Center of mass for the
illustrated coordinate system.

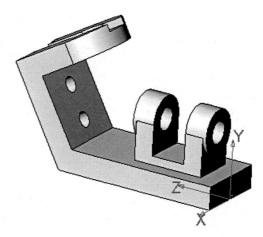

Where do you start? Build the illustrated model
as you did in the Tutorial: Advanced Part 9-6.
Create Coordinate System1 to locate the Center
of mass for the model.

1. **Open** Advanced Part 9-6 from your
    SolidWorks folder.

Create the illustrated Coordinate system.

2. Click the **Coordinate System** tool from the
    Consolidated Reference Geometry toolbar.
    The Coordinate System PropertyManager is
    displayed.

3. Click the **bottom midpoint** of Extrude-
    Thin1 as illustrated. Point<1> is displayed in
    the Origin box.

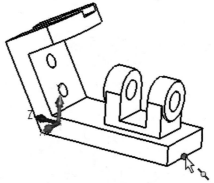

4. Click **OK** from the Coordinate System
    PropertyManager. Coordinate System1 is
    displayed.

```
Mass = 2536.59 grams

Volume = 352304.50 cubic millimeters

Surface area = 61252.90 millimeters^2

Center of mass: ( millimeters )
     X = 0.00
     Y = 34.97
     Z = 93.33
```

5. **Locate** the Center of mass
    based on the location of the
    illustrated coordinate system.
    Select Coordinate System1.

*   X: 0.00 millimeters

*   Y: 34.97 millimeters

*   Z: 93.33 millimeters

6. **Save** the part and name it
    Advanced Part 9-6A.

7. **View** the Center of mass with
    the default coordinate system.

8. **Close** the model.

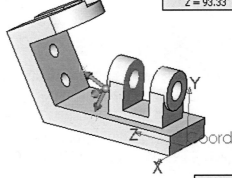

Coordinate System1

```
Mass = 2536.59 grams

Volume = 352304.50 cubic millimeters

Surface area = 61252.90 millimeters^2

Center of mass: ( millimeters )
     X = 0.00
     Y = 34.97
     Z = -46.67
```

Tutorial: Advanced part 9-7

An exam question in this category could read: Build this part. Calculate the overall mass and locate the Center of mass of the illustrated model.

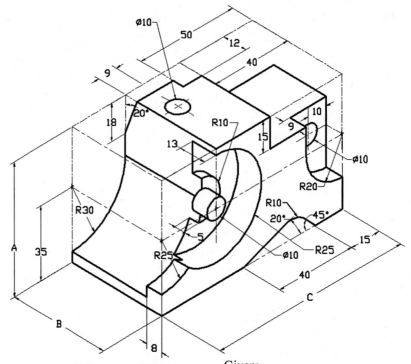

1. **Create** a New part in SolidWorks.

2. **Build** the illustrated dimensioned model. Insert thirteen features: Extruded Base, nine Extruded Cuts, two Extruded Bosses and a Chamfer.
   Note: The center point of the top hole is located 30mm from the top right edge.

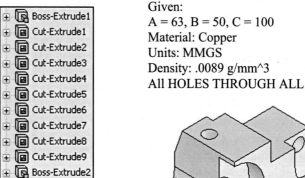

Given:
A = 63, B = 50, C = 100
Material: Copper
Units: MMGS
Density: .0089 g/mm^3
All HOLES THROUGH ALL

Think about the steps that you would take to build the illustrated part. Review the centerlines that outline the overall size of the part.

3. **Set** the document properties for the model.

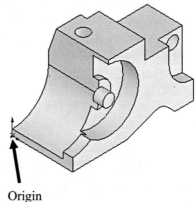

4. Create **Sketch1**. Sketch1 is the Base sketch. Select the Right Plane as the Sketch plane. Sketch a rectangle. Insert the required geometric relations and dimensions. The part Origin is located in the bottom left corner of the sketch.

Origin

5. Create the **Extruded Base** feature. Blind is the default End Condition in Direction 1.
   Depth = 50mm. Boss-Extrude1 is the Base feature.

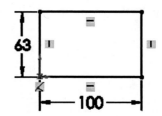

6. Create **Sketch2**. Select the right face of Extrude1 as the Sketch plane. Sketch a 90deg tangent arc. Sketch three lines to complete the sketch. Insert the required geometric relations and dimensions.

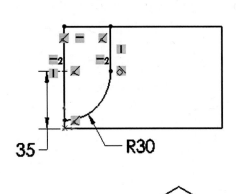

7. Create the first **Extruded Cut** feature. Offset the extrude feature. Select the Offset Start Condition. Offset value = 8.0mm. Blind is the default End Condition. Depth = 50mm.

💡 The default Start Condition in the Extrude PropertyManager is Sketch Plane. The Offset start condition starts the extrude feature on a plane that is offset from the current Sketch plane.

8. Create **Sketch3**. Select the right face as the Sketch plane. Create the Extrude profile. Insert the required geometric relations and dimensions.

9. Create the second **Extruded Cut** feature. Select Through All for End Condition in Direction 1.

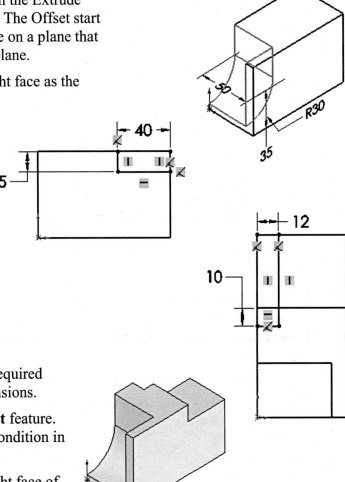

10. Create **Sketch4**. Select the top face of the Extrude feature as the Sketch Plane. Select the top edge to reference the 10mm dimension. Insert the required geometric relations and dimensions.

11. Create the third **Extruded Cut** feature. Select Through All for End Condition in Direction 1.

12. Create **Sketch5**. Select the right face of the Extrude feature as the Sketch Plane. Apply construction geometry. Sketch a 90deg tangent arc. Sketch three lines to complete the sketch. Insert the required geometric relations and dimensions.

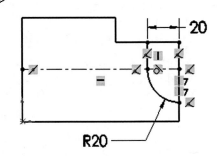

13. Create the forth **Extruded Cut** feature. Blind is the default End Condition. Depth = 9mm.

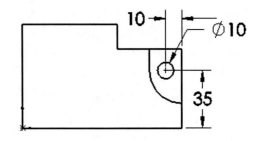

14. Create **Sketch6**. Select the right face of of the Extrude feature as the Sketch plane. Sketch a circle. Insert the required dimensions.

15. Create the fifth **Extruded Cut** feature. Select Through All for End Condition in Direction 1.

16. Create **Sketch7**. Select the top face of Extrude1 as the Sketch Plane. Sketch a circle. Insert the required dimensions and relations.

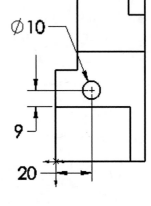

17. Create the sixth **Extruded Cut** feature. Select Through All for End Condition in Direction 1.

There are numerous ways to create the models in this chapter. The goal is to display different design intents and techniques.

18. Create **Sketch8**. Select the right face of Extrude1 as the Sketch plane. Insert a tangent arc as illustrated. Complete the sketch. Insert the required relations and dimensions.

19. Create the seventh **Extruded Cut** feature. Apply symmetry. Select the Through All End Condition in Direction 1 and Direction 2.

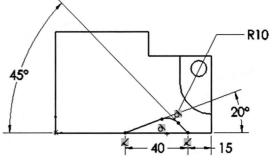

20. Create **Sketch9**. Select the right face of Extrude1 as the Sketch plane. Select Hidden Lines Visible. Sketch two construction circles centered about the end point of the arc. Apply the 3 Point Arc Sketch tool. Complete the sketch. Insert the required relations and dimensions.

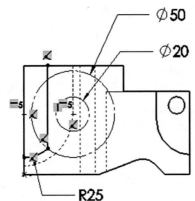

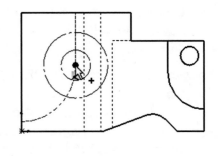

21. Create the eight **Extruded Cut** feature. Select the
    Through All End Condition in Direction 1 and Direction
    2. Note the direction of the extrude feature from the
    illustration.

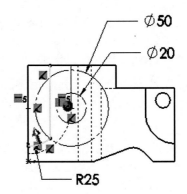

22. Create **Sketch10**. Select the right face of Extrude1 as
    the Sketch plane. Sketch a circle centered at the end
    point of the arc as illustrated. Apply the Trim Entities
    Sketch tool. Display Sketch9. Complete the sketch.
    Insert the required geometric relations.

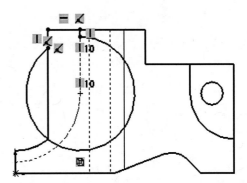

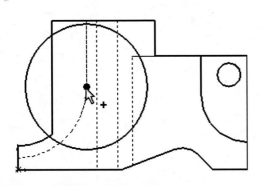

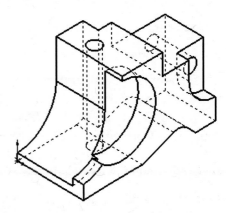

23. Create the ninth **Extruded Cut** feature. Blind is
    the default End Condition in Direction 1.
    Depth = 13mm. The feature is displayed.

24. Create **Sketch11**. Select the right face of the
    Extrude feature as the Sketch plane. Select the
    construction circle from Sketch9, the left arc, and
    the left edge as illustrated. Apply the Convert
    Entities Sketch tool. Apply the Trim Sketch tool.
    Insert the required relations.

25. Create the **Extruded Boss** feature. Blind is the
    default End Condition in Direction 1.
    Depth = 5.00mm.

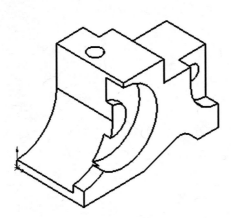

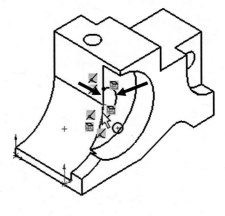

26. Create **Sketch12**. Select the right face of the Extrude feature as the Sketch plane. Sketch a circle. Insert the require relation and dimension.

27. Create the **Extruded Boss** feature. Select the Up To Surface End Condition in Direction 1. Select the right face of Extrude1 for Direction 1.

28. Create the **Chamfer** feature. Chamfer the left edge as illustrated. Distance = 18mm. Angle = 20deg.

29. **Assign** the material to the part.

30. **Calculate** the overall mass of the part. The overall mass = 1280.33 grams.

31. **Locate** the Center of mass relative to the part Origin:

- X: 26.81 millimeters

- Y: 25.80 millimeters

- Z: -56.06 millimeters

32. **Save** the part and name it Advanced Part 9-7.

33. **Close** the model.

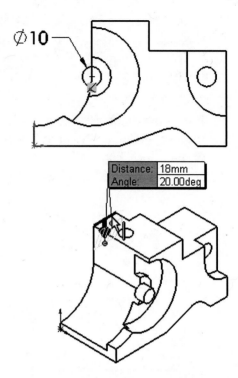

This example was taken from the SolidWorks website, www.solidworks.com/cswa as an example of an Advanced Part on the CSWA exam. This model has thirteen features and twelve sketches. As stated throughout this book, there are numerous ways to create the models in these chapters.

One of the goals in this book is to display different design intents and techniques, and to provide you with the ability to successfully address the provided models in the given time frame of the CSWA exam.

Mass = 1280.33 grams

Volume = 143857.58 cubic millimeters

Surface area = 26112.48 millimeters^2

Center of mass: (millimeters)
    X = 26.81
    Y = 25.80
    Z = -56.06

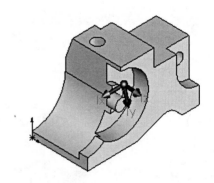

Summary

Advanced Part Modeling is one of the five categories on the CSWA exam. The main difference between the Advanced Part Modeling and the Simple Part Modeling category is the complexity of the sketches and the number of dimensions and geometric relations along with an increase in the number of features.

There is one question on the CSWA exam in this category. The question is worth twenty (20) points and is in a multiple choice single answer format. You are required to create a model, with eight or more features and to answer a question either on the location of the Center of mass relative to part Origin or to a new created coordinate system and all of the mass properties provided in the Mass Properties dialog box. Spend no more than 40 minutes on the question in this category. This is a timed exam. Manage your time.

At this time, there are no sheet metal questions, or questions on Loft, Swept, or Shell features on the exam.

Assembly Modeling (Bottom-up) is the next chapter in this book. Up to this point, a simple or advanced part was the focus. The Assembly Modeling category addresses an assembly with numerous sub-components. This chapter covers the general concepts and terminology used in Assembly Modeling and then addresses the core elements that are aligned to the exam. Knowledge of Standard mates is required in this category. There is one question on the CSWA exam in this category. The question is worth thirty (30) points. The question is in a multiple choice single answer format.

View sample screen shots from an older CSWA exam for an Advanced Modeling part at the end of the Homework section in this chapter.

Questions

1. In Tutorial: Advanced Part 9-1 you created the illustrated part. Modify the Base flange thickness from .40in to .50in. Modify the Chamfer feature angle from 45deg to 33deg. Modify the Fillet feature radius from .10in to .125in. Modify the material from 1060 Alloy to Nickel.

Calculate the overall mass of the part, volume, and locate the Center of mass with the provided information.

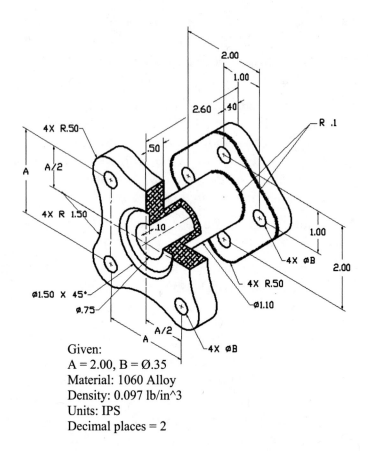

Given:
A = 2.00, B = Ø.35
Material: 1060 Alloy
Density: 0.097 lb/in^3
Units: IPS
Decimal places = 2

2. In Tutorial: Advanced Part 9-2 you created the illustrated part. Modify the CirPattern1 feature. Modify the number of instances from 6 to 8. Modify the seed feature from an 8mm diameter to a 6mm diameter.

Calculate the overall mass, volume, and the location of the Center of mass relative to the part Origin.

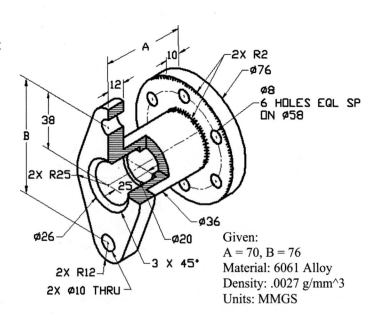

Given:
A = 70, B = 76
Material: 6061 Alloy
Density: .0027 g/mm^3
Units: MMGS

3. In Tutorial: Advanced Part 9-3 you created the illustrated part. Modify the material from 6061 Alloy to Copper. Modify the B dimension from 4.000in. to 3.500in. Modify the Fillet radius from .12in to .14in. Modify the unit system from IPS to MMGS.

Calculate the volume of the part and the location of the Center of mass. Save the part and name it Advance Part 9-3 Copper.

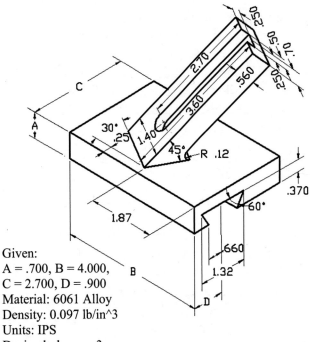

Given:
A = .700, B = 4.000,
C = 2.700, D = .900
Material: 6061 Alloy
Density: 0.097 lb/in^3
Units: IPS
Decimal places = 3

4. Build this illustrated model. Set document properties, identify the correct Sketch planes, apply the correct Sketch and Feature tools, and apply material. Calculate the overall mass of the part, volume and locate the Center of mass with the provided information.

- Material: 6061 Alloy

- Units: MMGS

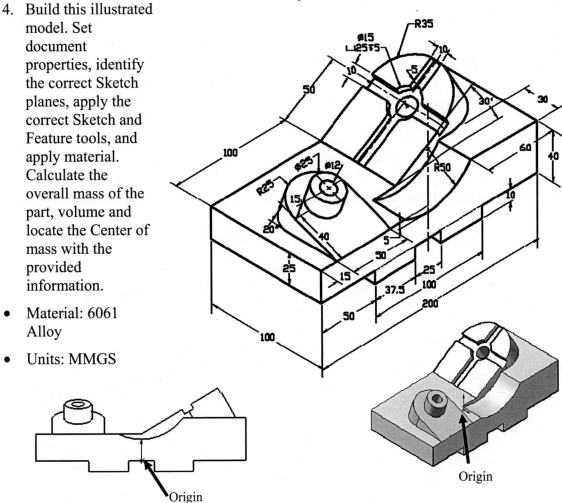

Origin

Origin

5. Build this illustrated model. Calculate the overall mass of the part, volume and locate the Center of mass with the provided information. Where do you start? Build the model, as you did in the above exercise. Create Coordinate System1 to locate the Center of mass for the model.

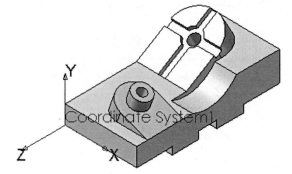

- Material: 6061 Alloy

- Units: MMGS

6. Build this illustrated model. Calculate the overall mass of the part, volume, and locate the Center of mass with the provided information.

- Material: 6061 Alloy

- Units: MMGS

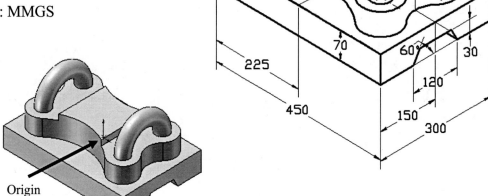

Origin

7. Build this model. Calculate the overall mass of the part, volume and locate the Center of mass with the provided information. Where do you start? Build the illustrated model, as you did in the above exercise. Create Coordinate System1 to locate the Center of mass for the model

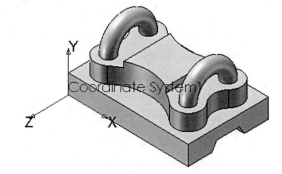

- Material: 6061 Alloy

- Units: MMGS

☀ Sample screen shots from an older CSWA exam for an Advanced Modeling part. Click on the additional views to understand the part and provided information. Read each question carefully. Understand the dimensions, center of mass and units. Apply needed materials.

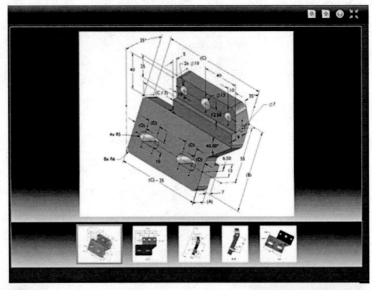

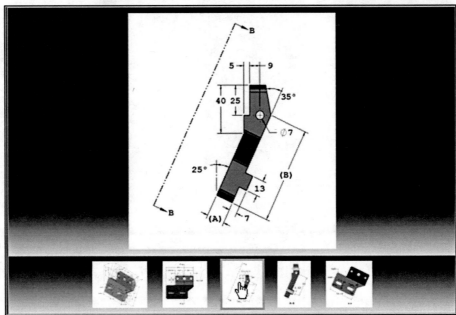

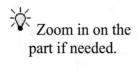 Zoom in on the part if needed.

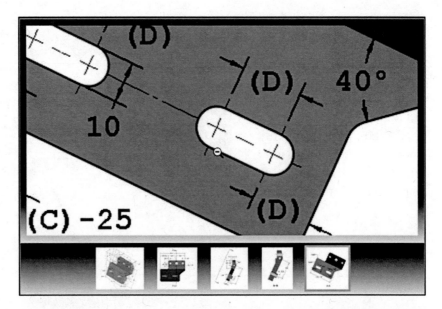

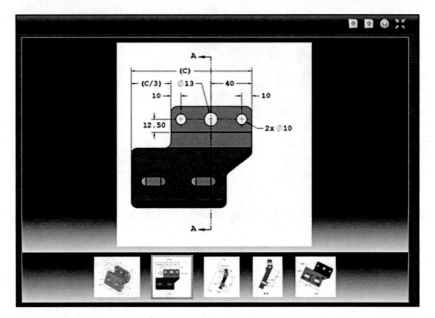

Chapter 10
Assembly Modeling

Objectives

Assembly Modeling is one of the five categories on the CSWA exam. In the last two chapters, a simple or advanced part was the focus. The Assembly Modeling (Bottom-up) category addresses an assembly with numerous sub-components.

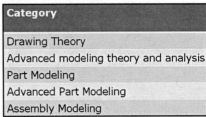

This chapter covers the general concepts and terminology used in Assembly modeling and then addresses the core elements that are aligned to the CSWA exam. Knowledge to build simples parts and to insert Standard mates is required in this category.

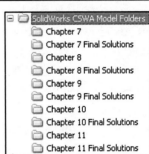

There is one question on the CSWA exam in this category. The question is worth thirty (30) points. The question is in a multiple choice single answer format.

On the completion of the chapter, you will be able to:

- Specify Document Properties

- Identify and build the components to construct the assembly from a detailed illustration using the following features:

  - Extruded Boss/Base, Extruded Cut, Fillet, Mirror, Revolved Cut, Revolved Boss/Base, Linear Pattern, Chamfer, and Hole Wizard

- Identify the first fixed component in an assembly

- Build a bottom-up assembly with the following Standard mates:

  - Coincident, Concentric, Perpendicular, Parallel, Tangent, Distance, Angle, and Aligned, Anti-Aligned options

- Apply the Mirror Component tool

- Locate the Center of mass relative to the assembly Origin

- Create a coordinate system location

- Locate the Center of mass relative to a created coordinate system

In the Simple Part Modeling, Advanced Part Modeling and Assembly Modeling categories, you are required to read and interpret all types of drawing views.

- Calculate the overall mass and volume for the created assembly

- Mate the first component with respect to the assembly reference planes

 At this time, Advance Mates and Mechanical Mates are not on the CSWA exam.

Assembly Modeling

There are two key Assembly Modeling techniques:

- Top-down, "In-Context" assembly modeling

- Bottom-up assembly modeling

In Top-down assembly modeling, one or more features of a part are defined by something in an assembly, such as a sketch or the geometry of another component. The design intent comes from the top, and moves down into the individual components, hence the name Top-down assembly modeling.

 Whenever you create a part or feature using top-down assembly modeling techniques, external references are created.

 At this time, Sheet metal assemblies are not on the CSWA exam.

Bottom-up assembly modeling is a traditional method that combines individual components. Based on design criteria, the components are developed independently. The three major steps in a Bottom-up design approach are:

1. Create each part independent of any other component in the assembly.

2. Insert the parts into the assembly.

3. Mate the components in the assembly as they relate to the physical constraints of your design.

 To modify a component in an assembly using the bottom-up assembly approach, you must edit the individually part.

The Bottom-up assembly modeling approach is used in this book to address the models in the Assembly Modeling category of the CSWA exam.

Build an assembly from a detailed dimensioned illustration

An exam question in this category could read: Build this assembly. Locate the Center of mass of the model with respect to the illustrated coordinate system.

The assembly contains the following: One Clevis component, three Axle components, two 5 Hole Link components, two 3 Hole Link components, and six Collar components. All holes Ø.190 THRU unless otherwise noted. Angle A = 150deg. Angle B = 120deg. Note: The location of the illustrated coordinate system: (+X, +Y, +Z).

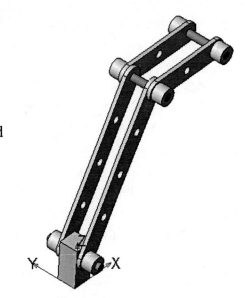

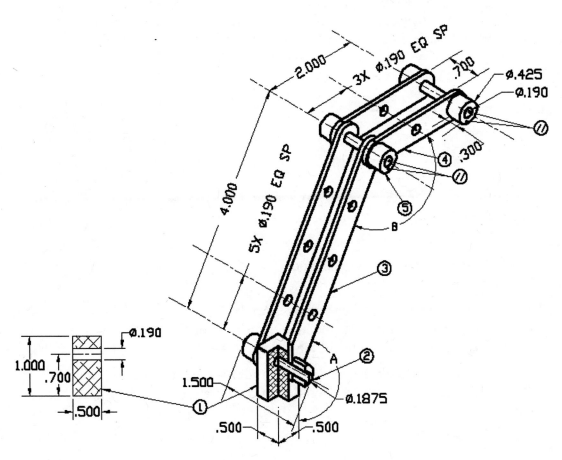

- Clevis, (Item 1): Material: 6061 Alloy. The two five (5) Hole Link components are positioned with equal Angle mates, (150 deg) to the Clevis component.

- Axle, (Item 2): Material: AISI 304. The first Axle component is mated Concentric and Coincident to the Clevis. The second and third Axle components are mated Concentric and Coincident to the 5 Hole Link and the 3 Hole Link components respectively.

- 5 Hole Link, (Item 3): Material: 6061 Alloy. Material thickness = .100in. Radius = .250in. Five holes located 1in. on center. The 5 Hole Link components are position with equal Angle mates, (120 deg) to the 3 Hole Link components.

- 3 Hole Link, (Item 4): Material: 6061 Alloy. Material thickness = .100in. Radius = .250in. Three holes located 1in. on center. The 3 Hole Link components are positioned with equal Angle mates, (120 deg) to the 5 Hole Link components.

- Collar, (Item 5): Material: 6061 Alloy. The Collar components are mated Concentric and Coincident to the Axle and the 5 Hole Link and 3 Hole Link components respectively.

Think about the steps that you would take to build the illustrated assembly. Identify and build the required parts. Identify the first fixed component. Position the Base component features in the part so they are in the correct orientation in the assembly. Insert the required Standard mates. Locate the Center of mass of the model with respect to the illustrated coordinate system. In this example, start with the Clevis part.

Tutorial Assembly model 10-1

Build the Clevis part.

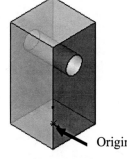
Origin

1. **Create** a New part in SolidWorks.

2. **Build** the illustrated Clevis part. Insert two features: Extruded Base, Extruded Cut. Think about the steps that you would take to build this part. Identify the location of the part Origin. Reflect back to the assembly illustration.

3. **Set** the document properties for the model.

4. Create **Sketch1**. Sketch1 is the Base sketch. Select the Top Plane as the Sketch plane. Sketch a square. Apply construction geometry. Insert the required geometric relations and dimension. Note the location of the Origin.

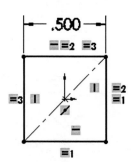

5. Create the **Extruded Base** feature. Boss-Extrude1 is the Base feature. Blind is the default End Condition in Direction 1. Depth = 1.000in.

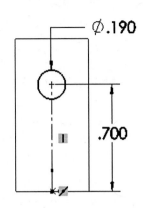

There are numerous ways to create the models in this chapter. The goal is to display different design intents and techniques.

6. Create **Sketch2**. Select the right face of Boss-Extrude1 as the Sketch plane. Sketch a circle. Insert the required geometric relation and dimensions.

7. Create the **Extruded Cut** feature. Select Through All for End Condition in Direction 1.

8. **Assign** 6061 Alloy material to the part.

9. **Save** the part and name it Clevis.

Leave the created models open. This will save time when you build the assembly during the exam. Open models are displayed in the Insert Components PropertyManager.

There are numerous ways to build the models in this chapter. The goal is to display different design intents and techniques.

Build the Axle part.

1. **Create** a New part in SolidWorks.

2. **Build** the illustrated Axle part. Think about the steps that you would take to build this part. Identify the location of the part Origin.

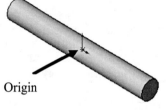

Origin

3. **Set** the document properties for the model.

4. Create **Sketch1**. Sketch1 is the Base sketch. Select the Right Plane as the Sketch plane. Sketch a circle. Insert the required dimension. Note the location of the Origin.

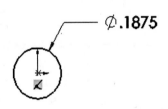

5. Create the **Boss-Extrude1** feature. Boss-Extrude1 is the Base feature. Select Mid Plane for End Condition in Direction 1. Depth = 1.500in.

6. **Assign** AISI 304 material to the part.

7. **Save** the part and name it Axle.

Create the 3 Hole Link part.

1. **Create** a New part in SolidWorks.

2. **Build** the illustrated 3 Hole Link part. Insert three features: Extruded Base, Extruded Cut and Linear Pattern. Identify the location of the part Origin.

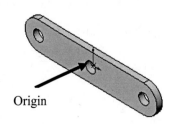

Origin

3. **Set** the document properties for the model.

4. Create **Sketch1**. Sketch1 is the Base sketch. Select the Front Plane as the Sketch plane. Apply construction geometry. Use the Tangent Arc and Line Sketch tool. Insert the required geometric relations and dimensions.
Note: You can also apply the Slot tool to save time.

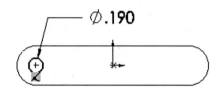

— R.250

— 2.000 —

5. Create the **Extruded Base** feature. Boss-Extrude1 is the Base feature. Select Mid Plane for End Condition in Direction 1. Depth = .100in.

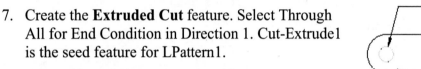

Ø.190

6. Create **Sketch2**. Select the front face of Boss-Extrude1 as the Sketch plane. Sketch a circle centered at the left tangent arc. Insert the required geometric relation and dimension.

7. Create the **Extruded Cut** feature. Select Through All for End Condition in Direction 1. Cut-Extrude1 is the seed feature for LPattern1.

Ø.190

8. Create the **Linear Pattern** feature. Spacing = 1.000in. Instances = 3.

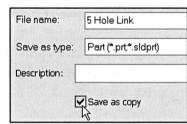

Direction 1	
Spacing:	1.000in
Instances:	3

9. **Assign** 6061 Alloy material to the part.

10. **Save** the part and name it 3 Hole Link.

Create the 5 Hole Link part.

1. Apply the **Save as Copy** command to save the 5 Hole Link. The CSWA exam is a timed exam. Conserve design time. You can either: create a new part, apply the ConfigurationManager, or use the Save as Copy command to modify the existing 3 Hole Link to the 5 Hole Link part.

File name:	5 Hole Link
Save as type:	Part (*.prt*.sldprt)
Description:	

☑ Save as copy

2. **Open** the 5 Hole Link part.

3. **Edit** Sketch1. Modify the dimension as illustrated for the 5 Hole Link part.

4. **Edit** LPattern1. Modify the number of Instances for the 5 Hole Link part. Instances = 5.

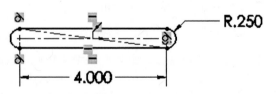

— R.250

— 4.000 —

5. **Save** the 5 Hole Link part. Note: Do not overwrite the 3 Hole Link part.

Create the Collar part.

1. **Create** a New part in SolidWorks.

2. **Build** the illustrated Collar part. Insert a Boss-Extrude1 feature. Apply symmetry. Identify the location of the part Origin.

3. **Set** the document properties for the model.

4. Create **Sketch1**. Sketch1 is the Base sketch. Select the Right Plane as the Sketch plane. Sketch two circles centered about the Origin. Insert the required dimensions.

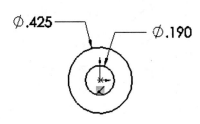

5. Create the **Extruded Base** feature. Boss-Extrude1 is the Base feature. Apply Symmetry. Select Mid Plane for End Condition in Direction 1. Depth = .300in.

6. **Assign** 6061 Alloy material to the part.

7. **Save** the part and name it Collar.

Create the assembly. The illustrated assembly contains the following: One Clevis component, three Axle components, two 5 Hole Link components, two 3 Hole Link components, and six Collar component s. All holes Ø.190 THRU unless otherwise noted. Angle A = 150deg. Angle B = 120deg.

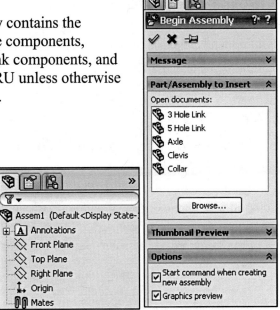

1. **Create** a New assembly in SolidWorks. The created models are displayed in the Open documents box.

   Click Cancel ✖ from the Begin Assembly PropertyManager. Assem1 is the default document name. Assembly documents end with the extension; .sldasm.

🔆 There are numerous ways to insert components to a new or existing assembly.

🔆 During the exam, various engineering symbols will be provided in the illustration of the part or assembly, such as parallelism.

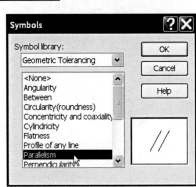

2. **Set** the document properties for the model.

3. **Insert** the Clevis part. Display the Origin.

4. **Fix** the component to the assembly Origin. Click OK from the Insert Component PropertyManager. The Clevis is displayed in the Assembly FeatureManager and in the Graphics window.

🔆 Fix the position of a component so that it cannot move with respect to the assembly Origin. By default, the first part in an assembly is fixed; however, you can float it at any time.

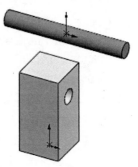

🔆 To remove the fixed state, Right-click a **component name** in the FeatureManager. Click **Float**. The component is free to move.

🔆 Select **Insert Components** from the Assembly toolbar, or click **Insert, Component, Existing Part/Assembly** from the Menu bar menu.

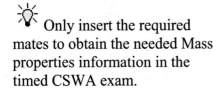

🔆 Only insert the required mates to obtain the needed Mass properties information in the timed CSWA exam.

5. **Insert** the Axle part above the Clevis component as illustrated.

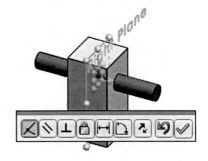

6. **Insert** a Concentric mate between the inside cylindrical face of the Clevis and the outside cylindrical face of the Axle. The selected face entities are displayed in the Mate Selections box. Concentric1 is created.

7. **Insert** a Coincident mate between the Right Plane of the Clevis and the Right Plane of the Axle. Coincident1 mate is created.

8. **Insert** the 5 Hole Link part. Locate and rotate the component as illustrated. Note the location of the Origin.

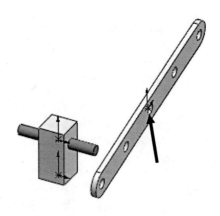

9. **Insert** a Concentric mate between the outside cylindrical face of the Axle and the inside cylindrical face of the 5 Hole Link. Concentric2 is created.

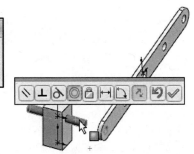

10. **Insert** a Coincident mate between the right face of the Clevis and the left face of the 5 Hole Link. Coincident2 is created.

11. **Insert** an Angle mate between the bottom face of the 5 Hole Link and the back face of the Clevis. Angle = 30deg. The selected faces are displayed in the Mate Selections box. Angle1 is created. Flip direction if needed.

Depending on the component orientation, select the Flip direction option and or enter the supplement of the angle.

12. **Insert** the second Axle part. Locate the second Axle component near the end of the 5 Hole Link as illustrated.

13. **Insert** a Concentric mate between the inside cylindrical face of the 5 Hole Link and the outside cylindrical face of the Axle. Concentric3 is created.

14. **Insert** a Coincident mate between the Right Plane of the assembly and the Right Plane of the Axle. Coincident3 is created.

15. **Insert** the 3 Hole Link part. Locate and rotate the component as illustrated. Note the location of the Origin.

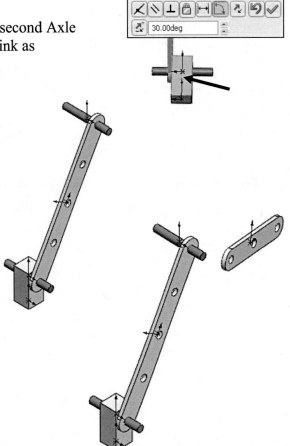

16. **Insert** a Concentric mate between the outside cylindrical face of the Axle and the inside cylindrical face of the 3 Hole Link. Concentric4 is created.

17. **Insert** a Coincident mate between the right face of the 5 Hole Link and the left face of the 3 Hole Link.

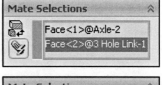

18. **Insert** an Angle mate between the bottom face of the 5 Hole Link and the bottom face of the 3 Hole Link. Angle = 60deg. Angle2 is created.

☀ Depending on the component orientation, select the Flip direction option and or enter the supplement of the angle when needed.

☀ Apply the Measure tool to check the angle. In this case, the Measure tool provides the supplemental angle.

19. **Insert** the third Axle part.

20. **Insert** a Concentric mate between the inside cylindrical face of the 3 Hole Link and the outside cylindrical face of the Axle.

21. **Insert** a Coincident mate between the Right Plane of the assembly and the Right Plane of the Axle.

22. **Insert** the Collar part. Locate the Collar near the first Axle component.

23. **Insert** a Concentric mate between the inside cylindrical face of the Collar and the outside cylindrical face of the first Axle.

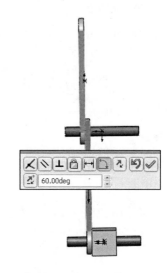

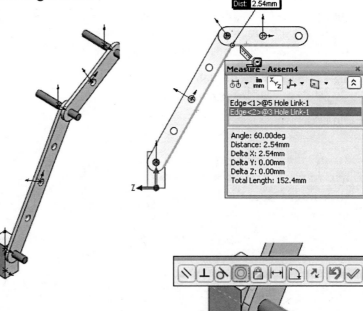

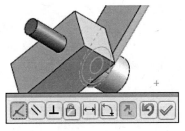

24. **Insert** a Coincident mate between the right face of the 5 Hole Link and the left face of the Collar.

25. **Insert** the second Collar part. Locate the Collar near the second Axle component

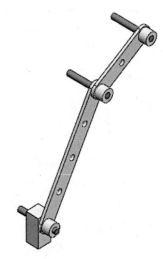

26. **Insert** a Concentric mate between the inside circular face of the second Collar and the outside circular face of the second Axle.

27. **Insert** a Coincident mate between the right face of the 3 Hole Link and the left face of the second Collar.

28. **Insert** the third Collar part. Locate the Collar near the third Axle component.

29. **Insert** a Concentric mate between the inside cylindrical face of the Collar and the outside cylindrical face of the third Axle.

30. **Insert** a Coincident mate between the right face of the 3 Hole Link and the left face of the third Collar.

31. **Mirror** the components. Mirror the three Collars, 5 Hole Link and 3 Hole Link about the Right Plane. Do not check any components in the Components to Mirror box. Check the Recreate mates to new components box. Click Next in the Mirror Components PropertyManager. Check the Preview instanced components box.

✵ Click **Insert, Mirror Components** from the Menu bar menu or click the **Mirror Components** tool from the Linear Component Pattern Consolidated toolbar.

✵ No check marks in the Components to Mirror box indicates that the components are copied. The geometry of a copied component is unchanged from the original, only the orientation of the component is different.

💡 Check marks in the Components to Mirror box indicates that the selected is mirrored. The geometry of the mirrored component changes to create a truly mirrored component.

💡 To preserve any mates between the selected components when you mirror more than one component, select **Recreate mates to new components**.

Create the coordinate system location for the assembly.

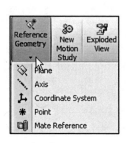

32. Select the front right **vertex** of the Clevis component as illustrated.

33. Click the **Coordinate System** tool from the Reference Geometry Consolidated toolbar. The Coordinate System PropertyManager is displayed.

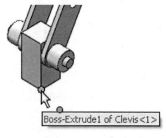

34. Click the **right bottom edge** of the Clevis component.

35. Click the **front bottom edge** of the Clevis component as illustrated.

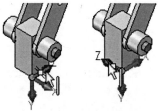

36. Address the **direction** for X, Y, Z as illustrated.

37. Click **OK** from the Coordinate System PropertyManager. Coordinate System1 is displayed

38. **Locate** the Center of mass based on the location of the illustrated coordinate system. Select Coordinate System1.

- X: 1.79 inches
- Y: 0.25 inches
- Z: 2.61 inches

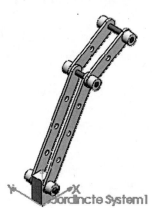

39. **Save** the part and name it Assembly Modeling 10-1.

40. **Close** the model.

Mass = 0.14 pounds

Volume = 1.20 cubic inches

Surface area = 27.04 inches^2

Center of mass: (inches)
 X = 1.79
 Y = 0.25
 Z = 2.61

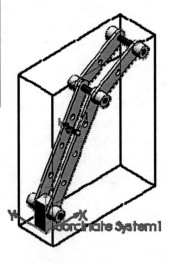

💡 There are numerous ways to create the models in this chapter. A goal is to display different design intents and techniques.

Tutorial: Assembly model 10-2

An exam question in this category could read: Build this
assembly. Locate the Center of mass of the model with the
illustrated coordinate system.

The assembly contains the following: two U-Bracket
components, four Pin components and one Square block
component.

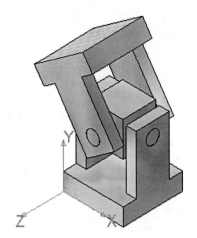

- U-Bracket, (Item 1): Material: AISI 304. Two
  U-Bracket components are combined together
  Concentric to opposite holes of the Square block
  component. The second U-Bracket component is
  positioned with an Angle mate, to the right face of the
  first U-Bracket and a Parallel mate between the top face
  of the first U-Bracket and the top face of the Square
  block component. Angle A = 125deg.

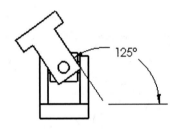

- Square block, (Item 2): Material: AISI 304. The Pin
  components are mated Concentric and Coincident to the
  4 holes in the Square block, (no clearance). The depth of
  each hole = 10mm.

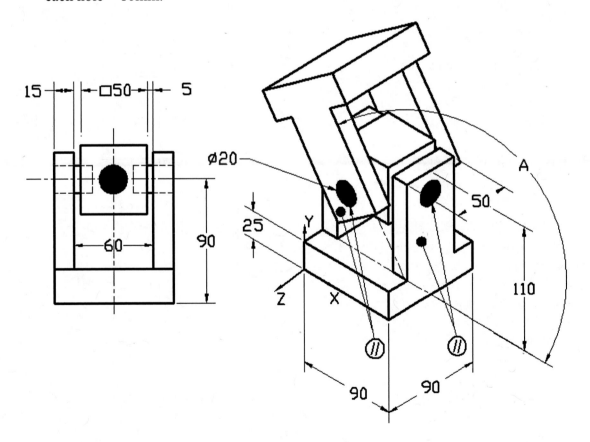

- Pin, (Item 3): Material: AISI 304. The Pin components are mated Concentric to the hole, (no clearance). The end face of the Pin components are Coincident to the outer face of the U-Bracket components. The Pin component has a 5mm spacing between the Square block component and the two U-Bracket components.

Think about the steps that you would take to build the illustrated assembly. Identify and build the required parts. Identify the first fixed component. This is the Base component of the assembly. Position the Base component features in the part so they are in the correct orientation in the assembly. Insert the required Standard mates. Locate the Center of mass of the model with respect to the illustrated coordinate system. In this example, start with the U-Bracket part.

Build the U-Bracket part.

1. **Create** a New part in SolidWorks.

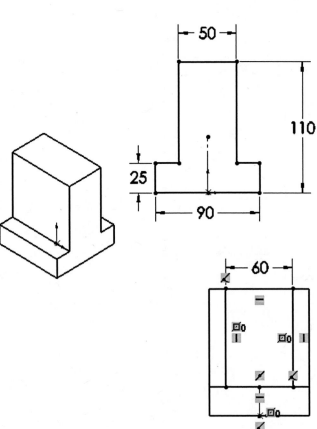

2. **Build** the illustrated U-Bracket part. Insert three features: Extruded Base and two Extruded Cuts. Think about the steps that you would take to build this part. Identify the location of the part Origin.

Origin

3. **Set** the document properties for the model.

4. Create **Sketch1**. Sketch1 is the Base sketch. Select the Right Plane as the Sketch plane. Apply symmetry. Insert the required geometry relations and dimensions.

5. Create the **Extruded Base** feature. Boss-Extrude1 is the Base feature. Apply Symmetry. Select Mid Plane for End Condition. Depth = 90mm.

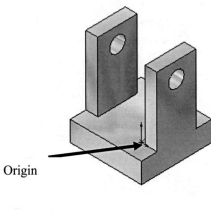

6. Create **Sketch2**. Select the Front Plane as the Sketch plane. Sketch a rectangle. Apply construction reference geometry. Insert the required geometry relations and dimension.

7. Create the first **Extruded Cut** feature. Select Through All for the End Condition in Direction 1 and Direction 2.

8. Create **Sketch3**. Select the right flat face of Boss-Extrude1 as the Sketch plane. Sketch a circle. Apply construction geometry. Insert the required relation and dimensions.

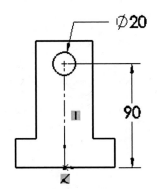

9. Create the second **Extruded Cut** feature. Select Through All for the End Condition in Direction 1. Two holes are created.

10. **Assign** AISI 304 material to the part.

11. **Save** the part and name it U-Bracket.

Create the Pin part.

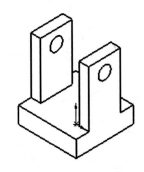

1. **Create** a New part in SolidWorks.

2. **Build** the illustrated Pin part. Insert a Boss-Extrude1 feature. Identify the location of the part Origin.

3. **Set** the document properties for the model.

4. Create **Sketch1**. Sketch1 is the Base sketch. Select the Front Plane as the Sketch plane. Sketch a circle. The Origin is located in the center of the sketch. Insert the required geometry relation and dimension.

Origin

5. Create the **Extruded Base** feature. Boss-Extrude1 is the Base feature. Blind is the default End Condition. Depth = 30mm. Note: The direction of the extrude feature.

6. **Assign** AISI 304 material to the part.

7. **Save** the part and name it Pin.

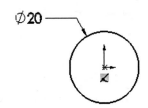

Create the Square block part.

1. **Create** a New part in SolidWorks.

2. **Build** the illustrated Square block part. Insert five features: Extruded Base, two Extruded Cuts and two Mirror. Identify the location of the part Origin.

3. **Set** the document properties for the model.

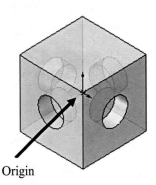

Origin

4. Create **Sketch1**. Sketch1 is the Base sketch. Select the Front Plane as the Sketch plane. Sketch a square. Apply construction reference geometry. Insert the required geometry relation and dimensions.

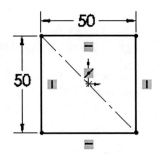

5. Create the **Extruded Base** feature. Boss-Extrude1 is the Base feature. Apply Symmetry. Select Mid Plane for End Condition. Depth = 50mm.

6. Create **Sketch2**. Select the front face as the Sketch plane. Sketch a circle centered about the Origin. Insert the required dimension.

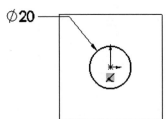

7. Create the first **Extruded Cut** feature. Blind is the default End Condition in Direction 1. Depth = 10mm.

8. Create **Sketch3**. Select the right face of Boss-Extrude1 as the Sketch plane. Sketch a circle centered about the Origin. Insert the required dimension.

9. Create the second **Extruded Cut** feature. Blind is the default End Condition in Direction 1. Depth = 10mm.

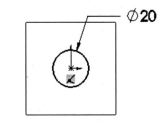

10. Create the first **Mirror** feature. Mirror the second Extruded Cut feature about the Right Plane.

11. Create the second **Mirror** feature. Mirror the first Extruded Cut feature about the Front Plane. Four holes are displayed in the Boss-Extrude1 feature.

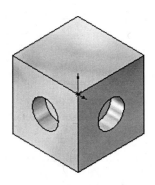

12. **Assign** AISI 304 material to the part.

13. **Save** the part and name it Square block.

Create the assembly. The illustrated assembly contains the following: Two U-Bracket components, four Pin components and one Square block component.

1. **Create** a New assembly in SolidWorks. The created models are displayed in the Open documents box.

2. Click **Cancel** ✖ from the Begin Assembly PropertyManager.

3. **Set** the document properties for the model.

4. **Insert** the first U-Bracket.

5. **Fix** the component to the assembly Origin. Click OK from the PropertyManager. The U-Bracket is displayed in the Assembly FeatureManager and in the Graphics window.

6. **Insert** the Square block above the U-Bracket component as illustrated.

7. **Insert** the first Pin part. Locate the first Pin to the front of the Square block.

8. **Insert** the second Pin part. Locate the second Pin to the back of the Square block.

9. **Insert** the third Pin part. Locate the third Pin to the left side of the Square block. Rotate the Pin.

10. **Insert** the fourth Pin part. Locate the fourth Pin to the right side of the Square block. Rotate the Pin.

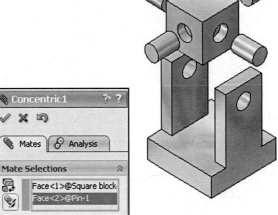

11. **Insert** a Concentric mate between the inside cylindrical face of the Square block and the outside cylindrical face of the first Pin. The selected face entities are displayed in the Mate Selections box. Concentric1 is created.

12. **Insert** a Coincident mate between the inside back circular face of the Square block and the flat back face of the first Pin. Coincident1 mate is created.

13. **Insert** a Concentric mate between the inside cylindrical face of the Square block and the outside cylindrical face of the second Pin. The selected face sketch entities are displayed in the Mate Selections box. Concentric2 is created.

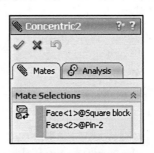

14. **Insert** a Coincident mate between the inside back circular face of the Square block and the front flat face of the second Pin. Coincident2 mate is created.

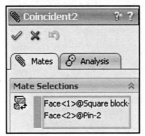

15. **Insert** a Concentric mate between the inside cylindrical face of the Square block and the outside cylindrical face of the third Pin. The selected face sketch entities are displayed in the Mate Selections box. Concentric3 is created.

16. **Insert** a Coincident mate between the inside back circular face of the Square block and the right flat face of the third Pin. Coincident3 mate is created.

17. **Insert** a Concentric mate between the inside circular face of the Square block and the outside cylindrical face of the fourth Pin. The selected face entities are displayed in the Mate Selections box. Concentric4 is created.

18. **Insert** a Coincident mate between the inside back circular face of the Square block and the left flat face of the fourth Pin. Coincident4 mate is created.

19. **Insert** a Concentric mate between the inside left cylindrical face of the Extrude feature on U-Bracket and the outside cylindrical face of the left Pin. Concentric5 is created.

20. **Insert** a Coincident mate between the Right Plane of the Square block and the Right Plane of the assembly. Coincident5 is created.

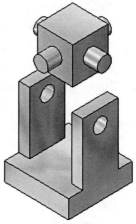

21. **Insert** the second U-Bracket part above the assembly. Position the U-Bracket as illustrated.

22. **Insert** a Concentric mate between the inside cylindrical face of the second U-Bracket component and the outside cylindrical face of the second Pin. The mate is created.

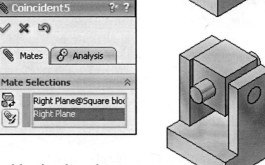

23. **Insert** a Coincident mate between the outside circular edge of the second U-Bracket and the back flat face of the second Pin. The mate is created.

There are numerous ways to mate the models in this chapter. The goal is to display different design intents and techniques.

24. **Insert** an Angle mate between the top flat face of the first U-Bracket component and the right narrow face of the second U-Bracket component as illustrated. Angle1 is created. An Angle mate is required to obtain the correct Center of mass.

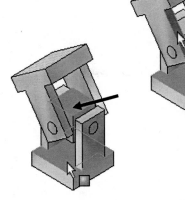

25. **Insert** a Parallel mate between the top flat face of the first U-Bracket and the top flat face of the Square block component.

26. **Expand** the Mates folder and the components from the FeatureManager. View the created mates.

Create the coordinate location for the assembly.

27. Select the front bottom left **vertex** of the first U-Bracket component as illustrated.

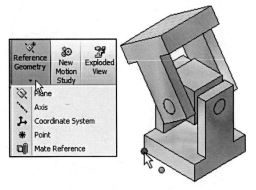

28. Click the **Coordinate System** tool from the Reference Geometry Consolidated toolbar. The Coordinate System PropertyManager is displayed.

29. Click **OK** from the Coordinate System PropertyManager. Coordinate System1 is displayed.

30. **Locate** the Center of mass based on the location of the illustrated coordinate system. Select Coordinate System1.

- X: 31.54 millimeters

- Y: 85.76 millimeters

- Z: -45.00 millimeters

31. **Save** the part and name it Assembly Modeling 10-2.

32. **Close** the model.

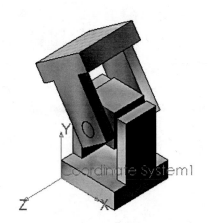

☀ At this time, there are no assembly configuration questions on the CSWA exam.

Mass = 6330.27 grams

Volume = 791283.19 cubic millimeters

Surface area = 123423.01 millimeters^2

Center of mass: (millimeters)
   X = 31.54
   Y = 85.76
   Z = -45.00

Tutorial: Assembly model 10-3

An exam question in this category could read:
Build this assembly.
Locate the Center of mass using the illustrated coordinate system.

The assembly contains the following: One WheelPlate component, two Bracket100 components, one Axle40 component, one Wheel1 component and four Pin-4 components.

- WheelPlate, (Item 1): Material: AISI 304. The WheelPlate contains 4-Ø10 holes. The holes are aligned to the left Bracket100 and the right Bracket100 components. All holes are THRU ALL. The thickness of the WheelPlate = 10 mm.

- Bracket100, (Item 2): Material: AISI 304. The Bracket100 component contains 2-Ø10 holes and 1- Ø16 hole. All holes are through-all.

- Wheel1, (Item 3): Material AISI 304: The center hole of the Wheel1 component is Concentric with the Axle40 component. There is a 3mm gap between the inside faces of the Bracket100 components and the end faces of the Wheel hub.

- Axle40, (Item 4): Material AISI 304: The end faces of the Axle40 are Coincident with the outside faces of the Bracket100 components.

- Pin-4, (Item 5): Material AISI 304: The Pin-4 components are mated Concentric to the holes of the Bracket100 components, (no clearance). The end faces are Coincident to the WheelPlate bottom face and the Bracket100 top face.

Identify and build the required parts. Identify the first fixed component. This is the Base component of the assembly. Position the Base component features in the part so they are in the correct orientation in the assembly. Insert the required Standard mates. Locate the Center of mass of the illustrated model with respect to the referenced coordinate system. The referenced coordinate system is located at the bottom, right, midpoint of the Wheelplate. In this example, start with the WheelPlate part.

Build the WheelPlate part.

1. **Create** a New part in SolidWorks.

2. **Build** the illustrated WheelPlate part. Insert four features: Extruded Base, Fillet, Extruded Cut and a Linear Pattern. Think about the steps that you would take to build this part. Identify the location of the part Origin.

3. **Set** the document properties for the model.

4. Create **Sketch1**. Sketch1 is the Base sketch. Select the Top Plane as the Sketch plane. Sketch a rectangle. Insert the required geometry relations and dimensions. The Origin is located in the middle of the sketch.

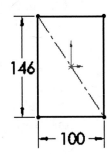

146

100

5. Create the **Extruded Base** feature. Boss-Extrude1 is the Base feature. Blind is the default End Condition in Direction 1. Depth = 10mm.

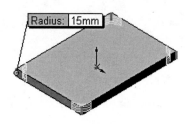

6. Create the **Fillet** feature. Fillet the four outside edges. Radius = 15mm.

7. Create **Sketch2**. Select the top face of Boss-Extrude1 as the Sketch plane. Sketch a circle. Insert the required geometric relations and dimensions.

🔆 In a timed exam, do not insert note annotation. It will not affect your answer for the exam.

8. Create the **Extruded Cut** feature. Select Through All for End Condition in Direction 1. This is the seed feature.

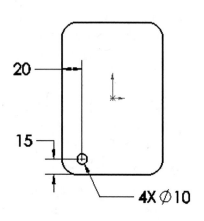

9. Create the **Linear Pattern** feature. Create a vertical and horizontal hole pattern. Cut-Extrude1 is the seed feature. Spacing = 116mm in Direction 1. Spacing = 60mm in Direction 2.

10. **Assign** AISI 304 material to the part.

11. **Save** the part and name it WheelPlate.

Create the Bracket100 part for the assembly. There are two Bracket100 components in the assembly.

1. **Create** a New part in SolidWorks.

2. **Build** the illustrated Bracket100 part. Insert seven features: Extruded Base, two Extruded Bosses, Extruded Cut, Hole Wizard, Mirror and Fillet. Think about the steps that you would take to build this part. Identify the location of the part Origin.

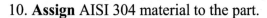

3. **Set** the document properties for the model.

4. Create **Sketch1**. Sketch1 is the Base sketch. Select the Top Plane as the Sketch plane. Sketch a rectangle. Insert the required geometric relations and dimensions. Note the location of the Origin.

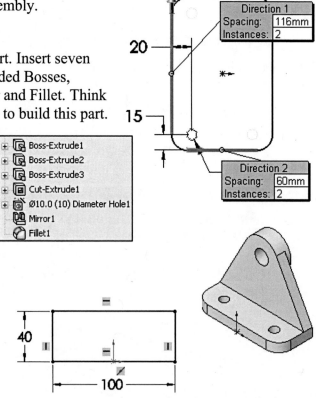

5. Create the **Extruded Base** feature. Boss-Extrude1 is the Base feature. Blind is the default End Condition. Depth = 10mm.

6. Create **Sketch2**. Select the back face of Boss-Extrude1 as the Sketch plane. Apply the Tangent Arc Sketch tool. Complete the sketch. Insert the required relations and dimensions.

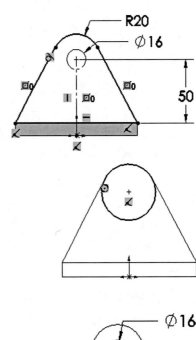

7. Create the first **Extruded Boss** (Boss-Extrude2) feature. Blind is the default End Condition in Direction 1. Depth = 10mm.

8. Create **Sketch3**. Select the front face of Boss-Extrude2 as the Sketch plane. Wake-up the centerpoint of the tangent arc. Sketch a circle Coradial and Coincident to the tangent arc.

9. Create the second **Extruded Boss** (Boss-Extrude3) feature. Blind is the default End Condition in Direction 1. Depth = 15mm. Note the direction of the extrude feature, towards the back.

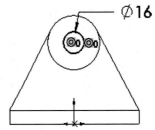

10. Create **Sketch4**. Select the back face of the Extrude feature as the Sketch plane. Sketch a circle. Insert the required relations and dimension.

11. Create the **Extrude Cut** feature. Select Through All for End Condition in Direction 1.

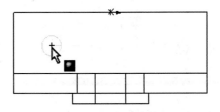

12. Create **Sketch5**. Select the bottom face of Boss-Extrude1 for the Sketch plane. Select a location as illustrated for the first hole. Sketch5 is the profile for the Hole Wizard feature.

13. Create the **Hole Wizard** feature. Select Hole for Hole Specification type. Select Ansi Metric for Standard. Select Drill sizes for Type. Select Ø10.0 for Size. Select Through All for End Condition. Click the Positions tab. Insert the required dimensions.

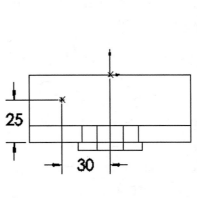

The Hole Wizard PropertyManager is displayed when you create a Hole Wizard hole. Two tabs are displayed in the Hole Wizard PropertyManager:

- Type (default). Sets the hole type parameters.

- Positions. Locates the Hole Wizard holes on planar or non-planar faces. Use the dimension and other sketch tools to position the center of the holes.

14. Create the **Mirror** feature. Mirror the Ø10.0mm hole about the Right Plane.

15. Create the **Fillet** feature. Fillet the two front edges. Radius = 15mm.

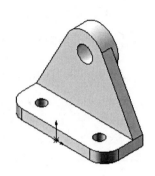

16. **Assign** AISI 304 material to the part.

17. **Save** the part and name it Bracket100.

Create the Axle40 part for the assembly.

1. **Create** a New part in SolidWorks.

2. **Build** the illustrated Axle40 part. Insert two features: Revolved Base and Chamfer. Identify the location of the part Origin.

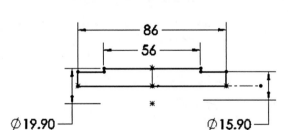

3. **Set** the document properties for the model.

4. Create **Sketch1**. Sketch1 is the Base sketch. Select the Right Plane as the Sketch plane. Apply construction reference geometry. Insert the required geometric relations and dimensions. Note the location of the Origin.

5. Create the **Revolved Base** feature. Revolve1 is an Angel-distance feature. Revolve1 is the Base feature for Axle40. 360deg is the default angle. Apply construction geometry for Axis of revolution.

6. Create the **Chamfer** feature. Chamfer the two outside edges. Distance = 2mm. Angle = 45deg.

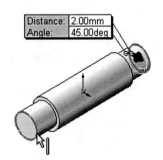

7. **Assign** AISI 304 material to the part.

8. **Save** the part and name it Axle40.

There are numerous ways to create the models in this chapter. The goal is to display different design intents and techniques.

A Revolve feature adds or removes material by revolving one or more profiles about a centerline. You can create Revolved Boss/Bases, Revolved Cuts, or Revolved Surfaces. The Revolve feature can be a solid, a thin feature, or a surface.

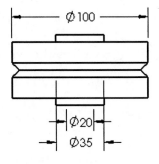

Create the Wheel1 part for the assembly.

1. **Create** a New part in SolidWorks.

2. **Build** the illustrated Wheel1 part. Insert two features: Revolved Base and Revolved Cut. Think about the steps that you would take to build this part. Identify the location of the part Origin.

3. **Set** the document properties for the model.

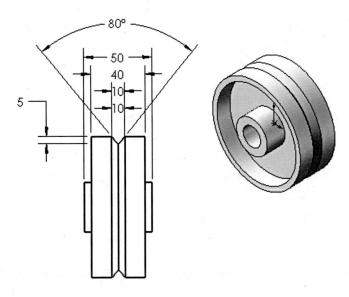

4. Create **Sketch1**. Sketch1 is the Base sketch. Select the Right Plane as the Sketch plane. Apply construction reference geometry. Apply symmetry. Insert the required geometric relations and dimensions. Note the location of the Origin.

5. Create the **Revolved Base** feature. Revolve1 is the Base feature for Wheel1. 360deg is the default angle. Select the horizontal construction geometry line for the Axis of Revolution.

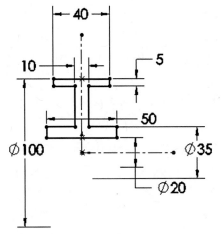

6. Create **Sketch2**. Select the Right Plane as the Sketch plane. Apply construction reference geometry. Sketch a triangle for the groove in the wheel. Insert the required geometric relations and dimensions.

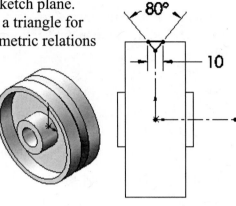

7. Create the **Revolved Cut** feature. 360deg is the default angle. Select the horizontal reference construction geometry line for the Axis of Revolution.

8. **Assign** AISI 304 material to the part.

9. **Save** the part and name it Wheel1.

Create the Pin-4 part for the assembly.

1. **Create** a New part in SolidWorks.

2. **Build** the illustrated Pin-4 part. Insert a Boss-Extrude1 feature. Think about the steps that you would take to build this part. Identify the location of the part Origin.

3. **Set** the document properties for the model.

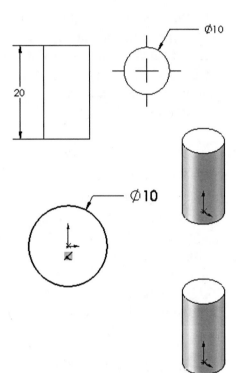

4. Create **Sketch1**. Sketch1 is the Base sketch. Select the Top Plane as the Sketch plane. Sketch a circle. Insert the required geometric relation and dimension. Note the location of the Origin.

5. Create the **Boss-Extrude1** feature. Boss-Extrude1 is the Base feature. Blind is the default End Condition. Depth = 20mm.

6. **Assign** AISI 304 material to the part.

7. **Save** the part and name it Pin-4.

Create the assembly. The assembly contains the following: one WheelPlate component, two Bracket100 components, one Axle40 component, one Wheel1 component, and four Pin-4 components.

1. **Create** a New assembly in SolidWorks. The created models are displayed in the Open documents box.

2. Click **Cancel** ✖ from the Begin Assembly PropertyManager.

3. **Set** the document properties for the model.

4. **Insert** the first component. Insert the WheelPlate. Fix the component to the assembly Origin. The WheelPlate is displayed in the Assembly FeatureManager and in the Graphics window. The WheelPlate component is fixed.

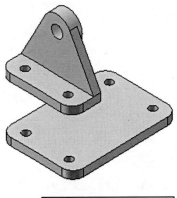

5. **Insert** the first Bracket100 part above the WheelPlate component as illustrated.

6. **Insert** a Concentric mate between the inside front left cylindrical face of the Bracket100 component and the inside front left cylindrical face of the WheelPlate. Concentric1 is created.

7. **Insert** a Concentric mate between the inside front right cylindrical face of the Bracket100 component and the inside front right cylindrical face of the WheelPlate. Concentric2 is created.

8. **Insert** a Coincident mate between the bottom flat face of the Bracket100 component and the top flat face of the WheelPlate component. Coincident1 is created.

9. **Insert** the Axle40 part above the first Bracket100 component as illustrated.

10. **Insert** a Concentric mate between the outside cylindrical face of the Axle40 component and the inside cylindrical face of the Bracket100 component. Concentric3 is created.

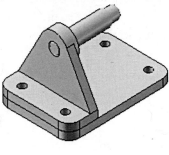

11. **Insert** a Coincident mate between the flat face of the Axle40 component and the front outside edge of the first Bracket100 component. Coincident2 is created.

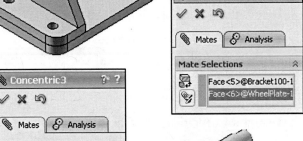

To verify that the distance between holes of mating components is equal, utilize Concentric mates between pairs of cylindrical hole faces.

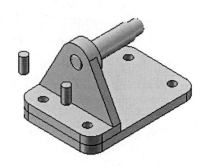

12. **Insert** the first Pin-4 part above the Bracket100 component.

13. **Insert** the second Pin-4 part above the Bracket100 component.

14. **Insert** a Concentric mate between the outside cylindrical face of the first Pin-4 component and the inside front left cylindrical face of the Bracket100 component. Concentric4 is created.

15. **Insert** a Coincident mate between the flat top face of the first Pin-4 component and the top face of the first Bracket100 component. Coincident3 is created.

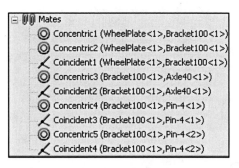

16. **Insert** a Concentric mate between the outside cylindrical face of the second Pin-4 component and the inside front right cylindrical face of the Bracket100 component. Concentric5 is created.

17. **Insert** a Coincident mate between the flat top face of the second Pin-4 component and the top face of the first Bracket100 component. Coincident4 is created.

18. **Insert** the Wheel1 part as illustrated.

19. **Insert** a Concentric mate between the outside cylindrical face of Axle40 and the inside front cylindrical face of the Wheel1 component. Concentric6 is created.

20. **Insert** a Coincident mate between the Front Plane of Axle40 and the Front Plane of Wheel1. Coincident5 is created.

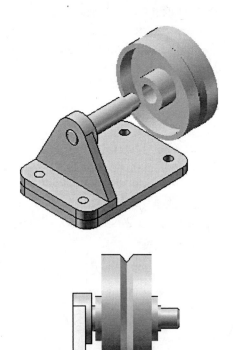

21. **Mirror** the components. Mirror the Bracket100, and the two Pin-4 components about the Front Plane. Do not check any components in the Components to Mirror box. Check the Recreate mates to new components box. Click Next in the PropertyManager. Check the Preview instanced components box.

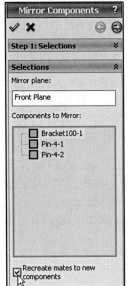

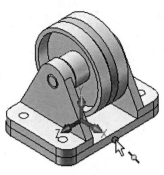

Click the **Mirror Component** tool from the Linear Component Pattern Consolidated toolbar to activate the Mirror Components PropertyManager.

Create the coordinate location for the assembly.

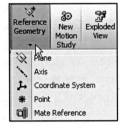

22. Click the **Coordinate System** tool from the Reference Geometry Consolidated toolbar. The Coordinate System PropertyManager is displayed.

23. **Select** the right bottom midpoint as the Origin location as illustrated.

24. **Select** the bottom right edge as the X axis direction reference as illustrated.

25. Click **OK** from the Coordinate System PropertyManager. Coordinate System1 is displayed.

26. **Locate** the Center of mass based on the location of the illustrated coordinate system. Select Coordinate System1.

- X: = 0.00 millimeters

- Y: = 37.14 millimeters

- Z: = -50.00 millimeters

27. **Save** the part and name it Assembly Modeling 10-3.

28. **Close** the model.

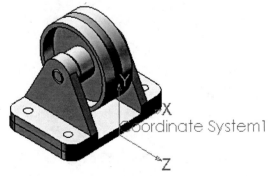

Mate the first component with respect to the assembly reference planes

You can fix the position of a component so that it cannot move with respect to the assembly Origin. By default, the first part in an assembly is fixed - however, you can float it at any time.

It is recommended that at least one assembly component is either fixed, or mated to the assembly planes or Origin. This provides a frame of reference for all other mates, and prevents unexpected movement of components when mates are added.

Up to this point, you identified the first fixed component, and built the required Base component of the assembly. The component features were orientated correctly to the illustrated assembly. In the exam, what if you created the Base component where the component features were not orientated correctly to the illustrated assembly.

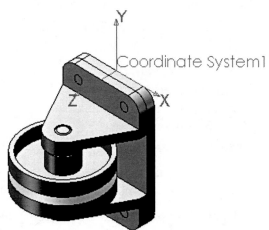

In the next tutorial, build the illustrated assembly. Insert the Base component, float the component, then mate the first component with respect to the assembly reference planes. Complete the assembly with the components from the Tutorial: Assembly model 10-3.

Tutorial: Assembly model 10-4

1. **Create** a New assembly in SolidWorks.

2. **Insert** the illustrated WheelPlate part that you built in Tutorial: Assembly model 10-3.

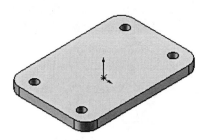

3. **Float** the WheelPlate component from the FeatureManager.

4. **Insert** a Coincident mate between the Front Plane of the assembly and the bottom flat face of the WheelPlate. Coincident1 is created.

5. **Insert** a Coincident mate between the Right Plane of the assembly and the Right Plane of the WheelPlate. Coincident2 is created.

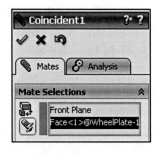

6. **Insert** a Coincident mate between the Top Plane of the assembly and the Front Plane of the WheelPlate. Coincident3 is created.

☀ When the Base component is mated to three assembly reference planes, no component status symbol is displayed in the Assembly FeatureManager.

7. **Insert** the first Bracket100 part as illustrated. Rotate the component if required.

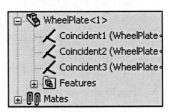

8. **Insert** a Concentric mate between the inside back left circular face of the Bracket100 component and the inside top left circular face of the WheelPlate. Concentric1 is created.

9. **Insert** a Concentric mate between the inside back right cylindrical face of the Bracket100 component and the inside top right cylindrical face of the WheelPlate. Concentric2 is created.

10. **Insert** a Coincident mate between the flat back face of the Bracket100 component and the front flat face of the WheelPlate component. Coincident4 is created.

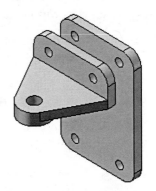

11. **Insert** the Axle40 part as illustrated. Rotate the component if required.

12. **Insert** a Concentric mate between the outside cylindrical face of the Axle40 component and the inside cylindrical face of the Bracket100 component. Concentric3 is created.

13. **Insert** a Coincident mate between the top flat face of the Axle40 component and the top outside circular edge of the Bracket100 component. Coincident5 is created.

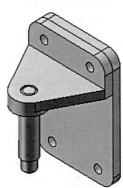

14. **Insert** the first Pin-4 part above the Bracket100 component. Rotate the component.

15. **Insert** the second Pin-4 part above the Bracket100 component. Rotate the component.

16. **Insert** a Concentric mate between the outside cylindrical face of the first Pin-4 component and the inside front left cylindrical face of the Bracket100 component. Concentric4 is created.

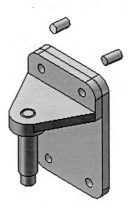

17. **Insert** a Coincident mate between the flat front face of the first Pin-4 component and the top flat front face of the Bracket100 component. Coincident6 is created.

18. **Insert** a Concentric mate between the outside cylindrical face of the second Pin-4 component and the inside front right cylindrical face of the Bracket100 component. Concentric5 is created.

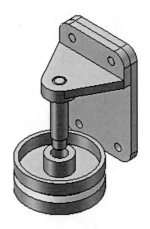

19. **Insert** a Coincident mate between the flat front face of the second Pin-4 component and the top flat front face of the Bracket100 component. Coincident7 is created.

20. **Insert** the Wheel1 part as illustrated.

21. **Insert** a Concentric mate between the outside cylindrical face of Axle40 and the inside top cylindrical face of the Wheel1 component. Concentric6 is created.

22. **Insert** a Coincident mate between the Right Plane of Axle40 and the Right Plane of the Wheel1 component. Coincident8 is created.

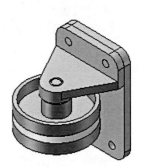

23. **Insert** a Coincident mate between the Front Plane of Axle40 and the Front Plane of the Wheel1 component. Coincident9 is created.

24. **Mirror** the components. Mirror the Bracket100, and the two Pin-4 components about the Top Plane. Do not check any components in the Components to Mirror box. Check the Recreate mates to new components box. Click Next in the PropertyManager. Check the Preview instanced components box.

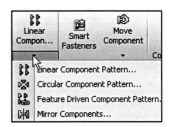

Create the coordinate location for the assembly.

25. Click the **Coordinate System** tool from the Reference Geometry Consolidated toolbar. The Coordinate System PropertyManager is displayed.

26. **Select** the top back midpoint for the Origin location as illustrated.

27. Click **OK** from the Coordinate System PropertyManager. Coordinate System1 is displayed.

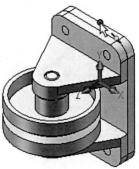

28. **Locate** the Center of mass based on the location of the illustrated coordinate system. Select Coordinate System1.

- X: = 0.00 millimeters

- Y: = -73.00 millimeters

- Z: = 37.14 millimeters

29. **Save** the part and name it Assembly Modeling 10-4.

30. **Close** the model.

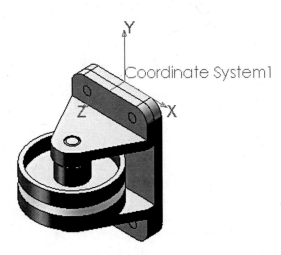

Mass = 3797.32 grams

Volume = 474665.19 cubic millimeters

Surface area = 130119.83 millimeters^2

Center of mass: (millimeters)
    X = 0.00
    Y = -73.00
    Z = 37.14

Summary

Assembly Modeling (Bottom-up) is one of the five categories on the CSWA exam. The Assembly Modeling category addresses an assembly with numerous sub-components. Each sub-component is a simple part. Knowledge is required to know and understand how to insert Standard mates between the components to build an assembly. This chapter covered the general concepts and terminology used in Assembly Modeling and then addressed the core elements that are aligned to the exam. Only insert the required mates to obtain the needed Mass properties information in the timed CSWA exam.

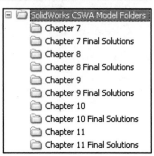

There is one question on the CSWA exam in this category. The question is worth thirty (30) points. The question is in a multiple choice single answer format. Spend no more than 40 minutes on the question in this category. This is a timed exam. Manage your time. At this time, there are no sheet metal assembly questions or questions on Advanced or Mechanical mates on the CSWA exam.

Advanced Modeling Theory and Analysis is the next chapter in this book. The chapter covers the general concepts and terminology used in SimulationXpress / COSMOSXpress and then addresses the core elements that are aligned to the exam.

There are two questions on the CSWA exam in this category. Each question is worth five (5) points. The two questions are in a multiple choice single answer format and requires general terminology used in Engineering analysis and provides the needed knowledge of SimulationXpress / COSMOSXpress that is aligned to the exam. Note: You are *not* required to perform an analysis on a part or assembly.

☼ View sample screen shots from an older CSWA exam for an Assembly Model at the end of the Homework section in this chapter.

Questions

1: Build this assembly. Calculate the overall mass and volume of the assembly. Locate the Center of mass using the illustrated coordinate system. The assembly contains the following: one Base100 component, one Yoke component, and one AdjustingPin component. Apply the MMGS unit system.

- Base100, (Item 1): Material 1060 Alloy. The distance between the front face of the Base100 component and the front face of the Yoke = 60mm.
- Yoke, (Item 2): Material 1060 Alloy. The Yoke fits inside the left and right square channels of the Base100 component, (no clearance). The top face of the Yoke contains a Ø12mm through all hole.

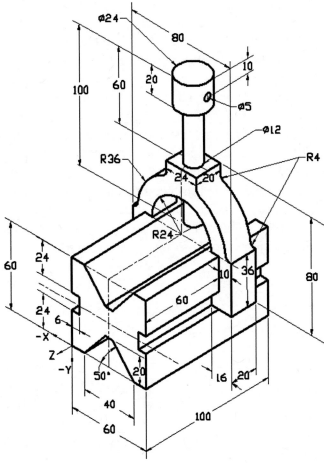

- AdjustingPin, (Item 3): Material 1060 alloy. The bottom face of the AdjustingPin head is located 40mm from the top face of the Yoke component. The AdjustingPin component contains an Ø5mm Though All hole.

☀ The coordinate system is located in the lower left corner of the Base100 component. The X axis points to the right.

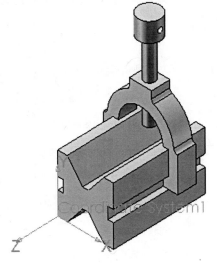

2. Build this assembly. Calculate the overall mass and volume of the assembly. Locate the Center of mass using the illustrated coordinate system. The assembly contains the following: three MachinedBracket components, and two Pin-5 components. Apply the MMGS unit system.

Insert the Base component, float the component, then mate the first component with respect to the assembly reference planes.

- MachinedBracket, (Item 1): Material 6061 Alloy. The MachineBracket component contains two Ø10mm through all holes. Each MachinedBracket component is mated with two Angle mates. The Angle mate = 45deg. The top edge of the notch is located 20mm from the top edge of the MachinedBracket.
- Pin-5, (Item 2): Material Titanium. The Pin-5 component is 5mms in length and equal in diameter. The Pin-5 component is mated Concentric to the MachinedBracket, (no clearance). The end faces of the Pin-5 component is Coincident with the outer faces of the MachinedBracket. There is a 1mm gap between the Machined Bracket components.

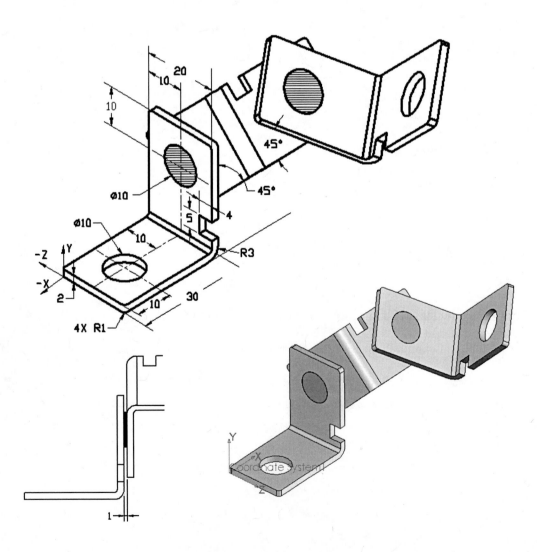

3. Build this assembly. Use the dimensions from the second Check your understanding problem in this chapter. Calculate the overall mass and volume of the assembly. Locate the Center of mass using the illustrated coordinate system. The illustrated assembly contains the following components: three Machined-Bracket components, and two Pin-6 components. Apply the MMGS unit system.

Insert the Base component, float the component, then mate the first component with respect to the assembly reference planes.

- Machined-Bracket, (Item 1): Material 6061 Alloy. The Machine-Bracket component contains two Ø10mm through all holes. Each Machined-Bracket component is mated with two Angle mates. The Angle mate = 45deg. The top edge of the notch is located 20mm from the top edge of the MachinedBracket.
- Pin-6, (Item 2): Material Titanium. The Pin-6 component is 5mms in length and equal in diameter. The Pin-5 component is mated Concentric to the Machined-Bracket, (no clearance). The end faces of the Pin-6 component is Coincident with the outer faces of the Machined-Bracket. There is a 1mm gap between the Machined-Bracket components.

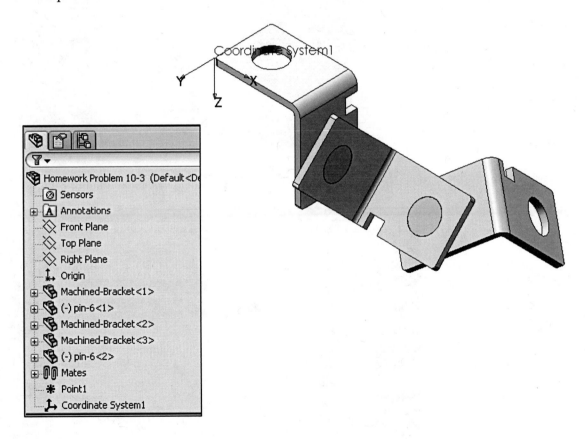

💡 Sample screen shots from an older CSWA exam for an assembly. Click on the additional views to understand the assembly and provided information. Read each question carefully. Understand the dimensions, center of mass and units. Apply needed materials.

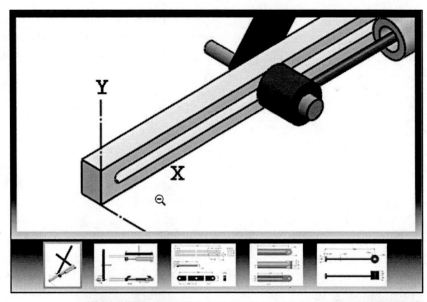

💡 Zoom in on the part if needed.

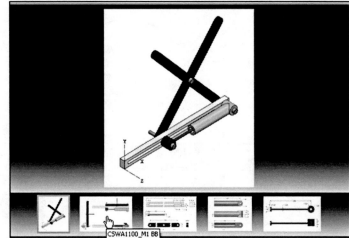

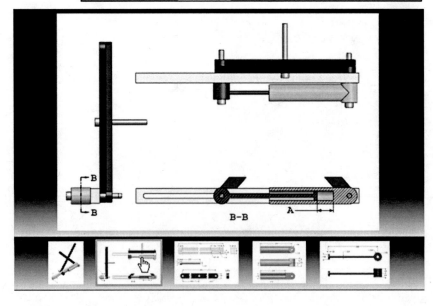

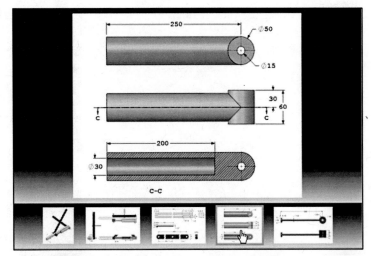

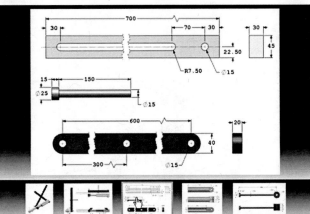

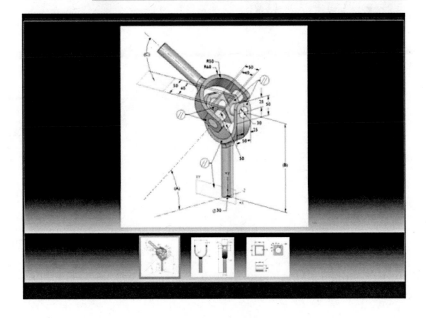

Zoom in on the part if needed.

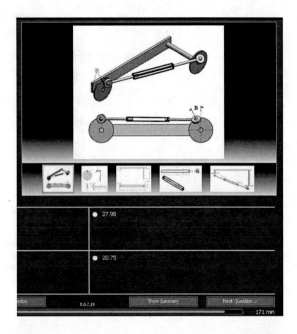

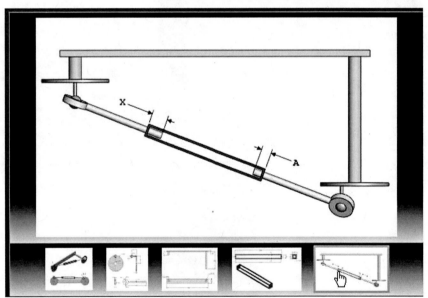

Chapter 11
Advanced Modeling Theory and Analysis

Objectives

Advanced Modeling Theory and Analysis is one of the five categories on the CSWA exam. This chapter covers general terminology used in Engineering analysis and provides the knowledge of SimulationXpress / COSMOSXpress that is aligned to the exam.

There are two questions on the CSWA exam in this category. Each question is worth five (5) points. The two questions are in a multiple choice single answer format.

In this category of the exam, you are not required to perform an analysis on a part or assembly, but are required to understand general engineering analysis terminology and how SimulationXpress / COSMOSXpress works.

On the completion of the chapter, you will be able to:

- Comprehend basic Engineering analysis definitions

- Wisdom of the SolidWorks SimulationXpress Wizard interface

- Skill to apply SolidWorks SimulationXpress to a simple part

Category
Drawing Theory
Advanced modeling theory and analysis
Part Modeling
Advanced Part Modeling
Assembly Modeling

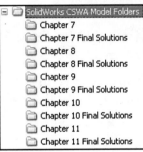

General Definitions

Buckling:

A failure mode characterized by a sudden failure of a structural member subjected to high compressive stresses, where the actual compressive stresses at failure are smaller than the ultimate compressive stresses that the material is capable of withstanding. This mode of failure is also described as failure due to elastic instability.

Coefficient of Thermal Expansion:

Defined as the change in length per unit length per one degree change in temperature (change in normal strain per unit temperature).

Creep:

Term used to describe the tendency of a solid material to slowly move or deform permanently under the influence of stresses. It occurs as a result of long term exposure to levels of stress that are below the yield strength or ultimate strength of the material. Creep is more severe in materials that are subjected to heat for long periods, and near the melting point.

Degrees of Freedom:

Are the set of independent displacements and/or rotations that specify completely the displaced or deformed position and orientation of the body or system. This is a fundamental concept relating to systems of moving bodies in mechanical engineering, aeronautical engineering, robotics, structural engineering, etc. There are six degrees of freedom: Three translations and three rotations.

Density:

Mass per unit volume. Density units are lb/in^3 in the English system and kg/m^3 in the SI system.

Density is used in static, nonlinear, frequency, dynamic, buckling, and thermal analyses. Static and buckling analyses use this property only if you define body forces (gravity and/or centrifugal).

Ductile:

Mechanical property which describes how a material lends itself to be formed into rod-like shapes before fracture occurs. Examples of highly ductile metals are silver, gold, copper, and aluminum. The ductility of steel varies depending on the alloying constituents. Increasing levels of carbon decreases ductility, i.e. the steel becomes more brittle.

Elastic Modulus:

For a linear elastic material, the elastic modulus is the stress required to cause a unit strain in the material. In other words stress divided by the associated strain. The modulus of elasticity was first introduced by Young and is often called the Young's Modulus.

Fatigue:

Progressive and localized structural damage that occurs when a material is subjected to cyclic loading. The maximum stress values are less than the ultimate tensile stress limit, and may be below the yield stress limit of the material.

Fixed Restraint:

For solids: restraint/fixture type sets all translational degrees of freedom to zero. For shells and beams: sets the translational and the rotational degrees of freedom to zero. For truss joints: sets the translational degrees of freedom to zero. When using this restraint type, no reference geometry is needed.

Force:

Is a push or pull upon an object resulting from the object's interaction with another object. Whenever there is an interaction between two objects, there is a force upon each of the objects. When the interaction ceases, the two objects no longer experience the force. Forces only exist as a result of an interaction.

For example, if you select three (3) faces and specify a 50 lb force, SimulationXpress applies a total force of 150 lbs (50 lbs on each face).

Knowing how a design will perform under different conditions allows engineers to make changes prior to physical prototyping, thus saving both time and money.

Linear Static Analysis:

Linear static analysis allows engineers to test different load conditions and their resulting stresses and deformation. What is stress? Stress is a measure of the average amount of force exerted per unit area. It is a measure of the intensity of the total internal forces acting within a body across imaginary internal surfaces, as a reaction to external applied forces and body forces.

Deformation is a change in shape due to an applied force. This can be a result of tensile (pulling) forces, compressive (pushing) forces, shear, bending or torsion (twisting). Deformation is often described in terms of strain.

When loads are applied to a body, the body deforms and the effect of loads is transmitted throughout the body. The external loads induce internal forces and reactions to render the body into a state of equilibrium.

Linear Static analysis calculates *displacements*, *strains*, *stresses*, and *reaction forces* under the effect of applied loads. Linear static analysis makes the following assumptions:

1. The induced response is directly proportional to the applied loads.

2. The highest stress is in the linear range of the stress-strain curve characterized by a straight line starting from the origin.

3. The maximum calculated displacement is considerably smaller than the characteristic dimension of the part. For example, the maximum displacement of a plate must be considerably smaller than its thickness and the maximum displacement of a beam must be considerably smaller than the smallest dimension of its cross-section. Inertia is neglected.

4. Loads are applied slowly and gradually until they reach their full magnitudes. Suddenly applied loads cause additional displacements, strains, and stresses.

Below are three simple graphics of Stress vs. Strain:

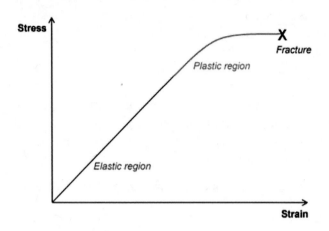

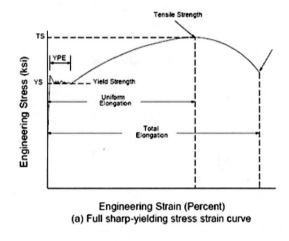

(a) Full sharp-yielding stress strain curve

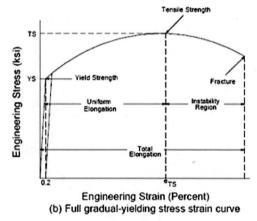

(b) Full gradual-yielding stress strain curve

Inertia:

Describes the motion of matter and how it is affected by applied forces. The principle of inertia as described by Newton in Newton's First Law of Motion states: An object that is not subject to any outside forces moves at a constant velocity, covering equal distances in equal times along a straight-line path. In even simpler terms, inertia means "body in motion tends to remain in motion; a body at rest tends to remain at rest."

Material Strength:

In materials science, the strength of a material refers to the material's ability to resist an applied force.

Mohr-Columb Stress Criterion:

The Mohr-Columb stress criterion is based on the Mohr-Columb theory also known as the Internal Friction theory. This criterion is used for brittle materials with different tensile and compressive properties. Brittle materials do not have a specific yield point and hence it is not recommended to use the yield strength to define the limit stress for this criterion.

Orthotropic Material:

A material is orthotropic if its mechanical or thermal properties are unique and independent in three mutually perpendicular directions. Examples of orthotropic materials are wood, many crystals, and rolled metals. For example, the mechanical properties of wood at a point are described in the longitudinal, radial, and tangential directions. The longitudinal axis (1) is parallel to the grain (fiber) direction; the radial axis (2) is normal to the growth rings; and the tangential axis (3) is tangent to the growth rings.

Poisson's Ratio:

Extension of the material in the longitudinal direction is accompanied by shrinking in the lateral directions. For example, if a body is subjected to a tensile stress in the X-direction, then Poisson's Ratio NUXY is defined as the ratio of lateral strain in the Y-direction divided by the longitudinal strain in the X-direction. Poisson's ratios are dimensionless quantities. If not defined, the program assumes a default value of 0.

Shear Modulus:

Also called modulus of rigidity, is the ratio between the shearing stress in a plane divided by the associated shearing strain. Shear Moduli are used in static, nonlinear, frequency, dynamic and buckling analyses.

Thermal Conductivity:

Indicates the effectiveness of a material in transferring heat energy by conduction. It is defined as the rate of heat transfer through a unit thickness of the material per unit temperature difference. The units of thermal conductivity are Btu/in sec $^{\circ}$F in the English system and W/m $^{\circ}$K in the SI system.

Thermal conductivity is used in steady state and transient thermal analyses.

Tensile Strength:

Tensile strength is the maximum load sustained by the specimen in the tension test, divided by the original cross sectional area.

von Mises yield Criterion:

A scalar stress value that can be computed from the stress. In this case, a material is said to start yielding when its von Mises stress reaches a critical value known as the yield strength. The von Mises stress is used to predict yielding of materials under any loading condition from results of simple un-axial tensile tests. The von Mises stress satisfies the property that two stress states with equal distortion energy have equal von Mises stress.

Yield Strength:

The stress at which the material yields or becomes permanently deformed is an important design parameter. This stress is the elastic limit below which no permanent shape changes will occur.

The elastic limit is approximated by the yield strength of the material, and the strain that occurs before the elastic limit is reached is called the elastic strain. The yield strength is define in three ways, depending on the stress-strain characteristics of the steel as it begins to yield per the procedures in SAE J416, ASTM E8 and ASTM A370.

SimulationXpress uses this material property to calculate the factor of safety distribution. SimulationXpress assumes that the material starts yielding when the equivalent (von Mises) stress reaches this value.

All questions on the exam are in a multiple choice single answer format. In this category, Advanced Modeling Theory and Analysis an exam question could read:

Question 1: Yield strength is typically determined at _____ strain.

- A = 0.1%

- B = 0.2%

- C = 0.02%

- D = 0.002%

The correct answer is B.

The stress-strain curve is a graphical representation of the relationship between stress, derived from measuring the load applied on the sample, and strain, derived from measuring the deformation of the sample, i.e. elongation, compression, or distortion. The nature of the curve varies from material to material.

Question 2: There are four key assumptions made in Linear Static Analysis: 1: Effects of inertia and damping is neglected, 2. The response of the system is directly proportional to the applied loads, 3: Loads are applied slowly and gradually, and_____ .

- A = Displacements are very small. The highest stress is in the linear range of the stress-strain curve.

- B = There are no loads

- C = Material is not elastic

- D = Loads are applied quickly

The correct answer is A.

Question 3: How many degrees of freedom does a physical structure have?

- A = Zero.

- B = Three – Rotational only

- C = Three – Translational only

- D = Six – Three translational and three rotational

The correct answer is D.

Question 4: Brittle materials has little tendency to deform (or strain) before fracture and does not have a specific yield point. It is not recommended to apply the yield strength analysis as a failure criterion on brittle material. Which of the following failure theories is appropriate for brittle materials?

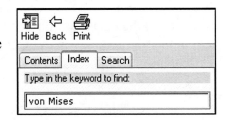

- A = Mohr-Columb stress criterion

- B = Maximum shear stress criterion

- C = Maximum von Mises stress criterion

- D = Minimum shear stress criterion

The correct answer is A.

Question 5: You are performing an analysis on your model. You select three faces and apply a 40 lb load. What is the total force applied to the model?

- A = 40 lbs

- B = 20 lbs

- C = 120 lbs

- D: Additional information is required.

The correct answer is C.

Question 6: In an engineering analysis, you select a face to Fix. What is the affect?

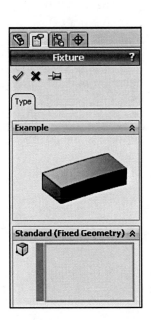

- A = The face will not translate but can rotate

- B = The face will rotate but can not translate

- C = You can not apply a restraint to a face

- D = The face will not rotate and will not translate

The correction answer is D.

Question 7: A material is orthotropic if its mechanical or thermal properties are not unique and independent in three mutually perpendicular directions.

- A = True

- B = False

The correction answer is B.

During the exam, use SolidWorks Help and SimulationXpress / COSMOSXpress help in the SimulationXpress / COSMOSXpress dialog box to review and understand various engineering terms.

SolidWorks SimulationXpress

SolidWorks SimulationXpress offers an easy-to-use first pass stress-analysis tool for SolidWorks users. This tool displays the effects of a force applied to a part, and simulates the design cycle and provides stress results. It also displays critical areas and safety levels at various regions in the selected part.

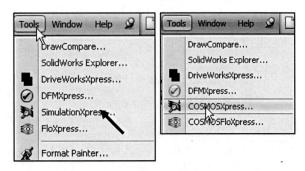

Based on these results, you can strengthen unsafe regions and remove material from over designed areas.

SolidWorks SimulationXpress calculates displacements, strains and stresses, but it only displays stresses and displacements.

The accuracy of the results of the analysis depends on selected material properties, fixtures and loads. For results to be valid, the specified material properties must accurately represent the part material, and the fixtures and loads must accurately represent the part working conditions.

SolidWorks SimulationXpress User Interface

SolidWorks SimulationXpress guides you through various default steps to define fixtures, loads, material properties, analyze the model, view the results and the optional Optimization process.

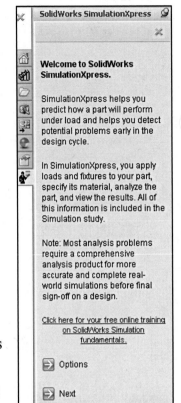

The SimulationXpress interface consists of the following options:

- **Welcome tab**: Allows you to set the default units, specify a folder for saving the analysis results, and to start a new analysis.

- **Fixtures tab**: Applies fixtures to faces of the part.

- **Loads tab**: Applies forces and pressures to faces of the part.

- **Material tab**: Applies material properties to the part. The material can be assigned from the material library or you can input the material properties.

- **Run tab**: Provides the ability to either display the analysis with the default settings or to change the settings.

- **Results tab**: Displays the analysis results in the following ways:

  - Shows critical areas where the factor of safety is less than a specified value.

  - Displays the stress distribution in the model with or without annotation for the maximum and minimum stress values.

  - Displays resultant displacement distribution in the model with or without annotation for the maximum and minimum displacement values.

  - Shows deformed shape of the model.

  - Generates an HTML report.

  - Generates eDrawing files for the analysis results.

- **Optimize tab**: Optimizes a model dimension based on a specified criterion.

- **Start Over button**: Deletes existing analysis data and results, and starts a new analysis session.

☀ SimulationXpress automatically saves the analysis information and closes the current analysis session.

Tutorial: SimulationXpress 11-1

Close all parts, assemblies and drawings.

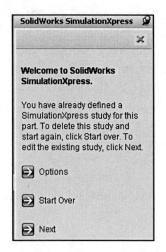

1. **Open** the SimulationXpress-Bent Bar part from the SolidWorks CSWA Model Folders\Chapter 11 location.

2. **Activate** SimulationXpress from the Menu bar menu. The Welcome box is displayed. The SolidWorks Simulation Wizard is displayed.

3. Click the **Options** button to select the system units and to specify a save in folder.

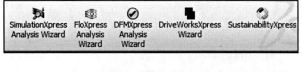

4. Select **SI (MMGS)** for unit system.

5. Select **folder** location.

6. Click **OK** from the SimulationXpress Options dialog box.

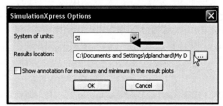

7. Add Fixtures to your model. Click **Next**. The Fixtures tab is highlighted. You can add, delete or edit a fixture. View your options.

8. Click the **Add a fixture** button. The Fixture PropertyManager is displayed.

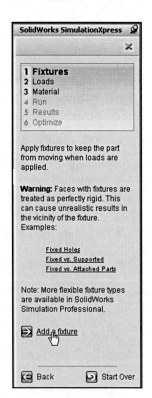

☀ You can specify multiples sets of fixtures for a part. Each set of fixtures can have multiple faces.

9. **Select** the two illustrated end faces of the Bend Bar to be Fixed. Face1 and Face2 are displayed in the dialog box.

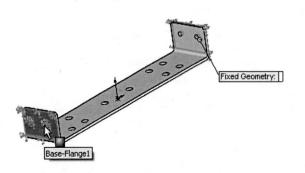

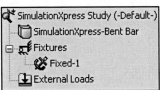

10. Click **OK** from the Fixture PropertyManager. View the updated SimulationXpress Study tree. This is a new feature in SolidWorks 2010.

11. Apply a Load. Click **Next**.

12. The Loads tab is highlighted. The load section provides the ability to input information of the load acting on the part. You can specify multiple loads in force or pressure.

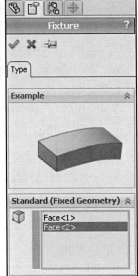

💡 You can apply multiple forces to a single face or to multiple faces.

💡 You can apply multiple pressures to a single face or to multiple faces. SimulationXpress applies pressure loads normal to each face.

13. Click the **Add a force** button. The Force PropertyManager is displayed. View your options.

14. Select **SI**.

15. Click the **top flat face** of the model as illustrated.

16. Enter **5**N for Force Value. Normal is selected by default.

17. Click **OK** from the Force PropertyManager. View the updated Study tree.

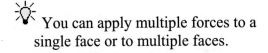

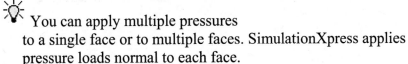

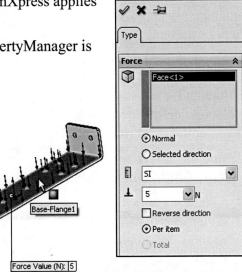

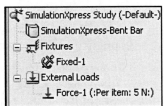

18. Apply Material to the part. Click **Next**.

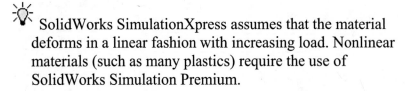

☀ SolidWorks SimulationXpress assumes that the material deforms in a linear fashion with increasing load. Nonlinear materials (such as many plastics) require the use of SolidWorks Simulation Premium.

19. Click the **Choose Material** button. The Material dialog box is displayed.

20. Select **6061 Alloy**. View your options and the supplied material information.

21. Click **Apply**.

22. Click **Close**. View the updated Study tree. A green check indicates material is applied to the part.

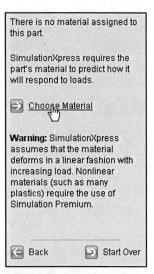

☀ Brittle materials do not have a specific yield point and hence it is not recommended to use the yield strength to define the limit stress for the criterion.

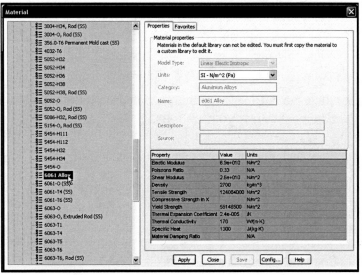

23. Run the analysis. Click **Next**. View your options.

24. Click the **Change settings** button. The Change settings option provides the ability to modify the mesh density of the run. The Mesh density determines the precision of the solution. A finer mesh improves stress results in local areas, but can make the simulation take considerably longer to run. View the provided examples.

25. Click the **Back** button to run the simulation with the default mesh setting.

26. Click the **Run Simulation** button. The analysis starts. This may take a few seconds.

27. **View** the results in the Study tree and the animation of the model in the Graphics window.

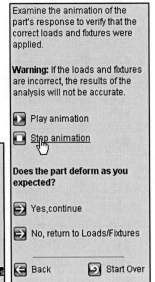

28. Click the **Stop animation** button.

29. Double-click the **Stress** folder. View the results.

30. Double click the **Displacement** folder. View the results.

31. Double click the **Deformation** folder. View the results.

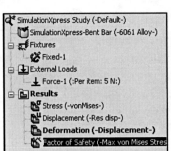

32. Double click the **Factor of Safety** folder. View the results. The plot displays in red, where the FOS is less than 1. The plot displays in blue, where the FOS is greater than one.

33. **Return** to the Stress folder.

34. Continue with the study. Click the **Yes, continue** button.

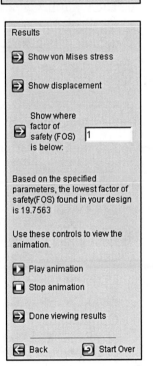

35. **View** the results. The Factor of safety for the specified parameters is approximately 19.75. What does this mean? This indicates that the current design is safe or maybe overdesigned. What can you do? You can decrease the part thickness, modify the part material, modify the applied load, select different fixed points, or perform a variation of all of the above.

The Factor of Safety is a ratio between the material strength and the calculated stress.

Interpretation of factor of safety values:

- A factor of safety less than 1.0 at a location indicates that the material at that location has yielded and that the design is not safe.

- A factor of safety of 1.0 at a location indicates that the material at that location has just started to yield.

- A factor of safety greater than 1.0 at a location indicates that the material at that location has not yielded.

- The material at a location will start to yield if you apply new loads equal to the current loads multiplied by the resulting factor of safety.

36. View the areas when the FOS is 3 or below. Enter **3**.

37. Click **Show where factor of safety (FOS) is below**. View the results in the Graphics window.

38. Click the **Done viewing results** button. View your options.

39. In this section, you can generate an HTML report, generate an eDrawings file, move to the next task (Optimize), or go back to modify the part. Explore each option. Click **Next**.

40. The Optimize your design options are displayed. Yes is selected by default. Click **Next**.

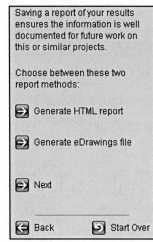

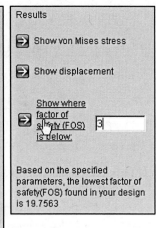

☀ Although SolidWorks SimulationXpress calculates displacements, strains and stresses, it only allows you to view stresses and displacement.

Modify the Bent Bar part thickness and re-run SimulationXpress. The Add Parameters dialog box and Optimization table is displayed.

Select a Dimension.

41. **Rotate** the part and click the thickness of **2.5mm** as illustrated.

42. Click **OK** from the Add Parameters dialog. View the updated Optimization table. Accept the Min (1.25mm) and Max (3.75mm) default values.

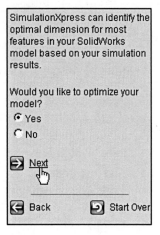

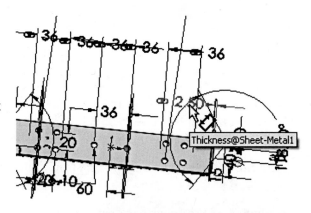

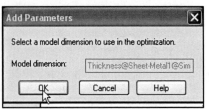

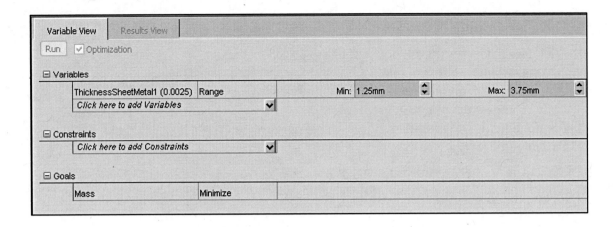

Optimize the model using the Factor of Safety.

43. Click **Next**. View the dialog box.

44. Click **Next**. Set the Constraint in the next step.

45. Click **Specify the constraint**. Note your options.

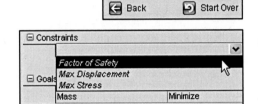

46. Select **Factor of Safety** from the Constraints drop-down menu as illustrated.

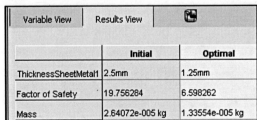

47. Accept the default: Is greater than. Enter **6** in the for Min of Factor of Safety box.

48. Click **Next**.

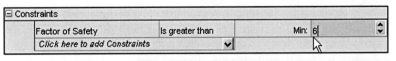

49. Click **Run the optimization**. Note: This may take 2- 3 minutes. View the results.

	Initial	Optimal
ThicknessSheetMetal1	2.5mm	1.25mm
Factor of Safety	19.756284	6.598262
Mass	2.64072e-005 kg	1.33554e-005 kg

50. Check the **Optimal Value** box.

51. Click **Next**. The results are now out of date because the study parameters have changed. You must rerun the study to update the plot results (**Stress**, **Displacement**, **Deformation**, and **Factor of Safety**).

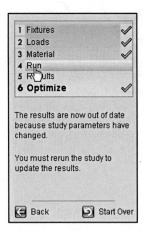

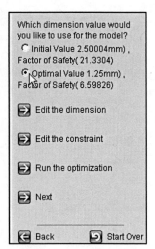

52. Click **Run** in the Wizard window.

53. Re-run the Simulation. Click **Run Simulation**.

The SolidWorks SimulationXpress Wizard window is updated. Generate an HTML report.

54. Click **Generate HTML report**.

55. View your options. **Fill out** the needed fields.

56. **Close** the report.

57. **Save** the part.

58. Click **Sheet-Metal1** in the FeatureManager. View the new updated thickness.

59. **Close** the model. You just performed a SolidWorks SimulationXpress study on a simple part using the Optimization tool.

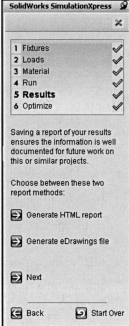

All questions on the exam are in a multiple choice single answer format. In this category, an exam question could read:

Question 1: SimulationXpress is used to analyze?

- A = Drawings

- B = Parts and Drawings

- C = Assemblies and Parts

- D = Parts

- E = All of the above

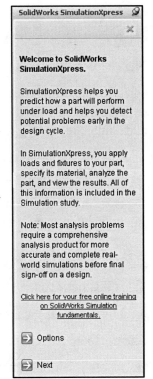

The correct answer is D.

Question 2: Under what SimulationXpress menu tab do you set system units?

- A = Fixtures tab

- B = Loads tab

- C = Welcome tab

- D = Run tab

The correct answer is C. Either SI or the IPS system units.

Question 3: Under what SimulationXpress tab can you modify the Mesh period of the part?

- A = Fixtures tab

- B = Material tab

- C = Run tab

- D = Results tab

The correct answer is C.

Question 4: Under what SimulationXpress menu tab can you set the direction for a Load?

- A = Fixtures tab

- B = Loads tab

- C = Run tab

- D = None of the above

The correct answer is B.

Question 5: An increase in the number of elements in a mesh for a part will_____.

- A = Decrease calculation accuracy and time

- B = Increase calculation accuracy and time

- C = Have no effect on the calculation

- D = Change the FOS below 1

The correct answer is B.

Question 6: SimulationXpress uses the von Mises Yield Criterion to calculate the Factor of Safety of many ductile materials. According to the criterion:

- A = Material yields when the von Mises stress in the model equals the yield strength of the material.

- B = Material yields when the von Mises stress in the model to 5 times greater that the minimum tensile strength of the material.

- C = Material yields when the von Mises stress in the model is 3 times greater than the FOS of the material.

- D = None of the above.

The correct answer is A.

Question 7: SimulationXpress calculates structural failure on:

- A = Buckling

- B = Fatigue

- C = Creep

- D = Material yield

The correct answer is D.

Question 8: Identify the loading types supported by SimulationXpress:

- A = Force with respect to a selected direction

- B = Force normal to a selected face

- C = Pressure normal to a selected face

- D =Pressure with respect to reference geometry

The correct answer is A, B, C and D.

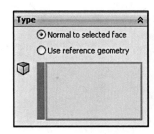

Mesh density determines the precision of the solution. The default setting should provide an accurate deformation solution and a reasonably accurate stress distribution. A finer mesh improves stress results in local areas, but can make the simulation take considerably longer to run. Examples

Consider rerunning the simulation with a finer mesh if the results indicate that the stress is close to exceeding acceptable limits.

Change mesh density

Continue

Back   Start Over

Question 9: Apply a uniform total force of 200 lbs on two faces of a model. The two faces have different areas. How do you apply the load using SimulationXpress?

- A = Select the two faces and input a normal to direction force of 200 lbs on each face.

- B = Select the two faces and a reference plane. Apply 100 lbs on each face.

- C = Apply equal pressure to the two faces. The force on each face is the total force divided by the total area of the two faces.

- D = None of the above.

The correct answer is C.

Question 10: SimulationXpress provides the ability to select a _____ to apply loads and fixtures.

- A = Faces and Edges

- B = Faces, Edges and Vertices

- C = Edges only

- D = Faces only

The correct answer is D.

Question 11: Can you apply a material to the part directly in SimulationXpress?

- A = Yes

- B = No

The correct answer is A

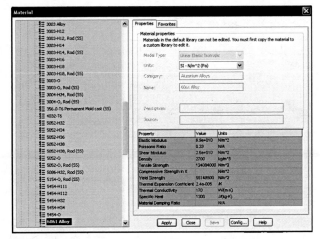

Question 12: A material was applied to a part in SolidWorks. You apply a new material in SimulationXpress. What happens to the material properties?

- A = A material can't be directly applied in SimulationXpress.

- B = The material applied in SimulationXpress is used only in the analysis. The material applied in SolidWorks stays the same.

- C = The part material in SolidWorks changes to the material type that you applied in SimulationXpress.

- D = None of the above

The correct answer is C

Question 13: Maximum and Minimum value indicators are displayed on Stress and Displacement plots in SimulationXpress.

- A = True

- B = False

The correct answer is B.

Question 14: You can store your Run results from SimulationXpress.

- A = True

- B = False

The correct answer is A.

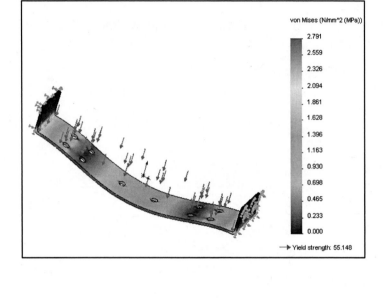

Question 15: Where are the Run results stored in SimulationXpress?

- A = They are not stored

- B = By default, in the active SolidWorks model folder

- C = A temporary directory folder

- D = In a specified folder location under, (Welcome, Options, Results location).

The correction answer is D.

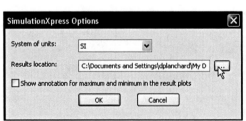

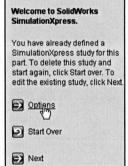

Summary

Advanced Modeling Theory and Analysis is one of the five categories on the CSWA exam. This chapter covered the general terminology used in Engineering analysis and general knowledge of SimulationXpress / COSMOSXpress that is aligned to the exam.

There are two questions on the CSWA exam in this category. Each question is worth five (5) points. The two questions are in a multiple choice single answer format.

In this category of the exam, you are not required to perform an analysis on a part or assembly, but are required to understand general Engineering analysis terminology and how to apply the SimulationXpress tool.

Spend no more than 10 minutes on each question in this category. This is a timed exam. Manage your time. Apply the SolidWorks Help Topics tool during the exam, if needed to obtain answers to this section. Also, use the Help button in the SimulationXpress dialog box.

View sample screen shots from an older CSWA exam for an Advanced Modeling Theory and Analysis question at the end of the Homework section in this chapter.

Questions

1: SimulationXpress is used to analyze?

- A = Drawings
- B = Parts and Drawings
- C = Assemblies and Parts
- D = Parts
- E = All of the above

2: At what percent Strain is Yield Strength normally determined.

- A = 0.002%
- B: 0.20%
- C: 0.02%
- D: 0.01%

3: Under what SimulationXpress menu tab do you set system units?

- A = Material tab
- B = Fixtures tab
- C = Welcome tab
- D = None of the above
- E = All of the above

4: Under what SimulationXpress tab can you modify the Mesh period of the part?

- A = Fixtures tab
- B = Material tab
- C = Run tab
- D = None of the above

5: An increase Mesh period for a part will?

- A = Decrease calculation accuracy
- B = Increase calculation accuracy
- C = Have no effect
- D = Change the FOS below 1

6: How many degrees of freedom does a physical structure have?

- A = Zero

- B = Three – Rotations only

- C = Three – Translations only

- D = Six – Three translations and three rotations

7: Brittle materials has little tendency to deform (or strain) before fracture and does not have a specific yield point. It is not recommended to apply the yield strength analysis as a failure criterion on brittle material. Which of the following failure theories is appropriate for brittle materials?

- A = Mohr-Columb stress criterion

- B = Maximum shear stress criterion

- C = Maximum von Mises stress criterion

- D = Minimum shear stress criterion

8: A material is orthotropic if its mechanical or thermal properties are not unique and independent in three mutually perpendicular directions.

- A = True

- B = False

9: You are performing an analysis on your model. You select three faces and apply a 40lb load. What is the total force applied to the model?

- A = 40lbs

- B = 20lbs

- C = 120lbs

- D = Additional information is required

10. SimulationXpress supports the analysis of the following?

- A = Solid, single-body part

- B = Assemblies

- C = Surface models

- D = Multi-body parts

11: What are the available system units in SimulationXpress?

- A = SI

- B = IPS

- C = RPT

- D = SI and IPS

12: Under what SimulationXpress menu tab can you modify the Element size and Element tolerance for the Mesh period?

- A = Fixtures tab

- B = Material tab

- C = Run tab

- D = None of the above

13: The Maximum normal stress criterion is also known as the?

- A = Mohr-Coulomb's criterion

- B = Maximum von Mises stress criterion

- C= Maximum shear stress criterion

- D = None of the above

14: SimulationXpress uses the vonMises Yield Criterion to calculate the Factor of Safety of many ductile materials. According to the criterion:

- A = Material yields when the vonMises stress in the model equals the yield strength of the material

- B = Material yields when the vonMises stress in the model to 5 times greater that the minimum tensile strength of the material

- C = Material yields when the vonMises stress in the model is 3 times greater than the FOS of the material

- D = None of the above

15: SimulationXpress calculates structural failure on:

- A = Buckling

- B = Fatigue

- C = Creep

- D = Material yield

16: In an engineering analysis, you select a face to Fix. What is the affect?

- A = The face will not translate but can rotate

- B = The face will rotate but can not translate

- C = You can not apply a restraint to a face

- D = The face will not rotate and will not translate

17: Is it possible using SimulationXpress to know the X,Y, Z coordinate location where the minimum and maximum stress or the displacements occur on the model?

- A = No

- B = Yes. Export the results in HTML report format. The X,Y,Z locations are displayed in the Stress and Displacement section.

Sample screen shots from an older CSWA exam. Read each question carefully. Use SolidWorks (SimulationXpress) help if needed.

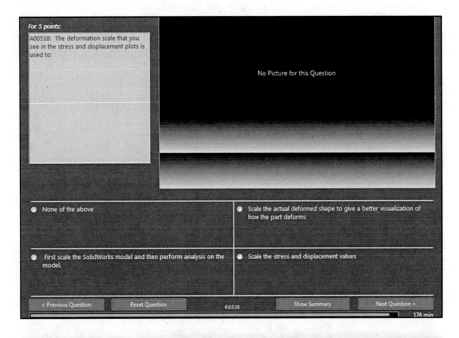

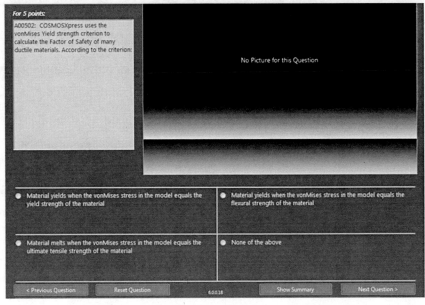

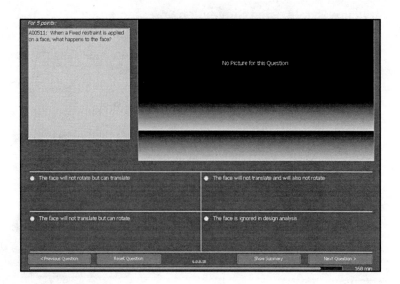

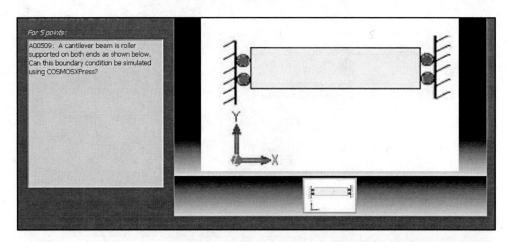

Appendix

Engineering Changer Order (ECO)

D&M Engineering Change Order		ECO # _____ Page 1 of __

Product Line	☐ Hardware ☐ Software ☐ Quality ☐ Tech Pubs	Author Date Authorized Mgr. Date

Change Tested By

Reason for ECO(Describe the existing problem, symptom and impact on field)

D&M Part No.	Rev From/To	Part Description	Description	Owner

ECO Implementation/Class		Departments	Approvals	Date	
All in Field	☐	Engineering			
All in Test	☐	Manufacturing			
All in Assembly	☐	Technical Support			
All in Stock	☐	Marketing			
All on Order	☐	DOC Control			
All Future					
Material Disposition		ECO Cost			
Rework	☐	DO NOT WRITE BELOW THIS LINE (ECO BOARD ONLY)			
Scrap	☐	Effective Date			
Use as is	☐	Incorporated Date			
None	☐	Board Approval			
See Attached	☐	Board Date			

This text follows the ASME Y14 Engineering Drawing and Related Documentation Practices for drawings. Display of dimensions and tolerances are as follows:

TYPES of DECIMAL DIMENSIONS (ASME Y14.5M)			
Description:	UNITS: MM	Description:	UNITS: INCH
Dimension is less than 1mm. Zero precedes the decimal point.	0.9 0.95	Dimension is less than 1 inch. Zero is not used before the decimal point.	.5 .56
Dimension is a whole number. Display no decimal point. Display no zero after decimal point.	19	Express dimension to the same number of decimal places as its tolerance. Add zeros to the right of the decimal point. If the tolerance is expressed to 3 places, then the dimension contains 3 places to the right of the decimal point.	1.750
Dimension exceeds a whole number by a decimal fraction of a millimeter. Display no zero to the right of the decimal.	11.5 11.51		

TABLE 1

TOLERANCE DISPLAY FOR INCH AND METRIC DIMENSIONS (ASME Y14.5M)

DISPLAY:	UNITS: INCH:	UNITS: METRIC:
Dimensions less than 1	.5	0.5
Unilateral Tolerance	$1.417^{+.005}_{-.000}$	$36^{0}_{-0.5}$
Bilateral Tolerance	$1.417^{+.010}_{-.020}$	$36^{+0.25}_{-0.50}$
Limit Tolerance	.571 .463	14.50 11.50

SolidWorks Keyboard Shortcuts

Listed below are some of the pre-defined keyboard shortcuts in SolidWorks:

Action:	Key Combination:
Model Views	
Rotate the model horizontally or vertically:	**Arrow** keys
Rotate the model horizontally or vertically 90 degrees.	**Shift** + **Arrow** keys
Rotate the model clockwise or counterclockwise	**Alt** + left of right **Arrow** keys
Pan the model	**Ctrl** + **Arrow** keys
Magnifying glass	**g**
Zoom in	**Shift + z**
Zoom out	**z**
Zoom to fit	**f**
Previous view	**Ctrl + Shift + z**
View Orientation	
View Orientation menu	**Spacebar**
Front view	**Ctrl + 1**
Back view	**Ctrl + 2**
Left view	**Ctrl + 3**
Right view	**Ctrl + 4**
Top view	**Ctrl + 5**
Bottom view	**Ctrl + 6**
Isometric view	**Ctrl + 7**
NormalTo view	**Ctrl + 8**
Selection Filters	
Filter edges	**e**
Filter vertices	**v**
Filter faces	**x**
Toggle Selection Filter toolbar	**F5**
Toggle selection filters on/off	**F6**
File menu items	
New SolidWorks document	**Ctrl + n**
Open document	**Ctrl + o**
Open From Web Folder	**Ctrl + w**
Make Drawing from Part	**Ctrl + d**
Make Assembly from Part	**Ctrl + a**
Save	**Ctrl +s**
Print	**Ctrl + p**
Additional shortcuts	
Access online help inside of PropertyManager or dialog box	**F1**
Rename an item in the FeatureManager design tree	**F2**
Rebuild the model	**Ctrl + b**
Force rebuild – Rebuild the model and all its features	**Ctrl + q**
Redraw the screen	**Ctrl + r**

Cycle between open SolidWorks document	**Ctrl + Tab**
Line to arc/arc to line in the Sketch	**a**
Undo	**Ctrl + z**
Redo	**Ctrl + y**
Cut	**Ctrl + x**
Copy	**Ctrl + c**
Additional shortcuts	
Paste	**Ctrl + v**
Delete	**Delete**
Next window	**Ctrl + F6**
Close window	**Ctrl + F4**
View previous tools	**s**
Selects all text inside an Annotations text box	**Ctrl + a**

 In a sketch, the **Esc** key un-selects geometry items currently selected in the Properties box and Add Relations box. In the model, the **Esc** key closes the PropertyManager and cancels the selections.

Use the **g** key to activate the Magnifying glass tool. Use the Magnifying glass tool to inspect a model and make selections without changing the overall view.

Use the **s** key to view/access previous command tools in the Graphics window.

Windows Shortcuts

Listed below are some of the pre-defined keyboard shortcuts in Microsoft Windows:

Action:	**Keyboard Combination:**
Open the Start menu	Windows Logo key
Open Windows Explorer	Windows Logo key + E
Minimize all open windows	Windows Logo key + M
Open a Search window	Windows Logo key + F
Open Windows Help	Windows Logo key + F1
Select multiple geometry items in a SolidWorks document	Ctrl key (Hold the Ctrl key down. Select items.) Release the Ctrl key.

Helpful On-Line Information

The SolidWorks URL: http://www.solidworks.com contains information on Local Resellers, Solution Partners, Certifications, SolidWorks users groups, and more.

Access 3D ContentCentral using the Task Pane to obtain engineering electronic catalog model and part information.

Use the SolidWorks Resources tab in the Task Pane to obtain access to Customer Portals, Discussion Forums, User Groups, Manufacturers, Solution Partners, Labs, and more.

Helpful on-line SolidWorks information is available from the following URLs:

- http://www.dmeducation.net

    Information on the CSWA Certification, software updates, design tips, and new book releases.

- http://www.mechengineer.com/snug/

    News group access and local user group information.

- http://www.nhcad.com

    Configuration information and other tips and tricks.

- http://www.solidworktips.com

    Helpful tips, tricks on SolidWorks and API.

- http://www.topica.com/lists/SW

    Independent News Group for SolidWorks discussions, questions and answers.

Certified SolidWorks Professionals (CSWP) URLs provide additional helpful on-line information.

- http://www.scottjbaugh.com   Scott J. Baugh

- http://www.3-ddesignsolutions.com   Devon Sowell

- http://www.zxys.com   Paul Salvador

- http://www.mikejwilson.com   Mike J. Wilson

- http://www.dimontegroup.com   Gene Dimonte & Ed Eaton

*On-line tutorials are for educational purposes only. Tutorials are copyrighted by their respective owners.

Appendix: Check your understanding answer key

This appendix contains the answers to the Check your understanding review questions at the end of each chapter.

Chapter 7

1. Identify the following Drawing View icon .

The correct answer is D: Crop View.

2. Identify the following Drawing View icon .

The correct answer is D: Aligned Section View

3. Identify the following Drawing View icon .

The correct answer is B: Standard 3 View.

4. Identify the illustrated Drawing view.

The correct answer is B: Alternative Position View

5. Identify the illustrated Drawing view.

The correct answer is B: Break View.

6. Identify the illustrated Drawing view.

The correct answer is A: Section View.

7. Identify the view procedure. To create the following view, you need to insert a:

The correct answer is B: Closed Profile: Spline.

8. Identify the view procedure. To create the following view, you need to insert a:

The correct answer is B: Closed Profile: Spline.

9. Identify the illustrated view type.

The correct answer is A: Crop View.

Chapter 8

1. Calculate the overall mass of the part, volume, and locate the Center of mass with the provided information using the provided Option 1 FeatureManager.

   - Overall mass of the part = 1105.00 grams
   - Volume of the part = 130000.00 cubic millimeters

- Center of Mass Location: X = 43.46 millimeters, Y = 15.00 millimeters, Z = -37.69 millimeters

2. Calculate the overall mass of the part, volume, and locate the Center of mass with the provided information using the provided Option 3 FeatureManager.

  - Overall mass of the part = 269.50 grams

  - Volume of the part = 192500.00 cubic millimeters

  - Center of Mass Location: X = 35.70 millimeters, Y = 27.91 millimeters, Z = -146 millimeters

3. Calculate the overall mass of the part, volume, and locate the Center of mass with the provided information.

  - Overall mass of the part = 1.76 pounds

  - Volume of the part = 17.99 cubic inches

  - Center of Mass Location: X = 0.04 inches, Y = 0.72 inches, Z = 0.00 inches

4. Calculate the overall mass of the part, volume, and locate the Center of mass with the provided illustrated information.

  - Overall mass of the part = 1280.91 grams

  - Volume of the part = 474411.54 cubic millimeters

  - Center of Mass Location: X = 0.00 millimeters, Y = -29.17 millimeters, Z = 3.18 millimeters

5. Calculate the overall mass of the part, volume, and locate the Center of mass with the provided information.

  - Overall mass of the part = 248.04 grams

  - Volume of the part = 91868.29 cubic millimeters

  - Center of Mass Location: X = -51.88 millimeters, Y = 24.70 millimeters, Z = 29.47 millimeters

6. Calculate the overall mass of the part with the provided information.

  - Overall mass of the part =3015.53 grams

7. Calculate the overall mass of the part with the provided information.

  - Overall mass of the part = 319.13 grams

8. Calculate the overall mass of the part, volume, and locate the Center of mass with the provided information.

  - Overall mass of the part = 0.45 pounds, Volume of the part = 4.60 cubic inches and the Center of Mass Location: X = 0.17 inches, Y = 0.39 inches, Z = 0.00 inches

9. Calculate the overall mass of the part, volume, and locate the Center of mass with the provided information.

    - Overall mass of the part = 0.28 pounds, Volume of the part = 2.86 cubic inches and the Center of Mass Location: X = 0.70 inches, Y = 0.06 inches, Z = 0.00 inches

Chapter 9

1. Calculate the overall mass of the part, volume, and locate the Center of mass with the provided information.

    - Overall mass of the part = 1.99 pounds

    - Volume of the part = 6.47 cubic inches

    - Center of Mass Location: X = 0.00 inches, Y = 0.00 inches, Z = 1.49 inches

2. Calculate the overall mass of the part, volume, and locate the Center of mass with the provided information.

    - Overall mass of the part = 279.00 grams

    - Volume of the part = 103333.73 cubic millimeters

    - Center of Mass Location: X = 0.00 millimeters, Y = 0.00 millimeters, Z = 21.75 millimeters

3. Calculate the overall mass of the part, volume, and locate the Center of mass with the provided information.

    - Overall mass of the part = 1087.56 grams

    - Volume of the part = 122198.22 cubic millimeters

    - Center of Mass Location: X = 44.81 millimeters, Y = 21.02 millimeters, Z = -41.04 millimeters

4. Calculate the overall mass of the part, volume and locate the Center of mass with the provided information.

    - Overall mass of the part = 2040.57 grams

    - Volume of the part = 755765.04 cubic millimeters

    - Center of Mass Location: X = -0.71 millimeters, Y = 16.66 millimeters, Z = -9.31 millimeters

5. Calculate the overall mass of the part, volume and locate the Center of mass with the provided information. Create Coordinate System1 to locate the Center of mass for the model.

    - Overall mass of the part = 2040.57 grams

    - Volume of the part = 755765.04 cubic millimeters

- Center of Mass Location: X = 49.29 millimeters, Y = 16.66 millimeters, Z = -109.31 millimeters

6. Calculate the overall mass of the part, volume and locate the Center of mass with the provided information.

   - Overall mass of the part = 37021.48 grams

   - Volume of the part = 13711657.53 cubic millimeters

   - Center of Mass Location: X = 0.00 millimeters, Y = 0.11 millimeters, Z = 0.00 millimeters

7. Calculate the overall mass of the part, volume and locate the Center of mass with the provided information.

   - Overall mass of the part = 37021.48 grams

   - Volume of the part = 13711657.53 cubic millimeters

   - Center of Mass Location: X = 225.00 millimeters, Y = 70.11 millimeters, Z = -150.00 millimeters

Chapter 10

1. Calculate the overall mass and volume of the assembly. Locate the Center of mass using the illustrated coordinate system.

   - Overall mass of the assembly = 843.22 grams

   - Volume of the assembly = 312304.62 cubic millimeters

   - Center of Mass Location: X = 30.00 millimeters, Y = 40.16 millimeters, Z = -53.82 millimeters

2. Calculate the overall mass and volume of the assembly. Locate the Center of mass using the illustrated coordinate system.

   - Overall mass of the assembly = 19.24 grams

   - Volume of the assembly = 6574.76 cubic millimeters

   - Center of Mass Location: X = 40.24, Y = 24.33, Z = 20.75

3. Calculate the overall mass and volume of the assembly. Locate the Center of mass using the illustrated coordinate system.

   - Overall mass of the assembly = 19.24 grams

   - Volume of the assembly = 6574.76 cubic millimeters

   - Center of Mass Location: X = 40.24, Y = -20.75, Z = 24.33

Chapter 11

1. SimulationXpress is used to analyze?

The correct answer is D: Parts. SimulationXpress supports the analysis of a single solid body. For multibody parts, you can analyze one body at a time. For assemblies, you can analyze the effect of Physical Simulation one component at a time. Surface bodies are not supported.

2. At what percent Strain is Yield Strength normally determined?

The correct answer is B: 0.20%. View the graph in the chapter for details.

3. Under what SimulationXpress menu tab can you set system units?

The correct answer is C. Welcome tab. Allows you to set default analysis units; SI or IPS (English) and to specify a folder for saving analysis results.

4. Under what SimulationXpress menu tab can you modify the Mesh period of the part?

The correct answer is C: Run tab. Select to analyze with the system default settings or change the settings.

5. An increase Mesh period for a part will?

The correct answer is B: Increase calculation accuracy. SimulationXpress sub divides the model into a mesh of small shapes called elements. Specifying a smaller element size provides a more accurate result, but requires additional time and resources.

6. How many degrees of freedom does a physical structure have?

The correct answer is D: Six – Three translations and three rotations.

7. Brittle materials has little tendency to deform (or strain) before fracture and does not have a specific yield point. It is not recommended to apply the yield strength analysis as a failure criterion on brittle material. Which of the following failure theories is appropriate for brittle materials?

The correct answer is A: Mohr-Columb stress criterion.

8. A material is Orthotropic if its mechanical or thermal properties are not unique and independent in three mutually perpendicular directions.

The correct answer is B: False.

9. You are performing an analysis on your model. You select three faces and apply a 40lb load. What is the total force applied to the model?

The correct answer is C: 120lbs.

10. SimulationXpress supports the analysis of the following.

The correct answer is A: Solid, single-body parts.

11. What are the available system units in SimulationXpress?

The correct answer is D: Select SI (International System of Units), or IPS (English). Setting the preferred system of units does not restrict you from entering data in other units, the dialog boxes of loads and boundary conditions let you override the default preferred units. The preferred units will be used by default to display the results, but you can choose to display the results in other units. For example you can choose the SI system as your default unit system, but still can apply pressure in psi and displacements in millimeters.

12. Under what SimulationXpress menu tab can you modify the Element size and Element tolerance for the Mesh period?

The correct answer is C: Run tab. Select to analyze with the system default settings or change the settings.

13. The Maximum normal stress criterion is also known as?

- A = Mohr-Coulomb's criterion

- B = Maximum von Mises stress criterion

- C= Maximum shear stress criterion

- D = None of the above

The correct answer is A: Mohr-Coulomb's criterion. The Mohr-Coulomb stress criterion is based on the Mohr-Coulomb theory also known as the Internal Friction theory. This criterion is used for brittle materials with different tensile and compressive properties. Brittle materials do not have a specific yield point and it is not recommended to use the yield strength to define the limit stress for this criterion.

14. SimulationXpress uses the vonMises Yield Criterion to calculate the Factor of Safety of many ductile materials. According to the criterion:

The correct answer is A: Material yields when the vonMises stress in the model equals the yield strength of the material.

15. SimulationXpress calculates structural failure on:

The correct answer is D: Material yield

16. In an engineering analysis, you select a face to restrain. What is the affect?

The correct answer is D: The face will not rotate and will not translate.

17. Is it possible using SimulationXpress to know the X,Y, Z coordinate location where the minimum and maximum stress or the displacements occur on the model?

The correct answer is A: Yes. Export the results in HTML report format. The X,Y,Z locations are displayed in the Stress and Displacement section.

CSWP

SolidWorks offers other advance levels of Certification after the CSWA.

The CSWP (Certified SolidWorks Professional) is an individual that has successfully passed the advanced skills examination. Each CSWP has proven their ability to design and analyze parametric parts and moveable assemblies using a variety of complex features in SolidWorks. Visit the SolidWorks website to find additional information on advance 3D CAD industry certifications.

CSWP
A Certified SolidWorks Professional is an individual that has successfully passed our advanced skills examination. Each CSWP has proven their ability to design and analyze parametric parts and moveable assemblies using a variety of complex features in SolidWorks.

CSWP-Sheet Metal
The completion of the Certified SolidWorks Professional Sheet Metal exam shows that an individual has successfully passed a skills test that demonstrates their ability to use the sheet metal tools inside of SolidWorks. Employers can be confidant that an individual possessing this certification understands the set of tools inside SolidWorks that will aid in the design of sheet metal components.

CSWP-Surfacing
SolidWorks software includes many advanced surfacing tools. The Certified SolidWorks Professional Surfacing Specialist exam is used to gauge someone's ability to utilize these tools in the creation of complex surfaces. Successful completion of this exam also shows the user's ability to troubleshoot and fix broken surface bodies, or imported bodies that are incorrect.

CSWSP-FEA
The Certified SolidWorks Professional Simulation Specialist exam is designed to test an individual's complete understanding of Simulation tools inside SolidWorks. Candidates who successfully pass this certification exam have demonstrated the ability to set up, run, and examine the results of various types of Simulation scenarios. They also have demonstrated the ability to interpret the various results available to them in SolidWorks Simulation.

Index

3 Point Arc Sketch tool, 4-18
3D Drawing View, 1-10
3D Sketch, 2-82
3HOLE-SHAFTCOLLAR Assembly - Insert SHAFT-COLLAR, 5-12
3HOLE-SHAFTCOLLAR Assembly, 5-12
5HOLE-SHAFTCOLLAR Assembly, 5-13

A

A (ANSI) Landscape, 3-7
A-ANSI-MM, 3-19
Accelerator Keys, 1-14
Add a Dimension, 1-25, 1-33
Add Drawing Sheet, 3-51
Advance Mates, 1-47
    Angle, 1-47
    Distance, 1-47
    Linear/Linear Coupler, 1-47
    Path, 1-47
    Symmetric, 1-47
    Width, 1-47
Advance Mode, 1-19
Aligned Dimension, 2-38
Angle Decimal place, 1-23
Angle Mate, 1-46
ANGLE-13HOLE Part, 2-15
ANGLE-13HOLE Part - Boss-Extrude1 Feature, 2-19
ANGLE-13HOLE Part - Fillet Feature, 2-23
ANGLE-13HOLE Part - First Extruded Cut Feature, 2-20
ANGLE-13HOLE Part - First Linear Pattern Feature, 2-22
ANGLE-13HOLE Part - Second Extruded Cut Feature, 2-24
ANGLE-13HOLE Part - Second Linear Pattern Feature, 2-25
ANGLE-13HOLE Part - Third Extruded Cut Feature, 2-26
Annotation tab, 3-8
Annotation toolbar, 3-8
ANSI Overall Drafting Standard, 1-22, 1-32, 1-40, 2-10, 2-17, 2-33, 3-9
Appearance tool, 1-27, 1-36
Apply Scene tool, 1-10

Arc Condition, 4-19
    Center, 4-19
    Max, 4-19
    Min, 4-19
Arrow Leader direction, 3-14
Arrow Size, 3-10
ASME Y14.3M, 2-6, 2-8
AssemblyXpert tool, 5-24
AssemblyXpress, 5-24
Auto Balloons drawing tool, 3-50
Auto Dimension Scheme, 1-14
Axis PropertyManager, 4-40
Axis tool, 4-40
AXLE Part, 1-22
AXLE Part - Boss- Extrude1 Feature, 1-23, 1-25
AXLE Part - Edit Color, 1-27
AXLE Part - View Modes, 1-28
AXLE-3000 Part, 4-48

B

Begin Assembly PropertyManager, 1-49
Bill of Materials PropertyManager, 3-48
Bill of Materials tool, 3-48
Blind End Condition, 1-42, 2-36
BOM, 3-48
Boss-Extrude PropertyManager, 1-25, 1-26, 1-33, 2-13
Boss-Extrude1 Feature, 1-25, 1-42, 2-19

C

Cam Mate, 1-47
Center Rectangle Sketch tool, 4-9, 4-10
Centerline Sketch tool, 1-42, 2-26, 2-34, 4-35, 4-37
Centerline Sketch tool, 2-26
Centerpoint Arc Sketch tool, 4-16
Centerpoint Straight Slot Sketch tool, 1-40
Chamfer Feature, 2-54
Circle Sketch tool, 1-24, 1-33, 1-43, 2-11, 2-37, 4-29
Circular Pattern Feature, 2-44, 2-53, 4-39
Circular Pattern Feature - Number of Instances, 2-53, 4-39
Circular Pattern PropertyManager, 2-44, 2-53, 4-39
Close all Documents, 1-46

Coincident Mate, 1-46, 1-55, 1-56, 2-59, 2-61
Coincident Relation, 2-14, 2-40, 2-43
Coincident SmartMate, 2-64
Collapse items, 1-13
Collinear Relation, 4-32
Color, 1-27
CommandManager, 1-11
    DimXpert tab, 1-11
    Evaluate tab, 1-11
    Features tab, 1-11
    Office Products tab, 1-11
    Sketch tab, 1-11
Company Logo, 3-15
Component Patterns in the Assembly, 5-46
Component Properties, 5-56
Concentric / Coincident SmartMate, 2-64
Concentric Mate, 1-57, 2-28, 2-58, 2-60, 2-61
Concentric Relation, 2-28
ConfigurationManager, 1-12, 3-37, 3-44
Confirmation Corner, 1-9
Consolidated Circle PropertyManager, 1-24
Consolidated drop-down menu, 1-8
Consolidated Rectangle Sketch tool, 1-40
Consolidated Slot toolbar, 2-27
Consolidated toolbar, 1-8
Constant Radius Fillet type, 2-23
Construction Line, 4-34, 4-37
Convert Entities Sketch tool, 2-51, 4-23
Copy a drawing view, 3-59
Copy Scheme, 1-14
Corner Rectangle Sketch tool, 1-40, 2-27,
    2-39
Cosmetic Thread, 2-14, 2-15, 2-79, 2-80
Create a New Part, 1-18
Create a Part Template, 4-8
Custom Properties, 3-12, 3-37
Customize CommandManager, 1-12, 1-21
Customize FeatureManager, 1-13
Cut-Revolve PropertyManager, 4-33
Cut-Sweep PropertyManager, 4-25

D
Deactivate Planes, 1-10
Default Datum Planes, 2-5
Default Reference Planes, 1-20
    Front, 1-20
    Right, 1-20
    Top, 1-20
Define Drawing Material Property, 3-37
Define Drawing property, 3-37
Design Library, 1-15

Design Table, 3-55, 3-64
Detail Drawing, 3-28
Detail View Drawing tool, 3-54
Diameter Dimension, 2-38
Dimension Cursor icon, 1-8
Dimension Font, 3-10
Dimension Precision, 3-32
Dimension PropertyManager - Leaders tab,
    4-19
Dimensioning Standard, 1-22
DimXpert tab, 1-11
DimXpert toolbar, 1-11
DimXpertManager tab, 1-12, 1-14
    Copy Scheme, 1-14
    Dimension Scheme, 1-14
    Show Tolerance Status, 1-14
    TolAnalyst Study,   1-14
Display Grid box, 1-10
Display Styles, 1-29
    Hidden Lines Removed, 1-30
    Hidden Lines Visible, 1-30
    Shaded With Edges, 1-29
    Shaded, 1-29
    Wireframe, 1-30
Display Toolbars, 1-21
Distance Mate, 1-47, 2-62
Document Properties, 1-22, 1-32, 1-40, 2-10,
    2-17
Document Recovery, 1-17
Document Units, 1-23, 1-40
Dome Feature, 4-21
Dome PropertyManager, 4-21
Draw1, 3-8
Drawing - Leader arrow direction, 4-7
Drawing Custom Property, 3-12
Drawing Dimension text, 3-32
Drawing Document Properties, 3-10
Drawing Radius text, 3-35
Drawing Template, 3-5
Drawing View Component Properties, 3-26
Drawing View Edge Properties, 3-26
Drawing View Properties, 3-26
Drop-down menu, 1-8
Dual Dimensions, 1-22
Dynamic Mirror Sketch tool, 2-27, 2-34, 2-37

E
Edge Cursor icon, 1-8
Edit Color, 1-27, 1-36
Edit Feature, 2-23, 4-43, 5-10
Edit Sheet Format mode, 3-5

Edit Sheet mode, 3-5
Edit Sketch, 2-13, 2-50, 4-10
Edit the Design Table, 3-57
End Chain, 2-33, 2-34
End Condition - Blind, 1-42, 2-36
End Condition - Mid Plane, 1-25, 1-33, 2-53, 4-30
End Condition - Through All, 1-25, 1-35, 1-43, 2-21, 2-25, 4-13
Equal Relation, 1-42, 2-18, 2-28, 2-38, 2-40, 2-42, 4-32
Evaluate tab, 1-11
Evaluate toolbar, 1-11
Exploded View tool, 3-44
Extended State, 5-59, 5-60
Extruded Boss/Base Feature, 1-25
Extruded Cut Feature, 1-34, 1-44, 2-20, 4-13
Extruded Cut PropertyManager, 1-35, 1-43, 2-21
Extruded Thin Feature, 2-16, 2-18

F
Face Cursor icon, 1-8
Feature - 1-18
Feature Driven Component Pattern Assembly tool, 5-47
FeatureManager - Customize, 1-13
FeatureManager - Rollback bar, 1-13
FeatureManager Design tree, 1-12
Features tab, 1-11
Features toolbar, 1-11
File Explorer, 1-16
Fillet Feature, 2-23, 2-53
Fillet PropertyManager, 2-23
Fillet PropertyManager - FilletXpert tab, 2-23
Fillet PropertyManager - Manual tab, 2-23
FilletXpert tab, 2-23
Filter, 1-13, 4-13
First Angle Projection, 2-7, 2-8
Fit model to Graphics window, 1-26
Fixed Component, 1-51, 2-57
FLATBAR Drawing, 3-21
FLATBAR Drawing - Front, Top, and Right view, 3-22
FLATBAR Drawing - Insert Annotations, 3-30
FLATBAR Drawing - Insert Dimensions, 3-30
FLATBAR Drawing - Isometric view, 3-23
FLATBAR Drawing - Linked Note, 3-38
FLATBAR Drawing - Position views, 3-27
FLATBAR Drawing - Sheet2, 3-59
FLATBAR Part, 1-39
FLATBAR Part - Boss-Extrude Feature, 1-43

FLATBAR Part - Design Table, 3-55
FLATBAR Part - Extruded Cut Feature, 1-44
FLATBAR Part - Linear Pattern Feature, 1-45
FLATBAR Sub-assemblies, 5-9
FLATBAR-SHAFTCOLLAR Assembly, 3-61
FLATBAR-SHAFTCOLLAR Assembly - Insert First SHAFTCOLLAR, 3-62
FLATBAR-SHAFTCOLLAR Assembly - Insert FLATBAR, 3-61
FLATBAR-SHAFTCOLLAR Assembly - Insert Second SHAFTCOLLAR, 3-63
Flexible State, 5-58, 5-59, 5-60
Flip Arrows, 1-25
Float Component, 2-57
Fly-out FeatureManager, 1-14
For Construction, 4-34, 4-37
Formatting Dialog box, 3-12
Front Plane, 1-20, 1-23
Front View, 1-28, 1-42
FRONT-SUPPORT Assembly, 2-56
FRONT-SUPPORT Assembly - Insert ANGLE-13HOLE, 2-56
FRONT-SUPPORT Assembly - Insert First HEX-STANDOFF, 2-58
FRONT-SUPPORT Assembly - Insert First SCREW, 2-64
FRONT-SUPPORT Assembly - Insert Fourth SCREW, 2-64
FRONT-SUPPORT Assembly - Insert Second HEX-STANDOFF, 2-60
FRONT-SUPPORT Assembly - Insert Second SCREW, 2-65
FRONT-SUPPORT Assembly - Insert Third SCREW, 2-64
FRONT-SUPPORT Assembly - Insert TRIANGLE, 2-62
Fully Defined Sketch, 1-27

G
Geometric Relation, 1-42
Geometric Relation - Coincident, 2-14, 2-40, 2-43
Geometric Relation - Collinear, 4-32
Geometric Relation - Concentric, 2-28
Geometric Relation - Equal, 1-42, 2-18, 2-28, 2-38, 4-33
Geometric Relation - Horizontal, 2-12, 2-28, 4-19, 4-31
Geometric Relation - Make Equal, 2-18
Geometric Relation - Make Horizontal, 2-12
Geometric Relation - Midpoint, 1-42
Geometric Relation - Parallel, 2-43
Geometric Relation - Pierce, 4-20, 4-24

Geometric Relation - Tangent 2-29, 2-40, 2-44, 4-18
Geometric Relation - Vertical, 4-17
Geometry Pattern, 1-44, 2-41
Graphics window, 1-20
Grid/Snap tool, 1-22

H
Heads-up View toolbar, 1-9
    3D Drawing View, 1-10
    Apply Scene, 1-10
    Display Style, 1-10
    Edit Appearance, 1-10
    Hide/Show Items, 1-10
    Previous View, 1-9
    Rotate, 1-10
    Section View, 1-9
    View Orientation, 1-10
    View Setting, 1-10
    Zoom to Area, 1-9
    Zoom to Fit, 1-9
Helix/Spiral Feature, 4-24
Help, 1-37
HEX-STANDOFF Part, 2-9
HEX-ADAPTER Part - Extruded Boss Feature, 4-45
HEX-ADAPTER Part - Extruded Cut Feature, 4-45
HEX-ADAPTER Part, 4-42
HEX-STANDOFF Part - Base Feature, 2-13
HEX-STANDOFF Part - Hole Wizard Feature, 2-14
Hidden Lines Removed, 1-30, 1-34, 1-42
Hidden Lines Visible, 1-30
Hide Components, 5-50
Hide Drawing Dimensions, 3-33
Hide Drawing View, 3-33
Hide FeatureManager Tree Area tab, 1-12
Hide Origin, 3-24
Hide Sketch, 2-44
Hide tool, 2-44, 4-14, 4-24
Hide/Show Items tool, 1-10
Hinge Mate, 1-47
Hole Specification PropertyManager, 2-14, 4-44
Hole Wizard Feature, 2-14, 2-82, 4-43
HOOK Part, 4-14
HOOK Part - Dome Feature, 4-21
HOOK Part - Helix/Spiral Feature, 4-23
HOOK Part - Swept Base Feature, 4-21
HOOK Part - Swept Cut Feature, 4-22

Horizontal Relation, 2-12, 2-28, 4-19, 4-30

I - J - K
Insert a Coincident Mate, 1-52
Insert a Parallel Mate, 1-55
Insert a Plane, 4-9, 4-22
Insert Axis, 4-40
Insert Component, 2-61
Insert Components Assembly tool, 1-50, 1-52, 1-56, 2-58
Instant3D tool, 1-11, 1-30
IPS - (inch, pound, second), 1-32, 1-40, 2-17, 2-33, 4-7
Isometric View, 1-29

L
Leader Arrow direction, 4-7
Length Basic Units, 1-23
Line Sketch tool, 2-18, 4-17, 4-32
Linear Component Pattern Assembly tool, 5-48
Linear Pattern Feature, 1-44, 2-22, 2-25
Linear Pattern Feature - Number of Instances, 1-44, 2-22, 2-26
Linear Pattern Feature - Reverse Direction, 1-44
Linear Pattern Feature - Spacing, 1-44, 2-22, 2-26
Link notes, 3-36
Link to Property tool, 3-39
LINKAGE Assembly, 1-45, 1-50
LINKAGE Assembly - Basic Motion, 1-59
LINKAGE Assembly - Insert AirCylinder, 1-49
LINKAGE Assembly - Insert AXLE, 1-51
LINKAGE Assembly - Insert First FLATBAR, 1-52
LINKAGE Assembly - Insert First HEX-STANDOFF Part, 5-34
LINKAGE Assembly - Insert First SHAFT-COLLAR, 1-56
LINKAGE Assembly - Insert Fourth SHAFT-COLLAR Part, 5-40
LINKAGE Assembly - Insert Second AXLE Part, 5-37
LINKAGE Assembly - Insert Second FLATBAR, 1-54
LINKAGE Assembly - Insert Second HEX-STANDOFF Part, 5-36
LINKAGE Assembly - Insert Second SHAFT-COLLAR, 1-57
LINKAGE Assembly - Insert Third SHAFT-COLLAR Part,
LINKAGE Assembly - Insert Third SHAFT-

COLLAR Part, 5-39
LINKAGE Assembly Drawing, 3-41
LINKAGE Assembly Drawing - Animation, 3-47
LINKAGE Assembly Drawing - Automatic Balloons, 3-50
LINKAGE Assembly Drawing - Bill of Materials, 3-48
LINKAGE Assembly Drawing - Sheet1, 3-41
LINKAGE Assembly Drawing - Sheet2 - Detail view, 3-54
LINKAGE Assembly Drawing - Sheet2 - Section view, 3-53
LINKAGE Assembly Drawing - Sheet2, 3-51
Linked Note, 3-38
Lock Mate, 1-46
Loft Boss/Base Feature, 4-12
Loft Feature, 4-12
Logo, 3-15
LPattern Feature, 2-22, 2-26

M
Magnifying Glass tool, 1-14
Make Assembly from Part/Assembly, 3-25
Make Drawing from Part/Assembly, 3-25
Make Equal Relation, 1-42, 2-18
Make Horizontal Relation, 2-12
Make Midpoint Relation, 1-42
Manipulator Points, 1-30
Mate Error, 5-14
Mate Pop-up toolbar, 1-51
Mate Selections box, 1-51, 1-52
Mate tool, 1-50, 1-53, 1-54, 2-58
Mate Types, 1-46
    Advance Mates, 1-47
    Mechanical Mates, 1-47
    Standard Mates, 1-46
Mating Techniques,
Max Arc Condition, 4-20
Measure tool, 5-23
Mechanical Mates, 1-47
    Cam, 1-47
    Gear, 1-47
    Rack Pinion, 1-47
    Screw, 1-47
    Joint, 1-47
Menu bar menu, 1-7
Menu bar toolbar, 1-7
    New, 1-7
    Open, 1-7
    Options, 1-7

Print, 1-7
Rebuild, 1-7
Save, 1-7
Select, 1-7
Undo, 1-7
Mid Plane End Condition, 1-25, 1-33, 2-19, 2-53, 4-30
Midpoint Relation, 1-42
Mirror Components Assembly tool, 5-52
Mirror Components PropertyManager, 5-53
Mirror Feature, 2-41
MMGS - (millimeter, gram, second), 1-32, 1-40, 2-17, 2-33, 3-9
Model Items tool, 3-30
Model View PropertyManager, 3-7, 3-22
Model View tool, 3-52
Modify a Feature, 3-34,
Modify a Part, 4-42
Modify Arc Condition, 4-19
Modify Dialog box, 1-25
Modify Dimensions, 1-35, 2-20, 4-50
Modify Drawing Dimension text, 3-32
Modify Drawing Radius text, 3-35
Motion Study tab, 1-17, 1-18, 1-59
Motion Study - Animation, 1-18, 1-59
Motion Study - Basic Motion, 1-18, 1-59
Motor PropertyManager, 1-60
Move Drawing Views, 3-25
Move with Triad, 5-19, 5-21
Multiple Drawing views, 3-22

N
New Assembly document, 1-49, 2-57, 2-56, 5-9
New Document, 1-7, 1-31, 2-10, 2-17
New Drawing Document, 3-7, 3-20
New Motion Study tool, 1-18
New Part, 1-18, 1-19, 1-31, 1-39, 2-10, 2-17, 2-33, 4-7
New Sketch, 1-33, 2-11
New SolidWorks Document Dialog box, 1-19
New View tool, 1-10
Note tool, 3-32
Novice Mode, 1-19
Number of Instances, 1-45

O
Office Products tab, 1-11
Office Products toolbar, 1-11
Offset Entities Sketch tool, 2-35
Offset Sketch, 2-35

Open Document, 1-7
Options, 1-8
Origin, 1-20, 1-24, 1-33, 2-11, 2-12
Orthographic projection, 1-28, 2-5, 2-6, 2-7
Over Defined Sketch, 1-27
Overall Drafting Standard, 1-22

P - Q
Parallel Mate, 1-46, 1-55, 2-61, 2-63, 2-59,
   2-61, 2-63, 5-30, 5-35
Parallel Relation, 2-28
Parallelogram Sketch tool, 2-42
Parametric Notes, 3-31
Part Document properties, 1-22
Part Origin, 1-20, 1-21, 1-23
Part Template, 4-8
PART-ANSI-IN, 4-7
Paste a Drawing view, 3-59
Path Mate, 1-47
Pattern Direction box, 2-25
Perpendicular Mate, 1-46
Pierce Relation, 4-20, 4-24
Pin tool, 1-7
Plane Feature, 4-9, 4-22
Plane PropertyManager, 4-9, 4-22
Pneumatic Test Module Layout, 5-7
PNEUMATIC-TEST-MODULE, 5-7, 5-32
PNEUMATIC-TEST-MODULE - Component
   Pattern Assembly tool, 5-46
PNEUMATIC-TEST-MODULE - Feature
   Driven Component Pattern, 5-47
PNEUMATIC-TEST-MODULE - Insert AIR-
   RESERVOIR-SUPPORT, 5-44
PNEUMATIC-TEST-MODULE - Insert FLAT-
   PLATE, 5-33
PNEUMATIC-TEST-MODULE - Insert
   FRONT-SUPPORT Assembly, 5-50
PNEUMATIC-TEST-MODULE - Insert HEX-
   STANDOFF Part, 5-34
PNEUMATIC-TEST-MODULE - Insert
   LINKAGE Assembly, 5-42
PNEUMATIC-TEST-MODULE - Insert
   WHEEL-AND-AXLE Assembly, 5-56
PNEUMATIC-TEST-MODULE - Linear
   Component Pattern tool, 5-48
PNEUMATIC-TEST-MODULE - Mirror
   Components tool, 5-52, 5-53
PNEUMATIC-TEST-MODULE -
   MirrorFRONT-SUPPORT, 5-55
Polygon Sketch tool, 2-11, 4-29
Previous View tool, 1-9
Primary Datum plane, 2-5
Primary Units, 1-22

Print Document, 1-7
Print tool, 1-7
Properties of a Drawing Sheet, 3-25
Properties PropertyManager, 1-41
PropertyManager tab, 1-12

R
Rapid Sketch tool, 1-11
Rebuild Document, 1-7, 1-8, 3-19
Rebuild tool, 1-7, 3-19
Recover from a Mate error, 4-61, 5-15
Reference Axis, 4-40
Reference Geometry Plane, 4-23
Reference Planes, 1-10, 1-20, 2-5
Rename Feature, 4-14
Rename Sketch, 4-11,
Reorder Features, 4-47
Replace Components tool, 5-13
Replace PropertyManager, 5-13
Revolved Base Feature tool, 2-49
Revolved Cut Feature, 4-33
Ridge State, 5-58
Right Plane, 1-20
Right View, 1-28
Right-click Pop-up menu, 1-8
Right-click Select, 1-42, 2-18
Right-click, 1-8
ROBOT Assembly, 5-64
ROBOT Assembly Insert basic_integration,
   5-67
ROBOT Assembly Insert HEX-STANDOFF,
   5-66
ROBOT Assembly Insert PNEUMATIC-
   TEST-MODULE, 5-65
ROBOT Assembly Insert Robot-platform,
   5-65
Rollback Bar, 1-12, 1-13
Rotary Motor box, 1-60
Rotate the model, 1-29
Rotate tool, 1-10

S
Save an Assembly, 1-49
Save Animation, 1-61
Save as copy, 4-43, 5-13
Save As Drawing Template, 3-18
Save As, 1-26, 1-39, 2-11, 4-42
Save Document, 1-7
Save Drawing Template, 3-19
Save Part Template, 4-7
Save Part, 1-26, 1-36

Save Sheet Format, 3-18
Save tool, 1-7
Screw Mate, 1-47
SCREW Part, 2-45
SCREW Part - Chamfer Feature, 2-54
SCREW Part - Circular Pattern Feature, 2-53
SCREW Part - Extruded Cut Feature, 2-51
SCREW Part - Fillet Feature, 2-53
SCREW Part - Revolved Base Feature, 2-47
Secondary Datum plane, 2-5
Secondary Units, 1-22
Section View Drawing tool, 3-53
Section View PropertyManager, 3-53
Section View, 1-9, 4-47
Select - Menu bar toolbar, 1-7
Selection Filter toolbar, 4-14
Sensors tool, 1-12
Set Lightweight to Resolved, 1-48
Shaded With Edges, 1-29, 1-35
Shaded, 1-29
SHAFT-COLLAR Part, 1-31
SHAFT-COLLAR Part - Boss-Extrude
    Feature, 1-33
SHAFT-COLLAR Part - Edit color, 1-36
SHAFT-COLLAR Part - Extruded Cut
    Feature, 1-34
SHAFT-COLLAR Part - Modify dimensions,
    1-35
SHAFTCOLLAR-500 Part, 4-49
Sheet Format, 3-5
Sheet Format/Size Dialog box, 3-7
Sheet Properties, 3-9, 3-24, 3-26
Sheet Scale, 3-9
Sheet1, 3-8
Short Cut keys, 1-14
Shortcut toolbar, 1-23, 1-40
Show Components tool, 5-55
Show Features Dimensions tool,
Show Tolerance Status, 1-14
Show, 2-37, 4-8, 4-34
Sketch Fillet Sketch tool, 2-36
Sketch Plane, 1-2, 1-23, 1-33, 1-40, 2-5
Sketch Point tool, 2-14
Sketch State, 1-27
    Cannot be solved, 1-27
    Fully Defined, 1-27
    Over Defined, 1-27
    Under Defined, 1-27
Sketch tab, 1-11

Sketch tool, 1-11
    3 Point Arc, 4-18
    Center Rectangle, 4-9, 4-10
    Centerline, 1-42, 2-26, 2-34, 2-37, 2-47
    Centerpoint Arc, 4-16
    Centerpoint Straight Slot, 1-40
    Circle, 1-24, 2-11, 1-43, 2-20, 2-37, 4-29
    Convert Entities, 2-51, 4-23
    Corner Rectangle, 1-40, 2-39, 2-27
    Dynamic Mirror, 2-27, 2-34, 2-37
    Exit Sketch, 4-10
    Line, 2-18, 2-52, 4-16, 4-31
    Offset Entities, 2-35
    Parallelogram, 2-42
    Polygon, 2-11, 4-29
    Sketch Fillet, 2-36
    Smart Dimension, 1-25, 1-33, 2-35
    Straight Slot, 1-39, 1-40, 2-27, 2-42
    Tangent Arc, 1-41, 2-40, 2-27, 2-50, 4-3
    Trim Entities, 2-27, 2-39, 2-50, 2-52
SketchXpert PropertyManager, 1-28
SketchXpert, 1-28
Slot PropertyManager, 2-27
Smart Dimension Sketch tool, 1-25, 1-33,
    2-35
SmartMate, 2-63, 5-12
SolidWorks 2010 icon, 1-6
SolidWorks DFMXpress Wizard, 6-24
SolidWorks DFMXpress, 6-24
SolidWorks graphics window, 1-20
SolidWorks Help, 1-37
SolidWorks Resources, 1-15
SolidWorks Search, 1-16
SolidWorks SimulationXpress, 6-8
SolidWorks SimulationXpress Wizard, 6-12
    Fixtures, 6-12
    Loads, 6-12
    Material, 6-12
    Optimize, 6-12
    Results, 6-12
    Run, 6-12
    Welcome, 6-12
SolidWorks Tutorials, 1-38
SolidWorks User Interface, 1-7
    CommandManager, 1-11
    Confirmation Corner, 1-9
    Drop-down menu, 1-8
    FeatureManager Design Tree, 1-12
    Fly-out FeatureManager, 1-14
    Fly-out tool buttons, 1-8

Heads-up View toolbar, 1-9
Menu bar menu, 1-7
Menu bar toolbar, 1-7
Motion Study tab, 1-17
Right-click Pop-up menu, 1-8
System Feedback icons, 1-8
Tags, 1-13
Task Pane, 1-15
SolidWorks Web Help, 1-37
Split bar, 1-13
Split ConfigurationManager, 1-14
Standard Mate, 1-46
Angle Mate, 1-46
Coincident Mate, 1-46
Concentric Mate, 1-46
Distance Mate, 1-46
Lock Mate, 1-46
Parallel Mate, 1-46, 5-30, 5-35
Perpendicular Mate, 1-46
Standard Sheet size, 3-7
Standard Views toolbar, 1-9
Start a SolidWorks session, 1-6
Start screen, 1-6
Straight Slot Sketch tool, 1-39, 1-40, 2-27,
2-42
Straight Slot Sketch tool, 1-39, 1-40, 2-27,
2-42
Suppress, 2-54
Swept Base Feature, 4-15
Swept Boss/Base Feature, 4-14, 4-21
Swept Cut Feature, 4-22, 4-25
Swept Path, 4-15
Swept Profile, 4-15
Symbol Dialog box, 3-14
Symmetric Mate, 1-47
System feedback icons, 1-8
Dimension, 1-8
Edge, 1-8
Face, 1-8
Vertex, 1-8
System Options - File Locations, 3-19

T
Tags, 1-13, 1-20
Tangent Arc Sketch tool, 1-41, 2-27, 2-40,
2-50, 4-31
Tangent Edges Removed, 3-43
Tangent Edges Visible, 3-43
Tangent Edges with Font, 3-43
Tangent Relation, 2-29, 2-40, 2-44, 4-18

Task Pane, 1-15
Appearances/Scenes, 1-17
Custom Properties, 1-17
Design Library, 1-15
Document Recovery, 1-17
File Explorer, 1-16
Search, 1-16
SolidWorks Resources, 1-15
View Palette, 1-16
Templates tab, 1-19
Temporary Axis, 2-43, 2-53, 4-40
Tertiary Datum plane, 2-5
Text Format box, 3-39
Third Angle Projection, 2-7, 2-8, 3-6, 3-9
Thread Profile, 4-25
Through All End Condition, 1-35, 1-43, 2-25,
4-13
Tile Horizontally, 2-65
Title Block, 3-10
TolAnalyst Study, 1-14
Tolerance Block, 3-13
Tolerance/Precision box, 3-32
Toolbars, 1-21
Top Plane, 1-20
Top View, 1-28
Trailing Zeroes, 3-30
TRIANGLE Part, 2-31
TRIANGLE Part - Boss-Extrude Feature,
2-36
TRIANGLE Part - Circular Pattern Feature,
2-44
TRIANGLE Part - First Extruded Cut Feature,
2-37
TRIANGLE Part - Mirror Feature, 2-41
TRIANGLE Part - Second Extruded Cut
Feature, 2-39
TRIANGLE Part - Third Extruded Cut
Feature, 2-42
Trim Entities Sketch tool, 1-41, 2-27, 2-39,
2-50, 2-52
Trim lines, 2-39
Trim PropertyManager, 1-41
Trim to closest, 1-41, 2-39, 2-50
Trimetric View, 1-35
Tutorial tab, 1-19
Type of Projection, 3-9

U
Under Defined sketch, 1-27
Undo Document, 1-7
Undo tool, 1-35
Units, 1-23, 1-32, 1-40, 2-10

Universal Joint Mate, 1-47
User Specified Name, 3-37, 3-49
User-Defined tags, 1-13

V
Vertex Cursor icon, 1-8
Vertical Relation, 4-17, 4-33
View Axis, 5-26
View Layout tab, 3-8
View Layout toolbar, 3-8
View Modes, 1-28
        Front View, 1-28
        Isometric View, 1-29
        Right View, 1-28
        Top View, 1-28
View Orientation tool, 1-10
View Origins, 1-21, 1-32
View Palette, 1-16, 3-23

View Reference Axis, 4-73
View Setting tool, 1-10
View Sketch Relations, 1-41
View Temporary Axes, 2-44, 2-53, 5-26
View toolbar, 1-9

W - X - Y
Wake up, 1-42
Web Help, 1-37
WEIGHT Part, 4-6
WEIGHT Part - Extruded Cut Feature, 4-13
WEIGHT Part - Lofted Feature, 4-12
What are features, 1-18

What's Wrong dialog box, 5-14
WHEEL Part, 4-27
WHEEL Part - Boss-Extrude Feature, 4-30
WHEEL Part - Circular Pattern Feature, 4-39
WHEEL Part - First Extruded Cut Feature,
    4-34
WHEEL Part - Revolved Cut Feature, 4-33
WHEEL Part - Second Extruded Cut Feature,
    4-36
WHEEL-AND-AXLE Assembly, 5-25
WHEEL-AND-AXLE Assembly - Insert AXLE-
    3000 Part, 5-25
WHEEL-AND-AXLE Assembly - Insert HEX-
    ADAPTER Part, 5-28
WHEEL-AND-AXLE Assembly - Insert
    SHAFTCOLLAR-500 Part, 5-30
WHEEL-FLATBAR Assembly - Insert
    3HOLE-SHAFTCOLLAR, 5-19
WHEEL-FLATBAR Assembly - Insert
    5HOLE-SHAFTCOLLOR, 5-21
WHEEL-FLATBAR Assembly, 5-16
WHEEL-FLATBAR Assembly - Insert
    WHEEL, 5-17
Width Mate, 1-47
Window-select, 1-41
Wireframe, 1-30, 2-27

Z
Zoom In, 1-29
Zoom Out, 1-29
Zoom to Area, 1-9
Zoom to Fit, 1-9, 1-29